UNIX

Concepts and Applications

Third Edition

About the Author

Sumitabha Das has a degree in electronics engineering from Calcutta University (1977). He picked up his interest in UNIX when working at the Ministry of Defence. Today, he teaches UNIX, Java and Systems Programming at BE College, Howrah. He is ably supported by his wife and 10-year old daughter.

UNIX

Concepts and Applications

Third Edition

Sumitabha Das

Faculty Consultant

PDSIT, Bengal Engineering College

Howrah

Tata McGraw-Hill Publishing Company Limited

NEW DELHI

McGraw-Hill Offices

New Delhi New York St Louis San Francisco Auckland Bogotá Caracas
Kuala Lumpur Lisbon London Madrid Mexico City Milan Montreal
San Juan Santiago Singapore Sydney Tokyo Toronto

Information contained in this work has been obtained by Tata McGraw-Hill, from sources believed to be reliable. However, neither Tata McGraw-Hill nor its authors guarantee the accuracy or completeness of any information published herein, and neither Tata McGraw-Hill nor its authors shall be responsible for any errors, omissions, or damages arising out of use of this information. This work is published with the understanding that Tata McGraw-Hill and its authors are supplying information but are not attempting to render engineering or other professional services. If such services are required, the assistance of an appropriate professional should be sought.

Eighth reprint 2005
DZLQCRCBRALRY

ISBN 0-07-053475-6

Published by Tata McGraw-Hill Publishing Company Limited, 7 West Patel Nagar, New Delhi 110 008, and printed at Pashupati Printers Pvt. Ltd., Delhi 110 095

Cover: SDR

The McGraw-Hill Companies

To

Julie *and* ***Sonu***

for their whole-hearted customization

of the UNIX authoring environment

A language is not worth knowing unless it teaches you to think differently.

—Larry Wall & Randal Schwartz

Contents

Preface

This book has been around for ten years now, a period that saw its steady consolidation and acceptance in the Indian market. This period was also punctuated by an initiative of McGraw-Hill Higher Education, USA to publish an adapted version of the book for the North American market. This adaptation was an extensive and time-consuming exercise that didn't just stop with the release of the book, but culminated in a translation into Mandarin for the Chinese market as well. The release of the third edition of this book was consequently delayed, but finally it's here at last—with major revisions, moderate additions and minor deletions. The total changes are significant enough to justify a small change of title yet again.

The UNIX spirit lives on as it has done for the last 25 years. While there is today a select community of people who swear by the name of UNIX, this operating system has also had its share of detractors—mostly people who have not been able to embrace its ideals owing to inadequate understanding. They have grown so used to seeing the mouse "doing" things that they are unable to lift the veil and look beyond the big picture. This is an unfortunate development because it induced a lot of intelligent people to miss the UNIX bus—people who would have loved to work in this environment but instead developed "bad" habits. This book endeavors to correct this viewpoint—and the habits.

UNIX is not "friendly" enough, that's what we have been hearing for a long time. Perceptions however differ; what is unfriendly to one can be quite friendly to another. A computer professional desiring to excel must understand why UNIX was deliberately designed to appear "unfriendly". Even though all UNIX systems offer a graphical environment, the power of UNIX lies in the programming environment with its rich collection of tools. A smart programmer uses this environment and its tools to turn out programs faster—and better.

Why UNIX Still Remains Important

UNIX and C changed the way people used and learned about computers. Even though technology changes fast—sometimes, every month—certain approaches to technology retain a sort of permanence. UNIX is one of them; it has survived the test of time. It's no wonder that theoretical courses on operating systems often use the UNIX system to illustrate key features. Thanks partly to Linux, things should remain this way in the foreseeable future too.

Even though UNIX was created by the engineering and scientific community, its robustness and absence of any comparable alternative led to its widespread acceptance in the commercial market. UNIX today is available on every hardware platform—from handhelds to supercomputers. More work is done on improving and enhancing the power of UNIX than on any other operating system. With so many people today having access to its source code, we can expect UNIX to only get better.

With the client-server framework splitting the computing environment into two (often, three) distinct parts, UNIX today is firmly entrenched as the operating system of choice for the server community—the backend where all the action is. Enterprise databases run on UNIX, and Oracle runs with full vigor on UNIX systems. Moreover, Internet Service Providers (ISP) use UNIX machines and UNIX remains the preferred platform for Web servers and electronic commerce. Think big and you'll have to think of UNIX.

UNIX has two of the best text editors in the world (**vi** and **emacs**). Its text processing utilities are simply unmatched. They can run as standalone applications but it's only by using these tools in combination that complex text manipulation problems are solved in UNIX. Add the shell's programming features, and you can at once develop noninteractive applications—and even schedule them to run at specific times. Once you start using all these tools that often require you to use only a line or two of code, you'll realize that UNIX actually encourages you to innovate. You'll join the privileged club who love to take up the numerous challenges offered by this operating system.

These years have also seen the phenomenal growth of the Linux cult—the free UNIX that today represents the most important manifestation of the Open Source movement. Today, we no longer believe that free software is not reliable enough. In fact, they are often better than commercial versions. However, let's make no mistake: Linux is a flavor of UNIX just as Solaris and HP-UX are. A UNIX programmer feels equally comfortable in the Linux environment—sometimes, more so. It's Linux that people are using today as a gateway to the world of UNIX. I see a great future ahead for Linux, the reason why this book also discusses Linux.

Another reason why people shied away from UNIX was its fragmentation. Vendors often modified the basic product which led to incompatibilities. This problem has now been addressed by standards bodies like POSIX and The Open Group. Today, we have a single standard, The Single UNIX Specification, Version 3, that lays down once and for all what an operating system must offer to be properly called UNIX. This single reference allows you to develop applications that will run without modification on all UNIX systems.

What's New in this Edition and What's Not

One of the unchanged features of this book is the two-part structure that has been carried over from the previous edition. The fundamental aspects of the system have been treated in Part I covering the first 17 chapters. The intermediate and experienced user may still find something worthwhile in Part I, but would be mostly reading the eleven chapters in Part II starting with Chapter 18. If you are studying UNIX as it is prescribed in the latest syllabus of DOE 'A' Level, then you'll need to study most of Part I, some of Part II and Appendix B.

I have always felt that it's most important for the reader to be aware of what to know now and what to pick up later. While the fundamentals of UNIX haven't changed much in all these years, its details and my perceptions of this operating system have. Different authors have different views of what is important and what is not. Time changes perceptions; some of the topics I considered as advanced material in the previous edition have now become essential and have been moved to Part I.

I am of the view that while beginners' interests are of paramount importance, this book must also provide an opportunity to explore further. As a result, concepts are probed deeply this time. Hopefully, by the time you have completed Part I, you'll be forced to ask this question:

How do all these things happen?

This edition answers many of the perceived questions, partly by gross additions to content. There are two new chapters this time and one appendix:

- Systems Programming I—The File (Chapter 25)
- Systems Programming II—Process Control (Chapter 26)
- Programming Tools—**make** and **ar** (Appendix B)

The two chapters on Systems Programming feature in Part II, and are the longest chapters in the book (around 90 pages) containing around 30 programs. You'll experience a certain thrill in being able to manipulate file descriptors and create and control processes "by hand". The other features to note are:

- Updated coverage on the Internet and the HTTP protocol.
- Increased coverage on Linux.
- All file attributes including umask, symbolic links, SUID and sticky bit have been moved to Part I.
- Shell programming is covered with increased depth and with better examples. The **expr** command has been moved to Part I.
- The **sed** command now features in Part I along with **grep**.
- File system internals no longer form a separate chapter but have been merged with system administration in Part II.
- TCP/IP network administration has been taken out of overall system administration and converted to a separate chapter in Part II.
- The pedagogical features—the Note, Tip and Caution asides and the end-of-chapter questions—have been given a major face-lift.

UNIX versions can be broadly divided into two schools—the *System V* school from AT&T Bell Laboratories and the *Berkeley* school from the University of California, Berkeley. More specifically, versions tend to be looked at as being either based on *SVR4* (System V Release 4—AT&T's last release before winding up its UNIX operations) or on *BSD UNIX* (Berkeley Software Distribution). While many of the features of UNIX are common to all systems, I have focused this time on two major versions—Solaris and Linux.

Unfortunately, UNIX gets greatly fragmented when it comes to system administration, and covering the features of all the major UNIX flavors requires a separate book by itself. The redeeming feature is that you'll generally find that commands, devices and their configuration files conform to either of the two schools that were just described. There is also a significant amount of overlap between the two schools. Coverage of UNIX system and network administration is spread across three chapters (17, 27, and 28).

There are plenty of end-of-chapter questions. In this edition, these questions have been grouped into two categories. The section entitled *Test Your Understanding* contains mostly simple questions, but you should try to solve them before you switch chapters. The answers to these questions are available in Appendix C. The more involved questions feature in *Flex Your Brains*, whose answers are provided on the book's Web site, *but available only to the adopters of the book*.

All examples should run on most UNIX and Linux systems, and you'll find suitable indications in the heading when a system-specific feature is encountered. Don't forget to read *Conventions Used in This Book* before you move into the UNIX mainstream beginning with Chapter 1.

It's quite possible that you may be using an older (or newer) release, and some commands may either not be available or throw out different messages. You have to take this in your stride, and need not automatically conclude that the system has bugs. Nevertheless, bugs in these examples are still possible, and I welcome ones (along with suggestions) that you may suddenly hit upon. I can be reached at *sumit@cal.vsnl.net.in*.

Acknowledgements

J.P. Mathew deserves thanks for the pains undertaken to examine the chapters on Systems Programming and the helpful suggestions offered. A. Gurusankar wrested the initiative from me to provide the answers to all questions that feature in Chapters 15 and 16. Numerous suggestions have been received from other quarters too.

My editor, Vibha Mahajan, has been most cooperative in ensuring that I had the necessary inputs to proceed with this major revision work. I also thank Mini Narayanan for some of the useful suggestions related to typesetting that enabled me to produce (hopefully) more attractive camera-ready-copy of this text. Need I mention again how and why Dr. Subrahmanyam still remains a constant driving force? I think not.

And on this note, I wish you an exciting journey to the UNIX world!

SUMITABHA DAS

Conventions Used in This Book

The following conventions have been used in this book:

- Commands, program names, user input in examples and system calls are shown in bold constant width font:

  Many commands in **`more`** including **`f`** and **`b`** use a repeat factor.

  The shell features three types of loops—**`while`**, **`until`** and **`for`**.

  Enter your name: **`henry`**

  The forking mechanism uses the **`fork`** system call to create a process.

- Apart from command output, filenames, command options, strings, expressions and symbols are shown in constant width font:

  Most commands are located in `/bin` and `/usr/bin`.

  Try doing that with the name `jai sharma`.

  There's adequate scope of using the `-e` and `-f` options.

  The shell looks for the characters `>`, `<` and `<<` in the command line.

- Machine and domain names, email addresses and URLs are displayed in italics:

  This copies a file from the remote machine *saturn*.

  User kumar on this host can be addressed as *kumar@calcs.heavens.com*.

  Google offers comprehensive News services at *http://groups.google.com*.

- Placeholders for filenames, terms, menu options and explanatory comments within examples are displayed in italics:

  When compiled with **`cc`** *filename*, it produces a file named **`a.out`**.

  .... to develop a set of standard rules (*protocols*)

  Use *Edit>Preferences* to configure Netscape.

  `$ cd ../..`   *Moves two levels up*

- The following abbreviations, shortcuts and symbols have been used:

  SVR4—System V Release 4

  `sh`—Bourne shell

  `csh`—C shell

  `ksh`—Korn shell

  `$HOME`/*flname*—The file *flname* in the home directory

  ~/*flname*—The file *flname* in the home directory

  `foo` and `bar`—Generic file and directory names as used on USENET

PART I

For the beginner ...

1

Getting Started

UNIX was never designed for the world. It is usual for a beginner to feel overwhelmed by the sheer weight of the system. The most common problem faced by her (even when she is an experienced computer professional) is in not knowing where to begin, or how much to learn. The system unfortunately wasn't conceived with the novice in mind. It has an unusual history which probably is responsible for most of its apparent incoherence.

This chapter begins the tour of the UNIX universe. To understand UNIX, we'll first have to know what an operating system is, why a computer needs one and how UNIX is vastly different from other operating systems that came before—and after. Through a hands-on session, we'll learn to play with the UNIX system and acquire familiarity with some of its commands that we need to use everyday for interacting with the system. The experience of the introductory session will help us understand the concepts presented in the next chapter.

UNIX is a system developed by programmers for their own use, and thus many things appeared quite obvious to them that don't appear to us. However, that doesn't imply in any way that it is unconquerable. If you are willing to put in some *guided* effort, you'll gradually see the UNIX story unfolding with indisputable clarity and simplicity. Focus your attention on the essentials and try to understand the designers' minds and their objectives. Everything will then fall into place automatically.

WHAT YOU WILL LEARN

- What an operating system is and how UNIX more than fulfills that role.
- Know the location of the special characters on the keyboard.
- Log in and out of a UNIX system using a username and password.
- Run a few commands like **date**, **who** and **cal**.
- View the *processes* with **ps**, and *files* with **ls**.
- Use a special character like the * to match multiple filenames.
- The role of the *shell* in interpreting all these special characters (*metacharacters*).

TOPICS OF SPECIAL INTEREST

- Examination of the sequence of steps followed by the shell in executing the command **ls > list** to save command output in a file.
- A similar examination of the sequence **ls | wc** to connect two commands to form a *pipeline*.

1.1 THE OPERATING SYSTEM

We use computers freely, but most of us never bother to know what's inside the box. Why should we? After all, we also use TV and never care to find out how this idiot box manages to convert invisible radio waves to real-life colorful pictures. Yes, you can certainly use spreadsheets and word processors, and probably even databases, without knowing how these programs access the machine's resources. As long as you continue to get all those reports and charts, do you really need to know anything else?

Then the inevitable happens. The great crash occurs, the machine refuses to boot. The expert tells you that the *operating system* has to be reloaded. You are taken by surprise. You've heard of software, and you have used lots of them. But, what is this thing called the operating system: Is this just another piece of software?

Relax, it is. But, it's not just any ordinary software that writes your letters for you, but a special one—one that gives life to a machine. Every computer needs some basic intelligence to start with. Unlike mortals, a computer is not born with any. This intelligence is used to provide the essential services for programs that run under its auspices—like using the CPU, allocating memory and accessing devices like your hard disk for reading and writing files.

The computer provides yet another type of service, this time for you—the user. You'll always need to copy or delete a file, or create a directory to house all these files. You'll need to know the people who are working in the network, or send a mail message to a friend. As a system administrator, you'll also have to back up files. No word processor will do all this for you, neither will your Web browser. All this belongs rightly to the domain of what is known as the *operating system*.

Without an operating system, the most powerful computer in the world would be a useless monster. No matter how powerful and elegant your programs are, they simply can't function without the assistance of an operating system. It's like saying that the most efficient chef can't display his talents if a properly furnished kitchen is not provided to him.

There have been lots of these operating systems in the past, one at least from each hardware vendor. They all contributed in their own way to the chaotic situation that made programs written on one machine totally incapable of running on another. Vendors required consumers to purchase expensive proprietary hardware and software if two dissimilar machines needed to talk to each other. We also had DOS and Windows (in all its manifestations) on our desktop computers providing us with a cheaper and user-friendly way of computing.

1.2 THE UNIX OPERATING SYSTEM

Like DOS and Windows, there's another operating system called UNIX. It arrived earlier than the other two, and stayed back late enough to give us the Internet. UNIX is a giant operating system, and is way ahead of them in sheer power. It has practically everything an operating system should have, and several features which other operating systems never had. It has a number of profound and diverse concepts developed and perfected over a period of time. Its richness and elegance go beyond the commands and tools that constitute it, while simplicity permeates the entire system. It runs on practically every hardware and today champions the cause of the Open Source movement.

However, UNIX also makes many demands of the user. It requires a different type of commitment to understand the subject, even when the user is an experienced computer professional. It introduces certain concepts not known to the computing community before, and uses numerous symbols whose meanings are anything but obvious. It achieves unusual tasks with a few keystrokes, but it takes time to devise a sequence of them for a specific task. Often, it doesn't tell you whether you are right or wrong, and doesn't warn you of the consequences of your actions. That is probably the reason why many people still prefer to stay away from UNIX.

Kernighan and Pike (*The UNIX Programming Environment*, Prentice-Hall) lamented long ago that "as the UNIX system has spread, the fraction of its users who are skilled in its application has decreased." Many people still use the system as they would use any other operating system, and continue to write comprehensive programs that have already been written before. Beginners with some experience in DOS and Windows think of UNIX in terms of them, quite oblivious of the fact that UNIX has much more to offer. Though references to DOS/Windows have often been made whenever a similar feature was encountered, the similarities end there too. You should not let them get in the way of the UNIX experience. The capabilities of UNIX are limited only by your imagination.

1.3 KNOWING YOUR MACHINE

Unlike DOS and Windows, UNIX can be used by several users concurrently. In other words, a *single* copy of the operating system installed on a single disk can serve the needs of hundreds of users. If you have access to such a *multiuser* system, then in all probability you'll be sitting with just a terminal, i.e., a monitor (the thing that looks more like a portable TV) and a keyboard. Like you, there will be others working on similar terminals. The rest of the equipment will probably be located in a separate room with restricted access. In this arrangement, you are expected to simply hook onto your account, perform your work, disconnect and leave quietly.

Things are quite different, however, when you are the sole user of the system. This could happen if you work on a desktop machine that has its own *CPU* (the Central Processor Unit), *RAM* (Random Access Memory—the memory), hard disk, floppy and CD-ROM drives, printer and the controllers of these devices. If you own the machine, then you are directly responsible for its startup, shutdown and maintenance. If you lose a file, it's your job to get it from a backup. If things don't work properly, you have to try all possible means to set them right before you decide to call the maintenance person.

1.3.1 The Keyboard

Before you start working, you need to know right now the functions of a number of keys on the keyboard. Many of these keys are either not used by DOS and Windows, or have different functions there. The portion of the keyboard at the left having the *QWERTY* layout resembles your typewriter. You need to be familiar with this section of the keyboard initially, in addition to some other keys in its immediate vicinity. If you know typing, you are on familiar terrain, and keyboard phobia should not get in your way.

Apart from the alphanumeric keys, you'll observe a number of symbols as shown below:

` ~ ! @ # $ % ^ & * ( ) - _ = + \ | [ ] { } ; : ' " , . < > / ?

Each alphabet, number or symbol is known as a *character*, which represents the smallest piece of information that you can deal with. All these characters have unique values assigned to them, called the *ASCII* value (ASCII—American Standard Code for Information Interchange). For instance, the letter `A` has the ASCII value 65, while the bang or exclamation mark (`!`) has the value 21.

There are some keys that have no counterparts in the typewriter. Note the key *[Enter]* at the right which is used to terminate a line. On some machines this key may be labeled *[Return]*. The significance of this key is taken up in Section 1.4.4.

When you look at a blank screen, you'll see a blinking object called a *cursor*. When you key in a character, it shows up at the location of the cursor, while moving the cursor itself right. Directly above the *[Enter]* key is the key shown with a ← or labeled *[Backspace]*. You have to press this key to erase one or more characters that you have just entered, using a feature known as *backspacing*. When this key is pressed, the cursor moves over the character placed on its left and removes it from sight.

Another important key is the one labeled *[Ctrl]* (called Control) which you'll find in duplicate on the lower side of the keyboard. This key is never used singly but always in combination with other keys. We'll be using this key several times in this book. For instance, whenever you are advised to use *[Ctrl-s]* to stop a scrolling display, you should first press the *[Ctrl]* key and then the key labeled `s`, while *[Ctrl]* is still kept pressed.

At the top-left corner, you can see the *[Esc]* key (called Escape), which you'll require to use when performing file editing with a text editor such as **`vi`**. This key often takes you to the previous menu in a menu-based program. Then there is the *[Delete]* key, which some systems (like SCO UNIX) use to interrupt a program in the same way *[Ctrl-c]* is used on other UNIX systems (and DOS). On a system running Solaris or Linux, you'll probably be using *[Ctrl-c]*, rather than *[Delete]*, for interrupting a program.

In the same line as the *[Esc]* key are the twelve function keys labeled *[F1]*, *[F2]*, etc., up to *[F12]*. You won't require these keys initially, but much later (for mapping keys in **`vi`**, for example). The cursor control keys (the ones with four arrows) are required for recalling previous commands in the Bash shell.

1.4 A BRIEF SESSION

Irrespective of what the textbooks may preach (including this one), a personal interaction with the system has definite advantages. Seeing is believing as they say, so without further ado, let's get down to business and see what a UNIX session is really like. If you are migrating from the DOS/Windows environment, then you have quite a bit of mental preparation to do before you start feeling comfortable.

UNIX isn't very friendly, and the messages that it throws up on the screen can sometimes be confusing. Sometimes there are no messages at all, and you'll then have to figure out yourself whether the command worked properly. Absorb as much as you can from this session, think for a while, and then move on to the other chapters.

1.4.1 Logging in with Username and Password

UNIX is security-conscious, and can be used only by those persons who maintain an *account* with the computer system. This list of accounts is maintained separately in the computer. You can't simply sit down at any terminal and start banging away if your name doesn't feature in the list. That's both inadvisable and an impossible thing to do.

Because the system can be used by many users, someone has to be given charge of administration of the system. This person is known as the *system administrator*, and he is the person who will grant you the authority to use the system. He opens an account with a name for your use, and gives you a secret code that you have to enter when the system prompts you for it. If you are running UNIX on your desktop, then remember that you are the administrator of the machine.

If you have the name kumar for this account, you'll be expected to enter this name when you see a *prompt* similar to this on the terminal:

```
SunOS 5.8                         A Sun machine running Solaris 8

login:
```

The prompt here is preceded by the version of the operating system, SunOS 5.8, which is the operating system of Solaris 8. This is a flavor (brand) of UNIX offered by Sun Microsystems, but your system could show a different string here (if at all). The prompt itself could have a prefix showing the machine name. (Yes, every machine has a name in UNIX.)

The login prompt indicates that the terminal is available for someone to *log in* (i.e., connect to the machine). This message also indicates that the previous user has *logged out* (i.e., finished her work and disconnected). Since you now have an account named kumar, enter this string at the prompt. Then press the *[Enter]* key after the string:

```
login: kumar[Enter]
Password:
```

The system now requests you to enter the secret code that was handed to you by your administrator. This code should be known to none except yourself. (The administrator doesn't need to know!) It's something like the personnel identification number (PIN) that you have to key in before withdrawing cash from an automatic teller machine. Type the secret code, and then press the *[Enter]* key:

```
login: kumar
Password: *********[Enter]                    Entry not displayed
```

You may be surprised to observe that the string that you enter at the Password: prompt isn't displayed on the screen. This is another security feature built into the system that doesn't let someone standing beside you see what you have entered (unless, of course, she has been meticulously monitoring your finger movements!).

If you make mistakes while typing, simply press *[Enter]* one or two times till the login prompt reappears on the screen. Be sure to terminate your responses with *[Enter]* to make the system "see" the input that you have entered.

The string that you entered at the first prompt (login:) is known variously as your *login name*, *user-id*, or *username*, and these names will be used interchangeably throughout this book. The secret code that you entered at the next prompt (Password:) is known as the *password*. If you enter either of them incorrectly, the system flashes the following message:

```
Login incorrect
login:
```

Another level of security! You simply don't know what went wrong—your login name or your password. The message Login incorrect is in fact quite deceptive. In most cases, it's the password that's the culprit. Go back to your secret diary where the password should have been noted and restart the session. When you get both these parameters correct, this is what you could be seeing on a Solaris system:

```
Last login: Thu May  9 06:48:39 from saturn.heavens.com
$ _                                   The cursor shown by the _ character
```

The system now shows the $ as the *prompt*, with the cursor constantly blinking beside it. This is a typical UNIX prompt, and many UNIX systems use the $ as the default prompt string. For some users, you might see the % instead of the $, and the system administrator will in all probability be using the #. UNIX allows you to customize the prompt, and it's not unusual to see prompts like these:

```
[/home/kumar] _
kumar@saturn:/home/kumar > _
```

Both prompts show your "location" in the file system. This should be familiar to users who have worked in DOS and used the statement PROMPT [pg] in their AUTOEXEC.BAT to customize their prompt string. A customized prompt, as you'll see later, helps in a number of ways. For the time being, be content with whatever prompt you have to work with; it won't cause you any harm.

> **Note** As soon as you log in, a program called the *shell* starts to run at your terminal, and keeps running till you terminate the session. The shell is your system's *command interpreter*. It displays the prompt and accepts all your input from the keyboard. The UNIX system offers a variety of shells (like Bourne shell, C shell, Korn shell and Bash) for you to choose from. Whether your prompt can display your "location" entirely depends on the shell you use. When the administrator opens a user account, he also sets a specific shell for the user.

Caution On your first login, the system may force you to change your password. It's also not unusual for the system not to prompt for the password at all, in which case you'll be taken to the prompt straightaway. This presents a security breach, and you should immediately assign a password to your own account. If others have acquired knowledge of your password; you should change it. Both assignment and change of password can be done with a command named **passwd** *(4.7)*. You'll also learn later the terrible consequences that you may have to face if people with mischievous intent somehow come to know what your password is.

1.4.2 The Command

We have now been able to successfully log on to a UNIX system. What do we do now? Let's enter something from the keyboard, press *[Enter]*, and then see what happens:

```
$ unix[Enter]
ksh: unix: command not found              A message from the shell
$ _                                       Shell returns prompt
```

What the system expected was a *command* that it knows, and **unix** doesn't appear to be a legitimate command. Nevertheless, the prompt returns to accept the next command. UNIX has a large family of commands, some of them quite powerful, and a UNIX expert is expected to know many of them. We'll now acquaint ourselves with a few of these commands.

1.4.3 date: Displaying Both Date and Time

Now that the previous command was rejected by the system, let's use one that it recognizes. UNIX has a **date** command that shows the date and time in the form used on the Internet. Type the four characters in **date** and press *[Enter]*:

```
$ date[Enter]
Tue Nov 19 21:37:51 IST 2002
$ _
```

date is a valid command, and it displays both the date and the time. Notice another security feature of UNIX; the command doesn't prompt you to change either the date or the time. This facility is available only to the administrator, and the strange thing is that he uses the same command *(17.2.1)* to do it!

So what is **date**? It's simply one of several hundred commands available on the UNIX system. Whatever you input through the keyboard is interpreted by the system as a command, and when you use one, you are in fact commanding the machine to do something. The **date** command instructs the machine to display the current date and time. Incidentally, most UNIX commands are represented as *files* in the system.

Caution Tampering with the system date can have adverse effects on a UNIX system. There are many processes that go on in the background without your knowledge, and they are scheduled to start at certain specific times. If a nonprivileged (ordinary) user (The system administrator is known as the *superuser* simply because he's blessed with enormous powers!) is allowed to change the date and time at will, chaos will ensue.

1.4.4 Two Important Observations

You have had your first interaction with the system by running two commands after logging in. Even though one command worked and the other didn't, you had to terminate each by hitting the *[Enter]* key. The text that you type at the terminal remains hidden from the system until this key is pressed. First-time users often fail to appreciate this point because there's no "[Enter] key" in the human information system. Humans register speech or text, as it is being spoken or read, in a continuous manner. In this respect, this key resembles the shutter of a camera; nothing gets into the film until the shutter is pressed.

Also note that the completion of a command, successful or otherwise, is indicated by the return of the prompt (here, a $). The return of the prompt indicates that all work relating to the previous command has been completed, and the system is ready to accept the next command. Henceforth, we'll not indicate the *[Enter]* key or the return of the prompt except in not-so-obvious circumstances.

1.4.5 `tput clear`: Clearing the Screen

All UNIX systems offer the **tput** command to clear the screen. This is something you'd often like to do to avoid getting distracted by the output or error messages of previous commands. However, when you use **tput** as it is, (i.e., without any additional words), this is what UNIX has to say:

```
$ tput
usage:   tput [-T [term]] capname [parm argument...]
OR:      tput -S <<
```

This message makes little sense to a beginner, so we won't attempt to interpret it right now. However, one thing is obvious; **tput** requires some additional material to work properly. To make **tput** work, follow `tput` with the word `clear`:

```
tput clear                                    clear is an argument to tput
```

You'll now find that whatever has been typed so far has vanished from your view, and the prompt and cursor are positioned at the top-left corner of the screen. Some systems also offer the **clear** command, but the standard UNIX specifications (like POSIX) don't require UNIX systems to offer this command. You must remember to use **tput clear** to clear the screen because we won't be discussing this command again in this text.

> **Note** The additional word used with **tput** isn't a command, but is referred to as an *argument*. Here, `clear` is an argument to **tput**, and the fact that **tput** refused to work alone indicates that it always requires an argument (sometimes more). And, if `clear` is one argument, then there could be others. We'll often refer to the *default* behavior of a command to mean the effect of a using a command without any arguments.

1.4.6 `cal`: The Calendar

cal is a handy tool that you can invoke any time to see the calendar of any specific month, or a complete year. To see the calendar for the month of April, 2003, provide the month number and year as two arguments to **cal**:

```
$ cal 4 2003
     April 2003
 S  M Tu  W Th  F  S
       1  2  3  4  5
 6  7  8  9 10 11 12
13 14 15 16 17 18 19
20 21 22 23 24 25 26
27 28 29 30
```

Command run with two arguments

With **cal**, you can produce the calendar for any month or year between the years 1 and 9999. This should serve our requirements for some time, right? We'll see more of this command later.

1.4.7 who: Who Are the Users?

UNIX is a system that can be concurrently used by multiple users, and you might be interested in knowing the people who are also using the system like you. Use the **who** command:

```
$ who
kumar       console      May  9 09:31    (:0)
vipul       pts/4        May  9 09:31    (:0.0)
raghav      pts/5        May  9 09:32    (saturn.heavens.com)
```

There are currently three users—kumar, vipul and raghav. These are actually the user-ids or usernames they used to log in. The output also includes the username, kumar, which you entered at the login: prompt to gain entry to the system. The second column shows the name of the terminal the user is working on. Just as all users have names, all terminals, disks and printers also have names. You'll see later that these names are represented as *files* on the system. The date and time of login are also shown in the output. Ignore the last column for the time being.

Observe also that the output of **who** doesn't include any headers to indicate what the various columns mean. This is an extremely important feature of the system, and is in some measure responsible for the unfriendly image that UNIX has acquired. After you have completed Chapter 9, you'll discover that it is actually a blessing in disguise.

> **Note** You logged in with the name kumar, so the system addresses you by this name and associates kumar with whatever work you do. Create a file and the system will make kumar the owner of the file. Execute a program and kumar will be the owner of the *process* (next topic) associated with your program. Send mail to another user and the system will inform the recipient that mail has arrived from kumar.

1.4.8 ps: Viewing the Processes

We observed that the shell program is always running at your terminal. Every command that you run gives rise to a *process*, and the shell is a process as well. To view all processes that you are responsible for creating, run the **ps** command:

```
$ ps
  PID TTY      TIME CMD
  364 console  0:00 ksh
```

Shell running all the time!

Unlike **who**, **ps** generates a header followed by a line containing the details of the **ksh** process. When you run several programs, there will be multiple lines in the **ps** output. **ksh** represents the Korn shell (an advanced shell from AT&T) and is constantly running at this terminal. This process has a unique number 364 (called the *process-id* or PID), and when you log out, this process is killed.

> **Note** Even though we are using the Korn shell here, you could be using another shell. Instead of **ksh**, you could see **sh** (the primitive Bourne shell), **csh** (C shell—still popular today) or **bash** (Bash shell—a very powerful shell and recommended for use). Throughout this book, we'll be comparing the features of these shells and discover features that are available in one shell but not in another. If a command doesn't produce output as explained in this text, it can often be attributed to the shell.

1.4.9 ls: Listing Files

Your UNIX system has a large number of files that control its functioning, and users also create files on their own. These files are organized in separate folders called *directories*. You can list the names of the files available in this directory with the **ls** command:

```
$ ls
README                                         Uppercase first
chap01
chap02
chap03
helpdir
progs
```

ls displays a list of six files, three of which actually contain the chapters of this textbook. Note that the files are arranged alphabetically with uppercase having precedence over lower (which we call the *ASCII collating sequence*).

Since the files containing the first three chapters have similar filenames, UNIX lets you use a special short-hand notation (*) to access them:

```
$ ls chap*
chap01
chap02
chap03
```

Sometimes, just displaying a list of filenames isn't enough; you need to know more about these files. For that **ls** has to be used with an *option*, -l, between the command and the filenames:

```
$ ls -l chap*                                  -l is an option
-rw-r--r--   1 kumar    users       5609 Apr 23 09:30 chap01
-rw-r--r--   1 kumar    users      26129 May 14 18:55 chap02
-rw-r--r--   1 kumar    users      37385 May 15 10:30 chap03
```

The argument beginning with a hyphen is known as an *option*. The characteristic feature of most command options is that they begin with a - (hyphen). An option changes the default behavior (i.e. when used without options) of a command, so if **ls** prints a columnar list of files, the -l option makes it display some of the attributes as well.

1.4.10 Directing Output to a File

UNIX has simple symbols (called *metacharacters*) for creating and storing information in files. Instead of viewing the output of the **ls** command on the terminal, you can save the information in a file, `list`, by using a special symbol, > (the right chevron character on your keyboard):

```
$ ls > list
$ _                                      Prompt returns—no display on the terminal
```

You see nothing on the terminal except the return of the prompt. The shell is at work here. It has a mechanism of *redirecting* any output, normally coming to the terminal, to a disk file. To check whether the shell has actually done the job, use the **cat** command with the filename as argument:

```
$ cat list                               cat displays a file's contents
README
chap01
chap02
chap03
helpdir
progs
```

Here you have a glimpse of the UNIX magic. The shell sees the > *before* **ls** runs, so it gets to act first. It then opens the file following the > (here, `list`). **ls** runs next and it looks up the "table of contents" of the directory to find out the filenames in it. But the shell has already manipulated things in such a way that the **ls** output doesn't come to the terminal but to the file opened by the shell on its behalf. And all this is done using only a single line of code!

> **Note** You list files in the directory with **ls** and display file contents with **cat**. You can get more details of a file using the `-l` option with **ls**.

1.4.11 wc: Counting Number of Lines in a File

How many lines are there in the file? The **wc** command answers this question:

```
$ wc list
      6       6      42 list
```

Observe once again the brevity that typically characterizes UNIX; it merely echoes three numbers along with the filename. You have to have the manual or this text in front of you to know that the file `list` contains 6 lines, 6 words and 42 characters.

1.4.12 Feeding Output of One Command to Another

Now you should see something that is often hailed as the finest feature of the system. Previously, you used **ls** to list files, and then the > symbol to save the output in the file `list`. You then counted the number of lines, words and characters of this file with **wc**. In this way, you could *indirectly* count the number of files in the directory. The shell can do better; its manipulative capability enables a *direct* count without creating an intermediate file. Using the | symbol, it connects two commands to create a *pipeline*:

```
$ ls | wc
       6       6      42                    No filename this time!
```

See how you can arrive at the same result (except for the filename), this time by simply connecting the output of **ls** to the input of **wc**. No intermediate file is now needed. On seeing the symbol, | (known as a *pipe*), the shell performs the job of connecting the two commands. If you can connect a number of UNIX commands in this way, you can perform difficult tasks quite easily.

1.4.13 Programming with the Shell

The system also features a programming facility. You can assign a value to a variable at the prompt:

```
$ x=5                                       No spaces on either side of =
$ _
```

and then evaluate the value of this variable with the **echo** command and prefixing the variable name with a $:

```
$ echo $x                                   A $ required during evaluation
5
```

Apart from playing with variables, UNIX also provides control structures like conditionals and loops, and you'll see a great deal of that in later chapters.

1.4.14 exit: Signing Off

So far, what you have seen is only a small fragment of the UNIX giant, though you have already been exposed to some of its key features. Most of these commands will be considered in some detail in subsequent chapters, and it's a good idea to suspend the session for the time being. You should use the **exit** command to do that:

```
$ exit
login:
```

Alternatively, you *may* be able to use *[Ctrl-d]* (generated by pressing the *[Ctrl]* key and the character d on the keyboard) to quit the session. The login: message confirms that the session has been terminated, thus making it available for the next user.

> **Note** Depending on how your environment has been set, you may not be able to use *[Ctrl-d]* to exit the session. In case you are unable to exit with *[Ctrl-d]*, try the **logout** command, and if that fails, use the **exit** command. This command will *always* work.

1.5 CONCLUSION

In this chapter you logged on to a UNIX machine and invoked some of its commands. You also used some special characters like the > and | to alter the destination of command output. We have many more commands to discuss and many special characters to understand. Because you may not see commands behaving exactly in the same way as they are described here, you need to acquaint yourself with the evolutionary path followed by UNIX. In the next chapter, we take up the important landmarks in this path before we examine the subsystems that support UNIX.

WRAP UP

A computer needs an *operating system* to provide all programs with essential services that involve use of the machine's resources. UNIX is also an operating system but it has more features than is expected out of an operating system.

UNIX can be used by multiple users concurrently. You enter a UNIX system by entering a username, assigned by the system administrator, and a password. The password is not displayed on the screen for security reasons. You can terminate a session by using the **`exit`** command or pressing *[Ctrl-d]*.

UNIX features a prompt, which could be a $, % or a customized string. You can enter any legitimate command at this prompt, followed by the *[Enter]* key. The prompt is produced by the *shell*, a program that constantly runs at the terminal as long as the user is logged in.

`date` tells you the date and time, **`tput clear`** clears the screen, **`cal`** displays the calendar, **`who`** shows the users at work and **`ps`** displays the processes. **`wc`** counts the number of characters, words and lines and **`ls`** lists files of a directory.

You can use the * to capture a number of filenames with a simple pattern. The > symbol is used to save the output coming on the screen in a file, while | feeds output of one command as input to another command.

TEST YOUR UNDERSTANDING

1.1 Every character has a value associated with it. What is it called?

1.2 Why is the password string not displayed on the terminal?

1.3 How do you come to know when a command has completed execution?

1.4 Enter this sequence: **`> user.lst`**. Note what happens. Repeat the process by removing the space after the >. Does it make any difference?

1.5 Enter this command sequence: **`ls | wc -l`**. What do you think the output represents?

1.6 Enter the two commands: **`echo *`** and **`ls`**. What do you think **`echo`** did?

1.7 Enter these commands: **`echo "$SHELL"`** and **`echo '$SHELL'`**. What difference do you notice?

1.8 When you enter a command, what processing does it go through before it is executed?

FLEX YOUR BRAIN

1.1 Why does a machine need an operating system?

1.2 When you log in, a program starts executing at your terminal. What is this program known as? Name four types of this program that are available on a system.

1.3 With which commands do you display filenames and processes?

1.4 What exactly happens when you enter this sequence: **`ls > list`**?

1.5 What is the significance of your username? Where in the system is the name used?

1.6 Attempt the variable assignment x=10 by providing a space on either end of the =. Why doesn't it work?

1.7 Name some of the duties of the system administrator that you have encountered so far.

2

A Conceptual Background

UNIX has had a rather turbulent background. Knowing this background will help us understand the objectives that guided its development. Even though UNIX owes its origin to AT&T, present-day UNIX systems incorporate several contributions made by the academic community and industry. While this has led both to the enrichment and fragmentation of UNIX, it would be helpful to know the role played by the standards bodies that makes it possible today to write programs that run on all UNIX systems.

To appreciate the material presented in the remaining chapters, you must understand the UNIX architecture. We present in this chapter the key features of UNIX as well. UNIX is now more than 25 years old, but fortunately the essentials remain the same. Some of these concepts may seem a little abstract, but you shouldn't be deterred if you haven't understood them initially. UNIX is very well documented, so there's hardly a way that a problem can remain unsolved for long.

WHAT YOU WILL LEARN

- A brief background of UNIX that led to its fragmentation across various flavors including Linux.
- What *system calls* are and how they enrich the UNIX programming environment.
- The *multiprogramming*, *multiuser* and *multitasking* nature of UNIX.
- How UNIX encourages the use of modular tools that can be connected together to form complex tasks.
- The other features of UNIX—its vast collection of tools, pattern matching and wide variety of its documentation sources.

TOPICS OF SPECIAL INTEREST

- The significance of the POSIX and Single UNIX Specification standards.
- The UNIX architecture and how two programs—the *kernel* and *shell*—work in a cooperative manner to handle everything.
- The significance of the two abstractions—the *file* and *process*—in the UNIX system.

2.1 HOW IT ALL CLICKED

Till UNIX came on the scene, operating systems were designed with a particular machine in mind. They were invariably written in a low-level language (like assembler, which uses humanly unreadable code). The systems were fast but were restricted to the hardware they were designed for. Programs designed for one system simply wouldn't run on another. That was the status of the computer industry when Ken Thompson and Dennis Ritchie, of AT&T fame, authored the UNIX system.

In 1969, AT&T withdrew its team from the MULTICS project, which was engaged in the development of a flexible operating system that would run continuously and be used remotely. Thompson and Ritchie then designed and built a small system having an elegant file system, a command interpreter (the shell) and a set of utilities. However, what they wanted was a general operating system running on more than one type of hardware. In 1973, they rewrote the entire system in C—a high-level language (more readable than assembler) that was invented by Ritchie himself. Portability became one of the strong features of UNIX.

AT&T's earlier products were first known as "Editions", then changed to "Systems". In 1982, they had System III, which became System V Release 3.0 in 1987, and finally Release 3.2 before a grand unification took place.

2.1.1 Berkeley: The Second School

A U.S. government decree (subsequently revoked) prevented AT&T from selling computer software. The company had no option but to distribute the product to academic and research institutions at a nominal fee, but without any support. The University of California, Berkeley (UCB), created a UNIX of its own. They called it *BSD UNIX* (Berkeley Software Distribution). These versions became quite popular worldwide, especially in universities and engineering circles. Later, UCB gave up all development work on UNIX.

Berkeley filled the gaps left behind by AT&T, and then later decided to rewrite the whole operating system in the way they wanted. They created the standard editor of the UNIX system (`vi`) and a popular shell (C shell). Berkeley also created a better file system, a more versatile mail feature and a better method of linking files (symbolic links). Later, they also offered with their standard distribution a networking protocol software (TCP/IP) that made the Internet possible. Like AT&T, they also offered it practically free to many companies.

2.1.2 The Others

When computer science graduates left academics for the commercial world, they took their UNIX aspirations with them. It was just a matter of time before business circles developed interest in the product, and they too joined in its development in a spree of unparalleled innovation. UNIX had turned commercial.

Sun used the BSD System as a foundation for developing their own brand of UNIX (then *SunOS*). Today, their version of UNIX is known as *Solaris*. Others had their own brands; IBM had *AIX*, HP offered *HP-UX*, while DEC produced *Digital UNIX*—and now *Tru64 UNIX*. Then the Linux wave arrived, and most of these vendors are offering Linux too. Today, most supercomputers run UNIX, and handheld devices are increasingly using Linux. By making itself available on most hardware, UNIX now gives the customer the "freedom of choice", as opposed to the "freedom from choice" (the way Scott McNealy, the CEO of Sun Microsystems, describes it). The notable UNIX flavors are listed in Table 2.1.

As each vendor modified and enhanced UNIX to create its own version, the original UNIX lost its identity as a separate product. The BSD releases were much different from the AT&T System V releases, and the incompatibilities steadily mounted. While standards were being developed as to what a product had to satisfy to be called UNIX, AT&T took it upon themselves to rework mainly the BSD product, and ultimately unify their own System V 3.2, BSD, SunOS and XENIX flavors into its last release—*System V Release 4* (SVR4). Shortly thereafter, AT&T sold its UNIX business to Novell, who later turned over the UNIX trademark to a standards body called X/OPEN, now merged with The Open Group.

Table 2.1 The UNIX Flavors

Product	*Company*	*Remarks*
Xenix	Microsoft Corporation	Now discontinued
FreeBSD, NetBSD and OpenBSD	Berkeley Software Design	Commercial venture started by some of the people who created BSD UNIX
Solaris	Sun Microsystems	Has a version that runs on PC
AIX	IBM	
HP-UX	Hewlett-Packard	
Digital UNIX	Digital Equipment Corporation	
Tru64 UNIX	Digital Equipment Corporation	
IRIX	Silicon Graphics	
SCO Open Server	Santa Cruz Operation	Now discontinued; replaced by SCO UnixWare
SCO UnixWare	Santa Cruz Operation	Runs on PC (like Open Server)
Linux	Red Hat, SuSE, Caldera and many other companies	A UNIX clone that has gained enormous popularity

2.1.3 The Internet

Even before the advent of SVR4, big things were happening in the U.S. Defense Department. DARPA, a wing of this department, engaged several vendors to develop a reliable communication system using computer technology. Through some brilliant work done by Vinton Cerf and Robert Kahn, DARPA's ARPANET network was made to work using packet-switching technology. In this scenario, data is split into packets, which can take different routes and yet be reassembled in the right order. That was the birth of *TCP/IP*—a set of protocols (rules) used by the Internet for communication.

DARPA commissioned UCB to implement TCP/IP on BSD UNIX. ARPANET converted to TCP/IP in 1983, and in the same year, Berkeley released the first version of UNIX which had TCP/IP built-in. The computer science research community were all using BSD UNIX, and the network expanded like wild fire. The incorporation of TCP/IP into UNIX and its use as the basis of development were two key factors in the rapid growth of the Internet (and UNIX).

2.1.4 The Windows Threat

In the meantime, however, Microsoft was making it big with Windows—a *graphical user interface* (GUI) that uses the mouse rather than arcane and complex command options to execute a job. Options could be selected from drop-down menu boxes and radio buttons, which made handling some of the basic operating system functions easier. Windows first swept the desktop market (with Windows 3.1/95/98) and then made significant inroads into the server market (with Windows NT/ 2000) which had for long been dominated by UNIX.

When UNIX badly needed a Windows-type interface for its survival, the Massachusetts Institute of Technology (MIT) introduced *X Window*—the first windowing system for UNIX. X Window has many of the important features of Microsoft Windows plus a lot more. Every flavor of UNIX now has X along with a host of other tools that can not only handle files and directories but also update the system's configuration files.

All said and done, the power of UNIX is derived from all the commands and their multiple options that one has to remember or look up. No graphical tool can ever replace the **find** command that looks for files having all sorts of attributes using elaborate matching schemes.

2.2 POSIX AND THE SINGLE UNIX SPECIFICATION

Dennis Ritchie's decision to rewrite UNIX in C didn't quite make UNIX very portable. UNIX fragmentation adversely affected the development of applications that could be moved freely across different UNIX systems. Initially, this could also be attributed to the absence of a single conforming standard, but until recently, UNIX standards were nearly as numerous as its variants.

In the early days, AT&T published a document called the *System V Interface Definition* (SVID). X/Open (now The Open Group), a consortium of vendors and users, had one too in the *X/Open Portability Guide* (XPG). In the U.S., yet another set of standards (and one that is cited most), named the *Portable Operating System Interface for Computer Environments* (POSIX), were developed at the behest of the Institution of Electrical and Electronics Engineers (IEEE).

The POSIX standard refers to a group of related standards for operating systems in general, but was based on UNIX because UNIX was supposedly free from bias on account of its vendor-neutrality. Two of the most-cited standards from the POSIX family are known as *POSIX.1* and *POSIX.2*. POSIX.1 specifies the C application program interface—the system calls (considered in Part II of this book). POSIX.2 deals with the shell and utilities. POSIX had a lot in common with XPG, but there were differences as well.

In 1998, X/Open and IEEE undertook an ambitious program of unifying the two standards. In 2001, this joint initiative resulted in what people had been waiting for in all these years—a single specification that could be published by both standards bodies. This is the *Single UNIX Specification, Version 3*, (SUSV3) that is also known as *IEEE 1003.1:2001* (POSIX.1). That was a glorious event in the history of UNIX, but the final moment of triumph arrived in 2002, when the International Organisation of Standardisation (ISO) approved SUSV3 and IEEE 1003.1:2001 as an International Standard. The ISO standard is known as *ISO/IEC 9945:2002*.

Most UNIX vendors actively cooperate with The Open Group and also build products based on the UNIX standard. The "write once, adopt everywhere" approach to the development of specifications means that once software has been developed on any POSIX-compliant UNIX system, it can be easily ported to another POSIX-compliant UNIX machine with minimum modifications. We make references to POSIX throughout this text, but these references should be interpreted to mean the SUSV3 as well.

> **Tip** The Single UNIX Specification, Version 3 is available at *http://www.unix.org/version3/pr.html*. You must frequently consult this document when you use a command, an option or a system call to confirm whether the usage is mandated by the specification.

2.3 LINUX AND GNU

Although UNIX finally turned commercial, Richard Stallman and Linus Torvalds had different ideas. Torvalds is the father of Linux, the free UNIX that has swept the computer world by storm. Stallman runs the Free Software Foundation (formerly known as GNU—a recursive acronym that stands for "GNU's Not Unix"!). Many of the important Linux tools were written and supplied free by GNU.

Linux is distributed under the GNU General Public License which makes it mandatory for developers and sellers to make the source code public. Linux is particularly strong in networking and Internet features, and is an extremely cost-effective solution in setting up an Internet server or a local internet. Today, development on Linux is carried out at several locations across the globe at the behest of the Free Software Foundation.

The most popular GNU/Linux flavors include Red Hat, Caldera, SuSE, Debian and Mandrake. These distributions, which are shipped on multiple CD-ROMs, include a plethora of software—from C and C++ compilers to Java, interpreters like **perl**, **python** and **tcl**, browsers like Netscape, Internet servers, and multimedia software. Much of the software can also be downloaded free from the Internet. All the major computer vendors (barring Microsoft) have committed to support Linux, and many of them have ported their software to this platform. This book also discusses Linux.

2.4 THE UNIX ARCHITECTURE

The entire UNIX system is supported by a handful of essentially simple, though somewhat abstract concepts. The success of UNIX, according to Thompson and Ritchie, "lies not so much in new inventions but rather in the full exploitation of a carefully selected set of fertile ideas, and especially in showing that they can be keys to the implementation of a small and yet powerful operating system." UNIX is no longer a small system, but it certainly is a powerful one. Before we examine the features of UNIX, we need to understand its software architecture—its foundation.

2.4.1 Division of Labor: Kernel and Shell

Foremost among these "fertile ideas" is the division of labor between two agencies—the *kernel* and the *shell*. The kernel interacts with the machine's hardware, and the shell with the user. You have seen both of them in action in the hands-on session though the kernel wasn't mentioned by name. Their relationship is depicted in Fig. 2.1.

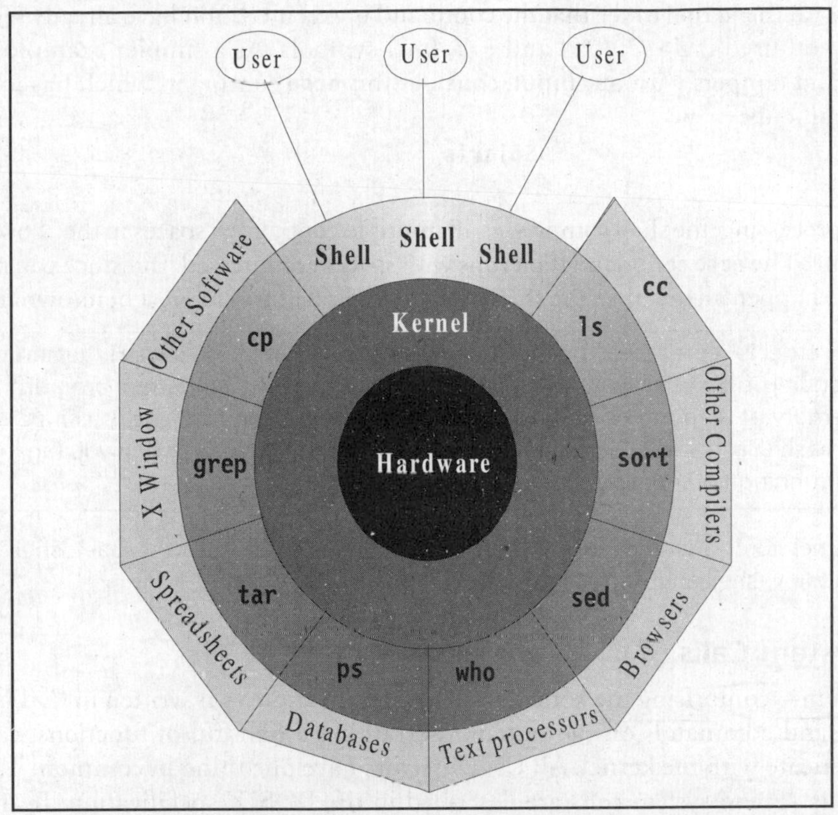

Fig. 2.1 Kernel-Shell-User Relationship

The kernel is the core of the operating system—a collection of routines mostly written in C. These routines communicate with the hardware directly. It is that part of the UNIX system that is loaded into memory when the system is booted. User programs (the applications) that need to communicate with the hardware (like the hard disk or the terminal) use the services of the kernel, which performs the job on the user's behalf. These programs access the kernel through a set of functions called *system calls*, which are taken up shortly.

Apart from providing support to user programs, the kernel has a great deal of housekeeping to do. It manages the system's memory, schedules processes, decides their priorities, and performs other tasks which you wouldn't like to bother about. The kernel has to do a lot of this work even if no user program is running. It is often called *the* operating system—a program's gateway to the computer's resources.

Computers don't have any inherent capability of translating commands into action. That requires an interpreter, and that job in UNIX is handled by the "outer part" of the operating system—the *shell*. It is actually the interface between the user and the kernel. Even though there's only one kernel running on the system, there could be several shells in action—one for each user who is logged in.

When you enter a command through the keyboard, the shell thoroughly examines the keyboard input for special characters. If it finds any, it rebuilds a simplified command line, and finally communicates with the kernel to see that the command is executed. You have already seen the shell in action when you used the > *(1.4.10)* and | *(1.4.12)* symbols. As a simpler example of how the shell examines and tampers with our input, consider this **echo** command which has lots of spaces between the arguments:

```
$ echo Sun                              Solaris
Sun Solaris
```

In the course of processing, the shell compresses all multiple contiguous spaces in the above command line to a single one. The **echo** command then runs with spaces compressed. But since you may not like this tampering to happen all the time, the shell itself provides features to prevent its own interference.

> **Note** The kernel is represented by the file **/stand/unix**, **/unix** or **/kernel/genunix** (Solaris), depending on the system you are using. The system's bootstrap program loads the kernel into memory at startup. The shell is represented by **sh** (Bourne shell), **csh** (C shell), **ksh** (Korn shell) or **bash** (Bash shell). One of these shells will run to serve you when you log in. To know the one that is running for you, use the command **echo $SHELL**.

> **LINUX:** The kernel is represented by the file **/boot/vmlinuz**. Linux uses the Bash shell by default, though it offers the C shell and Korn shell as well.

2.4.2 The System Calls

The UNIX system—comprising the kernel, shell and applications—is written in C. Though there are over a thousand commands on the system, they all use a handful of functions, called *system calls*, to communicate with the kernel. All UNIX flavors have one thing in common: They use the same system calls. These system calls are described in the POSIX specification. If an operating system used different system calls, then it wouldn't be UNIX.

A typical UNIX command writes a file with the **write** system call without going into the innards that actually achieve the write operation. Often the same system call can access both a file and a device; the **open** system call opens both. These system calls are built into the kernel, and interaction through them represents an efficient means of communication with the system. This also means that once software has been developed on one UNIX system, it can be easily ported to another UNIX machine.

C programmers on a Windows system use the *standard library functions* for everything. You can't use the **write** system call on a Windows system, you'll need to use a library function like **fprintf** for the purpose. In contrast, the C programmer in the UNIX environment has complete access to the entire system call library as well as the standard library functions. Chapters 25 and 26 deal with the basic system calls that you need to know to program in the UNIX environment.

2.5 FEATURES OF UNIX

UNIX is an operating system, so it has all the features an operating system is expected to have. However, UNIX also looks at a few things differently and possesses features unique to itself. Its text manipulation and pattern matching facilities are unmatched by any other system. The following sections present the major features of this operating system.

2.5.1 The File and Process

Two simple entities support the UNIX system—the *file* and *process*—and Kaare Christian (*The UNIX Operating System*, John Wiley) detects two powerful illusions in them: "Files have places and processes have life." You can consider a file as being situated in space, so you should be able to locate it with reference to a predetermined place. A file is also related to another by being part of a single hierarchical structure. Moreover, you too can be "placed" at a specific location in this hierarchy (the file system), and you can also "move" from one place to another. This real-life model makes the UNIX file system easily comprehensible.

UNIX doesn't really care to know the type of file you are using. It considers even directories and devices as members of the file system. A file to UNIX is just an array of bytes and can contain virtually anything—text, object code or a directory structure. The dominant file type is text, and the behavior of the system is mainly controlled by text files. UNIX provides a vast array of text manipulation tools that can edit these files without using an editor. The file system, its attributes and the text manipulation tools are discussed in several chapters.

The second entity is the process, which is the name given to a file when it is executed as a program. You could say that a process is simply the "time image" of an executable file. We treat processes as living organisms which have parents, children and grandchildren, and are born, even reborn and die. Like files, processes also belong to a separate hierarchical tree structure. UNIX provides the tools that allow us to control processes, move them between foreground and background, and even kill them. The basics of the process management system are discussed in Chapter 10.

2.5.2 UNIX: A Multiuser System

From a fundamental point of view, UNIX is a *multiprogramming* system. It permits multiple programs to run and compete for the attention of the CPU. This can happen in two ways: Multiple users can run separate jobs that share the system's CPU and resources, but a single user can also run multiple jobs. In fact, you'll see several processes constantly running on a UNIX system.

The feature of multiple users working on a single system often baffles Windows users. Windows is essentially a single-user system where the CPU, memory and hard disk are all dedicated to a single user. In UNIX, the resources are actually shared between all users; UNIX is also a *multiuser system*. Multiuser technology is the great socializer that has time for everyone.

For creating the illusory effect, the computer breaks up a unit of time into several segments, and each user is allotted a segment. So at any point in time, the machine will be doing the job of a single user. The moment the allocated time expires, the previous job is kept in abeyance and the next user's job is taken up. This process goes on till the clock has turned full-circle and the first user's job is taken up once again. This the kernel does several times in one second and keeps all ignorant and happy.

2.5.3 UNIX: A Multitasking System Too

A single user can also run multiple tasks concurrently; UNIX is a *multitasking* system. It is usual for a user to edit a file, print another one on the printer, send email to a friend and browse the World Wide Web—all without leaving any of the applications. The kernel is designed to handle a user's multiple needs.

In a multitasking environment, a user sees one job running in the *foreground*; the rest run in the *background*. You can switch jobs between background and foreground, suspend, or even terminate them. Programmers can use this feature in a very productive way. You can edit a C program, then suspend it to run the compiler; you don't have to quit the editor to do that. This feature is provided by most shells (except the original Bourne shell).

Note Today, we have machines with multiple CPUs that make it possible to actually earmark an entire processor for a single program (in a single-user and single-tasking situation).

2.5.4 The Building-block Approach

The designers never attempted to pack too many features into a few tools. Instead, they felt "small is beautiful," and developed a few hundred commands each of which performed one simple job only. You have already seen *(1.4.12)* how two commands (**ls** and **wc**) were used with the | (pipe) to count the number of files in your directory. No separate command was designed to perform the job. The commands that can be connected in this way are called *filters* because they filter or manipulate the data in different ways.

It's through pipes and filters that UNIX implements the small-is-beautiful philosophy. Today, many UNIX tools are designed with the requirement that the output of one tool be used as input to another. That's why the architects of UNIX had to make sure that commands didn't throw out excessive verbiage and clutter the output—one reason why UNIX programs are not interactive. If the output of the **ls** command contained column headers, or if it prompted the user for specific information, this output couldn't have been used as useful input to the **wc** command.

By interconnecting a number of tools, you can have an large number of combinations of their usage. That's why it's better to have a command handling a specialized function rather than one that tries to solve all problems itself. *Though UNIX started with this concept, it was somewhat forgotten when tools were added to the system later*.

2.5.5 The UNIX Toolkit

By one definition, UNIX represents the kernel, but the kernel by itself can't do anything that can benefit the user. To properly exploit the power of UNIX, you need to use the host of applications that are shipped with every UNIX system. These applications are quite diverse in scope; there are general-purpose tools, text manipulation utilities (called filters), compilers and interpreters, networked applications and system administration tools. You'll also have a choice of shells.

This is one area that's constantly changing with every UNIX release. New tools are being added and the older ones are being removed or modified. The shell and utilities form part of the POSIX specification. There are open-source versions for most of these utilities, which you should be able to download and configure to run on your machine.

2.5.6 Pattern Matching

UNIX features very sophisticated pattern matching features. You listed the chapters of the text *(1.4.19)* by using the **ls** command with an unusual argument (chap*) instead of specifying all the filenames explicitly. The * is a special character used by the system to indicate that it can match a number of filenames. If you choose your filenames carefully, you can use a simple expression to access a whole lot of them.

The * (known as a *metacharacter*) isn't the only special character used by the UNIX system; there are several others. UNIX features elaborate pattern matching schemes that use several characters from this metacharacter set. The matching isn't confined to filenames only. Some of the most advanced and useful tools also use a special expression called a *regular expression* that is framed with characters from this set. This book heavily emphasizes the importance of regular expressions, and shows how you can perform complex pattern matching tasks using them.

2.5.7 Programming Facility

The UNIX shell is also a programming language; it was designed for a programmer, not a casual end user. It has all the necessary ingredients, like control structures, loops and variables, that establish it as a powerful programming language in its own right. These features are used to design *shell scripts*—programs that also include UNIX commands in their syntax.

Many of the system's functions can be controlled and automated by using these shell scripts. If you intend taking up system administration as a career, then you'll have to know the shell's programming features very well. Proficient UNIX programmers seldom take recourse to any other language (except **perl**) for text manipulation problems. Shell programming is taken up in Chapters 16 and 24.

2.5.8 Documentation

UNIX documentation is no longer the sore point it once was. Even though it's sometimes uneven, at most times the treatment is quite lucid. The principal on-line help facility available is the **man** command, which remains the most important reference for commands and their configuration files. Thanks to O'Reilly & Associates, one can safely say that there's no feature of UNIX on which a separate textbook is not available. UNIX documentation and the man facility are discussed in Chapter 3.

Apart from the on-line documentation, there's a vast ocean of UNIX resources available on the Internet. There are several *newsgroups* on UNIX where you can fire your queries in case you are stranded with a problem—be it a problem related to shell programming or a network configuration issue. The *FAQ* (Frequently Asked Questions)—a document that addresses common problems—is also widely available on the Net. Then there are numerous articles published in magazines and journals and lecture notes made available by the universities on their Web sites. UNIX is easily tamed today.

2.6 CONCLUSION

With the goal of building a comfortable relationship with the machine, Thomson and Ritchie designed a system for their own use rather than for others. They could afford to do this because UNIX wasn't initially developed as a commercial product, and the project didn't have any predefined objective. They acknowledge this fact too: "We have not been faced with the need to satisfy someone else's requirements, and for this freedom we are grateful."

UNIX is a command-based system, and you have used a number of them already in the hands-on session. These commands have varied usage and often have a large number of options and arguments. Before we take up each UNIX subsystem along with its associated commands, you need to know more about the general characteristics of commands and the documentation associated with them. The next chapter addresses this issue.

WRAP UP

UNIX was developed at AT&T Bell Laboratories by Ken Thompson and Dennis Ritchie with the intention of creating a portable operating system. It was finally written in C, and now runs on all machines from handhelds to supercomputers.

Significant work was also done at the University of California, Berkeley (UCB) in their BSD distributions. UCB is responsible for the C shell, a better file system, the vi editor and the TCP/IP suite of networking utilities.

All UNIX flavors today offer a graphical user interface (GUI) in the X Window system. But the strength of UNIX lies in its commands and options.

AT&T introduced System V Release 4 (SVR4) to merge their own version, the Berkeley and other variants. Vendors like Sun, IBM and HP also made enhancements to UNIX, which also led to its fragmentation. UNIX now is a trademark of The Open Group. Two merged standards, *POSIX* and the *Single UNIX Specification*, are today used as guidance for development work on UNIX.

Linux today is a very popular UNIX flavor—the free UNIX that is constantly growing with contributions from the Free Software Foundation (formerly, GNU). Linux has a vast collection of tools and is rich in Internet-related features.

All work is shared by the *kernel*, which addresses the hardware directly, and the *shell*, which interacts with the user. The shell processes the entered command, scans it for special characters and rebuilds it in a form that the kernel can understand. The shell and applications communicate with the kernel using *system calls*, which are special routines built into the kernel.

The *file* and *process* are the two basic entities that support the UNIX system. UNIX considers everything as a file and has special tools to manipulate text files. A process represents a program (a file) in execution, and is similar to a file in many ways.

Several users can use the system together (multiuser), and a single user can also run multiple jobs concurrently (multitask).

UNIX uses a building-block approach in the design of some of its tools. Some UNIX commands are designed to perform simple jobs. UNIX lets you develop complex command routines by connecting these tools. UNIX offers a vast arsenal of applications and features extensive pattern-matching facilities.

On-line help is available in the **man** command. Other documentation is available on the Internet in newsgroups, FAQs, articles and university lecture notes.

TEST YOUR UNDERSTANDING

2.1 Why is UNIX more portable than other operating systems?

2.2 Who owns the UNIX trademark today? What are the two major specifications that relate to UNIX?

2.3 Name some of the contributions made by Berkeley in the development of UNIX.

2.4 Identify the companies associated with the following brands—Solaris, AIX, Tru64 UNIX.

2.5 What is the windowing system of UNIX known as?

2.6 What is the role of the Free Software Foundation in the development of Linux? Who developed the Linux kernel?

2.7 To obtain help on any feature of the system, what are the possible help sources available to you?

FLEX YOUR BRAIN

2.1 The wc command was designed to count characters, lines and words *only* in files. Explain whether the statement is true or not with a suitable example.

2.2 Describe briefly the UNIX architecture explaining the role played by the kernel and shell in sharing the workload.

2.3 What are the two schools of UNIX that initially guided its development? Mention the outcome of the standardization efforts that are currently in force today.

2.4 Explain briefly the significance of a UNIX file, and the relation it has to a process. Why do UNIX systems predominantly use text files?

2.5 What do *multiprogramming*, *multiuser* and *multitasking* mean?

2.6 Why are many UNIX commands designed to perform simple rather than complex tasks?

2.7 Why are UNIX commands noninteractive, and why is their output not usually preceded by header information?

2.8 What are *system calls*, and what role do they play in the system? How is C programming so different and powerful in the UNIX environment compared to Windows?

3

Understanding the UNIX Command

The UNIX system is command-based, i.e., you have to type in a few characters to frame a command. The terse syntax of its commands makes them initially difficult to use. This is not the case with Microsoft Windows, which is "friendlier", being primarily GUI-based *(2.1.4)*. You command a Windows machine by clicking on an icon, responding to an alert, or selecting a check box. You don't have to know the command Windows internally executes when you click on a button. If you use UNIX that way, then you would be shielding yourself from knowledge of the sheer power of the operating system, the file system and the tools. *Sometimes, it's just impossible to get a job done that way.*

Generally, Windows programs are interactive; UNIX commands are not. To exploit the power for which UNIX is well-known, you must know the syntax of these commands. The command you key in could be long enough to wrap around the next line of your terminal. The non-interactive feature of UNIX commands allows you to place the entire command sequence in a file. Next time you need to run the command, simply execute the file containing the command sequence. Windows, by contrast, requires your constant attention; you have to be always there waiting to answer a question, even though it may be the same answer every time.

WHAT YOU WILL LEARN

- How the shell uses the `PATH` variable to locate commands.
- The difference between *external* and *internal* commands.
- The breakup of a command into its *arguments* and *options*.
- How multiple commands can be executed without waiting for the return of the shell prompt.
- The use of the **`man`** command to look up the documentation of a command.
- Obtain contextual information on any topic using the **`apropos`** and **`whatis`** commands.

TOPICS OF SPECIAL INTEREST

- How to use the man documentation in an effective way and interpret the symbols used.
- The use of keyboard sequences to restore normal operation when commands don't work properly.

3.1 LOCATING COMMANDS

The system was designed to ensure that the minimum number of keystrokes achieve the maximum amount of work. That's why UNIX commands are seldom more than four characters long. All UNIX commands are single words like **ls**, **cat**, **who** etc. These names are all in lowercase, and you must start shedding your old DOS habits of being indifferent to case. For instance, if you enter **LS** instead of **ls**, this is how the system will respond:

```
$ LS
bash: LS: command not found
```

This message is from the shell (here, the Bash shell). There's obviously no command named **LS** on the UNIX system. This seems to suggest that there's a "predetermined" list of such commands that the shell first searches before it flashes the message above. These commands are essentially *files* (We'll take up files in Chapter 5.) containing programs, mainly written in C. These files are stored in certain *directories*. For instance, the **ls** command is a file (or program) to be found in the directory /bin.

The easiest way of knowing the location of an executable program is to use the **type** command:

```
$ type ls                                    Won't work in the C shell
ls is /bin/ls
```

When you execute the **ls** command, the shell locates this file in the /bin directory and makes arrangements to execute it. **type** looks up only the directories specified in the PATH variable (discussed next).

3.1.1 The PATH

The sequence of directories that the shell searches to look for a command is specified in its own PATH variable. If you evaluate the value of this variable, you'll find a directory list separated by colons:

```
$ echo $PATH
/bin:/usr/bin:/usr/local/bin:/usr/ccs/bin:/usr/local/java/bin:.
```

There are six directories in this colon-separated list, and when you issue a command, the shell searches this list *in the sequence specified* to locate and execute it. Note that this list also includes the current directory indicated by a singular dot at the end.

> **Note** The essential UNIX commands for general use are located in the directories /bin and /usr/bin. In Solaris, they are all in /usr/bin.

3.2 INTERNAL AND EXTERNAL COMMANDS

Since **ls** is a program or file having an independent existence in the /bin directory (or /usr/bin), it is branded as an *external command*. Most commands are external in nature, but there are some which are not really found anywhere, and some which are normally not executed even if they are in one of the directories specified by PATH. Take for instance the **echo** command:

```
$ type echo
echo is a shell builtin
```

echo isn't an external command in the sense that, when you type `echo`, the shell won't look in its `PATH` to locate it (even if it is there in `/bin`). Rather, it will execute it from its own set of built-in commands that are not stored as separate files. These built-in commands, of which **echo** is a member, are known as *internal commands*.

You must have noted that it's the shell that actually does all this work. This program starts running for you when you log in, and dies when you log out. The shell is an external command with a difference; it possesses its own set of internal commands. So if a command exists both as an internal command of the shell as well as an external one (in `/bin` or `/usr/bin`), the shell will accord top priority to its own internal command of the same name.

This is exactly the case with **echo**, which is also found in `/bin`, but rarely ever executed because the shell builtin almost always makes sure that the internal **echo** command takes precedence over the external. We'll take up the shell in great detail later.

3.3 COMMAND STRUCTURE

You have already entered commands that appeared to have multiple words (like **`tput clear`** and **`cat list`**). The first word (viz., `tput` and `cat`) is actually the command; the additional words are called *arguments*. That is to say, `clear` is an argument of the **tput** command. Because a command often accepts several types of arguments, it can be made to behave in numerous ways.

Commands and arguments have to be separated by spaces or tabs to enable the system to interpret them as *words*. You can use any number of them to separate the words that form a command. A contiguous string of spaces and tabs together form what is known as *whitespace*. Where the system permits the use of one whitespace character to separate words, it generally permits several, as in this command:

```
cat                README
```

The shell possesses a special mechanism of compressing these multiple consecutive spaces or tabs into a single space. You have already seen this happen in the previous chapter *(2.4.1)*.

UNIX arguments range from the simple to the complex. They consist of options, expressions, instructions, filenames, etc. The vast majority of commands have simple arguments, but some like **dd** and **find** can make you feel uneasy for a while. You'll have a taste of all these types as you proceed.

> **Note** Whitespace refers to a contiguous set of spaces, tabs and newline characters. The tab character is generated by hitting the *[Tab]* key on your keyboard, or using [*Ctrl-i*] in case *[Tab]* doesn't work. The newline character is generated by hitting the *[Enter]* key.

3.3.1 Options

There's a special type of argument that's mostly used with a - sign. For instance, when you use

```
ls -l note
```

`-l` is an argument to **ls** by definition, but more importantly, it's a special argument known as an *option*. An option is normally preceded by a minus sign (-) to distinguish it from filenames.

There must not be any whitespace between - and l. If you inadvertently provide that, many commands could land you in a great deal of trouble!

Options are also arguments, but given a special name because their list is predetermined. When we use **echo hello dolly**, hello and dolly are also arguments, but they are not predetermined. In fact, you can use millions of words legitimately with **echo** and they'll still remain arguments and not options.

LINUX: While most UNIX options use a single - as the option prefix (e.g. -l), Linux also offers options that use two hyphens and a multicharacter word. For instance, it offers the synonym **ls --all** in addition to **ls -a**. Though it means more typing load for the user, the words are quite meaningful and easy to remember; it's easier to remember --all than -a.

If you use a command with a wrong option, the shell locates the command all right, but the *command* this time finds the option to be wrong:

```
$ ls -z note
ls: illegal option -- z                    Message from ls, not shell
usage: ls -1RaAdCxmnlogrtucpFbqisfL [files]
```

The above message has been generated by the command, and not by the shell. **ls** does have a large number of options (over 20), but it seems that -z is not one of them. Many commands provide the right syntax and options to use when you use them wrongly.

Some commands have a large number of options. You don't need to know most of them—at least for now. What you need to keep in mind is something that beginners often forget—the necessity of providing spaces between the command and the argument. If you have used **DIR/P** instead of **DIR /P** in DOS, don't expect UNIX to be equally accommodating:

```
$ ls-l
bash: ls-l: command not found
```

Options can normally be combined with only one - sign, i.e., instead of using

```
ls -l -a -t
```

you might as well use

```
ls -lat                                    Same as ls -l -a -t
```

to obtain the same output. This facility reduces your typing load, which becomes significant when you use commands with several options. The shell *parses* (breaks up) the option combination into separate options.

Because UNIX was developed by people who had their own ideas as to what options should look like, there will invariably be exceptions to whatever rules we try to formulate. Some commands won't let you combine options in the way you did just now. There are some that use + as an option prefix instead of a -. Some even use the =! Let this not deter you; you would have already built up a lot of muscle before you take on these commands.

3.3.2 Filename Arguments

Many UNIX commands use a filename as argument so the command can take input from the file. If a command uses a filename as argument at all, it will generally be its last argument—and after all options. It's also quite common to see many commands working with multiple filenames as arguments:

```
ls -lat chap01 chap02 chap03
cp chap01 chap02 progs                              cp copies files
rm chap01 chap02                                    rm removes files
```

The command with its arguments and options is known as the *command line.* This line can be considered complete only after the user has hit *[Enter]*. The complete line is then fed to the shell as its input for interpretation and execution.

3.3.3 Exceptions

There are, of course, exceptions to the general syntax of commands that has been mentioned above. There are few commands (**pwd**) that don't accept any arguments, and some (**who**) that may or may not be specified with arguments. The **ls** command can also be executed without any arguments (**ls**), by using only options (**ls -l**), with only filenames (**ls chap01 chap02**), or using a combination of both (**ls -la chap01 chap02**). The word *option* turns out to be a misnomer in some instances; some commands compulsorily have to use one (**cut**).

There are some characters in the command line that are not really treated as arguments—the |, > and <, for instance. In Chapter 9, you'll see how some of them can even be placed before a command. Later on, you'll find that the arguments can take the form of an expression (in **grep**), a set of instructions (in **sed**), or a program (in **awk** and **perl**). It's simply not possible to specify a generalized syntax for a command, the syntax pertaining to a specific command is best taken from the UNIX manual. The syntax for some commands have been explicitly specified in this book.

3.4 FLEXIBILITY OF COMMAND USAGE

The UNIX system provides a certain degree of flexibility in the usage of commands. A command can often be entered in more than one way, and if you use it judiciously, you can restrict the number of keystrokes to a minimum. In this section, we'll see how permissive the shell is to command usage.

3.4.1 Combining Commands

So far, you have been executing commands separately; each command was first processed and executed before the next could be entered. Also, UNIX allows you to specify more than one command in the same command line. Each command has to be separated from the other by a ; (semicolon):

```
wc note ; ls -l note
```

When you learn to redirect the output of these commands *(9.5.2)*, you may even like to group them together within parentheses:

```
( wc note ; ls -l note ) > newlist
```

The combined output of the two commands is now sent to the file `newlist`. Whitespace is provided here only for better readability. You might reduce a few keystrokes like this:

```
(wc note;ls -l note)>newlist
```

When a command line contains a semicolon, the shell understands that the command on each side of it needs to be processed separately. The ; here is known as a *metacharacter*, and you'll come across several metacharacters that have special meaning to the shell.

3.4.2 A Command Line Can Overflow or Be Split into Multiple Lines

A command is normally entered in a line by typing from the keyboard. Though the terminal width is restricted to 80 characters, that doesn't prevent you from entering a command, or a sequence of them, in one line even though the total width may exceed 80 characters. The command simply overflows to the next line though it is still in a single *logical* line.

Some commands have a lengthy syntax, and you may often find it desirable, and sometimes compulsory, to split the command line into multiple lines. In that case, the shell will issue a *secondary* prompt, usually >, to indicate to you that the command line isn't complete. This is easily shown with the **echo** command:

```
$ echo "This is
> a three-line                    A second prompt (>) appears
> text message"
This is
a three-line
text message
```

> **Tip** Whenever you find the > appearing after you have pressed *[Enter]*, it will generally be due to the absence of a matching quote or parenthesis. In case you find that the problem persists even after providing it, just kill the command line with either *[Ctrl-c]* or *[Ctrl-u]*.

3.4.3 Entering a Command Before Previous Command has Finished

UNIX provides a full-duplex terminal which lets you type a command at any time, and feel satisfied that the system will interpret it. When you run a long program, the prompt won't appear till program execution is complete. Subsequent commands can be entered at the keyboard (as many commands as you wish) without waiting for the prompt; they may not be even displayed on your screen!

The reason why that happens is this: the command that you key in isn't seen by the shell as its input when it is busy running another program. The input remains stored in a *buffer* (a temporary storage in memory) that's maintained by the kernel for all keyboard input. The command is passed on to the shell for interpretation after the previous program has completed its run. If you type correctly, simply don't bother even if the output from the previous program garbles the display!

3.5 man: BROWSING THE MANUAL PAGES ON-LINE

All said and done, the syntax of some UNIX commands can still be confusing—even to the expert. You may not remember either the command or the required option that will perform a specific job. This is quite understandable considering that there are several hundred commands in `/bin` and `/usr/bin` on any UNIX system (around 600 in Solaris).

UNIX offers an on-line help facility in the **man** command. **man** displays the documentation—often called the *man documentation*— of practically every command on the system. For example, to seek help on the **wc** command, simply run **man** with `wc` as argument:

```
man wc                                        Help on the wc command
```

The entire man page for **wc** is dumped on the screen (Fig. 3.1). **man** presents the first page and pauses. It does this by sending its output to a *pager* program, which displays the contents of a file one page (screen) at a time. The pager is actually a UNIX command, and **man** is always preconfigured to be used with a specific pager. UNIX systems currently use these pager programs:

- **more**, Berkeley's pager, that's now available universally as a superior alternative to the original AT&T **pg** command (now obsolete). We'll be considering **more** in this text.
- **less**, the standard pager used on Linux systems, but also available for all UNIX platforms. **less** is modeled on the **vi** editor and is more powerful than **more** because it replicates many of **vi**'s navigational and search functions. The features of **less** are described briefly in Section 6.5.

One a man page that uses **more** as the pager, you'll see a prompt at the bottom-left of the screen which looks something like this:

```
--More--(26%)                                 less shows a : as the prompt
```

At this prompt you can press a key to perform navigation or search for a string. The key you press can be considered to be one of **man**'s (rather, the pager's) *internal commands*, and the character represented by the key often doesn't show up on the screen. Many UNIX utilities like **vi** and **mail** also have their own internal commands. A set of internal commands used by **more** is listed in Table 6.1. We'll discuss only a few of them related to navigation and string search.

To quit the pager, and ultimately **man**, press **q**. You'll be returned the shell's prompt.

3.5.1 Navigation and Search

The navigation commands are numerous and often vary across UNIX implementations. For the time being, you should know these two commands which should work on all systems:

f or spacebar, which advances the display by one screen of text at a time.
b, which moves back one screen.

The man documentation is sometimes quite extensive, and the search facility lets you locate a page containing a keyword quite easily. For example, you can call up the page containing the word `clobber` by following the **/** (frontslash) with the term:

```
/clobber[Enter]
```

The / and search string show up on the screen this time, and when you press *[Enter]*, you are taken to the page containing `clobber`. If that's not the page you are looking for, you can repeat the search by pressing **n**. Some pager versions even highlight the search term in reverse video.

3.6 UNDERSTANDING THE man DOCUMENTATION

Vendors organize the man documentation differently, but in general you could see eight sections of the UNIX manual (Table 3.1). Later enhancements have added subsections (like 1C, 1M, 3N etc.), but we'll ignore them in this text. Occasional references to other sections can also be reflected in the SEE ALSO section of a man page. You can see from the table that the documentation is not restricted to commands; important system files used by these commands also have separate man pages.

Most of the commands discussed in this text are available in Section 1, and **man** searches the manuals starting from Section 1. If it locates a command in one section it won't continue the search even if the command also occurs in another section. When a keyword is found in multiple sections, you should use the section number additionally as an argument. Depending on the UNIX flavor you are using, you may also need to prefix the `-s` option to the section number:

```
man 4 passwd                    passwd also occurs in Section 4
man -s4 passwd                  Solaris uses the -s option
```

This displays the documentation for a configuration file named `/etc/passwd`, from Section 4. There's also an entry for **passwd** in Section 1, but if we had used **man passwd** (without the section number), **man** would have looked up Section 1 only and wouldn't have looked at Section 4 at all.

> **Note** There are two chapters in this text featuring the important system calls and some standard library functions. Sections 2 and 3 provide detailed documentation on their usage. To look up the **read** system call, you'll have to use **man 2 read** or **man -s2 read**.

3.6.1 Understanding a man Page

A man page is divided into a number of compulsory and optional sections. Every command doesn't have all sections but the first three (NAME, SYNOPSIS and DESCRIPTION) are generally seen in all man pages. NAME presents a one-line introduction to the command. SYNOPSIS shows the syntax used by the command, and DESCRIPTION (often the largest section) provides a detailed description.

The SYNOPSIS Section is the one that we need to examine closely, and we'll do that with reference to the man page of the **wc** command shown in Fig. 3.1. Here you'll find the syntax—the options and arguments used with the command. The SYNOPSIS follows certain conventions and rules which every user must understand:

- If a command argument is enclosed in rectangular brackets, then it is optional; otherwise, the argument is required. The **wc** man page shows all its arguments enclosed in three such groups. This means that **wc** can be used without arguments.
- The ellipsis (a set of three dots) implies that there can be more instances of the preceding word. The expression [`file ...`] signifies that **wc** can be used with more than one filename as argument.

```
User Commands                                                    wc(1)

NAME
     wc - display a count of lines, words and characters in a file

SYNOPSIS
     wc [ -c | -m | -C ]  [ -lw ]  [ file ... ]

DESCRIPTION
     The wc utility  reads  one   or  more  input  files and,  by
     default,  writes the number of newline characters, words and
     bytes contained in  each input file to the standard output.

     The utility also writes a total count for all named  files,
     if more than one input file is specified.

     wc considers a word to be a non-zero-length string  of  char-
     acters  delimited by white space (for example, SPACE, TAB ).
     See iswspace(3C) or isspace(3C).

OPTIONS
     The following options are supported:
     -c        Count bytes.
     -m        Count characters.
     -C        Same as -m.
     -l        Count lines.
     -w        Count words delimited by white space characters or new
               line  characters.  Delimiting  characters are Extended
               Unix Code (EUC) characters from any code  set  defined
               by iswspace().

     If  no option is specified the default is -lwc (count  lines,
     words, and  bytes.)

OPERANDS
     The following operand is supported:
     file  A path name of an input file. If no file operands  are
           specified, the standard input will be used.
USAGE
     See largefile(5) for the description of the behavior of wc when
     encountering files greater than or equal to 2 Gbyte (2 **31 bytes).

EXIT STATUS
     The following exit values are returned:
     0      Successful completion.
     >0     An error occurred.

SEE ALSO
     cksum(1),      isspace(3C),      iswalpha(3C),      iswspace(3C),
     setlocale(3C), attributes(5), environ(5), largefile(5)
```

Fig. 3.1 man page for **wc** (Solaris)

- If you find a | character in any of these areas, it means that only one of the options shown on either side of the pipe can be used. Here, only one of the options, `-c`, `-m` and `-C`, can be used.

All options used by the command are listed in the OPTIONS section. Often, difficult options are supported by suitable examples. There's a separate section named EXIT STATUS which lists possible error conditions and their numeric representation. You need to understand the significance of these numbers when writing shell scripts in order to determine the actual cause of termination of a command.

3.6.2 Using `man` to Understand `man`

Since **`man`** is also a UNIX command like **`ls`** or **`cat`**, you'll probably first like to know how **`man`** itself is used. Use the same command to view its own documentation:

```
man man                                   Viewing man pages with man
```

From this man page you'll know that you can choose your pager too. The variable, `PAGER`, controls the pager **`man`** uses, and if you set it to `less`, then **`man`** will use **`less`** as its pager. This is how you set `PAGER` at the command prompt before you invoke **`man`**:

```
PAGER=less ; export PAGER                 Set this shell variable and export it
man wc                                    and then run man
```

To evaluate the value of `PAGER`, use the command **`echo $PAGER`**. This setting is valid only for the current session. In later chapters, you'll understand the significance of the **`export`** statement and also learn to make this setting permanent so that its assigned value remains valid for all sessions.

Note On some systems, **`echo $PAGER`** may not show you any value at all, in which case **`man`** is using a default pager. Some systems set this variable in the file `/etc/default/man` instead.

Table 3.1 Organization of the man Documentation

Section	*Subject (SVR4)*	*Subject (Linux)*
1	User programs	User programs
2	Kernel's system calls	Kernel's system calls
3	Library functions	Library functions
4	Administrative file formats	Special files (in `/dev`)
5	Miscellaneous	Administrative file formats
6	Games	Games
7	Special files (in `/dev`)	Macro packages and conventions
8	Administration commands	Administration commands

3.7 FURTHER HELP WITH `man -k`, `apropos` AND `whatis`

The POSIX specification requires **`man`** to support only one option (`-k`). Most UNIX systems also offer the **`apropos`** command that emulates **`man -k`**. When used with this option, **`man`** searches a summary database and prints a one-line description of the command. To know what **`awk`** does, use **`man`** like this:

```
$ man -k awk                                          Same as apropos awk
awk             awk (1)         - pattern scanning and processing language
nawk            nawk (1)        - pattern scanning and processing language
```

man locates its argument from the NAME line of all man pages. **nawk** is a "newer" version of **awk** (has been new for a long time) that is generally found on all modern UNIX systems. Once you know that **awk** is a processing language, you can use **man awk** to obtain the detailed documentation for this command. Note that both **awk** and **nawk** are found in Section 1. There's a separate chapter in this textbook that discusses **awk**.

Wanting to know what a command does is one thing, but to find out the commands and files associated with a keyword is quite another. What is FTP? Let's use the **apropos** command this time:

```
$ apropos FTP
ftp             ftp (1)         - file transfer program
ftpd            in.ftpd (1m)    - file transfer protocol server
ftpusers        ftpusers (4)    - file listing users to be disallowed ftp login
privileges
in.ftpd         in.ftpd (1m)    - file transfer protocol server
netrc           netrc (4)       - file for ftp remote login data
```

apropos lists the commands and files associated with FTP—the protocol used to transfer files between two machines connected in a network. There are two commands here, **ftp**and **in.ftpd**, who cooperate with each other for effecting file transfer. There are also two text files, ftpusers and netrc (actually, .netrc), that are looked up by these commands for authenticating users. Don't worry if you don't understand all this now; we still have some way to go before we take on FTP.

The **whatis** command is also available on many UNIX systems. **man** uses the -f option to emulate **whatis** behavior. The command also lists one-liners for a command:

```
$ whatis cp
cp              cp (1)          - copy files
```

This is the command you have to use to copy a file (or directory).

> **Note**
>
> **Note:** If you don't have the **apropos** command on your system, you can use **man -k**. You can also use **man -f** in place of **whatis**. The commands don't actually search the man pages but a database that is built separately from man pages. It may or may not be installed on your system. **apropos** and **whatis** are not included in the POSIX specification, but **man -k** is (but not -f).

LINUX: Some commands have just too many options, and sometimes a quick lookup facility is what you need. Most Linux commands offer the --help option that displays a compact listing of all options. You can spot the **find** option you are looking for by using this:

```
$ find --help
Usage: find [path...] [expression]
default path is the current directory; default expression is -print
expression may consist of:
operators (decreasing precedence; -and is implicit where no others are given):
      ( EXPR ) ! EXPR -not EXPR EXPR1 -a EXPR2 EXPR1 -and EXPR2
```

```
     EXPR1 -o EXPR2 EXPR1 -or EXPR2 EXPR1 , EXPR2
options (always true): -daystart -depth -follow --help
     -maxdepth LEVELS -mindepth LEVELS -mount -noleaf --version -xdev
tests (N can be +N or -N or N): -amin N -anewer FILE -atime N -cmin N
     -cnewer FILE -ctime N -empty -false -fstype TYPE -gid N -group NAME
     -ilname PATTERN -iname PATTERN -inum N -ipath PATTERN -iregex PATTERN
     -links N -lname PATTERN -mmin N -mtime N -name PATTERN -newer FILE
     -nouser -nogroup -path PATTERN -perm [+-]MODE -regex PATTERN
     -size N[bckw] -true -type [bcdpfls] -uid N -used N -user NAME
     -xtype [bcdpfls]
actions: -exec COMMAND ; -fprint FILE -fprint0 FILE -fprintf FILE FORMAT
     -ok COMMAND ; -print -print0 -printf FORMAT -prune -ls
```

A Linux command invariably offers far more options than its UNIX counterpart. You'll find this lookup facility quite useful when you know the usage of the options but can't recollect the one you require.

3.8 WHEN THINGS GO WRONG

Terminals and keyboards have no uniform behavioral pattern. Terminal settings directly impact keyboard operation, and you may sometimes need to check the value of the TERM variable. We'll discuss TERM later, but as of now, you should at least be able to wriggle out of some common traps. You must know which keys to press when things don't quite work as expected.

Table 3.2 Keyboard Commands to Try When Things Go Wrong

Keystroke or Command	*Function*
[Ctrl-h]	Erases text (The *erase* character)
[Ctrl-c] or *[Delete]*	Interrupts a command (The *interrupt* character)
[Ctrl-d]	Terminates login session or a program that expects its input from the keyboard (The *eof* character)
[Ctrl-s]	Stops scrolling of screen output and locks keyboard
[Ctrl-q]	Resumes scrolling of screen output and unlocks keyboard
[Ctrl-u]	Kills command line without executing it (The *line-kill* character)
[Ctrl-\]	Kills running command but creates a core file containing the memory image of the program (The *quit* character)
[Ctrl-z]	Suspends process and returns shell prompt; use **fg** to resume job (The *suspend* character)
[Ctrl-j]	Alternative to *[Enter]*
[Ctrl-m]	As above
`stty sane`	Restores terminal to normal status (a UNIX command)

Backspacing Doesn't Work Consider that you misspelled passwd (a legitimate command) as password, and when you pressed the backspace key to erase the last three characters, you saw this:

```
$ password^H^H^H
```

Backspacing is not working here; that's why you see the symbol ^H every time you press the key. This often happens when you log on to a remote machine whose terminal settings are different from your local one. In that case you should try these two key sequences; one of them should see you through:

[Ctrl-h] or *[Delete]* *The erase character*

Killing a Line If the command line contains many mistakes, you could prefer to kill the line altogether without executing it. In that case, use

[Ctrl-u] *The line-kill character*

The line-kill character erases everything in the line and returns the cursor to the beginning of the line.

Interrupting a Command Sometimes, a program goes on running for an hour and doesn't seem to complete. You can interrupt the program and bring back the prompt by using either of the two sequences:

[Ctrl-c] or *[Delete]* *The interrupt character*

This is an important key sequence, and in this book, you'll often be advised to use the *interrupt key*. Note, however, that if *[Delete]* works as the erase character on your machine, it can't also be the interrupt character at the same time.

Terminating a Command's Input You know that the **cat** command is used with an argument representing the filename *(1.4.10)*. What happens if you omit the filename and simply press *[Enter]*?

$ **cat***[Enter]*

Nothing happens; the command simply waits for you to enter something. Even if you do some text entry, you must know how to terminate your input. For commands that expect user input, enter a *[Ctrl-d]* to bring back the prompt:

```
$ cat
[Ctrl-d]                                   The end-of-file or eof character
$ _
```

This is another important key sequence; we'll often refer to *[Ctrl-d]* as the *eof* or end-of-file character. Sometimes pressing the interrupt key also works in this situation.

The Keyboard is Locked When this happens, you won't be able to key in anything. It could probably be due to the accidental pressing of the key sequence *[Ctrl-s]*. Try using *[Ctrl-q]* to release the lock and restore normal keyboard operation. These two sequences are actually used by the system to control the flow of command output.

At times, you may consciously like to use *[Ctrl-s]* and *[Ctrl-q]*. If the display from a command is scrolling too fast for you to see on the terminal, you can halt the output temporarily by pressing *[Ctrl-s]*. To resume scrolling, press *[Ctrl-q]*. With modern hardware where the output scrolls off very fast, this facility is now practically ineffective, but it pays to know what they do because inadvertent pressing of *[Ctrl-s]* can lock your terminal.

The [Enter] Key Doesn't Work This key is used to complete the command line. If it doesn't work, you can use either *[Ctrl-j]* or *[Ctrl-m]*. These key sequences generate the linefeed and carriage return characters, respectively.

The Terminal Behaves in an Erratic Manner Your terminal settings could be disturbed; it may display everything in uppercase or simply garbage when you press the printable keys. Try using the command **stty sane** to restore sanity. Since the *[Enter]* key may not work either in these situations, use *[Ctrl-j]* or *[Ctrl-m]* to simulate *[Enter]*.

These key functions are summarized in Table 3.2. We have provided names to some of these key sequences (like eof and interrupt), but don't be surprised if you find some of them behaving differently on your system. Much of UNIX is configurable by the user, and you'll learn later to use the **stty** command to change these settings. If you have problems, seek the assistance of the system administrator.

Tip At this early stage, it may not be possible for you to remember all these key sequences. But do keep these two keys in mind: *[Ctrl-c]*, the interrupt character, used to interrupt a running program and *[Ctrl-d]*, the eof character, used to terminate a program that's expecting input from the terminal. On machines running Solaris or Linux, *[Ctrl-c]* can interrupt a command even when it is expecting input.

Also keep in mind that some UNIX programs (like **mailx** and **pine**) are interactive and have their own set of internal commands (those understood only by the program). These commands have specific key sequences for termination. You may not remember them, so try using **q**, **quit**, **exit** or *[Ctrl-d]*; one of them might just work.

3.9 CONCLUSION

This chapter should prepare you well for the forthcoming tour of UNIX. You can now expect to encounter UNIX commands used with a wide variety of options and arguments. The man documentation will be your most valuable help tool and you must develop the habit of looking it up whenever you are stranded with a problem related to command usage. Also, things will go wrong and keyboard sequences won't sometimes work as expected. So don't forget to look up Section 3.8 for remedial action when that happens.

WRAP UP

UNIX is a command-based system. The system commands used by all users are located in the directories /bin and /usr/bin. The shell variable, PATH, specifies the search list of directories for locating commands.

External commands exist on disk as separate files. An *internal command* is built into the shell, and is normally executed even if there's an external command of the same name.

A command is used with *options* and *arguments*, and many commands are used with files. An option usually begins with a - and changes the default behavior of a command. Commands and arguments must be separated by any number of spaces or tabs (*whitespace*).

More than one command can be entered in one line, and a command sequence can be split into multiple lines. You don't have to wait for the previous command to complete before you enter another one.

If you have problems with command usage, use the **man** command. You can search for a string using the / and repeat the search with **n**. Most commands are found in Section 1. However, you'll find system calls and library functions in Sections 2 and 3, and to look them up, you'll have to provide the section number as argument to **man**.

A man page is divided into several sections, and the SYNOPSIS section features the syntax using some special symbols. Anything in [ ] is optional. The ellipsis (`...`) indicates that there can be more instances of the expression preceding it. The | delimits alternatives; `-a|-b|-c` means that only one of the three options can be used.

There are various key sequences that you can use when things go wrong. They are listed in Table 3.2.

TEST YOUR UNDERSTANDING

3.1 Can you run UNIX commands in uppercase?

3.2 Why are the directories `/bin` and `/usr/bin` usually found first in the output of **`echo $PATH`**?

3.3 How is the current directory indicated in the value of PATH?

3.4 Use the **type** command with the following arguments—**cd**, **date**, **pwd** and **ls**. Which are the internal commands in the list?

3.5 What is the difference between an *argument* and an *option*?

3.6 What does the secondary prompt look like and when does it appear?

3.7 What is a pager? Name the two standard pagers used by **man**.

3.8 If the command **`ls --all`** works on your system, which flavor of UNIX could you be using?

3.9 If a command doesn't seem to complete, which key will you press to interrupt it?

FLEX YOUR BRAIN

3.1 A program file named `foo` exists in the current directory, but when we try to execute it by entering **foo**, we see the message `foo: command not found`. Explain how that can happen.

3.2 What is *whitespace*? Explain the treatment the shell metes out to a command that contains a lot of whitespace.

3.3 Explain the difference between an *external* and *internal* command. How will you determine whether a command is external or not? Name two programs that have their own internal commands.

3.4 Is **cd** an external or an internal command? How will you find that out?

3.5 Reduce the number of keystrokes to execute this command: **`tar -t -v -f /dev/fd0`**.

3.6 If a command, filename and system call have the same name and are available in Sections 1, 5 and 2 respectively, how will you display the man pages of each one of them?

3.7 Explain the significance of the various symbols used in the SYNOPSIS section of a man page.

3.8 Explain why it is possible to key in the next command before the previous command has completed execution.

3.9 Explain the significance of the interrupt and eof characters. With which keys are they associated on your system?

3.10 How do you direct **man** to use a specific pager, say, **less**?

4

General-Purpose Utilities

The best way to start acquiring knowledge of the UNIX command set is to try your hand at some of the general-purpose utilities of the system. These commands have diverse functions, but can be broadly divided into two categories. Some commands act as handy accessories that can display the system date, for instance. Others tell you the state the system is in, or even manipulate it. You should know what your machine's operating system is and be able to change the terminal settings.

Every command featured in this chapter is useful, and has not been included here for cosmetic effect. Many of them have been reused in later chapters, especially in shell programming. A few are true dark horses. You'll need these commands in all situations in your daily life at the machine. The commands are simple to use, have very few options (except for **stty**), and don't require you to know much about the files they may access.

WHAT YOU WILL LEARN

- Display the calendar of a month or a year with **cal**.
- Display the current system date and time in a variety of formats using **date**.
- Use **echo** with escape sequences to display a message on the terminal.
- Use **bc** as a calculator with a decimal, octal or hexadecimal number as base.
- Change your password with **passwd**.
- Display the list of users currently working on the system with **who**.
- Display the characteristics of your operating system with **uname**.
- Display the filename of your terminal with **tty**.
- Use **stty** to display and change your terminal's settings.

TOPICS OF SPECIAL INTEREST

- Features of the POSIX-recommended **printf** command as a portable replacement of **echo**.
- Record your login session including all your keystrokes with **script**.

4.1 cal: THE CALENDAR

You can invoke the **cal** command to see the calendar of any specific month or a complete year. The facility is totally accurate and takes into account the leap year adjustments that took place in the year 1752. Let's have a look at its syntax drawn from the Solaris man page:

```
cal [ [ month ] year ]
```

Everything within rectangular brackets is optional, so we are told *(3.6.1)*. So **cal** can be used without arguments, in which case it displays the calendar of the current month:

```
$ cal
   December 2002
 S  M Tu  W Th  F  S
 1  2  3  4  5  6  7
 8  9 10 11 12 13 14
15 16 17 18 19 20 21
22 23 24 25 26 27 28
29 30 31
```

The syntax also tells us that when **cal** is used with arguments, the month is optional but the year is not. To see the calendar for the month of March 2003, you need two arguments:

```
$ cal 03 2003
    March 2003
 S  M Tu  W Th  F  S
                   1
 2  3  4  5  6  7  8
 9 10 11 12 13 14 15
16 17 18 19 20 21 22
23 24 25 26 27 28 29
30 31
```

You can't hold the calendar of an entire year on one page of the screen; it scrolls off too rapidly before you can use *[Ctrl-s]* to make it pause. To make **cal** pause in the same way **man** pauses, use **cal** with a pager (**more** or **less**) using the | symbol to connect them. A single argument to **cal** is interpreted as the year:

```
cal 2003 | more                                    Or use less instead of more
```

The | symbol connects two commands (in a pipeline) where **more** takes input from the **cal** command. We have used the same symbol in Chapter 1 to connect the **ls** and **wc** commands *(1.4.12)*. You can now scroll forward by pressing the spacebar, or move back using **b**.

4.2 date: DISPLAYING THE SYSTEM DATE

The UNIX system maintains an internal clock meant to run perpetually. When the system is shut down, a battery backup keeps the clock ticking. This clock actually stores the number of seconds elapsed since the *Epoch*; this is January 1, 1970. A 32-bit counter stores these seconds (except on 64-bit machines), and the counter will overflow sometime in 2038.

You can display the current date with the **date** command, which shows the date and time to the nearest second:

```
$ date
Tue Dec 10 18:52:24 IST 2002                    Time zone here is IST
```

The command can also be used with suitable format specifiers as arguments. Each format is preceded by a + symbol, followed by the % operator, and a single character describing the format. For instance, you can print only the month, using the format +%m:

```
$ date +%m
12
```

or the month name:

```
$ date +%h
Dec
```

or you can combine them in one command:

```
$ date +"%h %m"
Dec 12
```

There are many other format specifiers, and the useful ones are listed below:

d— he day of the month (1 to 31).
y—The last two digits of the year.
H, M and S—The hour, minute and second, respectively.
D—The date in the format *mm/dd/yy*.
T—The time in the format *hh:mm:ss*.

When you use multiple format specifiers (as in the previous example), you must enclose them within quotes (single or double), and use a single + symbol before it.

Note You can't change the date as an ordinary user, but the system administrator uses the same command with a different syntax to set the system date! This is discussed in Chapter 17.

4.3 echo: DISPLAYING A MESSAGE

We have used the **echo** command a number of times already in this text. This command is often used in shell scripts to display diagnostic messages on the terminal, or to issue prompts for taking user input. So far, we have used it in two ways:

- To display a message (like **echo Sun Solaris**).
- To evaluate shell variables (**echo $SHELL**).

Originally, **echo** was an external command *(3.2)*, but today all shells have **echo** built-in. There are some differences in **echo**'s behavior across the shells, and most of these differences relate to the way **echo** interprets certain strings known as *escape sequences*.

An escape sequence is generally a two character-string beginning with a \ (backslash). For instance, \c is an escape sequence. When it is placed at the end of a string used as an argument to **echo**, the command interprets the sequence as a directive to place the cursor and prompt in the same line that displays the output:

```
$ echo "Enter filename: \c"
Enter filename: $ _                    Prompt and cursor in same line
```

This is how **echo** is used in a shell script to accept input from the terminal. Like \c, there are other escape sequences (Table 4.1). Here are two commonly used ones:

\t—A tab which pushes text to the right by eight character positions.
\n—A newline which creates the effect of pressing *[Enter]*.

All escape sequences are not two-character strings. ASCII characters can also be represented by their octal values (numbers using the base 8 contrasted with the standard decimal system which uses the base 10). **echo** interprets a number as octal when it is preceded by \0. For instance, *[Ctrl-g]*, which results in the sounding of a beep, has the octal value 7 (i.e., \07). You can use this value as an argument to **echo**, but only after preceding it with \0:

```
$ echo '\07'                           Double quotes will also do
..... beep heard .....
```

This is the first time we see ASCII octal values used by a UNIX command. Later, you'll see the **tr**, **awk** and **perl** commands also using octal values.

> **Tip** Always use quotes around **echo**'s arguments. We have used both single and double quotes in the preceding examples. When using simple strings, you can choose either type, but when using variables and other special characters, you'll be forced to use one and not the other. Quotes also protect multiple contiguous spaces in a string, and all these features are discussed in Section 9.4.2.

Table 4.1 Escape Sequences Used by **echo** and **printf**

Escape Sequence	*Significance*
\a	Bell
\b	Backspace
\c	No newline (cursor in same line)
\f	Formfeed
\n	Newline
\r	Carriage return
\t	Tab
\v	Vertical tab
\\	Backslash
\0*n*	ASCII character represented by the octal value *n*, where *n* can't exceed 0377 (decimal value 255)

LINUX: Bash, the standard shell used in Linux, interprets the escape sequences only when **echo** is used with the -e option:

```
echo -e "Enter your name:\c"
```

However, Bash also uses the -n option as a substitute for \c, but Korn doesn't use -n. **echo**'s behavior varies so much across shells that POSIX recommends the use of **printf** as a portable replacement of **echo**.

4.4 printf: AN ALTERNATIVE TO echo

The **printf** command is available on most modern UNIX systems, and is the one you should use instead of **echo** (unless you have to maintain a lot of legacy code that use **echo**). Like **echo**, it exists as an external command; it's only the Bash shell that has **printf** built-in. The command in its simplest form can be used in the same way as **echo**:

```
$ printf "No filename entered\n"                    \n is explicitly specified
No filename entered
$ _
```

printf also accepts all escape sequences used by **echo**, but unlike **echo**, it doesn't automatically insert a newline unless the \n is used explicitly. Though we don't need to use quotes in this example, it's good discipline to use them. **printf** also uses formatted strings in the same way the C language function of the same name uses them:

```
$ printf "My current shell is %s\n" $SHELL          No comma after "
My current shell is /usr/bin/bash
```

The %s format string acts as a placeholder for the value of $SHELL (the argument), and **printf** replaces %s with the value of $SHELL. %s is the standard format used for printing strings. **printf** uses many of the formats used by C's **printf** function. Here are some of the commonly used ones:

%s String
%30s As above but printed in a space 30 characters wide
%d Decimal integer
%6d As above but printed in a space 6 characters wide
%o Octal integer
%x Hexadecimal integer
%f Floating point number

Note that the formats also optionally use a number to specify the width that should be used when printing a string or a number. You can also use multiple formats in a single **printf** command. But then you'll have to specify as many arguments as there are format strings—and in the right order.

While **printf** can do everything that **echo** does, some of its format strings can convert data from one form to another. Here's how the number 255 is interpreted in octal (base 8) and hexadecimal (base 16):

```
$ printf "The value of 255 is %o in octal and %x in hexadecimal\n" 255 255
The value of 255 is 377 in octal and ff in hexadecimal
```

The %o and %x format strings are also used by **awk** and **perl** (and by C) to convert a decimal integer to octal and hex, respectively; it's good to know them. Note that we specified 255 twice to represent the two arguments because it's the same number that we want to convert to octal and hex.

The discussion on **printf** should prepare you well for eventually using the **printf** function in C, but remember that the C **printf** uses many format specifiers not used by the **printf** command.

> **Note** C language users should note some syntactical differences in **printf** usage. **printf** is a function in C and hence uses the parentheses to enclose its arguments. Moreover, arguments are separated from one another as well as from the format string by commas. Here's how the previous command line is implemented as a C statement:
>
> ```
> printf("The value of 255 is %o in octal and %x in hexadecimal\n", 255, 255);
> ```

4.5 bc: THE CALCULATOR

UNIX provides two types of calculators—a graphical object (the **xcalc** command) that looks like one, and the text-based **bc** command. The former is available in the X Window system and is quite easy to use. The other one is less friendly, extremely powerful and remains one of the UNIX system's neglected tools.

When you invoke **bc** without arguments, the cursor keeps on blinking and nothing seems to happen. **bc** belongs to a family of commands (called *filters*) that expect input from the keyboard when used without an argument. Key in the following arithmetic expression and then use *[Ctrl-d]* to quit **bc**:

```
$ bc
12 + 5
17                                  Value displayed after computation
[Ctrl-d]                            The eof character
$ _
```

bc shows the output of the computation in the next line. Start **bc** again and then make multiple calculations in the same line, using the ; as delimiter. The output of each computation is, however, shown in a separate line:

```
12*12 ; 2^32                        ^ indicates "to the power of"
144
4294967296                          Maximum memory possible on a 32-bit machine
```

bc performs only integer computation and truncates the decimal portion that it sees—either in its input or in the computed result. This shows up clearly when you divide two numbers:

```
9/5
1                                   Decimal portion truncated
```

To enable floating-point computation, you have to set scale to the number of digits of precision before you key in the expression:

```
scale=2                             Truncates to 2 decimal places
17/7
2.42                                Not rounded off, result is actually 2.42857.....
```

bc is quite useful in converting numbers from one base to another. For instance, when setting IP addresses *(19.1.3)* in a network, you may need to convert binary numbers to decimal. Set ibase (input base) to 2 before you provide the number:

```
ibase=2
11001010
202                                   Output in decimal—base 10
```

The reverse is also possible, this time with obase:

```
obase=2
14
1110                                  Binary of 14
```

In this way, you can convert from one base to the other (not exceeding 16). **bc** also handles hexadecimal numbers perfectly well:

```
obase=16
14
E                                     Hexadecimal value of 14
```

bc is a pseudo-programming language featuring arrays, functions, conditionals (**if**) and loops (**for** and **while**). It also comes with a library for performing scientific calculations. It can handle very, very large numbers. If a computation results in a 900-digit number, **bc** will show each and every digit!

4.6 script: RECORDING YOUR SESSION

This command, virtually unknown to many UNIX users, lets you "record" your login session in a file. This command is not included in POSIX, but you'll find it useful to store in a file all commands that you invoke, their output and error messages. You can later view the file. If you are doing some important work and wish to keep a log of all your activities, then you should invoke this command immediately after you log in:

```
$ script
Script started, file is typescript
$ _                                   Another shell—child of login shell
```

The prompt returns and all your keystrokes (including the one used to backspace) that you now enter here get recorded in the file typescript. After your recording is over, you can terminate the session by entering **exit**:

```
$ exit                                Or use [Ctrl-d]
Script done, file is typescript
$ _                                   Back to login shell
```

You can now view this file with the **cat** command. **script** overwrites any previous typescript that may exist. If you want to append to it, or want to use a different log file, then you can consider using these arguments:

```
script -a                 Appends activities to existing file typescript
script logfile            Logs activities to file logfile
```

There are some activities that won't be recorded properly, for instance, the commands used in the full-screen mode (like **vi** and **pine**).

4.7 passwd: CHANGING YOUR PASSWORD

The remaining commands in this chapter relate to our UNIX system, and we'll first take up the command that changes the user's password. In Chapter 1, you have seen how keying in a wrong password prevents you from accessing the system. If your account doesn't have a password or has one that is already known to others, you should change it immediately. This is done with the **passwd** command:

```
$ passwd
passwd:  Changing password for kumar
Enter login password: *******                    Asks for old password
New password: ********
Re-enter new password: ********
passwd (SYSTEM): passwd successfully changed for kumar
```

passwd (note the spelling) expects you to respond three times. First, it prompts for the old password. Next, it checks whether you have entered a valid password, and if you have, it then prompts for the new password. Enter the new password using the password naming rules applicable to your system. Finally, **passwd** asks you to reenter the new password.

If everything goes smoothly, the new password is registered by the system. Next time you log in, you'll need to enter the new password. Since you are expected to be the custodian of your password name, remember it as long as you don't change it again. If you still forget it, then rush to your system administrator.

When you enter a password, the string is *encrypted* by the system. Encryption generates a string of seemingly random characters that UNIX subsequently uses to determine the authenticity of a password. This encryption is stored in a file named `shadow` in the `/etc` directory. Even if a user is able to see the encryption in the file, she can't work backwards and derive the original password string from the encryption.

> **Note** This is the first time you have changed the *state* of the system; you have indirectly modified a file (`shadow`) *that is otherwise not available to you for direct editing.* There's a special feature of UNIX that allows you to do that, and we'll be examining it at the end of Part I of this text.

4.7.1 Password Framing Rules and Discipline

Depending on the way they are configured, many systems conduct certain checks on the string that you enter as password. There is often a minimum length of the string. Many systems insist on using a mix of letters with numerals. They may either disallow you from framing easy-to-remember passwords or advise you against choosing a bad password. The following messages are quite common:

```
passwd(SYSTEM): Password too short - must be at least 6 characters.
passwd(SYSTEM): Passwords must differ by at least 3 positions
passwd(SYSTEM): The first 6 characters of the password must contain at least
two alphabetic characters and at least one numeric or special character.
BAD PASSWORD: it is based on a dictionary word
```

```
BAD PASSWORD: is too similar to the old one
passwd(SYSTEM): Too many failures - try later.
```

These messages suggest that you are not able to choose any password you like. These are some of the rules that you are expected to follow when handling your own password:

- Don't choose a password similar to the old one.
- Don't use commonly used names like names of friends, relatives, pets and so forth. A system may check with its own dictionary and throw out those passwords that are easily guessed.
- Use a mix of alphabetic or numeric characters. Enterprise UNIX systems won't allow passwords that are wholly alphabetic or numeric.
- Don't write down the password in an easily accessible document.
- Change the password regularly.

You'll learn later of the terrible consequences that you may have to face if people with mischievous intent somehow come to know what your password is. The command also behaves differently when used by the system administrator; it doesn't ask for the old password. The **passwd** command is revisited in Chapter 17.

4.8 who: WHO ARE THE USERS?

UNIX maintains an account of all users who are logged on to the system. It's often a good idea to know their login names so that you can mail them messages or set up a chat session with them. The **who** command displays an informative listing of these users:

```
$ who
root       console      Aug  1 07:51    (:0)
kumar      pts/10       Aug  1 07:56    (pc123.heavens.com)
sharma     pts/6        Aug  1 02:10    (pc125.heavens.com)
project    pts/8        Aug  1 02:16    (pc125.heavens.com)
sachin     pts/14       Aug  1 08:36    (mercury.heavens.com)
```

The first column shows the usernames (or user ids) of the five users currently working on the system. The second column shows the device names of their respective terminals. These are actually the filenames associated with the terminals. kumar's terminal has the name pts/10 (a file named 10 in the pts directory). The third, fourth and fifth columns show the date and time of logging in. The last column shows the machine name from where the user logged in. Users can log in remotely to a UNIX system, and all users here except root have logged in remotely from four different machines.

While it's a general feature of most UNIX commands to avoid cluttering the display with header information, this command does have a header option (-H). This option prints the column headers, and when combined with the -u option, provides a more detailed list:

```
$ who -Hu
NAME       LINE         TIME            IDLE    PID  COMMENTS
root       console      Aug  1 07:51    0:48  11040       (:0)
kumar      pts/10       Aug  1 07:56    0:33  11200       (pc123.heavens.com)
sachin     pts/14       Aug  1 08:36     .    13678       (mercury.heavens.com)
```

Two users have logged out, so it seems. The first five columns are the same as before, but it's the sixth one (IDLE) that is interesting. A . against sachin shows that activity has occurred in the last one minute before the command was invoked. kumar seems to be idling for the last 33 minutes. The PID is the process-id, a number that uniquely identifies a process. You have seen it when you used the **ps** command in Section 1.4.18 to list processes that are running at your terminal.

One of the users shown in the first column is obviously the user who invoked the **who** command. To know that specifically, use the arguments am and i with **who**:

```
$ who am i
kumar      pts/10       Aug  1 07:56     (pc123.heavens.com)
```

4.9 uname: KNOWING YOUR MACHINE'S CHARACTERISTICS

The **uname** command displays certain features of the operating system running on your machine. By default, it simply displays the name of the operating system:

```
$ uname
SunOS                                          Linux shows Linux
```

This is the operating system used by Sun's Solaris. Linux systems simply show the name Linux. Using suitable options, you can display certain key features of the operating system, and also the name of the machine. The output will depend on the system you are using.

The Current Release and Implementation Name (-r and -s) Since UNIX comes in many flavors, vendors have customized a number of commands to behave in the way they want, and not as AT&T decreed. A UNIX command often varies across versions so much so that you'll need to use the -r option to find out the version of your operating system:

```
$ uname -r
5.8                                            This is SunOS 5.8
```

The implementation name of this operating system can be obtained with the -s option:

```
$ uname -s
SunOS
```

The complete name of the operating system is actually a combination of the output of the two options. This is a machine running SunOS 5.8, the name given to the operating system used by the Solaris 8 environment. If a command doesn't work properly, it could either belong to a different "implementation" (could be BSD) or a different "release" (may be 4.0, i.e., System V Release 4 of AT&T).

The Machine Name (-n) If your machine is connected to a network, then it must have a name (called *hostname*). If your network is connected to the Internet, then this hostname is a component of your machine's *domain name* (a series of words separated by dots, like *mercury.heavens.com*). The -n option tells you the hostname:

```
$ uname -n
mercury                                        The first word of the domain name
```

The same output would be obtained with the **hostname** command. Many UNIX networking utilities use the hostname as an argument. To copy files from a remote machine named *mercury*, you have to run **ftp mercury**.

LINUX: **uname -n** may show either the host name (like `mercury`) or the complete domain name (like `mercury.heavens.com`), depending on the flavor of Linux you are using. **uname** and **uname -r** display the operating system name and version number of the kernel, respectively:

```
$ uname
Linux
$ uname -r
2.4.18-14                              Kernel version is 2.4
```

The first two numbers of the kernel version (here, 2.4) is something every Linux user must remember. Before installing software, the documentation may require you to use a kernel that is "at least" 2.2. The same software should run on this machine whose kernel version is 2.4.

4.10 tty: KNOWING YOUR TERMINAL

Since UNIX treats even terminals as files, it's reasonable to expect a command that tells you the filename of the terminal you are using. It's the **tty** (teletype) command, an obvious reference to the device that has now become obsolete. The command is simple and needs no arguments:

```
$ tty
/dev/pts/10
```

The terminal filename is 10 (a file named 10) resident in the pts directory. This directory in turn is under the /dev directory. These terminal names were seen on a Solaris machine; your terminal names could be different (say, `/dev/tty01`).

You can use **tty** in a shell script to control the behavior of the script depending on the terminal it is invoked from. If a program must run from only one specified terminal, the script logic must use **tty** to make this decision.

4.11 stty: DISPLAYING AND SETTING TERMINAL CHARACTERISTICS

Different terminals have different characteristics and it's possible that your terminal may not behave in the way you expect it to. For instance, command interruption may not be possible with *[Ctrl-c]* on your system. Sometimes you may like to change the settings to match the ones used at your previous place of work. The **stty** command helps straighten these things out; it both displays and changes settings.

stty uses a very large number of *keywords* (options that look different), but we'll consider only a handful of them. The -a (all) option displays the current settings. A trimmed output is presented below:

```
$ stty -a
speed 38400 baud; rows = 25; columns = 80; ypixels = 0; xpixels = 0;
intr = ^c; quit = ^\; erase = ^?; kill = ^u;
eof = ^d; eol = <undef>; eol2 = <undef>; swtch = <undef>;
start = ^q; stop = ^s; susp = ^z; dsusp = ^y;
-parenb -parodd cs8 -cstopb -hupcl cread -clocal -loblk -crtscts -crtsxoff -pare
xt
-ignbrk brkint ignpar -parmrk -inpck -istrip -inlcr -igncr icrnl -iuclc
ixon -ixany -ixoff imaxbel
isig icanon -xcase echo echoe echok -echonl -noflsh
-tostop echoctl -echoprt echoke -defecho -flusho -pendin iexten
opost -olcuc onlcr -ocrnl -onocr -onlret -ofill -ofdel tab3
```

The output shows, among other things, the baud rate (the speed) of the terminal—in this case 38,400. It also shows many of the parameters that were discussed in the previous chapter *(3.8)*. The setting `intr = ^c` signifies that *[Ctrl-c]* interrupts a program. The erase character is *[Ctrl-h]* and the kill character is *[Ctrl-u]*.

Of special significance is the eof (end-of-file) character which here is set to *[Ctrl-d]*. You used this key sequence with the **cat** command *(3.8)* and also with **bc** *(4.5)*. For commands that accept input from the keyboard, this key signifies the end of input.

Following the fourth line, you see a series of keywords with a - prefixed to some of them. When an option doesn't have the -, it means that the option is turned on. We'll now use **stty** to set and unset these options.

4.11.1 Changing the Settings

Whether Backspacing Should Erase Character (echoe) If you have worked on a number of terminals, you would have noticed that backspacing over a character sometimes removes it from sight and sometimes doesn't. This is decided by the keyword echoe. Since it is set here (no - prefix to it), backspacing removes the character from display.

You can use the same keyword to reverse this setting. Here you need to prefix a - to the echoe keyword:

```
stty -echoe
```

Backspacing now doesn't remove a character from sight. This setting is inoperative on some systems.

Entering a Password through a Shell Script (echo) The echo setting has to be manipulated to let shell programs accept a password-like string that must not be displayed on the screen. By default, the option is turned on, but you can turn it off in this way:

```
stty -echo                          Turns off keyboard input
```

With this setting, keyboard entry is not echoed. You should turn it off after the entry is complete by using **stty echo**, which again is not displayed, but makes sure that all subsequent input is.

Changing the Interrupt Key (intr) **stty** also sets the functions for some of the keys. For instance, if you like to use *[Ctrl-c]* as the interrupt key instead of *[Delete]*, then you'll have to use

```
stty intr \^c                       ^ and c
```

Here, the keyword intr is followed by a space, the \ (backslash) character, a ^ (caret), and finally the character c. This is the way **stty** indicates to the system that the interrupt character is *[Ctrl-c]*.

When you insert control characters into a file, you'll see a ^ symbol apparently prefixed to the character. For example, *[Ctrl-l]* is seen as ^l (or ^L). However, it's actually a single character, occupying two slots on the terminal; no caret is actually present. However, for using a control character in an **stty** setting, you'll have to use a literal caret preceded by a backslash.

Changing the End-of-File Key (`eof`) When using **bc**, you used *[Ctrl-d]* to terminate input. This eof character is also selectable. Instead of *[Ctrl-d]*, you can use *[Ctrl-a]* as the eof character:

```
stty eof \^a
```

[Ctrl-a] will now terminate input for those commands that expect input from the keyboard when invoked in a particular way. The **cat** and **bc** commands can be made to work in this way.

When Everything Else Fails (`sane`) **stty** also provides another argument to set the terminal characteristics to values that will work on most terminals. Use the word `sane` as a single argument to the command:

```
stty sane                                    Restores sanity to the terminal
```

There are other options, but you are advised against tampering with too many settings.

4.12 CONCLUSION

The commands featured in this chapter were used in standalone mode. But UNIX provides a number of commands (called *filters*) to extract data from command output for further processing. For instance, you can use the **cut** command (a filter) to obtain a list of users by taking out only the first column from **who**'s output. The ability to combine commands to perform tasks that are not possible to achieve using a single command is what makes UNIX so different from other operating systems. We'll be combining commands several times in this text to perform useful tasks.

The next four chapters examine one of the two illusions *(2.5.1)* that support the UNIX system—files.

WRAP UP

cal produces the calendar of a month or year.

date can display any component of the system date and time in a number of formats.

echo displays a message on the screen. It can work with escape sequences like `\c` and `\t` as well as octal numbers like `\007`. The command has portability problems, the reason why **printf** should be used. **printf** works like **echo** but can also use format specifiers like `%d` and `%s`.

bc is the calculator. You can use any numbering system or degree of precision you want. You can also store intermediate results in variables.

script is the UNIX system's recorder which logs all activities of a user in a separate file.

passwd is used to change a user's password but is not displayed on the screen. The command prompts for the old password before the new one. The system administrator doesn't need to know anyone's password to be able to change it.

who shows you the users working on the system. It also shows their time of logging in and the time they have been idling.

uname reveals details of your machine's operating system (`-r` and `-s`). It also displays the hostname (`-n`) that is used by networking commands.

tty tells you the device name of your terminal.

stty displays (`-a`) and sets various terminal attributes. You can define the key that interrupts a program (`intr`) and marks the end-of-file (`eof`). To enable a password to be entered through a shell script, you need to use **stty -echo**. Use **stty sane** to set the terminal to some standard values.

TEST YOUR UNDERSTANDING

4.1 Observe the calendar for the year 1752. Do you notice anything unusual?

4.2 How will you browse the above output, moving forward and back as necessary?

4.3 Display the current date in the form *dd/mm/yyyy*.

4.4 *[Ctrl-g]* sounds a beep. How do you use escape sequences in **echo** to do the same?

4.5 Can you have the same login name more than once in the **who** output?

4.6 Where is the password stored and in what form?

4.7 How will you ensure that **bc** displays the results of all divisions using 3 decimal places?

4.8 How will you record your login session in the file `session.lst`?

4.9 If you find that your keystrokes are not being echoed, what remedies will you try?

FLEX YOUR BRAIN

4.1 How do you display both date and time in the format *dd-mm-yy/hh:mm:ss*?

4.2 What is an *escape sequence*? Name three escape sequences used by the **echo** command, and explain the significance of each.

4.3 Why doesn't this command run in the way it is meant to? **printf "Filename: %s\n", fname**

4.4 Convert the decimal number 192 to octal and hexadecimal using i) **bc** and ii) **printf**. Which one will you use to display the number in binary?

4.5 You need to accept a secret code through a shell script. What command will you run in the script to make sure that your keyboard input is not displayed? How do you then revert to the normal setting?

4.6 How will you find out the name of your machine and operating system?

4.7 How do you determine the erase, kill and eof characters on your system?

4.8 What will you do to ensure that *[Ctrl-c]* interrupts any program? Will it work the next time you log in?

5

The File System

In this chapter, we begin our study of one of the two pillars that support UNIX—the file system. UNIX looks at everything as a file and any UNIX system has thousands of files. If you write a program, you add one more file to the system. When you compile it, you add some more. Files grow rapidly, and if they are not organized properly, you'll find it difficult to locate them. Proper file organization requires a directory-based storage system. Just as an office has separate file cabinets to group files of a similar nature, UNIX also organizes its own files in directories and expects you to do that as well.

The file system in UNIX is one of its simple and conceptually clean features. It lets users access other files not belonging to them, and without infringing on security. It also offers an adequate security mechanism so that outsiders are not able to tamper with a file's contents. In this chapter you'll learn to create directories, move around within the system, and list filenames in these directories. We'll deal with file attributes, including the ones that relate to security, in a later chapter.

WHAT YOU WILL LEARN

- The initial categorization of files into three types—*ordinary*, *directory* and *device*.
- The features of a UNIX filename and whether UNIX files need to have extensions.
- The hierarchical structure in which files and directories are arranged and the parent–child relationship that exists between them.
- The significance of the *home directory* and HOME variable.
- Navigate the file system with the **cd** and **pwd** commands.
- Create and remove directories with **mkdir** and **rmdir**.
- The significance of *absolute* and *relative* pathnames.
- Use **ls** to list filenames in a directory in different formats.

TOPIC OF SPECIAL INTEREST

- The significance of the important directories of the UNIX file system from a functional point of view.

5.1 THE FILE

The *file* is a container for storing information. As a first approximation, we can treat it simply as a sequence of characters. If you name a file `foo` and write three characters `a`, `b` and `c` into it, then `foo` will contain only the string `abc` and nothing else. Unlike the old DOS files, a UNIX file doesn't contain the eof (end-of-file) mark. A file's size is not stored in the file, nor even its name. All file attributes are kept in a separate area of the hard disk, not directly accessible to humans, but only to the kernel.

UNIX treats directories and devices as files as well. A directory is simply a folder where you store files and other directories. All physical devices like the hard disk, memory, CD-ROM, printer and modem are treated as files. The shell is also a file, and so is the kernel. And if you are wondering how UNIX treats the main memory in your system, it's a file too!

So we have already divided files into three categories:

- *Ordinary file*—Also known as *regular file*. It contains only data as a stream of characters.
- *Directory file*—We mentioned that a directory contains files and other directories, but strictly speaking, it contains their names and a number associated with each name.
- *Device file*—All devices and peripherals are represented by files. To read or write a device, you have to perform these operations on its associated file.

There are other types of files, but we'll stick to these three for the time being. The reason why we make this distinction between file types is that the significance of a file's attributes often depends on its type. Read permission for an ordinary file means something quite different from that for a directory or a device. Moreover, you can't directly put something into a directory file, and a device file isn't really a stream of characters. While the vast majority of commands work with all types of files, some don't. For a proper understanding of the file system you must understand the significance of these files.

5.1.1 Ordinary (Regular) File

This is the most common file type. All programs you write belong to this type. An ordinary file itself can be divided into two types:

- Text file
- Binary file

A *text file* contains only printable characters, and you can often view the contents and make sense out of them. All C and Java program sources, shell and **`perl`** scripts are text files. A text file contains lines of characters where every line is terminated with the *newline* character, also known as *linefeed* (LF). When you press *[Enter]* while inserting text, the LF character is appended to every line. You won't see this character normally, but there is a command (**`od`**) which can make it visible.

A *binary file*, on the other hand, contains both printable and unprintable characters that cover the entire ASCII range (ASCII value range—0 to 255). Most UNIX commands are binary files, and the object code and executables that you produce by compiling C programs are also binary files. Picture, sound and video files are binary files as well. Displaying such files with a simple **`cat`** command produces unreadable output and may even disturb your terminal's settings.

5.1.2 Directory File

A *directory* contains no data, but keeps some details of the files and subdirectories that it contains. The UNIX file system is organized with a number of directories and subdirectories, and you can also create them as and when you need. You often require to do that to group a set of files pertaining to a specific application. This allows two or more files in separate directories to have the same filename.

A directory file contains an entry for every file and subdirectory that it houses. If you have 20 files in a directory, there will be 20 entries in the directory. Each entry has two components:

- The filename.
- A unique identification number for the file or directory (called the *inode number*).

If a directory `bar` contains an entry for a file `foo`, we commonly (and loosely) say that the directory `bar` contains the file `foo`. Though we'll often be using the phrase "contains the file" rather than "contains the filename", you must not interpret the statement literally. A directory contains the filename and not the file's contents.

You can't, however, write a directory file, but you can perform some action that makes the kernel write a directory. For instance, when you create or remove a file, the kernel automatically updates its corresponding directory by adding or removing the entry (inode number and filename) associated with the file. The directory file is further discussed in Sections 7.6 and 13.4.

Note The name of a file can only be found in its directory; the file itself doesn't contain its own name or any of its attributes, like its size or access rights.

5.1.3 Device File

You'll also be printing files, installing software from CD-ROMs or backing up files to tape. All these activities are performed by reading or writing the file representing the device. For instance, you print a file by writing the file (`lp0` in System V) representing the printer. When you restore files from tape, you read the file associated with the tape drive. The kernel takes care of this "reflection" by mapping these special files to their respective devices. It is advantageous to treat devices as files as some of the commands used to access an ordinary file also work with device files.

Device filenames are generally found inside a single directory structure, `/dev`. A device file is indeed special; it's not really a stream of characters. *In fact, it doesn't contain anything at all*. You'll soon learn that every file has some attributes that are not stored in the file but elsewhere on the disk. It's the attributes of a device file that entirely govern the operation of the device. The kernel identifies a device from its attributes and then uses them to operate the device.

Now that you understand the three types of files, you shouldn't feel baffled by subsequent use of the word in the book. The term "file" will often be used in this book to refer to any of these types, though it will mostly be used to mean an ordinary file. The real meaning of the term should be evident from its context.

5.2 WHAT'S IN A (FILE)NAME?

On most UNIX systems today, a filename can consist of up to 255 characters though this figure is normally never reached. Files may or may not have extensions, and can consist of practically any ASCII character except the / and the Null character (ASCII value 0). You are permitted to use control characters or other unprintable characters in a filename. The following are valid filenames in UNIX:

```
.last_time    list.    ^V^B^D-++bcd    -{}[]    @#$%*abcd    a.b.c.d.e
```

The third filename contains three control characters (*[Ctrl-v]* being the first). These characters should definitely be avoided in framing filenames. Moreover, since the UNIX system has a special treatment for characters like $, `, ?, *, & among others, it is recommended that only the following characters be used in filenames:

- Alphabets and numerals.
- The period (.), hyphen (-) and underscore (_).

UNIX imposes no restrictions on the extension, if any, that a file should have. A shell script doesn't need to have the `.sh` extension, even though it helps in identification. In all cases, it's the application that imposes this restriction. Thus the C compiler expects C program filenames to end with `.c`, Oracle requires SQL scripts to have the `.sql` extension, and so forth. DOS/Windows users must also keep these two points in mind:

- A file can have as many dots embedded in its name; `a.b.c.d.e` is a perfectly valid filename. A filename can also begin with a dot or end with one.
- UNIX is sensitive to case; `chap01`, `Chap01` and `CHAP01` are three different filenames, and it's possible for them to coexist in the same directory.

Caution Avoid using any characters other than alphabets, numerals, the dot, hyphen and underscore character in framing a filename. Never use a - at the beginning of a filename; if you do that, then be assured of a tough time in getting rid of it!

5.3 THE PARENT–CHILD RELATIONSHIP

All files in UNIX are "related" to one another. The file system in UNIX is a collection of all these related files (ordinary, directory and device files) organized in a hierarchical (an inverted tree) structure. This system has also been adopted by DOS and Windows, and is visually represented in Fig. 5.1.

The implicit feature of every UNIX file system is that there is a top, which serves as the reference point for all files. This top is called *root* and is represented by a / (frontslash). root is actually a directory. It is conceptually different from the user-id root used by the system administrator to log in. In this text, we'll be using both the name "root" and the symbol / to represent the root directory.

The root directory (/) has a number of subdirectories under it. These subdirectories, in turn, have more subdirectories and other files under them. For instance, `bin` and `usr` are two directories directly under /, while a second `bin` and `sbin` are subdirectories under `usr`.

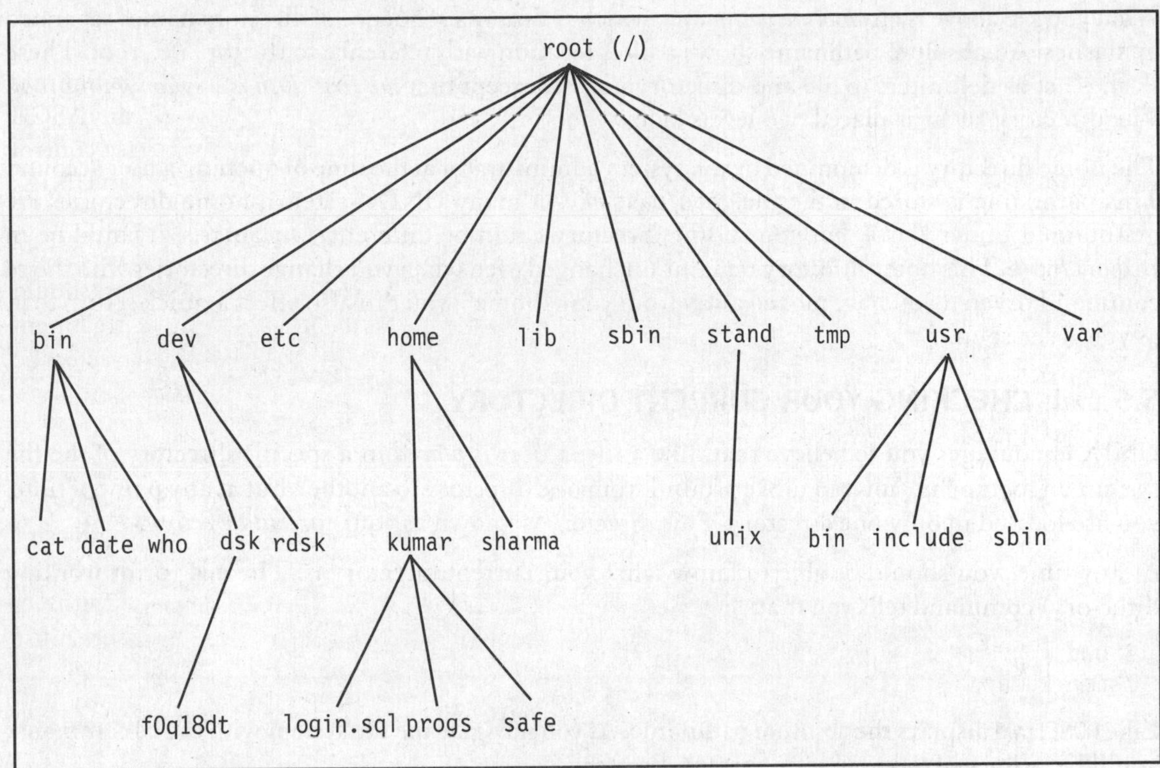

Fig. 5.1 The UNIX File System Tree

Every file, apart from root, must have a parent, and it should be possible to trace the ultimate parentage of a file to root. This should be easy for you to understand as we all have our own families with similar grandparent–parent–child relationships. Thus, the `home` directory is the parent of `kumar`, while / is the parent of `home`, and the grandparent of `kumar`. If you create a file `login.sql` under the `kumar` directory, then `kumar` will be the parent of this file.

It's also obvious that, in these parent–child relationships, the parent is always a directory. `home` and `kumar` are both directories as they are both parents of at least one file or directory. `login.sql` is simply an ordinary file; it can't have any directory under it.

5.4 THE HOME VARIABLE: THE HOME DIRECTORY

When you log on to the system, UNIX automatically places you in a directory called the *home directory*. It is created by the system when a user account is opened. If you log in using the login name kumar, you'll land up in a directory that could have the pathname `/home/kumar` (or something else). You can change your home directory when you like, but you can also effect a quick return to it, as you'll see soon.

The shell variable `HOME` knows your home directory:

```
$ echo $HOME
/home/kumar                          First / represents the root directory
```

What you see above is an *absolute pathname*, which is simply a sequence of directory names separated by slashes. An absolute pathname shows a file's location with reference to the top, i.e., root. These slashes act as delimiters to file and directory names, except that *the first slash is a synonym for root*. The directory `kumar` is placed two levels below root.

The home directory is determined by the system administrator at the time of opening a user account. This pathname is stored in the file `/etc/passwd`. On many UNIX systems, home directories are maintained under `/home`, but your home directory could be different. On Solaris, it could be in `/export/home`. This home directory remains unchanged even when you change directories with the **cd** command. Even if you have moved away from your "home", you can also effect a quick return to it, as you'll see soon.

5.5 pwd: CHECKING YOUR CURRENT DIRECTORY

UNIX encourages you to believe that, like a file, a user is *placed* in a specific directory of the file system on logging in. You can move around from one directory to another, but at any point of time, you are located in only one directory. This directory is known as your *current directory*.

At any time, you should be able to know what your current directory is. The **pwd** (print working directory) command tells you that:

```
$ pwd
/home/kumar
```

Like `HOME`, **pwd** displays the absolute pathname. As you navigate the file system with the **cd** command, you'll be using **pwd** to know your current directory.

> **Note** It's custom to refer to a file `foo` located in the home directory as `$HOME/foo`. Depending on the shell you use, it may be possible to even access `foo` as `~/foo`. One form is shell-dependent but the other isn't, but both naming conventions are followed throughout this text.

5.6 cd: CHANGING THE CURRENT DIRECTORY

You can move around in the file system by using the **cd** (change directory) command. When used with an argument, it changes the current directory to the directory specified as the argument, for instance, `progs`:

```
$ pwd
/home/kumar
$ cd progs                              progs must be in the current directory
$ pwd
/home/kumar/progs
```

Though **pwd** displays the absolute pathname, **cd** doesn't need to use one. The command **cd progs** here means this: "Change your subdirectory to `progs` under the current directory." Using a pathname causes no harm either; use **cd /home/kumar/progs** for the same effect.

When you need to switch to the `/bin` directory where most of the commonly used UNIX commands are kept, you should use the absolute pathname:

```
$ pwd
/home/kumar/progs
$ cd /bin                    Absolute pathname required here because
$ pwd                        bin isn't in current directory
/bin
```

We can also navigate to /bin (or any directory) using a different type of pathname; we are coming to that shortly.

cd can also be used without any arguments:

```
$ pwd
/home/kumar/progs
$ cd                         cd used without arguments
$ pwd                        reverts to the home directory
/home/kumar
```

Attention, DOS users! This command invoked without an argument doesn't indicate the current directory. It simply switches to the home directory, i.e., the directory where the user originally logged in. Therefore, if you wander around in the file system, you can force an immediate return to your home directory by simply using **cd**:

```
$ cd /home/sharma
$ pwd
/home/sharma
$ cd                         Returns to home directory
$ pwd
/home/kumar
```

The **cd** command can sometimes fail if you don't have proper permissions to access the directory. This doesn't normally happen unless you deliberately tamper with the permissions of the directory. The technique of doing that is described in Section 7.5.

> **Note**
>
> **Note:** Unlike in DOS, when **cd** is invoked without arguments, it simply reverts to its home directory. It doesn't show you the current directory!

5.7 mkdir: MAKING DIRECTORIES

Directories are created with the **mkdir** (make directory) command. The command is followed by the names of the directories to be created. A directory patch is created under the current directory like this:

```
mkdir patch
```

You can create a number of subdirectories with one **mkdir** command:

```
mkdir patch dbs doc                Three directories created
```

So far, simple enough, but the UNIX system goes further and lets you create directory trees with just one invocation of the command. For instance, the following command creates a directory tree:

```
mkdir pis pis/progs pis/data       Creates the directory tree
```

This creates three subdirectories—pis and two subdirectories under pis. The order of specifying the arguments is important; you obviously can't create a subdirectory before creation of its parent directory. For instance, you can't enter

```
$ mkdir pis/data pis/progs pis
mkdir: Failed to make directory "pis/data"; No such file or directory
mkdir: Failed to make directory "pis/progs"; No such file or directory
```

Note that even though the system failed to create the two subdirectories progs and data, it has still created the pis directory.

Sometimes, the system refuses to create a directory:

```
$ mkdir test
mkdir: Failed to make directory "test"; Permission denied
```

This can happen due to these reasons:

- The directory test may already exist.
- There may be an ordinary file by that name in the current directory.
- The permissions set for the current directory don't permit the creation of files and directories by the user. You'll most certainly get this message if you try to create a directory in /bin, /etc or any other directory that houses the UNIX system's files.

We'll take up file and directory permissions in Chapter 7 featuring file attributes.

5.8 rmdir: REMOVING DIRECTORIES

The **rmdir** (remove directory) command removes directories. You simply have to do this to remove the directory pis:

```
rmdir pis                                   Directory must be empty
```

Like **mkdir**, **rmdir** can also delete more than one directory in one shot. For instance, the three directories and subdirectories that were just created with **mkdir** can be removed by using **rmdir** with a reversed set of arguments:

```
rmdir pis/data pis/progs pis
```

Note that when you delete a directory and its subdirectories, a reverse logic has to be applied. The following directory sequence used by **mkdir** is invalid in **rmdir**:

```
$ rmdir pis pis/progs pis/data
rmdir: directory "pis": Directory not empty
```

Have you observed one thing from the error message? **rmdir** has silently deleted the lowest level subdirectories progs and data. This error message leads to two important rules that you should remember when deleting directories:

- You can't delete a directory *with* **rmdir** unless it is empty. In this case, the pis directory couldn't be removed because of the existence of the subdirectories, progs and data, under it.
- You can't remove a subdirectory unless you are placed in a directory which is hierarchically *above* the one you have chosen to remove.

The first rule follows logically from the example above, but the highlight on **rmdir** in the first bulleted observation has significance that will be explained later. (A directory can also be removed by other means.) To illustrate the second cardinal rule, try removing the progs directory by executing the command from the same directory itself:

```
$ cd progs
$ pwd
/home/kumar/pis/progs
$ rmdir /home/kumar/pis/progs                    Trying to remove the current directory
rmdir: directory "/home/kumar/pis/progs": Directory does not exist
```

To remove this directory, you must position yourself in the directory above progs, i.e., pis, and then remove it from there:

```
$ cd /home/kumar/pis
$ pwd
/home/kumar/pis
$ rmdir progs
```

The **mkdir** and **rmdir** commands work only in directories *owned* by the user. Generally, a user is the owner of her home directory, and she can create and remove subdirectories (as well as regular files) in this directory or in any subdirectories created by her. However, she normally won't be able to create or remove files and directories in other users' directories. The concept of ownership will be discussed in Section 7.3.

> **Note** A subdirectory can't be removed with **rmdir** unless it's empty, and one is positioned in its parent directory or above it. But we can remove a directory without using **rmdir** also (discussed later).

5.9 ABSOLUTE PATHNAMES

Many UNIX commands use file and directory names as arguments, which are presumed to exist in the current directory. For instance, the command

```
cat login.sql
```

will work only if the file login.sql exists in your current directory. However, if you are placed in /usr and want to access login.sql in /home/kumar, you can't obviously use the above command, but rather the pathname of the file:

```
cat /home/kumar/login.sql
```

As stated before, if the first character of a pathname is a /, the file's location must be determined with respect to root (the first /). Such a pathname, as the one above, is called an *absolute pathname.*

When you have more than one / in a pathname, for each such /, you have to descend one level in the file system. Thus, `kumar` is one level below `home`, and two levels below root.

When you specify a file by using frontslashes to demarcate the various levels, you have a mechanism of identifying a file uniquely. No two files in a UNIX system can have identical absolute pathnames. You can have two files with the same name, but in different directories; their pathnames will also be different. Thus, the file `/home/kumar/progs/c2f.pl` can coexist with the file `/home/kumar/safe/c2f.pl`.

5.9.1 Using the Absolute Pathname for a Command

A command often runs in UNIX by executing its disk file. When you specify the **date** command, the system has to locate the file `date` from a list of directories specified in the `PATH` variable, and then execute it. However, if you know the location of a particular command, you can precede its name with the complete path. Since **date** resides in `/bin` (or `/usr/bin`), you can also use the absolute pathname:

```
$ /bin/date
Fri Dec 20 19:06:51 IST 2002
```

Nobody runs the **date** command like that. For any command that resides in the directories specified in the `PATH` variable, you don't need to use the absolute pathname. This `PATH`, you'll recall *(3.1.1)*, invariably has the directories `/bin` and `/usr/bin` in its list. It also normally includes the current directory, the reason why a command in the current directory also doesn't need to be used with the absolute pathname.

If you execute programs residing in some other directory that isn't in the `PATH`, then the absolute pathname needs to be specified. For example, to execute the program **less** residing in `/usr/local/bin`, you need to enter the absolute pathname:

```
/usr/local/bin/less
```

If you are frequently accessing programs in a certain directory, then it's better to include the directory itself in the `PATH`. The technique of doing that is shown in Section 9.10.2.

5.10 RELATIVE PATHNAMES

You would have noted that in a previous example *(5.8)*, we didn't use an absolute pathname to move to the directory `progs`. Nor did we use one as an argument to **cat** *(5.9)*:

```
cd progs
cat login.sql
```

Here, both `progs` and `login.sql` are presumed to exist in the current directory. Now, if `progs` also contains a directory `scripts` under it, you still won't need an absolute pathname to change to that directory:

```
cd progs/scripts                                    progs is in current directory
```

Here we have a pathname that has a /, but it is not an absolute pathname because it doesn't begin with a /. In these three examples, we used a rudimentary form of relative pathnames though they are generally not labeled as such. Relative pathnames, in the sense they are known, are discussed next.

5.10.1 Using . and .. in Relative Pathnames

In a preceding example *(5.8)*, you changed your directory from /home/kumar/pis/progs to its parent directory (/home/kumar/pis) by using **cd** with an absolute pathname:

```
cd /home/kumar/pis
```

There's a better method of navigation available for moving between two directories that both point to a common ancestor (here, /home). UNIX offers a shortcut—the *relative pathname*—that uses either the current or parent directory as reference and specifies the path relative to it. A relative pathname uses one of these cryptic symbols:

- . (a single dot)—This represents the current directory.
- .. (two dots)—This represents the parent directory.

We'll now use the .. to frame relative pathnames. Assuming that you are placed in /home/kumar/progs/data/text, you can use .. as an argument to **cd**, to move to the parent directory, i.e., the directory /home/kumar/progs/data:

```
$ pwd
/home/kumar/progs/data/text
$ cd ..                                    Moves one level up
$ pwd
/home/kumar/progs/data
```

This method is compact and more useful when ascending the hierarchy. The command **cd ..** translates to this: "Change your directory to the parent of the current directory." You can combine any number of such sets of .. separated by /s. However, when a / is used with .. it acquires a different meaning; instead of moving down a level, it moves one level *up*. For instance, to move to /home, you can always use **cd /home**. Alternatively, you can also use a relative pathname:

```
$ pwd
/home/kumar/pis
$ cd ../..                                 Moves two levels up
$ pwd
/home
```

Now let's turn to the solitary dot that refers to the current directory. Any command which uses the current directory as an argument can also work with a single dot. This means that the **cp** command *(6.2)* which also uses a directory as the last argument can be used with a dot:

```
cp ../juliet/.profile .                    A filename can begin with a dot
```

This copies the file .profile to the current directory (.). Note that you didn't have to specify the filename of the copy; it's the same as the original one. This dot is implicitly included whenever we use a filename as argument, rather than a pathname. For instance, **cd progs** is the same as **cd ./progs**.

> **Note** Absolute pathnames can get very long if you are located a number of "generations" away from root. However, whether you should use one depends solely on the number of keystrokes required when compared to a relative pathname. In every case here, the relative pathname required fewer key depressions. Depending on where you are currently placed, an absolute pathname can be faster to type.

5.11 ls: LISTING DIRECTORY CONTENTS

You have already used the **ls** command *(1.4.9)* to obtain a list of all filenames in the current directory. Let's execute it again:

```
$ ls
08_packets.html                    Numerals first
TOC.sh                             Uppercase next
calendar                           Then lowercase
cptodos.sh
dept.lst
emp.lst
helpdir
progs
usdsk06x
usdsk07x
usdsk08x
```

What you see here is a complete list of filenames in the current directory arranged in *ASCII collating sequence* (numbers first, uppercase and then lowercase), with one filename in each line. It includes directories also, and if you are using Linux, you would probably see the directories and ordinary files in different colors.

> **LINUX**: If your Linux system doesn't show these colors, make sure that you create this alias after logging in:
>
> ```
> alias ls='ls --color=tty'
> ```

Directories often contain many files, and you may simply be interested in only knowing whether a particular file is available. In that case, just use **ls** with the filename:

```
$ ls calendar
calendar
```

and if **perl** isn't available, the system clearly says so:

```
$ ls perl
perl: No such file or directory
```

ls can also be used with multiple filenames and has options that list most of the file attributes. In the following sections, you'll see some of these options.

5.11.1 ls Options

ls has a very large number of options (Table 5.1), but in this chapter, we'll present a handful of them. The other options will be taken up in later chapters. The section numbers are appropriately indicated in the table.

Output in Multiple Columns (-x) When you have several files, it's better to display the filenames in multiple columns. Modern versions of **ls** do that by default (i.e., when used without options), but if that doesn't happen on your system, use the -x option to produce a multicolumnar output:

```
$ ls -x
08_packets.html  TOC.sh          calendar        cptodos.sh
dept.lst         emp.lst         helpdir         progs
usdsk06x         usdsk07x        usdsk08x        ux2nd06
```

This format is convenient for viewing filenames. If your system needs to use the `-x` option to display multicolumnar output, then you can later customize the command to display in this format by default *(11.2)*.

Identifying Directories and Executables (`-F`) The output of **ls** that you have seen so far merely showed the filenames. You didn't know how many of them, if any, were directory files. To identify directories and executable files, the `-F` option should be used. Combining this option with `-x` produces a multicolumnar output as well:

```
$ ls -Fx
08_packets.html   TOC.sh*          calendar*        cptodos.sh*
dept.lst          emp.lst          helpdir/         progs/
usdsk06x          usdsk07x         usdsk08x         ux2nd06
```

Note the use of two symbols that tag some of the filenames. The * indicates that the file contains executable code and the / refers to a directory. You can now identify the two subdirectories in the current directory—`helpdir` and `progs`.

Showing Hidden Files Also (`-a`) **ls** doesn't normally show all files in a directory. There are certain hidden files (filenames beginning with a dot) in every directory, especially in the home directory that normally don't show up in the listing. The `-a` option (all) lists all hidden files along with the other files:

```
$ ls -axF
./                ../               .exrc            .kshrc
.profile          .rhosts           .sh_history      .xdtsupCheck
.xinitrc          08_packets.html*  TOC.sh*          calendar*
 .....
```

Note there are a number of additional files that are shown this time—all beginning with a dot. The file `.profile` contains a set of instructions that are performed when a user logs in. It is conceptually similar to `AUTOEXEC.BAT` of DOS, and you'll know more about it later. The other file, `.exrc` contains a sequence of startup instructions for the **vi** editor.

While all these filenames beginning with a `.` are normally not displayed with **ls**, you can either use the `-a` option to include them, or ask for them specifically by using their filenames in the command line.

The first two files (`.` and `..`) are special directories. Recall that we used the same symbols in relative pathnames to represent the current and parent directories *(5.10.1)*. These symbols have the same meaning here. Whenever you create a subdirectory, these "invisible" directories are created automatically by the kernel. You can't remove them, nor can you write into them. They help in holding the file system together.

Table 5.1 Options to **ls** *(Section references shown in parentheses)*

Option	*Description*
-x	Multicolumnar output
-F	Marks executables with *, directories with / and symbolic links with @
-a	Shows all filenames beginning with a dot including . and ..
-R	Recursive list
-r	Sorts filenames in reverse order (ASCII collating sequence by default)
-1	One filename in each line
-l	Long listing in ASCII collating sequence showing seven attributes of a file *(7.1)*
-d *dirname*	Lists only *dirname* if *dirname* is a directory *(7.2)*
-t	Sorts filenames by last modification time *(13.6)*
-lt	Sorts listing by last modification time *(13.6)*
-u	Sorts filenames by last access time *(13.6)*
-lu	Sorts by ASCII collating sequence but listing shows last access time *(13.6)*
-lut	As above but sorted by last access time *(13.6)*
-i	Displays inode number *(13.1)*

Note All filenames beginning with a dot are displayed only when **ls** is used with the -a option. The directory . represents the current directory and .. signifies the parent directory.

Listing Directory Contents In the last example, you specified some ordinary filenames to **ls** to have a selective listing. However, the situation will be quite different if you specify the two directory names, helpdir and progs, instead:

```
$ ls -x helpdir progs
helpdir:
forms.obd     graphics.obd     reports.obd

progs:
array.pl     cent2fah.pl     n2words.pl     name.pl
```

This time the *contents* of the directories are listed, consisting of the Oracle documentation in the helpdir directory and a number of **perl** program files in progs. Note that **ls**, when used with directory names as arguments, doesn't simply show their names as it does with ordinary files.

Recursive Listing (-R) The -R (recursive) option lists all files and subdirectories in a directory tree. Similar to the **DIR /S** command of DOS, this traversal of the directory tree is done recursively till there are no subdirectories left:

```
$ ls -xR
08_packets.html  TOC.sh       calendar     cptodos.sh
dept.lst         emp.lst      helpdir      progs
usdsk06x         usdsk07x     usdsk08x     ux2nd06
```

```
./helpdir:
forms.hlp          graphics.hlp       reports.hlp

./progs:
array.pl           cent2fah.pl        n2words.pl         name.pl
```

The list shows the filenames in three sections—the ones under the home directory and those under the subdirectories `helpdir` and `progs`. Note the subdirectory naming conventions followed; `./helpdir` indicates that `helpdir` is a subdirectory under `.` (the current directory). Since `/home/kumar` happens to be the current directory, the absolute pathname of this file expands to `/home/kumar/helpdir`.

5.12 THE UNIX FILE SYSTEM

We have learned to use the basic command set for handling files and directories. Let's conclude this chapter by taking a cursory look at the structure of the UNIX file system. This structure has been changing constantly over the years until AT&T proposed one in its SVR4 release. Though vendor implementations vary in detail, broadly the SVR4 structure has been adopted by most vendors.

Refer to Fig. 5.1 which shows a heavily trimmed structure of a standard UNIX file system. In real life, the root directory has many more subdirectories under it than shown, but for our initial comprehension, we'll stick to the ones presented below. It helps, from the administrative point of view at least, to view the entire file system as comprising two groups of files. The first group contains the files that are made available during system installation:

- `/bin` and `/usr/bin`—These are the directories where all the commonly used UNIX commands (binaries, hence the name bin) are found. Note that the `PATH` variable always shows these directories in its list.
- `/sbin` and `/usr/sbin`—If there's a command that you can't execute but the system administrator can, then it would probably be in one of these directories. You won't be able to execute most (some, you can) commands in these directories. Only the system administrator's `PATH` shows these directories.
- `/etc`—This directory contains the configuration files of the system. You can change a very important aspect of system functioning by editing a text file in this directory. Your login name and password are stored in files `/etc/passwd` and `/etc/shadow`.
- `/dev`—This directory contains all device files. These files don't occupy space on disk. There could be more subdirectories like `pts`, `dsk` and `rdsk` in this directory.
- `/lib` and `/usr/lib`—Contain all library files in binary form. You'll require to link your C programs with files in these directories.
- `/usr/include`—Contains the standard header files used by C programs. The statement `#include <stdio.h>` used in most C programs refers to the file `stdio.h` in this directory.
- `/usr/share/man`—This is where the man pages are stored. There are separate subdirectories here (like `man1`, `man2`, etc.) that contain the pages for each section. For instance, the man page of **ls** can be found in `/usr/share/man/man1`, where the 1 in `man1` represents Section 1 of the UNIX manual. These subdirectories may have different names on your system (like `sman1`, `sman2`, etc. in Solaris).

Over time, the contents of these directories would change as more software and utilities are added to the system. Users also work with their own files; they write programs, send and receive mail and also create temporary files. These files are available in the second group shown below:

- `/tmp`—The directories where users are allowed to create temporary files. These files are wiped away regularly by the system.
- `/var`—The variable part of the file system. Contains all your print jobs and your outgoing and incoming mail.
- `/home`—On many systems, users are housed here. kumar would have his home directory in `/home/kumar`. However, your system may use a different location for home directories.

On a busy system, it's in directories belonging to the second group that you could experience rapid depletion of available disk space. You'll learn later to house some of these directory structures on separate *file systems* so that depletion of space in one file system doesn't affect other file systems. File system internals and administration are taken up toward the end of this text.

5.13 CONCLUSION

Though UNIX is known to make little distinction between the various types of files, that wasn't really established in this chapter. You used exclusive commands to handle directories (like **pwd**, **cd**, **mkdir** and **rmdir**). These commands have no relevance when applied to ordinary or device files. It appears that UNIX does care to some extent about the type of file it handles. In the next chapter, we look at ordinary files using yet another set of commands meant for them.

WRAP UP

Files have been assumed to be of three types. An *ordinary* file contains whatever you put in it. A *directory* groups a set of files, maintaining for each its inode number and name. A *device* file contains no data but the kernel uses the attributes of the file to operate the device. A file doesn't contain its attributes, nor does it contain the end-of-file mark.

A filename is restricted to 255 characters and can use practically any character. Executable files don't need any specific extensions.

The file system is a hierarchical structure resembling an inverted tree, and the top-most directory is called *root*. Files and directories have a parent-child relationship, and the parent of any file must be a directory. We represent a file's location with respect to root by an *absolute pathname*.

pwd tells you the current directory, and **cd** is used to change it. When used by itself, it switches to the *home* directory. The home directory is set in `/etc/passwd` and is available in the shell variable `HOME`. A file `foo` in the home directory is often referred to as `$HOME/foo` or `~/foo`.

mkdir and **rmdir** are used to create or remove directories. Multiple directories can also be created or removed with one invocation of the commands. To remove a directory `bar` with **rmdir**, `bar` must be empty and you must be positioned above `bar`.

A pathname is a sequence of directory and filenames separated by slashes. An *absolute* pathname begins with a/and denotes the file's location with respect to root. While two files may have the same name, they must have different absolute pathnames. A *relative* pathname uses the symbols `.` and `..` to represent the file's location relative to the current and parent directory, respectively.

By default, **ls** displays a list of filenames in *ASCII collating sequence*, which accords priority in this sequence—numbers, uppercase, lowercase. It can also display in multiple columns (-x), hidden filenames beginning with a dot (-a), a recursive list (-R) and also identify directories and executables (-F). However, when used with a directory name as argument, **ls** displays the *filenames* in the directory.

TEST YOUR UNDERSTANDING

5.1 How long can a UNIX filename be and which character can't be used in a filename?

5.2 In how many ways can you find out what your home directory is?

5.3 What is the easiest way of changing from `/var/spool/lp/admins` to `/var/spool/mail`?

5.4 What does **cd** do when used without arguments?

5.5 Use **man** to find out the easiest way of creating this directory structure—`share/man/cat1`.

5.6 If **rmdir c_progs** fails, what could be the possible reasons?

5.7 **echo** is a shell builtin. How do you then use the command of the same name that resides in `/bin`?

5.8 How do you run **ls** to mark directories and executables separately?

5.9 How will you obtain a complete listing of all files and directories in the whole system?

FLEX YOUR BRAIN

5.1 Name the two types of ordinary files and explain the difference between them. Provide three examples of each type of file.

5.2 Describe the contents of a directory, explaining the mechanism by which its entries are updated. Why is the size of a directory usually small?

5.3 How does the device file help in accessing the device?

5.4 Which of these commands will work? Explain with reasons: (i) **mkdir a/b/c** (ii) **mkdir a a/b** (iii) **rmdir a/b/c** (iv) **rmdir a a/b** (v) **mkdir /bin/foo**

5.5 If **mkdir test** fails, what could be the possible reasons?

5.6 Which of these files or directories can you create? Explain with reasons: `.`, `..`, `...` and `....`

5.7 The command **rmdir bar** fails with the message that the directory is not empty. On running **ls bar**, no files are displayed. Why did the **rmdir** command fail?

5.8 Suppose you have to develop a script that refers to a file in charlie's home directory. How will you specify the location of this file in your script to make sure that it works even when charlie's home directory changes?

5.9 Why do we sometimes run a command like this—**./update.sh** instead of **update.sh**?

5.10 The command **ls foo**, where `foo` is a directory, simply shows `foo` as the output. Explain how it can happen.

5.11 Assuming that you are positioned in the directory `/home/kumar`, what are these commands presumed to do and explain whether they will work at all: (i) **cd ../..** (ii) **mkdir ../bin** (iii) **rmdir ..** (iv) **ls ..**

6

Handling Ordinary Files

The last chapter examined the tools that handle directories. But users actually do most of their work with ordinary (or regular) files, and it's natural that the UNIX system should feature a host of commands to handle them. Although all these commands use filenames as arguments, they were not designed *only* to read files. In fact, many of them don't need to read a file at all. However, to understand their basic functionality, we'll use them with filenames in this chapter.

We'll first consider the common file-handling commands that the DOS environment also offers, except that the UNIX variety has more features. We'll also discuss those commands that show differences between two files and convert files between DOS and UNIX formats. Finally, we'll examine the important compression utilities with which we handle documents and software found on the Internet. As we progressively discover the shell's features in later chapters, we'll learn to use the same commands in other ways.

WHAT YOU WILL LEARN

- View text files with **`cat`** and **`more`** (or **`less`**), and use **`cat`** to create a file.
- The essential file functions—copy with **`cp`**, remove with **`rm`** and rename with **`mv`**.
- Print with **`lp`** (**`lpr`** in Linux).
- Classify files with **`file`**.
- Count the number of lines, words and characters with **`wc`**.
- Display the ASCII octal value of text with **`od`**.
- Compare two files with **`cmp`**, **`comm`** and **`diff`**.

TOPICS OF SPECIAL INTEREST

- A discussion on the issues related to file compression and archival.
- Compress and decompress files with **`gzip`** and **`gunzip`**.
- Create an *archive* comprising multiple files with **`tar`**.
- Perform both functions (compressing and archiving) with **`zip`** and **`unzip`**.
- Convert between UNIX and DOS files with **`unix2dos`** and **`dos2unix`**.

6.1 cat: DISPLAYING AND CREATING FILES

cat is one of the most well-known commands of the UNIX system. It is mainly used to display the contents of a small file on the terminal:

```
$ cat dept.lst
01|accounts|6213
02|progs|5423
03|marketing|6521
04|personnel|2365
05|production|9876
06|sales|1006
```

cat, like several other UNIX commands, also accepts more than one filename as arguments:

```
cat chap01 chap02
```

The contents of the second file are shown immediately after the first file without any header information. What **cat** has done here is to concatenate the two files—hence its name. Displaying a single file is only a special case of concatenation.

6.1.1 cat Options (-v and -n)

There are two **cat** options that you may find useful, though POSIX doesn't require **cat** to support either one.

Displaying Nonprinting Characters (`-v`) **cat** is normally used for displaying text files only. Executables, when seen with **cat**, simply display junk. If you have nonprinting ASCII characters in your input, you can use **cat** with the `-v` option to display these characters.

Numbering Lines (`-n`) The `-n` option numbers lines. C compilers indicate the line number where errors are detected, and this numbering facility often helps a programmer in debugging programs. But then your **vi** editor can show line numbers too, and if your version of **cat** doesn't support `-n`, you can use the **pr** *(14.2)* command to do the same job.

6.1.2 Using cat to Create a File

cat is also useful for creating a file. Though the significance of the following sequence can be appreciated only after reading Section 9.5.2, you should now know how to create small files. Enter the command **cat**, followed by the > (the right chevron) character and the filename (for example foo):

```
$ cat > foo
A > symbol following the command means that the
output goes to the filename following it. cat used
in this way represents a rudimentary editor.
[Ctrl-d]
$ _                                        Prompt returns
```

When the command line is terminated with *[Enter]*, the prompt vanishes. **cat** now waits to take input from the user. Enter the three lines, each followed by *[Enter]*. Finally press *[Ctrl-d]* to signify the end of input to the system. This is the eof character used by UNIX systems and is shown in the

stty output *(4.11)*. When this character is entered, the system understands that no further text input will be made. The file is written and the prompt returned. To verify this, simply "cat" this file:

```
$ cat foo
A > symbol following the command means that the
output goes to the filename following it. cat used
in this way represents a rudimentary editor.
```

> **Note** The *[Ctrl-d]* character is used to terminate input not only with **cat**, but with all commands that accept input from the keyboard.

cat is a versatile command. It can be used to create, display, concatenate and append to files. More important, it doesn't restrict itself to handling files only; it also acts on a *stream*. You can supply the input to **cat** not only by specifying a filename, but also from the output of another command. You'll learn about all this in the Chapter 9.

6.2 cp: COPYING A FILE

The **cp** (copy) command copies a file or a group of files. It creates an exact image of the file on disk with a different name. The syntax requires at least two filenames to be specified in the command line. When both are ordinary files, the first is copied to the second:

```
cp chap01 unit1
```

If the destination file (unit1) doesn't exist, it will first be created before copying takes place. If not, it will simply be overwritten without any warning from the system. So be careful when you choose your destination filename. Just check with the **ls** command whether or not the file exists.

If there is only one file to be copied, the destination can be either an ordinary or a directory file. You then have the option of choosing your destination filename. The following example shows two ways of copying a file to the progs directory:

```
cp chap01 progs/unit1          chap01 copied to unit1 under progs
cp chap01 progs                chap01 retains its name under progs
```

cp is often used with the shorthand notation, . (dot), to signify the current directory as the destination. For instance, to copy the file .profile from /home/sharma to your current directory, you can use either of the two commands:

```
cp /home/sharma/.profile .profile      Destination is a file
cp /home/sharma/.profile .             Destination is the current directory
```

Obviously, the second one is preferable because it requires fewer keystrokes.

cp can also be used to copy more than one file with a single invocation of the command. In that case, the last filename *must* be a directory. For instance, to copy the files chap01, chap02 and chap03 to the progs directory, you have to use **cp** like this:

```
cp chap01 chap02 chap03 progs
```

The files retain their original names in progs. If these files are already resident in progs, then they will be overwritten. For the above command to work, the progs directory must exist because **cp** won't create it.

You have already seen *(1.4.9)* how the UNIX system uses the * to frame a pattern for matching more than one filename. If there were only three filenames in the current directory having the common string chap, you can compress the above sequence using the * as a suffix to chap:

```
cp chap* progs                    Copies all files beginning with chap
```

> **Cautions** **cp** overwrites without warning the destination file if it exists! Run **ls** before you use **cp** unless you are sure that the destination file doesn't exist or deserves to be overwritten.

We'll continue to use the * as a shorthand for multiple filenames. There are other metacharacters too, and they are discussed in complete detail in Section 9.3.

6.2.1 cp Options

Interactive Copying (-i) The -i (interactive) option warns the user before overwriting the destination file. If unit1 exists, **cp** prompts for a response:

```
$ cp -i chap01 unit1
cp: overwrite unit1 (yes/no)? y
```

A y at this prompt overwrites the file, any other response leaves it uncopied.

Copying Directory Structures (-R) It's possible to copy an entire directory structure with the -R (recursive) option. The following command copies all files and subdirectories in progs to newprogs:

```
cp -R progs newprogs              newprogs must not exist
```

Attention! How **cp** behaves here depends on whether newprogs also exists as a directory. If newprogs doesn't exist, **cp** creates it along with the associated subdirectories, but if newprogs exists, progs becomes a subdirectory under newprogs. This means that the command run twice in succession will produce different results!

> **Cautions** Sometimes, it's not possible to copy a file. This can happen if it's read-protected or the destination file or directory is write-protected.

6.3 rm: DELETING FILES

Files can be deleted with **rm** (remove). It can delete more than one file with a single invocation. It normally operates silently and should be used with caution. The following command deletes the first three chapters of the book:

```
rm chap01 chap02 chap03           rm chap* could be dangerous to use!
```

A file once deleted can't be recovered. **rm** won't *normally* remove a directory, but it can remove files from one. You can remove the two chapters from the progs directory without having to "cd" to it:

```
rm progs/chap01 progs/chap02      Or rm progs/chap0[12]
```

You may sometimes require to delete all files in a directory as part of a cleanup operation. The *, when used by itself, represents all files, and you can then use **rm** like this:

```
$ rm *                                   All files gone!
$ _
```

DOS users, beware! When you delete files in this fashion, the system won't prompt you with the message `Are you sure?` before removing the files! The $ prompt will return silently; the work has been done. The * used here is equivalent to `*.*` used in DOS.

> **Note** **rm** works by removing the entry in the directory for the file that is removed. This entry comprises the inode number and filename *(5.1.2)*. Whether or not you are able to remove a file depends, not on the file's permissions but on the permissions you have for the *directory*. Directory permissions are taken up in Chapter 7.

6.3.1 rm Options

Interactive Deletion (`-i`) Like in **cp**, the `-i` (interactive) option makes the command ask the user for confirmation before removing each file:

```
$ rm -i chap01 chap02 chap03
rm: remove chap01 (yes/no)? ?y
rm: remove chap02 (yes/no)? ?n
rm: remove chap03 (yes/no)? [Enter]          No response—file not deleted
```

A y removes the file, any other response leaves the file undeleted.

Recursive Deletion (`-r` or `-R`) With the `-r` (or `-R`) option, **rm** performs a tree walk—a thorough recursive search for all subdirectories and files within these subdirectories. At each stage, it deletes everything it finds. **rm** *won't normally remove directories, but when used with this option, it will.* Therefore, when you issue the command

```
rm -r *                                  Behaves partially like rmdir
```

you'll delete all files in the current directory and all its subdirectories. If you don't have a backup, then these files will be lost forever.

Forcing Removal (`-f`) **rm** will prompt you for removal if a file is write-protected. The `-f` option overrides this minor protection also. It will force removal even if the files are write-protected. When you combine the `-r` option with it, it could be the most risky thing to do:

```
rm -rf *                 Deletes everything in current directory and below
```

> **Note** Unlike **rmdir**, **rm -r** can remove subdirectories even if they are not empty.

6.4 mv: RENAMING FILES

mv renames (moves) files. It has two functions:

- It renames a file (or directory).
- It moves a group of files to a different directory.

mv doesn't create a copy of the file; it merely renames it. No additional space is consumed on disk during renaming. To rename the file chap01 to man01, you should use

```
mv chap01 man01
```

If the destination file doesn't exist, it will be created. For the above example, **mv** simply replaces the filename in the existing directory entry with the new name. By default, **mv** doesn't prompt for overwriting the destination file if it exists. So be careful again.

Like **cp**, a group of files can be moved to a directory. The following command moves three files to the progs directory:

```
mv chap01 chap02 chap03 progs
```

mv can also be used to rename a directory, for instance, pis to perdir:

```
mv pis perdir
```

Like in **cp -R**, there's a difference in behavior depending on whether perdir exists or not. You can check that out for yourself.

There's a -i option available with **mv** also, and behaves exactly like in **cp**. The messages are the same and require a similar response.

6.5 more: PAGING OUTPUT

The **man** command displays its output a page at a time. This is possible because it sends its output to a pager program. UNIX offers the **more** pager (originally from Berkeley) which has today replaced **pg**, the original pager of UNIX. Linux also offers **more** but **less** is its standard pager. We'll discuss **more** in this section and note the exclusive features of **less** separately in the aside on Linux.

To view the file chap01, enter the command with the filename:

```
more chap01                                   Press q to exit
```

You'll see the contents of chap01 on the screen, one page at a time. At the bottom of the screen, you'll also see the filename and the percentage of the file that has been viewed:

```
--More--(17%)
```

more has a couple of internal commands of its own that don't show up on the screen when you invoke them. **q**, the command used to exit **more**, is an internal command.

The AT&T and BSD versions of **more** differ widely in their capabilities and command usage. The POSIX specification on **more** is based on the BSD version. You have to try out the commands shown in Table 6.1, as well as look up the man pages, to know whether they apply to your system. **more** has a fairly useful help screen too; hitting an **h** invokes this screen.

6.5.1 Navigation

Irrespective of version, **more** uses the spacebar to scroll forward a page at a time. You can also scroll by small and large increments of lines or screens. To move forward one page, use

f or the spacebar

and to move back one page, use

b

The Repeat Factor Many navigation commands in **more**, including **f** and **b**, use a *repeat factor*. This is the term used in **vi** *(8.1.1)* to prefix a number to a **vi** internal command. Use of the repeat factor as a command prefix simply repeats the command that many times. This means you can use **10f** for scrolling forward by 10 pages and **30b** for scrolling back 30 pages. Just remember that the commands themselves are not displayed on the screen—even for a moment.

Repeating The Last Command (.) **more** has a repeat command, the dot (same command used by **vi**), that repeats the last command you used. If you scroll forward with **10f**, you can scroll another 10 pages by simply pressing a dot. This is a great convenience available in **more**!

6.5.2 Searching for a Pattern

You can perform a search for a pattern with the **/** command followed by the string. For instance, to look for the first **while** loop in your program, you'll have to enter this:

```
/while                                    Press [Enter] also
```

You can repeat this search for viewing the next **while** loop section by pressing **n**, and you can do that repeatedly till you have scanned the entire file. Move back with **b** (using a repeat factor, if necessary) to arrive at the first page.

> **Note** Searching is not always confined to a string like while. Like **more**, many UNIX commands (**grep**, **sed** and **vi**) let you use an expression to match multiple similar strings. This expression that uses some special characters is termed a *regular expression*. Regular expressions are discussed in several chapters of this text beginning with Chapter 15.

6.5.3 Other Features

Using Multiple Filenames **more** also works with multiple filenames:

```
more chap01 chap02 chap03                 Same as more chap0[123]
```

You'll first see the contents of the first file. After you have finished viewing this file, you'll see a message similar to this:

```
--More--(Next file: chap02)
```

more moves over to the next file chap02 when you press **f** or the spacebar at this prompt. In this way, it sequentially displays all files, pausing additionally whenever a change of file occurs. In the middle of a session, you can switch to the next or previous file using these sequences:

`:n` Next file
`:p` Previous file

Using **more** *in a Pipeline* The **man** syntax doesn't indicate this (except mention that **more** is a filter), but we often use **more** to page the output of another command. The **ls** output won't fit on the screen if there are too many files, so the command has to be used like this:

```
ls | more
```
No filename with `more`*!*

We have a *pipeline* here of two commands where the output of one is used as the input of the other. Pipes are a feature of the shell and the topic is taken up in Chapter 9.

Tip You can start up the **vi** editor from inside **more** by pressing **v**. When you finish editing, exit from **vi** returns you to **more** once again.

Table 6.1 Internal Commands of **more** and **less**

more	less	*Action*
Spacebar or f	Spacebar or f or z	One page forward
20f	-	20 pages forward
[Enter]	j or *[Enter]*	One line forward
b	b	One page back
15b	-	15 pages back
-	k	One line back
-	p or 1G	Beginning of file
-	G	End of file
/*pat*	/*pat*	Search forward for expression *pat*
n	n	Repeat search forward
-	?*pat*	Search back for expression *pat*
:n	:n	Skip to next file specified in command line
:p	:p	Skip to previous file specified in command line
. (a dot)	-	Repeat last command
v	v	Start up **vi** editor
!*cmd*	!*cmd*	Execute UNIX command *cmd*
q	q	Quit
h	h	View Help

LINUX: less—The Standard Pager

Even though every Linux system also offers **more**, **less** is its standard pager. It's ironic that it bears such a name because it's more powerful than **more**. **less** is modeled on the **vi** editor, so learning **less** should be a breeze for **vi** users.

Navigation is **vi**-compatible. You have to work with these keys:

f, *[Ctrl-f]* or spacebar — Scroll forward one screen
b or *[Ctrl-b]* — Scroll backward one screen

j	One line up
k	One line down

Like **vi**, **less** uses the **G** command with a repeat factor to move to a specific line. For instance, **1G** takes you to the beginning of the file, **400G** goes to line number 400, while a singular **G** means the end of file.

Pattern searching techniques are similar. Unlike **more**, **less** can search for a pattern in the reverse direction also using the sequence **?***pattern*. But **less** does have one serious limitation. Unlike **more** (which uses the .), it can't repeat the last command.

6.6 THE lp SUBSYSTEM: PRINTING A FILE

No user is allowed direct access to the printer. Instead, one has to *spool* (line up) a job along with others in a print queue. Spooling ensures the orderly printing of jobs and relieves the user from the necessity of administering the print resources. The spooling facility in System V is provided by the **lp** (line printing) command. Systems derived from BSD (like Linux) use the **lpr** command instead.

The following **lp** command prints a single copy of the file `rfc822.ps` (a document containing an Internet specification in the form of a Request For Comment):

```
$ lp rfc822.ps                                   A Postscript file
request id is pr1-320 (1 file)
$ _
```

Note that the prompt is returned immediately after the job is submitted. The file isn't actually printed at the time the command is invoked, but later, depending on the number of jobs already lined up in the queue. Several users can print their files in this way without conflict.

lp notifies the request-id—a combination of the printer name (pr1) and the job number (320)—which can later be accessed with other commands. The hard copy of the file is often preceded by a title page mentioning the username, request-id and date.

6.6.1 lp Options

lp accepts the above request because a default printer has been defined by the administrator. If it is not, or if there is more than one printer in the system, you have to use the `-d` option with the printer name (say, laser):

```
lp -dlaser chap01.ps                             Can also provide space after -d
```

The `-t` (title) option, followed by the title string, prints the title on the first page:

```
lp -t"First chapter" chap01.ps                   Can also provide space after -t
```

You can notify the user with the `-m` (mail) option after the file has been printed. You can also print multiple copies (`-n`):

```
lp -n3 -m chap01.ps                    Prints three copies and mails user a message
```

Even though we used **lp** with filenames, this will not always be the case. You are aware that the shell's | symbol allows us to use **ls | more**. The same symbol also lets us use **ls | lp**.

6.6.2 Other Commands in the lp Subsystem

The print queue is viewed with the **lpstat** command. By viewing this list, you can use the **cancel** command to cancel any jobs submitted by you. **cancel** uses the request-id or printer name as argument:

```
cancel laser                    Cancels current job on printer laser
cancel pr1-320                  Cancels job with request-id pr1-320
```

You can cancel only those jobs that you own (i.e., you have submitted yourself), but the system administrator can cancel any job. **cancel** is effective only when a job remains in the print queue. If it is already being printed, **cancel** can't do a thing.

Note Most UNIX printers are of the *Postscript* variety, i.e., they can properly print files formatted in Postscript, like the files `rfc822.ps` and `chap01.ps` used in the examples. (Postscript files are easily identified by the extension `.ps`.) When you select *Print* from the *File* menu of any GUI program, the program converts the data to Postscript which serve as input to the printer. No such conversion takes place when you use **lp** to print a text file like `/etc/passwd`. If you have a text file to print, use a Postscript conversion utility before you use **lp**. On Solaris, you can use the program **/usr/lib/lp/postscript/postprint** before running **lp**.

LINUX: Printing with **lpr**, **lpq** and **lprm**

Linux uses Berkeley's printing system which supports the **lpr** command for printing. You must have your printer configured properly before you use **lpr**. The command normally doesn't throw out the job number:

```
lpr /etc/group
```

Linux has a rich set of tools that convert text files to Postscript. Check whether you have the programs **a2ps** or **enscript** on your system. Both eventually call up **lpr**; you don't have to do that on your own.

Like in System V, you can print a specific number of copies, choose the title and direct output to a specific printer. You can also mail the completion of the job:

```
lpr -P hp4500 foo.ps                 Prints on the printer hp4500
lpr -T "The List of RFCs" foo.ps     Uses this title
lpr -#3 foo.ps                       Prints 3 copies
lpr -m foo.ps                        Mails message after completion
```

lpq displays the print queue showing the job numbers. Using one or more job numbers as arguments to **lprm**, you can remove from the print queue only those jobs that are owned by you:

```
lprm 31                              Removes job number 31
lprm -                               Removes all jobs owned by the user
```

The **lpc** command is used by the administrator to configure the printer. We'll not discuss Linux printer administration in this text.

6.7 `file`: KNOWING THE FILE TYPES

Even though we know (so far) that files are of three types, you may often require to know more about these files. For instance, a regular file may contain plain text, a C program or executable code. UNIX provides the **file** command to determine the type of file, especially of an ordinary file.

You can use it with one or more filenames as arguments:

```
$ file archive.zip
archive.zip:     ZIP archive
```

file correctly identifies the basic file types (regular, directory or device). For a regular file, it attempts to classify it further. Using the * to signify all files, this is how **file** behaves on this system having regular files of varying types:

```
$ file *
CW6.Eval.exe:     DOS executable (EXE)
User_Guide.ps:    PostScript document
archive.tar.gz:  gzip compressed data - deflate method , original file name
create_user.sh:  commands text
fatal.o:          ELF 32-bit MSB relocatable SPARC Version 1
fork1.c:          c program text
os_Lec03.pdf:     Adobe Portable Document Format (PDF) v1.2
```

This command identifies the file type by examining the *magic number* that is embedded in the first few bytes of the file. Every file type has a unique magic number. **file** recognizes text files, and can distinguish between shell programs, C source and object code. It also identifies DOS executables, compressed files, PDF documents and even empty files. While this method of identifying files is not wholly accurate, it's a reliable indicator.

6.8 wc: COUNTING LINES, WORDS AND CHARACTERS

UNIX features a universal word-counting program. The command name is in fact a misnomer; it counts lines, words and characters, depending on the options used. It takes one or more filenames as its arguments, and displays a four-columnar output.

Before you use **wc** to make a count of the contents of the file `infile`, just use **cat** to have a look at its contents:

```
$ cat infile
I am the wc command
I count characters, words and lines
With options I can also make a selective count
```

You can now use **wc** without options to make a "word count" of the data in the file:

```
$ wc infile
      3      20      103 infile
```

wc counts 3 lines, 20 words and 103 characters. The filename has also been shown in the fourth column. The meanings of these terms should be clear to you as they are used throughout the book:

- A *line* is any group of characters not containing a newline.
- A *word* is a group of characters not containing a space, tab or newline.
- A *character* is the smallest unit of information, and includes a space, tab and newline.

wc offers three options to make a specific count. The `-l` option counts only the number of lines, while the `-w` and `-c` options count words and characters, respectively:

```
$ wc -l infile
      3 infile                              Number of lines
$ wc -w infile
     20 infile                              Number of words
$ wc -c infile
    103 infile                              Number of characters
```

When used with multiple filenames, **wc** produces a line for each file, as well as a total count:

```
$ wc chap01 chap02 chap03
    305    4058   23179 chap01
    550    4732   28132 chap02
    377    4500   25221 chap03
   1232   13290   76532 total                A total as a bonus
```

wc, like **cat**, doesn't work with only files; it also acts on a data stream. You'll learn all about these streams in Chapter 9.

6.9 od: DISPLAYING DATA IN OCTAL

Many files (especially executables) contain nonprinting characters, and most UNIX commands don't display them properly. The file `odfile` contains some of these characters that don't show up normally:

```
$ more odfile
White space includes a
The ^G character rings a bell
The ^L character skips a page
```

The apparently incomplete first line actually contains a tab (entered by hitting *[Tab]*). The **od** command makes these commands visible by displaying the ASCII octal value of its input (here, a file). The `-b` option displays this value for each character separately. Here's a trimmed output:

```
$ od -b odfile
0000000 127 150 151 164 145 040 163 160 141 143 145 040 151 156 143 154
0000020 165 144 145 163 040 141 040 011 012 124 150 145 040 007 040 143
    .....Other lines deleted....
```

Each line displays 16 bytes of data in octal, preceded by the offset (position) in the file of the first byte in the line. In the absence of proper mapping it's difficult to make sense out of this output, but when the `-b` and `-c` (character) options are combined, the output is friendlier:

```
$ od -bc odfile
0000000 127 150 151 164 145 040 163 160 141 143 145 040 151 156 143 154
          W   h   i   t   e       s   p   a   c   e       i   n   c   l
0000020 165 144 145 163 040 141 040 011 012 124 150 145 040 007 040 143
          u   d   e   s       a      \t  \n   T   h   e     007       c
0000040 150 141 162 141 143 164 145 162 040 162 151 156 147 163 040 141
          h   a   r   a   c   t   e   r       r   i   n   g   s       a
0000060 040 142 145 154 154 012 124 150 145 040 014 040 143 150 141 162
              b   e   l   l  \n   T   h   e      \f       c   h   a   r
    .....Other lines deleted....
```

Each line is now replaced with two. The octal representations are shown in the first line. The printable characters and escape sequences are shown in the second line. The first character in the first line is the letter W having the octal value 127. You'll recall having used some of the escape sequences with **echo** *(4.3)*. Let's have a look at their various representations:

- The tab character, *[Ctrl-i]*, is shown as \t and the octal value 011.
- The bell character, *[Ctrl-g]*, is shown as 007. Some systems show it as \a.
- The formfeed character, *[Ctrl-l]*, is shown as \f and 014.
- The LF (linefeed or newline) character, *[Ctrl-j]*, is shown as \n and 012. Note that **od** makes the newline character visible too.

Like **wc**, **od** also takes a command's output as its own input, and in Section 6.13, we'll use it to display nonprintable characters in filenames.

6.10 cmp: COMPARING TWO FILES

You may often require to know whether two files are identical so that one of them can be deleted. There are three commands in the UNIX system that can tell you that. In this section, we'll have a look at the **cmp** (compare) command. Obviously, it needs two filenames as arguments:

```
$ cmp chap01 chap02
chap01 chap02 differ: char 9, line 1
```

The two files are compared byte by byte, and the location of the first mismatch (in the ninth character of the first line) is echoed to the screen. **cmp**, by default, doesn't bother about possible subsequent mismatches.

The -l (list) option gives a detailed list of the byte number and the differing bytes in octal for each character that differs in both files:

```
$ cmp -l note1 note2
     3 143 145                     Third character has the ASCII values 143 and 145
     6 170 167
     7 171 170
     8 172 171
```

There are four differences in the two files. If two files are identical, **cmp** displays no message, but simply returns the prompt. You can try it out with two copies of the same file:

```
$ cmp chap01 chap01
$ _
```

This follows the UNIX tradition of quiet behavior. This behavior is also very important because the comparison has returned a *true* value, which can be subsequently used in a shell script to control the flow of a program.

6.11 comm: WHAT IS COMMON?

Suppose you have two lists of people and you are asked to find out the names available in one and not in the other, or even those common to both. **comm** is the command you need for this work. It requires two *sorted* files, and lists the differing entries in different columns. Let's try it on these two files:

```
$ cat file1                  $ cat file2
c.k. shukla                  anil aggarwal
chanchal singhvi             barun sengupta
s.n. dasgupta                c.k. shukla
sumit chakrobarty            lalit chowdury
                             s.n. dasgupta
```

Both files are sorted and have some differences. When you run **comm**, it displays a three-columnar output:

```
$ comm file[12]                          Comparing file1 and file2
        anil aggarwal
        barun sengupta
                c.k. shukla
chanchal singhvi
        lalit chowdury
                s.n. dasgupta
sumit chakrobarty
```

The first column contains two lines unique to the first file, and the second column shows three lines unique to the second file. The third column displays two lines common (hence its name) to both files.

This output provides a good summary to look at, but is not of much use to other commands that take **comm**'s output as their input. These commands require single-column output from **comm**, and **comm** can produce it using the options -1, -2 or -3. To drop a particular column, simply use its column number as an option prefix. You can also combine options and display only those lines that are common:

```
comm -3 foo1 foo2                        Selects lines not common to both files
comm -13 foo1 foo2                       Selects lines present only in second file
```

The last example and one more with the other matching option (-23) has more practical value than you may think, but we'll not discuss their application in this text.

6.12 diff: CONVERTING ONE FILE TO OTHER

diff is the third command that can be used to display file differences. Unlike its fellow members, **cmp** and **comm**, it also tells you which lines in one file have to be *changed* to make the two files identical. When used with the same files, it produces a detailed output:

```
$ diff file1 file2                       Or diff file[12]
0a1,2                                    Append after line 0 of first file
> anil aggarwal                          this line
> barun sengupta                         and this line
2c4                                      Change line 2 of first file
< chanchal singhvi                       Replacing this line
---                                      with
> lalit chowdury                         this line
4d5                                      Delete line 4 of first file
< sumit chakrobarty                      containing this line
```

diff uses certain special symbols and *instructions* to indicate the changes that are required to make two files identical. You should understand these instructions as they are used by the **sed** command, one of the most powerful commands on the system.

Each instruction uses an *address* combined with an *action* that is applied to the first file. **0a1,2** means appending two lines after line 0, which become lines 1 and 2 in the second file. **2c4** changes line 2 which is line 4 in the second file. **4d5** deletes line 4.

> **Tip** If you are simply interested in knowing whether two files are identical or not, use **cmp** without any options.

Maintaining Several Versions of a File (-e) **diff -e** produces a set of instructions only (similar to the above), but these instructions can be used with the **ed** editor (not discussed in this text) to convert one file to the other. This facility saves disk space by letting us store the oldest file in its entirety, and only the changes between consecutive versions. We have a better option of doing that in the *Source Code Control System* (SCCS), but **diff** remains quite useful if the differences are few.

6.13 dos2unix AND unix2dos: CONVERTING BETWEEN DOS AND UNIX

Life being the way it is, you'll encounter DOS/Windows files in the course of your work. Sometimes, you'll need to move files between Windows and UNIX systems. Windows files use the same format as DOS, where the end of line is signified by two characters—CR (\r) and LF (\n). UNIX files, on the other hand, use only LF. Here are two lines from a DOS file, foo, viewed on a UNIX system with the **vi** editor:

```
Line 1^M                                The [Ctrl-m] character at end
Line 2^M
```

There's a ^M (*[Ctrl-m]*) representing the CR sequence at the end of each line. An octal dump confirms this:

```
$ od -bc foo
0000000 114 151 156 145 040 061 015 012 114 151 156 145 040 062 015 012
          L   i   n   e       1  \r  \n   L   i   n   e       2  \r  \n
```

The CR-LF combination is represented by the octal values 015-012 and the escape sequence \r\n. Conversion of this file to UNIX is just a simple matter of removing the \r. This is often done automatically when downloading a UNIX file from a Windows machine using **ftp**, but sometimes you have to do that job yourself.

For this purpose, some UNIX systems feature two utilities—**dos2unix** and **unix2dos**—for converting files between DOS and UNIX. Sometimes, systems differ in their implementation. This is how we use **dos2unix** to convert this file foo to UNIX format on a Solaris system:

```
dos2unix foo foo.dos
```

The output is written to foo.dos. When you use **od** again, you'll find that the CR character is gone:

```
$ od -bc foo.dos
0000000 114 151 156 145 040 061 012 114 151 156 145 040 062 012
          L   i   n   e       1  \n   L   i   n   e       2  \n
```

One some systems (like Solaris), the first and second filenames could be the same. Others (like Linux) require only one filename, in which case the command rewrites the input file. Some may even require redirection. Browse through the man page to identify the form that works on your machine:

```
dos2unix foo foo                    foo rewritten in UNIX format
dos2unix foo                        Same
dos2unix foo > foo.dos              Taking shell's help
```

unix2dos inserts CR before every LF, and thus increases the file size by the number of lines in the file. The syntactical form that works for **dos2unix** would also work for **unix2dos**.

Tip You can use **dos2unix** to delete the ^M character that occurs at the end of every line in the file typescript. This is the file used by **script** to record a login session *(4.6)*.

Note If you view the UNIX file foo on Windows using Notepad but without performing the conversion, then you'll see a single line, Line 1Line2. In fact, whenever you see a single line on a Windows machine that should have been multiple lines, satisfy yourself that you are viewing an unconverted UNIX file.

Caution Never perform this conversion on a binary file. If you have downloaded a Windows program (say, a .EXE file) on a UNIX machine, the file must be transferred to the Windows machine without conversion. Otherwise, the program simply won't execute.

6.14 COMPRESSING AND ARCHIVING FILES

To conserve disk space you'll require to compress large and infrequently used files. Moreover, before sending a large file as an email attachment, it's good netiquette to compress the file first. A file can often be compressed to a fraction of its original size. Every UNIX system comes with some or all of the following compression and decompression utilities:

- **compress** and **uncompress** (.Z)
- **gzip** and **gunzip** (.gz)
- **bzip2** and **bunzip2** (.bz2)
- **zip** and **unzip** (.zip)

You'll find all these programs on Solaris and Linux. The extension acquired by the compressed filename is shown in parentheses. The degree of compression that can be achieved depends on the type of file, its size and the compression program used. Large text files compress more, but GIF and JPEG image files (the types used on the World Wide Web) compress very little because they hold data in compressed form.

We won't consider **compress** in this edition because it has been superseded by other programs. In case someone requires you to send a file in this format, use **compress** with the filename to create a .Z file. The **uncompress** command retrieves the original file. Very rarely, you'll come across software or documentation on the Internet that's available *only* in the .Z form.

Apart from compressing, you'll also require to group a set of files into a single file, called an *archive*. The **tar** and **zip** commands can pack an entire directory structure into an archive. You can send this archive as a single file, either using **ftp** or as an email attachment, to be used on a remote machine. An additional layer of compression helps to bring down the file size, the reason why **tar** is often used with **gzip** and **bzip2** for creating a compressed archive. **zip** handles both functions itself. In the next few sections, we'll be discussing these compression and archival utilities.

> **Note** Modern versions of WINZIP that run on Windows can read all these formats though it can write only in the ZIP format. So you can choose any of these formats for compressing and archiving files even if you have to restore them on a Windows system. However, do check the WINZIP documentation on the other system before you select the format to write an archive.

6.15 gzip AND gunzip: COMPRESSING AND DECOMPRESSING FILES

We'll monitor the size of two files, of type HTML and Postscript, as they go through a number of compression and archival agents. We'll start with **gzip**, a very popular program, that works with one or more filenames. It provides the extension .gz to the compressed filename and removes the original file.

How well do HTML files compress? In the following example, we run **gzip** on the file libc.html (documentation for the GNU C library). We also note the file size, both before and after compression, using **wc -c** which counts characters:

```
$ wc -c libc.html
   3875302 libc.html
$ gzip libc.html
$ wc -c libc.html.gz
    788096 libc.html.gz
```

We seem to have achieved very high compression here, but before we go in for the statistics, let's repeat the previous exercise on a Postscript file:

```
$ wc -c User_Guide.ps ; gzip User_Guide.ps ; wc -c User_Guide.ps.gz
    372267 User_Guide.ps                                    Before compression
    128341 User_Guide.ps.gz                                 After compression
```

How much compression did we actually achieve for both files? Use the -l option with the compressed or original filenames as arguments:

```
$ gzip -l libc.html.gz User_Guide.ps.gz                    .gz not necessary
compressed  uncompr. ratio uncompressed_name
   788096   3875302  79.6% libc.html
   128341    372267  65.5% User_Guide.ps
   916437   4247569  78.4% (totals)
```

HTML compressed better than Postscript (79.6% vs. 65.5%). This may not always be the case.

6.15.1 gzip Options

Uncompressing a "gzipped" File (-d) To restore the original and uncompressed file, you have two options: Use either **gzip -d** or **gunzip** with one or more filenames as arguments; the .gz extension is optional yet again:

```
gunzip libc.html.gz                          Retrieves lib.html
gzip -d libc.html                            Same—.gz assumed
gunzip libc.html.gz User_Guide.ps.gz         Works with multiple files
```

You can now browse the files with their respective viewers—a browser like Netscape for HTML files, and **gv** for Postscript documents.

Recursive Compression (-r) Like **cp**, you can also descend a directory structure and compress all files found in subdirectories. You need the -r option, and the arguments to **gzip** must comprise at least one directory:

```
gzip -r progs                                Compresses all files in progs
```

This option can be used for decompression also. To decompress all files in this directory you need to use **gunzip -r progs** or **gzip -dr** progs.

Writing to Terminal (-c) When used with **gzip**, this option doesn't create a compressed file, but sends the compressed output (as a stream) to the terminal. The same option used with **gunzip** also shows the uncompressed contents of a compressed file on the terminal. The original file remains unchanged.

> **Tip** To view compressed plain text files, you really don't need to "gunzip" (decompress) them. Use the **gzcat** and **gzmore** (or **zcat** and **zmore**) commands if they are available on your system. In most cases, the commands run **gunzip -c**.

> **Note** For some years, **gzip** reigned as the most favored compression agent. Today, we have a better agent in **bzip2** (and **bunzip2**). **bzip2** is slower than **gzip** and creates .bz2 files. We are beginning to see .bz2 files on the Internet. **bzip2** options are modeled on **gzip**, so if you know **gzip** you also know **bzip2**.

6.16 tar: THE ARCHIVAL PROGRAM

For creating a disk archive that contains a group of files or an entire directory structure, we need to use **tar**. The command is taken up in some detail in Chapter 17 to back up files to tape (or floppy), but in this section we need to know how the command is used to create a disk archive. For this minimal use of **tar** we need to know these *key* options:

-c	Create an archive
-x	Extract files from archive
-t	Display files in archive
-f *arch*	Name the archive *arch*

Only one these key options can be used at a time. We'll also learn to use **gzip** and **gunzip** to compress and decompress the archive created with **tar**.

6.16.1 Creating an Archive (-c)

To create an archive, we need to specify the name of the archive (with `-f`), the copy or write operation (`-c`) and the filenames as arguments. Additionally, we'll use the `-v` (verbose) option to display the progress while **tar** works. This is how we create a file archive, `archive.tar`, from the two uncompressed files used previously:

```
$ tar -cvf archive.tar libc.html User_Guide.ps
a libc.html 3785K                              -v (verbose) displays list
a User_Guide.ps 364K                           a indicates append
```

By convention, we use the `.tar` extension, so you'll remember to use the same **tar** command for extraction. We created an archive containing two ordinary files, but **tar** also behaves recursively to back up one or more directories. In the following example, **tar** fills the archive `progs.tar` with three directory structures:

```
tar -cvf progs.tar c_progs java_progs shell_scripts
```

We'll soon use the same **tar** command to extract files from this archive. But before we do that, let's see how we can compress this archive.

Using **gzip** *with* **tar** If the created archive is very big, you may like to compress it with **gzip**:

```
gzip archive.tar                               Archived and compressed
```

This creates a "tar-gzipped" file, `archive.tar.gz`. This file can now be sent out by **ftp** or as an email attachment to someone. A great deal of open-source UNIX and Linux software are available as `.tar.gz` files on the Internet. To use the files in this archive, the recipient needs to have both **tar** and **gzip** at her end.

6.16.2 Extracting Files from Archive (-x)

tar uses the `-x` option to extract files from an archive. You can use it right away on a `.tar` file, the one we just used to archive three directories:

```
tar -xvf progs.tar                             Extracts the three directories
```

But to extract files from a `.tar.gz` file (like `archive.tar.gz`), you must first use **gunzip** to decompress the archive and then run **tar**:

```
$ gunzip archive.tar.gz                        Retrieves archive.tar
$ tar -xvf archive.tar                         Extracts files
x libc.html, 3875302 bytes, 7569 tape blocks   x indicates extract
x User_Guide.ps, 372267 bytes, 728 tape blocks
```

You'll now find the two files in the current directory. Selective extraction is also possible. Just follow the above command line with one or more filenames that have to be extracted:

```
tar -xvf archive.tar User_guide.ps             Extracts only User_guide.ps
```

This extracts a single file from the archive. If you use a pathname, then it must be exactly in the same form that was used during the copying operation. This has been discussed later *(17.10.1)*.

6.16.3 Viewing the Archive (-t)

To view the contents of the archive, use the `-t` (table of contents) option. It doesn't extract files, but simply shows their attributes in a form that you'll see more often later:

```
$ tar -tvf archive.tar
-rw-r--r-- 102/10   3875302 Aug 24 19:49 2002 libc.html
-rw-r--r-- 102/10   372267 Aug 24 19:48 2002 User_Guide.ps
```

You'll understand the significance of these columns after you have learned to interpret the **ls -l** output *(7.1)*. But you can at least see the individual file size (third column) and their names (last column) in this output.

Both **tar** and **gzip** can be made to behave like *filters* (a group of programs whose input and output are quite flexible), and after you have understood the working of *filters*, you'll be able to perform both activities without creating an intermediate file.

LINUX: **tar** and **gzip** are so often used together that GNU **tar** has a `-z` option that compresses and archives together (and decompresses and extracts together). This dual activity is reflected in the following commands:

```
tar -cvzf archive.tar.gz libc.html User_Guide.ps        Compresses also
tar -xvzf archive.tar.gz                                Decompresses also
tar -xvzf archive.tar.gz User_Guide.ps                  Extracts one file only
tar -tvzf archive.tar.gz                                Displays list
```

Note that whether you should use the `-z` option with `-x` or `-t` depends on whether the archive was compressed in the first place with `-c`. The archive's extension (`.tar.gz`) should provide this hint, but that's no guarantee. A wrong extension could have been provided by the user at the time of archival.

GNU **tar** also has a `--bzip` option that uses **bzip2** for handling compression. If you decide to use it, then provide the extension `.tar.bz2` to the compressed archive so that the person at the other end knows how to handle it.

6.17 zip AND unzip: COMPRESSING AND ARCHIVING TOGETHER

Phil Katz's popular PKZIP and PKUNZIP programs are now available as **zip** and **unzip** on UNIX and Linux systems. **zip** generally doesn't compress as much as **gzip** but it combines the compressing function of **gzip** with the archival function of **tar**. So instead of using two commands to compress a directory structure, you can use only one—**zip**. All the letters of the alphabet are available as its options but we'll consider just a few of them.

zip requires the first argument to be the compressed filename; the remaining arguments are interpreted as files and directories to be compressed. The compression in the previous example could have been achieved with **zip** in the following way:

```
$ zip archive.zip libc.html User_Guide.ps
  adding: libc.html (deflated 80%)
  adding: User_Guide.ps (deflated 66%)
```

The unusual feature of this command is that it doesn't overwrite an existing compressed file. If `archive.zip` exists, files will either be updated or appended to the archive depending on whether they already exist in the archive.

Recursive Compression (`-r`) For recursive behavior, **zip** uses the `-r` option. It descends the tree structure in the same way **tar** does except that it also compresses files. You can easily compress your home directory in this way:

```
cd ; zip -r sumit_home.zip .                          cd is same as cd $HOME
```

Using **unzip** Files are restored with the **unzip** command, which in its simplest form, uses the compressed filename as argument. **unzip** does a noninteractive restoration if it doesn't overwrite any existing files:

```
$ unzip archive.zip
Archive:  archive.zip
  inflating: libc.html
  inflating: User_Guide.ps
```

But if the uncompressed file exists on disk, then **unzip** makes sure that it's doing the right thing by seeking user confirmation:

```
replace libc.html? [y]es, [n]o, [A]ll, [N]one, [r]ename: y
```

You can respond with `y` or `n`. You can also rename the file (`r`) to prevent overwriting or direct **unzip** to perform the decompression on the remaining files noninteractively (`A`).

Viewing the Archive (`-v`) You can view the compressed archive with the `-v` option. The list shows both the compressed and uncompressed size of each file in the archive along with the percentage of compression achieved:

```
$ unzip -v archive.zip
Archive:  archive.zip
 Length  Method   Size  Ratio   Date     Time   CRC-32     Name
 ------  ------   ----  -----   ----     ----   ------     ----
3875302  Defl:N 788068  80%  08-24-02  19:49  fae93ded    libc.html
 372267  Defl:N 128309  66%  08-24-02  19:48  7839e6b3    User_Guide.ps
 ------         ------  ---                               -------
4247569         916377  78%                               2 files
```

zip has a number of other useful options that you can explore them after you get comfortable with it. The `-t` and `-tt` options let you select files that have changed prior to or after a certain date (specified in the form *mmddyyyy*).

> **Tip** If you have to move files between UNIX and Windows machines, you can take advantage of the end-of-line conversion options offered by **zip**. Use `-l` to convert from LF to CR-LF, and `-ll` to do the opposite. However, use them only when there are no binary files in your archive.

6.18 CONCLUSION

The commands discussed in this chapter don't always take input from files. Some commands (like **more** and **lp**) use, as alternate sources of input, the keyboard or the output of another command. Most of the other commands (like **wc**, **cat**, **cmp**, **od**, **gzip** and **tar**) can also send output to a file or serve as input to another command. Some examples in this chapter (and previous ones) have shown this to be possible with the > and | symbols. The discussion on these techniques is taken up in Chapter 9.

You would have also noted that we can use **gzip -d** instead of **gunzip** to decompress files. You'll have to understand why two commands have been offered to do the same job when one of them would have sufficed. Are **gzip** and **gunzip** one and the same file? This question is related to file attributes, and we begin our discussion on file attributes in the next chapter.

WRAP-UP

cat is not only used to display one or more files but also to create a file. It can also display line numbers (-n).

You can copy files with **cp**, remove them with **rm**, and rename them with **mv**. All of them can be used interactively (-i), and the first two can be used to work on a complete directory tree (-r or -R) i.e., recursively. **rm -r** can remove a directory tree even if is not empty.

more is a pager that shows the output one page at a time. You can scroll both forward and backward, using a *repeat factor* if necessary. You can search for a pattern (/) and repeat the search (**n**). Linux offers **less** as a superior pager.

lp prints a file and can be used to print multiple copies (-n). You can cancel any submitted job with **cancel**. It can be *directly* used to print Postscript documents. Linux uses the **lpr** command instead of **lp**.

file identifies the file type beyond the normal three categories. **wc** counts the number of lines, words and characters. displays the octal value of each character and is used to display invisible characters.

We discussed three file comparison utilities. **cmp** tells you where the first difference was encountered. **comm** shows the lines that are common and optionally shows you lines unique to either or both *sorted* files. **diff** lists file differences as a sequence of **sed**-like instructions.

The **dos2unix** and **unix2dos** commands convert files between DOS and UNIX. DOS files use CR-LF as the line terminator, while UNIX uses only LF.

We also discussed several compression and archival tools. **gzip** and **gunzip** compresses and decompresses individual files (extension—.gz), and can also work recursively (-r). **tar** always works recursively to archive a group of files into an *archive*. **tar** and **gzip** are often used together to create compressed archives (extension—.tar.gz).

zip and **unzip** can perform all functions that are found in **gzip**, **gunzip** and **tar**. **zip** alone can create a compressed archive from directory structures (-r). It can also perform newline conversions (-l and -ll).

TEST YOUR UNDERSTANDING

6.1 What will **cat foo foo foo** display?

6.2 How will you copy a directory structure bar1 to bar2? Does it make any difference if bar2 exists?

6.3 Run the command **tty** and note the device name of your terminal. Now use this device name (say, /dev/pts/6) in the command, **cp /etc/passwd /dev/pts/6**. What do you observe?

6.4 How will you remove a directory tree even when it's not empty without using **rmdir**?

6.5 How does the command **mv bar1 bar2** behave, where both bar1 and bar2 are directories, when (i) bar2 exists and (ii) bar2 doesn't exist?

6.6 Print three copies of /etc/passwd on the printer named arjun.

6.7 How will you find out the ASCII octal values of the numerals and alphabets?

6.8 How will you display *only* the lines common to two files?

6.9 The command **cmp foo1 foo2** displays nothing. What does it indicate?

FLEX YOUR BRAIN

6.1 What is the difference between **cat foo** and **cat > foo**? Why do you have to use *[Ctrl-d]* in one and not in the other?

6.2 Will the command **cp foo bar** work if (i) foo is an ordinary file and bar is a directory (ii) both foo and bar are directories?

6.3 Assuming that bar is a directory, explain what the command **rm -rf bar** does. How is the command different from **rmdir bar**?

6.4 What is the significance of these commands? (i) **mv $HOME/include .** (ii) **cp -r bar1 bar2** (iii) **mv * ../bin**

6.5 Explain the significance of the repeat factor used in **more**. How do you search for the pattern include in a file and repeat the search? What is the difference between this repeat command and the dot command?

6.6 A file with the .ps extension should be a Postscript file, but how can you be sure? What is the importance of this file type in the printing subsystem?

6.7 A file foo contains a list of filenames, with one filename in each line. One of the filenames appears to have an embedded space. How will you (i) count the number of filenames (ii) check whether there's actually an embedded space in a filename?

6.8 How do DOS and UNIX text files differ? Name the utilities that convert files between these two formats?

6.9 You have two lists, foo1 and foo2, containing names of users. How do you create a third list of those users in foo2 who are absent in foo1? When will the command not work properly?

6.10 How do you use **tar** to add two files, foo.html and bar.html, to an archive and then compress the archive? How will you reverse the entire process and extract the files in their original uncompressed form?

6.11 Name three advantages **zip** has over **gzip**. How do you use **zip** to send a complete directory structure to someone by email? How does the recipient recreate the directory structure at her end?

6.12 What is meant by *recursive* behavior of a command? Name four commands, along with a suitable example of each, that can operate recursively.

7

Basic File Attributes

In the last two chapters, you created files and directories, navigated the file system, and copied, moved and removed files without any problem. In real life, however, matters may not be so rosy. You may have problems when handling a file or directory. Your file may be modified or even deleted by others. A restoration from a backup may be unable to write to your directory. You must know why these problems happen and how to rectify and prevent them.

The UNIX file system lets users access other files not belonging to them—without infringing on security. A file also has a number of *attributes* (properties) that are changeable by well-defined rules. In this chapter we'll use the **ls -l** command with additional options to display these attributes, which are all stored in the inode. We'll also consider two basic file attributes—permissions and ownership. The remaining attributes are taken up in Chapter 13.

WHAT YOU WILL LEARN

- Interpret the significance of the seven fields of the **ls -l** output (*listing*).
- How to obtain the listing of a specific directory.
- The importance of *ownership* and *group ownership* of a file and how they affect security.
- The significance of the nine permissions of a file as applied to different *categories* of users.
- Use **chmod** to change all file and directory permissions in a relative and absolute manner.
- Use **chown** and **chgrp** to change the owner and group owner of files on BSD and AT&T systems.

TOPICS OF SPECIAL INTEREST

- The importance of directory permissions (discussion on individual permissions deferred to Chapter 13).
- An introductory treatment of the relationship that exists between file ownership, file permissions and directory permissions.

7.1 ls -l: LISTING FILE ATTRIBUTES

We have already used the **ls** command with a number of options. It's the -l (long) option that reveals most. This option displays most attributes of a file—like its permissions, size and ownership details. The output in UNIX lingo is often referred to as the *listing*. Sometimes we combine this option with other options for displaying other attributes or ordering the list in a different sequence.

ls looks up the file's inode to fetch its attributes. Let's use **ls -l** to list seven attributes of all files in the current directory:

```
$ ls -l
total 72
-rw-r--r--   1 kumar    metal       19514 May 10 13:45 chap01
-rw-r--r--   1 kumar    metal        4174 May 10 15:01 chap02
-rw-rw-rw-   1 kumar    metal          84 Feb 12 12:30 dept.lst
-rw-r--r--   1 kumar    metal        9156 Mar 12  1999 genie.sh
drwxr-xr-x   2 kumar    metal         512 May  9 10:31 helpdir
drwxr-xr-x   2 kumar    metal         512 May  9 09:57 progs
```

The list is preceded by the words `total 72`, which indicates that a total of 72 blocks are occupied by these files in the disk, each block consisting of 512 bytes (1024 in Linux). We'll now briefly describe the significance of each field in the output.

File Type and Permissions The first column shows the type and *permissions* associated with each file. The first character in this column is mostly a -, which indicates that the file is an ordinary one. This is, however, not so for the directories `helpdir` and `progs`, where you see a `d` at the same position.

You then see a series of characters that can take the values `r`, `w`, `x` and `-`. In the UNIX system, a file can have three types of permissions—read, write and execute. You'll see how to interpret these permissions and also how to change them in Sections 7.4 and 7.5.

Links The second column indicates the number of *links* associated with the file. This is actually the number of filenames maintained by the system of that file. UNIX lets a file have as many names as you want it to have, even though there is a single file on disk. This attribute will be discussed in Chapter 13.

Note A link count greater than one indicates that the file has more than one name. That doesn't mean that there are two copies of the file.

Ownership When you create a file, you automatically become its *owner*. The third column shows kumar as the owner of all these files. The owner has full authority to tamper with a file's contents and permissions—a privilege not available with others except the root user. Similarly, you can create, modify or remove files in a directory if you are the owner of the directory.

Group Ownership When opening a user account, the system administrator also assigns the user to some group. The fourth column represents the *group owner* of the file. The concept of a group of users also owning a file has acquired importance today as group members often need to work on the same file. It's generally desirable that the group have a set of privileges distinct from others as well as the owner. Ownership and group ownership are elaborated in Section 7.3.

File Size The fifth column shows the size of the file in bytes, i.e., the amount of data it contains. The important thing to remember is that it is only a character count of the file and not a measure of the disk space that it occupies. The space occupied by a file in the disk is usually larger than this figure since files are written to disk in blocks of 1024 bytes or more. In other words, even though the file `dept.lst` contains 84 bytes, it would occupy 1024 bytes on the disk on systems that use a block size of 1024 bytes. We'll discuss the significance of block size much later in the text.

The two directories show smaller file sizes (512 bytes each). This is to be expected as a directory maintains a list of filenames along with an identification number (the inode number) for each file. The size of the directory file depends on the size of this list—whatever be the size of the files themselves.

Last Modification Time The sixth, seventh and eighth columns indicate the last modification time of the file, which is stored to the nearest second. A file is said to be modified only if its contents have changed in any way. If you change only the permissions or ownership of the file, the modification time remains unchanged. If the file is less than a year old since its last modification date, the year won't be displayed. Note that the file `genie.sh` has been modified more than a year ago.

You'll often need to run automated tools that take decisions based on a file's modification time. This column shows two other time stamps when **ls** is used with other options. The time stamps are discussed in Chapter 13.

Filename The last column displays the filenames arranged in ASCII collating sequence. You already know *(5.2)* that UNIX filenames can be very long (up to 255 characters). If you would like to see an important file at the top of the listing, then choose its name in uppercase—at least, its first letter.

The order of the list can be changed by combining the `-l` option with other options. In the rest of the chapter, we'll discuss permissions and ownership, and also learn how to change them.

7.2 THE -d OPTION: LISTING DIRECTORY ATTRIBUTES

You'll recall *(5.11.1)* that **ls**, when used with directory names, lists files in the directory, rather than the directory itself. To force **ls** to list the attributes of a directory, rather than its contents, you need to use the `-d` (directory) option:

```
$ ls -ld helpdir progs
drwxr-xr-x   2 kumar    metal           512 May  9 10:31 helpdir
drwxr-xr-x   2 kumar    metal           512 May  9 09:57 progs
```

Directories are easily identified from the listing by the first character of the first column, which here shows a `d`. For ordinary files, this slot always shows a `-` (hyphen), and for device files, either a `b` or `c`. The significance of the attributes of a directory differ a good deal from an ordinary file. Directories will be considered in some detail in Chapter 13.

> **Tip** To see the attributes of a directory rather than the files contained in it, use **ls -ld** with the directory name. Note that simply using **ls -d** will *not* list all subdirectories in the current directory.

7.3 FILE OWNERSHIP

Before we take up file permissions, you need to understand the significance of file ownership. When you create a file, your username shows up in the third column of the file's listing; you are the *owner* of the file. Your group name is seen in the fourth column; your group is the *group owner* of the file. If you copy someone else's file, you are the owner of the copy. If you can't create files in other users' home directories, it's because those directories are not owned by you (and the owner has not allowed you write access).

Several users may belong to a single group. People working on a project are generally assigned a common group, and all files created by group members (who have separate user-ids) will have the same group owner. However, make no mistake: The privileges of the group are set by the owner of the file and not by the group members.

When the system administrator creates a user account, he has to assign these parameters to the user:

- The user-id (UID)—both its name and numeric representation.
- The group-id (GID)—both its name and numeric representation. The administrator has to assign the group name also if the GID represents a new group.

The file `/etc/passwd` maintains the UID (both the number and name) and GID (but only the number). `/etc/group` contains the GID (both number and name). We'll discuss these two files when learning to add a user account in Chapter 17.

> **Tip** To know your own UID and GID without viewing `/etc/passwd` and `/etc/group`, use the **`id`** command:
>
> ```
> $ id
> uid=655537(kumar) gid=655535(metal)
> ```
>
> The uid is kumar, and if this name matches the one shown in the ownership field of the listing (**`ls -l`** output), then you are the owner of those files. It also means that you have the authority to change the file's attributes.

7.4 FILE PERMISSIONS

UNIX has a simple and well-defined system of assigning permissions to files. Issue the **`ls -l`** command once again to view the permissions of a few files:

```
$ ls -l chap02 dept.lst dateval.sh
-rwxr-xr--   1 kumar    metal       20500 May 10 19:21 chap02
-rwxr-xr-x   1 kumar    metal         890 Jan 29 23:17 dateval.sh
-rw-rw-rw-   1 kumar    metal          84 Feb 12 12:30 dept.lst
```

Observe the first column that represents the file permissions. These permissions are also different for the three files. UNIX follows a three-tiered file protection system that determines a file's access rights. To understand how this system works, let's break up the permissions string of the file `chap02` into three groups. The initial - (in the first column) represents an ordinary file and is left out of the permissions string:

```
     r w x     r - x     r - -
```

Each group here represents a *category* and contains three slots, representing the read, write and execute permissions of the file—in that order. `r` indicates read permission, which means **cat** can display the file. `w` indicates write permission; you can edit such a file with an editor. `x` indicates execute permission; the file can be executed as a program. The `-` shows the absence of the corresponding permission.

The first group (`rwx`) has all three permissions. The file is readable, writable and executable by the *owner* of the file, kumar. But do we know who the owner is? Yes we do. The third column shows kumar as the owner and the first permissions group applies to kumar. You have to log in with the username kumar for these privileges to apply to you.

The second group (`r-x`) has a hyphen in the middle slot, which indicates the absence of write permission by the *group owner* of the file. This group owner is metal, and all users belonging to the metal group have read and execute permissions only.

The third group (`r--`) has the write and execute bits absent. This set of permissions is applicable to *others*, i.e., those who are neither the owner kumar nor belong to the metal group. This category (others) is often referred to as the *world*. This file is not world-writable.

You can set different permissions for the three categories of users—owner, group and others. It's important that you understand them because a little learning here can be a dangerous thing. A faulty file permission is a sure recipe for disaster.

> **Note** The group permissions here don't apply to kumar (the owner) even if kumar belongs to the metal group. The owner has its own set of permissions that override the group owner's permissions. However, when kumar renounces the ownership of the file, the group permissions then apply to him.

7.5 chmod: CHANGING FILE PERMISSIONS

Before we take up **chmod**, let's decide to change a habit. Henceforth, we'll refer to the owner as *user* because that's how the **chmod** command (which changes file permissions) refers to the owner. In this section, whenever we use the term *user*, we'll actually mean *owner*.

A file or directory is created with a default set of permissions, and this default is determined by a simple setting (called *umask*), which we'll discuss later. Generally, the default setting write-protects a file from all except the user (new name for owner), though all users *may* have read access. However, this may not be so on your system. To know your system's default create a file `xstart`:

```
$ cat /usr/bin/startx > xstart                    Actually copies the file startx
$ ls -l xstart
-rw-r--r--    1 kumar    metal       1906 Sep  5 23:38 xstart
```

It seems that, by default, a file doesn't also have execute permission. So how does one execute such a file? To do that, the permissions of the file need to be changed. This is done with **chmod**.

The **chmod** (change mode) command is used to set the permissions of one or more files for all three categories of users (user, group and others). It can be run only by the user (the owner) and the superuser. The command can be used in two ways:

- In a relative manner by specifying the changes to the current permissions.
- In an absolute manner by specifying the final permissions.

We'll consider both ways of using **chmod** in the following sections.

7.5.1 Relative Permissions

When changing permissions in a relative manner, **chmod** only changes the permissions specified in the command line *and leaves the other permissions unchanged.* In this mode it uses the following syntax:

chmod *category operation permission filename(s)*

chmod takes as its argument an expression comprising some letters and symbols that completely describe the user category and the type of permission being assigned or removed. The expression contains three components:

- User *category* (user, group, others)
- The *operation* to be performed (assign or remove a permission)
- The type of *permission* (read, write, execute)

By using suitable abbreviations for each of these components, you can frame a compact expression and then use it as an argument to **chmod.** The abbreviations used for these three components are shown in Table 7.1.

Now let's consider an example. To assign execute permission to the user (We won't remind again that user here is the owner.) of the file xstart, we need to frame a suitable expression by using appropriate characters from each of the three columns of Table 7.1. Since the file needs to be executable only by the user, the expression required is u+x:

```
$ chmod u+x xstart
$ ls -l xstart
-rwxr--r--    1 kumar    metal          1906 May 10 20:30 xstart
```

The command assigns (+) execute (x) permission to the user (u), but other permissions remain unchanged. You can now execute the file if you are the owner of the file but the other categories (i.e., group and others) still can't. To enable all of them to execute this file, you have to use multiple characters to represent the user category (ugo):

```
$ chmod ugo+x xstart ; ls -l xstart
-rwxr-xr-x    1 kumar    metal          1906 May 10 20:30 xstart
```

The string ugo combines all three categories—user, group and others. UNIX also offers a shorthand symbol a (all) to act as a synonym for the string. And, as if that wasn't enough, there's an even shorter form that combines these three categories. When it is not specified, the permission applies to all categories. So the previous sequence can be replaced by either of the following:

```
chmod a+x xstart                              a implies ugo
chmod +x xstart                               By default, a is implied
```

chmod also accepts more than one filename in the command line. When you need to assign the same set of permissions to a group of files, all the filenames have to be specified with a single **chmod** command:

```
chmod u+x note note1 note3
```

Permissions are removed with the - operator. To remove the read permission from both group and others, use the expression go-r:

```
$ ls -l xstart
-rwxr-xr-x   1 kumar    metal          1906 May 10 20:30 xstart
$ chmod go-r xstart ; ls -l xstart
-rwx--x--x   1 kumar    metal          1906 May 10 20:30 xstart
```

chmod also accepts multiple expressions delimited by commas. For instance, to restore the original permissions to the file xstart, you have to remove the execute permission from all (a-x) and assign read permission to group and others (go+r):

```
$ chmod a-x,go+r xstart ; ls -l xstart
-rw-r--r--   1 kumar    metal          1906 May 10 20:30 xstart
```

More than one permission can also be set; u+rwx is a valid **chmod** expression. So setting write and execute permissions for others is no problem:

```
$ chmod o+wx xstart ; ls -l xstart
-rw-r--rwx   1 kumar    metal          1906 May 10 20:30 xstart
```

We described relative permissions here, but **chmod** also uses an absolute assignment system, which is taken up in the next topic.

Table 7.1 Abbreviations Used by **chmod**

Category	*Operation*	*Permission*
u—User	+ —Assigns permission	r—Read permission
g—Group	- —Removes permission	w—Write permission
o—Others	= —Assigns absolute permission	x—Execute permission
a—All (ugo)		

7.5.2 Absolute Permissions

Sometimes you don't need to know what a file's current permissions are, but want to set all nine permission bits explicitly. The expression used by **chmod** here is a string of three octal numbers (base 8). Each type of permission is assigned a number as shown:

- Read permission—4
- Write permission—2
- Execute permission—1

For each category we add the numbers that represent the assigned permissions. For instance, 6 represents read and write permissions, and 7 represents all permissions.

To take a simple example, if a file has read and write permissions for the user, the octal representation of the user's permissions will be 4 + 2 = 6. When this exercise is repeated for the other categories, the result will be a three-character string representing three octal digits, with each octal digit indicating the permissions for the category. The sequence followed is user, group and others.

You can use this method to assign read and write permission to all three categories. Without octal numbers, you should normally be using **chmod a+rw xstart** to achieve the task (assuming there was no execute permission initially). Now you can use a different method:

```
$ chmod 666 xstart ; ls -l xstart
-rw-rw-rw-    1 kumar    metal        1906 May 10 20:30 xstart
```

The 6 indicates read and write permissions (4 + 2). To restore the original permissions to the file, you need to remove the write permission (2) from group and others:

```
$ chmod 644 xstart ; ls -l xstart
-rw-r--r--    1 kumar    metal        1906 May 10 20:30 xstart
```

To assign all permissions to the owner, read and write permissions to the group, and only execute permission to the others, use this:

```
chmod 761 xstart
```

Now it should be quite easy for you to understand that the expression 777 signifies all permissions for all categories, while 000 indicates absence of all permissions for all categories.

Note Remember that a file's permissions can only be changed by the owner (understood by **chmod** as *user*) of the file. One user can't change the protection modes of files belonging to another user. However, the system administrator can tamper with all file attributes including permissions, irrespective of their ownership.

7.5.3 The Security Implications

To understand the security implications behind these permissions and the role played by **chmod**, consider the default permissions of the file xstart that was shown at the beginning of Section 7.5:

```
-rw-r--r--    1 kumar    metal        1906 May 10 20:30 xstart
```

These permissions are fairly safe; only the user can edit the file. What are the implications if we remove all permissions in either of these ways?

```
chmod u-rw,go-r xstart
chmod 000 xstart
```

The listing in either case will look like this:

```
----------    1 kumar    metal        1906 May 10 20:30 xstart
```

This setting renders the file virtually useless; you simply can't do anything useful with it. *But the user can still delete this file!* To understand why that can happen, you need to understand directory permissions and how they are related to file permissions.

On the other hand, you must not be too generous (and careless, too) to have all permissions enabled for all categories of users, using either of these commands:

```
chmod a+rwx xstart
chmod 777 xstart
```

The resulting permissions setting is simply dangerous:

```
-rwxrwxrwx   1 kumar    metal         1906 May 10 20:30 xstart
```

It's the universal write permission here that concerns us most. This file can be written by all. You shouldn't be able to read, write or execute every file. If that were possible, you can never have a secure system. The UNIX system, by default, never allows that, and no sensible user will compromise security so easily.

> **Note** We ignored the directory permissions in our discussions, but they also have a major role to play in setting a file's access rights. No matter how careful you are with your file permissions, a faulty directory permission will affect the security of all files housed in that directory. It doesn't matter who owns the file or whether the file itself has write permission for that user. The directory is taken up first in Section 7.6 and then again in Chapter 13.

7.5.4 Using chmod Recursively (-R)

It's possible to make **chmod** descend a directory hierarchy and apply the expression to every file and subdirectory it finds. This is done with the -R (recursive) option:

```
chmod -R a+x shell_scripts
```

This makes all files and subdirectories found in the tree-walk (that commences from the shell_scripts directory) executable by all users. You can provide multiple directory and filenames, and if you want to use **chmod** on your home directory tree, then "cd" to it and use it in one of these ways:

```
chmod -R 755 .                                   Works on hidden files also
chmod -R a+x *                                   Leaves out hidden files
```

Even though the . and * seem to be equivalent, there's a subtle difference. When you know the shell metacharacters well, you'll appreciate that the * doesn't match files beginning with a dot. If you want **chmod** to work on the dot files also, the . would be a safer bet.

7.6 DIRECTORY PERMISSIONS

Directories also have their own permissions and the significance of these permissions differ a great deal from those of ordinary files. You may not have expected this, but be aware that read and write access to an ordinary file are also influenced by the permissions of the directory housing them. It's possible that a file can't be accessed even though it has read permission, and can be removed even when it's write-protected. In fact, it's very easy to make it behave that way.

If the default directory permissions are not altered, the **chmod** theory still applies. However, if they are changed, unusual things can happen. Though directory permissions are taken up later *(13.4)*, it's worthwhile to know what the default permissions are on your system:

```
$ mkdir c_progs; ls -ld c_progs
drwxr-xr-x   2 kumar    metal         512 May  9 09:57 c_progs
```

The default permissions of a directory on this system are `rwxr-xr-x` (or 755); that's what they should be. *A directory must never be writable by group and others.* If you find that your files are being tampered with even though they appear to be protected, check up the directory permissions. If the permissions differ from what you see here, then look up Chapter 13 for remedial action.

Caution If a directory has write permission for group and others also, then be assured that every user can remove every file in the directory! As a rule, you must not make directories universally writable unless you have definite reasons to do so.

Note The default file and directory permissions on your machine could be different from what has been assumed here. The defaults are determined by the *umask* setting of your shell. This topic is discussed in Section 13.5.

7.7 CHANGING FILE OWNERSHIP

File ownership is a feature often ignored by many users. By now you know well enough that when a user kumar of the metal group creates a file `foo`, he becomes the owner of `foo`, and metal becomes the group owner. It's only kumar who can change the major file attributes like its permissions and group ownership. No member of the metal group (except kumar) can change these attributes. However, when sharma copies `foo`, the ownership of the copy is transferred to sharma, and he can then manipulate the attributes of the copy at will.

There are two commands meant to change the ownership of a file or directory—**chown** and **chgrp**. UNIX systems differ in the way they restrict the usage of these two commands. On BSD-based systems, only the system administrator can change a file's owner with **chown**. On the same systems, the restrictions are less severe when it comes to changing groups with **chgrp**. On other systems, only the owner can change both.

7.7.1 chown: Changing File Owner

We'll first consider the behavior of BSD-based **chown** (change owner) that has been adopted by many systems including Solaris and Linux. The command is used in this way:

```
chown options owner [:group]  file(s)
```

chown transfers ownership of a file to a user, and it seems that it can optionally change the group as well. The command requires the user-id (UID) of the recipient, followed by one or more filenames. Changing ownership requires superuser permission, so let's first change our status to that of superuser with the **su** command:

```
$ su
Password: ********                    This is the root password!
# _                                   This is another shell
```

After the password is successfully entered, **su** returns a # prompt, the same prompt used by root. **su** let's us acquire superuser status if we know the root password. To now renounce the ownership of the file note to sharma, use **chown** in the following way:

```
# ls -l note
-rwxr----x   1 kumar    metal         347 May 10 20:30 note
# chown sharma note ; ls -l note
-rwxr----x   1 sharma   metal         347 May 10 20:30 note
# exit                                Switches from superuser's shell
$ _                                   to user's login shell
```

Once ownership of the file has been given away to sharma, the user file permissions that previously applied to kumar now apply to sharma. Thus, kumar can no longer edit note since there's no write privilege for group and others. He can't get back the ownership either. But he can copy the file to his own directory, in which case he becomes the owner of the copy.

7.7.2 chgrp: Changing Group Owner

By default, the group owner of a file is the group to which the owner belongs. The **chgrp** (change group) command changes a file's group owner. On systems that implement the BSD version of **chgrp** (like Solaris and Linux), a user can change the group owner of a file, but only to a group to which she also belongs. Yes, a user can belong to more than one group, and the one shown in /etc/passwd is the user's main group. We'll discuss supplementary groups in Chapter 17 featuring system administration.

chgrp shares a similar syntax with **chown**. In the following example, kumar changes the group ownership of dept.lst to dba (no superuser permission required):

```
$ ls -l dept.lst
-rw-r--r--   1 kumar    metal         139 Jun  8 16:43 dept.lst
$ chgrp dba dept.lst ; ls -l dept.lst
-rw-r--r--   1 kumar    dba           139 Jun  8 16:43 dept.lst
```

This command will work on a BSD-based system if kumar is also a member of the dba group. If he is not, then only the superuser can make the command work. Note that kumar can reverse this action and restore the previous group ownership (to metal) because he is still owner of the file and consequently retains all rights related to it.

Using **chown** *to Do Both* As an added benefit, UNIX allows the administrator to use only **chown** to change both owner and group. The syntax requires the two arguments to be separated by a :

```
chown sharma:dba dept.lst             Ownership to sharma, group to dba
```

Like **chmod**, both **chown** and **chgrp** use the -R option to perform their operations in a recursive manner.

7.8 CONCLUSION

In this chapter we considered two important file attributes—permissions and ownership. After we complete our first round of discussions related to files, we'll take up the other file attributes—the links and time stamps (Chapter 13). We also need to examine the inode that stores all these attributes. By the time you complete this text, you should be able to access and manipulate files and inode information with both UNIX commands and system calls used in C programs. In the next chapter, we'll discuss file editing with the **vi** editor.

WRAP UP

The UNIX file has a number of attributes and seven of them are listed with **ls -l**, often called the *listing*. **ls -ld** used with a directory name lists directory attributes.

A file can have more than one *link*, i.e., more than one name without having multiple copies on disk.

A file has an *owner*, usually the name of the user (UID) who creates the file. A file is also owned by a group (GID), by default, the group to which the user belongs. Both UID and GID are maintained in /etc/passwd. Apart from the superuser, it's only the owner who can change all file attributes.

Other fields in the listing include the date and time of last modification of the file and the file size in bytes. The size is not the actual space the file occupies on disk, but the number of bytes it contains.

A file can have read (r), write (w) or execute (x) permission, and there are three sets of such permissions for the *user* (u), *group* (g) and *others* (o).

A file's owner uses **chmod** to alter file permissions. The permissions can be *relative* when used with the + or - symbols, or *absolute* when used with octal numbers. The octal digit 7 includes read (4), write (2) and execute permissions (1).

For security reasons, a regular file shouldn't normally have write permission for group and others. The significance of directory permissions differs from those of ordinary files. A file's access rights are also influenced by the permissions of its directory. Usually a directory has read and execute permission for all three categories.

chown and **chgrp** are used to transfer ownership and group ownership, respectively. They can be used by the owner of the file on AT&T systems. On BSD systems, **chown** can be used only by the superuser, and a user can use **chgrp** to change her group to another to which she also belongs.

TEST YOUR UNDERSTANDING

7.1 A file contains 1026 bytes. How many bytes of disk space will it occupy?

7.2 Show the octal representation of these permissions: (i) rwxr-xrw- (ii) rw-r----- (iii) --x-w-r--

7.3 What will the permissions string look like for these octal values? (i) 567 (ii) 623 (iii) 421

7.4 If a file's permissions are 000, can the superuser still read and write the file?

7.5 Which important file attribute changes when you copy a file from some other user account?

7.6 Try creating a directory in the system directories /bin and /tmp. What do you notice and why does that happen?

7.7 If the owner doesn't have write permission on a file but her group has, can she edit it?

7.8 How is **chown** different from **chgrp** when it comes to renouncing ownership?

7.9 Explain with reference to the dot and * what the following commands do: (i) **`chown -R project .`** (ii) **`chgrp -R project *`**

FLEX YOUR BRAIN

7.1 How will you obtain a complete listing of all files and directories in the whole system and save the output in a file?

7.2 Explain briefly the significance of the first four fields of the **`ls -l`** output. Who can change these attributes? Is there any attribute that can be changed *only* by the superuser?

7.3 Explain the significance of the following commands: (i) **`ls -ld .`** (ii) **`ls -l ..`**

7.4 The commands **`ls bar`** and **`ls -d bar`** display the same output—the string `bar`. This can happen in two ways. Explain.

7.5 Create a file `foo`. How do you assign all permissions to the owner and remove all permissions from others using (i) relative assignment and (ii) absolute assignment? Do you need to make any assumptions about `foo`'s default permissions?

7.6 Explain the consequences, from the security viewpoint, of a file having the permissions (i) 000 and (ii) 777.

7.7 Examine the output of the two commands below. Explain whether kumar can (i) edit (ii) delete (iii) change permissions (iv) change ownership of `foo`:

```
$ who am i ; ls -l foo
kumar
-r--rw----    1 sumit    kumar         78 Jan 27 16:57 foo
```

7.8 Assuming that a file's current permissions are `rw-r-xr--`, specify the **chmod** expression required to change them to (i) `rwxrwxrwx` (ii) `r--r-----` (iii) `--r--r--` (iv) `--------`, using both the relative and absolute methods of assigning permissions.

7.9 Use **`chmod -w .`** and then try to create and remove a file in the current directory. Can you do that? Is the command same as **`chmod a-w foo`**?

7.10 How will you determine whether your system uses the BSD or AT&T version of **chown** and **chgrp**?

8

The vi Editor

No matter what work you do with the UNIX system, you'll eventually write some C programs or shell (or **perl**) scripts. You may have to edit some of the system files at times. For all this you must learn to use an editor, and UNIX provides a very versatile one—**vi**. Bill Joy created this editor for the BSD system. The program is now standard on all UNIX systems. Bram Moolenaar improved it and called it **vim** (vi improved). In this text we discuss the **vi** editor and also note the features of **vim** available in Linux.

Like any editor, **vi** uses a number of internal commands to navigate to any point in a text file and edit the text there. It also allows you to copy and move text within a file and also from one file to another. **vi** offers cryptic, and sometimes mnemonic, internal commands for editing work. It makes complete use of the keyboard where practically every key has a function. **vi** has numerous features but you don't need to master **vi** right now; a working knowledge is all that is required initially. The advanced features of **vi** are taken up in Part II of this book.

WHAT YOU WILL LEARN

- The three modes in which **vi** operates for sharing the workload.
- Use the *repeat factor* to repeat a command multiple times.
- Use the *Input Mode* to insert and replace text.
- Use the *ex Mode* to save the buffer and quit the editor.
- Use the *Command Mode* to perform navigation in a relative and absolute manner.
- Use the *word* as a navigation unit for movement along a line.
- Delete, yank (copy) and move text using *operators*.
- Undo last editing action and repeat the last command.
- Search for a pattern and repeat the search both forward and backward.
- Use the ex Mode to perform substitution—replacing one string with another.

TOPICS OF SPECIAL INTEREST

- Master the technique of using a three-function sequence to (i) search for a pattern (ii) take some action and (iii) repeat the search and action.
- Learn to use the two powerful features available in **vim**—word completion and multiple undoing.

8.1 vi BASICS

For a quick tour of **vi** let's add some text to a file. Invoke **vi** with the filename sometext:

```
vi sometext
```

In all probability, the file doesn't exist, and **vi** presents you a full screen with the filename shown at the bottom with the qualifier, [New File]. The cursor is positioned at the top and all remaining lines of the screen (except the last) show a ~. You can't take your cursor there yet; they are nonexistent lines. The last line is reserved for commands that you can enter to act on the text. This line is also used by the system to display messages.

You are now in the *Command Mode*, one of the three modes used by **vi**. This is the mode where you can pass commands to act on text, using most of the keys of the keyboard. Pressing a key doesn't show it on screen but may perform a function like moving the cursor to the next line, or deleting a line. You can't use the Command Mode to enter or replace text.

For text editing, **vi** uses 24 of the 25 lines that are normally available in a terminal. To enter text, you must switch to the *Input Mode*. First press the key marked i, and you are in this mode ready to input text. Subsequent key depressions will then show up on the screen as text input. Start inserting a few lines of text, each line followed by *[Enter]*, as shown in Fig. 8.1.

```
This is the vi editor[Enter]
It is slow in getting started but is quite powerful[Enter]
It operates in three modes[Enter]
All the features of ex are also available[Enter]
You can even escape to the UNIX shell[Enter]
It maintains 26 buffers for storing chunks of text
~
~
~
~
~
```

Fig. 8.1 Inserting Some Text

After text entry is complete, the cursor is positioned on the last character of the last line. This is known as the *current line* and the character where the cursor is stationed is the *current cursor position*. If you see something that shouldn't be there, use the *[Backspace]* key to wipe it out. If a word has been misspelled, use *[Ctrl-w]* to erase the entire word.

Now press the *[Esc]* key to revert to *Command Mode*. Press it again and you'll hear a beep; a beep in **vi** indicates that a key has been pressed unnecessarily.

The text that you entered hasn't been saved on disk yet. In our case, the file sometext doesn't exist yet. The entered text exists in some temporary storage called a *buffer*. To save the entered text, you must switch to the *ex Mode* or *Last Line Mode* (the third mode). Invoke the ex Mode from the

Command Mode by entering a **:** (colon), which shows up in the last line. Enter an **x** and press *[Enter]*:

```
:x[Enter]
"sometext" 6 lines, 232 characters
$ _                                        Quits editor—back to shell prompt
```

The file is saved on disk and **vi** returns the shell prompt. To modify this file, you'll have to invoke **vi sometext** again. But before moving ahead, let's summarize the modes used by **vi**:

- *Command Mode*—The default mode of the editor where every key pressed is interpreted as a command to run on text. You'll have to be in this mode to copy and delete text. Unnecessary pressing of *[Esc]* in this mode sounds a beep but also confirms that you are in this mode.
- *Input Mode*—Every key pressed after switching to this mode actually shows up as text. This mode is invoked by pressing one of the keys shown in Table 8.1. Pressing *[Esc]* in this mode takes **vi** to Command Mode.
- *ex Mode* or *Last Line Mode*—The mode used to handle files (like for saving) and perform substitution (replacing one string with another). Pressing a **:** in the Command Mode invokes this mode. You then enter an ex Mode command followed by *[Enter]*. After the command is run, you are back to the default Command Mode.

Much of the chapter deals with Command Mode commands where most of the action is. Some of these commands also have ex Mode equivalents which are sometimes easier to use. But all three modes also have their own exclusive features and an editing session in **vi** involves constant switching between modes as depicted in Fig. 8.2.

8.1.1 The Repeat Factor

When discussing **more** *(6.5.1)*, we introduced the *repeat factor* as a command prefix to repeat the command as many times as the prefix. **vi** also provides the repeat factor with many of its Command Mode and Input Mode commands. So if the Command Mode command **k** moves the cursor up one line, then **10k** moves it up 10 lines. The repeat factor thus speeds up operations. You'll be using it several times in this chapter.

8.1.2 The File .exrc

The default behavior of **vi** is adequate for novices, but as you get comfortable with it, you'll feel the need to customize it to behave in a way that makes writing programs and documents easier. **vi** reads the file `$HOME/.exrc` (same as `~/.exrc` in some shells) on startup. If **ls -a** doesn't show this file in your home directory, then you can create or copy one. Linux users must note that **vim** generally doesn't use `.exrc`, but only `.vimrc`.

Many ex Mode commands can be placed in this file so they are available in every session. You can create abbreviations, redefine your keys to behave differently and also make variable settings. Your `.exrc` will progressively develop into an exclusive "library" containing all shortcuts and settings that you use regularly. It could be your most prized possession, so always keep a backup of this file.

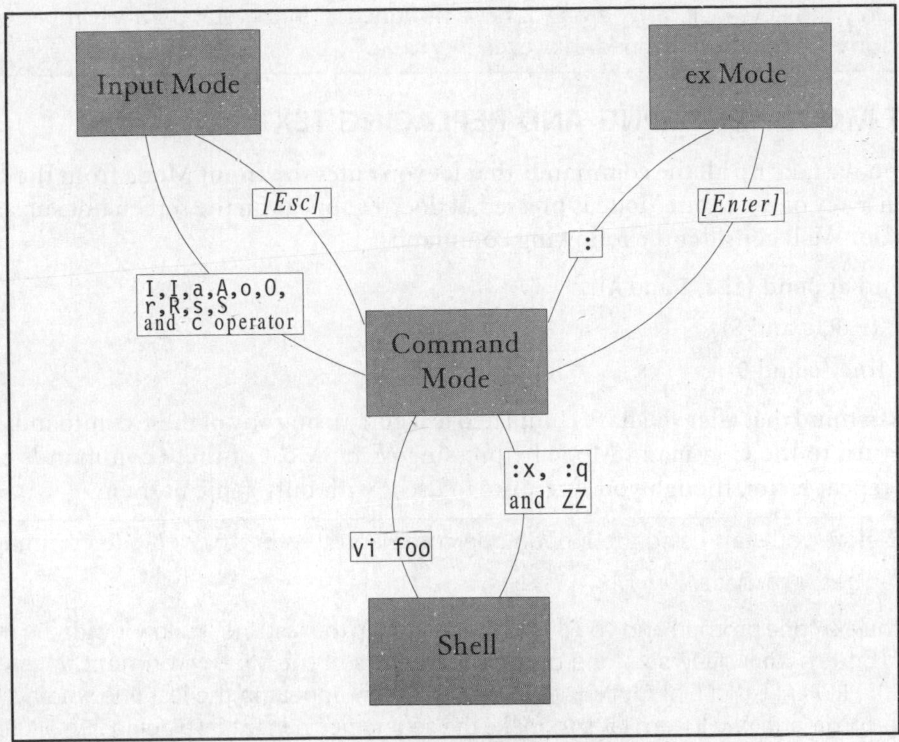

Fig. 8.2 The Three Modes

8.1.3 A Few Tips First

We are about to take off, but before we do that, a few tips at this stage will stand you in good stead. You must keep them in mind at all times when you are doing work with `vi`:

- *Clearing the Screen* If the screen gets garbled for some reason, use *[Ctrl-l]* (el) in the Command Mode to redraw the screen. If you hit *[Ctrl-l]* in the Input Mode, you'll see the symbol `^L` on the screen. Use the backspace key to wipe it out, press *[Esc]* and then hit *[Ctrl-l]*.
- *Don't Use [CapsLock]* Make sure that the *[CapsLock]* key is not activated on most occasions. `vi` commands are case-sensitive; `a` and `A` are different Input Mode commands. Even if you have to activate this key to enter a large block of text in uppercase, make sure you deactivate the key after text entry is complete.
- *Avoid Using the PC Navigation Keys* As far as possible, avoid using all the standard navigation keys like Up, Down, Left and Right, *[PageUp]* and *[PageDown]*. They can't take you to a specific line number and many of them could fail when you use `vi` over a network connection. `vi` provides an elaborate set of keys for navigation purposes.
- `vi` reads the `TERM` variable to determine the file that contains the terminal's characteristics. As discussed later *(11.1.1)*, `vi` actually reads a file in a specific directory to know the control sequences that apply to the terminal name assigned to `TERM`. You should always check `TERM` whenever `vi` behaves in an awkward manner.

> **Note** Only the keys **g**, **K**, **q**, **v**, **V** and **Z** have no function in the standard **vi** implementation. Some of them are defined, however, in **vim**.

8.2 INPUT MODE—ENTERING AND REPLACING TEXT

In this section we take up all the commands that let you enter the Input Mode from the Command Mode. When a key of the Input Mode is pressed, it doesn't appear on the screen but subsequent key depressions do. We'll consider the following commands:

- Insert and append (**i**, **a**, **I** and **A**),
- Replace (**r**, **R**, **s** and **S**),
- Open a line (**o** and **O**).

Always keep in mind that after you have completed text entry using any of these commands (except **r**), you must return to the Command Mode by pressing *[Esc]*. Most of these commands can also be used with a repeat factor, though you'll require to use it with only some of them.

> **Tip** Before you start using the Input Mode commands, enter this ex Mode command:
>
> `:set showmode`*[Enter]*
>
> Enter a **:** (the ex Mode prompt) and you'll see it appearing in the last line. Follow it with the two words and press *[Enter]*. `showmode` sets one of the parameters of the **vi** environment. Messages like `INSERT MODE`, `REPLACE MODE` or `CHANGE MODE`, etc. will now appear in the last line when you run an Input Mode command. We'll learn later to make the setting permanent by placing it in `$HOME/.exrc`.

8.2.1 Insertion of Text (i and a)

The simplest type of input is insertion of text. Whether the file contains any text or not, when **vi** is invoked, the cursor is always positioned on the first character of the first line. To insert text at this position, press

`i` *Existing text will be shifted right*

Pressing this key changes the mode from Command to Input. Since the showmode setting was made at the beginning (with **:set showmode**), you'll see the words `INSERT MODE` at the bottom-right corner of the screen. Further key depressions will result in text being entered and displayed on the screen.

If the **i** command is invoked with the cursor positioned on existing text, text on its right will be shifted further without being overwritten. The insertion of text with **i** is shown in Fig. 8.3, along with the position of the cursor.

There are other methods of inputting text. To append text to the right of the cursor position, use

`a` *Existing text will also be shifted right*

followed by the text you wish to key in (Fig. 8.4). After you have finished editing, press *[Esc]*. With **i** and **a**, you can append several lines of text in this way.

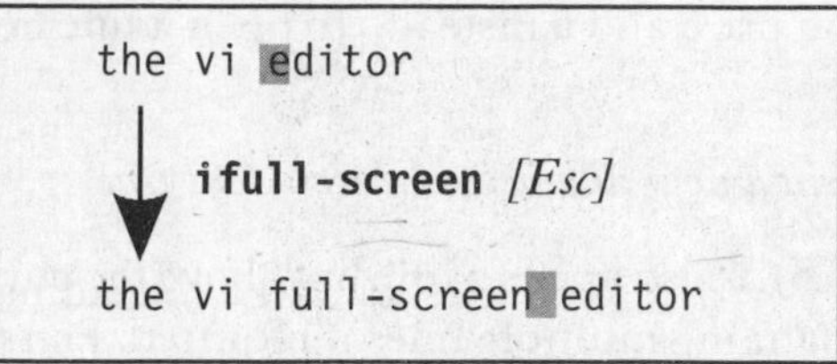

Fig. 8.3 Text Insertion with `i`

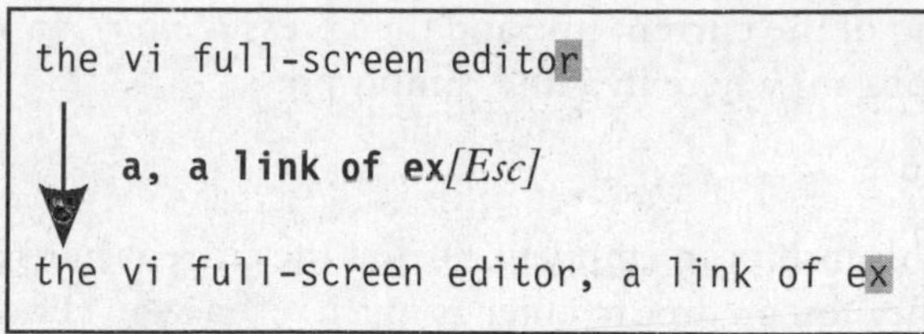

Fig. 8.4 Text Appending with `a`

8.2.2 Insertion of Text at Line Extremes (I and A)

I and **A** behave somewhat like **i** and **a** except that they work at line extremes by performing the necessary navigation to move there:

`I`	Inserts text at beginning of line.
`A`	Appends text at end of line.

These two commands are suitable for converting code to comment lines in a C program (Fig 8.5). A comment line in C is of the form /* *comment* */. Use **I** on an existing line that you now wish to convert to a comment, and then enter the symbols /*. After pressing *[Esc]*, use **A** to append */ at the end of the line and press *[Esc]* again. A document author often needs to use **A** to continue text entry from the point work was suspended—adding a sentence to a paragraph, for instance.

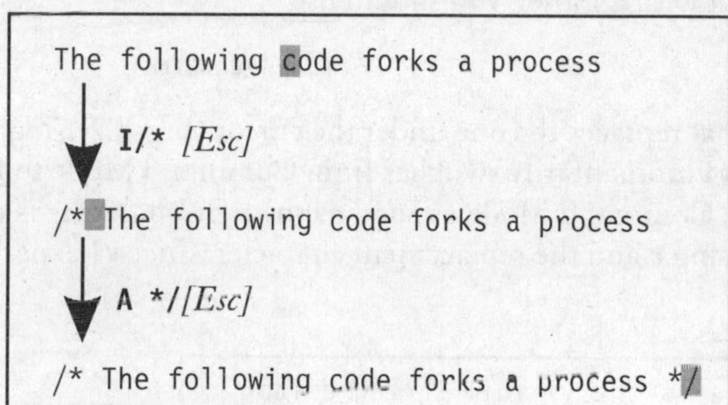

Fig. 8.5 Using `I` and `A` to Create a Comment Line in a C Program

> **Tip** C language programmers sometimes precede a block of comment lines with a pattern like this:
>
> ```
> /**********************************************************************
> ```
>
> It seems that there are 70 asterisks here, and to draw them you should use a repeat factor. After you have entered / in the Input Mode, press *[Esc]*, and then enter **70a***[Esc]. You'll see 70 asterisks appended to the /.

8.2.3 Opening a New Line (o and O)

Many a time it has been observed that people migrating from a word-processing environment use a convoluted sequence to open a new line below the current line. They move the cursor past the end of the current line and then press *[Enter]*. In **vi**, you use **o** and **O** instead. To open a line below from anywhere in a line, simply press

o *Opens a new line below the current line*

This inserts an empty line below the current line (Fig. 8.6). **O** also opens a line but above the current line. You are free to enter as much text as you choose, spanning multiple lines if required. Press the *[Esc]* key after completing text input.

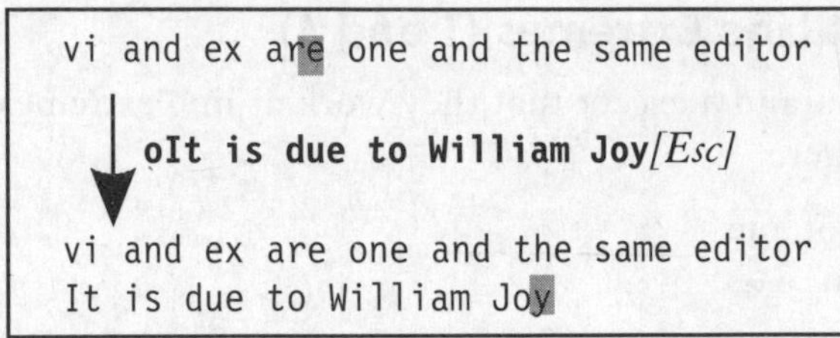

Fig. 8.6 Opening a New Line with **o**

8.2.4 Replacing Text (r, s, R and S)

To change existing text, **vi** provides mainly four commands (actually, more) as shown in the heading. To replace a single character with another, you should use

r *No [Esc] required*

followed by the character that replaces the one under the cursor (Fig. 8.7). You can replace a single character only in this way. **vi** momentarily switches from Command Mode to Input Mode when **r** is pressed. It returns to the Command Mode as soon as the new character is entered. There's no need to press *[Esc]* when using **r** and the replacement character, since **vi** expects a single character anyway.

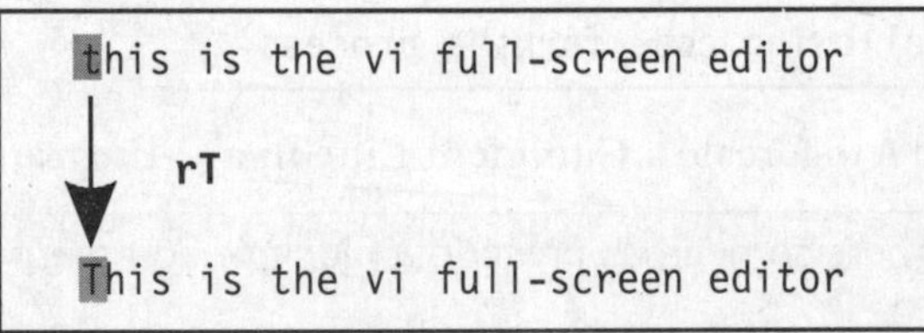

Fig. 8.7 Replacing a Single Character with **r**

When you want to replace the letter d with 10f in a **printf** statement in C, you need to replace one character with three. In that case, press

s *Replaces one character with many*

vi deletes the character under the cursor and switches to Input Mode. It may also show a $ at that location to indicate that replacement will not affect text on its right. Now enter **10f** and press *[Esc]*.

To replace multiple characters, use a repeat factor. **3s** replaces three characters with new text. Use of **s** is shown in Fig. 8.8.

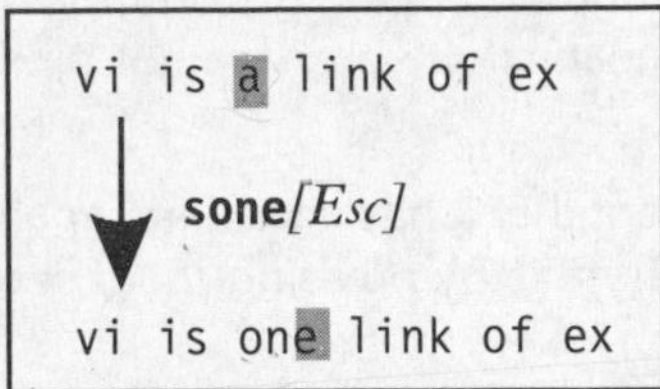

Fig. 8.8 Replacing Text with **s**

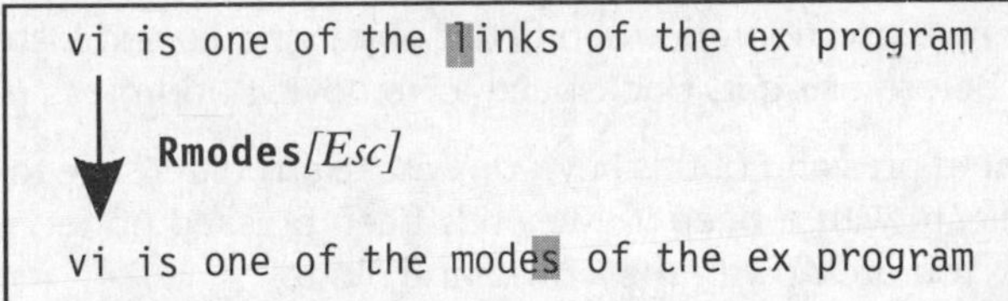

Fig. 8.9 Replacing Text with **R**

R and **S** act in a similar manner compared to their lowercase ones except that they act on a larger group of characters:

- `R` Replaces all text on the right of the cursor position.
- `S` Replaces the entire line irrespective of the cursor position. (Existing line disappears)

Try using the repeat factor with **R** and **S** and see whether you can take advantage of this feature. Use of **R** is shown in Fig. 8.9.

You have now been able to enter the Input Mode in ten ways. The functions of these ten keys are summarized in Table 8.1.

> **LINUX:** A superb text completion feature is available in **vim**. If the string `printf` is available in the file, you don't need to enter the entire string eve. Just key in as much as is necessary to make the string unique (say, up to `pr`), and then press
>
> *[Ctrl-p]*   `vim` *attempts to complete string*
>
> **vim** expands `pr` to `printf` if this is the *only* word beginning with `pr`. In case there are other words, repeated pressing of the key shows all matching words in turn. In case you have to view the list backwards, use *[Ctrl-n]*.

Table 8.1 Input Mode Commands

Command	*Function*
`i`	Inserts text to left of cursor (Existing text shifted right)
`a`	Appends text to right of cursor (Existing text shifted right)
`I`	Inserts text at beginning of line (Existing text shifted right)
`A`	Appends text at end of line
`o`	Opens line below
`O`	Opens line above
`r`*ch*	Replaces single character under cursor with *ch* (No *[Esc]* required)
`R`	Replaces text from cursor to right (Existing text overwritten)
`s`	Replaces single character under cursor with any number of characters
`S`	Replaces entire line

Note At the cost of repetition, it's emphasized yet again that you must press *[Esc]* after you have keyed in text. Although **i**, **a**, **o**, etc. are Input Mode commands, they actually *take* you to that mode. However, they are actually invoked from the Command Mode. If you press **i** to begin text insertion and then find it appearing as text instead, it means that you have not pressed *[Esc]* before using it. Backspace to remove it and press *[Esc]*.

Repeated pressing of this key won't make any difference to **vi**, except that it has a built-in capability to indicate with a beep if a key has been pressed unnecessarily. Try this by pressing *[Esc]* several times. You are now in the Command Mode.

8.3 SAVING TEXT AND QUITTING—THE ex MODE

When you edit a file using **vi**—or for that matter, any editor—the original file isn't disturbed as such, but only a copy of it that is placed in a *buffer* (a temporary form of storage). From time to time, you should save your work by writing the buffer contents to disk to keep the disk file current (or, as we say, in *sync*). When we talk of saving a file, we actually mean saving this buffer. You may also need to quit **vi** after or without saving the buffer. These features are adequately handled by the ex Mode. The basic file handling features are shown in Table 8.2.

8.3.1 Saving Your Work (:w)

We have already used the ex Mode command, **x**, to save the buffer and exit the editor *(8.1)*. For extended sessions with **vi**, you must able to save the buffer and *remain* in the editor. From time to time, you must use the **w** command to write the buffer to disk. Enter a **:**, which appears at the last line of the screen, then **w**, and finally *[Enter]*:

```
:w[Enter]
"sometext", 8 lines, 275 characters
```

You can now continue your editing work normally, only make sure that you execute this command regularly. With the **w** command you can optionally specify a filename as well. In that case, the contents are separately written to another file.

8.3.2 Saving and Quitting (:x and :wq)

The above command returns you to the Command Mode so you can continue editing. However, to save and quit the editor (i.e., return to the shell), use the **x** (exit) command instead:

```
:x[Enter]
"sometext", 8 lines, 303 characters
$ _
```

You can also use **:wq** to save and quit the editor. But that requires an additional keystroke and is not recommended for use.

Tip The best way to save and quit the editor is to use **ZZ**, a Command Mode command, instead of **:x** or **:wq**.

8.3.3 Aborting Editing (:q)

It's also possible to abort the editing process and quit the editing mode without saving the buffer. The **q** (quit) command is used to do that:

```
:q[Enter]                                   Won't work if buffer is unsaved
$ _
```

vi also has a safety mechanism that prevents you from aborting accidentally if you have modified the file (buffer) in any way. The following message is typical when you try to do so:

```
No write since last change (:quit! overrides)
```

If the buffer has been changed and you still want to abandon the changes, then use

```
:q!                                         Ignores all changes made and quits
```

to return you to the prompt irrespective of the status of the buffer—no questions asked. The **!** makes its appearance in the editor's message every time **vi** feels that you could be doing something that is potentially unsafe.

8.3.4 Writing Selected Lines

The **w** command is an abbreviated way of executing the ex Mode instruction **1,$w**. **w** can be prefixed by one or two *addresses* separated by a comma. The command

```
:10,50w n2words.pl                          Writes 41 lines to another file
```

saves lines 10 through 50 to the file `n2words.pl`. You can save a single line as well:

```
:5w n2words.pl                              Writes 5th line to another file
```

There are two symbols used with `w` that have special significance—the dot and $. The dot represents the current line while $ represents the last line of the file. You can use them singly or in combination:

```
:.w tempfile                                Saves current line (where cursor is positioned)
:$w tempfile                                Saves last line
:.,$w tempfile                              Saves current line through end
```

If `tempfile` exists and is writable by you, **vi** issues yet another warning:

```
"tempfile" File exists - use "w! tempfile" to overwrite
```

The message is clear: **vi** is telling you to suffix the ! to the **w** command to overwrite `tempfile`. The ! is the universal overriding operator in the ex Mode and you'll be using it often.

> **Note** In the ex Mode, the current line number is represented by **.** (dot) and the last line is denoted by $. **w** is the same as **1,$w**. Both commands address the entire file.

Table 8.2 Save and Exit Commands of the ex Mode

Command	*Action*
`:w`	Saves file and remains in editing mode
`:x`	Saves file and quits editing mode
`:wq`	As above
`:w n2w.pl`	Like *Save As* ..... in Microsoft Windows
`:w! n2w.pl`	As above, but overwrites existing file
`:q`	Quits editing mode when no changes are made to file
`:q!`	Quits editing mode but after abandoning changes
`:`*n1*`,`*n2*`w build.sql`	Writes lines *n1* to *n2* to file `build.sql`
`:.w build.sql`	Writes current line to file `build.sql`
`:$w build.sql`	Writes last line to file `build.sql`
`:sh`	Escapes to UNIX shell
`:recover`	Recovers file from a crash

8.3.5 Escape to the UNIX Shell (:sh and *[Ctrl-z]*)

How do do you edit and compile your C program repeatedly? You need to make a temporary escape to the shell to run the **cc** command. There are two ways; the first method is to use the ex Mode command, **sh**:

```
:sh
$ _                                          You haven't quit vi yet
```

This returns a shell prompt. Execute **cc** or any UNIX command here and then return to the editor using *[Ctrl-d]* or **exit**. Don't make the mistake of running **vi** once again, as you'll then have two instances of **vi**—an undesirable situation.

If your shell supports *job control* (which most shells do), then you can also *suspend* the current **vi** session. Just press *[Ctrl-z]* and you'll be returned a shell prompt. Run your commands and then use the **fg** command to return to the editor. Job control is discussed in Section 10.9.

8.3.6 Recovering from a Crash (:recover and -r)

Accidents can and will happen. The power can go off, leaving work unsaved. However, don't panic, **vi** stores most of its buffer information in a hidden swap file. Even though **vi** removes this file on successful exit, a power glitch or an improper shutdown procedure lets this swap file remain on disk. **vi** will then complain the next time you invoke it with the same file.

The complaint usually also contains some advice regarding the salvage operation. You'll be advised to use either the ex Mode command **:recover**, or **vi -r foo** to recover as much of `foo` as possible. After you have done that, have a look at the buffer's contents and satisfy yourself of the success of the damage control exercise. If everything seems fine, save the buffer and remove the swap file if **vi** doesn't do that on its own.

> **Note** You can't be assured of complete recovery every time. Sometimes, **vi** may show you absolute junk when using the -r option (or **:recover**). In that case, don't save the file and simply quit (with **:q!**). Start **vi** again normally; recovery is not possible here. Linux users should note that in these situations, they need to delete the file having a .swp extension manually; otherwise the file will not be editable.

8.4 NAVIGATION

We'll now consider the functions of the Command Mode. This is the mode you come to when you have finished entering or changing your text. A Command Mode command doesn't show up on screen but simply performs a function. We begin with navigation. Don't forget to avoid the cursor control keys for navigation as advised in Section 8.1.3.

8.4.1 Movement in the Four Directions (h, j, k and l)

vi provides the keys **h**, **j**, **k** and **l** to move the cursor in the four directions. These keys are placed adjacent to one another in the middle row of the keyboard. Without a repeat factor, they move the cursor by one position. Use these keys for moving the cursor vertically:

k Moves cursor up
j Moves cursor down

To move the cursor along a line, use these commands:

h Moves cursor left
l Moves cursor right

The repeat factor can be used as a command prefix with all these four commands. Thus, **4k** moves the cursor 4 lines up and **20h** takes it 20 characters to the left. Navigation with the four keys is shown in Fig. 8.10. Note that this motion is relative; you can't move to a specific line number with these keys.

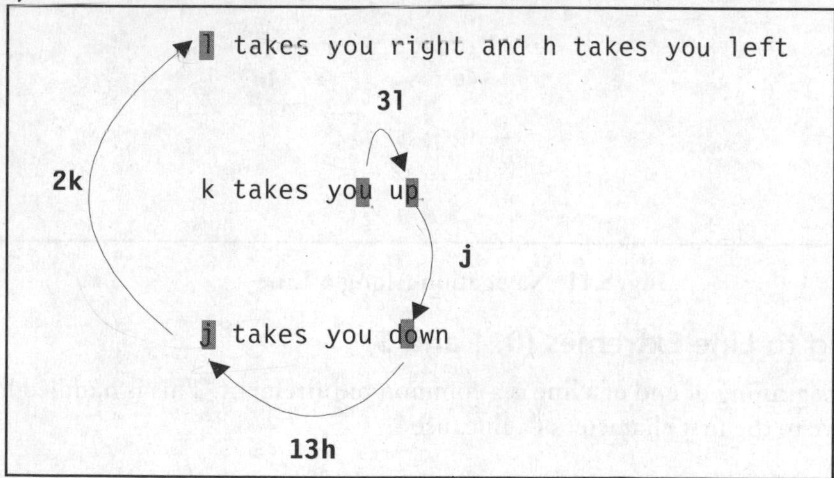

Fig. 8.10 Relative Navigation with **h**, **j**, **k** and **l**

Tip To remember the keys that move the cursor left or right, observe these four keys on your keyboard. The left-most key, **h**, moves the cursor to the left, and the right-most key, **l** (el), moves it right.

8.4.2 Word Navigation (b, e and w)

Moving by one character is not always enough, and you'll often need to move faster along a line. **vi** understands a *word* as a navigation unit which can be defined in two ways, depending on the key pressed. If your cursor is a number of words away from your desired position, you can use the word-navigation commands to go there directly. There are three basic commands:

b	Moves back to the beginning of word
w	Moves forward to the beginning of word
e	Moves forward to the end of word

A repeat factor speeds up cursor movement along a line. For example, **5b** takes the cursor five words back, while **3w** takes the cursor three words forward. A word here is simply a string of alphanumeric characters and the _ (underscore). Bash is one word; so is sh_profile. tcp-ip is three words; the hyphen by definition becomes a word too.

The keys **B**, **E** and **W** perform functions similar to those of their lowercase counterparts except that punctuation is skipped. A word here becomes a string of non-whitespace characters, i.e., those not containing a space or tab.

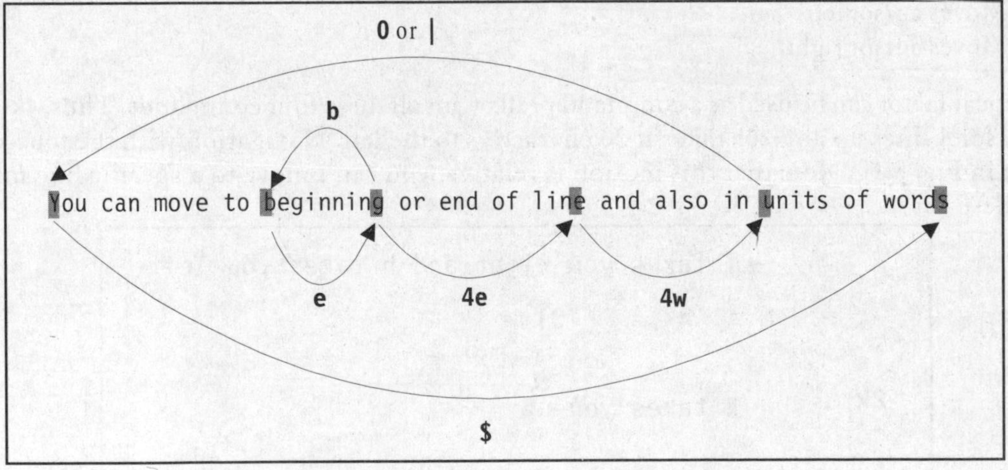

Fig. 8.11 Navigation Along a Line

8.4.3 Moving to Line Extremes (0, | and $)

Moving to the beginning or end of a line is a common requirement. This is handled by the keys **0**, **|** and **$**. To move to the first character of a line, use

0 *or* | 30| *moves the cursor to column 30*

The | takes a repeat factor and using that, you can position the cursor on a certain column. To position the cursor on column 30, use **30|**.

We used $ as the line address in the ex Mode to represent the last line of the file. The same symbol in the Command Mode represents the end of line. To move to the end of the current line, use

```
$                                    Moves to end of line
```

The use of these two commands along with those that use units of words (**b**, **e** and **w**) is shown in Fig. 8.11.

> **Note** When you use the keys **b**, **e** and **w**, remember that a word is simply a string of alphanumeric characters and the _ (underscore).

8.4.4 Scrolling (*[Ctrl-f]*, *[Ctrl-b]*, *[Ctrl-d]* and *[Ctrl-u]*)

Faster movement can be achieved by scrolling text in the window using the control keys. The two commands for scrolling a page at a time are

[Ctrl-f] Scrolls forward
[Ctrl-b] Scrolls backward

You can use the repeat factor, like in **10***[Ctrl-f]*, to scroll 10 pages and navigate faster in the process. You can scroll by half a page as well:

[Ctrl-d] Scrolls half page forward
[Ctrl-u] Scrolls half page backward

The repeat factor can also be used here.

8.4.5 Absolute Movement (G)

Upon startup, **vi** displays the total number of lines in the last line. At any time, you can press *[Ctrl-g]* to know the current line number:

```
"/etc/passwd" [Read only] line 89 of 179 --49%--
```

The cursor is on line 89 (49% of 179), and this read-protected file has 179 lines in all. Compilers also indicate line numbers in their error messages. You need to use the **G** command with the line number as repeat factor to locate the offending lines. To move to the 40th line, use

```
40G                                  Goes to line number 40
```

and to move to the beginning of the file, use

```
1G                                   Goes to line number 1
```

The end of the file is reached by simply using

```
G                                    Goes to end of file
```

> **Note** The ex Mode offers equivalent commands for moving between lines. The previous three commands can be replaced by **:40**, **:1** and **:$**, respectively (along with *[Enter]*).

8.5 EDITING TEXT

The editing facilities in **vi** are very elaborate and involve the use of *operators*. Though we'll be taking up operators in Part II of this text, for performing some of the essential editing functions that are considered in the following sections, we'll only be using a special mode of these two operators:

d Delete
y Yank (copy)

d and **y** are not commands, but they can be used (as **dd** and **yy**) for deletion and copying entire lines. The "pasting" operation is performed by the **p** and **P** commands. We'll now use these commands for editing operations.

8.5.1 Deleting Text (x and dd)

The simplest text deletion is achieved with the **x** command. This command deletes the character under the cursor. Move the cursor to the character that needs to be deleted and then press

x *Deletes a single character*

The character under the cursor gets deleted, and the text on the right shifts left to fill up the space. A repeat factor also applies here, so **4x** deletes the current character as well as three characters from the *right* (Fig. 8.12).

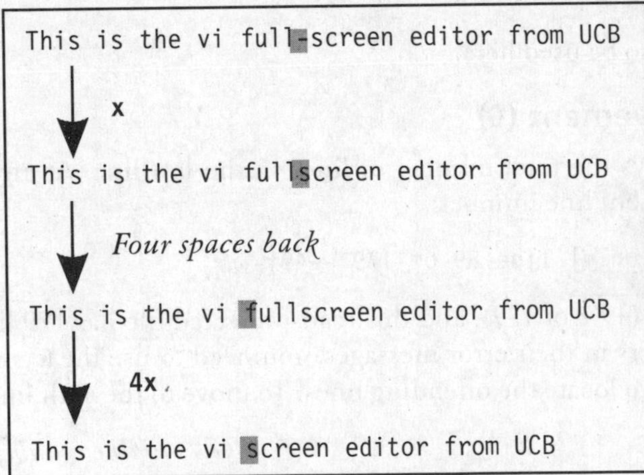

Fig. 8.12 Deleting Text with **x**

A Windows Notepad user would be surprised to note that when the cursor is at the end of a line, **x** doesn't pull up the following line but works instead on text on the *left* of the cursor. Deletion of text from the left is otherwise handled by the **X** command. Keep it pressed, and you'll see that you have erased all text to the beginning of the line.

Entire lines are removed with the **dd** "command" (rather a doubled operator). Move the cursor to any line and then press

```
dd                                    Cursor can be anywhere in line
```

6dd deletes the current line and five lines below. Fig. 8.13 illustrates the use of **dd** both with and without a repeat factor. There are other forms of deletion available in **vi** and you'll know them all after you have understood the **d** operator well *(23.1.1)*.

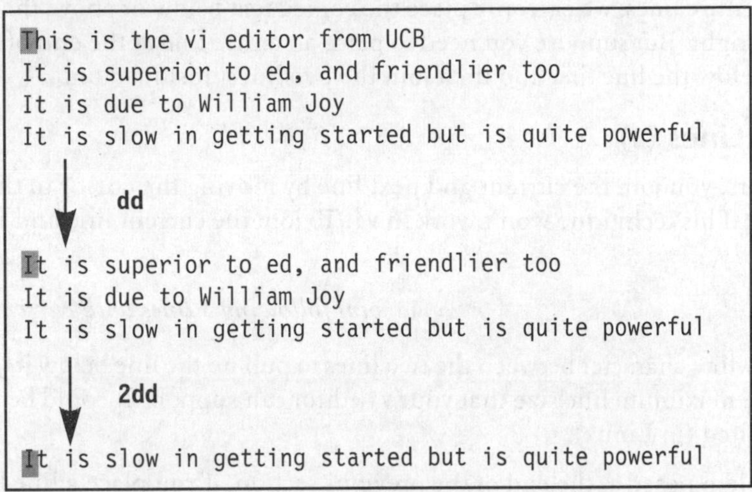

```
This is the vi editor from UCB
It is superior to ed, and friendlier too
It is due to William Joy
It is slow in getting started but is quite powerful
        dd
It is superior to ed, and friendlier too
It is due to William Joy
It is slow in getting started but is quite powerful
        2dd
It is slow in getting started but is quite powerful
```

Fig. 8.13 Deleting Lines with **dd**

8.5.2 Moving Text (p)

Text movement requires you to perform an additional task: Put the text at the new location with **p** or **P**. **vi** uses these two commands for all "put" operations that follow delete or copy operations. The significance of **p** and **P** depends on whether they are used on parts of lines or complete lines. We need some examples to illustrate their behavior.

For instance, to correct sdtio.h to stdio.h, you'll have to transpose the characters d and t, i.e. delete the d and put it after the t. Move your cursor to the d in sdtio.h and use these two commands:

```
x        sdtio.h becomes stio.h—cursor on t
p        d put on right—stio.h becomes stdio.h
```

Since we worked on parts of lines, associate the word "right" with **p** and "left" with **P**. **P** places text on the left of the cursor.

To put entire (deleted) lines at a different location, you'll need to use the same commands, except that we have to think in terms of "below" and "above" the current line. **p** places text below the current line and **P** places text above.

Note **p** and **P** place text on left and right only when you delete parts of lines. But the same keys get associated with "above" and "below" when you delete complete lines.

8.5.3 Copying Text (y and p)

vi uses the term "yanking" for copying text, the reason why the operator is named **y**. The principles are exactly the same as compared to deletion with **d**. For instance, to copy (or yank) one or more lines, use the **yy** "command":

```
yy          Yanks current line
10yy        Yanks current line and 9 lines below
```

This yanked text has to be placed at the new location. The put commands are the same—**p** and **P**. Since we copied entire lines, we can only place the copied text below or above the current line, and not on the left or right. But suppose you need to place an entire line at the end of another line. You have to place it below the line first and then join the two lines. Just read on.

8.5.4 Joining Lines (J)

In word processors, you join the current and next line by moving the cursor to the end of line and pressing *[Delete]*. This technique won't work in **vi**. To join the current line and the line following it, use

```
J           4J joins following 3 lines with current one
```

J removes the newline character between the two lines to pull up the line below it. Joining, however, is restricted to the maximum line size that your **vi** editor can support. It could be below 2000 (as in Solaris) or unlimited (in Linux).

To solve the problem posed at the end of the previous section, if you place a line below the current line with **p**, you can use **J** to join the two lines.

8.6 UNDOING LAST EDITING INSTRUCTIONS (u and U)

If you have inadvertently made an editing change that you shouldn't have, **vi** provides the **u** command to undo the last change made. Before you do anything else, reverse the last change you made to the buffer by pressing

```
u           Must use in Command Mode; press [Esc] if necessary
```

This will undo the most recent single editing change by restoring the position before the change. Another **u** at this stage will undo this too, i.e., restore the original status (doesn't apply to Linux). This facility is very useful, especially for beginners, who may accidentally delete a group of lines. Any deletion can be undone with **u** provided it is pressed *immediately* after deletion, and before fresh editing action has been performed.

When a number of editing changes have been made to a single line, **vi** allows you to discard all the changes *before you move away from the line.* The command

```
U           Don't move away from current line
```

reverses all changes made to the current line, i.e., all modifications that have been made since the cursor was moved to this line.

Caution Make sure the cursor has not been moved to another line before invoking **U**, in which case it won't work.

LINUX: *Multiple Undoing and Redoing* **vim** lets you undo and redo multiple editing instructions. **u** behaves differently here; repeated use of this key progressively undoes your previous actions. You could even have the original file in front of you! Further, **10u** reverses your last 10 editing actions. The function of **U** remains the same.

You may overshoot the desired mark when you keep **u** pressed, in which case use *[Ctrl-r]* to redo your undone actions. Further, undoing with **10u** can be completely reversed with **10***[Ctrl-r]*. The undoing limit is set by the ex Mode command **:set undolevels=***n*, where *n* is set to 1000 by default.

8.7 REPEATING THE LAST COMMAND (.)

Indentation

Most editors don't have the facility to repeat the last *editing* instruction, but **vi** has. The **.** (dot) key is used for repeating both Input and Command Mode commands. The principle is this: Use the actual command only once, and then repeat it at other places with the dot command.

To take a simple example, if you have deleted two lines of text with **2dd**, then to repeat this operation elsewhere, all you have to do is to position the cursor at the desired location and press

. *Use* `u` *to undo this repeat*

This will repeat the last editing instruction performed, i.e., it will also delete two lines of text.

The **.** command is indeed a very handy tool. As another example, consider that you have to indent a group of lines by inserting a tab at the beginning of each line. You need to use **i***[Tab][Esc]* only once, say on the first line. You can then move to each line in turn by hitting *[Enter]*, and simply press the dot. A group of lines can be indented in no time. The dot is specially suited for substitution work also, as you'll see in Section 8.8.1.

The **.** key can be used to repeat only the most recent *editing* operation— be it insertion, deletion or any other action that modifies the buffer. This, obviously, doesn't include the search commands (that don't modify the buffer contents in any way) which have their own set of characters for repeating a search. It doesn't also include the navigation or paging commands because they don't alter the buffer either.

Note The dot command can be applied to repeat the last editing instruction only, i.e., an instruction that changes the contents of a file. The dot retains its meaning even after undoing, so you can use it again at another location.

8.8 SEARCHING FOR A PATTERN (/ and ?)

vi is extremely strong in search and replacement activities. Searching can be made in both forward and reverse directions and can be repeated. It is initiated from the Command Mode by pressing a /, which shows up in the last line. For example, if you are looking for the string `printf`, enter this string after the /:

`/printf`*[Enter]* *Searches forward*

The search begins forward to position the cursor on the first instance of the word. **vi** searches the entire file, so if the pattern can't be located till the end of file is reached, the search *wraps around* to resume from the beginning of the file. If the search still fails, **vi** responds with the message `Pattern not found.`

Likewise, the sequence

?pattern[Enter]

searches backward for the most previous instance of the pattern. The wraparound feature also applies here but in the reverse manner.

8.8.1 Repeating the Last Pattern Search (n and N)

The **n** and **N** commands repeat a search where **n** and **N** don't exactly play the roles you'd expect them to. For repeating a search in the direction the previous search was made with **/** or **?**, use

`n` *Repeats search in same direction of original search*

The cursor will be positioned at the beginning of the pattern. In this way, you can press **n** repeatedly to scan all instances of the string. **N** reverses the direction pursued by **n**, which means you can use it to retrace your search path. The search and repeat actions are illustrated in Fig. 8.14 and the commands are summarized in Table 8.3.

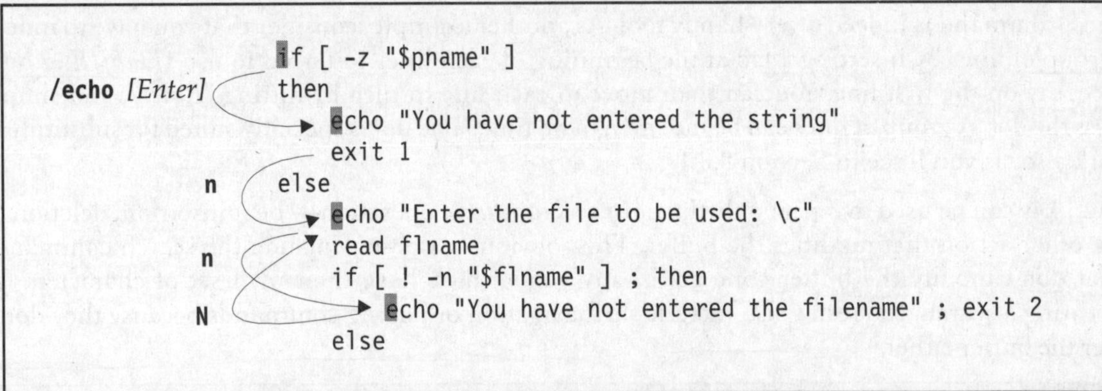

Fig. 8.14 Search and Repeat with / and n

> **Note** **n** doesn't necessarily repeat a search in the forward direction; the direction depends on the search command used. If you used **?printf** to search in the reverse direction in the first place, then **n** also follows the same direction. In that case, **N** will repeat the search in the forward direction, and not **n**.

Tip The three commands, / (search), **n** (repeat search) and **.** (repeat last editing command), form a wonderful trio of search—search-repeat—edit-repeat commands. You'll often be tempted to use this trio in many situations where you want the same change to be carried out at a number of places.

For instance, if you want to replace some occurrences of int with double, then first search for `int` with **/int**, change `int` to double with **3s**, repeat the search with **n**, and press the **.** wherever you want the replacement to take place. Yes, you wouldn't like `printf` to also show up (`int` is embedded there), which means you need to use *regular expressions* to throw `printf` out. Like **more**, **vi** also recognizes regular expressions as search patterns; these expressions are first discussed in Section 15.2.

Note You can start up **vi** by specifying a pattern. Use the +/ symbols before the pattern:

```
vi +/scheduling chap01                    Cursor at scheduling
```

The cursor will be located at the first instance of the pattern. You can then use **n** and **N** in the usual way for locating the next instance of the string. If the pattern contains multiple words, surround them with quotes.

Table 8.3 Search and Repeat Commands

Command	*Function*
/*pat*	Searches forward for pattern *pat*
?*pat*	Searches backward for pattern *pat*
n	Repeats search in same direction along which previous search was made
N	Repeats search in direction opposite to that along which previous search was made

8.9 SUBSTITUTION—SEARCH AND REPLACE (:s)

vi offers yet another powerful feature, that of substitution, which is achieved with the ex Mode's **s** (substitute) command. It lets you replace a pattern in the file with something else. The syntax is shown below:

:*address/source_pattern/target_pattern/flags*

The *source_pattern* here is replaced with *target_pattern* in all lines specified by *address*. The *address* can be one or a pair of numbers, separated by a comma. For instance, **1,$** addresses all lines in a file. The most commonly used flag is g, which carries out the substitution for all occurrences of the pattern in a line. The following example shows a typical substitution command:

```
:1,$s/director/member/g                   Can also use % instead of 1,$
```

Here, `director` is replaced with `member` globally throughout the file. If the pattern can't be found, **vi** responds with the message `Substitute pattern match failed`. If you leave out the g, then the substitution will be carried out for the *first* occurrence in each addressed line.

The target pattern is optional. If you leave it out, then you'll delete all instances of the source pattern in all lines matched by the address:

```
:1,50s/unsigned//g
```
Deletes `unsigned` *everywhere in lines 1 to 50*

As shown above, you can choose the range of lines that are to be affected by the substitution. The following examples should make addressing clear:

`:3,10s/director/member/g`	*Substitute lines 3 through 10*
`:.s/director/member/g`	*Only the current line*
`:$s/director/member/g`	*Only the last line*

Interactive Substitution Sometimes you may like to selectively replace a string. In that case, add the `c` (confirmatory) parameter as the flag at the end:

```
:1,$s/director/member/gc
```

Each line is selected in turn, followed by a sequence of carets in the next line, just below the pattern that requires substitution. The cursor is positioned at the end of this caret sequence, waiting for your response:

```
9876|jai sharma       |director |production|03/12/50|7000
                       ^^^^^^^^y
2365|barun sengupta   |director |personnel |05/11/47|7800
                       ^^^^^^^^n
1006|chanchal singhvi |director |sales     |09/03/38|6700
                       ^^^^^^^^y
6521|lalit chowdury   |director |marketing |09/26/45|8200
                       ^^^^^^^^n
```

A `y` performs the substitution, any other response doesn't. This sequence is repeated for each of the matched lines in turn. In the present case, the substitution is performed for only two of the four lines.

LINUX: The interactive substitution feature in **`vim`** is both friendlier and more powerful than its UNIX counterpart. The string to be replaced is shown in reverse video, and a prompt appears in the last line of the screen:

```
replace with msg (y/n/a/q/^E/^Y)?
```

Apart from responding with `y` or `n`, you have the option of aborting (`q`) the substitution process or making it noninteractive (`a`).

8.10 CONCLUSION

The features of **`vi`** that have been highlighted so far are good enough for a beginner who shouldn't proceed any further before mastering most of them. There are many more functions that make **`vi`** a very powerful editor. Can you copy three words or even the entire file using simple keystrokes? Can you copy or move multiple sections of text from one file to another in a single file switch? How do you compile your C and Java programs without leaving the editor? **`vi`** can do all that, and if you already know this editor quite well, then skip to Chapter 23.

With the completion of the first round of discussions on files, we need to examine the other areas of UNIX. The shell is taken up in the next chapter.

WRAP UP

vi operates in three modes for performing different functions. The *Command Mode* is used to enter commands that operate on text or control cursor motion. The *Input Mode* is used to enter text. The *ex Mode* (or *Last Line Mode*) is used for file handling and substitution. Most of the Input and Command Mode commands also work with a *repeat factor* which generally performs the command multiple times.

The Input Mode is used to insert (**i** and **I**), append (**a** and **A**), replace (**r** and **R**), change (**s** or **S**) text and open a line (**o** and **O**). The mode is terminated by pressing *[Esc]*.

The ex Mode is invoked by pressing a **:** in the Command Mode. You can save your work (**:w**), exit the editor after saving (**:x**) and quit without saving (**:q** and **:q!**). You can write selected lines to a separate file by using the line addresses with **:w**. The current line in this mode is represented by a dot and the last line by a $. Sometimes you'll need to escape to a shell (**:sh**) without quitting the editor.

Navigation is performed in the Command Mode. You can move in the four directions (**h**, **j**, **k** and **l**) or move along a line, using a *word* as a navigation unit. You can move back (**b**) and forward (**w**) to the beginning of a word. Beginning of a line is reached with **0** and end of a line with **$**. You can know your current line number (*[Ctrl-g]*) and go to a specific line number (**G**). You can use the Control keys to page forward and back.

You can also perform the editing functions in the Command Mode. You can delete characters (**x** and **X**) and lines (**dd**) and yank or copy lines (**yy**). Deleted and yanked text can be put at another location (**p** and **P**).

vi can repeat (**.**) and undo (**u**) the last editing instruction. You can undo all changes made to the current line (**U**). **vim** in Linux can perform multiple levels of undo and redo with **u** and *[Ctrl-r]*, respectively.

You can search for a pattern (**/** and **?**) and also repeat (**n** and **N**) the search in both directions. The **/**, **n** and **.** commands form a very useful trio for interactive replacement work.

The ex Mode is also used for substitution (**:s**) with or without addresses. Substitution can be global (g flag) or confirmatory (c flag). Both search and replace operations also use *regular expressions* for matching multiple patterns.

TEST YOUR UNDERSTANDING

8.1 How will you replace has with have in the current line?

8.2 How will you insert a line (i) above the current line (ii) below the current line?

8.3 How do you abort an editing session?

8.4 Name three ways exiting a **vi** session after saving your work.

8.5 How will you locate the 40th character of a line?

8.6 How will you quickly move to the fifth word of a line and replace its four characters with the string `counter`?

8.7 Find out the number of words in this string as interpreted by (i) **vi** and (ii) **wc**—`29.02.2000 is_last_day_of_February`.

8.8 Explain which of the following commands can be repeated or undone: (i) **40k** (ii) *[Ctrl-f]* (iii) **5x** iv) **J**

8.9 You have wrongly entered the word `Comptuer`. How will you correct it to `Computer`?

8.10 How do you combine five lines into a single line?

8.11 What is the significance of the **n** and **N** commands?

8.12 Every time you press a **.** (dot), you see a blank line inserted below your current line. Why does that happen?

FLEX YOUR BRAIN

8.1 Name the three modes of **vi** and how you can switch from one mode to another.

8.2 You pressed **50k** to move the cursor 50 lines up but you see 50k input as text. What mistake did you make and how do you remove the three characters?

8.3 How will you add /* at the beginning of a line and */ at the end?

8.4 How do you remove the characters that you just inserted above?

8.5 **vi** refuses to quit with **:q**. What does that indicate and how do you exit anyway?

8.6 Explain what the following commands do: (i) **:.,10w foo** (ii) **:$w! foo**. In which mode are the commands executed and what difference does it make if `foo` already exists?

8.7 In the midst of your work, how can you see the list of users logged in? If you have a number of UNIX commands to execute, which course of action will you take?

8.8 Name the sequence of commands to execute to move to the line containing the string `#include`, deleting four lines there, and then placing the deleted lines at the beginning of the file.

8.9 Mention the sequence of commands to execute that will replace `printf(` with `fprintf(stderr,`? How will you repeat the action globally?

8.10 How will you search for a pattern `printf` and then repeat the search in the opposite direction the original search was made?

8.11 How do **u** and **U** differ? When will **U** fail to work?

8.12 Name the commands required to noninteractively replace all occurrences of `cnt` with `count` in (i) the first 10 lines (ii) the current line (iii) all lines. How do you repeat the exercise in an interactive manner?

8.13 If the power to the machine is cut off while a **vi** session is active, how does it affect your work? What salvage operation will you try?

8.14 How do you move to line number 100 and then write the remaining lines (including that line) to a separate file?

9

The Shell

This chapter introduces the agency that sits between the user and the UNIX system. It is called the *shell*. All the wonderful things that you can do with UNIX are possible because the shell does a lot of work on our behalf that could be tedious for us to do on our own. The shell looks for some special symbols in the command line, performs the tasks associated with them and finally executes the command. For example, it opens a file to save command output whenever it sees the > symbol.

The shell is a unique and multi-faceted program. It is a command interpreter and a programming language rolled into one. From another viewpoint, it is also a process that creates an environment for you to work in. All these features deserve separate chapters for discussion, and you'll find the shell discussed at a number of places in this book. In this chapter, we focus on the shell's basic interpretive activities. We have seen some of these activities in previous chapters (like **rm *** or **ls | wc**), but it is here that we need to examine them closely.

WHAT YOU WILL LEARN

- An overview of the shell's interpretive cycle.
- The significance of *metacharacters* and their use in *wild-cards* for matching multiple filenames.
- The use of *escaping* and *quoting* to remove the meaning of a metacharacter.
- The difference between use of double and single quotes.
- The significance of the three *standard files (streams)* that are available to every command.
- How the shell manipulates the default source and destination of these streams to implement *redirection* and *pipelines*.
- Understand what *filters* are and why they are so important in UNIX.
- The significance of the files `/dev/null` and `/dev/tty`.
- The use of *command substitution* to obtain the arguments of a command from the standard output of another.
- Shell variables and why they are so useful.

TOPIC OF SPECIAL INTEREST

- The importance of making the command ignorant of the source of its input and destination of its output.

9.1 THE SHELL'S INTERPRETIVE CYCLE

When you log on to a UNIX machine, you first see a prompt. This prompt remains there till you key in something. Even though it may appear that the system is idling, a UNIX command is in fact running at the terminal. But this command is special; it's with you all the time and never terminates unless you log out. This command is the *shell*.

Even though the shell appears not to be doing anything meaningful when there's no activity at the terminal, it swings into action the moment you key in something through your keyboard. If you provide this input in the form of a **ps** command (that shows processes owned by you), you'll see the shell running:

```
$ ps
   PID TTY        TIME CMD
   328 pts/2      0:00 bash                    Bash shell running
```

The Bash shell is running at the terminal `/dev/pts/2`. When you key in a command, it goes as input to the shell. The shell first scans the command line for *metacharacters*. These are special characters that mean nothing to the command, but mean something special to the shell. The previous example (**ps**) had none of these characters, but we did encounter these characters before (section numbers shown in parentheses):

```
cat > foo           (6.1.2)
rm -r *             (6.3.1)
ls | more           (6.5.3)
comm file[12]       (6.11)
```

So what does the shell do with input like these? When it sees metacharacters like the >, |, *, etc. in the command line, it performs all actions represented by the symbols *before* the command can be executed. For instance, the * makes no sense to **rm**, so the shell replaces it with all filenames in the current directory. **rm** ultimately runs with these filenames as arguments. The > means nothing to **cat**, so the shell creates the file `foo` and connects **cat**'s output to it.

When all pre-processing is complete, the shell passes on the command line to the kernel for ultimate execution. The command line now has none of the metacharacters that were originally seen by the shell. While the command is running, the shell has to wait for notice of its termination from the kernel. After the command has completed execution, the shell once again issues the prompt to take up your next command.

To summarize, the following activities are typically performed by the shell in its interpretive cycle:

- The shell issues the prompt and waits for you to enter a command.
- After a command is entered, the shell scans the command line for metacharacters and expands abbreviations (like the * in **rm ***) to recreate a simplified command line.
- It then passes on the command line to the kernel for execution.
- The shell waits for the command to complete and normally can't do any work while the command is running.
- After command execution is complete, the prompt reappears and the shell returns to its waiting role to start the next cycle. You are now free to enter another command.

You can change this behavior and instruct the shell not to wait so you can fire one job after another without waiting for the previous one to complete. We'll be discussing the role of the & metacharacter in running jobs in the background later in the chapter.

9.2 SHELL OFFERINGS

Your UNIX system offers a variety of shells for you to choose from. Over time, shells have become more powerful by the progressive addition of new features. The shells we consider in this text can be grouped into two categories:

- The Bourne family comprising the Bourne shell (**/bin/sh**) and its derivatives—the Korn shell (**/bin/ksh**) and Bash (**/bin/bash**).
- The C Shell (**/bin/csh**) and its derivative, Tcsh (**/bin/tcsh**).

The absolute pathname of the shell's command file is shown in parentheses. This chapter discusses the common features of the Bourne family of shells. Everything that applies to Bourne also applies to its supersets, Korn and Bash. However, just a few of the shell's features discussed in this chapter don't apply to the C shell. We note the shell-specific features in separate asides in this text.

When you run **echo $SHELL**, the output displays the absolute pathname of the shell's command file. If $SHELL evaluates to /bin/bash, your login shell is Bash. Bash is near POSIX-compliant and is probably the best shell to use. Korn should be the next choice. Decide on the shell you would like to use for interpretive work and make that your login shell.

Note Some systems (like Linux) offer the **chsh** command that can change your login shell. In case you don't find it on your system, you'll have to ask the administrator to make the change for you. He'll either use the **usermod** command or directly edit the last field in the relevant line of /etc/passwd. You may not like to know all this right now, but it does pay at this stage to know the shell that you are using or one that you should henceforth use.

9.3 PATTERN MATCHING—THE WILD-CARDS

We begin with the special set of characters that the shell uses to match filenames. In previous chapters, you used commands with more than one filename as arguments (e.g., **cat chap01 chap02**). Often, you may require to enter multiple filenames in a command line. To illustrate this point, try listing all filenames beginning with chap. The most obvious solution is to specify all the filenames separately:

```
ls chap chap01 chap02 chap03 chap04 chapx chapy chapz
```

Since the filenames have a common string, viz. chap, the lengthy command line that uses this string repeatedly looks rather wasteful. If filenames are similar, the shell offers a facility of representing them by a single pattern or model. For instance, the pattern chap* represents all filenames beginning with chap. This pattern is framed with ordinary characters (like chap) and some metacharacters (like *) using well-defined rules. The pattern can then be used as an argument to the command, and the shell will expand it suitably *before the command is executed*.

The metacharacters that are used to construct the generalized pattern for matching filenames belong to a category called *wild-cards* (something like the joker that can match any card). In the following sections, we'll discuss the significance of the various metacharacters in the wild-card set that are listed in Table 9.1.

Table 9.1 The Shell's Wild-cards

Wild-Card	*Matches*
*	Any number of characters including none
?	A single character
[*ijk*]	A single character—either an *i*, *j* or *k*
[x-z]	A single character that is within the ASCII range of the characters x and z
[!*ijk*]	A single character that is not an *i*, *j* or *k* (Not in C shell)
[!x-z]	A single character that is not within the ASCII range of the characters x and z (Not in C shell)
{*pat1*,*pat2*...}	*pat1*, *pat2*, etc. (Not in Bourne Shell)

9.3.1 The * and ?

In the first chapter you used the command **ls chap*** *(1.4.9)* to list some filenames beginning with chap. The metacharacter, *, is one of the characters of the shell's wild-card set. It matches any number of characters (including none). It thus matches all filenames specified in the previous command line which can now be shortened in this way:

```
$ ls chap*
chap   chap01  chap02  chap03  chap04  chap15  chap16  chap17  chapx  chapy
chapz
```

Observe that chap* also matches the string chap. When the shell encounters this command line, it identifies the * immediately as a wild-card. It then looks in the current directory and recreates the command line as below from the filenames that match the pattern chap*:

```
ls chap chap01 chap02 chap03 chap04 chap15 chap16 chap17 chapx chapy chapz
```

The shell now hands over this command line to the kernel which uses its process creation facilities to run the command.

What happens when you use **echo** with only the * as argument?

```
$ echo *
array.pl back.sh calendar cent2fah.pl chap chap01 chap02 chap03 chap04 chap15 ch
ap16 chap17 chapx chapy chapz count.pl date_array.pl dept.lst desig.lst n2words.
pl name.pl name2.pl odfile operator.pl profile.sam rdbnew.lst rep1.pl
```

You simply see a list of files! All filenames in the current directory match a solitary *, so you see all of them in the output. If you use **rm *** in this directory, all these files will be deleted.

Note DOS/Windows users may be surprised to know that the * may occur anywhere in a filename and not merely at the end. Thus, `*chap*` matches all the following filenames—`chap newchap chap03 chap03.txt`.

Caution Be careful when you use the * with **rm** to remove files. You could land yourself in a real mess if, instead of typing **rm *.o** which removes all the C object files, you inadvertently introduce a space between * and `.o`:

```
$ rm * .o                                    Very dangerous!
rm: .o: No such file or directory
```

The error message here masks a disaster that has just occurred; **rm** has removed all files in this directory! In such situations, you should pause and check the command line before you finally press *[Enter]*.

The next wild-card is the ?, which matches a single character. When used with same string `chap` (`chap?`), the shell matches all five-character filenames beginning with `chap`. Appending another ? creates the pattern `chap??`, which matches six-character filenames. Use both expressions separately, and the meaning becomes obvious:

```
$ ls chap?
chapx  chapy  chapz
$ ls chap??
chap01  chap02  chap03  chap04  chap15  chap16  chap17
```

Both the * and ? operate with some restrictions that are taken up in the next topic.

9.3.2 Matching the Dot

The behavior of the * and ? in relation to the dot isn't as straightforward as it may seem. The * doesn't match all files *beginning* with a . (dot) or the / of a pathname. If you want to list all hidden filenames in your directory having at least three characters after the dot, then the dot must be matched explicitly:

```
$ ls .???*
.bash_profile   .exrc   .netscape  .profile
```

However, if the filename contains a dot anywhere but at the beginning, it need not be matched explicitly. For example, the expression `emp*lst` matches a dot embedded in the filename:

```
$ ls emp*lst
emp.lst    emp1.lst   emp22lst  emp2.lst    empn.lst
```

Note There are two things that the * can't match. First, it doesn't match a filename beginning with a dot, but it can match any number of embedded dots. For instance, `apache*gz` matches `apache_1.3.20.tar.gz`. Second, the * doesn't match the / in a pathname. You can't use **cd /usr*local** to switch to `/usr/local`.

9.3.3 The Character Class

The patterns framed in the preceding examples are not very restrictive. With the knowledge we have, it's not easy to list only chapy and chapz. Nor is it easy to match only the first four chapters from the numbered list. You can frame more restrictive patterns with the *character class*.

The character class comprises a set of characters enclosed by the rectangular brackets [and], but it matches a *single* character in the class. The pattern [abcd] is a character class, and it matches a single character—an a, b, c, or d. This can be combined with any string or another wild-card expression, so that selecting the files chap01, chap02 and chap04 now becomes a simple matter:

```
$ ls chap0[124]
chap01  chap02  chap04
```

Range specification is also possible inside the class with a - (hyphen); the two characters on either side of it form the range of the characters to be matched. Here are two examples:

```
ls chap0[1-4]        Lists chap01, chap02, chap03 and chap04
ls chap[x-z]         Lists chapx, chapy and chapz
```

A valid range specification requires that the character on the left have a lower ASCII value than the one on the right.

> **Note** The expression [a-zA-Z]* matches all filenames beginning with an alphabet, irrespective of case.

Negating the Character Class (!) How about framing a pattern that reverses the above matching criteria? The solution that we prescribe here unfortunately doesn't work with the C shell, but with the other shells, you can use the ! as the first character in the class to negate the class. The two examples below should make this point amply clear:

```
*.[!co]      Matches all filenames with a single-character extension but not the .c or .o files.
[!a-zA-Z]*   Matches all filenames that don't begin with an alphabetic character.
```

Even though the character class is meant to be used with a group of characters, it's the only way you can negate a match for a single character. Thus to match all files except those ending with .o (i.e., C object files), you have to use a character class as a "dummy class":

```
*.[!o]       Not the .o files
```

> **C Shell** The ! can't be used to negate a character class at all. In fact, the C shell has no mechanism for doing so.

9.3.4 Matching Totally Dissimilar Patterns

This feature, not available in the Bourne shell, enables us to match totally dissimilar patterns. How does one copy all the C and Java source programs from another directory? Delimit the patterns with a comma, and then put curly braces around them (no spaces please!):

```
cp $HOME/prog_sources/*.{c,java} .        Won't work in Bourne shell
```

This works in the Korn, Bash and C shells. The Bourne shell would require two separate invocations of **cp** to do this job. Using the curly brace form, you can also access multiple directories:

```
cp /home/kumar/{project,html,scripts}/*                Won't work in Bourne shell
```

This copies all files from three directories (project, html and scripts) to the current directory. Isn't this convenient?

> **Note** Wild-cards mean nothing to a command but only to the shell. The shell interprets the wild-cards and produces a clean list of filenames, which is easily understood by the command.

9.3.5 Rounding Up

Some of the wild-card characters have different meanings depending on where they are placed in the pattern. The * and ? lose their meaning when used inside the class, and are matched literally. Similarly, - and ! also lose their significance when placed outside the class. There are other restrictions but we can ignore them for now.

Whether or not you are able to devise a suitable pattern that matches a group of filenames depends, apart from your ingenuity, on the way the filenames were chosen in the first instance. When organizing information in groups of files, you should choose these names with care so you don't require to use too many patterns to match them. If you don't do that, be prepared to specify them separately every time you use a command that accesses all of them!

To summarize what has been discussed so far, a sample set of command lines is presented below:

`ls *.c`	Lists all files with extension `.c`.
`mv * ../bin`	Moves all files to `bin` subdirectory of parent directory.
`cp foo foo*`	Copies `foo` to `foo*` (* loses meaning here).
`cp ?????? progs`	Copies to `progs` directory all files with six-character names.
`lp note[0-1][0-9]`	Prints files `note00`, `note01` ..... through `note19`.
`rm *.[!l][!o][!g]`	Removes all files with three-character extensions except the ones with the `.log` extension.
`cp -r /{include,lib,bin} .`	Copies recursively the three directories, `include`, `lib` and `bin` from / to the current directory. (Not in Bourne shell)

It's the shell that interprets these expressions. Sometimes we don't want this interpretation to take place. This could be on account of a mistake that has occurred (like creating a file name `foo*`) but there could be other reasons as well. In the next topic we discuss two techniques of removing the special meaning of metacharacters.

9.4 ESCAPING AND QUOTING

At this stage, you might well think that if the shell uses some special characters to match filenames, then the filenames themselves must not contain any of these characters. That's right thinking but the real world is far from perfect. One of the sample lines featured in the previous section shows how easy it is to actually create a file named `foo*`. Because the pattern `foo*` also matches the filename `foo*`, the shell will include it in its list if it actually finds a file with this name:

```
$ ls chap*
chap   chap*  chap01  chap02  chap03  chap04  chap15  chap16  chap17  chapx
chapy  chapz
```

This file can be a great nuisance and should be removed immediately. But that won't be easy. Trying **rm chap*** could be dangerous; there could be other filenames beginning with chap (as here), and they would be removed too. We must be able to protect all special characters (including wild-cards) so the shell is not able to interpret them. The shell provides two solutions to prevent its own interference:

- *Escaping*—Providing a \ (backslash) before the wild-card to remove (escape) its special meaning.
- *Quoting*—Enclosing the wild-card, or even the entire pattern, within quotes (like "chap*"). Anything within these quotes (barring few exceptions) are left alone by the shell and not interpreted.

In most cases you can use either mechanism, but some situations warrant the use of quotes. Sometimes you also need to make a distinction between single and double quotes, but more of that later.

9.4.1 Escaping

Let's take up escaping first. When we use the \ immediately before a metacharacter, it turns off its special meaning. In the pattern *, the \ tells the shell that the asterisk has to be treated and matched literally instead of being interpreted as a metacharacter. This means that we can remove the file chap* without affecting the other filenames that also begin with chap by using

```
rm chap\*                                   Doesn't remove chap1, chap2
```

The \ suppresses the wild-card nature of the *, thus preventing the shell from performing filename expansion on it. This feature is known as *escaping*. You'll see this concept of using the \ in other areas also.

To consider another example, if you have files chap01, chap02 and chap03 in your current directory, and still dare to create a file chap0[1-3] by using

```
echo > chap0[1-3]                           Creates a file chap0[1-3]
```

then you should escape the two rectangular brackets when accessing the file:

```
$ ls chap0\[1-3\]                           Must escape the [ and ]
chap0[1-3]
$ rm chap0\[1-3\]
$ ls chap0\[1-3\]
chap0[1-3] not found                        File removed
```

Escaping the Space Apart from metacharacters, there are other characters that are special—like the space character. The shell uses it to delimit command line arguments. So to remove the file My Document.doc which has a space embedded, a similar reasoning should be followed:

```
rm My\ Document.doc                         Without the \ rm would see two files
```

Escaping the \ Itself Sometimes you may need to interpret the \ itself literally. You need another \ before it, that's all:

```
$ echo \\
\
$ echo The newline character is \\n
The newline character is \n
```

Escaping the Newline Character The newline character is also special; it marks the end of the command line. Some command lines that use several arguments can be long enough to overflow to the next line. To ensure better readability, you need to split the wrapped line into two lines, but make sure that you input a \ before you press *[Enter]*:

```
$ find /usr/local/bin /usr/bin -name "*.pl" -mtime +7 -size +1024 \[Enter]
> -size -2048 -atime +25 -print                                   Note the >
```

This is the **find** command at work, a command often used with several arguments. The \ here escapes the meaning of the newline character generated by *[Enter]*. It also produces the second prompt (which could be a > or a ?), which indicates that the command line is incomplete. Command lines involving multiple commands (as in pipelines) can also be very long. For better readability, you should split them into multiple lines wherever possible.

> **Note** The space, \ and LF (the newline character generated by *[Enter]*) are also special and need to be escaped if the shell is to be prevented from interpreting them in the way it normally does.

9.4.2 Quoting

There's another way to turn off the meaning of a metacharacter. When a command argument is enclosed in quotes, the meanings of all enclosed special characters are turned off. Here's how we can run some of the previous commands, using a mix of single- and double-quoting this time:

```
echo '\'                          Displays a \
rm 'chap*'                        Removes file chap*
rm "My Document.doc"              Removes file My Document.doc
```

Escaping also turns out to be a tedious affair when there are just too many characters to protect. Quoting is often a better solution. The following example shows the protection of four special characters using single quotes:

```
$ echo 'The characters |, <, > and $ are also special'
The characters |, <, > and $ are also special
```

We could have used escaping here, but then we would need to use four \s in front of each of these four metacharacters. We used single quotes because they protect all special characters (except the single quote). Double quotes are more permissive; they don't protect (apart from the double quote itself) the $ and the ` (backquote):

```
$ echo "Command substitution uses `` while TERM is evaluated using $TERM"
Command substitution uses  while TERM is evaluated using vt100
```

Observe that the pair of backquote characters (``) and the variable $TERM have been interpreted by the shell inside double quotes. $TERM is vt100 for this terminal, and `` evaluated to a null command. Now try out the same example using single quotes:

```
$ echo 'Command substitution uses `` while TERM is evaluated using $TERM'
Command substitution uses `` while TERM is evaluated using $TERM
```

> **Note** It's often crucial to select the right type of quote, so bear in mind that single quotes protect all special characters. Double quotes, however, let a pair of backquotes (``) be interpreted as *command substitution* characters, and the $ as a variable prefix. There is also a reciprocal relationship between the two types of quotes; double quotes protect single quotes, and single quotes protect the double.

9.4.3 Escaping in echo

We used **echo** in Section 4.3 with escape sequences like \n and \t. The \ has a reverse meaning there; it treats the characters n and t as special rather than remove their special meanings because n and t don't have special meanings. These escape sequences are always used within quotes to keep the shell out. But what is **echo**?

```
$ type echo
echo is a shell builtin
```

It's a funny situation that we have here. We quoted **echo**'s arguments to keep the shell out of the picture only to learn that **echo** is built into the shell! For this purpose, the shell treats **echo** as an external command (which it once was).

9.5 REDIRECTION: THE THREE STANDARD FILES

Before we commence our discussions on redirection, let's first understand what the term "terminal" means since we'll be using it often. In the context of redirection, the terminal is a generic name that represents the screen, display or keyboard (or even an X window that emulates a terminal). Just as we refer to a directory as a file, we'll also sometimes refer to the keyboard as a terminal.

We see command output and error messages on the terminal (display), and we sometimes provide command input through the terminal (keyboard). The shell associates three files with the terminal—two for the display and one for the keyboard. Even though our terminal is also represented by a specific device name (/dev/tty), commands don't usually read from or write to this file. They perform all terminal-related activity with the three files that the shell makes available to every command.

These special files are actually *streams* of characters which many commands see as input and output. A stream is simply a sequence of bytes. When a user logs in, the shell makes available three files representing three streams. Each stream is associated with a default device, and—generically speaking—this device is the terminal:

- *Standard Input*—The file (or stream) representing input, which is connected to the keyboard.
- *Standard Output*—The file (or stream) representing output, which is connected to the display.
- *Standard Error*—The file (or stream) representing error messages that emanate from the command or shell. This is also connected to the display.

Every command that uses streams will always find these files open and available. The files are closed when the user logs out. Even though the shell associates each of these files with a default physical device, this association is not permanent. The shell can easily unhook a stream from its default device and connect it to a disk file (or to any command) the moment it sees some special characters in the command line. You, as user, have to instruct the shell to do that by using symbols like > and < in the command line.

9.5.1 Standard Input

We have used the **cat** and **wc** commands to read disk files. These commands have an additional method of taking input. When they are used without arguments, they read the file representing the *standard input*. This file is indeed special; it can represent three input sources:

- The keyboard, the default source.
- A file using redirection with the < symbol (a metacharacter).
- Another program using a pipeline (to be taken up later).

When you use **wc** without an argument and have no special symbols like the < and | in the command line, **wc** obtains its input from the default source. You have to provide this input from the keyboard and mark the end of input with *[Ctrl-d]*:

```
$ wc
Standard input can be redirected
It can come from a file
or a pipeline
[Ctrl-d]
      3      14      71
```

This situation is similar to the one encountered when creating a file with **cat** *(6.1.2)*. Enter the three lines of text and signify the end of input with *[Ctrl-d]*. **wc**, which takes the stream from standard input, immediately counts 3 lines, 14 words and 71 characters. We have used **wc** before *(1.4.11)*, but then it showed the filename in the fourth column. This time no filename was specified, so no filename was output. And yet it remains true that **wc** read a file—the standard input file.

The shell's manipulative nature finds place here. It can reassign the standard input file to a disk file. This means it can *redirect* the standard input to originate from a file on disk. This reassignment or redirection requires the < symbol:

```
$ wc < sample.txt                              File containing the above 3 lines
      3      14      71
```

The filename is missing once again, which means that **wc** didn't open `sample.txt`. It read the standard input file as a stream but only after the shell made a reassignment of this stream to a disk file. The important thing here is that **wc** has no idea where the stream came from; it is not even aware that the shell had to open the file `sample.txt` on its behalf!

You may have already framed your next question. Why bother to redirect the standard input from a file if the command can read the file itself? After all, **wc** can also use a filename as argument!

The answer is that there are times when you need to keep the command *ignorant* of the source of its input. This aspect, representing one of the most deep-seated features of the system, will gradually expose itself as you progress through these chapters.

> **Note** When the standard input is redirected to come from a file (with <), it's the shell that opens the file. The command here is totally ignorant of what the shell is doing to provide it with input. However, when you invoke a command with a filename as argument, it's the command that opens the file and not the shell.

Taking Input Both from File and Standard Input When a command takes input from multiple sources—say a file and standard input, the - symbol must be used to indicate the sequence of taking input. The meaning of the following sequences should be quite obvious:

```
cat - foo          First from standard input and then from foo
cat foo - bar      First from foo, then standard input, and then bar
```

The third source of standard input is the pipe, which is discussed later *(9.7)*. There's a fourth form of standard input which we have not mentioned here. It's the *here document* that has application in shell programming and hence discussed in Chapter 16.

9.5.2 Standard Output

All commands displaying output on the terminal actually write to the *standard output* file as a stream of characters, and not *directly* to the terminal as such. There are three possible destinations of this stream:

- The terminal, the default destination.
- A file, using the redirection symbols > and >>.
- As input to another program using a pipeline (to be taken up later).

The shell can effect redirection of this stream when it sees the > or >> symbols in the command line. You can replace the default destination (the terminal) with any file by using the > (right chevron) operator, followed by the filename:

```
$ wc sample.txt > newfile
$ cat newfile
       3      14      71  sample.txt
```

The first command sends the word count of `sample.txt` to `newfile`; nothing appears on the terminal screen. The sequence works like this: On seeing the >, the shell opens the disk file, `newfile`, for writing. It also unplugs the standard output file from its default source and assigns it to `newfile`. Next, **wc** (and not the shell) opens the file `sample.txt` for reading and writes to standard output which has earlier been reassigned by the shell to `newfile`. And all this happens without **wc** knowing that it is in fact writing to `newfile`! Any command that uses standard output is ignorant about the destination of its output also.

If the output file doesn't exist, the shell creates it before executing the command. If it exists, the shell overwrites it, so use this operator with caution. The shell also provides the >> symbol (the right chevron used twice) to append to a file:

```
wc sample.txt >>newfile                    Doesn't disturb existing contents
```

Redirection also becomes a useful feature when concatenating the standard output of a number of files. The following example that uses a wild-card saves all C programs in a single file:

```
cat *.c > c_progs_all.txt
```

This concatenated output stream provides no visual indication of the name of the files, so we can do somewhat better by preceding this output with a list of filenames. A single > does the job, but this requires the use of the (and) symbols for grouping commands:

```
( ls -x *.c ; echo ; cat *.c ) > c_progs_all.txt
```

The **echo** command in the middle serves to insert a blank line between the multicolumn file list and the code listings. The program names now feature in the front page, so you have a table of contents preceding your code listings. But better still would be to precede each program listing with its filename. You can do this using a loop construct after you have learned shell programming.

The standard output of one command can also be used by another command as its standard input. This is the third destination of standard output and is taken up in the discussion on pipes *(9.7)*.

> **Note** When the output of a command is redirected to a file, the output file is created by the shell before the command is executed. Any idea what **cat foo > foo** does?

9.5.3 Standard Error

Before we proceed any further, you should know that each of the three standard files is represented by a number, called a *file descriptor*. A file is opened by referring to its pathname, but subsequent read and write operations identify the file by this file descriptor. The kernel maintains a table of file descriptors for every process running in the system. The first three slots are generally allocated to the three standard streams in this manner:

0—Standard input
1—Standard output
2—Standard error

These descriptors are *implicitly* prefixed to the redirection symbols. For instance, > and 1> mean the same thing to the shell, while < and 0< also are identical. If your program opens a file, in all probability, the file will be allocated the descriptor 3.

We need to explicitly use one of these descriptors when handling the standard error stream. When you enter an incorrect command or try to open a nonexistent file, certain diagnostic messages show up on the screen. This is the *standard error* stream whose default destination is the terminal. Trying to "cat" a nonexistent file produces the error stream:

```
$ cat foo
cat: cannot open foo
```

cat fails to open the file, and writes to the standard error. If you are not using the C shell, you can redirect this stream to a file. Using the symbol for standard output obviously won't do:

```
$ cat foo > errorfile
cat: cannot open foo
```
Error stream can't be captured with >

The diagnostic output has not been sent to `errorfile`. It's obvious that standard error can't be redirected in the same way the standard output can (with > or >>). Even though standard output and standard error use the terminal as the default destination, the shell possesses a mechanism for capturing them individually. Redirecting standard error requires the use of the 2> symbols:

```
$ cat foo 2>errorfile
$ cat errorfile
cat: cannot open foo
```

This works. You can also append diagnostic output in a manner similar to the one in which you append standard output:

```
cat foo 2>> errorfile
```

If you have a program that runs for a long time and is not error-free, you can direct the standard error to a separate file and then stay away from the terminal. On return, you can examine this file for errors.

C Shell The standard error is handled differently by the C shell, so the examples of this section won't work with it. In fact, the C shell merges the standard error with the standard output; it has no separate symbol for handling standard error only. The command **`cat foo >& bar`** saves both standard output and standard error in `bar`.

Now that you have separate symbols for the output and error streams, you can redirect them separately:

```
foo.sh > bar1 2>bar2
```

What about saving both streams in the same file? You need to use the stream merging mechanism (which uses the symbols 1>&2 and 2>&1), but these are required in shell scripts and are appropriately taken up in Chapter 24.

9.5.4 Filters—Using Both Standard Input and Standard Output

We return to the input and output streams to ask ourselves this question: Do all commands use the features of standard input and standard output? No, certainly not. From this viewpoint, the UNIX commands can be grouped into four categories:

- Directory-oriented commands like **`mkdir`**, **`rmdir`** and **`cd`**, and basic file handling commands like **`cp`**, **`mv`** and **`rm`** take neither standard input nor standard output.
- Commands like **`ls`**, **`pwd`**, **`who`**, etc. don't take any standard input but they send their output to the standard output.
- **`lp`** uses standard input but produces no standard output.
- Commands like **`cat`**, **`wc`**, **`od`**, **`cmp`**, **`gzip`**, etc. that use both standard input and standard output.

Commands in the fourth category are called, in UNIX parlance, *filters*, and the dual stream-handling feature makes filters powerful text manipulators. Note that most filters can also read *directly* from files whose names are provided as arguments. Four separate chapters are earmarked for filters in this text.

Some of the commands discussed in previous chapters are actually filters. To see how their capabilities get enhanced when used as filters, let's use the **bc** command as a filter this time. Consider this file containing some arithmetic expressions:

```
$ cat calc.txt
2^32                              Maximum memory on a 32-bit computer
25*50
30*25 + 15^2
```

You can redirect **bc**'s standard input to come from this file and save the output in yet another:

```
$ bc < calc.txt > result.txt      Using both standard input and output
$ cat result.txt
4294967296                        This is 2^32
1250                              This is 25*50
975                               This is 30*25 + 15^2
```

bc obtained the expressions from redirected standard input, processed them and sent out the results to a redirected output stream. Though we used the < first and then the >, there's no restriction in the sequence we use or in the use of whitespace around the symbols:

```
bc > result.txt < calc.txt
bc>result.txt<calc.txt            No whitespace!
> result.txt < calc.txt bc        As above, but command at end
```

The last example illustrates a departure from the statement made previously *(3.3)* that the first word in the command line is the command. In the last example, **bc** is the last word in the command line. Rather than use these combinations, you'll find it more convenient to stick to the first form.

The indifference of a command to the source of its input and destination of its output is one of the most profound features of the UNIX system. It raises the possibility of commands "talking" to one another so that the output of one command can be used as the input to another. Very soon we'll discuss pipes, when you'll see how two or more commands communicate with one another.

9.6 /dev/null AND /dev/tty: TWO SPECIAL FILES

`/dev/null` Quite often, and especially in shell programming, you'll like to check whether a program runs successfully without seeing its output on the screen. You may not want to save this output in a file either. You have a special file that simply accepts any stream without growing in size—the file /dev/null:

```
$ cmp foo1 foo2 >/dev/null
$ cat /dev/null
$ _                               Size is always zero
```

Check the file size; it's always zero. /dev/null simply incinerates all output written to it. No matter whether you direct or append output to this file, its size always remains zero. This facility is useful in redirecting error messages away from the terminal so they don't appear on the screen. /dev/null is actually a pseudo-device because, unlike all other device files, it's not associated with any physical device.

Why did we run cmp to compare two files if we are not interested in its output? Later, you'll learn how to examine a special shell variable ($?) to know whether two files are identical or not. It's this value that we are often interested in and not the actual output that lists the differences.

/dev/tty The second special file in the UNIX system is the one indicating one's terminal—/dev/tty. But make no mistake: *This is not the file that represents standard output or standard error*. Commands generally don't write to this file, but you'll require to redirect some statements in shell scripts to this file.

Consider, for instance, that romeo is working on terminal /dev/pts/1 and juliet on /dev/pts/2. However, both romeo and juliet can refer to their own terminals with the same filename—/dev/tty. Thus, if romeo issues the command

```
who >/dev/tty
```

the list of current users is sent to the terminal he is currently using—/dev/pts/1. Similarly, juliet can use an identical command to see the output on her terminal, /dev/pts/2. Like /dev/null, /dev/tty can be accessed independently by several users without conflict.

You may ask why one should need to specifically redirect output to one's own terminal since the default output goes to the terminal anyway. The answer is that sometimes you need to specify that explicitly as the following real-world example suggests.

Consider redirecting a shell script to a file, say, by using **foo.sh > redirect.txt**. Redirecting a script implies redirecting the standard output of all statements in the script. That's not always desirable. Your script may contain some **echo** commands that provide helpful messages for the user, and you would obviously like to see them on the terminal. If these statements are explicitly redirected to /dev/tty inside the script, redirecting the script won't affect these statements. We'll use this feature later in our shell scripts.

Apart from its use in redirection, /dev/tty can also be used as an argument to some UNIX commands. Section 9.8 makes use of this feature, while some situations are presented in Chapter 16 (featuring shell programming).

Note The size of /dev/null is always zero and all terminals can be represented by /dev/tty.

9.7 PIPES

Standard input and standard output constitute two separate streams that can be individually manipulated by the shell. If that be so, can't the shell connect these streams together so that one command takes input from the other? That is not only possible, but forms the cornerstone of the building-block approach that UNIX advocates to solve all text manipulation problems.

You know the **who** command produces a list of users, one user per line. Let's use redirection to save this output in a file:

```
$ who > user.txt
$ cat user.txt
root      console     Aug  1 07:51    (:0)
romeo     pts/10      Aug  1 07:56    (pc123.heavens.com)
juliet    pts/6       Aug  1 02:10    (pc125.heavens.com)
project   pts/8       Aug  1 02:16    (pc125.heavens.com)
andrew    pts/14      Aug  1 08:36    (mercury.heavens.com)
```

Let's now use **wc** to make a complete count of this file's contents. We'll use the `-l` option to count the number of lines only, and redirect **wc**'s input so that the filename doesn't appear in the output:

```
$ wc -l < user.txt
      5                                          Counts the number of users
```

Using an intermediate file (`user.txt`), wc effectively counted the number of users. This method of running two commands separately has two obvious disadvantages:

- For long-running commands, this process can be slow. The second command can't act unless the first has completed its job.
- You require an intermediate file that has to be removed after completion of the job. When handling large files, temporary files can build up easily and eat up disk space in no time.

Here, **who**'s standard output was redirected, and so was **wc**'s standard input, and both used the same disk file. The shell can connect these streams using a special operator—the | (pipe) and avoid the creation of the disk file. You can make **who** and **wc** work in tandem so that one takes input from the other:

```
$ who | wc -l                                    No intermediate files created
      5
```

Here, the output of **who** has been passed directly to the input of **wc**, and **who** is said to be *piped* to **wc**. When a sequence of commands is combined together in this way, a *pipeline* is said to be formed. It's the shell that sets up this interconnection and the commands have no knowledge of it.

The pipe is the third source and destination of standard input and standard output, respectively. You can now use one to count the number of files in the current directory:

```
$ ls | wc -l
     15
```

Note that no separate command was designed to tell you that, though the designers could easily have provided another option to **ls** to perform this operation. And because **wc** uses standard output, you can redirect this output to a file:

```
ls | wc -l > fkount
```

There's no restriction on the number of commands you can use in a pipeline. But you must know the behavioral properties of these commands to place them there. Consider this command sequence which prints the man page of **grep** on the printer:

```
man grep | col -b | lp
```

The online man pages of a command often show the keywords in boldface. These pages contain a number of control characters which are removed here by the **col -b** command. Like **col**, **lp** also reads its standard input from **col**'s output and prints the file. For a pipeline like this to be feasible, the leftmost command (here, **man**) must be able to write to standard output while the rightmost command (here, **lp**) must be able to read from standard input. Intermediate commands (here, **col**) must be able to do both.

In a pipeline, all programs run simultaneously. A pipe also has a built-in mechanism to control the flow of the stream. Since a pipe is both being read and written, the reader and writer have to act in unison. If one operates faster than the other, then the appropriate driver has to readjust the flow. This happens when you use the following command sequence:

```
ls | more
```

Since the standard output from more freezes as long as you don't scroll forward, the kernel makes sure that **ls** writes to the pipe only as much as **more** can absorb at a time.

9.7.1 When a Command Needs to Be Ignorant of Its Source

We mentioned several times about a command being ignorant of its source and destination. When and why is this ignorance essential for us? To appreciate this point, let's use the **wc** command to display the *total* size of all C programs:

```
$ wc -c *.c
   2078 backtalk.c
    231 beyond_array.c
    .......                                    Output trimmed here
   1944 dog.c
    884 hexdump.c
    214 swap.c
 940101 total
```

The display shows the total usage at 940,101 bytes, but it also shows the usage for each file. We are not interested in individual statistics this time, what we need is a single figure representing the total size. To be able to do that, you must make **wc** ignorant of its input source. You can do that by feeding the concatenated output stream of all these files to **wc -c** as its input:

```
$ cat *.c | wc -c
940101
```

Since **wc** acts on a stream this time, it displays a single figure. When do we need a single figure? We can use this command sequence as a control command in a shell script to determine whether the files will fit in a floppy diskette:

```
if [ `cat *.c | wc -c` -lt 1474560 ] ; then
   echo 'These files will fit in a single 3.5" diskette'
fi
```

Note how the single quotes protect the double quote in the **echo** statement. We'll learn to use the **if** construct in Chapter 16 that features shell programming. The two backquotes (``) denote command substitution and is discussed shortly.

> **Note** In a pipeline, the command on the left of the | must use standard output and the one on the right must use standard input.

The feature of pipelining represents one of the most important aspects of the UNIX system. It implements the UNIX philosophy that difficult jobs can be done by combining some tools that do simple jobs in isolation. The UNIX manual doesn't tell you the combinations of commands required for each task, and this makes pipelines difficult to conceive initially. A lot is left to knowledge of filters, perseverance and imagination.

9.8 tee: CREATING A TEE

tee is an external command and not a feature of the shell. It handles a character stream by splitting its input into two components. It saves one component in a file and writes the other to the standard output. Being also a filter (which uses standard input and standard output), **tee** can be placed anywhere in a pipeline. **tee** doesn't perform any filtering action on its input; it gives out exactly what it takes.

The following command sequence uses **tee** to display the output of **who** and saves this output in a file as well:

```
$ who | tee user.txt
romeo     pts/2        Sep  7 08:41   (pc123.heavens.com)
juliet    pts/3        Sep  7 17:58   (pc122.heavens.com)
sumit     pts/5        Sep  7 18:01   (mercury.heavens.com)
```

user.txt also contains this output, but how can we be sure without using **cat** to view user.txt? Since **cmp** compares two files and one of them can be represented by the standard input file, we can arrange to provide this input from the output of **who**:

```
$ who | cmp user.txt -                      Second file is standard input
$ _
```

The comparison *succeeded*, so **who**'s output and the contents saved earlier by **tee** are identical. We'll later understand what "success" here means.

How do you use **tee** to display both the list of users and its count on the terminal? Since the terminal is also a file, you can use the device name /dev/tty as an argument to **tee**:

```
$ who | tee /dev/tty | wc -l               /dev/tty used as command argument
romeo     pts/2        Sep  7 08:41   (pc123.heavens.com)
juliet    pts/3        Sep  7 17:58   (pc122.heavens.com)
sumit     pts/5        Sep  7 18:01   (mercury.heavens.com)
       3                                   It's like running who | wc -l
```

tee "saved" the **who** output in /dev/tty, thus effectively showing it on screen. **wc -l** counted the other stream. The advantage of treating the terminal as a file is apparent from the above example.

You couldn't have done this if **tee** (or for that matter, any UNIX command) had placed restrictions on the type of file it could handle.

9.9 COMMAND SUBSTITUTION

The shell enables the connecting of two commands in yet another way. While a pipe enables a command to obtain its standard input from the standard output of another command, the shell enables one or more command *arguments* to be obtained from the standard output of another command. This feature is called *command substitution.*

To consider a simple example, suppose you need to display today's date with a statement like this:

```
The date today is Sat Sep  7 19:01:16 IST 2002
```

The last part of the statement (beginning from Sat) represents the output of the **date** command. How does one incorporate **date**'s output into the **echo** statement? With command substitution it's a simple matter. Use the expression `` `date` `` as an argument to **echo**:

```
$ echo The date today is `date`
The date today is Sat Sep  7 19:01:56 IST 2002
```

When scanning the command line, the ` (backquote or backtick) is another metacharacter that the shell looks for. There's a special key on your keyboard (generally at the top-left) that generates this character, and it should not be confused with the single quote ('). The shell then executes the enclosed command and replaces the enclosed command line with the output of the command. For command substitution to work, the command so "backquoted" must use standard output. **date** does; that's why command substitution worked.

You can use this feature to generate useful messages. For example, you can use two commands in a pipeline and then use the output as the argument to a third:

```
$ echo "There are `ls | wc -l` files in the current directory"
There are 58 files in the current directory
```

The command worked properly even though the arguments were double-quoted. It's a different story altogether when single quotes are used:

```
$ echo 'There are `ls | wc -l` files in the current directory'
There are `ls | wc -l` files in the current directory
```

This was to be expected because we had already tried out a similar exercise earlier *(9.4.2)*. The ` is one of the few characters interpreted by the shell when placed within double quotes. If you want to echo a literal `, you have to use single quotes.

Command substitution has wide application in shell scripts. The **for** loop works with a list and this list can be obtained from the output of the **cat** command using command substitution:

```
for fname in `cat flist` ; do
   cp $fname $fname.bak
done
```

The file `flist` presumably contains a list of filenames, and each filename is assigned to the variable `fname` in turn. This simple three-line construct makes a copy of each file in the list by providing `.bak` extension to the existing filename. Without command substitution we would have had to write additional code to do this.

> **Korn Shell, Bash Shell** POSIX recommends the use of the form `$(`*command*`)` rather than the archaic `` ` ``*command*`` ` `` for command substitution. The Korn and Bash shells offer both forms. The POSIX form requires you to place the command inside parentheses and have a $ before them:
>
> ```
> $ echo The date today is $(date)
> The date today is Sat Sep  7 19:15:33 IST 2002
> ```
>
> Whether or not you should use the POSIX notation is something you have to decide for yourself. Make sure that you don't have to run your shell scripts with the Bourne shell before you decide to adopt this form.

9.10 SHELL VARIABLES

The shell supports variables that are useful both in the command line and shell scripts. You have already encountered some of them like `TERM` and `SHELL`. Variable usage in the Bourne family differs from that in the C shell. In this section and elsewhere, we discuss Bourne-type variables. The features of C shell variables are noted in the aside at the end of this section.

A variable assignment is of the form *variable=value* (no spaces around =), but its evaluation requires the $ as prefix to the variable name:

```
$ count=5                                  No $ required for assignment
$ echo $count                              but needed for evaluation
5
```

A variable can also be assigned the value of another variable:

```
$ total=$count                             Assigning a value to another variable
$ echo $total
5
```

When the shell reads the command line, it interprets any word preceded by a $ as a variable, and replaces the word by the value of the variable. Programmers must note that there must not be any whitespace on either side of the = symbol. The command line `x =5` is interpreted by the shell as the `x` command running with the `=5` argument!

Variable names begin with a letter but can contain numerals and the _ as the other characters. Names are case-sensitive; `x` and `X` are two different variables. Unlike in programming languages, shell variables are not typed; you don't need to use a `char`, `int` or `long` prefix when you define them. In fact, you don't even have to declare them before you can use them. All shell variables are of the string type, which means even a number like 123 is stored as a string rather than in binary. (This may not remain true in future.)

All shell variables are initialized to null strings by default. While explicit assignment of null strings with x="" or x='' is possible, you can also use this as a shorthand:

```
x=                                      A null string
```

A variable can be removed with **unset** and protected from reassignment by **readonly**. Both are shell internal commands:

```
unset x                                 x is now undefined
readonly x                              x can't be reassigned
```

Tip By convention, variable names used by the UNIX system and software packages are in uppercase. You are advised to use lowercase variable names in your shell scripts simply to distinguish them from system variables.

C Shell **C Shell:** The C shell uses the **set** statement to set variables. There either has to be whitespace on both sides of the = or none at all:

```
set count = 1                           Both statements are valid
set count=1                             but set count= 1 won't work
```

The evaluation is done in the normal manner (**echo $count**). The C shell uses another statement, **setenv**, to set an *environment variable*. These variables are discussed in Chapter 11.

9.10.1 Effects of Quoting and Escaping

To assign a multiword string to a variable, you can escape each space character, but quoting (single or double) is the preferred solution:

```
message=You\ didn't\ enter\ the\ filename
message="You didn't enter the filename"
```

Now that you have another special character ($) that is gobbled up by the shell, you may still require to interpret it literally without it being evaluated. This time we have escaping and single-quoting as our options:

```
$ echo The average pay is \$1000
The average pay is $1000
$ echo 'The average pay is $1000'
The average pay is $1000
```

Like the backquote, the $ is also evaluated by the shell when it is double-quoted. Here are two examples:

```
$ echo "The PATH is $PATH and the current directory is `pwd`"
The PATH is /bin:/usr/bin:. and the current directory is /home/kumar/workc
$ echo "The average pay is $1000"
The average pay is 000
```

The first example shows both command substitution and variable evaluation at work, but have a look at the second example. Here, the shell evaluated a "variable" $1. It is not defined, so a null string was output. $1 belongs to a set of parameters that are called *positional parameters*, *(16.3)* signifying the arguments that you pass to a script.

> **Note** Whether you should use double quotes or single quotes depends on whether you want command substitution and variable evaluation to be enabled or not. Double quotes permit their evaluation but single quotes don't.

9.10.2 Where to Use Shell Variables

Setting Pathnames If a pathname is used several times in a script, then you should assign it to a variable. You can then use it as an argument to any command. Let's use it with **cd** in this manner:

```
$ progs='/home/kumar/c_progs'
$ cd $progs ; pwd
/home/kumar/c_progs
```

A shell script would generally contain this definition at the beginning, and then it could be used everywhere—both in the script and in other scripts run from that script. It means lesser typing, but there's another advantage. In a later reorganization, if the location of `c_progs` changes to, say, `/export/home/kumar/c_progs`, then you simply need to change the variable definition, and everything will work in just the same way as before.

Using Command Substitution You can also use the feature of command substitution to set variables:

```
$ mydir=`pwd` ; echo $mydir
/home/kumar/c_progs
```

You can store the size of a file in a variable too:

```
size=`wc -c < foo.txt`
```

We used the < symbol to leave out the filename in the value assigned to size. If we had used `foo.txt` as an argument instead, then `size` would have contained a two-word string.

Concatenating Variables and Strings You'll often require to concatenate a variable with another variable or string in your shell scripts. In a later chapter, we'll use this feature to change a file's extension. To concatenate two variables you can either place them side by side:

```
base=foo ; ext=.c                    Two assignments in one line
file=$base$ext                       This is foo.c
```

or use curly braces to delimit them:

```
file=${base}$ext
```

In either case, you can finally run a compilation command in this way:

```
cc -o $base $file                    Creates executable foo from foo.c
```

A similar technique can be used to concatenate a variable and a string. Note that some situations require you to use quotes:

```
file=$base'.c'          This is foo.c; quotes not required
file=${base}.c          Same but more readable
file=$base'01'          This is foo01; quotes required
```

> **Note** This concatenation feature finds application in adding a directory name to the shell's PATH variable. You can append a directory to the existing PATH in this way:
>
> ```
> PATH=$PATH:/usr/local/bin
> ```
>
> You can make this assignment at the prompt in which case the setting will be valid only for the current session. Later, you'll learn to make this setting permanent.

The UNIX system also uses a number of variables to control its behavior. There are variables that tell you the type of terminal you are using, the prompt string that you use or the directory where incoming mail is kept. These variables are often called *environment variables* because they can alter the operation of the environment in many ways. A detailed discussion of the significance of these special shell (environment) variables will be taken up in Chapter 11.

9.11 CONCLUSION

Now that you have seen the major interpretive features of the shell, it's time we made a summary of these activities. After the command line is terminated by hitting the *[Enter]* key, the shell goes ahead with processing the command line in one or more passes. The sequence varies with the shell you use, but broadly assumes the following order:

- *Parsing* The shell first breaks up the command line into words using spaces and tabs as delimiters, unless quoted. All consecutive occurrences of a space or tab are replaced here with a single space.
- *Variable evaluation* All words preceded by a $ are evaluated as variables, unless quoted or escaped.
- *Command substitution* Any command surrounded by backquotes is executed by the shell, which then replaces the standard output of the command into the command line.
- *Redirection* The shell then looks for the characters >, < and >> to open the files they point to.
- *Wild-card interpretation* The shell finally scans the command line for wild-cards (the characters *, ?, [and]). Any word containing a wild-card is replaced by a sorted list of filenames that match the pattern. The list of these filenames then forms the arguments to the command.
- *PATH evaluation* It finally looks for the PATH variable to determine the sequence of directories it has to search in order to hunt for the command.

The preceding sequence can be considered as a simplistic treatment of the shell's behavioral pattern. There are many more characters that the shell looks for that have been ignored here. And the shell itself can be viewed from different perspectives. The next chapter examines the process; the shell is also a process. Later chapters discuss the shell's environment (Chapter 11) and its programming features (Chapters 16 and 24).

WRAP UP

The shell is a process that runs when a user logs in and terminates when she logs out. It issues a prompt and scans the command you enter for some special characters (*metacharacters*). It rebuilds the command line before turning it over to the kernel for execution, and then waits for the command to terminate.

The shell matches filenames with *wild-cards* that have to be expanded before the command is executed. It can match any character (*) or a single one (?). It can also match a range ([ ]) and negate a match ([!]). The * doesn't match a filename beginning with a dot though it matches embedded dots.

A wild-card is *escaped* with a \ to be treated literally, and if there are a number of them, then they should be *quoted*. These techniques also work on the space, the newline and the \, which the shell interprets specially.

The shell makes available three files representing *standard input*, *standard output* and *standard error* to every command that it runs. It uses the < and > symbols to manipulate the default source and destination of the input and output streams by assigning them to disk files. Standard error is redirected with 2>. These files are accessed with small integers called *file descriptors*.

The file `/dev/null` never grows in size and every user can access her own terminal as `/dev/tty`.

Pipes connect the standard output of one command to the standard input of another. Commands using standard output and standard input are called *filters*, which serve as powerful text manipulators.

Command substitution enables a command's output to become the arguments of another command. The shell supports *variables* which are evaluated by prefixing a $ to the variable name. Single quotes protect all special characters, while double quotes enable command substitution and variable evaluation.

This text book discusses the Bourne shell (**sh**) and its two supersets, the Korn shell (**ksh**) and Bash shell (**bash**). It also highlights the C shell (**csh**). You should use either Korn or Bash as your login shell.

TEST YOUR UNDERSTANDING

9.1 What is the significance of the command **ls *.***?

9.2 How do you remove only the hidden files of your directory? Does **rm** * remove these files as well?

9.3 Match the filenames chapa, chapb, chapc, chapx, chapy and chapz with a wild-card expression.

9.4 Is the wild-card expression [3-h]* valid?

9.5 Frame a wild-card model where the last character is not numeric.

9.6 When will **cd** * work?

9.7 Name the three sources of standard input and standard output.

9.8 How do you save your entire home directory structure including the hidden files in a file?

9.9 The commands, **cat** and **bc**, when used without arguments don't seem to do anything. What does that indicate and how do you return the shell prompt?

9.10 How will you create a filename containing just one space character? How will you later confirm from the **`ls`** output that it indeed contains a space?

9.11 Command substitution requires the command to use (i) standard input (ii) standard output (iii) both (iv) none of these.

9.12 To append `.c` to a variable `x`, you have to use the expression (i) `$x.c` (ii) `$x".c"` (iii) `${x}.c` (iv) any of these (v) only the first two.

FLEX YOUR BRAIN

9.1 When the shell finds metacharacters in the command line what does it do? When is the command finally executed?

9.2 Devise suitable wild-card patterns to match the following filenames: (i) `foo1`, `foo2` and `foo5` (ii) `quit.c`, `quit.o` and `quit.h` (iii) `tutorial.ps` and `tutorial.pdf` (iv) all filenames beginning with a dot and ending with `.swp`.

9.3 Frame a wild-card pattern to match all filenames where the first character is numeric and the last character is not alphabetic.

9.4 Devise a command that copies all files named `chap01`, `chap02`, `chap03` and so forth, and up to `chap26` to the parent directory. Can a single wild-card pattern match them all?

9.5 You have a file named * and a directory named `My Documents` in the current directory. How do you remove them?

9.6 Explain the significance of single- and double-quoting explaining clearly when one is to be used in preference to the other.

9.7 How do the commands **`wc foo`** and **`wc < foo`** differ? Who opens the file in each case?

9.8 You want to concatenate two files, `foo1` and `foo2`, but also insert some text after `foo1` and before `foo2` from the terminal. How will you do this?

9.9 Execute the command **`ls > newlist`**. What interesting observation can you make from the contents of `newlist`?

9.10 What are *file descriptors* and why is 2> used as the redirection symbol for standard error?

9.11 What are the conditions that need to be satisfied to make this sequence work?

prog1 | prog2 | prog3

9.12 How do you find out the number of users logged in?

9.13 Using command substitution, write a command sequence that always prints the calendar of the current month.

9.14 How will you store the total size of all C source files (`.c`) in the variable `count`?

10

The Process

Everything, they say, in UNIX is a file. In this chapter, we look at everything as a process. A process is a UNIX abstraction that enables us to look at files and programs in another way. A file is treated as a simple file when it lies in a dormant state on disk. It can also be understood as a process when it is executed. Like living organisms, processes are born, they give birth to other processes and also die. Processes make things "happen" in UNIX.

UNIX being a multitasking system, hundreds or even thousands of processes can run on a large system. Processes belong to the domain of the kernel, which is responsible for their management. We'll examine the process attributes and understand the process creation mechanism. We must also be able to control these processes by moving them between foreground and background and killing them when they get out of control. We'll also examine the process scheduling facilities offered by UNIX.

WHAT YOU WILL LEARN

- An overview of the kernel's role in process management and the similarities between files and processes.
- Examine the process attributes and the inheritance mechanism at work.
- View the process attributes with **ps**.
- Run a job in the background with & and prevent its termination with **nohup**.
- Reduce the priority of a job with **nice**.
- Use **kill** to terminate processes.
- Use the *job control* commands to switch control from one job to another.
- Schedule jobs for one-time execution with **at** and **batch**.
- Use the **cron** scheduler and examine the *crontab* file to schedule jobs to run periodically.
- Time a process with **time**, noting also the time spent by the kernel on the user's behalf.

TOPICS OF SPECIAL INTEREST

- How a process is created using three primitives—*fork*, *exec* and *wait*.
- Understand how the shell is created using these primitives.
- A brief introduction to *signals* whose coverage is expanded in Chapter 26.

10.1 PROCESS BASICS

A process is simply an instance of a running program. A process is said to be *born* when the program starts execution and remains alive as long as the program is active. After execution is complete, the process is said to *die*. A process also has a name, usually the name of the program being executed. For example, when you execute the **grep** command, a process named **grep** is created. However, a process can't be considered synonymous with a *program*. When two users run the same program, there's one program on disk but two processes in memory.

It's the kernel (and not the shell) that is ultimately responsible for the management of these processes. It determines the time and priorities that are allocated to processes so that multiple processes are able to share CPU resources. It provides a mechanism by which a process is able to execute for a finite period of time and then relinquish control to another process. The kernel has to sometimes store pages (sections) of these processes in the swap area of the disk before calling them again for running. All this happens more than once a second, making the user transparent to the switching process.

Files have attributes and so do processes. Some attributes of every process are maintained by the kernel in memory in a separate structure called the *process table*. You could say that the process table is the inode for processes. Two important attributes of a process are:

- The *Process-id* (PID) Each process is uniquely identified by a unique integer called the *Process-id* (PID) that is allotted by the kernel when the process is born. We need this PID to control a process, for instance, to kill it.
- The *Parent PID* (PPID) The PID of the parent is also available as a process attribute. When several processes have the same PPID, it often makes sense to kill the parent rather than all its children separately.

The other attributes are inherited by the child from its parent and are discussed in Section 10.4.

Things do go wrong at times. A process may go berserk and multiply rapidly, bringing the system to a complete standstill. A process may not complete in the expected time, and you may decide to suspend it, move it to the background, or even kill it. UNIX provides us with the tools to understand the process hierarchy and also control these processes.

10.1.1 The Shell Process

When you log on to a UNIX system, a process is immediately set up by the kernel. This process represents a UNIX command which may be **sh** (Bourne shell), **ksh** (Korn shell), **csh** (C shell) or **bash** (Bash). Any command that you type in at the prompt is actually the standard input to the shell process. This process remains alive until you log out, when it is killed by the kernel. We'll mostly assume and use the Bash shell for the examples of this chapter.

The shell maintains a set of environment variables, and you have already encountered some of them like PATH and SHELL. The shell's pathname is stored in SHELL, but its PID is stored in a special "variable", $$. To know the PID of your current shell, type

```
$ echo $$                                    The PID of the current shell
291
```

The PID of your login shell can't obviously change as long as you are logged in. A low PID indicates that the process was initiated quite early. When you log out and log in again, your login shell will be assigned a different PID. Knowledge of the PID is often necessary to control the activities at your terminal, especially when things go wrong.

10.1.2 Parents and Children

Just as a file has a parent, every process also has one. This *parent* itself is another process, and a process born from it is said to be its *child*. When you run the command

```
cat emp.lst
```

from the keyboard, a process representing the **cat** command, is started by the shell process. This **cat** process remains active as long as the command is active. The shell (which could be **sh**, **ksh**, **bash** or **csh**) is said to be the parent of **cat**, while **cat** is said to be the child of the shell.

Since every process has a parent, you can't have an "orphaned" process (though a process can remain in this condition for a small moment). The ancestry of every process can be traced to one ultimate process that happens to be the first process (PID 0) that is set up when the system is booted. It's like the root directory of the file system.

The analogy with files and directories doesn't stop here. Like a file, a process can have only one parent. Moreover, just as a directory can have more than one file under it, the multitasking nature of UNIX permits a process to generate (or *spawn*) one or more children. The command

```
cat emp.lst | grep 'director'
```

sets up two processes for the two commands. These processes have the names **cat** and **grep**, and both are spawned by the shell.

10.1.3 Wait or Not Wait?

While the analogy between processes and mortals is striking, you could be amused by two different attitudes that can be taken by the parent toward its child:

- It may wait for the child to die so that it can spawn the next process. The death is informed by the kernel to the parent. When you execute a command from the shell, the shell process waits for the command to die before it returns the prompt to take up the next command.
- It may not wait for the child to die at all and may continue to spawn other processes. This is what the **init** process does, the reason why **init** is the parent of several processes. Your shell can also create a process without waiting for it to die.

We'll consider instances of both attitudes that are displayed by the shell in this chapter.

Note All commands don't set up processes. Built-in commands of the shell like **pwd**, **cd** etc. don't create processes.

10.2 ps: PROCESS STATUS

Let's now use the **ps** command to display some process attributes. **ps** can be seen as the process counterpart of the file system's `ls` command. The command reads through the kernel's data structures and process tables to fetch the characteristics of processes.

By default, **ps** displays the processes associated with a user at the terminal. If you execute the command immediately after logging in, what you see could look like this:

```
$ ps
  PID TTY       TIME CMD
  291 console   0:00 bash                    The login shell of this user
```

Like **who**, **ps** also generates header information. Each line (here, only one) shows the PID, the terminal (TTY) with which the process is associated (the *controlling terminal*), the cumulative processor time (TIME) that has been consumed since the process has been started, and the process name (CMD).

You can see that your login shell (**bash**) has the PID 291, the same number echoed by the special variable, $$. On some systems, you might see the ps command itself in the output. Since the login shell isn't doing much work, its CPU usage is negligible. Here, the user is running the Bash shell; your shell could be different.

10.2.1 ps Options

ps is a highly variant command; its actual output varies across different UNIX flavors. BSD and System V are at war here; there are hardly any options common to both systems. For instance, **ps -e** on System V *approximates* to **ps aux** (no hyphens) on BSD. Solaris uses the System V version while Linux accepts both type of options. Table 10.1 shows the options used by both systems, showing their equivalence wherever possible.

Full Listing (`-f`) To get a detailed listing which also shows the parent of every process, use the `-f` (full) option:

```
$ ps -f
     UID   PID  PPID  C    STIME TTY         TIME CMD
   sumit   367   291  0 12:35:16 console     0:00 vi create_user.sh
   sumit   291     1  0 10:24:58 console     0:00 -bash
   sumit   368   367  0 12:35:18 console     0:00 /usr/bin/bash -i
```

Now you can see the parent (PPID) and owner (UID) of every process. The login shell (PID 291) has the PPID 1, the second process of the system. (The first process has the PID 0). This is **init**, the creator of all login shells and parent of all services offered by the system. We'll be discussing **init** soon.

Apart from the **vi** editor, there are two shells running here, and the `-f` option easily identifies a login shell by the hyphen preceding the command name. We'll ignore the C header for the time being. STIME shows the time the process started. CMD this time displays the full command line with its arguments.

Caution The display of the entire command line by the `-f` option lets one user know what the other is doing. This can arguably be considered as a serious demerit of the system. When a user is working on a file, it's difficult for her to keep the filename a closely guarded secret.

Table 10.1 Options to **ps**

POSIX Option	*BSD Option*	*Significance*
`-f`	`f`	Full listing showing the PPID of each process
`-e` or `-A`	`aux`	All processes including user and system processes
`-u` *usr*	`U` *usr*	Processes of user *usr* only
`-a`		Processes of all users excluding processes not associated with terminal
`-l`	`l`	A long listing showing memory-related information
`-t` *term*	`t` *term*	Processes running on terminal *term* (say, `/dev/console`)

Displaying Processes of a User (`-u`) The system administrator needs to use the `-u` (user) option to know the activities of any user. The following output shows a user working on the X Window system rather than a character terminal and X running a number of processes on the user's behalf:

```
$ ps -u sumit
   PID TTY      TIME CMD
   378 ?        0:05 Xsun
   403 ?        0:00 Xsession
   339 pts/3    0:00 bash
   346 pts/3    0:00 vi
   347 pts/3    0:00 bash
   478 ?        0:00 dtfile
   460 pts/5    0:00 dtsessio
   467 ?        0:01 dtwm                      The window manager of CDE
   479 ??       0:00 dtterm                    A terminal window in CDE
```

It's the Common Desktop Environment (CDE) that's running as X Window on this Solaris machine. All commands beginning with the string `dt` are components of CDE. You'll learn about some of these commands in Chapter 18 that features X Window and CDE. The terminal name `pts/3` refers to a pseudo-terminal, like an **xterm** window that runs under X.

Displaying All User Processes (`-a`) The `-a` (all) option lists the processes of all users but doesn't display the system processes:

```
$ ps -a
  PID     TTY        TIME CMD
  662     pts/01  00:00:00 ksh
  705     pts/04  00:00:00 sh
 1005     pts/01  00:00:00 ksh
 1017     pts/01  00:00:04 vi
  680     pts/03  00:00:00 ksh
 1056     pts/02  00:00:00 sort
 1058     pts/05  00:00:00 bash
 1069     pts/02  00:00:00 ps
```

Several users are at work here, as evident from the terminal names displayed. Most of them seem to be users of the Korn shell. Not much work seem to be going on here except for sorting and a file editing operation with **vi**. The list is usually much larger than this but has been condensed here for obvious reasons.

10.3 SYSTEM PROCESSES (-e or -A)

Apart from the processes a user generates, a number of system processes keep running all the time. Most of them are not associated with any terminal (having no controlling terminal). They are spawned during system startup and some of them start when the system goes to the multiuser state. To list all processes running on your machine, use the -e or -A option. On a busy system, this list could be very long; we produce below a trimmed and annotated list showing some important system processes:

```
$ ps -e
   PID TTY      TIME CMD
     0 ?        0:01 sched        Takes care of swapping
     1 ?        0:00 init         Parent of all shells
     2 ?        0:00 pageout      Part of the kernel—not exec'd
     3 ?        4:36 fsflush      Part of the kernel—not exec'd
   194 ?        0:00 syslogd      Logs all system messages
   170 ?        0:00 inetd        Server side of Ftp and Telnet
   231 ?        0:00 lpsched      The printer daemon
   200 ?        0:00 cron         Schedules your jobs
   247 ?        0:00 sendmail     Handles all your mail
  2931 ?        0:00 in.telne     Serves your telnet requests
   292 ?        0:00 dtlogin
  1436 ?        0:00 in.rlogi     Serves your rlogin requests
  3054 pts/2    0:00 bash
  3006 ?        0:01 dtwm         Handles windows on X Window
  2908 pts/4    0:00 vi
  2993 pts/6    0:00 bash
```

System processes are easily identified by the ? in the TTY column; they generally don't have a *controlling terminal* (term used twice before). This means that the standard input and standard output of these processes are not connected to the terminal. You can't press *[Ctrl-c]* to interrupt these processes either. These processes are known as *daemons* because they are called without a specific request from a user. Many of these daemons are actually sleeping and wake up only when they receive input.

Daemons do important work for the system. The **lpsched** daemon controls all printing activity. **sendmail** handles both your incoming and outgoing mail. Your TCP/IP network won't run Ftp and Telnet without the **inetd** daemon. **cron** looks at its control file once a minute to decide what it should do. You'll learn about some of these daemons and other system processes in subsequent chapters. We'll consider the **cron** daemon in this chapter.

> **Note** Many system daemons act as *server* components of a TCP/IP network. They listen at certain *ports* for user requests and then wake up when they receive input. For each of these daemons, there's a corresponding *client* component (another program) that a user may run on another machine. For instance, the **ftp** command on your machine communicates with the **inetd** daemon (server). Your mail handling program like **pine** or Netscape connects to **sendmail** to send out mail.

10.4 MECHANISM OF PROCESS CREATION

There are three distinct phases in the creation of a process and uses three important system calls—*fork*, *exec* and *wait*. Knowledge of the process creation cycle will enable you to write programs that create processes (Chapter 26) and also help you debug shell scripts. The three phases are discussed below:

- *Fork* A process in UNIX is created with the **fork** system call, which creates a copy of the process that invokes it. The process image is practically identical to that of the calling process, except for a few parameters like the PID. When a process is *forked* in this way, the child gets a new PID. The forking mechanism is responsible for the multiplication of processes in the system.
- *Exec* The child then overwrites the image that it has just created with the copy of the program that has to be executed. This is done with a system call belonging to the *exec* family (which has six functions), and the parent is said to *exec* this process. No additional process is created here; the existing program is simply replaced (or *overlaid*) with the new program. This process has the same PID as the child that was just forked.
- *Wait* The parent then executes the **wait** system call to *wait* for the child process to complete. It picks up the *exit status* of the child (explained shortly) and then continues with its other functions. As observed before *(10.1.3)*, a parent may not decide to wait for the death of its child.

All this means that when you run a command (say, **cat**) from the shell, the shell first forks another shell process. The newly forked shell then overlays itself with the executable image of **cat**, which then starts to run. The parent (the shell) waits for **cat** to terminate and then picks up the exit status of the child. This is a number returned by the child to the kernel, and has great significance in both shell programming and systems programming. You'll meet the exit status in Chapters 16 and 26; the latter chapter discusses the entire process creation scheme in detail.

When a process is forked, the child has a different PID and PPID from its parent. However, it inherits most of the environment of its parent. The important attributes that are inherited are:

- The *real* UID and *real* GID of the process. These are attributes that we relate to a file, but here they represent the UID and GID of the user running the program (and not of the file that is executed). These parameters are stored in the entry for the user in `/etc/passwd`.
- The *effective* UID and *effective* GID of the process. These are generally the same as their "real" cousins.
- The priority with which the process runs.

- The current directory from where the process was run. This is something you must remember to understand why you can't create a process to change your current directory.
- The descriptors of all files opened by the parent process. Recall that these are small integers that are used to identify a file *(9.5.3)*. Note that normally, the file descriptor table reserves the first three slots (0, 1 and 2) for the shell's standard streams.
- Some environment variables (like HOME and PATH). Every process knows the user's home directory and the path used by the shell to look for commands.

Some conclusions are inescapable. First, by virtue of ownership, one user can't kill or otherwise control another user's process. However, this doesn't apply to the root user, who can manipulate every user process. Moreover, inheritance here implies that the child has its own *copy* of these parameters and can thus alter the operating environment it has inherited. However, in that case, the modified environment is not available to the parent process and disappears as soon as the child dies.

The use of the two qualifiers, *real* and *effective*, used with UID and GID raises some obvious questions, but we'll have to postpone the answers till Chapter 25. For the time being it's the effective UID and GID that are important for us. In most cases, they are the same as the real ones. We'll later come across a situation *(17.3.2)* when they are not.

> **Note** A process remembers the directory from where it was run. This attribute acquires importance when a process also changes a directory.

10.4.1 How the Shell is Created

With this knowledge of the elements of process creation, let's now see how the shell itself is created. When the system moves to multiuser mode, **init** forks and execs a **getty** for every active communication port (or line). Each one of these **getty**s prints the login prompt on the respective terminal and then goes off to sleep.

When a user attempts to log in, **getty** wakes up and fork-execs the **login** program to verify the login name and the password entered. On successful login, **login** forks-execs the process representing the login shell. Repeated overlaying ultimately results in **init** becoming the immediate ancestor of the shell as can be seen from this sequence:

```
init  ====>  getty  ====>  login  ====>  shell
      fork         fork-exec       fork-exec
```

init goes off to sleep, waiting for the death of its children. The other processes **getty** and **login** have extinguished themselves by overlaying. When the user logs out, her shell is killed, and the death is intimated to **init**. **init** then wakes up, and spawns another **getty** for that line to monitor the next login. We'll see in Chapter 27 how all this is implemented in /etc/inittab, the configuration file used by **init**.

10.5 INTERNAL AND EXTERNAL COMMANDS

From the process viewpoint, the shell recognizes three types of commands:

- *External Commands*—The most commonly used ones are the UNIX utilities and programs, like **cat**, **ls** etc. The shell creates a process for each of these commands that it executes while remaining their parent.
- *Shell Scripts*—The shell executes these scripts by spawning another shell, which then executes the commands listed in the script. The child shell becomes the parent of the commands that feature in the script.
- *Internal Commands*—The shell has a number of built-in commands as well. Some of them like **cd** and **echo** don't generate a process, and are executed directly by the shell. Similarly, variable assignment with the statement `x=5`, for instance, doesn't generate a process either.

Why a Change of Directory Can't be Made in a Separate Process It's just as well that certain commands are built into the shell itself because it would be either difficult or impossible to implement them as separate external commands. You know that a child process inherits the current working directory from its parent as one of its environmental parameters. This inheritance has important consequences for the **cd** command.

It's necessary for the **cd** command not to spawn a child to achieve a change of directory. If it did so through a separate child process, then after **cd** had finished, control would revert to the parent and the original directory would be restored. It would then be impossible to change directories.

10.6 RUNNING JOBS IN BACKGROUND

A multitasking system lets a user do more than one job at a time. Since there can be only one job in the *foreground*, the rest of the jobs have to run in the *background*. There are two ways of doing this—with the shell's `&` operator and the **nohup** command. The latter permits you to log out while your jobs are running, but the former doesn't allow that (except in the C shell and Bash).

10.6.1 &: No Logging Out

The `&` is the shell's operator used to run a process in the background. The parent in this case doesn't wait for the child's death. Just terminate the command line with an `&`; the command will run in the background:

```
$ sort -o emp.lst emp.lst &
550                                    The job's PID
```

The shell immediately returns a number—the PID of the invoked command (550). The prompt is returned and the shell is ready to accept another command even though the previous command has not been terminated yet. The shell, however, remains the parent of the background process. Using an `&` you can run as many jobs in the background as the system load permits.

Depending on the shell you are using, the standard output and standard error of a job running in the background may or may not come to the terminal. If they do, then make sure both streams are redirected suitably, using `/dev/null`, if necessary. This precaution has to be taken when you are using the C shell. This shell, along with Bash, allows you to log out without aborting the job.

Background execution of a job is a useful feature that you should utilize to relegate time-consuming or low-priority jobs to the background, and run the important ones in the foreground. Here, discipline is very important as significant deterioration of CPU performance can occur. It can also be a disservice to other users who might find the machine practically at a standstill owing to the multiplicity of these processes. UNIX can't prevent users from running multiple jobs.

10.6.2 nohup: Log Out Safely

Background jobs cease to run, however, when a user logs out (the C shell and Bash excepted). That happens because her shell is killed. And when the parent is killed, its children are also normally killed (subject to certain conditions). The UNIX system permits a variation in this default behavior. The **nohup** (no hangup) command, when prefixed to a command, permits execution of the process even after the user has logged out. You must use the `&` with it as well:

```
$ nohup sort emp.lst &
586
Sending output to nohup.out
```

The shell returns the PID this time too, and some shells display this message as well. When the **nohup** command is run in these shells, **nohup** sends the standard output of the command to the file `nohup.out`. If you don't get this message, then make sure that you have taken care of redirection or provided an output filename, wherever possible. You can now safely log out of the system without aborting the command.

When you use the **ps** command after using **nohup** from another terminal (and if it has not been completed already), you'll notice something quite significant:

```
$ ps -f -u kumar
   UID   PID  PPID  C    STIME TTY  TIME COMMAND
 kumar   586     1 45 14:52:09  01  0:13 sort emp.lst
```

Look what's happened this time. The shell died (rather, was killed) on logging out but its child (**sort**) didn't; it turned into an *orphan*. The kernel handles such situations by reassigning the PPID of the orphan (**sort**) to the system's **init** process (PID 1)—the parent of all shells. When the user logs out, **init** takes over the parentage of any process run with **nohup**. *In this way, you can kill a parent (the shell) without killing its child* (**sort**).

If you run more than one command in a pipeline, then you should use the **nohup** command at the beginning of each command in the pipeline:

```
nohup grep 'director' emp.lst & | nohup sort &
```

C Shell, Bash Shell Jobs run in the background continue to send their standard output and standard error to the terminal, and have to be redirected to avoid screen clutter. The jobs are not aborted even after the user has logged out. This is not the case with the Bourne and Korn shells. Moreover, the **nohup** command in the C shell doesn't send the standard output of the command to `nohup.out`. It has to be separately redirected to a file.

10.7 `nice`: JOB EXECUTION WITH LOW PRIORITY

Processes in the UNIX system are usually executed with equal priority. This is not always desirable since high-priority jobs must be completed at the earliest. UNIX offers the **nice** command, which is used with the & operator to *reduce* the priority of jobs. More important jobs can then have greater access to the system resources (being "nice" to your neighbors).

To run a job with a low priority, the command name should be prefixed with **nice**:

```
nice wc -l uxmanual
```

or better still with

```
nice wc -l uxmanual &
```

nice is a built-in command in the C shell. nice values are system-dependent and typically range from 1 to 19. Commands execute with a nice value that is generally in the middle of the range—usually 10. A higher nice value implies a lower priority. **nice** reduces the priority of any process, thereby raising its nice value. You can also specify the nice value explicitly with the -n option:

```
nice -n 5 wc -l uxmanual &          Nice value increased by 5 units
```

A nonprivileged user can't increase the priority of a process; that power is reserved for the superuser. The nice value is displayed with the **ps -o nice** command.

10.8 KILLING PROCESSES WITH SIGNALS

The UNIX system often requires to communicate the occurrence of an event to a process. This is done by sending a *signal* to the process. Each signal is identified by a number and designed to perform a specific function. Because the same signal number may represent two different signals on two different machines, signals are better represented by their symbolic names having the SIG prefix. They can be generated from the keyboard or by the **kill** command, which we'll be discussing soon.

If a program is running longer than you anticipated and you want to terminate it, you normally press the interrupt key. This sends the process the SIGINT signal (numbered 2). The *default* action of this signal is to kill the process. A process may also ignore a signal or execute some user-defined code written to handle that signal. Chapter 26 discusses all these options in detail; in this chapter we are concerned with a signal's default action only.

Irrespective of what you do, there's one signal (actually, two) that a process can't ignore or run user-defined code to handle it; it's the SIGKILL (9) signal which terminates a process immediately. We'll now learn to use the **kill** command to send specific signals to processes.

10.8.1 `kill`: Premature Termination of a Process

The **kill** command sends a signal *usually* with the intention of killing the process. **kill** is an internal command in most shells; the external **/bin/kill** is executed only when the shell lacks the kill capability. The command uses one or more PIDs as its arguments, and by default uses the SIGTERM (15) signal. Thus,

```
kill 105                                    It's like using kill -s TERM 105
```

terminates the job having PID 105. To facilitate premature termination, the & operator displays the PID of the process that's run in the background. If you don't remember the PID, then use the **ps** command to find out and then use **kill**.

If you run more than one job—either in the background or in different windows in the X Window system, then you can kill them all with a single **kill** statement. Just specify all their PIDs with **kill**:

```
kill 121 122 125 132 138 144
```

If all these processes have the same parent, you may simply kill the parent in order to kill all its children. However, when you use **nohup** with a set of commands and log out, you can't kill the parent as **init** acquires their parentage. You then have to kill the processes individually because you can't kill **init**.

> **Note** Like files, you also own those processes spawned by commands you execute. It's natural that you can kill only those processes that you own, and you can't kill processes of other users. Moreover, certain system processes having the PIDs 0, 1, 2, 3 and 4 simply can't be killed in this manner.

Killing the Last Background Job For most shells, the system variable $! stores the PID of the last background job—the same number seen when the & is affixed to a command. So you can kill the last background process without using the **ps** command to find out its PID:

```
$ sort -o emp.lst emp.lst &
345
$ kill $!                                   Kills the sort command
```

If your shell supports job control (as most shells do), you can use **kill** with a slightly different syntax to terminate a job. We'll be discussing job control shortly.

*Using **kill** with Other Signals* By default, **kill** uses the SIGTERM signal (15) to terminate the process. You would have noticed that some programs simply ignore it and continue execution normally. In that case, the process can be killed with the SIGKILL signal (9). This signal can't be generated at the press of a key, so you must use **kill** with the signal name (without the SIG) prefixed with the -s option:

```
kill -s KILL 121                            Recommended way of using kill
kill -9 121                                 Same as above but not recommended
```

A simple **kill** command (with TERM) won't kill the login shell. You can kill your login shell by using any of these commands:

```
kill -9 $$                                  $$ stores PID of current shell
kill -s KILL 0                              Kills all processes including the login shell
```

> **Tip** To view the list of all signal names and numbers that are available on your machine, use the command **kill -l** (list) or view the file /usr/include/sys/signal.h.

> **Note** In early days, **kill** was used only to terminate a process. Today, with so many signals available, the name "kill" today has turned a misnomer; all signals don't kill a process. In Chapter 26, we'll examine the **kill** system call to learn that **kill** can also suspend a job or even direct a suspended job to continue!

10.9 JOB CONTROL

A *job* is the name given to a group of processes. The easiest way of creating a job is to run a pipeline of two or more commands. Now consider that you expect a job to complete in 10 minutes and it goes on for half an hour. If you kill the job now, then you'll lose a lot of work. If you are using the C shell, Korn shell or Bash, you can use their *job control* facilities to manipulate jobs. Job control in these shells means that you can

- Relegate a job to the background (**bg**).
- Bring it back to the foreground (**fg**).
- List the active jobs (**jobs**).
- Suspend a foreground job (*[Ctrl-z]*).
- Kill a job (**kill**).

The commands needed to perform these activities are shown in parentheses. To begin our discussion, if you have invoked a command and the prompt hasn't yet returned, you can suspend the job by pressing *[Ctrl-z]*. You'll then see the following message:

```
[1] + Stopped                     spell uxtip02 > uxtip02.spell
```

Observe that the job has not been terminated yet; it's only suspended ("stopped"). You can now use the **bg** command to push the current foreground job to the background:

```
$ bg
[1]      spell uxtip02 > uxtip02.spell&                    A single-process job
```

The & at the end of the line indicates that the job is now running in the background. So a foreground job goes to the background, first with *[Ctrl-z]*, and then with the **bg** command. You can start more jobs in the background any time:

```
$ sort permuted.index > sorted.index &
[2]     530     [2] indicates second job
$ wc -l uxtip?? > word_count &
[3]    540
```

All these jobs comprise one process each. Now that you have three jobs running, you can have a listing of their status with the **jobs** command:

```
$ jobs
[3] +  Running                  wc -l uxtip?? > word_count &
[1] -  Running                  spell uxtip02 > uxtip02.spell &
[2]    Running                  sort permuted.index > sorted.index &
```

You can now bring any of the background jobs to the foreground with the **fg** command. To bring the current (most recent) job to the foreground, use

```
fg
```

This will bring the **wc** command in the foreground. The **fg** and **bg** commands can also be used with the job number, job name or a string as arguments, prefixed by the % symbol:

`fg %1`	*Brings first job to foreground*
`fg %sort`	*Brings sort job to foreground*
`bg %2`	*Sends second job to background*
`bg %?perm`	*Sends to background job containing string* perm

At any time, however, you can terminate a job with the **kill** command using the same identifiers as above. Thus, **kill %1** kills the first background job with SIGTERM, while **kill -s KILL %spell** terminates the spell-checking program with SIGKILL.

At this point, it must be mentioned that the reason why we used *[Ctrl-z]* for suspending a job is that, by default, this is the character set by the **stty** command *(4.11)* for this purpose. When you use this command in those shells supporting job control, you'll probably see a line of output similar to this:

```
start = ^q; stop = ^s; susp = ^z; dsusp = ^y;
```

The third assignment shows the suspend character as ^z, which is **stty**'s way of representing *[Ctrl-z]*. You can change it if you want but that normally won't be necessary.

10.10 at AND batch: EXECUTE LATER

UNIX provides sophisticated facilities to schedule a job to run at a specified time of day. If the system load varies greatly throughout the day, it makes sense to schedule less urgent jobs at a time when the system overheads are low. The **at** and **batch** commands make such scheduling possible.

10.10.1 at: ONE-TIME EXECUTION

at takes as its argument the time the job is to be executed and displays the at> prompt. Input has to be supplied from the standard input:

```
$ at 14:08
at> empawk2.sh
[Ctrl-d]
commands will be executed using /usr/bin/bash
job 1041188880.a at Sun Dec 29 14:08:00 2002
```

The job goes to the queue, and at 2:08 p.m. today, the script file **empawk2.sh** will be executed. **at** shows the job number, the date and time of scheduled execution. This job number is derived from the number of seconds that have elapsed since the Epoch. It's the most meaningful method of making such numbers unique across several years.

at doesn't indicate the name of the script to be executed; that is something the user has to remember. The standard output and standard error of this shell script will be mailed to the user, who can use any mail reading program to view it. Alternatively, a user may prefer to redirect the output of the command itself:

```
at 15:08
empawk2.sh > rep.lst
```

You can also use the `-f` option to take commands from a file. However, any error messages that may be generated when executing a program will, in the absence of redirection, continue to be mailed to the user. To mail job completion to the user, use the `-m` option.

at also offers the key words `now`, `noon`, `midnight`, `today` and `tomorrow`. Moreover, it accepts the `+` symbol to act as an operator. The words that can be used with this operator include `hours`, `days`, `weeks`, `months` and `years`. The following forms show the use of some of the key words and operators:

```
at 15                        24-hour format assumed
at 5pm
at 3:08pm
at noon                      At 12:00 hours today
at now + 1 year              At the current time after one year
at 3:08pm + 1 day            At 3:08 p.m. tomorrow
at 15:08 December 18, 2001
at 9am tomorrow
```

The month name and day of the week, when used at all, must be either fully spelled out or abbreviated to three letters.

Jobs can be listed with the **at -l** command and removed with **at -r**. Unfortunately, there's no way you can find out the name of the program scheduled to be executed. This can create problems, especially when you are unable to recall whether a specific job has actually been scheduled for later execution.

10.10.2 batch: Execute in Batch Queue

The **batch** command also schedules jobs for later execution, but unlike **at**, jobs are executed as soon as the system load permits. The command doesn't take any arguments but uses an internal algorithm to determine the execution time. This prevents too many CPU-hungry jobs from running at the same time. The response of **batch** is similar to at otherwise:

```
$ batch < empawk2.sh
commands will be executed using /usr/bin/bash
job 1041185673.b at Sun Dec 29 13:14:33 2002
```

Any job scheduled with **batch** goes to a special at queue, and can also be removed with **at -r**.

> **Note** The system administrator controls the use of **at** and **batch** on your system. For details, look up Section 17.2.4.

10.11 cron: RUNNING JOBS PERIODICALLY

The **ps -e** command always shows the **cron** daemon running. This is the UNIX system's chronograph, ticking away every minute. Unlike **at** and **batch** that are meant for one-time execution, **cron** executes programs at regular intervals. It is mostly dormant, but every minute it wakes up and looks in a control file (the *crontab* file) in /var/spool/cron/crontabs for instructions to be performed at that instant. After executing them, it goes back to sleep, only to wake up the next minute.

A user may also be permitted to place a crontab file named after her login name in crontabs directory. kumar has to place his crontab commands in the file /var/spool/cron/crontabs/kumar. This location is, however, system-dependent. A specimen entry in the file /var/spool/cron/crontabs/kumar can look like this:

```
00-10 17 * 3,6,9,12 5  find / -newer .last_time -print > backuplist
```

Each line contains a set of six fields separated by whitespace. The complete command line is shown in the last field. All these fields together determine when and how often the command will be executed. **cron** uses an unusual number matching system for matching fields. A set of numbers is delimited by a comma. A * used in any of the first five fields implies that the command is to be executed every period depending on the field where it is placed.

The first field (legal values 00 to 59) specifies the number of minutes after the hour when the command is to be executed. The range 00-10 schedules execution every minute in the first 10 minutes of the hour. The second field (17, i.e., 5 p.m.) indicates the hour in 24-hour format for scheduling (legal values 1 to 24).

The third field (legal values 1 to 31) controls the day of the month. This field (here, an asterisk), read with the other two, implies that the command is to be executed every minute, for the first 10 minutes, starting at 5 p.m. every day. The fourth field (3,6,9,12) specifies the month (legal values 1 to 12). The fifth field (5—Friday) indicates the days of the week (legal values 0 to 6), Sunday having the value 0.

So what is the frequency of execution of this command? Even though the third field uses a * to indicate execution every day, the fifth field overrides the entry and limits execution to every Friday. The **find** command will thus be executed every minute in the first 10 minutes after 5 p.m., every Friday of the months March, June, September and December (of every year).

> **LINUX:** Linux additionally looks up the file /etc/crontab, which has the instructions in a different format.

10.11.1 crontab: Creating a crontab File

You can also create your own crontab files with **vi** in the format shown previously. You'll then need to use the **crontab** command to place the file in the directory containing crontab files for **cron** to read the file again:

```
crontab cron.txt                                  cron.txt contains cron commands
```

If kumar runs this command, a file named kumar will be created in /var/spool/cron/crontabs containing the contents of cron.txt. In this way, different users can have crontab files named after their user-ids.

It's also possible to enter **cron** commands by using **crontab** with the `-e` option. **crontab** calls up the editor defined in the `EDITOR` variable (often, **vi**). After you have edited your commands and quit **vi**, the commands are automatically scheduled for execution.

You can see the contents of your crontab file with **crontab -l** and remove them with **crontab -r**.

cron is mainly used by the system administrator to perform housekeeping chores, like removing outdated files or collecting data on system performance. It's also extremely useful to periodically dial up to an Internet mail server to send and retrieve mail.

> **Note** Like **at** and **batch**, the use of **cron** is controlled by some system files, which can be edited only by the system administrator *(17.2.4)*.

10.12 `time`: TIMING PROCESSES

When you have multiple versions of a program, you'll want to find out how efficiently they use the system resources. The **time** command accepts the entire command line to be timed as its argument and does this work. It executes the program and also displays the time usage on the terminal. This enables programmers to tune their programs to keep CPU usage at an optimum level.

You can find out the time taken to perform a sorting operation by preceding the **sort** command with **time**:

```
$ time sort -o newlist invoice.lst
real     0m29.811s
user     0m1.370s
sys      0m9.990s
```

The `real` time shown is the clock elapsed time from the invocation of the command till its termination. The `user` time shows the time spent by the program in executing itself. In Chapter 25, you'll see how control shifts to the kernel when a program executes a system call, and `sys` indicates the time used by the kernel in doing work on behalf of the user process. The sum of the user time and the sys time actually represents the CPU time. This could be significantly less than the real time on a heavily loaded system (as is the case above).

10.13 CONCLUSION

This chapter examined the relationship between files and processes—the key subsystems of the UNIX operating system. We discussed the process creation mechanism, the process attributes and how one can send signals to a process. We also learned to schedule these processes. We briefly examined the job control mechanism without discussing *process groups*. Fortunately, the basic process subsystem uses only a handful of system calls to achieve all these tasks and we have already been introduced to these primitives—**fork**, the exec family and **wait**.

In Chapter 26, we'll have a second look at processes and use these system calls to actually create them, run external commands and wait for their death. We'll also have a close look at the signaling facility to change the default signal-handling behavior of these processes. Knowledge of processes is also key to customizing the shell's operating environment, and that is what we are going to take up in the next chapter.

WRAP UP

A process is an instance of a running program. It is identified by the *process-id* (PID), and its *parent PID* (PPID). The kernel decides which process to run and for how long before another process is given a chance. Process attributes are maintained in the *process table* and other structures in memory.

A process is created by another process and gives rise to a parent-child relationship. Because of multitasking, a process can *spawn* multiple processes. The login shell is a process that keeps running as long as the user is logged in. Its PID is stored in the parameter $$.

You can list your own processes with **ps**, view the process ancestry (-f), all users' processes (-a) and all system processes (-e). BSD uses a different set of options. System processes, often called *daemons*, are generally not attached to a terminal and not invoked specifically by a user. They often act as *servers* in a client-server framework that requires two processes to communicate with each other.

A process is created with the **fork** system call, which creates a copy (a child) of itself. The child then uses an exec function to overwrite itself with the image of the program to be run. The parent normally waits to pick up the *exit status* of the child's termination by issuing the **wait** system call.

The child's environment inherits some parameters from the parent, like the real and effective UID and GID, the file descriptors, the current directory and environment variables. However, changes in the child are *not* made available in the parent. Built-in shell commands like **pwd** and **cd** don't fork a separate process. Shell scripts use a sub-shell to run the commands in a script.

A job can be run in the background by affixing an & at the end of the command line. **nohup** ensures that a background job remains alive even after the user has logged out. Premature death of the parent makes the child an *orphan*, and **init** takes over the parentage of all orphans. The **nice** command is used to reduce the priority of a process. Only the superuser can increase this value.

The UNIX kernel communicates with a process by sending it a *signal*. Signals can be generated from the keyboard or by the **kill** command. You can kill a process with **kill**, and use **kill -s KILL** if a simple **kill** doesn't do the job. The last background process is killed with **kill $!**.

A *job* is a collection of processes, often resulting from a pipeline. The C shell, Korn and Bash shells enable job control. You can move jobs between foreground and background (**fg** and **bg**) and suspend (*[Ctrl-z]*) them. You can list jobs (**jobs**) and also kill them (**kill**) using their job numbers as identifiers.

You can schedule a job for one-time execution with **at**, or run it when the system load permits with **batch**. **cron** lets you schedule jobs so that they run repeatedly. It takes input from a user's *crontab* file where the schedule and frequency of execution is specified by five fields using a special number matching system.

Jobs are timed with **time**, a useful tool for the programmer for making comparisons between different versions of a program.

TEST YOUR UNDERSTANDING

10.1 What is the significance of the PID and PPID?

10.2 Which process do you think may have the maximum number of children?

10.3 How do you display all processes running on your system?

10.4 Which programs are executed by spawning a shell?

10.5 Name some commands that don't require a separate process.

10.6 How do you find out the complete command line of a process run by user timothy?

10.7 How will you use **kill** to ensure that a process is killed?

10.8 How will you kill the last background job without knowing its PID?

10.9 How do you display the signal list?

10.10 You are editing a file with **vi**, and you want to make a temporary exit to the shell. How will you do it and then come back to **vi** again?

10.11 Interpret the following crontab entry without examining the **find** command line:

```
30 21 * * * find /tmp /usr/tmp -atime +30  -exec rm -f {} \;
```

10.12 How do you compare the efficiency of the programs foo1 and foo2?

FLEX YOUR BRAIN

10.1 Mention the significance of the two shell parameters, $$ and $!.

10.2 Mention the similarities that you find between processes and files.

10.3 What are the two options available to a parent after it has spawned a child? How can the shell be made to behave in both ways?

10.4 Explain what *daemon* processes are and their behavioral pattern. Name three examples of daemons and the tasks they perform. How do you use **ps** to identify these processes?

10.5 How is a process created? Mention briefly the role of the **fork** and **exec** system calls in process creation.

10.6 Name five important process attributes that are inherited by the child from its parent.

10.7 Explain the sequence of steps followed by **init** that allows us to log in and work at the shell prompt. What does **init** do when a user logs out?

10.8 How does the shell execute a shell script?

10.9 What is the difference between a process run with & and one run with **nohup**?

10.10 What are *signals* and name a way of generating a signal from the keyboard. Why should we use **kill** with signal names rather than their numbers?

10.11 The **jobs** command issued the message `jobs: not found`. When does that normally happen?

10.12 What is the difference between a *job* and a *process*? How do you (i) suspend the foreground job (ii) move a suspended job to the background (iii) bring back a suspended job to the foreground?

10.13 Interpret these crontab entries and explain if they will work: (i) `* * * * * dial.sh` (ii) `00-60 22-24 30 2 * find.sh`

10.14 Frame a crontab entry to execute the **connect.sh** script every 30 minutes on every Monday, Wednesday and Friday between the times 8 a.m. and 6 p.m.

11

Customizing the Environment

Interaction with the operating system takes away a significant chunk of the user's time. She has to constantly change directories, list files, edit and compile programs and repeat previous commands. Incorrect or inconvenient environmental settings can also make life miserable for the UNIX programmer. As a user, you must strive to set a pleasant environment for yourself. The task is not difficult at all as UNIX is second to none in environment control.

UNIX can be highly customized by manipulating the settings of the shell alone. Commands can be made to change their default behavior. You can recall, edit and reexecute previous commands. You can devise shortcuts to commands or make the shell complete commands and filenames for you. You can also make these settings permanent so they are always available when you log in. The degree of customization possible depends mainly on the shell you use.

The Bourne shell has the minimum number of features, but its derivatives—the Korn shell and Bash—are feature-rich and highly customizable. You'll have a headstart over others if you select one of the two as your login shell. After reading this chapter, you may want to make this decision.

WHAT YOU WILL LEARN

- The significance of environment variables like `HOME`, `SHELL`, `MAIL`, and so forth.
- How to customize the prompt string in Bash and Korn.
- Use *aliases* to invoke commands with short names.
- Use the *history* mechanism to recall, edit and run previously executed commands.
- Prevent accidental overwriting of files and logging out with *[Ctrl-d]* using **`set -o`**.
- Use the *tilde substitution* feature to shorten pathnames that refer to the home directory.
- How the initialization scripts function in the various shells while noting the distinction between the *profiles* and *rc* scripts.

TOPICS OF SPECIAL INTEREST

- Use the history mechanism to repeatedly edit and compile a program using the minimum number of keystrokes.
- Use the $_ shortcut with any command to represent the last argument of the previous command.
- Edit any previous command line using the **`vi`**-like *in-line editing* feature.

11.1 ENVIRONMENT VARIABLES

The UNIX system is controlled by a number of shell variables that are separately set by the system—some during the boot sequence and some after logging in. These variables are called *environment variables* or *system variables.* You need to know the significance of many of them because they determine the environment in which you work. You can even alter their values to your liking.

We begin our study by examining the environment variables that are common to the Bourne family of shells (**sh**, **bash** and **ksh**). Later, we'll examine some variables specific to Bash and Korn.

11.1.1 Common Variables

The **set** statement displays a complete list of all environment variables (A concise list is displayed here.):

```
$ set
HOME=/home/henry
IFS='
'
LOGNAME=henry
MAIL=/var/mail/henry
MAILCHECK=60
PATH=/bin:/usr/bin:.:/usr/ccs/bin
PS1='$ '
PS2='> '
SHELL=/usr/bin/bash
TERM=xterm
```

By convention, such built-in variable names are defined in uppercase. If you use variables of your own, then for the purpose of distinguishing them from the ones built in, it is preferable to use lowercase names only. The significance of some of the important system variables is presented next.

The Command Search Path (PATH) The PATH variable instructs the shell about the route it should follow to locate any executable command. This has already been discussed *(3.1.1)*. Its current value as displayed by **set** shows a list of four directories. If you wish to include the directory /usr/xpg4/bin in your search list, then you'll have to reassign this variable:

```
PATH=$PATH:/usr/xpg4/bin          Adding new value to old value—OK
```

> **Note** If there are two commands having the same name in two different directories, that command will be executed whose directory name appears first in the PATH list.

Your Home Directory (HOME) When you log in, UNIX normally places you in a directory named after your login name. This directory is called the home or login directory *(5.4)* and is available in the variable HOME:

```
$ echo $HOME
/home/henry
```

The home directory ($HOME) for a user is set by the system administrator in /etc/passwd. The line for this user could look like this:

```
henry:x:208:50::/home/henry:/bin/ksh
```

Note that the home directory has been set in the last but one field. This file can be edited by the system administrator, either manually, or by invoking the **useradd** or **usermod** commands. You only have to tell the administrator if you desire a change of HOME.

You can change the value of this variable, but it will *not* change the home directory as such, but only the directory that **cd** switches to when used without arguments. This happens because a simple **cd** implies **cd $HOME**.

Mailbox Location and How Often Checked (MAIL *and* MAILCHECK) The UNIX mail handling system doesn't inform the user that mail has arrived; that job has to be done by the shell. It knows the location of a user's mailbox from MAIL. This mailbox is generally /var/mail or /var/spool/mail (Linux). henry's mail is saved in /var/mail/henry on an SVR4 system.

MAILCHECK determines how often the shell checks the file for the arrival of new mail (The **set** output shows 60). If the shell finds the file modified since the last check, it informs the user with this familiar message:

```
You have mail in /var/mail/henry
```

The Prompt Strings (PS1 *and* PS2) The shell has two prompts stored in PS1 and PS2. The primary prompt string PS1 is the one you normally see. You have also seen when discussing the **echo** command *(3.4.2)*, how a multiline command makes the shell respond with a >. The > is the secondary prompt string stored in PS2. Normally, PS1 and PS2 in the Bourne shell are set to the characters $ and >, respectively.

You can change the primary prompt string to C> if you find the Windows environment more reassuring:

```
$ PS1="C> "
C> _
```

While the $ is the primary prompt string for nonprivileged users, the system administrator uses the # as the prompt. We have something more to discuss about PS1 when we take up the Bash and Korn shells.

Shell Used by Commands with Shell Escapes (SHELL) SHELL tells you the shell you are using. There are some programs like **more** and **vi** that provide you with a *shell escape* to let you run a UNIX command. SHELL determines the shell these programs use.

The system administrator usually sets up your login shell in /etc/passwd when creating a user account, though he can change it whenever you make a request. Just have a look at the sample line in the discussion on the HOME variable; the last field sets the value of SHELL.

The Terminal Type (TERM) TERM indicates the terminal type that is used. Every terminal has certain characteristics that are defined in a separate control file in the terminfo directory (in

/usr/lib or /usr/share/lib). This directory contains a number of subdirectories named after the letters of the alphabet. A terminal's control file is available in a directory having a one-letter name that is the same as the first letter of the terminal name. For instance, vt100 terminals use the file /usr/share/lib/terminfo/v/vt100.

Some utilities like the **vi** editor are terminal-dependent, and they need to know the type of terminal you are using. If TERM isn't set correctly, **vi** won't work and the display will be faulty. TERM is also important when you log on to a remote machine.

Your Username (LOGNAME) This variable shows your username. When you wander around in the file system, you may sometimes forget your login name. (It's strange, but it happens when you have multiple accounts!) From time to time, just make sure you know which account you logged in to:

```
$ echo $LOGNAME                                  Or try who am i
henry
```

Where else can you use this variable? You can use it in a shell script which does different things depending on the user actually invoking the script.

Field Separator for Command and Arguments (IFS) IFS contains a string of characters that are used as word separators in the command line. The string normally consists of the space, tab and the newline characters. All these characters are invisible but the blank line following it suggests that the newline character is part of this string. You can confirm the contents of this variable by taking its octal dump:

```
$ echo "$IFS" | od -bc
0000000  040 011 012 012
              \t  \n  \n
0000004
```

You can see the three whitespace characters that comprise IFS. You normally don't need to change this variable, but advanced shell programmers sometimes need to make a temporary change to IFS. We'll also do that in Chapter 24.

11.1.2 Variables Used in Bash and Korn

Current Directory in Prompt (PWD *and* PS1) Bash and Korn dispense with the need to use the **pwd** command which displays the current directory. They offer a separate variable PWD whose value can be assigned to PS1:

```
$ PS1='[$PWD] '                                  Value to be enclosed within quotes
[/home/henry] _
```

See how the prompt changes from $ to [/home/henry]. If you change your directory now to tulec2, the prompt changes to reflect the new directory:

```
[/home/henry] cd tulec2
[/home/henry/tulec2] _
```

PWD is a rather unusual variable; it is reevaluated every time the working directory changes. The prompt accordingly changes to reflect the new value of PWD.

Using Event Number in PS1 *(!)* Bash and Korn also support a *history* facility that treats a previous command as an *event* and attaches a number to it. You can then recall and execute previous commands by their event numbers. Using the !, you can set the PS1 prompt to show the current event number:

```
$ PS1='[!] '                              Bash requires \ before !
[42] _
```

or better still, include the PWD variable to also reflect the current directory:

```
$ PS1='[! $PWD] '                         Variable evaluation within single quotes!
[43 /home/henry/tulec2]
```

Every time you execute a command, the event number is incremented (here, from 42 to 43). Knowledge of the event number is quite useful because you can reexecute a previous command by referring to this number.

Customizing PS1 in Bash Bash uses a number of escape sequences to make your prompt string as informative as possible. For instance, the \h string shows the hostname of your computer:

```
$ PS1="\h> "
saturn> _                                 saturn is the machine's name
```

When you use **telnet** to get into other machines in the network, you often get confused as to where you actually are. This prompt keeps you informed at all times. If you set PS1 to include your hostname and see some other name in the prompt string, then you must be logged on to a remote machine. Look up the Bash documentation for the other escape sequences.

The other variables used by Bash and Korn will be discussed in later sections that feature the history facility, in-line editing and the startup files.

11.2 ALIASES (bash and ksh)

Bash and Korn support the use of *aliases* that let you assign shorthand names for frequently used commands. For instance, many people customize the **ls** command to always execute **ls -xF**. Aliasing is done with the **alias** statement and an alias is defined in the same way as a variable.

A UNIX user often uses the **ls -l** command, so if you don't have the **ll** command or alias on your system, then you can create an alias:

```
alias ll='ls -l'                          Quoting necessary for multiple words
```

As with shell variables, there must not be any whitespace on either side of the = symbol. Once the alias is defined, you can execute the **ls -l** command simply by using

```
ll                                        This executes ls -l
```

To consider another example, we often use the **cd** command with long pathnames. If there's a sequence that you use often, then it would be sensible to convert it into an alias like this:

```
alias cdsys="cd /usr/include/sys"
```

Now you can simply invoke **cdsys** to change to this directory. You can also use aliasing to redefine an existing command so that it is always invoked with certain options. Here are two useful aliases:

```
alias cp="cp -i"
alias rm="rm -i"
```

The **cp -i** command behaves interactively when the destination file exists. **rm -i** always behaves interactively. With aliases now defined for them, every time you invoke these commands, their aliased versions are executed. How can you now use the original external commands? Just precede the command with a \. This means that you have to use **\cp foo1 foo2** to override the alias.

You can display an alias definition by using **alias** with the name:

```
$ alias cp
cp='cp -i'                                    Bash output differs a little
```

Let's briefly examine the other features of aliases. An alias is recursive, which means that if **a** is aliased to **b** and **b** is aliased to **c**, **a** should run **c**. You can list all aliases by using **alias** without arguments and unset an alias with the **unalias** statement. To unset the alias **cp**, use **unalias cp**.

Exercise some restraint in using aliases; too much aliasing can be confusing and difficult to remember. Moreover, aliases have been entirely superseded by *shell functions (24.10)*, which offer a superior form of aliasing. Aliases are good to begin with but eventually you'll be using shell functions.

> **Note** If the alias **cp** works with two filenames as arguments, don't interpret that to mean that the alias accepts arguments. It's just that the shell expands the alias before running the command line. Bash and Korn aliases don't use arguments, but C shell aliases do.

11.3 COMMAND HISTORY (bash and ksh)

A serious drawback of the Bourne shell is that a command has to be retyped to be reexecuted. Bash and Korn support a versatile *history* feature that lets you recall previous commands (even those executed in previous sessions), edit them if required and reexecute them. The shell assigns each command an event number and may (depending on the shell used) save all commands in a history file.

The **history** command displays the history list showing the event number of every previously executed command. A command is recalled by using this event number with a symbol like **!** or **r**. The maximum size and name of this file are determined by two shell-specific variables.

While Bash displays the complete history list with **history**, Korn lists the 16 commands most recently used, but we can easily find out the last five commands by using a numeric argument:

```
history 5                                Bash
history -5                               Korn
```

In either case, the output would show the event number and the command associated with that number, and it could look like this:

```
35 set -o ignoreeof
36 exit
37 alias l='ls -l'
38 tar cvf /dev/fd0 *.doc
39 fc -l
40 history                               Also includes command invoked to obtain list
```

By default, Bash stores all previous commands in the file `$HOME/.bash_history` (`sh_history` in Korn). When a command is entered and executed it is appended to the list.

Knowing the event number may not be enough; you may need to repeat a previous command. Sometimes you may also have to edit it a bit before reexecuting it. Both Bash and Korn allow you to do that, and these features are taken up in the following sections.

11.3.1 Accessing Previous Commands by Event Numbers (! and r)

The **!** symbol (**r** in Korn) is used to repeat previous commands. For repeating the last command, you have to use this:

```
!!                                     Repeats previous command—Bash
r                                      Same—Korn
```

Just one or two characters, nothing could be simpler than that! You can repeat other commands using **!** or **r**, but with the event number as argument:

```
$ !38                                  Use r 38 in Korn
38 tar cvf /dev/fd0 *.c
```

The command line is displayed and executed. Working like this, you might execute a wrong command (like **rm**), so by using the p (print) modifier, you can display the command without executing it. However, this works only in Bash:

```
$ !38:p                                Use fc -l 38 38 in Korn
38 tar cvf /dev/fd0 *.doc              Copies files from disk to diskette
```

This **tar** command copies files between disk and diskette. You should make sure of what you are doing by using the `:p` modifier first. If the command you recalled had `xvf` instead of `cvf` as arguments, data would flow in the reverse direction—from diskette to disk *(17.10.2)*. But if the above command line is the one you want to run again, simply use **!!**.

Relative Addressing If you don't know the event number but want to execute the command prior to the previous one, then you can use a negative argument with **!** or **r**:

```
!-2                                    Bash—no space between ! and -
r -2                                   Korn
```

> **Tip** Programmers will find this form of relative addressing very useful for repeatedly editing and compiling programs. For instance, if you use the command **vi appl.c** and **cc appl.c** alternately, you need to explicitly invoke the commands only once. Subsequently, you can continue using **!-2** (**r -2** in Korn) till the compilation generates no errors.

11.3.2 Executing Previous Commands by Context

You probably won't remember the event numbers of the commands except for the immediately preceding two or three, but you could at least remember that the command started with a specific letter or a string. If you know that the last command name *beginning* with v was the **vi** command, you can use **!** or **r** with either v or vi to repeat the last **vi** command:

```
!v                          Repeats last command beginning with v—Bash
r v                         Same—Korn
```

Like in the previous example discussed in the Tip, you can also use **!c** for compiling a C program and **!v** for editing (**r c** and **r v** in Korn); this is even simpler!

11.3.3 Substitution in Previous Commands

Often you require to execute a previous command but only after replacing a string in the command line with another. The same history symbols (**!** in Bash and **r** in Korn) allow you to do that by following the normal repeat command with a substitution instruction. This instruction takes on different forms in Bash and Korn.

Bash uses the **vi**-style **:s** command and the / as delimiter of the old and new patterns. Korn uses the form *old=new*. So if you want to repeat the previous **tar** command, but this time using the .bak instead of the .doc files, you have to replace doc with bak in this way:

```
!tar:s/doc/bak              Bash—vi also uses :s for substitution
r tar doc=bak               Korn
```

You can well guess that to perform a substitution on the immediately previous command, you only have to use **!!** or **r** with the substitution instruction. However, Bash offers an additional shortcut; its the ^ (caret). Restore the original command line by replacing bak with doc in this way:

```
!!:s/bak/doc                Bash—Substitution in previous command
^bak^doc                    Bash—Same; a shortcut
r bak-doc                   Korn
```

Note that this substitution is made only for the *first* occurrence in a line; two or more substitutions are not permitted in Korn. However, Bash permits global substitution also.

11.3.4 Using Last Argument of Previous Command ($_)

We often run several commands on the same file, and instead of specifying the filename every time, we can now use $_ as the abbreviated filename. This expression signifies the *last* argument of the previous command. For instance, we create a directory with **mkdir bar** and then change to it with **cd bar**. We can use $_ as a shorthand feature to represent the directory used by the previous command:

```
mkdir progs
cd $_                              Changes directory to progs
```

To consider another example, if you have edited a shell script **cronfind.sh** with **vi**, you can execute this file by simply entering this:

```
$_                                 Executes cronfind.sh
```

What better way can you imagine of executing a shell or **perl** script that you just edited with **vi**! Bash has several other parameters that can access every argument of any previous command, but that's beyond the scope of this text. For details on these parameters, look up this author's *Your UNIX: The Ultimate Guide* (Tata McGraw-Hill).

11.3.5 The History Variables

There are a few environment variables that influence the behavior of the history mechanism in Bash and Korn. First, the `HISTFILE` variable determines the filename that saves the history list. If it is not set, then Bash and Korn use these as the default history files in the home directory:

```
.bash_history                     Bash
.sh_history                       Korn
```

The history list is maintained in memory also. Bash uses two separate variables, `HISTSIZE` and `HISTFILESIZE`, for setting the size of the history list in memory and on disk. Korn uses simply `HISTSIZE` for both purposes. Here are two examples:

```
HISTSIZE=500                      Bash and Korn
HISTFILESIZE=1000                 Bash only—determines size of disk file
```

With memory and disk space going cheap today, you should set these variables to large values so that you can store commands of multiple login sessions.

11.4 IN-LINE COMMAND EDITING (bash and ksh)

Bash and Korn provide a "**vi**-like" capability of editing the command line, both of the current command and its predecessors in the history list. Before you are able to do that, you have to make the following setting:

```
set -o vi                         Use set +o vi to reverse this setting
```

You can switch off either mode by using the `+o` option instead. The editing features of the **vi** editor are built into the Bash and Korn shells, and this setting enables their use for *in-line editing*. Since you are familiar with the editing commands used in **vi**, you would be delighted to be able to use them without specifically invoking **vi**.

11.4.1 Editing a Command Line

In **vi** jargon, when you enter a command, you are always in the Input Mode, i.e., the mode where every key pressed is entered as text. With in-line editing enabled, if you notice a mistake anywhere in the current command line, you need no longer erase all previous text to take the cursor to that point. All you have to do is to press *[Esc]*. This key, you'll recall, takes you to the Command Mode. After you have done that, you can use all **vi** navigation commands to move across a line, using a repeat factor too, if necessary and relevant.

For instance, you can invoke the commands used to enter the Input Mode, like **i**, **a**, **A**, etc. You can also delete a character with **x** and three characters with **3x**. You can even put this word elsewhere with **p** or **P**! Once all changes are made, the command can be executed by hitting *[Enter]*.

To edit previous commands, recall that the **k** command in **vi** takes the cursor one line up. However, when the same command is used for in-line editing, the previous command is presented. And since the repeat factor applies here too, you can also use **5k** to present the fifth-most recent command (barring the present). If that's not the command you are looking for, then use **j** to show the next line. Once you have located the line, you can navigate along it and make the necessary changes.

Tip To recall a previous command, first press *[Esc]* and then **k** as many times as required till you locate the command. If you overshoot, use **j** till you get the line you are looking for.

11.4.2 Searching History List for Previous Commands

You can use **vi**'s search techniques to recall previous commands from the history list. Even though the search is in the reverse direction, you'll have to use the */pattern* sequence:

`/cvf`*[Enter]*	*Locates last occurrence of string* `cvf`

You can use *?pattern* only when you have already conducted a search backward and now want to conduct a forward search. You can repeat the search by pressing **n** repeatedly. If you overshoot, come back with **N**. Edit the line and run it again. Now, isn't this something!

Tip A proficient **vi** user will easily exploit these editing facilities to run a command with selected arguments of previous commands. If you remember having executed the command **vi foo1 foo2 foo3 foo4**, then you can easily run the **gzip** command with some or all of these arguments. Press *[Esc]*, search for the command with **/vi**, change `vi` to `gzip` with **2s**, and hit *[Enter]*. If you need to delete the last argument, move to the fourth argument with **4w** and press **d$**. It's as simple as that!

11.5 MISCELLANEOUS FEATURES (bash and ksh)

Before moving on to the shell's initialization scripts, let's consider a few features available in Bash and Korn which you'll find quite useful. Two of them use the shell's **set** statement. We'll also consider the significance of the ~ (tilde) in these shells.

11.5.1 Using set -o

The **set** statement by default displays the environment variables *(11.1)*, but in Bash and Korn, it can make several environment settings with the `-o` option, followed by a keyword. This option takes care of some of the common hazards faced by users, like overwriting files and accidental logging out.

File Overwriting (`noclobber`*)* The shell's > symbol overwrites (clobbers) an existing file, and to prevent such accidental overwriting, you have to use the `noclobber` argument in this way:

`set -o noclobber`	*No more overwriting files with >*

This means that if you redirect output to an existing file `foo`, the shell will retort with a message:

`bash: foo: cannot overwrite existing file`	*Bash*
`ksh: foo: file already exists`	*Korn*

To override this protection feature, use the | after the >:

```
head -5 emp.lst >| foo
```

Accidental Logging Out (ignoreeof) Users often inadvertently press *[Ctrl-d]* with intent to terminate the standard input, but end up logging out of the system. The ignoreeof keyword offers protection from accidental logging out:

```
set -o ignoreeof                        [Ctrl-d] won't log you out
```

Now, when you use *[Ctrl-d]* to terminate your session, here's a typical response from the shell:

```
Use 'exit' to terminate this shell
```

You now have to use the **exit** command to take you out of the session; *[Ctrl-d]* won't do any more (unless executed repeatedly!).

A **set** option is turned off with **set +o** *keyword*. To reverse the noclobber feature, use **set +o noclobber**. The complete list of **set**'s special options is obtained by using **set -o** or **set +o** without any additional arguments.

11.5.2 Tilde Substitution

The ~ acts as a shorthand representation of the home directory. When the ~ is followed by a login name, the shell understands the entire argument as the absolute pathname of the login directory referred to. Thus, when the shell encounters the following command line

```
cd ~sharma                              Effectively becomes $HOME/sharma
```

it switches to sharma's home directory. If the value of $HOME is /home/sharma/tulec1, then this is the directory where **cd ~sharma** switches to.

Interestingly, the ~ when used by itself or when immediately followed by a /, refers to the home directory of the user using it. If you have logged in as juliet, you can access the html directory under your home directory by using **cd ~/html**. That's why we often find a configuration file like .profile referred to both as $HOME/.profile and ~/.profile. The former works in the Bourne shell also but not the latter.

You can also toggle between the directory that you switched to most recently and your current directory. This is done with the ~- symbols (or simply -). For instance, either of the commands

```
cd ~-                                   Change to your previous directory
cd -                                    Same
```

changes your current working directory to the one you used most recently. Here's how you use it:

```
[/home/image] cd /bin                   Changes to /bin from /home/image
[/bin] cd -                             Reverts to /home/image
/home/image                             Shell displays this
[/home/image] _                         Current directory shown by PS1
```

This toggling effect is like the button many TV remote units have to let you alternate between the current and last visited channels.

11.6 THE INITIALIZATION SCRIPTS

We have assigned values to many of the environment variables, defined aliases and used **set** options. These settings are applicable only for the session; they revert to their default values when the user logs out. To make these settings permanent, you'll have to place them in certain startup scripts.

Every shell uses at least one startup script in the user's home directory—much like the `AUTOEXEC.BAT` file of DOS. This script is executed when the user logs in. Some shells also make use of a separate file that is run before logging out. Look in your home directory with **ls -a** and you'll find one or more of these files:

- `.profile` (Bourne shell)
- `.profile` and `.kshrc` (Korn Shell)
- `.bash_profile` (or `.profile` or `.bash_login`) and `.bashrc` (Bash)

Bash has an elaborate startup system, but the system is not as complex as it may appear. We have two types of files here—the "profiles" and "rc" files. The profiles are executed only once, upon login. The rc files are designed to be executed every time a separate shell is created. Let's now examine these files and consider the entries that we can place in them.

11.6.1 The Profile (.profile and .bash_profile)

The Bourne family uses `.profile` as the login script. As an added feature, the profile used by Bash can have one of three names—`.bash_profile`, `.profile` and `.bash_login`. Bash looks for one of these files in the sequence specified and identifies the one it spots first as its profile.

Issue the **ls -a** command and see whether you can locate one of these files in your home directory. This login script should be added to your home directory at the time of user creation, but you can create one even if it's not there. It is really a shell script that is executed by the shell when one logs on to the system. These "profiles" can be quite large depending on users' requirements, but an abridged one should do for initial comprehension:

```
$ cat .profile
# User $HOME/.profile - commands executed at login time
MAIL=/var/mail/$LOGNAME                                    # mailbox location
PATH=$PATH:$HOME/bin:/usr/ucb:.
PS1='$ '
PS2=>
TERM=vt100
MOZILLA_HOME=/opt/netscape ; export MOZILLA_HOME
mesg y
stty stop ^S intr ^C erase ^?
echo "Today's date is `date`"
```

The profile contains commands that are meant to be executed only *once* in a session. Some of the system variables have been assigned in this script. The later statements show that the file has been edited to taste. The PATH has been modified to contain three more directories. **mesg y** expresses your willingness to receive messages from people using the **talk** command *(12.2)*. Some **stty** settings have also been made here. All these commands and variables are understood by the Bourne shell, so this script will work in all shells of the Bourne family.

The .profile lets you customize your operating environment to suit your requirements. This environment remains in effect throughout the login session. Every time you make changes to it, you should either log out and log in again or use a special command (called dot) to execute it:

```
. .profile                                    Used by the Bourne family
```

Additionally, Bash offers the use of the C shell-styled **source** command, so you can also use **source .profile.** Both **source** and **.** execute a script in a special way—without creating a separate process (like **cd**). That's why there are certain things you can do with this file that are difficult or impossible to do otherwise.

> **Note** The .profile must be located in your home directory and it is executed after /etc/profile, the universal profile for all users. Universal environment settings are kept by the administrator in /etc/profile so they are available to all users.

11.6.2 The rc File (bash and ksh)

There's no rc file in Bourne, but Bash and Korn use one. This file is defined by an environment variable (BASH_ENV in Bash and ENV in Korn), which should be specified in the profile (.profile or .bash_profile). You should have one of these settings in your profile depending on the shell you use:

```
export ENV=$HOME/.kshrc               Korn; can also use ENV=~/.kshrc
export BASH_ENV=$HOME/.bashrc         Bash; can also use BASH_ENV=~/.bashrc
```

This file is executed every time a second shell is called up (when running a shell script, for instance). However, there's a little difference in the way Bash and Korn use their rc file. Korn automatically executes .kshrc during login if ENV is defined in the way shown above. However, the above Bash definition merely ensures that a sub-shell executes this file. If the login shell also has to execute this file, then a separate statement must be added in the profile:

```
. ~/.bashrc                           Bash; can also use source ~/.bashrc
```

The environment file should be used to hold only Bash- or Korn-specific features. History list settings (like HISTSIZE and HISTFILE), command editing settings (like **set -o vi**) and alias definitions should all be made in the environment file. This is a cleaner arrangement because should you decide to change your shell any time later, you won't be saddled with a .profile ridden with irrelevant entries. Here are some sample entries:

```
alias cp="cp -i"
alias rm="rm -i"
set -o noclobber
set -o vi
set -o ignoreeof
```

This rc file will be executed after the profile. However, if the BASH_ENV or ENV variable isn't set, then the shell executes only the profile.

11.7 CONCLUSION

In this chapter, we had another look at the shell, this time at the environment it provides to the user. We looked at three shells, and we found the Bourne shell to be weak in features. Bash and Korn are supersets of Bourne, while Bash also has features borrowed from the C shell. Knowledge of these two shells only supplements your knowledge of Bourne and doesn't take anything away.

It's always advisable to use Bash or Korn as your default login shell. If you are convinced, ask your system administrator to set it that way. You are assured of a fruitful and rewarding experience. This experience will include the shell's other features. The shell is also a programming language and there are two chapters that examine this language. We are not done with the shell yet.

WRAP UP

The UNIX shell sets the user's environment and can be tailored to behave in the way you want. Bash and Korn are feature-rich and recommended for use.

The shell makes a number of *environment variables* available. You can set the command search path (PATH), your home directory (HOME), the terminal (TERM) and the prompts (PS1 and PS2). The prompt can display both the current directory and the event number in Bash and Korn. You can also set the location of your mailbox (MAIL) and the frequency of checking it (MAILCHECK).

Bash and Korn offer *aliases* that let you abbreviate any command sequence to a string. Aliases are also useful in redefining existing commands to always run with specific options.

These shells also offer a *history* feature that lets you recall, edit and reexecute previous commands without retyping them. Previous commands can be accessed by their *event number* or context (**!** and **r**), and substitution can be performed on them. Bash and Korn identify $_ as the last argument of the previous command. The history list is saved in a file (~/.bash_history or ~/.sh_history).

These shells also offer an *in-line editing* facility that lets us edit a previous command line with **vi**-like commands. The feature has to be enabled first with **set -o vi**.

Using **set -o** in Bash and Korn, you can protect your files from accidental overwriting (noclobber) and accidental logout (ignoreeof). *Tilde substitution* lets you access a file foo in the home directory with ~/foo, and use a shortcut like **cd ~henry** to switch to henry's home directory. The command **cd ~-** toggles between the current and previous directory.

The shell executes a "profile" on login (~/.profile or ~/.bash_profile). It also executes an "rc" file when a sub-shell is created. These files are executed without creating a process using the **.** or **source** commands. Commands to be executed only once are placed in the profile. Aliases, history settings and **set -o** commands should be kept in the rc file.

TEST YOUR UNDERSTANDING

11.1 How is the home directory set—by the HOME variable or /etc/passwd?

11.2 If TERM has the value vt220, where will you expect to find its control file?

11.3 How will you add the parent directory to your existing PATH?

11.4 Write a Korn or Bash alias to show *only* the hidden files of the current directory.

11.5 How will you repeat the last command in (i) Korn (ii) Bash?

11.6 You have just used the command **tar -cvf /dev/fd0 *.sh**. How will you repeat the command to use the .pl files this time in (i) Korn (ii) Bash?

11.7 To enable **vi**-like editing of the command line, what setting will you have to make first?

11.8 Suppose you have just viewed a file with **cat calc_km.java**. How will you now display it with **more** if you are using the Korn or Bash shells?

11.9 You don't know the absolute pathname of the home directory of *henry*. How will you "cd" to it in the Bash and Korn shells?

11.10 There is a file profile (no dot) in /etc. When is this file executed?

11.11 If you have the files .bash_profile and .profile in your home directory, will Bash read them both on login?

11.12 You repeatedly have to toggle between /usr/include and /usr/lib. How do you use a shortcut to do that repeatedly?

11.13 Can you copy all files from henry's home directory even if you don't know its absolute pathname?

FLEX YOUR BRAIN

11.1 Which two environment variables are set by reading /etc/passwd?

11.2 Explain the significance of the MAIL and MAILCHECK variables. How do you come to know that mail has arrived?

11.3 How can you create a prompt like this in Bash (user—henry, machine name—*jupiter* and current directory—project8? [jupiter-henry ~/project8]

11.4 Create an alias named **rm** that always deletes files recursively. How can you execute the original **rm** command without unaliasing it?

11.5 How can you prevent your files from being overwritten using the redirection symbols? Which shells support this feature? How will you overwrite these files?

11.6 What is the significance of these commands in Bash? (i) **!50** (ii) **!-2:p** (iii) **!!** (iv) **^doc^bak**. What are their equivalents in Korn?

11.7 In the Korn shell, the command **r ca** runs from the history list (i) the last command having ca embedded (ii) the first command beginning with ca (iii) the last command beginning with ca (iv) all commands beginning with ca.

11.8 Can you condense these sequences? (i) **cp *.c c_progs ; cd c_progs** (ii) **cmp foo foo.bak; cmp foo foo.doc**

11.9 Using the history facility, how can you repeatedly execute this sequence in (i) Korn (ii) Bash? **vi signal.c; cc signal.c**

11.10 You want to recall all the **tar** commands that you executed for viewing. How can you see them in turn by pressing a single key repeatedly in Korn and Bash?

11.11 Explain the significance of these commands: (i) **cd ~henry** (ii) **cd ~/henry** (iii) **cd ~-** (iv) **cd -**

11.12 Why do all shells use a profile as well as an rc file? What type of entries do you place in each?

11.13 Name two ways of making the changes you make to .profile available in the environment.

12

Communication and Electronic Mail

In a multiuser system, it's often necessary for one user to know what the other is doing. Communication through the system seems quite natural and necessary, especially when the users are located quite a distance apart. UNIX provides a few "real-time" communication tools and an impressive collection of email agents as offline communication tools. All these tools can be used to communicate with users on the same host, different hosts in a TCP/IP network or on any host on the Internet.

We'll discuss two offline tools (**finger** and **talk**), but our focus in this chapter is on email. This medium is fast replacing the fax and reducing the load of the post office. It's fast and cheap, and can be used to exchange graphics, sound and video files as well. To send an email message, one has to simply type it in, write the address (or probably select it from an address book) and then issue a send command or click on a button. The message is usually received in a few seconds, and certainly faster than post office mail (often referred to as "snail mail").

WHAT YOU WILL LEARN

- Look up user information with **finger**.
- Engage oneself in an online text chat with **talk**.
- Use **mesg** to enable and disable the use of **talk**.
- The basics of electronic mail and its addressing scheme.
- An examination of email message headers.
- Use **mailx** as an interactive and noninteractive mail client.
- Use **pine** as a menu-based mail client and its address book facility.
- The significance of two files, `$HOME/.forward` and `$HOME/.signature`, in forwarding a message and attaching user credentials.

TOPICS OF SPECIAL INTEREST

- The usefulness of the character-based mailers in their ability to send out mail noninteractively.
- The study of the *mailbox* and *mbox*, and how mail moves from one to the other.

12.1 finger: DETAILS OF USERS

Like **who**, the **finger** command also lists login details of a user, but is a more informative tool. It doesn't feature in the POSIX specification, but is considered here because it's a useful tool that is available on all UNIX systems. When used without arguments, it simply produces a list of all users logged on to the system:

```
$ finger
Login     Name             TTY  Idle  When       Where
henry     henry james      *01        Fri 08:56  mercury.heavens.com
tulec     tata infotech     03    16  Fri 09:26  saturn.heavens.com
root      Superuser        *04    32  Fri 08:59
sumit     sumitabha das    *05  1:07  Fri 09:24  jupiter.heavens.com
```

The second field shows the user's full name, the third field shows her terminal, preceded by an asterisk if the terminal doesn't have write permission. The fourth field shows the idle time—the time that has elapsed since the last keystroke was entered at that terminal. The last field shows the name of the machine from where the user logged in. The root user is local to the machine, while three users have logged in from three different machines.

Unlike **who**, **finger** can also provide details about a single user. This user is logged on to the same machine the command is run on:

```
$ finger sumit
Login name: sumit
Directory: /users1/home/staff/sumit        Shell: /usr/bin/ksh
On since Jan 13 12:58:37 on pts/4 from jupiter.heavens.com
Mail last read Mon Jan 13 17:24:37 2003
No Plan.
```

sumit is using the Korn shell and has "no plan". If the user is not logged in, the output will show the time of last login.

finger also runs in a network and it can obtain information about remote users. For instance, so you can get the details of user henry working on host *mercury* using **finger henry@mercury**. This addressing scheme uses the @ as the delimiter of username and host—the same used by the email system.

The `.plan` *and* `.project` *Files* It's the "plan" feature that makes **finger** a useful communication tool. It's often necessary to leave behind your schedule and other important information for others to see, especially if you are going on vacation. Since it's not possible to send mail to all users, you can keep your messages in two files, `$HOME/.project` (only one line) and `$HOME/.project` (multiple lines). When someone runs **finger** with your user-id as argument, the contents of these two files are displayed.

We'll enter one line of text in `.project` and two lines in `.plan`, and when someone "fingers" this user, this is what they'll see at the end of **finger**'s output:

```
Project:
The TMH project should be completed by March 31, 2003
Plan:
The CRCs will be submitted on CD-ROM this time.
The text should be out by April 15, 2003.
```

Many people resent the loss of privacy that **finger** causes. They feel that an individual's personal details must not be divulged to outsiders without her consent. Consequently, the **finger** service (see Note below) is disabled on many systems, especially on the Internet.

> **Note** **finger** belongs to a group of commands (called *clients*) that can't work alone; it needs to communicate with its counterpart (the *server*) to obtain user information. Most network tools like **ftp**, **telnet** and the Web browser also operate in this manner. For **finger** to work, it's obvious that the server (usually, **fingerd** or **in.fingerd**) has to run too. These servers are also called *daemons (10.3)* and they can only be controlled by the root user. Client-server tools are taken up in Part II of the book.

12.2 talk: ONLINE COMMUNICATION

talk is a popular communications program. It enables you to have a two-way communication with any person who is currently logged in. This conversation is actually text-based where text entered by one user appears on the terminal of the other—and in real time. **talk** makes obsolete the **write** command and is the ancestor of the Internet Relay Chat (both dropped from this edition).

You can use **talk** to exchange messages with another user on the same or a remote host. This is how henry invokes **talk** to communicate with user charlie on the same host:

```
talk charlie
```

henry's screen splits up into two and shows the message `[Waiting for your party to respond]`. At the other end, charlie, if logged in, should see this on his display:

```
Message from Talk_Daemon@arka.pdsit.becs.ac.in at 20:56 ...
talk: connection requested by henry@arka.pdsit.becs.ac.in.
talk: respond with:  talk henry@arka.pdsit.becs.ac.in
```

If charlie wants to communicate with henry, he too has to use the **talk** command in this way:

```
talk henry
```

Once charlie acknowledges henry's gesture, a connection is set up between the two users. charlie's screen also splits into two, so we now have two split windows on both machines (Fig. 12.1). Both displays would now show the message `[Connection established]`.

henry and charlie can now simultaneously send messages to each other. Outgoing messages appear in the top window while incoming messages show up in the bottom window. The conversation is in real-time; the message appears on each recipient's screen simultaneously as it is being typed. In this way, it is possible to continue a conversation until such time as one or both the users decide to terminate it. **talk** is terminated by either user pressing the interrupt key (usually, *[Ctrl-c]*).

Like **finger**, **talk** can also run in a network. If charlie is on host *jupiter*, henry, working on a different host, should use **talk charlie@jupiter**.

```
[Connection established]
What is that you wanted to say?



-----------------------------------------------------------------------------------------

Was just wondering whether you received the message from jim.
```

Fig. 12.1 A **talk** Screen

12.3 mesg: YOUR WILLINGNESS TO TALK

Online communication with **talk** can be disconcerting to a user who might be watching the output of an important program on her terminal at that instant. In that case, she can use the **mesg** command to prevent such intrusions. The command

```
mesg n
```

prevents other people from writing to the terminal. y enables receipt of such messages. If you want to know the status your terminal is in, simply use **mesg** without arguments:

```
$ mesg
is y                                                    Can receive messages
```

The **mesg** setting is typically kept in the `.profile` by users who won't mind being disturbed. If **talk** doesn't work, check the **mesg** setting.

12.4 E-MAIL BASICS

An email message never appears on your terminal the moment it is received. It is deposited in your *mailbox* even when you are not logged in. This is often an advantage over **talk**, where two users need to be logged in to communicate. The shell regularly checks this mailbox (as often as the `MAILCHECK` variable mandates, see Section 11.1.1), and when it detects the arrival of new mail, it issues a message similar to this:

```
You have new mail in /var/mail/romeo                    romeo is the user
```

You can see this message either when you log in or after a program run by you completes execution. It's good practice to see incoming mail immediately upon arrival rather than defer it for future viewing. After viewing it, you can do these things with it:

- Reply to the sender and all recipients.
- Forward it to others.
- Save it in a mailbox folder.
- Save it in a separate file.
- Delete it.
- Print it.
- Add the address of the sender and all recipients to the address book.
- Call up a helper application to view it if it is not in plain text format.

The characteristic feature of most character-based mail programs (like **mailx**, **mail**, **pine**, etc.) is that mail doesn't remain in the mailbox after it is viewed. The message moves from the mailbox to the *mbox* (a secondary file), where it remains till it is explicitly deleted.

12.4.1 Mail Addressing Scheme

A recipient is identified by her email address. The addressing scheme in the early days simply used the recipient's username (as registered in /etc/passwd) as the email address. However, in a single network, the email address is identical in form to the argument used by **finger** and **talk**. Here are the two forms:

```
mailx henry                henry on same host
mailx henry@saturn         henry on networked host saturn
```

The second example uses a combination of the username and hostname; this email address is unique in a network. A similar form is also used in Internet addressing except that the Internet uses *domain names* (called FQDNs) instead of simple hostnames:

```
mailx henry@heavens.com    Email address unique on the Internet
```

Because of the way domains (like *heavens*) are allotted, no two individuals or organizations can have the same email address on the Internet. We'll discuss domains in Chapter 20 that features the Internet.

12.4.2 Anatomy of a Mail Message

Every mail message consists of several lines of header information. You may or may not be able to see all the headers; that would depend on the application used to compose the message and the one used to transport it. However, a typical message shows at least the first four fields as shown below:

```
Subject: creating animations in macromedia director from GIF89a images
   Date: Fri, 08 Nov 2002 15:42:38 +0530
   From: joe winter <winterj@sasol.com>
     To: heinz@xs4all.nl
     Cc: psaha@earthlink.net
```

When you compose a mail message, the subject is optional, but it's good discipline to fill up the Subject: field, especially when you are trying to draw the attention of the recipient. The Date: and

`From:` fields are automatically filled in by the system. The `Cc:` field is used to copy a message to someone else; we call it a *carbon copy*. Some messages will also have a `Bcc:` header where its recipient receives a *blind carbon copy* (a fact not known to the `To:` and `Cc:` recipients).

The `From:` line in the example above shows the email address, *winterj@sasol.com*, appended to another string representing the full name of the sender (`joe winter`). On the Internet, we use email addresses of this form, though the minimal form also works there. The full name is not used for routing the mail, so mistakes here are permissible. In fact, you can use any name here. However, if there's a mistake in the actual email address, the mail will bounce.

Following the headers is the message body which is separated from the last header by a blank line. The message body contains the text of the message. You can send attachments with your message as a *multipart* message. Binary attachments are *encoded* (converted to printable characters) so that they can be saved in text format in the user's mailbox. Your mailer may not be able to handle some of these formats (like audio and video data), but it should be able to call up an external program (which could be a *plugin* or *helper application*) to handle them.

> **Tip** Irrespective of the mailer you use, you can consider the automatic forwarding facility to redirect all your incoming messages to another address. When you travel, you may want to use this facility. Simply place the address where you want all mail to be forwarded to in the file `$HOME/.forward`. This forwarding facility is a feature of **`sendmail`**—the program that delivers most of our mail on the Internet.

12.5 `mailx`: THE UNIVERSAL MAILER

One of the strengths of UNIX lies in its command line tools. Even though we may use a sophisticated mailer (like Netscape) for handling our mail, we also need a simple mail program that can run noninteractively from shell scripts. We should be able to execute this program with its various command line options, using redirection and piping, to generate mail headers and the message body on the fly. A few character-based mail agents can do that, like **`mail`** and **`mailx`**.

In this chapter, we discuss **`mailx`** and a superior menu-based program named **`pine`**. **`mailx`** finds place in the POSIX specification, which no longer requires UNIX systems to support the earliest mail agent of all—the **`mail`** command. Linux doesn't support **`mailx`**, so you must use **`mail`** or BSD-based **`Mail`**, which have a lot in common with **`mailx`**.

There are two ways of invoking **`mailx`**—in the sending and receiving modes. In the sending mode, **`mailx`** is used with the email address of the recipient as argument. In the receiving mode, you *generally* use it without arguments to handle your received mail. In this mode, you can perform all mail functions listed at the beginning of Section 12.4. In the following paragraphs, we'll be discussing both modes to communicate with another user on the same host.

12.5.1 Sending Mail

In the sending mode, **`mailx`** turns interactive, prompting for the subject first. You have to key it in first and then enter the message body. The same conventions apply: Use the standard input to key in your input and then use *[Ctrl-d]* (or a solitary `.`). This is how henry sends mail to charlie:

```
$ mailx charlie                                          charlie is on same host
Subject: New System
The new system will start functioning from next month.
Convert your files by next week - henry
[Ctrl-d]                                                 Some systems use a dot here
EOT                                                      System indicates end of text
```

Sending a message is as simple as this. The sent message doesn't directly appear on charlie's terminal but lands in his mailbox, which is usually `/var/mail/charlie`. How charlie handles this mail is considered shortly.

Sending Mail Noninteractively Since we often require to send mail from a shell script, we can use redirection to take the message body from a file and the `-s` option to specify the subject:

```
mailx -s "New System" charlie < message.txt
```

Though POSIX doesn't require **mailx** to support options that copy messages to other people, on most systems, **mailx** can be used to send copies. Use the `-c` option to send a carbon copy (recipient shown in the `Cc:` header) and the `-b` option to send a blind carbon copy (recipient shown in `Bcc:` header). Multiple recipients should be enclosed in quotes:

```
mailx -s "New System" -c "jpm,sumit" -b kumar charlie < message.txt
```

This command sends a message to charlie with carbon copies to jpm and sumit, and a blind carbon copy to kumar. If one can send a message like this from a shell script, you can well understand why UNIX is considered to be a versatile system.

Sending Mail to Self You can send mail to yourself also. In that case, you have to use your own login name as argument:

```
$ pwd
/home/henry
$ mail henry < imp.msg
```

When henry reads his mailbox, he will see the same message that he has addressed to himself. Mail sent to oneself in this way serves as a reminder service provided the user is disciplined enough to read all incoming mail immediately on logging in.

12.5.2 Receiving Mail

All incoming mail is *appended* to the mailbox. This is a text file named after the user-id of the recipient. UNIX systems maintain the mailbox in a directory defined by the `MAIL` variable, which is usually `/var/mail` (`/var/spool/mail` in Linux). charlie's mail is appended to `/var/mail/charlie`. By default, **mailx** reads this file for viewing received mail.

Referring to the message sent by henry, the shell on charlie's machine checks his mailbox as often as determined by `MAILCHECK` *(11.1.1)* to determine the receipt of new mail. If charlie is currently running a program, the shell waits for program execution to finish before flashing the following message:

```
You have new mail in /var/mail/charlie
```

When charlie logs in, he may also see this message. He now has to invoke the **mailx** command in the receiving mode (without using an argument) to see the mail henry has sent him. The system first displays the headers and some credentials of all incoming mail *that's still held in the mailbox*:

```
$ mailx
mailx version 5.0 Wed Jan  5 16:00:40 PST 2000  Type ? for help.
 "/var/mail/charlie": 5 messages 2 new 5 unread
 U  1 henry@jack.hill.com   Fri Apr  3 16:38  19/567    "sweet dreams"
 U  2 MAILER-DAEMON@jack.h  Sat Apr  4 16:33  69/2350   "Warning: could not se"
 U  3 MAILER-DAEMON@jack.h  Thu Apr  9 08:31  63/2066   "Returned mail: Cannot"
 N  4 henry@jack.hill.com   Thu Apr 30 10:02  17/515    "Away from work"
>N  5 henry@jack.hill.com   Thu Apr 30 10:39  69/1872   "New System"
? _                                                          The ? prompt
```

The pointer (>) is positioned at the fifth message—the *current message*. charlie can either press *[Enter]* or the number of the message showed in the second column to view the message body. The following message is typically seen on charlie's screen:

```
Message 5:
>From henry@saturn.heavens.com  Tue Jan 13 10:06:14 2003
Date: Tue, 13 Jan 2003 10:06:13 +0530
From: "henry blofeld" <henry@saturn.heavens.com>
To: charlie@saturn.heavens.com
Subject: New System

The new system will start functioning from next month.
Convert your files by next week - henry

? q                                                   Quitting mailx with q
Saved 1 message in /users1/home/staff/charlie/mbox
$ _
```

As we mentioned before, after a message has been seen by the recipient, it moves from the mailbox to the mbox—the secondary storage. The location of this file is defined by the `MBOX` environment variable, and by default it is `$HOME/mbox`. If charlie wants to view mail that has already moved to `mbox`, then he should invoke **mailx** with the `-f` option (**mailx -f mbox**).

> **Note** All mail handling commands are presumed to work in a network. That's why the sender's address shows `@saturn.heavens.com` appended. This is the sender's domain name whose significance is taken up in Chapter 20.

12.5.3 mailx Internal Commands

There are a number of internal commands (Table 12.1) that you can enter at the ? prompt. Enter **help** or a **?** at this prompt to seek online help. **mailx** then displays several screens featuring commands and options. We'll be considering the important ones in this section.

Once **mailx** responds with a ?, you can see the next message (if there is one) using the concept of *relative addressing*. Enter a **+** (or *[Enter]*) at the prompt to see further mail, and a **-** to display the immediately preceding message. Since they are all numbered, a message can also be accessed by simply entering the number itself:

```
3                                   Shows message number 3
```

Replying to mail The **r** (reply) command enables the recipient to reply when the sent message is on display at her terminal. **mailx** has a way of deducing the sender's details, and consequently, the **r** command is usually not used with an address:

```
? r
To: henry@saturn.heavens.com        Sender's address automatically inserted
Subject: Re: File Conversion

I am already through.
[Ctrl-d]
EOT
```

When charlie invokes the **r** command, **mailx** switches to the sending mode. The rules for replying to a message are the same as for sending.

Saving Messages Generally, all mail commands act on the current message by default. With the **w** command, you can save one or more messages in separate files rather than the default mbox ($HOME/mbox) used by the system:

```
w note3                             Appends current message to note3
w 1 2 3 note3                       Appends first three messages to note3
```

In either case, the message is saved without header information. With the **s** command, you can save mail messages with all headers:

```
s 1 3 4 mailfile                    Appends messages 1, 3 and 1 to mailfile
```

You can later view these messages with their headers using **mail -f mailfile**.

Deleting Mail To delete a file from the mailbox, use the **d** (delete) command. It actually *marks* mail for deletion; the mail actually gets deleted only after quitting **mailx**.

Like in **vi**, the **u** (undo) command undeletes any deleted mail, provided you don't exit **mailx** before using it. This command, by default, restores the message that was last deleted. Both **d** and **u** use message numbers as arguments as well.

You'll have either **mail** or **mailx** on your system. Neither offers an attractive user interface, which makes use of the program difficult for casual users.

Table 12.1 Internal Commands used by **mailx**

Command	*Action*
+	Prints next message
-	Prints previous message
N	Prints message numbered *N*
h	Prints headers of all messages
d *N*	Deletes message *N* (The current message if *N* is not specified)
u *N*	Undeletes message *N* (The current message if *N* is not specified)
s *flname*	Saves current message with headers in *flname* ($HOME/mbox if *flname* is not specified)
w *flname*	Saves current message without headers in *flname* ($HOME/mbox if *flname* is not specified)
m *user*	Forwards mail to *user*
r *N*	Replies to sender of message *N* (The current message if *N* is not specified)
q	Quits **mailx**
! *cmd*	Runs UNIX command *cmd*

12.6 pine: A FULL-SCREEN MAIL PROGRAM

pine, the program for Internet news and email, is arguably the most popular character-based mailer, and is widely used on the Internet. Developed at the University of Washington, it combines simplicity and power using a core set of minimal functions. **pine** is standard on Linux systems, but is not available on all UNIX systems. However, since **pine** is a free program, it can be downloaded from the Internet.

```
PINE 4.44   MAIN MENU                          Folder: INBOX  No Messages

           ?     HELP                -  Get help using Pine

           C     COMPOSE MESSAGE     -  Compose and send a message

           I     MESSAGE INDEX       -  View messages in current folder

           L     FOLDER LIST         -  Select a folder to view

           A     ADDRESS BOOK        -  Update address book

           S     SETUP               -  Configure Pine Options

           Q     QUIT                -  Leave the Pine program

     Copyright 1989-2002.  PINE is a trademark of the University of Washington.
                       [Folder "INBOX" opened with 0 messages]
? Help                   P PrevCmd                      R RelNotes
O OTHER CMDS > [ListFldrs] N NextCmd                    K KBLock
```

Fig. 12.2 The Opening Screen in **pine**

The mailer is invoked simply by entering **`pine`**. The interface (Fig. 12.2) looks so simple that you'll hardly realize its true power. The menu items are neatly laid out and one of them shows an *address book*—a feature missing in **`mailx`**.

12.6.1 Viewing Mail

`pine` breaks up incoming and outgoing mail into a number of folders. Pressing **`l`** or **`L`** shows the list:

```
                    Local folders in Mail/
----------------------------------------------------------------------
INBOX               sent-mail               saved-messages      Sent
received
```

You can highlight any of these five (sometimes, more) folders, and then press *[Enter]* for further details. The `INBOX` folder (same term used by Netscape) refers to the user's mailbox file in `/var/mail` (or `/var/spool/mail` in Linux). When you highlight this folder and press *[Enter]*, a screenful of headers (the message index) is displayed:

```
PINE 4.44   MESSAGE INDEX                  Folder: INBOX  Message 1 of 26  NEW

      1 Aug 23 isingh@elnet-31.com    (304) Mail server working fine
      2 Aug 22 sujit lala           (3,993) Fw: GOT IT
+ N   3 Aug 23 henry blofeld        (8,174) RE: RealAudio -- TCP or UDP?
      4 Aug 23 Kothari Pioneer     (15,561) KPMF InstaNAV 23.08.1999
      5 Aug 26 The Economist        (9,639) Politics This Week August 21st
... lines deleted ...

? Help          < FldrList   P PrevMsg     - PrevPage D Delete     R Reply
O OTHER CMDS > [ViewMsg]   N NextMsg   Spc NextPage U Undelete   F Forward
```

You can select a message with the cursor keys and then press *[Enter]* or **>** to show the message contents. Let's have a look at the only unread message (the one marked `+ N`) in this folder:

```
Date: Mon, 23 Aug 1999 13:12 +0500 (GMT)
From: henry blofeld <henry@vsnl.com>
To: joe winter <winterj@sasol.com>
Subject: RE: RealAudio -- TCP or UDP?

dear joe:

RealAudio has to come streaming in. If it has to wait for
retransmission of segments, will you ever hear the sound properly?
It has to use UDP.
... lines deleted ...

? Help          < MsgIndex   P PrevMsg      - PrevPage D Delete     R Reply
O OTHER CMDS > ViewAttch   N NextMsg    Spc NextPage U Undelete   F Forward
```

If you have more messages to view, you can use **n** to see them in turn, and **p** to view a previous one. Pressing **i** or **<** returns you to the message index.

> **Tip** The keys **>** and **<** are extremely useful and can make your work in **pine** very productive. Using **>** repeatedly, you can move from the folder list to the header list, and then to the screen featuring the message body. Use **<** to trace your path back—right up to **pine**'s opening screen.

12.6.2 Composing a Message

Pressing **c** from the main menu makes **pine** bring up its built-in Pico editor for composing a message. We'll send a copy of our message to a local user this time:

```
To      : bruno@elnet-31.com                    Someone on the Internet
Cc      : henry                                 User on the same host
Attchmnt:
Subject : how does one start Star Office?
---- Message Text -----
dear bruno:

i am unable to invoke Star Office from an ordinary user account. well,
henry is using some word processor on linux (I don't know which one), and
he may be able to help too. do either of u know?

sumit
....

^G Get Help  ^X Send     ^R Read File ^Y Prev Pg  ^K Cut Text  ^O Postpone
^C Cancel    ^J Justify  ^W Where is  ^V Next Pg  ^U UnCut Text^T To Spell
```

This editor is fairly easy to use. You can cut (**^K**) and paste (**^U**) text and search for a string (**^W**). After you have finished composing your text, you can use **^X** to send it. **pine** is built on the principle that the user must confirm every action that she can't undo later:

```
Send message?
```

pine also allows you to postpone (**^O**) transmission of a message. This is a useful feature (also available in Netscape) that lets you edit a message later before you are sure of sending it.

With the cursor positioned in the content section, you can use **^R** to insert a file's contents into your message, for instance, a program listing or its output. To send a file as an attachment, move the cursor to the appropriate header (`Attchmnt:`) and use **^J**.

You can also use **pine** with the address directly, in which case the composition window appears on the screen:

```
pine henry@heavens.com                          Can't use pine noninteractively
```

Tip You probably have seen details of a person's address and telephone number at the end some messages. Most mailers make use of the *signature* facility to affix a section of text to every message you send. **pine** includes the contents of `$HOMF/.signature` with all outgoing messages, so place your signature details in this file.

12.6.3 Replying and Forwarding

Use **r** and **f** for replying and forwarding messages from either the message index window or when viewing the message contents. **pine** asks you one or more of these questions when you decide to reply:

```
Include original message in Reply (using "> ")?
Use "Reply-To:" address instead of "From:" address?
Reply to all recipients?
```

The `Reply-To:` prompt appears when the sender's message contains this field. You can include as much of the original message in your reply. This often helps the recipient in correlating the messages; people do tend to forget what they had written.

12.6.4 The Address Book

An interesting feature of **pine** is its *address book* (also available in Netscape), where you enter a person's details just once so they can be picked up from the "book" subsequently. You can select the address book from the main menu and then press **@** to add a new entry:

```
Nickname  : bulumashi
Fullname  : sipra saha
Fcc       :
Comment   :
Addresses : sipra@intu.edu

Fill in the fields. It is ok to leave fields blank.
To form a list, just enter multiple comma-separated addresses.
Press "^X" to save the entry, "^C" to cancel, "^G" for help.
If you want to use quotation marks inside the Fullname field, it is best
to use single quotation marks; for example: George 'Husky' Washington.
```

A helpful message appears from **pine**. After you have saved the entry with **^X**, you can later pick up the address when composing a message. At the first prompt (`To:`), press **^T** to invoke the address book, then highlight the entry you want and select it with **s**. The field gets automatically filled in.

12.6.5 pine Options and Configuration

pine also has a number of options. The `-I` option lets you supply a sequence of keystrokes that **pine** will execute on startup. Since you press **c** at the main menu to open the composition window, you can have this window in front of you when you start **pine**:

```
pine -I c                                        Executes c command on startup
```

You can view the messages that **mailx** has saved in mbox:

```
pine -f mbox
```

pine can be configured from the main menu itself. It uses the startup files /etc/pine.conf for system-wide settings, and /etc/pine.conf.fixed for options that can't be overridden. **pine** also supports a user-specific file $HOME/.pinerc. The files are very well documented, and you'll have no problem editing them.

pine is used on the Internet for at least one reason: it can be used to send multimedia attachments. With the advent of the World Wide Web, its charm has somewhat declined because Netscape's Communicator software also handles email and attachments.

12.7 CONCLUSION

We discussed one user information lookup tool (**finger**) and one online communication tool (**talk**), but most of the chapter was devoted to email. We examined the structure of a mail message and the functioning of two mailers, but there's still a lot to know about email. The mailing mechanism isn't as simple as it may appear; in fact, two or more protocols—SMTP and POP—actually make the system work on a modern UNIX system. We need to examine this mechanism and also a heavy-duty mail client—Netscape—that has many of these features built-in. We'll take up email again and the way it is used on the Internet in Chapter 20.

WRAP UP

finger displays information about users who are logged in, but it can also display information of any user. **finger** also lets you leave your schedule behind when you go on leave so that others can see it. The messages have to be placed in two files—$HOME/.plan and $HOME/.project.

talk lets you have an online and interactive chat. It makes viewing the sender's text easier because it displays received and sent text in two separate windows. For this two-way dialog to be possible, you have to set **mesg** to y. **mesg n** disables use of **talk**.

Electronic mail can be used to send messages to a user on the same host, any host in a network or on the Internet. A mail message is appended to a *mailbox* from where it moves to *mbox* after it has been viewed. The network mail addressing scheme is of the form *username@domain_name*.

A message comprises a number of headers followed by the message body. It can be copied to other recipients. Attachments are sent as *multipart* messages and are *encoded*. Forwarding is enabled by placing the email address in $HOME/.forward.

mailx is a command line mail client that can also be used noninteractively from shell scripts. It is invoked with the email address of the recipient in the sending mode, and without arguments in the receiving mode. A message can be saved with or without headers (**s** and **w**), and you can reply (**r**) to the message while viewing it. You can delete mail (**d**) in your mailbox and undo deletions (**u**) before quitting **mailx**.

pine is a menu-based mail handler that can't be used noninteractively. You can postpone the transmission of a message and maintain an address book. **pine** also handles multimedia attachments.

TEST YOUR UNDERSTANDING

12.1 How will someone using **`finger`** know whether you are on vacation or not?

12.2 If you don't want to be disturbed by others using **`write`** and **`talk`**, what precautions should you take?

12.3 What is the default location of a user's mailbox on UNIX and Linux systems?

12.4 When do you use **`mailx`** with and without an argument?

12.5 Using **`mailx`**, how do you send the **`ps`** output showing all system processes to user charlie?

12.6 If you find a message in `$HOME/mbox`, what does that indicate?

12.7 How will you call up **`pine`** so that it first shows the address book and not the main menu?

12.8 Why is **`pine`** so useful on the Internet?

FLEX YOUR BRAIN

12.1 If **`finger henry`** doesn't display any output, what could be the possible reason?

12.2 How do you use **`talk`** to communicate with user brenda on host *uranus*?

12.3 Explain the significance of the terms *mailbox* and *mbox*.

12.4 How do you send mail to all users whose names are stored in a file `foo` and the message is stored in `message.txt`?

12.5 Name two features of **`pine`** not found in **`mailx`**.

12.6 Mention four common headers found in a mail message. What is the significance of the `Bcc:` header?

12.7 What is a *multipart* mail message?

12.8 How do you ensure that (i) all your outgoing messages show your credentials (ii) your incoming mail is forwarded to a different email address?

12.9 What are *plugins* and *helper applications*? When are they used by the mailer?

13

More File Attributes

Apart from permissions and ownership, a UNIX file has several other attributes, and in this chapter, we look at most of the remaining ones. A file also has properties related to its time stamps and links. It's important to know how these attributes are interpreted when applied to a directory or a device. You need to revisit the **ls** command and see some of its other options that reveal these attributes. We'll also discuss **find**—one of the most versatile attribute-handling tools of the UNIX system.

This chapter also introduces the concept of a *file system*. It also looks at the *inode*, the lookup table that contains almost all file attributes. Though a detailed treatment of file systems is taken up later, knowledge of its basics is essential to our understanding of the significance of some of the file attributes. Moreover, some administration tools act and report on individual file systems separately.

WHAT YOU WILL LEARN

- The concept of the *file system* and how multiple file systems are seen as one.
- The use of the *inode* to store file attributes and **ls** to display the inode number.
- Use **ln** to create a *hard link* by providing a file with a different name.
- The limitations of hard links and how they are overcome by *symbolic links*.
- The concept of the *user mask* and how **umask** changes the default file and directory permissions.
- How to display the listing in order of a file's time stamps.
- Use **touch** to change a file's modification and access times.

TOPICS OF SPECIAL INTEREST

- Three possible situations where hard links can be very useful.
- The significance of directory permissions and how they ultimately impact a file's access rights.
- The elaborate syntax used by **find** to match one or more file attributes, and take action on selected files.

13.1 FILE SYSTEMS AND INODES

We now need to have some idea of the way files are organized in a UNIX system. So far, we have been referring to the UNIX file hierarchy as a "file system" as if all files and directories are held together in one big superstructure. That is seldom the case, and never so in large systems. The hard disk is split up into distinct *partitions* (or *slices*), with a separate *file system* in each partition (or slice).

Every file system has a separate tree-like directory structure, each with its own root directory. If you have three file systems on one hard disk, then they will have three separate root directories. When the system is up, we only see a *single* file system with a single root directory.

Of these multiple file systems, one of them is considered to be the main one, and contains most of the essential files of the UNIX system. This is the *root* file system, which is more equal than others in at least one respect; its root directory is also the root directory of the combined UNIX system. At the time of booting, all secondary file systems *mount* (attach) themselves to the main file system, creating the illusion of a single file system to the user.

Every file is associated with a table that contains all that you could possibly need to know about a file—except its name and contents. This table is called the *inode* (shortened from index node) and is accessed by the *inode number*. The inode contains the following attributes of a file:

- File type (regular, directory, device, etc.).
- File permissions (the nine permissions and three more).
- Number of links (the number of aliases the file has).
- The UID of the owner.
- The GID of the group owner.
- File size in bytes.
- Date and time of last modification.
- Date and time of last access.
- Date and time of last change of the inode.
- An array of pointers that keep track of all disk blocks used by the file.

Observe that *neither the name of the file nor the inode number is stored in the inode*. It's the directory that stores the inode number along with the filename. When you use a command with a filename as argument, the kernel first locates the inode number of the file from the directory and then reads the inode to fetch data relevant to the file.

Every file system has a separate portion set aside for storing inodes, where they are laid out in a contiguous manner. This area is accessible only to the kernel. The inode number is actually the *position* of the inode in this area. The kernel can locate the inode number of any file using simple arithmetic. Since a UNIX machine usually comprises multiple file systems, you can conclude that the inode number for a file is unique in a *single* file system.

The **ls** command reads the inode to fetch a file's attributes, and it can list most of them using suitable options. One of them is the `-i` (inode) option that tells you the inode number of a file:

```
$ ls -il tulec05
9059 -rw-r--r--    1 kumar    metal         51813 Jan 31 11:15 tulec05
```

The file `tulec05` has the inode number 9059. No other file *in the same file system* can have this number unless the file is removed. In that case, the kernel will allocate it to a new file.

> **Note** The inode contains all attributes of a file except the filename. The filename is stored in the directory housing the file. The inode number is also not stored in the inode, but the kernel can locate any inode by its position, since it's size is fixed.

13.2 HARD LINKS

When a file is copied, both the original and copy occupy separate space on disk. UNIX allows a file to have more than one name and yet maintain a single copy on disk. The file is then said to have more than one *link*, i.e., it has more than one name. All names provided to a single file have one thing in common; they all have the same inode number.

The link count is displayed in the second column of the listing. This count is normally 1 (as shown in the previous listing), but the following files have two links:

```
-rwxr-xr--    2 kumar    metal        163 Jul 13 21:36 backup.sh
-rwxr-xr--    2 kumar    metal        163 Jul 13 21:36 restore.sh
```

All attributes seem to be identical, but the "files" could still be copies (which have different inode numbers). It's the link count that seems to suggest that the "files" are linked to each other. But this can only be confirmed by using the `-i` option to **ls**:

```
$ ls -li backup.sh restore.sh
    478274 -rwxr-xr--    2 kumar    metal         163 Jul 13 21:36 backup.sh
    478274 -rwxr-xr--    2 kumar    metal         163 Jul 13 21:36 restore.sh
```

Both "files" indeed have the same inode number, so there's actually only one file with a single copy on disk. We can't really refer to them as two "files", but only as two "filenames". This file simply has two aliases; changes made in one alias (link) are automatically available in the others. There are two entries for this file in the directory, both having the same inode number.

13.2.1 ln: Creating Hard Links

A file is linked with the **ln** (link) command, which takes two filenames as arguments. The command can create both a *hard* and a *soft* link (discussed later) and has a syntax similar to the one used by **cp**. The following command (hard) links `emp.lst` with `employee`:

```
ln emp.lst employee                                    employee must not exist
```

The `-i` option of **ls** shows that they have the same inode number, meaning that they are actually one and the same file:

```
$ ls -li emp.lst employee
29518 -rwxr-xr-x   2 kumar    metal         915 May  4 09:58 emp.lst
29518 -rwxr-xr-x   2 kumar    metal         915 May  4 09:58 employee
```

The link count, which is normally one for unlinked files, is shown to be two. You can link a third filename, emp.dat, and increase the number of links to three:

```
$ ln employee emp.dat ; ls -l emp*
29518 -rwxr-xr-x   3 kumar    metal         915 May  4 09:58 emp.dat
29518 -rwxr-xr-x   3 kumar    metal         915 May  4 09:58 emp.lst
29518 -rwxr-xr-x   3 kumar    metal         915 May  4 09:58 employee
```

You can link multiple files (i.e., create a link for each), but then the destination filename must be a directory. Here's how you create links for all the chapters of this text in the directory project8_dir:

```
ln chap?? project8_dir                    project8_dir is a directory
```

If chap?? matches 27 files, then there will be 27 linked filenames in project8_dir, i.e., there will be 27 entries in that directory. The **rm** command removes a file by removing its directory entry, so we expect the same command to remove a link also:

```
$ rm emp.dat ; ls -l emp.lst employee
-rwxr-xr-x   2 kumar    metal         915 May  4 09:58 emp.lst
-rwxr-xr-x   2 kumar    metal         915 May  4 09:58 employee
```

The link count has come down to two. Another **rm** will further bring it down to one. A file is considered to be completely removed from the system when its link count drops to zero.

Many UNIX commands are linked. Refer to Section 6.18, where we posed the question whether **gzip** and **gunzip** were two separate files. This question can now easily be answered by looking at their inode numbers:

```
13975 -r-xr-xr-x   3 root     bin      60916 Jan  5  2000 gunzip
13975 -r-xr-xr-x   3 root     bin      60916 Jan  5  2000 gzip
```

They are, in fact, one and the same file. The listing shows the existence of a third link as well, but how does one locate it? Doing an **ls -li** and then looking for entries with the same inode number isn't a practical approach. It may not also work since links could be spread across multiple directories. For this task, we need the **find** command which is discussed at the end of this chapter.

Tip **ln** returns an error when the destination file exists. Use the -f option to force the removal of the existing link before the creation of the new one.

13.2.2 Where to Use Hard Links

When do you require to link files? We can think of three situations straightaway:

- The most obvious use of a link is to "notionally place" a file in a specific directory where many programs expect it to find. For instance, you may have a number of **perl** programs expecting the **perl** interpreter in /usr/bin. In a later reorganization of the file system, you decide to move all GNU programs (of which **perl** is one), to /usr/local/bin. You can move the file to /usr/local/bin but leave a link in /usr/bin like this:

```
ln /usr/bin/perl /usr/local/bin/perl
```

With this link available, your existing programs will continue to find **perl**. It's more convenient to do this that modify all programs to point to the new path.

- Links provide some protection against accidental deletion, especially when they exist in different directories. By creating a link, you create a "backup". So even if you inadvertently delete one link, another will still be available; your file is not gone yet.
- Because of links, we don't need to maintain two programs as two separate disk files if there is very little difference between them. A file's name is available to a C program (as argv[0]) and to a shell script (as $0). A single file with two links can have its program logic make it behave in two different ways depending on the name by which it is called. There's a shell script using this feature in Section 16.10.

13.3 SYMBOLIC LINKS AND ln

We have seen how links let us have multiple names for a file. These links are often called *hard links*, and have two limitations:

- You can't have two linked filenames in two file systems. In other words, you can't link a filename in the /usr file system to another in the /home file system.
- You can't link a directory even within the same file system.

These serious limitations were overcome when *symbolic links* made their entry. Till now, we have divided files into three categories (ordinary, directory and device). The symbolic link is the fourth file type considered in this text. Unlike the hard link, a symbolic link doesn't have the file's contents, but simply provides the pathname of the file that actually has the contents. Being more flexible, a symbolic link is also known as a *soft link*. Windows shortcuts are more like symbolic links.

The **ln** command creates symbolic links also, except that you have to use the -s option. This time the listing tells you a different story:

```
$ ln -s note note.sym
$ ls -li note note.sym
9948 -rw-r--r--    1 kumar    group              80 Feb 16 14:52 note
9952 lrwxrwxrwx    1 kumar    group               4 Feb 16 15:07 note.sym -> note
```

You can identify symbolic links by the character l (el) seen in the permissions field. The pointer notation -> note suggests that note.sym contains the pathname for the filename note. It's note, and not note.sym, that actually contains the data. When you use **cat note.sym**, you don't actually open the symbolic link, note.sym, but the file the link points to. Observe that the size of the symbolic link is 4; this is the length of the pathname it contains (note).

It's important you realize that this time we indeed have two "files", and they are not identical. Removing note.sym won't affect us much because we can easily recreate the link. But if we remove note, we would lose the file containing the data. By pointing to a nonexistent file, note.sym would become a *dangling* symbolic link.

Symbolic links can also be used with relative pathnames. Unlike hard links, they can also span multiple file systems and also link directories. If you have to link a hundred filenames in one directory to another directory, it makes sense to simply link the directories. Like other files, a symbolic link has a separate directory entry with its own inode number. This means that **rm** can remove a symbolic link even if its points to a directory (or even a device).

LINUX: A symbolic link has an inode number separate from the file that it points to. In most cases, the pathname is stored in the symbolic link and occupies space on disk. However, Linux uses a *fast symbolic link* which stores the pathname in the inode itself provided it doesn't exceed 60 characters.

13.4 THE DIRECTORY

A directory has its own permissions, owners and links. However, the significance of the file attributes change a great deal when applied to a directory. For example, the size of a directory is in no way related to the size of the files that exist in the directory, but rather to the *number* of files housed by it. The higher the number, the larger is the directory.

Permissions too acquire a different meaning when the term is applied to a directory. Before we take up directory permissions, let's see what its default permissions are on this system:

```
$ ls -l -d progs
drwxr-xr-x   2 kumar    metal            320 May  9 09:57 progs
```

The default permissions are different from those of ordinary files. The user has all permissions, and group and others have read and executable permissions only. The permissions of a directory also impact the security of its files. To understand how that can happen, we must know what permissions for a directory really mean.

13.4.1 Read Permission

Read permission for a directory means that the *list* of filenames stored in that directory is accessible. Since **ls** reads the directory to display filenames, if a directory's read permission is removed, **ls** won't work. Consider removing the read permission first from the directory progs:

```
$ ls -ld progs
drwxr-xr-x   2 kumar    metal            128 Jun 18 22:41 progs
$ chmod -r progs ; ls progs
progs: Permission denied
total 2
```

Being unreadable, the progs directory couldn't be accessed by **ls**, and hence the error message. *However, this doesn't prevent you from reading the files separately if you know their names.*

13.4.2 Write Permission

Be aware that you can't write to a directory file; only the kernel can do that. If that were possible, then any user could destroy the integrity of the file system. Write permission for a directory implies that you are permitted to create or remove files in it (that would make the kernel modify the directory entries). To try that out, restore the read permission and remove the write permission from the directory before you try to copy a file to it:

```
$ chmod 555 progs ; ls -ld progs
dr-xr-xr-x   2 kumar    metal          128 Jun 18 22:41 progs
$ cp emp.lst progs
cp: cannot create progs/emp.lst: Permission denied
```

The directory doesn't have write permission; you can't create, copy or delete a file in it. But can you modify its existing files? This question often confuses beginners, and if you are confused too, then follow this line of reasoning:

- The write permission for a directory determines whether you can create or remove files in it because these actions modify the directory.
- Whether you can modify a file depends solely on whether the file itself has write permission. Changing a file doesn't in any way modify its directory entry.

Note The term "write-protected" has a limited meaning in the UNIX file system. A write-protected file can't be written, but it can be removed if the directory has write permission.

13.4.3 Execute Permission

Executing a directory just doesn't make any sense, so what does its execution privilege mean? It only means that a user can "pass through" the directory in searching for subdirectories. When you use a pathname with any command

```
cat /home/kumar/progs/emp.sh
```

you need to have executable permission for each of the directories involved in the complete pathname. The directory `home` contains the entry for `kumar`, and the directory `kumar` contains the entry for `progs`, and so forth. If a single directory in this pathname doesn't have execute permission, then it can't be searched for the name of the next directory. That's why the execution privilege of a directory is often referred to as the *search* permission.

A directory has to be searched for the next directory, so the **cd** command won't work if the search permission for the directory is turned off:

```
$ chmod 666 progs ; ls -ld progs
drw-rw-rw-   2 kumar    metal          128 Jun 18 22:41 progs
$ cd progs
bash: cd: progs: Permission denied
```

Like for regular files, directory permissions are extremely important because system security is heavily dependent upon them. If you tamper with the permissions of your directories, then make sure you set them correctly. If you don't, then be assured that an intelligent user could make life miserable for you!

Let's now add a qualifier to the two bulleted observations made above regarding write permission for a directory. To be able to create or remove files, write permission for the directory is not enough; the directory must have search (execute) permission as well.

> **Caution** Any file can be removed by a user having write permission for the directory housing the file. It doesn't matter whether the file itself has write permission. As a rule, you should never assign write permission to group and others for directories unless you have definite reasons to do so.

13.5 umask: DEFAULT FILE AND DIRECTORY PERMISSIONS

When you create files and directories, the permissions assigned to them depend on the system's default setting. The UNIX system has the following default permissions for all files and directories:

`rw-rw-rw-` (octal 666) for regular files.
`rwxrwxrwx` (octal 777) for directories.

However, you don't see these permissions when you create a file or a directory. Actually, this default is transformed by subtracting the *user mask* from it to remove one or more permissions. To understand what this means, let's evaluate the current value of the mask by using **umask** without arguments:

```
$ umask
022
```

This is an octal number which has to be subtracted from the system default to obtain the *actual* default. This becomes 644 (666 - 022) for ordinary files and 755 (777 - 022) for directories. When you create a file on this system, it will have the permissions `rw-r--r--`.

umask is a shell built-in command though it also exists as an external command. A user can also use this command to set a new default. Here's an extreme setting:

```
umask 000                                    All read-write permissions on
```

A umask value of 000 means that you haven't subtracted anything, and this could be dangerous. The system's default then applies (666 for files and 777 for directories). All files and directories are then writable by all; nothing could be worse than that! However, a mask value of 666 or 777 doesn't make much sense either; you'll then be creating files and directories with no permissions.

The important thing to remember is that, no one—not even the administrator—can turn on permissions not specified in the systemwide default settings. However, you can always use **chmod** as and when required. The systemwide umask setting is placed in one of the machine's startup scripts, and is automatically made available to all users.

13.6 MODIFICATION AND ACCESS TIMES

A UNIX file has three time stamps associated with it. In this section, we'll be discussing just two of them (the first two):

- Time of last file modification — *Shown by* `ls -l`
- Time of last access — *Shown by* `ls -lu`
- Time of last inode modification — *Shown by* `ls -lc`

Whenever you write to a file, the time of last modification is updated in the file's inode. A directory can be modified by changing its entries—by creating, removing and renaming files in the directory. Note that changing a file's contents only changes its last modification time but not that of its directory. `ls -l` displays the last modification time.

A file also has an access time, i.e., the last time someone read, wrote or executed the file. This time is distinctly different from the modification time that gets set only when the contents of the file are changed. For a directory, the access time is changed by a read operation only; creating or removing a file or doing a "cd" to a directory doesn't change its access time. The access time is displayed when `ls -l` is combined with the `-u` option.

Even though `ls -l` and `ls -lu` show the time of last modification and access, respectively, the sort order remains standard, i.e. ASCII. However, when you add the `-t` option to `-l` or `-lu`, the files are actually displayed in *order* of the respective time stamps:

`ls -lt`	Displays listing in order of their modification time
`ls -lut`	Displays listing in order of their access time

Knowledge of a file's modification and access times is extremely important for the system administrator. Many of the tools used by him look at these time stamps to decide whether a particular file will participate in a backup or not. A file is often incorrectly stamped when extracting it (using an option) from a backup with a file restoration utility (like **tar** or **cpio**). If that has happened to you, then you can use **touch** to reset the times to certain convenient values without actually modifying or accessing the file. **touch** is discussed next.

> **Note** It's possible to change the access time of a file without changing its modification time, but not vice versa. When you modify a file, you change its access time as well (not strictly true, see Test Your Understanding at the end of this chapter).

13.6.1 touch: Changing the Time Stamps

As has just been discussed, you may sometimes require to set the modification and access times to predefined values. The **touch** command changes these times, and is used in the following manner:

touch *options expression filename(s)*

When **touch** is used without *options* or *expression*, both times are set to the current time. The file is created if it doesn't exist:

```
touch emp.lst                                   Creates file if it doesn't exist
```

When **touch** is used without options but with *expression*, it changes both times. The *expression* consists of an eight-digit number using the format *MMDDhhmm* (month, day, hour and minute). Optionally, you can suffix a two- or four-digit year string:

```
$ touch 03161430 emp.lst ; ls -l emp.lst
-rw-r--r--   1 kumar   metal        870 Mar 16 14:30 emp.lst
```

```
$ ls -lu emp.lst
-rw-r--r--   1 kumar    metal          870 Mar 16 14:30 emp.lst
```

It's also possible to change the two times individually. The -m and -a options change the modification and access times, respectively:

```
$ touch -m 02281030 emp.lst ; ls -l emp.lst
-rw-r--r--   1 kumar    metal          870 Feb 28 10:30 emp.lst
$ touch -a 01261650 emp.lst ; ls -lu emp.lst
-rw-r--r--   1 kumar    metal          870 Jan 26 16:50 emp.lst
```

The system administrator often uses touch to "touch up" these times so a file may be included in or excluded from an *incremental backup* (that backs up only changed files). The **find** command then can be used to locate files that have changed or been accessed after the time set by **touch**. **find** is the last command we discuss in this chapter and is taken up next.

13.7 find: LOCATING FILES

find is one of the power tools of the UNIX system. It *recursively* examines a directory tree to look for files matching some criteria, and then takes some action on the selected files. It has a difficult command line, and if you have ever wondered why UNIX is hated by many, then you should look up the cryptic **find** documentation. However, **find** is easily tamed if you break up its arguments into three components:

find *path_list selection_criteria action*

This is how **find** operates:

- First, it recursively examines all files in the directories specified in *path_list*.
- It then matches each file for one or more *selection_criteria*.
- Finally, it takes some *action* on those selected files.

The *path_list* comprises one or more subdirectories separated by whitespace. There can also be a host of *selection_criteria* that you can use to match a file, and multiple *actions* to dispose of the file. This makes the command difficult to use initially, but it is a program that every user must master since it lets her make file selection under practically any condition.

As our first example, let's use **find** to locate all files named a.out (the executable file generated by the C compiler):

```
$ find / -name a.out -print
/home/kumar/scripts/a.out
/home/tiwary/scripts/reports/a.out
/home/sharma/a.out
```

The path list (/) indicates that the search should start from the root directory. Each file in the list is then matched against the selection criteria (-name a.out), which always consists of an expression in the form *-operator argument*. If the expression matches the file (i.e., the file has the name a.out), then the file is selected. The third section specifies the action (-print) to be taken on the files; in this case, a simple display on the terminal. All **find** operators start with a -, and the *path_list* can never contain one.

LINUX: `find` in UNIX displays the file list only if the `-print` operator is used. However, Linux doesn't need this option; it prints by default. Linux also doesn't need the path list; it uses the current directory by default. Linux even prints the entire file list when used without any options whatsoever! This behavior is not required by POSIX.

You can also use relative names (like the `.`) in the path list, and **`find`** will then output a list of relative pathnames. When **`find`** is used to match a group of filenames with a wild-card pattern, the pattern should be quoted to prevent the shell from looking at it:

```
find . -name "*.c" -print          All files with extension .c
find . -name '[A-Z]*' -print       Single quotes will also do
```

The first command looks for all C program source files in the current directory tree. The second one searches for all files whose names begin with an uppercase letter. You must not forget to use the `-print` option because without it, **`find`** on UNIX systems will look for files all right but won't print the list.

`-name` is not the only operator used in framing the selection criteria; there are many others (Table 13.1). The actual list is much longer, and takes into account practically every file attribute. Let's now take a look at some of the important ones. We'll consider the selection criteria first, and then the possible actions we can take on the selected files.

13.7.1 Selection Criteria

Locating a File by Inode Number (`-inum`) Refer to Section 13.2.1, where we found that **`gzip`** has three links and **`gunzip`** was one of them. **`find`** allows us to locate files by their inode number. Use the `-inum` option to find all filenames that have the same inode number:

```
$ find / -inum 13975 -print                 Inode number obtained from Section 13.2.1
find: cannot read dir /usr/lost+found: Permission denied
/usr/bin/gzip
/usr/bin/gunzip
/usr/bin/gzcat                              "Cats" a compressed file
```

Now we know what the three links are. Note that **`find`** throws an error message when it can't change to a directory. Sometimes, there will be so many of them on your screen that you would find it difficult to spot the files that actually show up as **`find`**'s output. To avoid these messages, simply redirect the standard error to `/dev/null`.

File Type and Permissions (`-type` and `-perm`) The `-type` option followed by the letter `f`, `d` or `l` selects files of the ordinary, directory and symbolic link type. Here's how you locate all directories of your home directory tree:

```
$ cd; find . -type d -print 2>/dev/null
.                                           Shows the . also
./.netscape                                 Displays hidden directories also
./java_progs
./c_progs
./c_progs/include
./c_progs/lib
./shell_scripts
./.ssh
```

Note the relative pathname **find** displays, but that's because the pathname itself was relative (.). **find** also doesn't necessarily display an ASCII sorted list. The sequence in which files are displayed depends on the internal organization of the file system.

The -perm option specifies the permissions to match. For instance, -perm 666 selects files having read and write permission for all categories of users. Such files are security hazards. You'll often want to use two options in combination to restrict the search to only directories:

```
find $HOME -perm 777 -type d -print
```

find uses an AND condition (an implied -a operator between -perm and -type) to select directories that provide all access rights to everyone. It selects files only if both selection criteria (-perm and -type) are fulfilled.

Finding Unused Files (-mtime *and* -atime*)* Files tend to build up incessantly on disk. Some of them remain unaccessed or unmodified for months—even years. **find**'s options can easily match a file's modification (-mtime) and access (-atime) times to select them. -mtime helps in backup operations by providing a list of those files that have been modified, say, in less than 2 days:

```
find . -mtime -2 -print
```

-2 here means *less* than 2 days. To select from the /home directory all files that have not been accessed for more than a year, a positive value has to be used with -atime:

```
find /home -atime +365 -print | mail root
```

Because **find** uses standard output, the list can be stored in a file or used to mail a message.

> **Note** +365 means greater than 365 days, -365 means less than 365 days. For specifying exactly 365, use 365.

13.7.2 The find Operators (!, -o and -a)

There are three operators that are commonly used with **find**. The ! operator is used before an option to negate its meaning. So,

```
find . ! -name "*.c" -print
```

selects all but the C program files. To look for both shell and **perl** scripts, use the -o operator which represents an OR condition. We need to use an escaped pair of parentheses here:

```
find /home \( -name "*.sh" -o -name "*.pl" \) -print
```

The (and) are special characters that are interpreted by the shell to group commands *(3.4.1)*. The same characters are used by **find** to group expressions using the -o and -a operators, the reason why they need to be escaped.

The -a represents the AND condition, and is implied by default whenever two selection criteria are placed together.

Table 13.1 Expressions Used by **find** (Meaning gets reversed when - is replaced by +, and vice versa)

Selection Criteria	*Selects File*
`-inum` *n*	having inode number *n*
`-type` *x*	if of type *x*; *x* can be `f` (ordinary file), `d` (directory) or `l` (symbolic link)
`-type f`	if an ordinary file
`-perm` *nnn*	if octal permissions match *nnn* completely
`-links` *n*	if having *n* links
`-user` *usname*	if owned by *usname*
`-group` *gname*	if owned by group *gname*
`-size +`*x*`[c]`	if size greater than *x* blocks (characters if `c` is also specified) *(Chapter 17)*
`-mtime -x`	if modified in less than *x* days
`-newer` *flname*	if modified after *flname (Chapter 27)*
`-mmin -`*x*	if modified in less than *x* minutes *(Linux only)*
`-atime +`*x*	if accessed in more than *x* days
`-amin +`*x*	if accessed in more than *x* minutes *(Linux only)*
`-name` *flname*	*flname*
`-iname` *flname*	As above, but match is case-insensitive *(Linux only)*
`-follow`	after following a symbolic link
`-prune`	but don't descend directory if matched
`-mount`	but don't look in other file systems *(Chapter 27)*
Action	***Significance***
`-print`	Prints selected file on standard output
`-ls`	Executes **`ls -lids`** command on selected files
`-exec` *cmd*	Executes UNIX command *cmd* followed by `{} \;`
`-ok` *cmd*	Like `-exec`, except that command is executed after user confirmation

13.7.3 Options Used by the Action Component

Displaying the Listing (`-ls`) The `-print` option belongs to the *action* component of the **find** syntax. In real life, you'll often want to take some action on the selected files and not just display the filenames. For instance, you may like to view the listing with the `-ls` option:

```
$ find . -type f -mtime +2 -mtime -5 -ls                    -a option implied
475336   1 -rw-r--r--   1 romeo     users    716 Aug 17 10:31 ./c_progs/fileinout.c
```

find here runs the **`ls -lids`** command to display a special listing of those regular files that are modified in more than two days and less than five days. In this example, we see two options in the selection criteria (both `-mtime`) simulating an AND condition. It's the same as using `\( -mtime +2 -a -mtime -5 \)`.

Taking Action on Selected Files (`-exec` *and* `-ok`) The `-exec` option is the dark horse of the **find** tool. It lets you take any action by running a UNIX command on the selected files. `-exec` takes the command to execute as its own argument, followed by `{}` and finally the rather cryptic symbols `\;` (backslash and semicolon). This is how you can reuse a previous **find** command quite meaningfully:

```
find $HOME -type f -atime +365 -exec rm {} \;
```
Note the usage

This will use **rm** to remove all ordinary files unaccessed for more than a year. This can be a risky thing to do, so you can consider using **rm**'s -i option. But all commands don't have interactive options, in which case, you should use **find**'s -ok option:

```
$ find $HOME -type f -atime +365 -ok mv {} $HOME/safe \;
< mv ... ./archive.tar.gz > ? y
< mv ... ./yourunix02.txt > ? n
< mv ... ./yourunix04.txt > ? y
  .......
```

mv turns interactive with -i but only if the destination file exists. Here, -ok seeks confirmation for every selected file to be moved to the $HOME/safe directory irrespective of whether the files exist at the destination or not. A y deletes the file.

find is the system administrator's tool, and in Chapter 17, you'll see it used for a number of tasks. It is specially suitable for backing up files and for use in tandem with the **xargs** command *(27.11.3)*.

> **Note** {} is a placeholder for a filename. So, -exec cp {} {}.bak provides a .bak extension to all selected files. Don't forget to use the \; symbols at the end of every -exec or -ok keyword.

13.8 CONCLUSION

This chapter is a sequel to Chapter 7, and examined practically all the UNIX attributes that concern a new user. We understood what a file system is, and we now have an adequate understanding of the way a file's attributes are separated from its contents. The inode is at the heart of it all, but it contains 12 permissions for a file, and not 9, as you might be tempted to think. We'll be examining the three remaining permission bits—the SUID, SGID and the sticky bit—in Chapter 17.

At this point we have covered most of the concepts, so it's time we applied them. The next chapter is the first of four chapters devoted to those powerful text manipulators that we call *filters*.

WRAP UP

The UNIX directory tree is actually a collection of multiple *file systems*, each with its own root directory. These file systems are *mounted* at boot time to appear as a single file system. Every file is identified by its *inode number* and has its attributes stored in the *inode*. The inode number is displayed with the -i option of **ls** and is unique in a single file system.

A file can have more than one name or *link*, and is linked with **ln**. Two linked filenames have the same inode number. Links provide protection against accidental deletion. A C or shell programmer takes advantage of the linking feature to write code that does different things depending on the name by which the file is invoked.

A *symbolic link* is a file which contains the pathname of another file or directory even if it is in another file system. Accidental deletion of the file pointed to is dangerous and creates a *dangling* symbolic link. Symbolic links are created with **ln -s**. **rm** removes both types of links.

Permissions have different significance for directories. Read permission means that the filenames stored in the directory are readable, which must be so for **ls** to work. Write permission implies that you are permitted to create or remove files in the directory. But write permission for a file means that you can modify the file. Execute (or *search*) permission means that you can change to that directory with the **cd** command.

The UNIX system creates files and directories with 666 and 777 as the default permissions. But this default is generally changed by **umask** in the system's startup scripts. A umask value of 022 changes the system default to 644 and 755 for a file and directory, respectively.

The inode stores the time of last modification and access of a file. **ls** can sort a file by its modification time (-t) or access time (-ut). You can use **touch** to change both these times to either the current time, by default, or to arbitrary values.

find looks for files by matching one or more file attributes. A file can be specified by type (-type), name (-name), permissions (-perm) or by its time stamps (-mtime and -atime). -print is the action commonly used, but any UNIX command can be run on the selected files (-ls, -exec and -ok) with or without user confirmation.

TEST YOUR UNDERSTANDING

13.1 Which important file attribute is not maintained in the inode? Where is it stored then?

13.2 How do you link all C source files in the current directory and place the links in another directory, bar?

13.3 The **rm** command removes only a hard link and not a symbolic link. True or false?

13.4 A symbolic link has the same inode number as the file it is linked to. True or false?

13.5 How do you link foo1 to foo2 using (i) a hard link (ii) a symbolic link? If you delete foo2, does it make any difference?

13.6 What do you do to make sure that no one is able see the names of the files you have?

13.7 A file was not writable by group and others and yet could be deleted by users of those categories. How?

13.8 How do you ensure that all files created by you will have the default permissions rw-rw----?

13.9 When you invoke **ls -l foo** the access time of foo changes. True or false?

13.10 What does the command **touch foo** do? Why is the command important for the system administrator?

13.11 How do you change the modification time of a file to Sep 30, 10:30 a.m.?

13.12 Find out from /bin and /usr/bin all filenames that (i) begin with z (ii) have the extension .html or .java.

13.13 How will you count the number of ordinary files in the directory tree, /home/henry?

13.14 Observe the access time of a file foo with **ls -lu foo**. Next, append the **date** command output to it and observe the access time of foo again. What do you see?

FLEX YOUR BRAIN

13.1 The UNIX file system has many root directories even though it actually shows one. True or False?

13.2 What are the three time stamps maintained in the inode and how do you display two of them for the file `foo`?

13.3 What change takes place in the inode and directory when a file is linked and later removed?

13.4 Explain when two files can't have the same inode number. If the **`ls -li`** command shows two filenames with the same inode number, what does that indicate?

13.5 What happens when you invoke the command **`ln foo bar`** if (i) `bar` doesn't exist (ii) `bar` exists as an ordinary file (iii) `bar` exists as a directory?

13.6 Explain two application areas of hard links. What are the two main disadvantages of the hard link?

13.7 Explain the significance of *fast symbolic links* and *dangling symbolic links*.

13.8 You have a number of programs in `$HOME/progs` which are called by other programs. You have now decided to move these programs to `$HOME/internet/progs`. How can you ensure that users don't notice this change?

13.9 The command **`cd bar`** failed. When can that happen even if `bar` exists?

13.10 If a file has the permissions 000, you may or may not be able to delete the file. Explain how both situations can happen. Does the execute permission have any role to play here?

13.11 If **`umask`** shows the value (i) 000 (ii) 002, what implications do they have from the security viewpoint?

13.12 Explain the difference between (i) **`ls -l`** and **`ls -lt`** (ii) **`ls -lu`** and **`ls -lut`**.

13.13 Use **`find`** to locate from your home directory tree all (i) files with the extension `.html` or `.HTML` (ii) files having the inode number 9076 (iii) directories having permissions 666 (iv) files modified yesterday. Will any of these commands fail?

13.14 Use *only* **`find`** to locate the file `login.sql` in the `/oracle` file system and copy it to your own directory.

13.15 Find out from the `/home` directory all files that have not been accessed for more than year and mail the list to root.

13.16 Locate all files named `a.out` or `core` in your home directory tree and remove them interactively.

14

Simple Filters

This chapter features the simple filters of the system—commands which accept data from standard input, manipulate it and write the results to standard output. Filters are the central tools of the UNIX tool kit, and each filter featured in this chapter performs a simple function. This chapter shows their use both in standalone mode and in combination with other tools using redirection and piping.

Many UNIX files have lines containing *fields*—strings of characters representing a meaningful entity. Some commands expect these fields to be separated by a suitable delimiter that's not used by the data. Typically this delimiter is a : (as in /etc/passwd and $PATH), but we have used the | (pipe) as delimiter for some of the sample files in this and other chapters. Many filters work well with delimited fields, and some simply won't work without them.

WHAT YOU WILL LEARN

- Format text to provide margins and headers, doublespacing and multiple column output with **pr**.
- Pick up lines from the beginning with **head**, and from the end with **tail**.
- Extract characters or fields vertically with **cut**.
- Join two files laterally, and multiple lines to a single line with **paste**.
- Sort, merge and remove repeated lines with **sort**.
- Find out the unique and nonunique lines with **uniq**.
- Change, delete or squeeze individual characters with **tr**.

TOPICS OF SPECIAL INTEREST

- A special feature of **paste** to form a singe line from multiple lines.
- The counting facility available in **uniq**.
- Use all these commands in an example to perform content manipulating tasks.

14.1 THE SAMPLE DATABASE

Henceforth, you'll be learning the features of several UNIX commands, including the advanced ones, text editing and shell programming with reference to a file `emp.lst`. It's a good idea to have a close look at the file now and understand the organization:

```
$ cat emp.lst
2233|a.k. shukla        |g.m.      |sales     |12/12/52|6000
9876|jai sharma         |director  |production|12/03/50|7000
5678|sumit chakrobarty  |d.g.m.    |marketing |19/04/43|6000
2365|barun sengupta     |director  |personnel |11/05/47|7800
5423|n.k. gupta         |chairman  |admin     |30/08/56|5400
1006|chanchal singhvi   |director  |sales     |03/09/38|6700
6213|karuna ganguly     |g.m.      |accounts  |05/06/62|6300
1265|s.n. dasgupta      |manager   |sales     |12/09/63|5600
4290|jayant Choudhury   |executive |production|07/09/50|6000
2476|anil aggarwal      |manager   |sales     |01/05/59|5000
6521|lalit chowdury     |director  |marketing |26/09/45|8200
3212|shyam saksena      |d.g.m.    |accounts  |12/12/55|6000
3564|sudhir Agarwal     |executive |personnel |06/07/47|7500
2345|j.b. saxena        |g.m.      |marketing |12/03/45|8000
0110|v.k. agrawal       |g.m.      |marketing |31/12/40|9000
```

This is a text file designed in fixed format containing a personnel database. There are 15 lines in the file, where each line has six fields separated from one another by the delimiter `|`. The details of an employee are stored in one line. A person is identified by the emp-id, name, designation, department, date of birth and salary, as indicated by the fields (in the same order). You'll be using this files, or ones derived from them, in various ways to see the extent of manipulation that is possible with the UNIX tool kit.

14.2 pr: PAGINATING FILES

The **pr** command prepares a file for printing by adding suitable headers, footers and formatted text. A simple invocation of the command is to use it with a filename as argument:

```
$ pr dept.lst

May 06 10:38 1997  dept.lst Page 1

01:accounts:6213
02:admin:5423
03:marketing:6521
04:personnel:2365
05:production:9876
06:sales:1006
...blank lines...
```

These six lines are the original contents of `dept.lst` *shown in Section 6.1*

pr adds five lines of margin at the top and five at the bottom. The lower portion of the page has not been shown in the examples for reasons of economy. The header shows the date and time of last modification of the file, along with the filename and page number.

14.2.1 pr Options

pr's *-k* option (where *k* is an integer) prints in *k* columns. If a program outputs a series of 20 numbers, one in each line, then this option can make good use of the screen's empty spaces. And because **pr** is a filter, it can obtain its input from the standard output of another program. Let's use the -t option also to suppress the headers and footers:

```
$ a.out | pr -t -5
0        4        8        12       16
1        5        9        13       17
2        6        10       14       18
3        7        11       15       19
```

If you are not using the -t option, then you can have a header of your choice with the -h option. This option is followed by the header string. There are some more options that programmers will find useful:

- -d Doublespaces input, reduces clutter.
- -n Numbers lines, which help in debugging code.
- -o *n* Offsets lines by *n* spaces; increases left margin of page.

Combine these various options to produce just the format you require:

```
$ pr -t -n -d -o 10 dept.lst
              1    01:accounts:6213

              2    02:admin:5423

              3    03:marketing:6521

              4    04:personnel:2365

              5    05:production:9876

              6    06:sales:1006
```

There's one option that uses a number prefixed by a + to print from a specific page number. Another option (-l) sets the page length:

```
pr +10 chap01                                   Starts printing from page 10
pr -l 54 chap01                                 Page set to 54 lines
```

Because **pr** formats its input by adding margins and a header, it's often used as a "pre-processor" before printing with the **lp** command:

```
pr -h "Department list" dept.lst | lp           Use lpr in Linux
```

Since **pr** output often lands up in the hard copy, **pr** and **lp** form a common pipeline sequence.

> **Note** For numbering lines, you can also use the **nl** command (not covered in this edition). It's more convenient to use **nl foo** than **pr -t -n foo**.

14.3 head: DISPLAYING THE BEGINNING OF A FILE

The **head** command, as the name implies, displays the top of the file. When used without an option, it displays the first ten lines of the file:

```
head emp.lst                                        Shows first ten lines
```

You can use the -n option (POSIX mandated) to specify a line count and display, say, the first three lines of the file:

```
$ head -n 3 emp.lst                      Or head -3 emp.lst on some systems
2233|a.k. shukla        |g.m.      |sales     |12/12/52|6000
9876|jai sharma         |director |production|12/03/50|7000
5678|sumit chakrobarty|d.g.m.     |marketing |19/04/43|6000
```

head can be used in imaginative ways. Consider that you are resuming an editing session the next day and find that you are unable to recall the name of the file you last edited. Since **ls -t** displays files in order of their modification time, picking up the first file from the list and using it as an argument to the **vi** editor should do the job. This requires command substitution:

```
vi `ls -t | head -n 1`                    Opens last modified file for editing
```

You can define this as an alias *(11.2)* so that the aliased command is always available for you to use.

14.4 tail: DISPLAYING THE END OF A FILE

Complementing its **head** counterpart, the **tail** command displays the end of the file. It provides an additional method of addressing lines, and like **head**, it displays the last ten lines when used without arguments. The last three lines are displayed in this way:

```
$ tail -3 emp.lst                          Or use tail -n 3 emp.lst
3564|sudhir Agarwal     |executive|personnel |06/07/47|7500
2345|j.b. saxena        |g.m.      |marketing |12/03/45|8000
0110|v.k. agrawal       |g.m.      |marketing |31/12/40|9000
```

You can also address lines from the beginning of the file instead of the end. The *+count* option allows you to do that, where *count* represents the line number from where the selection should begin. Since the file contains 15 lines, selecting the last five implies using

```
tail +11 emp.lst                   11th line onwards, possible with + symbol
```

14.4.1 tail Options

tail has more options than **head**, and can also extract in units of bytes rather than lines.

Monitoring File Growth (-f) Many UNIX programs constantly write to the system's log files as long as they are running. System administrators need to monitor the growth of these files to view the latest messages. **tail** offers the -f (follow) option for this purpose. This is how you can monitor the installation of Oracle by watching the growth of the log file install.log from another terminal:

```
tail -f /oracle/app/oracle/product/8.1/orainst/install.log
```

The prompt doesn't return even after the work is over. With this option, you have to use the interrupt key to abort the process and exit to the shell.

Extracting Bytes Rather than Lines (`-c`) POSIX requires **tail** to support the `-c` option followed by a positive or a negative integer depending on whether the extraction is performed relative to the beginning or end of a file. Solaris supports this option only in its XPG4 version, but this is no problem in Linux:

```
tail -c -512 foo          Copies last 512 bytes from foo
tail -c +512 foo          Copies everything after skipping 511 bytes
```

> **Tip** Use **tail -f** when you are running a program that continuously writes to a file, and you want to see how the file is growing. You have to terminate this command with the interrupt key.

14.5 cut: SLITTING A FILE VERTICALLY

The features of the **cut** and **paste** commands will be illustrated with specific reference to the file `shortlist`, which stores the first five lines of `emp.lst`:

```
$ head -n 5 emp.lst | tee shortlist
2233|a.k. shukla       |g.m.     |sales     |12/12/52|6000
9876|jai sharma        |director |production|03/12/50|7000
5678|sumit chakrobarty|d.g.m.   |marketing |04/19/43|6000
2365|barun sengupta    |director |personnel |05/11/47|7800
5423|n.k. gupta        |chairman |admin     |08/30/56|5400
```

Note the use of the **tee** facility that saves the output in `shortlist` and also displays it on the terminal. We can extract both columns and fields from this file with the **cut** command. Columns are specified with the `-c` option and fields with `-f`. We'll take up columns first.

14.5.1 Cutting Columns (-c)

To extract specific columns, you need to follow the `-c` option with a list of column numbers, delimited by a comma. Ranges can also be used using the hyphen. Here's how we extract the name and designation from `shortlist`:

```
$ cut -c 6-22,24-32 shortlist
a.k. shukla        g.m.
jai sharma         director
sumit chakrobartyd.g.m.
barun sengupta     director
n.k. gupta         chairman
```

Note that there should be no whitespace in the column list. Moreover, **cut** uses a special form for selecting a column from the beginning and up to the end of a line:

```
cut -c -3,6-22,28-34,55- shortlist          Must be an ascending list
```

The expression 55- indicates column number 55 to the end of the line. Similarly, -3 is the same as 1-3.

14.5.2 Cutting Fields (-f)

The -c option is useful for fixed-length lines. Most UNIX files (like /etc/passwd and /etc/group) don't contain fixed-length lines. To extract useful data from these files you'll need to cut fields rather than columns. **cut** uses the tab as the default field delimiter, but can also work with a different delimiter. Two options need to be used here— -d for the field delimiter and -f for the field list. This is how you cut the second and third fields of our sample file:

```
$ cut -d \| -f 2,3 shortlist | tee cutlist1
a.k. shukla       |g.m.
jai sharma        |director
sumit chakrobarty|d.g.m.
barun sengupta    |director
n.k. gupta        |chairman
```

The | was escaped to prevent the shell from interpreting it as the pipeline character; alternatively, it can also be quoted (-d"|"). To cut out fields numbered 1, 4, 5 and 6, and save the output in cutlist2, follow a similar procedure:

```
cut -d "|" -f 1,4- shortlist > cutlist2                Here | is quoted
```

Extracting User List from who *Output* **cut** can be used to extract the first word of a line by specifying the space as the delimiter. The example used in Section 4.8 now run in tandem with **cut** displays the list of users only:

```
$ who | cut -d " " -f1                                 Space is the delimiter
root
kumar
sharma
project
sachin
```

cut is a powerful text manipulator often used in combination with other commands or filters. You'll be using the command a number of times in this text.

> **Note** You must indicate to **cut** whether you are extracting fields or columns. One of the options -f and -c must be specified. These options are really not optional; one of them is compulsory.

14.6 paste: PASTING FILES

What you cut with **cut** can be pasted back with the **paste** command—but vertically rather than horizontally. You can view two files side by side by pasting them. In the previous topic, **cut** was used to create the two files cutlist1 and cutlist2 containing two cut-out portions of the same file. Using **paste**, you can fix them laterally:

```
$ paste cutlist1 cutlist2
a.k. shukla       |g.m.          2233|sales       |12/12/52|6000
jai sharma        |director      9876|production|12/03/50|7000
sumit chakrobarty|d.g.m.         5678|marketing  |19/04/43|6000
barun sengupta    |director      2365|personnel  |11/05/47|7800
n.k. gupta        |chairman      5423|admin      |30/08/56|5400
```

The original contents have been restored to some extent, except that the fields have different relative locations, and pasting has taken place on whitespace. Like **cut**, **paste** also uses the tab as the default delimiter, but you can specify *one or more delimiters* with -d:

```
$ paste -d"|" cutlist1 cutlist2
a.k. shukla         |g.m.     |2233|sales      |12/12/52|6000
jai sharma          |director |9876|production |12/03/50|7000
sumit chakrobarty|d.g.m.     |5678|marketing  |19/04/43|6000
barun sengupta      |director |2365|personnel  |11/05/47|7800
n.k. gupta          |chairman |5423|admin      |30/08/56|5400
```

Even though **paste** uses at least two files for concatenating lines, the data for one file can be supplied through the standard input. If, for instance, cutlist2 doesn't exist, you can provide the character stream by cutting out the necessary fields from shortlist and piping the output to **paste**:

```
$ cut -d \| -f 1,4- shortlist | paste -d "|" cutlist1 -
a.k. shukla         |g.m.     |2233|sales      |12/12/52|6000
jai sharma          |director |9876|production |12/03/50|7000
sumit chakrobarty|d.g.m.     |5678|marketing  |19/04/43|6000
barun sengupta      |director |2365|personnel  |11/05/47|7800
n.k. gupta          |chairman |5423|admin      |30/08/56|5400
```

You can also reverse the order of pasting by altering the location of the - sign:

```
cut -d "|" -f 1,4- shortlist | paste -d "|" - cutlist1
```

Joining Lines (-s) **paste** is more useful than you might think. Consider this address book that contains details of three persons, with three lines for each:

```
$ cat addressbook
anup kumar                                              Name
anup_k@yahoo.com                                        Email address
24569083                                                Telephone number
vinod sharma
vinod_sharma@hotmail.com
34586532
madhuri_bahl
madhuri@heavens.com
39034943
```

The -s option joins lines in the same way **vi**'s **J** command does *(8.5.4)*. Using this option on this file (with **paste -s addressbook**) would join all these nine lines to form a single line. This probably won't be of much use, but if we use the -d option with multiple delimiters (say, the string ||\n), then we can join three lines at a time. The delimiters then are used in a circular manner; the first and second lines would be joined with the | as delimiter, and the same would be true for the second and third line. The third and fourth line would be separated by a newline. After the list is exhausted it is reused. This is exactly what we want:

```
$ paste -s -d"||\n" addressbook
anup kumar|anup_k@yahoo.com|24569083
vinod sharma|vinod_sharma@hotmail.com|34586532
madhuri_bahl|madhuri@heavens.com|39034943
```

Just see how **paste** works (with a single file this time) to concatenate lines in a specified manner. Table data is often split with each column on a separate line, and it's in situations like these that **paste** can be so useful.

14.7 sort: ORDERING A FILE

sort orders a file. Like **cut**, it identifies fields and it can sort on specified fields. We'll consider the important **sort** options by sorting the file `shortlist` (created in Section 14.5) in different ways. By default, the entire line is sorted:

```
$ sort shortlist
2233|a.k. shukla        |g.m.     |sales     |12/12/52|6000
2365|barun sengupta     |director |personnel |11/05/47|7800
5423|n.k. gupta         |chairman |admin     |30/08/56|5400
5678|sumit chakrobarty  |d.g.m.   |marketing |19/04/43|6000
9876|jai sharma         |director |production|12/03/50|7000
```

By default, **sort** reorders lines in ASCII collating sequence—whitespace first, then numerals, uppercase letters and finally lowercase letters. This default sorting sequence can be altered by using certain options. You can sort on one or more keys (fields) or use a different ordering rule, and we are going to discuss them next.

14.7.1 sort Options

The important **sort** options are summarized in Table 14.1. In this edition, we'll be using the `-k` (key) POSIX option to identify *keys* (the fields) instead of the *+n* and *-n* forms (where *n* is the field number) that were used in the previous edition. Unlike **cut** and **paste**, **sort** uses the space as the default field separator (tab in **cut** and **paste**). We'll use the `-t` option to specify the delimiter.

Sorting on Primary Key (`-k`) Let's now use the `-k` option to sort on the second field (name). The option should be `-k 2`:

```
$ sort -t"|" -k 2 shortlist
2233|a.k. shukla        |g.m.     |sales     |12/12/52|6000
2365|barun sengupta     |director |personnel |11/05/47|7800
9876|jai sharma         |director |production|12/03/50|7000
5423|n.k. gupta         |chairman |admin     |30/08/56|5400
5678|sumit chakrobarty  |d.g.m.   |marketing |19/04/43|6000
```

The sort order can be reversed with the `-r` (reverse) option. The following sequence reverses a previous sorting order:

```
$ sort -t"|" -r -k 2 shortlist
5678|sumit chakrobarty  |d.g.m.   |marketing |19/04/43|6000
5423|n.k. gupta         |chairman |admin     |30/08/56|5400
9876|jai sharma         |director |production|12/03/50|7000
2365|barun sengupta     |director |personnel |11/05/47|7800
2233|a.k. shukla        |g.m.     |sales     |12/12/52|6000
```

sort combines options in a rather unusual way. The previous command sequence could also have been written as:

```
sort -t"|" -k 2r shortlist
```

Sorting on Secondary Key You can sort on more than one key, i.e., you can provide a secondary key to **sort**. If the primary key is the third field, and the secondary key the second field, then you need to specify for every -k option, where the sort ends. This is done in this way:

```
$ sort -t"|" -k 3,3 -k 2,2 shortlist
5423|n.k. gupta          |chairman |admin      |30/08/56|5400
5678|sumit chakrobarty|d.g.m.   |marketing  |19/04/43|6000
2365|barun sengupta     |director |personnel  |11/05/47|7800
9876|jai sharma         |director |production|12/03/50|7000
2233|a.k. shukla        |g.m.     |sales      |12/12/52|6000
```

This sorts the file by designation and name. -k 3,3 indicates that sorts atarts on the third field and ends on the same field.

Sorting on Columns You can also specify a character position within a field to be the beginning of sort. If you are to sort the file according to the year of birth, then you need to sort on the seventh and eighth column positions within the fifth field:

```
$ sort -t"|" -k 5.7,5.8 shortlist
5678|sumit chakrobarty|d.g.m.   |marketing  |19/04/43|6000
2365|barun sengupta     |director |personnel  |11/05/47|7800
9876|jai sharma         |director |production|12/03/50|7000
2233|a.k. shukla        |g.m.     |sales      |12/12/52|6000
5423|n.k. gupta          |chairman |admin      |30/08/56|5400
```

The -k option also uses the form -k *m*.*n* where *n* is the character position in the *m*th field. So, 5.7,5.8 means that sorting starts on column 7 of the fifth field and ends on column 8.

Numeric Sort (-n) When **sort** acts on numerals, strange things can happen. When you sort a file containing only numbers, you get a curious result:

```
$ sort numfile
10
2
27
4
```

This is probably not what you expected, but the ASCII collating sequence places 1 above 2, and 2 above 4. That's why 10 preceded 2 and 27 preceded 4. This can be overridden by the -n (numeric) option:

```
$ sort -n numfile
2
4
10
27
```

Removing Repeated Lines (-u) The -u (unique) option lets you purge repeated lines from a file. If you "cut" out the designation field from emp.lst, you can pipe it to **sort** to find out the unique designations that occur in the file:

```
$ cut -d"|" -f3 emp.lst | sort -u | tee desigx.lst
chairman
d.g.m.
director
executive
g.m.
manager
```

We used three commands to solve a text manipulation problem. Here, **cut** select the third field from `shortlist` for **sort** to work on.

Other **sort** *Options* Even though **sort**'s output can be redirected to a file, we can use its `-o` option to specify the output filename. Curiously enough, the input and output filenames can even be the same:

```
sort -o sortedlist -k 3 shortlist          Output stored in sortedlist
sort -o shortlist shortlist                Output stored in same file
```

To check whether the file has actually been sorted in the default order, use the `-c` (check) option:

```
$ sort -c shortlist
$ _                                        File is sorted
```

You can also add the `-k` option to the above to check whether a specific field is sorted:

```
$ sort -t"|" -c -k 2 shortlist
sort: shortlist:2: disorder: 2365|barun sengupta   |director |personnel |11/05/4
7|7800
```

When **sort** is used with multiple filenames as arguments, it concatenates them and sorts them collectively. When large files are sorted in this way, performance often suffers. The `-m` (merge) option can merge two or more files that are sorted individually:

```
sort -m foo1 foo2 foo3
```

This command will run faster than the one used without the `-m` option only if the three files are sorted.

Table 14.1 sort Options

Option	*Description*
`-t`*char*	Uses delimiter *char* to identify fields
`-k` *n*	Sorts on *n*th field
`-k` *m*`,`*n*	Starts sort on *m*th field and ends sort on *n*th field
`-k` *m*`.`*n*	Starts sort on *n*th column of *m*th field
`-u`	Removes repeated lines
`-n`	Sorts numerically
`-r`	Reverses sort order
`-f`	Folds lowercase to equivalent uppercase (case-insensitive sort)
`-m` *list*	Merges sorted files in *list*
`-c`	Checks if file is sorted
`-o` *flname*	Places output in file *flname*

14.8 uniq: LOCATE REPEATED AND NONREPEATED LINES

When you concatenate or merge files, you'll face the problem of duplicate entries creeping in. You saw how **sort** removes them with the -u option. UNIX offers a special tool to handle these lines—the **uniq** command. Consider a sorted file dept.lst that includes repeated lines:

```
$ cat dept.lst
01|accounts|6213
01|accounts|6213
02|admin|5423
03|marketing|6521
03|marketing|6521
03|marketing|6521
04|personnel|2365
05|production|9876
06|sales|1006
```

uniq simply fetches one copy of each line and writes it to the standard output:

```
$ uniq dept.lst
01|accounts|6213
02|admin|5423
03|marketing|6521
04|personnel|2365
05|production|9876
06|sales|1006
```

Since **uniq** requires a sorted file as input, the general procedure is to sort a file and pipe its output to **uniq**. The following pipeline also produces the same output, except that the output is saved in a file:

```
sort dept.lst | uniq -  uniqlist
```

uniq is indeed unique; if provided with two filenames as arguments, **uniq** will read the first file and write its output to the second. Here, it reads from the standard input and writes to uniqlist.

14.8.1 uniq Options

If **uniq** is to merely select unique lines, it is preferable to use **sort -u** that does this job with a single command. But **uniq** has a couple of useful options; they can be used to make simple database queries.

Selecting the Nonrepeated Lines (-u*)* To determine the designation that occurs uniquely in emp.lst, cut out the third field, sort it, and then pipe it to **uniq**. The -u (unique) option selects only lines that are not repeated:

```
$ cut -d"|" -f3 emp.lst | sort | uniq -u
chairman
```

Selecting the Duplicate Lines (-d*)* The -d (duplicate) option selects only one copy of the repeated lines:

```
$ cut -d"|" -f3 emp.lst | sort | uniq -d
d.g.m.
director
executive
g.m.
manager
```

Counting Frequency of Occurrence (-c) The -c (count) option displays the frequency of occurrence of all lines, along with the lines:

```
$ cut -d"|" -f3 emp.lst | sort | uniq -c
   1 chairman
   2 d.g.m.
   4 director
   2 executive
   4 g.m.
   2 manager
```

In SQL, you would be using this:
SELECT COUNT(*), JOB FROM EMP GROUP BY JOB ;

This is an extremely useful option, and we'll make best use of it in an example that we'll consider at the end of this chapter. It raises the possibility of printing a word-count list that displays the frequency of occurrence of each word.

> **Caution** Like **sort**, **uniq** also accepts the output filename as an argument, but without using an option (unlike -o in sort). If you use **uniq foo1 foo2**, **uniq** simply processes foo1 and overwrites foo2 with its output. Never use **uniq** with two filenames unless you know what you are doing.

14.9 tr: TRANSLATING CHARACTERS

So far, the commands have been handling either entire lines, or columns. The **tr** (translate) filter manipulates *individual characters* in a line. More specifically, it translates characters using one or two compact expressions:

tr *options expression1 expression2 standard input*

Note that **tr** takes input only from the standard input; it doesn't take a filename as argument. By default, it translates each character in *expression1* to its mapped counterpart in *expression2*. The first character in the first expression is replaced with the first character in the second expression, and similarly for the other characters.

Let's use **tr** to replace the | with a ~ (tilde) and the / with a -. Simply specify two expressions containing these characters in the proper sequence:

```
$ tr '|/' '~-' < emp.lst  | head -n 3
2233~a.k. shukla      ~g.m.     ~sales     ~12-12-52~6000
9876~jai sharma       ~director ~production~12-03-50~7000
5678~sumit chakrobarty~d.g.m.   ~marketing ~19-04-43~6000
```

Note that the lengths of the two expressions should be equal. If they are not, the longer expression will have unmapped characters (not in Linux). Single quotes are used here because no variable evaluation or command substitution is involved. It's just as easy to define the two expressions as two separate variables, and then evaluate them in double quotes:

```
exp1='|/' ; exp2='~-'
tr "$exp1" "$exp2" < emp.lst
```

Like wild-cards, **tr** also accepts ranges in the expressions. The same rules apply; the character on the right of the - must have an ASCII value higher than that of the character on the left. The escaping rules should also be obvious; the character [needs to be escaped if the special meaning is to be removed from it.

Changing Case of Text Since **tr** doesn't accept a filename as argument, the input has to be redirected from a file or a pipe. The following sequence changes the case of the first three lines from lower to upper:

```
$ head -n 3 emp.lst | tr '[a-z]' '[A-Z]'
2233|A.K. SHUKLA       |G.M.     |SALES     |12/12/52|6000
9876|JAI SHARMA        |DIRECTOR |PRODUCTION|12/03/50|7000
5678|SUMIT CHAKROBARTY|D.G.M.    |MARKETING |19/04/43|6000
```

Reversing the two expressions will convert case from upper to lower. **tr** is often used to change the case of a file's contents.

14.9.1 tr Options

Deleting Characters (-d) The file emp.lst has fields separated by delimiters and the date formatted in readable form with a /. In nondatabase setups, delimiters are not used, and the date is generally represented as a six-character field in the format *ddmmyy*. To convert this file to the traditional format, use the -d (delete) option to delete the characters | and / from the file. The following command does it for the first three lines:

```
$ tr -d '|/' < emp.lst | head -n 3
2233a.k. shukla       g.m.     sales     1212526000
9876jai sharma        director production1203507000
5678sumit chakrobartyd.g.m.    marketing 1904436000
```

Compressing Multiple Consecutive Characters (-s) UNIX tools work best with fields rather than columns (like above), so it's preferable to use files with delimited fields. In that case, lines need not be of fixed length; you can eliminate all redundant spaces with the -s (squeeze) option, which squeezes multiple consecutive occurrences of its argument to a single character. We can then have compressed output with lines in free format:

```
$ tr -s ' ' < emp.lst | head -n 3
2233|a.k. shukla |g.m. |sales |12/12/52|6000
9876|jai sharma |director |production|12/03/50|7000
5678|sumit chakrobarty|d.g.m. |marketing |19/04/43|6000
```

Tip You can use the -s option to compress all contiguous spaces in the output of several UNIX commands and then use **cut** to extract individual fields from this compressed output. For instance, you can "cut" out any field from the listing.

Complementing Values of Expression (-c) Finally, the -c (complement) option complements the set of characters in the expression. Thus, to delete all characters except the | and /, you can combine the -d and -c options:

```
$ tr -cd '|/' <emp.lst
||||//||||||//||||||//||||||//||||||//||||||//||||||//||||||//||||||//||||||//||||||//||||
|//||||||//||||||//||||||//||$ _
```

Unusual output indeed! **tr** has deleted all characters except the | and the / from the file. The appearance of the prompt at the immediate end of output shows that the newline character has also not been spared. We'll use the -c and -d options to place each word in a separate line in our examples section *(14.10)*.

Using ASCII Octal Values and Escape Sequences Like **echo**, **tr** also uses octal values and escape sequences to represent characters. This facility is specially suited for using nonprintable characters in the expression. So to have each field in a separate line, you can replace the | with the newline character (octal value 012):

```
$ tr '|' '\012' < emp.lst | head -n 6
2233
a.k. shukla
g.m.
sales
12/12/52
6000
```

Can also use \n *instead of* \012

If you reverse the two expressions, you'll make the newline character visible. Study these **tr** options closely, and you'll discover many areas where you can apply them. We'll be using some of the **tr** options in the example that's considered next.

14.10 AN EXAMPLE: DISPLAYING A WORD-COUNT LIST

Armed with knowledge of the basic UNIX filters, let's consider devising a command sequence that uses a number of them in a pipeline. Document authors sometimes like to view a list that displays the frequency of usage of each word in the document. For this to be possible, each word has to be placed in a separate line. **tr** can do that by converting all spaces and tabs (octal 011) to newlines:

```
tr "□\011" "\012\012" < foo1
```

Space is \040

There's a space before \011; we won't be displaying the symbol subsequently. If we define a word as a contiguous group of alphabetic characters, we have to use **tr** again to delete all nonalphabetic characters (apart from the newline) from the output of the first **tr** command. This requires the use of the complementary (-c) and delete (-d) options:

```
tr " \011" "\012\012" < foo1 | tr -cd "[a-zA-Z\012]"
```

You now have a list of words, with each word in a separate line. Now sort this output and pipe it to **uniq -c**:

```
$ tr " \011" "\012\012" < foo1 | tr -cd "[a-zA-Z\012]" | sort | uniq -c
     32 Apache                                              Apache used 32 times
     18 DNS
     10 Directory
     16 FQDN
     25 addresses
     56 directory
```

You had to use four commands to display the word usage. You'll need two more to sort the list in reverse numeric sequence and print it in three columns:

```
$ tr " \011" "\012\012" < foo1 | tr -cd "[a-zA-Z\012]" | sort | uniq -c \
>   | sort -nr | pr -t -3
     56 directory                25 addresses                16 FQDN
     32 Apache                   18 DNS                      10 Directory
```

This command line is pretty long, so for the sake of readability, we split it into two lines by using \ to escape the *[Enter]* key.

14.11 CONCLUSION

This chapter presented some of the commonly used filters available in the UNIX system. These filters mostly work on entire lines or fields; it's only **tr** that manipulates individual characters. These filters have limited use when they are used in the standalone mode. But you also used a number of them in pipelines to perform tasks that apparently seem so difficult to achieve by conventional means. We still have four other filters to discuss—**grep**, **sed**, **awk** and **perl**, but three of them actually deviate from the do-one-thing-well approach to UNIX tool building.

WRAP UP

The **pr** command formats input to print headings and page numbers but can also drop them (-t). The output can be numbered (-n), doublespaced (-d) and offset from the left (-o).

head displays the beginning of a file, while **tail** displays the end. Unlike **head**, **tail** can also be used with a line number (with the + option) from where extraction should begin. It is most useful in monitoring the growth of a file (-f).

cut selects columns (-c) from its input, as well as fields (-f). The field numbers have to be a comma-delimited sequence of ascending numbers with hyphens to denote ranges. You can join two files laterally with **paste**. By using the delimiter in a circular manner, **paste** can join multiple lines into one.

With **sort**, you can sort on one or more fields or keys (-k), and columns within these fields. You can sort numerically (-n), reverse the sort order (-r), make a case-insensitive sort (-f), merge two sorted files (-m) and remove repeated lines (-u).

uniq removes repeated lines, but can also select only nonrepeated lines, as well as only the repeated ones. The command is often combined with **sort** to order the input first.

tr translates characters using two expressions, but *only* accepts standard input. It can be used to change the case of letters. You can compress multiple consecutive occurrences (-s) and delete a specific character (-d). You can also use it with ASCII octal values and escape sequences to transform nonprintable characters.

TEST YOUR UNDERSTANDING

14.1 How will you doublespace a file?

14.2 How will you produce a list of all files in the current directory without headers, but in three columns?

14.3 What happens when you use **head** with multiple filenames?

14.4 You need to run a program, `a.out`, that continuously writes to a file. How will you run the program and then monitor the growth of this file from the same terminal?

14.5 Use **head** and **tail** to select lines 5 to 10 of a file.

14.6 Will this command work? **`cut -d: -c1 -f2 foo`**

14.7 Write a sort sequence to order `emp.lst` on the month of birth.

14.8 Produce from `emp.lst`, a list of the birth years, along with the number of people born in that year.

14.9 Generate a code list by selecting the departments from `emp.lst`.

14.10 Remove repeated lines from a file.

14.11 Convert the contents of the file `emp.lst` to uppercase.

FLEX YOUR BRAIN

14.1 How will you use **pr**, **sort** and **cut** to read a file's lines in reverse order?

14.2 Write a Korn or Bash shell alias that always brings up the last modified file for editing with **vi**.

14.3 How do you display the **date** output with each field in a separate line? How do now combine the fields back to get back the original output?

14.4 How will you find out the number of times the character ? occurs in a file?

14.5 Extract the names of the users from `/etc/passwd` after ignoring the first 10 entries.

14.6 Sort the file `/etc/passwd` on GID (primary) and UID (secondary) so that the users with the same GID are placed together. Users with a lower UID should be placed higher in the list.

14.7 Devise a pipeline sequence which lists the five largest files in the current directory. (HINT: Compress the spaces in the **`ls -l`** output first.)

14.8 Use a pipeline and command substitution to set the length of a line in `emp.lst` to a variable.

14.9 You have with you two files, `foo1` and `foo2`, copied from two /etc/passwd files on two machines. How do you print two lists of only users who are (i) present in `foo1` and not in `foo2` (ii) present in `foo2` and not in `foo1` (iii) present in both files?

14.10 Mail a sorted list of users currently logged in to root, taking account of the possibility that a user may be logged in more than once.

15

Filters Using Regular Expressions —grep and sed

You often need to search a file for a pattern, either to see the lines containing (or not containing) it or to have it replaced with something else. This chapter discusses two important filters that are specially suited for these tasks—**grep** and **sed**. **grep** takes care of all search requirements you may have. **sed** goes further and can even manipulate the individual characters in a line. In fact **sed** can do several things, some of them quite well.

This chapter also takes up one of the fascinating features of UNIX—*regular expressions*. When discussing **more** and **vi**, we observed that the search patterns in those programs can also take on special expressions. In this chapter, you'll see regular expressions in all their manifestations. This chapter should prepare you well for **awk** and **perl** because they too use these expressions.

WHAT YOU WILL LEARN

- Use **grep** to search a file for a pattern and display both matching and nonmatching lines.
- The various **grep** options to display a count, line numbers or filenames.
- The concept of a *regular expression* as a mechanism for matching multiple similar patterns.
- The significance of the characters of the *Basic Regular Expression* (BRE) set.
- The significance of the characters of the *Extended Regular Expression* (ERE) set.
- Use **sed** to edit an input stream and understand its addressing mechanism.
- The *substitution* feature and how it is enhanced when used with regular expressions.
- The significance of the *repeated* and *remembered* patterns.

TOPICS OF SPECIAL INTEREST

- Use the *interval regular expression* (IRE) to locate or replace patterns at specific locations.
- Use the *tagged regular expression* (TRE) to use *part* of the source pattern in the target pattern.

15.1 grep: SEARCHING FOR A PATTERN

grep scans its input for a pattern, and can display the selected pattern, the line numbers or the filenames where the pattern occurs. The command uses the following syntax:

```
grep options pattern filename(s)
```

grep searches for *pattern* in one or more *filenames*. The first argument (barring the option) is the pattern and ones remaining are filenames. Let's use **grep** to display lines containing the string sales from the file emp.lst; the contents of this file are shown in Section 14.1:

```
$ grep "sales" emp.lst
2233|a.k. shukla      |g.m.     |sales     |12/12/52|6000
1006|chanchal singhvi |director |sales     |03/09/38|6700
1265|s.n. dasgupta    |manager  |sales     |12/09/63|5600
2476|anil aggarwal    |manager  |sales     |01/05/59|5000
```

Because **grep** is also a filter, it can search its standard input for the pattern and store the output in a file:

```
who | grep kumar > foo
```

It's generally safe to quote the pattern, though we have used the pattern both with ("sales") and without quotes (kumar). Quoting is essential if the search string consists of more than one word, or uses any of the shell's characters like *, $ etc.

grep also silently returns the prompt in case the pattern can't be located:

```
$ grep president emp.lst                    No quoting necessary here
$ _                                         No president found
```

The command *failed* because the string president couldn't be located. Though the feature of scanning a file for a pattern is available in both **sed** and **awk**, these commands are *not* considered to fail if they can't locate the patterns in their input. The success or failure of a command is yet another important feature of the UNIX system, and you'll see in Chapter 16 (shell programming) how this feature is used in the command line of the shell's programming constructs.

When **grep** is used with multiple filenames, it displays the filenames along with the output. In the next example, **grep** searches two files. Don't bother about what they contain; just observe how each line is preceded by the filename:

```
$ grep "director" emp1.lst emp2.lst
emp1.lst:1006|chanchal singhvi |director|sales      |03/09/38|6700
emp1.lst:6521|lalit chowdury   |director|marketing  |26/09/45|8200
emp2.lst:9876|jai sharma       |director|production |12/03/50|7000
emp2.lst:2365|barun sengupta   |director|personnel  |11/05/47|7800
```

Though we need not have quoted the patterns in these examples, quoting is essential when the pattern contains multiple words:

```
$ grep 'jai sharma' emp.lst
9876|jai sharma       |director |production|12/03/50|7000
```

Though quotes are redundant in single-word fixed strings, it's better to enforce their use. It sets up a good habit with no adverse consequences. You can then use regular expressions inside them.

> **Note** Quote the pattern used with **grep** if it contains multiple words or special characters that can be interpreted otherwise by the shell. You can generally use either single or double quotes, but if the special characters in the pattern require command substitution or variable evaluation to be performed, you must use double quotes.

15.1.1 grep Options

grep is one of the most important UNIX commands, and you must know the options that POSIX requires **grep** to support. Table 15.1 shows only the POSIX options. Linux supports all these options, but Solaris has two versions of **grep** (in `/usr/bin` and `/usr/xpg4/bin`), and between them they support all POSIX options.

Ignoring Case (`-i`) When you look for a name, but are not sure of the case, **grep** offers the `-i` (ignore) option which ignores case for pattern matching:

```
$ grep -i 'agarwal' emp.lst
3564|sudhir Agarwal    |executive|personnel |06/07/47|7500
```

This locates the name `Agarwal`.

Deleting Lines (`-v`) **grep** can play an inverse role too; the `-v` (inverse) option selects all *except* lines containing the pattern. Thus, you can create a file `otherlist` containing all but directors:

```
$ grep -v 'director' emp.lst > otherlist
$ wc -l otherlist
    11 otherlist                                There were 4 directors initially
```

More often than not, when we use **grep -v**, we also redirect its output to a file as a means of getting rid of unwanted lines. Obviously, the lines haven't been deleted from the original file as such.

> **Note** The `-v` option removes lines from **grep**'s output, but doesn't actually change the argument file. This option is frequently used with redirection.

Displaying Line Numbers (`-n`) The `-n` (number) option displays the line numbers containing the pattern, along with the lines:

```
$ grep -n 'marketing' emp.lst
3:5678|sumit chakrobarty|d.g.m.    |marketing |19/04/43|6000
11:6521|lalit chowdury   |director |marketing |26/09/45|8200
14:2345|j.b. saxena      |g.m.     |marketing |12/03/45|8000
15:0110|v.k. agrawal     |g.m.     |marketing |31/12/40|9000
```

The line numbers are shown at the beginning of each line, separated from the actual line by a `:`. Now that you know how to use **cut**, it's a simple matter to extract only the line numbers from this output.

Counting Lines Containing Pattern (`-c`) How many directors are there in the file? The `-c` (count) option counts the number of lines containing the pattern (which is not the same as number of occurrences). The following example reveals that there are four of them:

```
$ grep -c 'director' emp.lst
4
```

If you use this command with multiple files, the filename is prefixed to the line count:

```
$ grep -c director emp*.lst
emp.lst:4
emp1.lst:2
emp2.lst:2
empold.lst:4
```

Sometimes, you need to get a single count from all these files so that you can use it in script logic. You have already handled a similar situation before *(9.7.1)*, and you should be able to use **grep** in a manner that drops the filenames from the output.

Displaying Filenames (`-l`) The `-l` (list) option displays only the names of files containing the pattern:

```
$ grep -l 'manager' *.lst
desig.lst
emp.lst
emp1.lst
empn.lst
```

So if you have forgotten the filename where you last saw something, just use this option to find out.

Matching Multiple Patterns (`-e`) With the `-e` option (Solaris has it only in the XPG4 version.), you can match the three *agarwals* by using **grep** like this:

```
$ grep -e "Agarwal" -e "aggarwal" -e "agrawal" emp.lst
2476|anil aggarwal    |manager   |sales     |05/01/59|5000
3564|sudhir Agarwal   |executive|personnel |07/06/47|7500
0110|v.k. agrawal     |g.m.      |marketing |12/31/40|9000
```

You could question the wisdom of entering such a long command line when the patterns don't differ much from one another. Yes, **grep** supports sophisticated pattern matching techniques that can display the same lines but with a *single* expression. This is the ideal forum for regular expressions to make their entry.

Taking Patterns from a File (`-f`) You can place all the three patterns in a separate file, one pattern per line. **grep** takes input from there with the `-f` option:

```
grep -f pattern.lst emp.lst
```

In Solaris, the `-f` option is available only in its XPG4 version. There's no problem with this option in Linux.

Table 15.1 Options Used by **grep**

Option	*Significance*
`-i`	Ignores case for matching
`-v`	Doesn't display lines matching expression
`-n`	Displays line numbers along with lines
`-c`	Displays count of number of occurrences
`-l`	Displays list of filenames only
`-e` *exp*	Specifies expression *exp* with this option. Can use multiple times. Also used for matching expression beginning with a hyphen.
`-x`	Matches pattern with entire line (doesn't match embedded patterns)
`-f` *file*	Takes patterns from *file*, one per line
`-E`	Treats pattern as an extended regular expression (ERE)
`-F`	Matches multiple fixed strings (in **fgrep**-style)

15.2 BASIC REGULAR EXPRESSIONS (BRE)—AN INTRODUCTION

View the file `emp.lst` *(14.1)* once again and locate all the *agarwal*s. On close examination, you'll see three lines containing similar, but not identical patterns—`Agarwal`, `aggarwal` and `agrawal`. It's tedious to specify each pattern separately with the `-e` option. This is where searches in UNIX become truly remarkable; you can locate an agarwal without knowing exactly how his name is spelled.

Like the shell's wild-cards *(9.3)* which match similar filenames with a single expression, **grep** uses an expression of a different sort to match a group of similar patterns. Unlike wild-cards, however, this expression is a feature of the *command* that uses it and has nothing to do with the shell. It uses an elaborate metacharacter set (Table 15.2), overshadowing the shell's wild-cards, and can perform amazing matches. If an expression uses any of these characters, it is termed a *regular expression*. Some of the characters used by regular expressions are also meaningful to the shell—enough reason why these expressions should be quoted.

Regular expressions take care of some common query and substitution requirements. You may want the system to present a list of similar names, so you can select exactly the one you require. Or you may want to replace multiple spaces with a single space, or display lines that begin with a #. You may even be looking for a string at a specific column position in a line. All this is possible (and much more) with regular expressions as you'll discover in the three rounds of discussions that feature the subject in this chapter.

POSIX identifies regular expressions as belonging to two categories—*basic* and *extended*. **grep** supports basic regular expressions (BRE) by default and extended regular expressions (ERE) with the `-E` option. **sed** supports only the BRE set. We'll first start with a minimal treatment of the BRE set and then take up the ERE set in the next section. We'll later expand the coverage of the BRE when we discuss **sed**.

Note Regular expressions are interpreted by the command and not by the shell. Quoting ensures that the shell isn't able to interfere and interpret the metacharacters in its own way.

Table 15.2 The Basic Regular Expression (BRE) Character Subset

Symbols or Expressions	*Matches*
`*`	Zero or more occurrences of the previous character
`g*`	Nothing or g, gg, ggg, etc.
`.`	A single character
`.*`	Nothing or any number of characters
[*pqr*]	A single character *p*, *q* or *r*
[*c1*-*c2*]	A single character within the ASCII range represented by *c1* and *c2*
`[1-3]`	A digit between 1 and 3
[^*pqr*]	A single character which is not a *p*, *q* or *r*
`[^a-zA-Z]`	A nonalphabetic character
^*pat*	Pattern *pat* at beginning of line
pat$	Pattern *pat* at end of line
`bash$`	`bash` at end of line
`^bash$`	`bash` as the only word in line
`^$`	Lines containing nothing

15.2.1 The Character Class

A regular expression lets you specify a group of characters enclosed within a pair of rectangular brackets, [ ]; the match is performed for any *single* character in the group. This form resembles the one used by the shell's wild-cards. Thus, the expression

```
[ra]
```

matches either an `r` or an `a`. The metacharacters `[` and `]` can now be used to match `Agarwal` and `agrawal`. The following regular expression

```
[aA]g[ar][ar]wal
```

matches the two names. The character class `[aA]` matches the letter `a` in both lowercase and uppercase. The model `[ar][ar]` matches any of the four patterns:

```
aa    ar    ra    rr
```

of which the second and third are relevant to the present problem. As a first step, let's use this regular expression with **grep**:

```
$ grep "[aA]g[ar][ar]wal" emp.lst
3564|sudhir Agarwal   |executive|personnel |07/06/47|7500
0110|v.k. agrawal     |g.m.     |marketing |12/31/40|9000
```

A single pattern has located two similar strings; that's what regular expressions are all about. You can also use ranges, both for alphabets and numerals. The pattern `[a-zA-Z0-9]` matches a single alphanumeric character. When you use a range, make sure that the character on the left of the hyphen has a lower ASCII value than the one on the right. Also bear in mind that uppercase precedes lowercase in the ASCII sequence.

Negating a Class (^) Regular expressions use the ^ (caret) to negate the character class, while the shell uses the ! (bang). When the character class *begins* with this character, all characters other than the ones grouped in the class, are matched. So, [^a-zA-Z] matches a single nonalphabetic character string.

> **Note** The character class feature is similar to the wild-cards except that negation of the class is done by a ^ (caret), while in the shell it's done by the ! (bang).

15.2.2 The *

The * (asterisk) refers to the *immediately preceding* character. However, its interpretation is the trickiest of the lot as it bears absolutely no resemblance whatsoever with the * used by wild-cards or DOS. Here, it indicates that the *previous* character can occur many times, or not at all. The pattern

```
g*
```

matches the single character g, and any number of gs. Because the previous character may not occur at all, it also matches a null string. Thus, apart from this null string, it also matches the following strings:

```
g    gg    ggg    gggg  .....
```

Mark the key words "zero or more occurrences of the previous character" that are used to describe the significance of the *. Don't make the mistake of using g* to match a string beginning with g; use gg* instead. The * used here has a different significance from the * used by wild-cards, where it doesn't relate to the previous character at all.

How do you then match all the three patterns? The third pattern aggarwal contains an extra g, while the other patterns don't. To include this string also, you can use the * to enhance the previous expression. Observe carefully that the regular expression

```
[aA]gg*[ar][ar]wal
```

matches all three patterns. Now use this expression with **grep**, and you'll find that it solves the problem:

```
$ grep "[aA]gg*[ar][ar]wal" emp.lst
2476|anil aggarwal     |manager  |sales      |05/01/59|5000
3564|sudhir Agarwal    |executive|personnel  |07/06/47|7500
0110|v.k. agrawal      |g.m.     |marketing  |12/31/40|9000
```

A simple regular expression matches all three names! You don't have to use the -e option three times to get this result. But note that these are not the only strings it can match; the expression is general enough to include other patterns. It would have also matched Agggaawal had there been such a pattern in the file.

> **Note** C programmers should note that the expression s*printf matches sprintf, ssprintf, sssprintf and so forth, but it also matches printf, because the previous character, s, which the * refers to, may not occur at all.

15.2.3 The Dot

A . matches a single character. The shell uses the ? character to indicate that. The pattern

```
2...
```

matches a four-character pattern beginning with a 2. The shell's equivalent pattern is 2???.

The Regular Expression .* The dot along with the * (.*) constitutes a very useful regular expression. It signifies any number of characters, or none. Consider that you want to look up the name j. saxena but are not sure whether it actually exists in the file as j.b. saxena or as joginder saxena. No problem, just embed the .* in the search string:

```
$ grep "j.*saxena" emp.lst
2345|j.b. saxena     |g.m.      |marketing |03/12/45|8000
```

Note that if you literally look for the name j.b. saxena, then the expression should be j\.b\.saxena. The dots need to be escaped here with the \, the same character you used in the shell *(9.4.1)* for despecializing the next character.

> **Note** A regular expression match is made for the longest possible string. Thus when you use the expression 03.*05, it will match 03 and 05 as close to the left and right of the line, respectively.

15.2.4 Specifying Pattern Locations (^ and $)

Most of the regular expression characters are used for matching patterns, but there are two that can match a pattern at the beginning or end of a line. Anchoring a pattern is often necessary when it can occur in more than one place in a line, and you are interested in its occurrence only at a particular location. These are the two characters that are used:

^ (caret) — For matching at the beginning of a line.
$ — For matching at the end of a line.

Consider a simple example. Try to extract those lines where the emp-id begins with a 2. What happens if you simply use

```
2...
```

as the expression? This won't do because the character 2, followed by three characters, can occur anywhere in the line. You must indicate to **grep** that the pattern occurs at the beginning of the line, and the ^ does it easily:

```
$ grep "^2" emp.lst
2233|a.k. shukla     |g.m.      |sales     |12/12/52|6000
2365|barun sengupta  |director  |personnel |05/11/47|7800
2476|anil aggarwal   |manager   |sales     |05/01/59|5000
2345|j.b. saxena     |g.m.      |marketing |03/12/45|8000
```

Similarly, to select those lines where the salary lies between 7000 and 7999, you have to use the $ at the end of the pattern:

```
$ grep "7...$" emp.lst
9876|jai sharma      |director |production|03/12/50|7000
2365|barun sengupta  |director |personnel |05/11/47|7800
3564|sudhir Agarwal  |executive|personnel |07/06/47|7500
```

How can you reverse the search and select only those lines where the emp-ids *don't* begin with a 2? You need the expression `^[^2]`:

```
grep "^[^2]" emp.lst
```

UNIX has no command that lists only directories. However, we can use a pipeline to "grep" those lines from the listing that begin with a d:

```
ls -l | grep "^d"                                    Shows only directories
```

You should convert this into an alias *(11.2)* or a *shell function (24.10)* so that it is always available for you to use.

> **Note** The caret has a triple role to play in regular expressions. When placed at the beginning of a character class (e.g. `[^a-z]`), it negates every character of the class. When placed outside it, and at the beginning of the expression (e.g. `^2...`), the pattern is matched at the beginning of the line. At any other location (e.g. `a^b`), it matches itself literally.

15.2.5 When Metacharacters Lose Their Meaning

It is possible that some of these special characters actually exist as part of the text. If a literal match has to be made for any of them, the "magic" of the characters should be turned off. Sometimes, that is automatically done if the characters violate the regular expression rules. Like the caret, the meaning of these characters can change depending on the place they occupy in the expression.

The - loses its meaning inside the character class if it's not enclosed on either side by a suitable character, or when placed outside the class. The . and * lose their meanings when placed inside the character class. The * is also matched literally if it's the first character of the expression. For instance, when you use **grep "*"**, you are in fact looking for an asterisk.

Sometimes, you may need to escape these characters, say, when looking for a pattern `g*`. In that case, **grep "g*"** won't do, and you have to use the \ for escaping. Similarly, to look for a [, you should use `\[`, and to look for the literal pattern `.*`, you should use `\.\*`.

Regular expressions are found everywhere in the UNIX system. Apart from **grep**, some of the most powerful UNIX commands like **vi**, **sed**, **awk**, **perl** and **expr** also use regular expressions, a reason why these commands have become indispensable to the UNIX tool kit. You must understand them because they hold the key to the mastery of the UNIX system.

15.3 EXTENDED REGULAR EXPRESSIONS (ERE) AND egrep

Extended regular expressions (ERE) make it possible to match dissimilar patterns with a single expression. This set uses some additional characters (Table 15.3) and POSIX-compliant versions of **grep** use them with the `-E` option. Linux **grep** has this option, but Solaris users must use

/usr/xpg4/bin/grep to use EREs. If your version of **grep** doesn't support this option, then use **egrep** but without the -E option.

15.3.1 The + and ?

The ERE set includes two special characters, + and ?. They are often used in place of the * to *restrict* the matching scope. They signify the following:

+ — Matches one or more occurrences of the previous character.
? — Matches zero or one occurrence of the previous character.

What all this means is that b+ matches b, bb, bbb, etc, but it doesn't match nothing—unlike b*. The expression b? matches either a single instance of b or nothing. These characters restrict the scope of match as compared to the *.

Using this extended set, you can now have a different regular expression for matching Agarwal and aggarwal. Note that the character g occurs only once or twice. So, gg? now restricts the expansion to one or two gs only. This time we need to use **grep**'s -E option to use an ERE:

```
$ grep -E "[aA]gg?arwal" emp.lst
2476|anil aggarwal    |manager  |sales     |01/05/59|5000
3564|sudhir Agarwal   |executive|personnel |06/07/47|7500
```

The + is a pretty useful character too. When you are looking for a multiword string like #include <stdio.h>, but don't know how many spaces separate the #include and <stdio.h>, you can use the expression #include +<stdio.h> to match them all. This expression matches the following patterns:

```
#include <stdio.h>        #include  <stdio.h>            #include      <stdio.h>
```

And if you are not sure whether there's a space between # and include, include the ? in the expression in this manner—# ?include +<stdio.h>. But there could be tabs here instead of spaces as well, so how does one handle them also?

15.3.2 Matching Multiple Patterns (|, (and))

The | is the delimiter of multiple patterns. Using it, we can locate both sengupta and dasgupta from the file without using the -e option twice:

```
$ grep -E 'sengupta|dasgupta' emp.lst
2365|barun sengupta   |director |personnel |11/05/47|7800
1265|s.n. dasgupta    |manager  |sales     |12/09/63|5600
```

The ERE thus handles the problem easily, but offers an even better alternative. The characters, (and), let you group patterns, and when you use the | inside the parentheses, you can frame an even more compact pattern:

```
$ grep -E '(sen|das)gupta' emp.lst
2365|barun sengupta   |director |personnel |11/05/47|7800
1265|s.n. dasgupta    |manager  |sales     |12/09/63|5600
```

EREs when combined with BREs form very powerful regular expressions. For instance, the expression `agg?[ar]+wal` contains characters from both sets. All EREs can also be placed in a file in exactly the same way they are used in the command line. You then have to use **grep** both with the `-E` and `-f` options to take the patterns from the file.

> **Note** If **grep** doesn't support the `-E` option on your machine, use **egrep** without the `-E` option for all examples considered in this section.

Table 15.3 The Extended Regular Expression (ERE) Set Used by **grep**, **egrep** and **awk**

Expression	*Significance*
ch+	Matches one or more occurrences of character *ch*
ch?	Matches zero or one occurrence of character *ch*
exp1|*exp2*	Matches *exp1* or *exp2*
GIF|JPEG	Matches GIF or JPEG
(*x1*|*x2*)*x3*	Matches *x1x3* or *x2x3*
(lock|ver)wood	Matches `lockwood` or `verwood`

15.4 sed:THE STREAM EDITOR

sed is a multipurpose tool which combines the work of several filters. It is derived from **ed**, the original UNIX editor (not discussed in this text). **sed** performs noninteractive operations on a data stream—hence its name. It uses very few options but has a host of features that allow you to select lines and run instructions on them. Learning **sed** will prepare you well for **perl** which uses many of these features.

sed uses *instructions* to act on text. An instruction combines an *address* for selecting lines, with an *action* to be taken on them, as shown by the syntax:

`sed` *options* `'`*address action*`'` *file(s)*

The address and action are enclosed within single quotes. Addressing in **sed** is done in two ways:

- By one or two line numbers (like `3,7`).
- By specifying a /-enclosed pattern which occurs in a line (like `/From:/`).

In the first form, *address* specifies either one line number to select a single line or a set of two (`3,7`) to select a group of contiguous lines. Likewise, the second form uses one or two patterns. The *action* component is drawn from **sed**'s family of internal commands (Table 15.4). It can either be a simple display (print) or an editing function like insertion, deletion or substitution of text. We'll refer to these actions as *commands*.

sed processes several instructions in a sequential manner. Each instruction operates on the output of the previous instruction. In this context, two options are relevant, and probably they are the only ones you'll use with **sed**—the `-e` option that lets you use multiple instructions, and the `-f` option to take instructions from a file. Both options are used by **grep** in identical manner.

15.5 LINE ADDRESSING

To consider *line addressing* first, the instruction **3q** can be broken down to the address 3 and the action **q** (quit). When this instruction is enclosed within quotes and followed by one or more filenames, you can simulate **head -n 3** in this way:

```
$ sed '3q' emp.lst                                    Quits after line number 3
2233|a.k. shukla       |g.m.      |sales      |12/12/52|6000
9876|jai sharma        |director  |production|03/12/50|7000
5678|sumit chakrobarty|d.g.m.    |marketing |04/19/43|6000
```

Generally, we'll be using the **p** (print) command to display lines. However, this command behaves in a seemingly strange manner; it outputs both the selected lines as well as *all* lines. So the selected lines appear twice. We must suppress this behavior with the -n option, and remember to use this option whenever we use the **p** command. Thus:

```
$ sed -n '1,2p' emp.lst
2233|a.k. shukla       |g.m.      |sales      |12/12/52|6000
9876|jai sharma        |director  |production|03/12/50|7000
```

prints the first two lines. To select the last line of the file, use the $:

```
$ sed -n '$p' emp.lst
0110|v.k. agrawal      |g.m.      |marketing |31/12/40|9000
```

Selecting Lines from Anywhere The two command invocations above emulate the **head** and **tail** commands, but **sed** can also select a contiguous group of lines from anywhere in the file. To select lines 9 through 11, you have to use the following command:

```
sed -n '9,11p' emp.lst
```

Selecting Multiple Groups of Lines **sed** is not restricted to selecting only one group of lines. You can select as many sections from just about anywhere:

```
sed -n '1,2p                           3 addresses in one command, using only a single
7,9p                                   pair of quotes
$p' emp.lst                            Selects the last line
```

In the next section, we'll be considering alternative methods of running the above **sed** command.

Negating the Action (!) **sed** also has a negation operator (!), which can be used with any action. For instance, selecting the first two lines is the same as *not* selecting lines 3 through the end. A previous command sequence (**1,2p**) can be written in this way too:

```
sed -n '3,$!p' emp.lst                 Don't print lines 3 to the end
```

The address and action are normally enclosed within a pair of single quotes. As you have already learned by now, you should use double quotes only when parameter evaluation or command substitution is embedded within the command.

> **Tip** Use the -n option whenever you use the **p** command, unless you deliberately want to select lines twice. Usually, that requirement doesn't arise.

15.6 USING MULTIPLE INSTRUCTIONS (-e and -f)

In the previous section we encountered multiple instructions in a single **sed** command, the one that selected three segments from a file. There's adequate scope of using the -e and -f options whenever **sed** is used with multiple instructions. The -e option allows you to enter as many instructions as you wish, each preceded by the option. We can repeat the command prior to the previous one with this:

```
sed -n -e '1,2p' -e '7,9p' -e '$p' emp.lst
```

When you have too many instructions to use or when you have a set of common instructions that you execute often, they are better stored in a file. For instance, the above three instructions can be stored in a file, with each instruction on a separate line:

```
$ cat instr.fil
1,2p
7,9p
$p
```

You can now use the -f option to direct **sed** to take its instructions from the file using the command **sed -n -f instr.fil emp.lst**.

sed is quite liberal in that it allows a great deal of freedom in using and repeating options. You can use the -f option with multiple files. You can also combine the -e and -f options as many times as you want:

```
sed -n -f instr.fil1 -f instr.fil2 emp.lst
sed -n -e '/saxena/p' -f instr.fil1 -f instr.fil2 emp?.lst
```

These are some of the features of **sed** that make it so versatile, and at the same time easy to work with. The second example uses context addressing (/saxena/) in an instruction. This is the other form of addressing used by **sed**, and is considered next.

15.7 CONTEXT ADDRESSING

The second form of addressing, called *context addressing*, lets you specify one or two patterns to locate lines. The pattern must be bounded by a / on either side. When you specify a single pattern, all lines containing the pattern are selected. You can "grep" the directors in this way:

```
$ sed -n '/director/p' emp.lst
9876|jai sharma       |director |production|03/12/50|7000
2365|barun sengupta   |director |personnel |05/11/47|7800
1006|chanchal singhvi |director |sales     |09/03/38|6700
6521|lalit chowdury   |director |marketing |09/26/45|8200
```

You can also specify a comma-separated pair of context addresses to select a group of lines. Line and context addresses can also be mixed:

```
sed -n '/dasgupta/,/saksena/p' emp.lst
sed -n '1,/dasgupta/p' emp.lst
```

Using Regular Expressions Context addresses also uses regular expressions, which you first saw used in **grep**. The following command lines should refresh your memory:

```
sed -n '/[aA]gg*[ar][ar]wal/p' emp.lst          All the agarwals
sed -n '/sa[kx]s*ena/p                          Either the saxenas or
        /gupta/p' emp.lst                       gupta
```

You can use the anchoring characters, ^ and $, as part of the regular expression syntax. This is how you locate all people born in the year 1950:

```
$ sed -n '/50.....$/p' emp.lst
9876|jai sharma        |director |production|03/12/50|7000
4290|jayant Choudhury  |executive|production|09/07/50|6000
```

Regular expressions in **grep** and **sed** are actually more powerful than the ones we have used so far. They use some more special characters, and we'll meet them in the third round of discussions at the end of the chapter.

> **Tip** C programmers should use the command **sed -n '/{/,/}/p' foo.c** to select the *first* block of code delimited by { and }. **sed** won't select the subsequent blocks.

> **Note** We used single quotes here, but if the pattern itself contains a single quote, then you must use double quotes. In that case, make sure that a $ (if present) in the pattern is not interpreted as a variable unless it has been used to be interpreted that way.

15.8 WRITING SELECTED LINES TO A FILE (w)

Irrespective of the way you select lines (by line or context addressing), you can use the **w** (write) command to write the selected lines to a separate file. Save the lines of directors in `dlist` in this way:

```
sed -n '/director/w dlist' emp.lst              No display when using -n option
```

Since **sed** accepts more than one address, you can perform a full context splitting of the file `emp.lst`. You can store the lines pertaining to the directors, managers and executives in three separate files:

```
sed -n '/director/w dlist
        /manager/w mlist
        /executive/w elist' emp.lst
```

The same applies to line addressing also. For a file `foo.main` containing 1000 lines, you can save the two halves separately:

```
sed -n '1,500w foo1                             Saves first 500 lines in foo1
501,$w foo2' foo.main                           and the rest in foo2
```

> **Note** The `-n` option is required with the **w** command only to suppress printing of all lines on the terminal. However, even without it, the selected lines will be written to the respective files.

15.9 TEXT EDITING

This section discusses some of the editing commands available in **sed**'s action component. **sed** can insert text and change existing text in a file. A **vi** user would be relieved to learn that the commands are also the same—**i** (insert), **a** (append), **c** (change) and **d** (delete). But there are important differences too.

15.9.1 Inserting and Changing Lines (i, a, c)

The **i** command inserts text. A C programmer can add two common "include" lines at the beginning of a program, foo.c in this way:

```
$ sed '1i\                      Need to use \ before [Enter] here ...
> #include <stdio.h>\           and here only
> #include <unistd.h>           Unclosed quote shows PS2
> ' foo.c > $$                  Redirect output to a temporary file
```

First enter the instruction **1i**, which inserts text at line number 1. Then enter a \ before pressing *[Enter]*. You can now key in as many lines as you wish. Each line *except the last* has to be terminated by the \ before hitting *[Enter]*. **sed** identifies the line without the \ as the last line of input. This technique has to be followed when using the **a** and **c** commands also.

The above command writes the concatenated output of the two lines of inserted text and the existing lines to the standard output, which we redirected to a temporary file, `$$`. We must move this file to foo.c to be able to use it. The first two lines show that the **i** command worked fine:

```
$ mv $$ foo.c ; head -2 foo.c
#include <stdio.h>
#include <unistd.h>
```

Doublespacing Text What is the consequence of not using an address with these commands? The inserted or changed text then is placed after or before *every* line of the file. The following command

```
sed 'a\                         Inserts after every line
                                this blank line
' emp.lst
```

inserts a blank line *after* each line of the file is printed. This is another way of doublespacing text *(14.2.1)*. Using **i** here would have inserted a blank line *before* each selected line.

15.9.2 Deleting Lines (d)

Using the **d** (delete) command, **sed** can emulate **grep**'s -v option to select lines not containing the pattern. Either of the following commands

```
sed '/director/d' emp.lst > olist           -n option not to be used with d
sed -n '/director/!p' emp.lst > olist
```

selects all lines except those containing director, and saves them in olist.

Deleting Blank Lines A blank line consists of any number of spaces, tabs or nothing. How do you delete these lines from a file? Frame a pattern which matches zero or more occurrences of a space or tab:

```
sed '/^[ ⇥]*$/d' foo
```
A space and a tab inside [ ]

You need to press the *[Tab]* key or *[Ctrl-i]* inside the character class—immediately after the space. Providing a ^ at the beginning and a $ at the end matches only lines that contain nothing but whitespace. Obviously, this expression also matches those lines that contain nothing.

15.10 SUBSTITUTION (s)

Substitution is easily the most important feature of **sed**, and this is one job that **sed** does exceedingly well. It lets you replace a pattern in its input with something else. The use of regular expressions enhances our pattern matching capabilities, and in this chapter we feature some more regular expression characters that make the use of **sed** so compelling. You have encountered the substitution syntax in **vi** before *(8.9)*:

*[address]*s/*expression1*/*expression2*/*flags*

Here, *expression1* (which can also be a regular expression) is replaced with *expression2* in all lines specified by *[address]*. Unlike in **vi**, however, if the address is not specified, the substitution is performed for all matching lines. This means that there's no need to use 1,$ as the address. To bring *flags* into the picture, let's first avoid its use and replace the | with a colon:

```
$ sed 's/|/:/' emp.lst | head -2
2233:a.k. shukla     |g.m.      |sales     |12/12/52|6000
9876:jai sharma      |director  |production|12/03/50|7000
```

Just look at what **sed** has done; only the first (left-most) instance of the | in a line has been replaced. You need to use the g (global) flag to replace all the pipes:

```
$ sed 's/|/:/g' emp.lst | head -2
2233:a.k. shukla     :g.m.      :sales     :12/12/52:6000
9876:jai sharma      :director  :production:12/03/50:7000
```

We used global substitution to replace all pipes with colons. **s** here is the same as **1,$s**. Though we are seeing two lines here, the substitution has been carried out for the entire file. You can limit the vertical boundaries too by specifying an address:

```
sed '1,3s/|/:/g' emp.lst
```
First three lines only

Substitution is not restricted to a single character; it can be any string. Let's replace the word director with member in the first five lines of emp.lst:

```
$ sed '1,5s/director/member  /' emp.lst
2233|a.k. shukla     |g.m.      |sales     |12/12/52|6000
9876|jai sharma      |member    |production|03/12/50|7000
5678|sumit chakrobarty|d.g.m.   |marketing |04/19/43|6000
2365|barun sengupta  |member    |personnel |05/11/47|7800
5423|n.k. gupta      |chairman  |admin     |08/30/56|5400
1006|chanchal singhvi |director |sales     |09/03/38|6700
```
....more lines....

sed also uses regular expressions for patterns to be substituted. To replace all occurrences of `agarwal`, `aggarwal` and `agrawal` with simply `Agarwal`, use the regular expression you had used earlier with **grep** *(15.2.2)*:

```
sed 's/[Aa]gg*[ar][ar]wal/Agarwal/g' emp.lst
```

You can also use the anchoring characters, ^ and $, with the same meaning. Further, when either is used as a sole character in the source pattern, it implies that the target pattern has to be placed at that location. This is how you can add the 2 prefix to all emp-ids:

```
$ sed 's/^/2/' emp.lst | head -n 1
22233|a.k. shukla     |g.m.      |sales     |12/12/52|6000
```

There are five digits now in the first field. Likewise, you can add the suffix `.00` to the salary:

```
$ sed 's/$/.00/' emp.lst | head -n 1
2233|a.k. shukla      |g.m.      |sales     |12/12/52|6000.00
```

Note When a `g` is used at the end of a substitution instruction, the change is performed globally along the line. Without it, only the left-most occurrence is replaced.

Performing Multiple Substitutions You can perform multiple substitutions with one invocation of **sed**. Simply press *[Enter]* at the end of each instruction, and then close the quote at the end. This is how you replace three HTML tags:

```
$ sed 's/<I>/<EM>/g
> s/<B>/<STRONG>/g
> s/<U>/<EM>/g' form.html
```

sed is a stream editor; it works on a data stream. This means that an instruction processes the output of the previous one. This is something users often forget; they don't get the sequence right. Note that the following sequence finally converts all `<I>` tags to `<STRONG>`:

```
$ sed 's/<I>/<EM>/g
> s/<EM>/<STRONG>/g' form.html
```

Tip When there are a group of instructions to execute, you should place these instructions in a file instead, and then use **sed** with the `-f` option.

Compressing Multiple Spaces How do you delete the trailing spaces from the second, third and fourth fields? The regular expression required in the source string needs to signify one or more occurrences of a space, followed by a |:

```
$ sed 's/  *|/|/g' emp.lst | tee empn.lst | head -n 3
2233|a.k. shukla|g.m.|sales|12/12/52|6000
9876|jai sharma|director|production|12/03/50|7000
5678|sumit chakrobarty|d.g.m.|marketing|19/04/43|6000
```

Most UNIX system files (like `/etc/passwd`) follow this variable-length format because the common filters can easily identify a field by seeing the delimiter. Using **tee**, we created the file `empn.lst`. This is the file you'll be using with the **awk** command later.

15.10.1 The Remembered Pattern (//)

So far, we've looked for a pattern and then replaced it with something else. Truly speaking, the three commands below do the same job:

```
sed 's/director/member/' emp.lst
sed '/director/s//member/' emp.lst
sed '/director/s/director/member/' emp.lst
```

The second form suggests that **sed** "remembers" the scanned pattern, and stores it in // (2 frontslashes). The // representing an empty (or null) regular expression is interpreted to mean that the search and substituted patterns are the same. We'll call it the *remembered pattern*.

However, when you use // in the target string, it means you are removing the pattern totally:

```
sed 's/|//g' emp.lst                    Removes every | from file
```

The address /director/ in the third form appears to be redundant. However, you must understand this form also because it widens the scope of substitution. It's possible that you may like to replace a string in all lines containing a different string:

```
$ sed -n '/marketing/s/director/member   /p' emp.lst
6521|lalit chowdury    |member     |marketing |09/26/45|8200
```

> **Note** The significance of // depends on its position in the instruction. If it is in the source string, it implies that the scanned pattern is stored there. If the target string is //, it means that the source pattern is to be removed.

15.11 BASIC REGULAR EXPRESSIONS REVISITED

To master **sed**, you must appreciate the numerous possibilities that regular expressions throw up with this command—more so than in **grep**. This third round of discussions feature some more characters from the BRE set. Both **grep** and **sed** use these characters, but **sed** simply exploits them to the hilt. This time be prepared to see and use a \ before every metacharacter discussed in this section, except the &. We'll learn to use three types of expressions:

- The *repeated pattern*—This uses a single symbol, &, to make the entire source pattern appear at the destination also.
- The *interval regular expression* (IRE)—This expression uses the characters { and } with a single or a pair of numbers between them.
- The *tagged regular expression* (TRE)—This expression groups patterns with (and) and represents them at the destination with numbered tags.

In the last two types of expressions, the metacharacters need escaping so the *command* understands them as special. The expressions themselves are quoted so the shell can't interpret them.

15.11.1 The Repeated Pattern (&)

We sometimes encounter situations when the source pattern also occurs at the destination. We can then use the special character & to represent it. All these commands do the same thing:

```
sed 's/director/executive director/' emp.lst
sed 's/director/executive &/' emp.lst
sed '/director/s//executive &/' emp.lst
```

All these commands replace `director` with `executive director`. The &, known as the *repeated pattern*, here expands to the entire source string. Apart from the numbered tag (discussed soon), the & is the only other special character you can use in the target expression.

15.11.2 Interval Regular Expression (IRE)

We have matched a pattern at the beginning and end of a line. But what about matching it at any specified location—or within a zone? **sed** and **grep** also use the *interval regular expression* (IRE) that uses an integer (or two) to specify the number of characters preceding a pattern. The IRE uses an escaped pair of curly braces and takes three forms:

- *ch*\{*m*\}—The metacharacter *ch* can occur *m* times.
- *ch*\{*m*,*n*\}—Here, *ch* can occur between *m* and *n* times.
- *ch*\{*m*,\}—Here, *ch* can occur at least *m* times.

All these forms have the single character regular expression *ch* as the first element. This can either be a literal character, a . (dot), or a character class. It is followed by a pair of escaped curly braces containing either a single number *m*, or a range of numbers lying between *m* and *n* to determine the number of times the character preceding it can occur. The values of *m* and *n* can't exceed 255.

To illustrate the first form, let's consider this small telephone directory where a person has either a wired phone (8 digits) or a mobile phone (10 digits):

```
$ cat teledir.txt
jai   sharma 25853670
chanchal singhvi 9831545629
anil   aggarwal 9830263298
shyam saksena 23217847
lalit chowdury 26688726
```

Let's use **grep** to select only those users who have a mobile phone. We must use an IRE to indicate that a numeral can occur 10 times:

```
$ grep '[0-9]\{10\}' teledir.txt
chanchal singhvi 9831545629
anil   aggarwal 9830263298
```

Let's now consider the second form of the IRE, using **sed** this time. Since this matches a pattern within a "zone," we can display the listing for those files that have the write bit set either for group or others:

```
$ ls -l | sed -n '/^.\{5,8\}w/p'
-r-xr-xrwx   3 sumit    dialout         426 Feb 26 19:58 comj
-r-xr-xrwx   3 sumit    dialout         426 Feb 26 19:58 runj
-r-xrw-r-x   1 sumit    dialout         527 Apr 23 07:42 valcode.sh
-r-xrw-r-x   2 sumit    dialout         289 Apr 23 07:42 vvi.sh
```

Extracting Lines Based on Length With the IRE, you can use the following commands to select lines longer than 100 characters. The second one additionally imposes a limit of 150 on the maximum length:

```
sed -n '/.\{101,\}/p' foo                    Line length at least 101
grep '^.\{101,150\}$' foo                    Line length between 101 and 150
```

The ^ and $ are required in the second example; otherwise lines longer than 150 characters would also be selected. *A regular expression always tries to match the longest pattern possible.*

15.11.3 The Tagged Regular Expression (TRE)

This is the most complex of all regular expressions, and possibly the finest. It relates to breaking up a line into groups and then extracting one or more of these groups. The tagged regular expression (TRE) requires two regular expression to be specified—one each for the source and target patterns.

This is how the TRE works. You have to identify the segments of a line that you wish to extract and enclose each segment with a matched pair of escaped parentheses. For instance, if you see a number, then you'll have to represent that number as `\([0-9]*\)`. A series of nonalphabetic characters can be represented as `\([^a-zA-Z]*\)`. Every grouped pattern automatically acquires the numeric label *n*, where *n* signifies the *n*th group from the left. To reproduce a group at the destination, you have to use the tag *n*. This means that the first group is represented as \1, the second one as \2 and so forth.

Let's illustrate this with a simple example. Consider the telephone directory that was considered in the previous section. Apart from telephone numbers, this file also contains names in the sequence *first_name last_name*. Some lines may have more than one space between the two name components, and our job is to use the TRE to take care of these imperfections.

We'll create a new list from this file that shows the surname first, followed by a , and then the first name and the rest of the line. For instance, the first name in the file should appear as `sharma, jai  5853670`. We'll have to frame two groups of alphabetic characters and then reverse them in the target pattern, while inserting a comma between them. This is how we can obtain a sorted list:

```
$ sed 's/\([a-z]*\) *\([a-z]*\)/\2, \1/' teledir.txt | sort
aggarwal, anil 9830263298
chowdury, lalit 6688726
saksena, shyam 3217847
sharma, jai  5853670
singhvi, chanchal 9831545629
```

The first group, `\([a-z]*\)`, represents zero or more occurrences of alphabetic characters; this effectively captures the first name. An identical pattern takes care of the surname. These two groups are separated by zero or more occurrences of space (□*). In the target pattern, we recreate these groups but in a reverse sequence with the tags \2 and \1. The comma between them is treated by **sed** literally.

Taking the cue from here, you can now add the century prefix to the year in the fifth field representing the date of birth in our sample database. We'll also convert the date format to *yyyymmdd*. To do that, consider the date field as comprising three pattern groups, representing the day, month and year. This group can be represented by \(..\). Now use the TRE to generate the *19yymmdd* format from the existing one:

```
$ sed 's^\(..\)/\(..\)/\(..\)^19\3\2\1^' emp.lst | head -n 3
2233|a.k. shukla       |g.m.      |sales      |19521212|6000
9876|jai sharma        |director  |production|19500312|7000
5678|sumit chakrobarty|d.g.m.     |marketing |19430419|6000
```

Each group is separated from the next one by /. In the target pattern, we added the string 19, dropped the /, and totally inverted the pattern groups (shown as \3\2\1).

You may be wondering what the ^ is doing here, when a / was expected. The fact is that **sed** doesn't compulsorily have to use a / to delimit patterns for substitution; *you can use any character provided it doesn't occur in the entire command line*. Choosing a different delimiter has allowed us to get away without escaping the / which actually occurs in the pattern.

You'll find numerous uses for the TRE when using **sed**. Though it's quite cryptic and difficult to comprehend initially, you must understand it if you want **sed** to serve as a gateway to learning **perl**. **perl** also uses these numbered tags, but in a more readable form.

Table 15.4 Internal Commands Used by **sed**

Command	*Description*
`i, a, c`	Inserts, appends and changes text
`d`	Deletes line(s)
`10q`	Quits after reading the first 10 lines
`p`	Prints line(s) on standard output
`3,$p`	Prints lines 3 to end (`-n` option required)
`$!p`	Prints all lines except last line (`-n` option required)
`/begin/,/end/p`	Prints lines enclosed between `begin` and `end` (`-n` option required)
`q`	Quits after reading up to addressed line
`r flname`	Places contents of file *flname* after line
`w flname`	Writes addressed lines to file *flname*
`=`	Prints line number addressed
`s/`*s1*`/`*s2*`/`	Replaces first occurrence of expression *s1* in all lines with expression *s2*
`10,20s/-/:/`	Replaces first occurrence of - in lines 10 to 20 with a :
`s/`*s1*`/`*s2*`/g`	Replaces all occurrences of expression *s1* in all lines with expression *s2*
`s/-/:/g`	Replaces all occurrences of - in all lines with a :

15.12 CONCLUSION

While **grep** is pretty to easy to comprehend, **sed** is best mastered by sheer practice, by repeated attempts to figure out the exact command sequence that will perform a specific job. You don't always get it right the first time, but don't worry; hardly anybody does—not with this command at least.

This completes our discussion on filters for Part I of this book. We'll visit filters and regular expressions again in Part II when we examine the two heavyweights—**awk** and **perl**. In the next chapter, you'll see how filters are used in shell scripts.

WRAP UP

The **grep** filter searches a file for a pattern. You can ignore case when performing a match (-i) and select lines not containing the pattern (-v). You can also display a count (-c), the filenames (-l) and line numbers (-n). Multiple patterns can also be specified (-e) in the command line or placed in a separate file (-f).

grep can also be used with a *regular expression* using two sets of metacharacters—the *basic regular expression* set (BRE) and the *extended regular expression set* (ERE). **sed** doesn't use the extended set. All regular expressions must be quoted to prevent the shell from interfering.

In the BRE set, the . matches a single character, while * matches zero or more occurrences of the *previous* character. The character class is similar to the one used by wild-cards except that the ^ negates the class. The pattern .* matches anything and is often embedded in a regular expression. The ^ and $ serve as anchoring characters, and match a pattern at the beginning and end of a line, respectively.

grep uses the ERE with the -E option, but **egrep** does the same without requiring this option. The ERE uses the | to delimit multiple patterns and the (and) to group patterns. The + and ? are similar to the * used in the BRE except that they are more restrictive.

A **sed** instruction comprises an *address* and an *action* (command). Lines can be addressed by one or two line numbers or context patterns enclosed by /s. **sed** accepts multiple instructions which can be used to print lines from various sections of a file.

The action **p** prints a file, and the -n option makes sure that lines are not printed twice. Lines can be inserted (**i**), appended (**a**), changed (**c**) and deleted (**d**). Different segments of a file can be written to separate files too (**w**).

sed is mostly used for substitution (**s**). The g flag at the end makes the substitution global. The search and substitution patterns can be regular expressions, but only of the BRE type. A set of two slashes (//) as the source pattern represents the expression used for scanning a pattern (the *remembered pattern*). The & reproduces the entire source pattern at the target (the *repeated pattern*).

The *interval regular expression* (IRE) uses a single or a pair of numbers surrounded by escaped curly braces—like *ch*\{*m*,*n*\}. The expression signifies that *ch* can occur between *m* and *n* times. The *tagged regular expression* (TRE) uses \(and \) to enclose a pattern. The grouped pattern gets a tag \1, \2, etc. The feature is useful in reproducing a portion of the source pattern at the target.

TEST YOUR UNDERSTANDING

15.1 What do these commands do? (i) **grep a b c** (ii) **grep <HTML> foo**

15.2 What does **grep "^*"** look for? Is the \ really necessary?

15.3 What do these regular expressions match? (i) `a.*b` (ii) `^}$`

15.4 How do you locate lines containing these patterns? (i) `saxena` or `saksena` (ii) `rajiv`, `rajeeb` or `rajeev` (iii) `SIGSTOP` or `SIGTSTP`

15.5 Devise a command sequence to locate the line containing the last occurrence of a pattern.

15.6 Find out the name and designation of the youngest person in `emp.lst` *(14.1)* who is not a director.

15.7 Use extended regular expressions to extract all section headers from this book. (Each section is numbered.)

15.8 Write a Korn or Bash alias which lists only directories in the current directory.

15.9 How will you display, from all files in the current directory, lines containing the string `printf` or `fprintf` without prefixing the filename to each line?

15.10 How will you select from a file (i) lines 3 to 10 (ii) all but the last line?

15.11 How will you replace - with _ and vice versa using **sed**, assuming that that file doesn't contain any numerals?

15.12 How will you replace the string `Linux` with `Red Hat Linux`?

15.13 How do you add two spaces to the beginning of every line?

15.14 Invert the name of the individual in `emp.lst` so that the surname occurs first.

FLEX YOUR BRAIN

15.1 What is the difference between a wild-card and a regular expression?

15.2 How will you list the *ordinary* files in your current directory that are not user-writable?

15.3 What is the significance of this command? **grep -l "`echo '\t'`" foo**

15.4 Set a variable `kount` to store a count of the number of lines containing the word `HTML` in the files `foo1`, `foo2` and `foo3`.

15.5 Use command substitution with **grep** to list the names of the persons from `emp.lst` who were born today.

15.6 How do these expressions differ? (i) `[0-9]*` and `[0-9][0-9]*` (ii) `^[^^]` and `^^^`

15.7 Frame regular expressions to match these patterns: (i) `jefferies jeffery jeffreys` (ii) `hitchen hitchin hitching` (iii) `Heard herd Hird` (iv) `dix dick dicks dickson dixon` (v) `Mcgee mcghee magee`

15.8 How will you remove blank lines from a file using (i) **grep** and (ii) **sed**? (A blank line may contain either nothing or only whitespace characters.)

15.9 How do you locate lines containing only `printf` but not `fprintf` using (i) **grep** (ii) **sed**? (Note that `printf` can also occur at the beginning of a line.)

15.10 Locate lines longer than 100 and smaller than 150 characters using (i) **grep** (ii) **sed**.

15.11 Find out the occurrences of three consecutive and identical word characters (like `aaa` or `bbb`) using (i) **grep** and (ii) **sed**.

15.12 **`grep -c ENCRYPTION foo`** outputs the number of lines containing `ENCRYPTION`, but if the pattern sometimes occurs more than once in a line, how do you then obtain a count of all these *occurrences*? (HINT: Use **sed** also.)

15.13 Frame a command sequence that looks at romeo's mailbox to tell him that either he has received a message from henry or the `Subject:` line contains the word `urgent` or `immediate` in lower- or uppercase.

15.14 How do add the tags <HTML> at the beginning and </HTML> at the end of a file?

15.15 How do you delete all leading and trailing spaces in all lines of a file?

15.16 Explain what these commands do and if there's anything wrong with them:

```
 (i) sed -e 's/print/printf/g' -e 's/printf/print/g' foo
(ii) sed -e 's/compute/calculate/g' -e 's/computer/host/g' foo
```

15.17 Every `<B>` tag in an HTML file has a closing `</B>` tag as well. Convert them to `<STRONG>` and `</STRONG>`, respectively, using **sed** with a *single* **s** command.

16

Essential Shell Programming

The activities of the shell are not restricted to command interpretation alone. The shell has a whole set of internal commands that can be strung together as a language—with its own variables, conditionals and loops. Most of its constructs are borrowed from C, but they are often used differently from C. What makes shell programs powerful is that the external UNIX commands blend easily with the shell's internal constructs.

We need two chapters to discuss the programming features of the shell in some detail and to put them to productive use in real-world situations. In this chapter, we focus on the Bourne shell—the lowest common denominator of all shells. We have reserved the discussion of the advanced features of the Korn and Bash shells for Part II of the book. However, everything discussed here applies to both these shells too. The C shell uses totally different programming constructs and has been separately treated in Appendix A.

A shell program runs in *interpretive* mode. It is not compiled to a separate executable file as a C program is. Each statement is loaded into memory when it is to be executed. Shell scripts consequently run slower than those written in high-level languages. Speed is not a factor in many jobs we do, and in many cases, using the shell is an advantage—especially in system administrative tasks. *The UNIX system administrator must be an accomplished shell programmer.*

WHAT YOU WILL LEARN

- How shell scripts are executed, and the role of the *interpreter line*.
- Make shell scripts interactive using **read**.
- Use *positional parameters* to read command line arguments.
- The role of the **exit** statement in terminating a script.
- Elementary decision making with the || and && operators.
- Comprehensive decision making with the **if** conditional.
- Use **if** in tandem with **test** to perform numeric and string comparison, and test a file's attributes.
- Use the wild-card pattern matching features of **case** for decision making.
- Integer computing and string handling using **expr**.
- Use a **while** loop to repeatedly execute a set of commands.

- Use a **for** loop with a list.
- Manipulate the positional parameters with the **set** and **shift** statements.
- Use **trap** to control the behavior of a shell script when it receives signals.

TOPICS OF SPECIAL INTEREST

- Redirect some statements to /dev/tty so that the other statements can be manipulated separately.
- Exploit the hard linking feature with $0 to make a script behave in different ways depending on the name by which it is invoked.
- Use a *here document* as the fourth source of standard input to run any interactive shell script noninteractively.

16.1 SHELL SCRIPTS

When a group of commands have to be executed regularly, they should be stored in a file, and the file itself executed as a *shell script* or *shell program*. Though it's not mandatory, we normally use the .sh extension for shell scripts. This makes it easy to match them with wild-cards.

Shell scripts are executed in a separate child shell process, and this sub-shell need not be the same as your login shell. In other words, even if your login shell is Bourne, you can use a Korn sub-shell to run your script. By default, the child and parent shells belong to the same type, but you can provide a special *interpreter line* in the first line of the script to specify a different shell for your script.

Cautions Unless otherwise stated, all scripts in this chapter run without problem in the Bourne and Korn shells. There's only one problem you'll face when you use Bash. Several scripts here use **echo** with the \c and \n escape sequences. Bash doesn't recognize them unless you use **echo** with the -e option.

Use your **vi** editor to create the shell script, **script.sh** (Fig. 16.1). The script runs three **echo** commands and shows the use of variable evaluation and command substitution. It also prints the calendar of the current month.

```
#!/bin/sh
# script.sh: Sample shell script
echo "Today's date: `date`"
echo "This month's calendar:"
cal `date "+%m 20%y"`                      # This month's calendar
echo "My shell: $SHELL"
```

Fig. 16.1 script.sh

Note the comment character (#) that can be placed anywhere in a line; the shell ignores all characters placed on its right. However, this doesn't apply to the first line which also begins with a #. This is the *interpreter line* that was mentioned previously. It always begins with #! and is followed by the pathname of the shell to be used for running the script. Here, this line specifies the Bourne shell.

To run the script, make it executable first and then invoke the script name:

```
$ chmod +x script.sh
$ script.sh                                        Make sure that . is in PATH;
Today's date: Mon Jan  6 10:02:42 IST 2003         else use ./script.sh
This month's calendar:
    January 2003
Su Mo Tu We Th Fr Sa
          1  2  3  4
5  6  7  8  9 10 11
12 13 14 15 16 17 18
19 20 21 22 23 24 25
26 27 28 29 30 31

My shell: /bin/sh
```

The script is just too simple to require any explanation—no inputs, no command line arguments and no control structures. We'll be progressively adding these features to our future scripts.

We mentioned that shell scripts are executed by a child shell. Strictly speaking, the child shell simply reads and executes each statement in sequence (in interpretive mode). You can also *explicitly* spawn a child of your choice with the script name as argument:

```
sh script.sh                                       Will spawn a Bourne shell
```

When used in this way, *the script doesn't need to have executable permission*. The interpreter line is not required either.

> **Note** The interpreter line is not mandatory, and if you don't provide it, the login shell will spawn a child of its own type to run the script—which may not be the shell you want. We'll make it a practice to use the interpreter line in all our scripts.

16.2 read: MAKING SCRIPTS INTERACTIVE

The **read** statement is the shell's internal tool for taking input from the user, i.e., making scripts interactive. It is used with one or more variables. Input supplied through the standard input is read into these variables. When you use a statement like

```
read name
```

the script pauses at that point to take input from the keyboard. Whatever you enter is stored in the variable name. Since this is a form of assignment, no $ is used before name. The script, **emp1.sh** (Fig. 16.2), uses **read** to take a search string and filename from the terminal.

Shell scripts accept comments prefixed by # anywhere in a line. You know what the sequence \c does *(4.3)*. Run the script and specify the inputs when the script pauses twice:

```
#!/bin/sh
# emp1.sh: Interactive version - uses read to take two inputs
#
echo "Enter the pattern to be searched: \c"       # No newline
read pname
echo "Enter the file to be used: \c"              # Use echo -e in Bash
read flname
echo "Searching for $pname from file $flname"
grep "$pname" $flname
echo "Selected records shown above"
```

Fig. 16.2 emp1.sh

```
$ emp1.sh
Enter the pattern to be searched: director
Enter the file to be used: emp.lst
Searching for director from file emp.lst
9876|jai sharma       |director |production|12/03/50|7000
2365|barun sengupta   |director |personnel |11/05/47|7800
Selected records shown above
```

The script first asks for a pattern to be entered. Input the string `director`, which is assigned to the variable `pname`. Next, the script asks for the filename; enter the string `emp.lst`, which is assigned to the variable `flname`. **grep** then runs with these two variables as its arguments.

A single **read** statement can be used with one or more variables to let you enter multiple arguments:

```
read pname flname
```

If the number of arguments supplied is less than the number of variables accepting them, any leftover variables will simply remain unassigned. However, when the number of arguments exceeds the number of variables, the remaining words are assigned to the *last* variable.

16.3 USING COMMAND LINE ARGUMENTS

Like UNIX commands (which are written in C), shell scripts also accept arguments from the command line. They can, therefore, run noninteractively and be used with redirection and pipelines. When arguments are specified with a shell script, they are assigned to certain special "variables"—rather *positional parameters*.

The first argument is read by the shell into the parameter $1, the second argument into $2, and so on. You can't technically call them shell variables because all variable names start with a letter. In addition to these positional parameters, there are a few other special parameters used by the shell. Their significance is noted below:

- $* — It stores the complete set of positional parameters as a single string.
- $# — It is set to the number of arguments specified. This lets you design scripts that check whether the right number of arguments have been entered.
- $0 — Holds the command name itself. You can link a shell script to be invoked by more than one name. The script logic can check $0 to behave differently depending on the name by which it is invoked.

```
#!/bin/sh
# emp2.sh: Non-interactive version  - uses command line arguments
#
echo "Program: $0                    # $0 contains the program name
The number of arguments specified is $#
The arguments are $*"                # All arguments stored in $*
grep "$1" $2
echo "\nJob Over"
```

Fig. 16.3 `emp2.sh`

The next script, **emp2.sh** (Fig. 16.3), runs **grep** with two positional parameters that are set by the script arguments, `director` and `emp.lst`:

```
$ emp2.sh director emp.lst
Program: emp2.sh
The number of arguments specified is 2
The arguments are director emp.lst
1006|chanchal singhvi |director |sales      |03/09/38|6700
6521|lalit chowdury   |director |marketing  |26/09/45|8200

Job Over
```

When arguments are specified in this way, the first word (the command itself) is assigned to $0, the second word (the first argument) to $1, and the third word (the second argument) to $2. You can use more positional parameters in this way up to $9 (and using the **shift** statement, you can go beyond).

When you use a multiword string to represent a single command line argument, you must quote it. To look for `chanchal singhvi`, use **emp2.sh "chanchal singhvi" emp.lst**. You have noted this quoting requirement when using **grep** also *(15.1)*.

All assignments to the positional and special parameters are made by the shell. You can't really tamper with their values, except in an indirect fashion, but you can use them to great advantage in several ways. They will be used over and over again in shell scripts, and are listed in Table 16.1.

Table 16.1 Special Parameters Used by the Shell

Shell Parameter	*Significance*
$1, $2...	Positional parameters representing command line arguments
$#	Number of arguments specified in command line
$0	Name of executed command
$*	Complete set of positional parameters as a single string
"$@"	Each quoted string treated as a separate argument (recommended over $*)
$?	Exit status of last command
$$	PID of the current shell *(10.1.1)*
$!	PID of the last background job *(10.8.1)*

16.4 exit AND EXIT STATUS OF COMMAND

C programs and shell scripts have a lot in common, and one of them is that they both use the same command (or function in C) to terminate a program. It has the name **exit** in the shell and **exit()** in C. We'll take up the **exit** function in Part II of this book, but in this section, we'll examine the shell's **exit** command. The command is generally run with a numeric argument:

```
exit 0                                  Used when everything went fine
exit 1                                  Used when something went wrong
```

These are two very common **exit** values. You don't need to place this statement at the end of every shell script because the shell understands when script execution is complete. Rather, it's quite often used with a command when it fails.

Once **grep** couldn't locate a pattern *(15.1)*; we said then that the command *failed*. What we meant was that the **exit** function in the **grep** code was invoked with a nonzero argument (**exit(1)**). This value (1) is communicated to the calling program, usually the shell.

It's through the **exit** command or function that every command returns an *exit status* to the caller. Further, a command is said to return a *true* exit status if it executes successfully, and *false* if it fails. The **cat** command as used below:

```
$ cat foo
cat: can't open foo
```

returns a nonzero exit status because it couldn't open the file. The shell offers a variable ($?) and a command (**test**) that evaluates a command's exit status.

The Parameter $? The parameter $? stores the exit status of the last command. It has the value 0 if the command succeeds and a nonzero value if it fails. This parameter is set by **exit**'s argument. If no exit status is specified, then $? is set to zero (true). Try using **grep** in these ways and you'll see it returning three different exit values:

```
$ grep director emp.lst >/dev/null; echo $?
0                                            Success
$ grep manager emp.lst >/dev/null; echo $?
1                                            Failure—in finding pattern
$ grep manager emp3.lst >/dev/null; echo $?
grep: can't open emp3.lst                    Failure—in opening file
2
```

The exit status is extremely important for programmers. They use it to devise program logic that branches into different paths depending on the success or failure of a command. For example, there's no point in continuing with script execution if an important file doesn't exist or can't be read.

> **Tip** To find out whether a command executed successfully or not, simply use **echo $?** after the command. 0 indicates success, other values point to failure.

16.5 THE LOGICAL OPERATORS && AND ||—CONDITIONAL EXECUTION

The script **emp1.sh** has no logic to prevent display of the message, `Selected lines shown above`, when the pattern search fails. That is because we didn't use **grep**'s exit status to control the flow of the program. The shell provides two operators that allow conditional execution—the && and ||, which typically have this syntax:

```
cmd1 && cmd2
cmd1 || cmd2
```

The && delimits two commands; the command *cmd2* is executed only when *cmd1* succeeds. You can use it with **grep** in this way:

```
$ grep 'director' emp.lst && echo "pattern found in file"
1006|chanchal singhvi |director |sales       |03/09/38|6700
6521|lalit chowdury   |director |marketing   |26/09/45|8200
pattern found in file
```

The || operator plays an inverse role; the second command is executed only when the first fails. If you "grep" a pattern from a file without success, you can notify the failure:

```
$ grep 'manager' emp.lst || echo "Pattern not found"
Pattern not found
```

The || goes pretty well with the **exit** command. You often like to terminate a script when a command fails. The script **emp2.sh** can be modified to include this feature. The following two lines ensure that the program is aborted when the **grep** command fails, and a message is printed if it succeeds:

```
grep "$1" $2  || exit 2                     No point continuing if search fails
echo "Pattern found - Job Over"             Executed only if grep succeeds
```

This segment makes rudimentary decisions which the previous scripts couldn't. In fact, the && and || operators are recommended for making simple decisions. When complex decision making is involved, they have to make way for the **if** statement.

16.6 THE if CONDITIONAL

The **if** statement makes two-way decisions depending on the fulfillment of a certain condition. In the shell, the statement uses the following forms, much like the one used in other languages:

Form 1	Form 2	Form 3

`if` *command is successful*
`then`
   execute commands
`else`
   execute commands
`fi`
	`if` *command is successful*
	`then`
	   execute commands
	`fi`
		`if` *command is successful*
		`then`
		   execute commands
		`elif` *command is successful*
		`then ...`
		`else ...`
		`fi`

As in BASIC, **if** also requires a **then**. It evaluates the success or failure of the *command* that is specified in its "command line." If *command* succeeds, the sequence of commands following it is executed. If *command* fails, then the **else** statement (if present) is executed. This statement is not always required, as shown in Form 2. Every **if** is closed with a corresponding **fi**, and you'll encounter an error if one is not present.

What makes shell programming so powerful is that a command's exit status solely determines the course of action pursued by many of the shell's important constructs like **if** and **while**. All commands return an exit status as we saw with **cat** and **grep**, so you can imagine where shell programming can lead us.

In the next script, **emp3.sh** (Fig. 16.4), **grep** is first executed and a simple if–else construct tests the exit status of **grep**. This time we'll search /etc/passwd for the existence of two users; one exists in the file and the other doesn't:

```
#!/bin/sh
# emp3.sh: Using if and else
if grep "^$1" /etc/passwd 2>/dev/null    # Search username at beginning of line
   then
        echo "Pattern found - Job Over"
   else
        echo "Pattern not found"
fi
```

Fig. 16.4 **emp3.sh**

```
$ emp3.sh ftp
ftp:*:325:15:FTP User:/users1/home/ftp:/bin/true
Pattern found - Job Over
$ emp3.sh mail
Pattern not found
```

We'll discuss the third form of the **if** statement when we discuss **test**. The condition placed in the command line of the **if** statement will henceforth be referred to as the *control command*. You can use **if** in this way with any executable program. Amazing power indeed!

16.7 USING test AND [ ] TO EVALUATE EXPRESSIONS

When you use **if** to evaluate expressions, you require the **test** statement because the true or false values returned by expressions can't be *directly* handled by **if**. **test** uses certain operators to evaluate the condition on its right and returns either a true or false exit status, which is then used by **if** for making decisions. **test** works in three ways:

- Compares two numbers.
- Compares two strings or a single one for a null value.
- Checks a file's attributes.

These tests can be made by **test** in association with the shell's other statements also, but for the present we'll stick with **if**. **test** doesn't display any output but simply returns a value that sets the parameter $?. In the following sections, we'll actually check this value.

16.7.1 Numeric Comparison

The numerical comparison operators (Table 16.2) used by **test** have a form different from what you would have seen anywhere. They always begin with a - (hyphen), followed by a two-character word, and enclosed on either side by whitespace. Here's a typical operator:

-ne Not equal

The operators are quite mnemonic; -eq implies equal to, -gt implies greater than, and so on. Numeric comparison in the shell is confined to integer values only; decimal values are simply truncated. To illustrate how numeric tests are performed, we'll assign some values to three variables and numerically compare them:

```
$ x=5; y=7; z=7.2
$ test $x -eq $y ; echo $?
1                                          Not equal
$ test $x -lt $y ; echo $?
0                                          True
$ test $z -gt $y ; echo $?
1                                          7.2 is not greater than 7!
$ test $z -eq $y ; echo $?
0                                          7.2 is equal to 7!
```

The last two tests prove conclusively that numeric comparison is restricted to integers only. Having used **test** as a standalone feature, you can now use it as **if**'s control command. The next script, **emp3a.sh** (Fig. 16.5) uses **test** in an if–elif–else–fi construct (Form 3) to evaluate the shell parameter, $#. It displays the usage when no arguments are input, runs **grep** if two arguments are entered and displays an error message otherwise.

```
#!/bin/sh
# emp3a.sh: Using test, $0 and $# in an if-elif-if construct
#
if test $# -eq 0 ; then
     echo "Usage: $0 pattern file" >/dev/tty
elif test $# -eq 2 ; then
     grep "$1" $2 || echo "$1 not found in $2" >/dev/tty
else
     echo "You didn't enter two arguments" >/dev/tty
fi
```

Fig. 16.5 emp3a.sh

Why did we redirect the **echo** output to /dev/tty? We would like to be able to redirect the script itself to capture the **grep** output. We obviously want the **echo** statements to appear on the terminal and not in the file. These statements are being used as "error" messages even though they are not directed to the standard error. Now run the script four times and redirect the output every time:

```
$ emp3a.sh > foo
Usage: emp3a.sh pattern file
$ emp3a.sh ftp > foo
You didn't enter two arguments
$ emp3a.sh henry /etc/passwd > foo
henry not found in /etc/passwd
$ emp3a.sh ftp /etc/passwd > foo
$ cat foo
ftp:*:325:15:FTP User:/users1/home/ftp:/bin/true
```

The importance of /dev/tty as a mechanism of explicitly redirecting an output stream shows up in this example. You must appreciate this and use this feature in shell scripts where you may like to have the redirection option open. The above script works just as well even if you don't redirect it.

> **Tip** It's often advantageous to be able to redirect a shell script itself, especially if the script contains multiple statements whose output you would like to capture. In that case, make sure that other statements (like **echo**) should have their output directed to /dev/tty inside the script.

Table 16.2 Numerical Comparison Operators Used by **test**

Operator	*Meaning*
-eq	Equal to
-ne	Not equal to
-gt	Greater than
-ge	Greater than or equal to
-lt	Less than
-le	Less than or equal to

Shorthand for **test** **test** is so widely used that fortunately there exists a shorthand method of executing it. A pair of rectangular brackets enclosing the expression can replace it. Thus, the following two forms are equivalent:

```
test $x -eq $y
[ $x -eq $y ]
```

Note that you must provide whitespace around the operators (like -eq), their operands (like $x) and inside the [and]. The second form is easier to handle and will be used henceforth. But don't forget to be liberal in the use of whitespace here!

> **Note** It is a feature of most programming languages that you can use a condition like **if (x)**, where x is a variable. If x is greater than 0, the statement is said to be true. We can also apply the same logic here and use **if [$x]** as a shorthand form of **if [$x -gt 0]**.

16.7.2 String Comparison

test can be used to compare strings with yet another set of operators (Table 16.3). Equality is performed with = and inequality with the C-type operator !=. Other **test** checks can be negated by the ! too. Thus, [! -z $string] negates [-z $string].

Our next script, **emp4.sh** (Fig. 16.6) behaves both interactively and noninteractively. When run without arguments, it turns interactive and takes two inputs from you. It then runs **emp3a.sh**, the script developed previously, with the supplied inputs as arguments to the script. However, when **emp4.sh** itself is run with at least one argument, it runs **emp3a.sh** with the same arguments. In either case, **emp3a.sh** is run, which finally checks for the actual number of arguments entered before making a search with **grep**.

```
#!/bin/sh
# emp4.sh: Checks user input for null values - Finally runs emp3a.sh
#                                              developed previously
if [ $# -eq 0 ] ; then
   echo "Enter the string to be searched: \c"
   read pname
   if [ -z "$pname" ] ; then          # -z checks for a null string
      echo "You have not entered the string" ; exit 1
   fi
   echo "Enter the filename to be used: \c"
   read flname
   if [ ! -n "$flname" ] ; then       # ! -n is the same as -z
      echo "You have not entered the filename" ; exit 2
   fi
   emp3a.sh "$pname" "$flname"        # Runs the script that will do the job
else
   emp3a.sh $*                        # We'll change $* to "$@" soon
fi
```

Fig. 16.6 emp4.sh

When the script runs in the interactive mode, the check for a null string is made with [-z "$pname"] as well as with [! -n "$flname"], since they are really two different ways of saying the same thing. Note the use of $* in the noninteractive mode; this is the way you can use the same set of arguments to run another script. Very soon, we'll find a good reason to change $* to "$@". Let's first run the script interactively:

```
$ emp4.sh
Enter the string to be searched: [Enter]
You have not entered the string
$ emp4.sh
Enter the string to be searched: root
Enter the filename to be used: /etc/passwd
root:x:0:1:Super-User:/:/usr/bin/bash                    From emp3a.sh
```

See how two scripts cooperated in displaying root's entry from /etc/passwd. When we run the script with arguments, **emp4.sh** bypasses all the above activities and calls **emp3a.sh** to perform all validation checks:

```
$ emp4.sh jai
You didn't enter two arguments
$ emp4.sh jai emp.lst
9876|jai sharma        |director |production|12/03/50|7000
$ emp4.sh "jai sharma" emp.lst
You didn't enter two arguments
```

The last message could take you by surprise as jai sharma should have been treated as a single argument by the script. Indeed it is, but $* doesn't understand it as such; jai and sharma are embedded in $* as separate arguments. $# thus makes a wrong argument count. The solution to this is simple: Replace $* in the script with "$@" (with quotes) and then run the script again:

```
$ emp4.sh "jai sharma" emp.lst
9876|jai sharma        |director |production|12/03/50|7000
```

Tip Always use "$@" instead of $*. When you employ multiword strings as arguments to a shell script, it's only "$@" that interprets each quoted argument as a separate argument. As the output above suggests, if you use $*, the shell makes a wrong count of the arguments.

test also permits the checking of more than one condition in the same line, using the -a (AND) and -o (OR) operators. You can now simplify the earlier script to illustrate this feature. Accept both inputs in succession and then make the check with a compound **if** statement:

```
if [ -n "$pname" -a -n "$flname" ] ; then
   emp3a.sh "$pname" "$flname"
else
   echo "At least one input was a null string" ; exit 1
fi
```

The **test** output is true only if both variables are nonnull strings, i.e., the user enters some nonwhitespace characters when the script pauses twice.

Table 16.3 String Tests Used by **test**

Test	*True if*
s1 = *s2*	String *s1* = *s2*
s1 != *s2*	String *s1* is not equal to *s2*
-n *stg*	String *stg* is not a null string
-z *stg*	String *stg* is a null string
stg	String *stg* is assigned and not null
s1 == *s2*	String *s1* = *s2* (Korn and Bash only)

Tip Observe that we have been quoting our variables wherever possible. Quoting is essential when you assign multiple words to a variable. To try that out, drop the quotes to use the statement `if [ -z $pname ]`. When you input two words, or even a null string to be assigned to `pname`, you'll often encounter an error. Quoting is safe with no adverse consequences.

16.7.3 File Tests

test can be used to test the various file attributes like its type (file, directory or symbolic link) or its permissions (read, write, execute, SUID, etc.). Both **perl** and the UNIX system call library also offer these facilities (Table 16.4). Let's test some attributes of the file `emp.lst` at the prompt:

```
$ ls -l emp.lst
-rw-rw-rw-   1 kumar    group         870 Jun  8 15:52 emp.lst
$ [ -f emp.lst ] ; echo $?
0                                              An ordinary file
$ [ -x emp.lst ] ; echo $?
1                                              Not an executable
$ [ ! -w emp.lst ] || echo "False that file is not writable"
False that file is not writable
```

The `!` negates a test, so `[ ! -w foo ]` negates `[ -w foo ]`. Using these features, you can design a script, **filetest.sh** (Fig. 16.7), that accepts a filename as argument, and then performs a number of tests on it.

```
#!/bin/sh
# filetest.sh: Tests file attributes
#
if [ ! -e $1 ] ; then
    echo "File does not exist"
elif [ ! -r $1 ] ; then
    echo "File is not readable"
elif [ ! -w $1 ] ; then
    echo "File is not writable"
else
    echo "File is both readable and writable"
fi
```

Fig. 16.7 **filetest.sh**

Test the script with two filenames—one that doesn't exist and one that does:

```
$ filetest.sh emp3.lst
File does not exist
$ filetest.sh emp.lst
File is both readable and writable
```

This completes the discussion on the three domains of **test**—numeric comparison, testing of strings and file attributes. Even though we used **test** with the **if** statement in all our examples, **test** returns an **exit** status only, and can thus be used with any shell construct that uses an exit status. **test** also finds wide application in the **while** statement.

Table 16.4 File-related Tests with **test**

Test	*True if*
`-f` *file*	*file* exists and is a regular file
`-r` *file*	*file* exists and is readable
`-w` *file*	*file* exists and is writable
`-x` *file*	*file* exists and is executable
`-d` *file*	*file* exists and is a directory
`-s` *file*	*file* exists and has a size greater than zero
`-e` *file*	*file* exists *(Korn and Bash only)*
`-u` *file*	*file* exists and has SUID bit set
`-k` *file*	*file* exists and has sticky bit set
`-L` *file*	*file* exists and is a symbolic link *(Korn and Bash only)*
f1 `-nt` *f2*	*f1* is newer than *f2 (Korn and Bash only)*
f1 `-ot` *f2*	*f1* is older than *f2 (Korn and Bash only)*
f1 `-ef` *f2*	*f1* is linked to *f2 (Korn and Bash only)*

16.8 THE case CONDITIONAL

The **case** statement is the second conditional offered by the shell. It doesn't have a parallel either in C (**switch** is similar) or **perl**. The statement matches an expression for more than one alternative, and uses a compact construct to permit multiway branching. **case** also handles string tests, but in a more efficient manner than **if**. The general syntax of the **case** statement is as follows:

```
case expression in
      pattern1) commands1 ;;
      pattern2) commands2 ;;
      pattern3) commands3 ;;
        ....
esac
```

case first matches *expression* with *pattern1*. If the match succeeds, then it executes *commands1*, which may be one or more commands. If the match fails, then *pattern2* is matched, and so forth. Each command list is terminated with a pair of semicolons, and the entire construct is closed with **esac** (reverse of **case**).

Consider a simple script, **menu.sh** (Fig. 16.8) that uses **case**. The script accepts values from 1 to 5, and performs some action depending on the number keyed in. The five menu choices are displayed with a multiline **echo** statement.

case matches the value of `$choice` with the strings 1, 2, 3, 4 and 5. If the user enters a 1, the **ls -l** command is executed. Option `5` quits the program. The last option (*) matches any option not matched by by the previous options. We'll make good use of the * later.

```
#!/bin/sh
# menu.sh: Uses case to offer 5-item menu
#
echo "          MENU\n
1. List of files\n2. Processes of user\n3. Today's Date
4. Users of system\n5. Quit to UNIX\nEnter your option: \c"
read choice
case "$choice" in
    1) ls -l ;;
    2) ps -f ;;
    3) date  ;;
    4) who   ;;
    5) exit  ;;
    *) echo "Invalid option"        # ;; not really required for the last option
esac
```

Fig. 16.8 menu.sh

You can see today's date by choosing the third option:

```
$ menu.sh
          MENU
1. List of files
2. Processes of user
3. Today's Date
4. Users of system
5. Quit to UNIX
Enter your option: 3
Tue Jan  7 18:03:06 IST 2003
```

case can't handle relational and file tests, but it matches strings with compact code. It is also very effective when the string is fetched by command substitution. If you cut out the first field from the **date** output, you can use this **case** construct to do different things, depending on the day of the week:

```
case `date | cut -d" " -f1` in                          Outputs three-character day string
    Mon) tar -cvf /dev/fd0 $HOME ;;
    Wed) rcp -r $HOME mercury:/home/henry ;;
    Fri) find $HOME -newer .last_full_backup_time -print > tarilist ;;
      *) ;;
esac
```

case can also handle numbers, but only by treating them as strings. Some of our previous programs used **if** and **test** to check the value of `$#`. You can use **case** to match `$#` *directly* (without using **test**) with specific values (0, 1, 2. etc.), but you can't use it to make numeric checks (of the type `$# -gt 2`).

16.8.1 Matching Multiple Patterns

case can also specify the same action for more than one pattern. Programmers frequently encounter a logic that has to test a user response for both y and Y (or n and N). Like **grep -E** and **egrep**, **case** uses the | to delimit multiple patterns. For instance, the expression y|Y can be used to match y in both upper and lowercase:

```
echo "Do you wish to continue? (y/n): \c"
read answer
case"$answer" in
    y|Y) ;;                                   Null statement, no action to be performed
    n|N) exit ;;
esac
```

The same logic would require a larger number of lines if implemented with **if**. **case** becomes an automatic choice when the number of matching options is high.

16.8.2 Wild-Cards: case Uses Them

case has a superb string matching feature that uses wild-cards. It uses the filename matching metacharacters *, ? and the character class *(9.3)—but only to match strings and not files in the current directory*. The revised **case** construct of a previous example lets the user answer the question in several ways:

```
case "$answer" in
        [yY][eE]*) ;;                         Matches YES, yes, Yes, YEs, yES, etc.
         [nN][oO]) exit ;;                    Matches NO, no, nO and No
                *) echo "Invalid response"    When everything else fails
esac
```

Wild-card usage in the first two options appears simple enough. Note that the * appears in two options. In the first option, it behaves like a normal wild-card. In the last option, it provides a refuge for all other nonmatched options. Note that the last **case** option doesn't need ;; but you can provide them if you want.

16.9 expr: COMPUTATION AND STRING HANDLING

The Bourne shell can check whether an integer is greater than another, but it doesn't have any computing features at all. It has to rely on the external **expr** command for that purpose. This command combines two functions in one:

- Performs arithmetic operations on integers.
- Manipulates strings.

We'll use **expr** to perform both these functions, but with not-very-readable code when it comes to string handling. If you are using the Korn shell or Bash, you have better ways of handling these things *(24.7)*, but you must also understand the helplessness of Bourne. It's quite possible that you have to debug someone else's script which contains **expr**.

16.9.1 Computation

expr can perform the four basic arithmetic operations, as well as the modulus (remainder) function:

```
$ x=3 y=5                    Multiple assignments without a ;
$ expr 3 + 5
8
$ expr $x - $y
-2
$ expr 3 \* 5                Asterisk has to be escaped
15
$ expr $y / $x
1                            Decimal portion truncated
$ expr 13 % 5
3
```

The operand, be it +, -, * etc., must be enclosed on either side by whitespace. Observe that the multiplication operand (*) has to be escaped to prevent the shell from interpreting it as the filename metacharacter. Since **expr** can handle only integers, division yields only the integral part.

expr is often used with command substitution to assign a variable. For example, you can set a variable z to the sum of two numbers:

```
$ x=6 y=2 ; z=`expr $x + $y`
$ echo $z
8
```

Perhaps the most common use of expr is in incrementing the value of a variable. All programming languages have a shorthand method of doing that, and it is natural that UNIX should also have its own:

```
$ x=5
$ x=`expr $x + 1`            This is the same as C's x++.
$ echo $x
6
```

If you are using the Korn shell or Bash, then you can turn to Section 24.5 for a discussion on the **let** statement that both shells use to handle computation.

16.9.2 String Handling

Though **expr**'s string handling facilities aren't exactly elegant, Bourne shell users hardly have any choice. For manipulating strings, **expr** uses two expressions separated by a colon. The string to be worked upon is placed on the left of the :, and a regular expression is placed on its right. Depending on the composition of the expression, **expr** can perform three important string functions:

- Determine the length of the string.
- Extract a substring.
- Locate the position of a character in a string.

The Length of a String The length of a string is a relatively simple matter; the regular expression .* signifies to **expr** that it has to print the number of characters matching the pattern, i.e., the length of the entire string:

```
$ expr "abcdefghijkl" : '.*'                    Space on either side of : required
12
```

Here, **expr** has counted the number of occurrences of any character (.*). This feature is useful in validating data entry. Consider that you want to validate the name of a person accepted through the keyboard so that it doesn't exceed, say, 20 characters in length. The following **expr** sequence can be quite useful for this task:

```
while echo "Enter your name: \c" ; do              echo always returns true
    read name
    if [ `expr "$name" : '.*'` -gt 20 ] ; then
        echo "Name too long"
    else
        break                                      break terminates a loop
    fi
done
```

Extracting a Substring **expr** can extract a string enclosed by the escaped characters \(and \). If you wish to extract the 2-digit year from a 4-digit string, you must create a pattern group and extract it this way:

```
$ stg=2003
$ expr "$stg" : '..\(..\)'                         Extracts last two characters
03
```

Note the pattern group \(..\). This is the tagged regular expression (TRE) used by **sed** *(15.11.3)*, but it is used here with a somewhat different meaning. It signifies that the first two characters in the value of $stg have to be ignored and two characters have to be extracted from the third character position. (There's no \1 and \2 here.)

Locating Position of a Character **expr** can also return the location of the first occurrence of a character inside a string. To locate the position of the character d in the string value of $stg, you have to count the number of characters which are not d ([^d]*), followed by a d:

```
$ stg=abcdefgh ; expr "$stg" : '[^d]*d'
4
```

expr also duplicates some of the features of the **test** statement, and also uses the relational operators in the same way. They are not pursued here because **test** is a built-in feature of the shell, and is consequently faster. The Korn shell and Bash have built-in string handling facilities; they don't need **expr**. These features are taken up in Chapter 24.

16.10 $0: CALLING A SCRIPT BY DIFFERENT NAMES

In our discussion on links *(13.2.2)*, we raised the possibility of calling a file by different names and doing different things depending on the name by which it is called. In fact, there are a number of UNIX commands that do exactly that. Now that we know how to extract a string with **expr**, it's time we designed a single script, **comc.sh** (Fig. 16.9), that compiles, edits or runs the last modified C program. The script file will have three more names, but before developing it, let's understand the compiling mechanism used by the **cc** or **gcc** compiler.

A C program has the `.c` extension. When compiled with **cc** *filename*, it produces an executable file named **a.out**. However, we can provide a different name to the executable using the `-o` option, For instance, **cc -o foo foo.c** creates an executable named **foo**. We must be able to extract the "base" filename after dropping the extension, and with **expr** it should be a simple matter.

```
#!/bin/sh
# comc.sh: Script that is called by different names
#
lastfile=`ls -t *.c | head -1`
command=$0                          # Assigning a special parameter to a variable - OK
executable=`expr $lastfile : '\(.*\).c'`        # Removes .c; foo.c becomes foo
case $command in
       *runc) $executable ;;                    # Runs the executable
        *vic) vi $lastfile ;;
       *comc) cc -o $executable $lastfile &&
              echo "$lastfile compiled successfully" ;;
esac
```

Fig. 16.9 `comc.sh`

First, we store the name of the C program that was last modified in the variable `lastfile`. Next, we extract the base filename by dropping the `.c` extension using the TRE feature of **expr**. The **case** conditional now checks the name (saved in the variable command) by which the program is invoked. Observe that the first option (runc) simply executes the value evaluated by the variable `executable`. The only thing left to do now is to create three links:

```
ln comc.sh comc
ln comc.sh runc
ln comc.sh vic
```

Now you can run **vic** to edit the program, **comc** to compile it and **runc** to execute the object code. We'll only compile it here:

```
$ comc
hello.c compiled successfully
```

Note that this script works only with a C program that is stored, along with any functions, in one file. If functions are stored in separate files, this script won't work. In that case, **make** is the solution. **make** is discussed in Appendix B.

16.11 while: LOOPING

None of the pattern scanning scripts developed so far offers the user another chance to rectify a faulty response. Loops let you perform a set of instructions repeatedly. The shell features three types of loops—**while**, **until** and **for**. All of them repeat the instruction set enclosed by certain keywords as often as their control command permits.

The **while** statement should be quite familiar to most programmers. It repeatedly performs a set of instructions till the control command returns a true exit status. The general syntax of this command is as follows:

```
while condition is true
do                                          Note the do keyword
    commands
done                                        Note the done keyword
```

The *commands* enclosed by **do** and **done** are executed repeatedly as long as *condition* remains true. You can use any UNIX command or **test** as the *condition*, as before.

We'll start with an orthodox **while** loop application. The script, **emp5.sh** (Fig. 16.10), accepts a code and description in the same line, and then writes the line to `newlist`. It then prompts you for more entries. The loop iteration is controlled by the value of `$answer`.

```
#!/bin/sh
# emp5.sh: Shows use of the while loop
#
answer=y                        # Must set it to y first to enter the loop
while [ "$answer" = "y" ]                           # The control command
do
    echo "Enter the code and description: \c" >/dev/tty
    read code description                           # Read both together
    echo "$code|$description" >> newlist      # Append a line to newlist
    echo "Enter any more (y/n)? \c" >/dev/tty
    read anymore
    case $anymore in
        y*|Y*) answer=y ;;                          # Also accepts yes, YES etc.
        n*|N*) answer=n ;;                          # Also accepts no, NO etc.
            *) answer=y ;;                          # Any other reply means y
    esac
done
```

Fig. 16.10 **emp5.sh**

We have redirected the output of two **echo** statements to `/dev/tty` for reasons that will be apparent later. We'll make a small, but significant modification later, but let's run it first:

```
$ emp5.sh
Enter the code and description: 03 analgesics
Enter any more (y/n)? y
Enter the code and description: 04 antibiotics
Enter any more (y/n)? [Enter]                       No response, assumed to be y
Enter the code and description: 05 OTC drugs
Enter any more (y/n)? n
```

When you see the file `newlist`, you'll know what you have actually achieved:

```
$ cat newlist
03|analgesics
04|antibiotics
05|OTC drugs
```

Did redirection with /dev/tty achieve anything here? No, nothing yet, but after we make a small change in the script, it will. Note that you added a record to newlist with the >> symbol. This causes newlist to be opened every time **echo** is called up. The shell avoids such multiple file openings and closures by providing a redirection facility at the **done** keyword itself:

```
done > newlist
```

Make this change in the script and remove the redirection provided with the >> symbols. This form of redirection speeds up execution time as newlist is opened and closed only once. Because this action redirects the standard output of all commands inside the loop, we redirected some statements to /dev/tty so that they can't be redirected again at the **done** keyword.

Note Redirection is also available at the **fi** and **esac** keywords, and includes input redirection and piping:

`done < param.lst`	*Statements in loop take input from* param.lst
`done | while true`	*Pipes output to a* while *loop*
`fi > foo`	*Affects statements between* if *and* fi
`esac > foo`	*Affects statements between* case *and* esac

16.11.1 Using while to Wait for a File

Let's now consider an interesting **while** loop application. There are situations when a program needs to read a file that is created by another program, but it also has to wait till the file is created. The script, **monitfile.sh** (Fig. 16.11), periodically monitors the disk for the existence of the file, and then executes the program once the file has been located. It makes use of the external **sleep** command that makes the script pause for the duration (in seconds) as specified in its argument.

```
#!/bin/sh
# monitfile.sh: Waits for a file to be created
#
while [ ! -r invoice.lst ]         # while the file invoice.lst can't be read
do
   sleep 60                          # Sleep for 60 seconds
done
alloc.pl              # Execute this program after exiting the while loop
```

Fig. 16.11 **monitfile.sh**

The loop executes as long as the file invoice.lst can't be read (! -r means not readable). If the file becomes readable, the loop is terminated and the program **alloc.pl** is executed. This script is an ideal candidate to be run in the background like this:

```
alloc.pl &
```

We used the **sleep** command to check every 60 seconds for the existence of the file. **sleep** is also quite useful in introducing some delay in shell scripts.

16.11.2 Setting Up an Infinite Loop

Suppose you, as the system administrator, want to see the free space available on your disks every five minutes. You need an infinite loop, and it's best implemented by using **true** as a dummy control command with **while**. **true** does nothing except return a true exit status. Another command named **false** returns a false value. You can set up this loop in the background as well:

```
while true ; do                      This form is also permitted
   df -t                             df reports the free space on the disk
   sleep 300
done &                               & after done runs loop in background
```

With the job now running in the background, you can continue your other work, except that every five minutes you could find your screen filled with **df** output *(17.6.1)*. You can't use the interrupt key to kill it; you'll have to use **kill $!**, which kills the last background job *(10.8.1)*.

> **Note** The shell also offers an **until** statement which operates with a reverse logic used in **while**. With **until**, the loop body is executed as long as the condition remains *false*. Some people would have preferred to have written a previous **while** control command as **until [-r invoice.lst]**. This form is easily intelligible.

16.12 for: LOOPING WITH A LIST

The shell's **for** loop differs in structure from the ones used in other programming languages. There is no three-part structure as used in C, **awk** and **perl**. Unlike **while** and **until**, **for** doesn't test a condition, but uses a list instead:

```
for variable in list
do
   commands                          Loop body
done
```

The loop body also uses the keywords **do** and **done**, but the additional parameters here are *variable* and *list*. Each whitespace-separated word in *list* is assigned to *variable* in turn, and *commands* are executed until *list* is exhausted. A simple example can help you understand things better:

```
$ for file in chap20 chap21 chap22 chap23 ; do
>     cp $file ${file}.bak
>     echo $file copied to $file.bak
> done
chap20 copied to chap20.bak
chap21 copied to chap21.bak
chap22 copied to chap22.bak
chap23 copied to chap23.bak
```

The *list* here comprises a series of character strings (chap20 and onwards, representing filenames) separated by whitespace. Each item in the list is assigned to the variable `file`. `file` first gets the value chap20, then chap21, and so on. Each file is copied with a `.bak` extension and the completion message displayed after every file is copied.

16.12.1 Possible Sources of the List

The list can consist of practically any of the expressions that the shell understands and processes. `for` is probably the most often used loop in the UNIX system, and it's important that you understand it thoroughly.

List from Variables You can use a series of variables in the command line. They are evaluated by the shell before executing the loop:

```
$ for var in $PATH $HOME $MAIL ; do echo "$var" ; done
/bin:/usr/bin:/home/local/bin:/usr/bin/X11:.:/oracle/bin
/home/henry
/var/mail/henry
```

You have to provide the semicolons at the right places if you want to enter the entire loop in a single line. The three output lines represent the values of the three environment variables.

List from Command Substitution You can also use command substitution to create the list. The following **for** command line picks up its list from the file `clist`:

```
for file in `cat clist`
```

This method is most suitable when the list is large and you don't consider it practicable to specify its contents individually. It's also a clean arrangement because you can change the list without having to change the script.

List from Wild-cards When the list consists of wild-cards, the shell interprets them as *filenames*. **for** is thus indispensable for making substitutions in a set of files with **sed**. Take for instance this loop which works on every HTML file in the current directory:

```
for file in *.htm *.html ; do
   sed 's/strong/STRONG/g
   s/img src/IMG SRC/g' $file > $$
   mv $$ $file
   gzip $file
done
```

In this loop, each HTML filename is assigned to the variable `file` in turn. **sed** performs some substitution on each file and writes the output to a temporary file. This filename is numeric—expanded from the variable $$ (the PID of the current shell). The temporary file is written back to the original file with **mv**, and the file is finally compressed with **gzip**.

List from Positional Parameters **for** is also used to process positional parameters that are assigned from command line arguments. The next script, **emp6.sh** (Fig. 16.12), scans a file repeatedly for each argument. It uses the shell parameter `"$@"` (and not `$*`) to represent all command line arguments.

```
#!/bin/sh
# emp6.sh -- Using a for loop with positional parameters
#
for pattern in "$@" ; do                    # Decided not to use $* - Section 16.7.2
   grep "$pattern" emp.lst || echo "Pattern $pattern not found"
done
```

Fig. 16.12 **emp6.sh**

Execute the script by passing four arguments, one of which is a multiword string:

```
$ emp6.sh 2345 1265 "jai sharma" 4379
2345|j.b. saxena      |g.m.     |marketing |12/03/45|8000
1265|s.n. dasgupta    |manager  |sales     |12/09/63|5600
9876|jai sharma       |director |production|12/03/50|7000
Pattern 4379 not found
```

Since **for** is mostly used with "$@" to access command line arguments, a blank list defaults to this parameter. Thus, these two statements mean the same thing:

```
for pattern in "$@"
for pattern                                         "$@" is implied
```

Note that the script won't work properly if we replaced "$@" with $*. Make this change and then see for yourself how the script behaves.

16.12.2 basename: Changing Filename Extensions

We'll discuss yet another external command, **basename**, only because it's most effective when used inside a **for** loop. Working in tandem, they are quite useful in changing the extensions of a group of files. **basename** extracts the "base" filename from an absolute pathname:

```
$ basename /home/henry/project3/dec2bin.pl
dec2bin.pl
```

When **basename** is used with a second argument, it strips off the string from the first argument:

```
$ basename ux2nd.txt txt
ux2nd.                                              txt stripped off
```

You can now use this feature to rename filename extensions from txt to doc:

```
for file in *.txt ; do
  leftname=`basename $file txt`                     Stores left part of filename
  mv $file ${leftname}doc
done
```

If **for** picks up seconds.txt as the first file, leftname stores seconds (without a dot). **mv** simply adds a .doc to the extracted string (seconds). You don't need **expr** for this job at all!

16.13 set AND shift: MANIPULATING THE POSITIONAL PARAMETERS

Some UNIX commands like **date** produce single-line output. We also pass command output through filters like **grep** and **head** to produce a single line. Recall that we had to use an external command (**cut**) to extract a field from the **date** output *(16.8)*:

```
case `date | cut -d" " -f1` in
```

This is overkill; the shell has an internal command to do this job––the **set** statement. It assigns the positional parameters $1, $2, and so on, to its arguments. This feature is especially useful for picking up individual fields from the output of a program. But before we do that, let's use **set** to convert its arguments to positional parameters:

```
$ set 9876 2345 6213
$ _
```

This assigns the value 9876 to the positional parameter $1, 2345 to $2 and 6213 to $3. It also sets the other parameters $# and $*. You can verify this by echoing each parameter in turn:

```
$ echo "\$1 is $1, \$2 is $2, \$3 is $3"
$1 is 9876, $2 is 2345, $3 is 6213
$ echo "The $# arguments are $*"
The 3 arguments are 9876 2345 6213
```

We'll now use command substitution to extract individual fields from the **date** output without using **cut**:

```
$ set `date`
$ echo $*
Wed Jan 8 09:40:35 IST 2003
$ echo "The date today is $2 $3, $6"
The date today is Jan 8, 2003
```

The day of the week is available in $1. Using the **set** feature, the **case** construct simplifies to **case $1 in**.

> **Tip** **set** parses its arguments on the delimiters specified in the environment variable `IFS`, which, by default, is whitespace. You can change the value of this variable to make **set** work on a different delimiter. This means that you can easily extract any field in a line from `/etc/passwd` without using **cut**! One of our sample validation scripts *(16.7.1)* makes use of this feature.

16.13.1 shift: Shifting Arguments Left

Many scripts use the first argument to indicate a separate entity—say a filename. The other arguments could then represent a series of strings—probably different patterns to be selected from a file. For this to be possible, `for` should start its iteration from the second parameter onwards. This is possible with the **shift** statement.

shift transfers the contents of a positional parameter to its immediate lower numbered one. This is done as many times as the statement is called. When called once, $2 becomes $1, $3 becomes $2, and so on. Try this on the positional parameters filled up with the **date** command:

```
$ echo "$@"                                    Here, "$@" and $* are interchangeable
Wed Jan 8 09:48:44 IST 2003
$ echo $1 $2 $3
Wed Jan 8
$ shift
$ echo $1 $2 $3
Jan 8 09:48:44
$ shift 2                                      Shifts 2 places
$ echo $1 $2 $3
09:48:44 IST 2003
```

Note that the contents of the leftmost parameter, $1, are lost every time **shift** is invoked. In this way, you can access $10 by first shifting it and converting it to $9. So if a script uses twelve arguments, you can shift thrice and then use the ninth parameter. We require the set–shift duo for the next script, **emp7.sh** (Fig. 16.13), which is run with a filename and a set of patterns as arguments.

```
#!/bin/sh
# emp7.sh: Script using shift -- Saves first argument; for works with rest
#
case $# in
    0|1) echo "Usage: $0 file pattern(s)" ; exit 2 ;;
      *) flname=$1                      # Store $1 as a variable before it gets lost
         shift
         for pattern in "$@" ; do       # Starts iteration with $2
             grep "$pattern" $flname || echo "Pattern $pattern not found"
         done ;;
esac
```

Fig. 16.13 emp7.sh

Since the script requires at least two arguments, you should verify their presence before you act on the patterns. We stored $1 in the variable flname because the next **shift** operation would throw it away. Now you can use the script with a variable number of arguments (not less than 2):

```
$ emp7.sh emp.lst
Insufficient number of arguments
$ emp7.sh emp.lst saxena 1006 9876
2345|j.b. saxena     |g.m.      |marketing |12/03/45|8000
1006|chanchal singhvi |director |sales     |03/09/38|6700
Pattern 9876 not found
```

Here flname stores emp.lst, and the **for** loop iterates with the three strings, saxena, 1006, 9876.

> **Tip** Every time you use **shift**, the leftmost variable gets lost; so it should be saved in a variable before using **shift**. If you have to start iteration from the fourth parameter, save the first three parameters and then use **shift 3**.

16.13.2 set --: Helps Command Substitution

You'll often need to use **set** with command substitution. There's a small problem though, especially when the output of the command begins with a -:

```
$ set `ls -l unit01`
-rw-r--r--: bad option(s)
```

Since the permissions string begins with a - (for regular files), **set** interprets it as an option and finds it to be a "bad" one. **set** creates another problem when its arguments evaluate to a null string. Consider this command:

```
set `grep PPP /etc/passwd`
```

If the string PPP can't be located in the file, **set** will operate with no arguments and puzzle the user by displaying all variables on the terminal (its default output)! The solution to both these problems lies in the use of -- (two hyphens) immediately after **set**:

```
set -- `ls -l unit01`                    The first - now taken care of
set -- `grep PPP /etc/passwd`            Null output is no problem
```

set now understands that the arguments following -- are not to be treated as options. The two hyphens also direct **set** to suppress its default behavior if the arguments evaluate to a null string.

16.14 THE *HERE DOCUMENT* (<<)

There are occasions when the data your program reads is fixed and fairly limited. The shell uses the << symbols to read data from the same file containing the script. This is referred to as a *here document*, signifying that the data is here rather than in a separate file. Any command using standard input can also take input from a here document.

This feature is useful when used with commands that don't accept a filename as argument (like the **mailx** command, for instance). If the message is short (which any mail message is normally expected to be), you can have both the command and message in the same script:

```
mailx sharma << MARK
Your program for printing the invoices has been executed
on `date`. Check the print queue              Command substitution permitted
The updated file is known as $flname          Variable evaluation too
MARK                                          No spaces permitted here
```

The here document symbol (<<) is followed by three lines of data and a delimiter (the string MARK). The shell treats every line following the command and delimited by MARK as input to the command. sharma at the other end will see the three lines of message text with the date inserted by command substitution and the evaluated filename. The word MARK itself doesn't show up. When this sequence is placed inside a script, execution is faster because **mailx** doesn't have to read an external file; it's here.

> **Note** The contents of a here document are interpreted and processed by the shell before it goes as input to a command. This means you can use command substitution and variables in its input. You can't do that with normal standard input.

16.14.1 Using the Here Document with Interactive Programs

Many commands require input from the user. Often, it's the same input that is keyed in response to a series of questions posed by the command. For instance, you may have to enter a y two or three times when the command pauses, but the questions may not come in quick succession. Rather than wait for the prompt, we can instruct the script to take input from a here document.

We'll now attempt something that has far-reaching consequences. Recall that we used an interactive script **emp1.sh** *(16.2)* by keying in two parameters. We can make that script work noninteractively by supplying the inputs through a here document:

```
$ emp1.sh << END
> director
> emp.lst
> END
Enter the pattern to be searched: Enter the file to be used: Searching for direc
tor from file emp.lst
9876|jai sharma      |director |production|12/03/50|7000
2365|barun sengupta  |director |personnel |11/05/47|7800
Selected records shown above
```

Even though the prompts are displayed in a single line, the important thing is that the script worked. We have been able to run an interactive script noninteractively!

Tip If you write a script that uses the **read** statement, and which often assumes a predefined set of replies, you can make the script behave noninteractively by supplying its input from a here document.

16.15 trap: INTERRUPTING A PROGRAM

By default, shell scripts terminate whenever the interrupt key is pressed. It's not always a good idea to terminate shell scripts in this way because that can leave a lot of temporary files on disk. The **trap** statement lets you do the things you want in case the script receives a signal. The statement is normally placed at the beginning of a shell script and uses two lists:

trap '*command_list*' *signal_list*

When a script is sent any of the signals in *signal_list*, **trap** executes the commands in *command_list*. The signal list can contain the integer values or names (without the SIG prefix) of one or more signals—the ones you use with the **kill** command. So instead of using 2 15 to represent the signal list, you can also use INT TERM (the recommended approach).

If you habitually create temporary files named after the PID number of the shell, you should use the services of **trap** to remove them whenever an interrupt occurs:

```
trap 'rm $$* ; echo "Program interrupted" ; exit' HUP INT TERM
```

trap is a signal handler. Here, it first removes all files expanded from $$*, echoes a message and finally terminates the script when the signals SIGHUP (1), SIGINT (2) or SIGTERM (15) are sent to the shell process running the script. When the interrupt key is pressed, it sends the signal number 2. It's a good idea to include this number in your scripts.

You may also like to ignore the signal and continue processing. In that case, you should make the script ignore such signals by using a null command list. A script containing the following **trap** statement will not be affected by three signals; this time we'll use the signal numbers:

```
trap '' 1 2 15                    Script can't be killed by normal means
```

The Korn and Bourne shells don't execute a file on logging out, but using **trap**, you can make them do that. You'll have to use the signal name EXIT (or 0) as a component of the signal list. These shells also use the statement **trap -** to reset the signals to their default values. You can also use multiple **trap** commands in a script; each one overrides the previous one.

> **Note** It's not mandatory to have a **trap** statement in your shell scripts. However, if you have one, don't forget to include the **exit** statement at the end of the command list unless you want the script to ignore the specific signals.

16.16 DEBUGGING SHELL SCRIPTS WITH set -x

Apart from assigning values to positional parameters, **set** serves as a useful debugging tool with its -x option. When used inside a script (or even at the $ prompt), it echoes each statement on the terminal, preceded by a + as it is executed. Modify any previous script to turn on the **set** option by placing the following statement at the beginning of the script:

```
set -x
```

set +x turns off **set -x**, and you can place the latter statement at the end of the script. This is what you'll see when you invoke the script, **emp7.sh**, in the following manner:

```
$ emp7.sh emp.lst 2233 1265 0110
+ flname=emp.lst
+ shift
+ grep 2233 emp.lst
2233|a.k. shukla      |g.m.     |sales      |12/12/52|6000
+ grep 1265 emp.lst
1265|s.n. dasgupta    |manager  |sales      |12/09/63|5600
+ grep 0110 emp.lst
0110|v.k. agrawal     |g.m.     |marketing  |31/12/40|9000
```

This is an ideal tool to use if you have trouble finding out why scripts don't work in the manner expected. Note how the shell prints each statement as it is being executed, affixing a + to each. It even shows you what the **grep** command line looks like at every iteration!

16.17 SAMPLE VALIDATION AND DATA ENTRY SCRIPTS

It's time to consolidate our knowledge by devising two interactive shell scripts that accept input from the user. One script looks up a code list while the other adds an entry to a text database.

16.17.1 valcode.sh: Script to Look Up a Code List

This script, **valcode.sh** (Fig. 16.14), uses the **set** and **shift** features to accept and validate a department code. It looks up a code list maintained as a here document in the script file itself, and flashes the department name on the terminal.

```
#!/bin/sh
# valcode.sh: Uses a here document to look up a code list
#
IFS="|"                       # Reset field separator to pipe
while echo "Enter department code   : \c" ; do
    read dcode
    set -- `grep "^$dcode" << limit
01|accounts|6213
02|admin|5423
03|marketing|6521
04|personnel|2365
05|production|9876
06|sales|1006
limit`                        # Closing ` marks end of standard input

    case $# in
        3) echo "Department name          : $2\nEmp-id of head of dept : $3\n"
           shift 3 ;;         # Flush out the positional parameters
        *) echo "Invalid code"  ; continue
    esac
done
```

Fig. 16.14 valcode.sh

Since **echo** always produces a true exit status, the statement issuing the prompt is itself used as the control command of the **while** loop. The pattern selected by **grep** is split up on the | delimiter by **set** into three positional parameters. This is done by changing the IFS setting that normally consists of whitespace. **shift 3** flushes the positional parameters before starting the next iteration.

When you execute the script, this is how it behaves:

```
$ valcode.sh
Enter department code  : 99
Invalid code
Enter department code  : 02
Department name        : admin
Emp-id of head of dept : 5423

Enter department code  : 04
Department name        : personnel
Emp-id of head of dept : 2365

Enter department code  : [Ctrl-c]
```

The script doesn't terminate normally, but you can use the interrupt key at any time to abort the program.

16.17.2 dentry1.sh: A Data Entry Script

Our final script, **dentry1.sh** (Fig. 16.15), accepts a designation code and its description from the terminal, performs some rudimentary validation checks, and then adds an entry to a file (desig.lst). It validates the code entered with the ones that already exist in the file. The script repeatedly prompts the user till the right response is obtained.

Before you examine the script, you must know two keywords, **break** and **continue**, which are used by the shell's loops. They have their counterparts in the C language with the same names. **continue** suspends execution of all statements following it, and switches control to the top of the loop for the next iteration. **break**, on the other hand, causes control to break out of the loop.

```
#!/bin/sh
# dentry1.sh: Data entry script - Runs in a loop
#
trap 'echo Not to be interrupted' INT          # [Ctrl-c] won't work
trap 'echo Signal received ; exit' HUP TERM   # but these two signals will
file=desig.lst                              # The file that is looked up and appended to
while echo "Designation code: \c"  >/dev/tty ; do
    read desig
    case "$desig" in                  # First check if the code exists
    [0-9][0-9]) if grep "^$desig" $file >/dev/null ; then
                    echo "Code exists"
                    continue            # Go to loop beginning
                fi ;;
             *) echo "Invalid code"
                continue ;;
    esac

    while echo "Description       : \c"  >/dev/tty ; do
        read desc
        case "$desc" in
      *[!\ a-zA-Z]*) echo "Can contain only alphabets and spaces"  >/dev/tty
                     continue ;;         # Go to inner loop beginning
                 "") echo "Description not entered"  >/dev/tty
                     continue ;;
                  *) echo "$desig|$desc"
                     break              # Terminate this inner loop
        esac
    done >> $file                       # Appends to same file that is looked up

    echo "\nWish to continue? (y/n): \c"
    read answer
    case "$answer" in
        [yY]*) continue ;;              # Go to outer loop beginning
            *) break ;;                 # Terminate outer loop
    esac
done

echo "Normal exit"
```

Fig. 16.15 **dentry1.sh**

The script prompts for two fields, the designation code and the description, and uses two **while** loops, one enclosed by the other. The code has to be reentered if it exists in the file or if it doesn't have a two-digit structure. Similarly, the description has to be reentered if it contains a nonalphabetic character other than a space (`*[!\ a-zA-Z]*`). The **continue** statements let you reenter the data or start a fresh cycle. The **break** statement in the inner loop quits the loop after adding the line.

The logic becomes convincing after you undertake a dialog with the script, but before that let's see the entries in `desig.lst`:

```
$ cat desig.lst
01|accounts
02|admin
03|marketing
04|personnel
05|production
06|sales
$ dentry1.sh
Designation code: 01
Code exists
Designation code: 07
Description     : security officer

Wish to continue? (y/n): Y
Designation code: 8
Invalid code
Designation code: 08
Description     : vice president 1
Can contain only alphabets and spaces
Description     : vice president

Wish to continue? (y/n): n
Normal exit
```

When you see the last two lines of `desig.lst`, you'll see the two appended entries:

```
$ tail -2 desig.lst
07|security officer
08|vice president
```

The **while** structure is ideal for developing data entry shell scripts with extensive validation features. You have had a taste of this in this section. If you have found this script difficult, you should flip back and reassimilate the material. It isn't difficult at all, be assured.

16.18 CONCLUSION

This chapter presented the essential programming constructs offered by the shell. If you have written C programs, you can realize that the domain of shell programming is quite different from that of any high-level language. Shell scripts are ideal for integrating your existing applications. You should now be able to write scripts up to moderate complexity. If you are the system administrator, you'll need the services of shell scripting to automate the routine functions, using `cron` scheduling when needed. In Part II, we revisit the shell to consider its advanced features.

WRAP UP

The shell is also a programming language that executes shell scripts in the *interpretive mode*—one line at a time. It's customary to place the *interpreter line* as the first line of a script to signify the sub-shell that is to be used to run the script.

The **read** statement is used with one or more variables to provide input to a script from the keyboard. Command line arguments passed to a script are read into *positional parameters* (like `$1`, `$2`, etc.). `$#` stores the number of arguments. Both `$*` and `"$@"` contain all arguments, but use of `"$@"` is preferred. `$0` contains the name of the script itself.

The **exit** statement terminates a script. The numeric argument used with it is available in the shell's special variable, `$?`, and signifies *success* or *failure* of the command or the script.

The && and || operators are used as simple conditionals. The **if** statement has three forms, and is normally used with the **test** statement or its synonym `[ ]`. **test** can be used with operators to compare numbers and strings, as well as check the various file attributes.

case is a compact string matching construct. It accepts the shell's wild-cards for matching patterns, and can also match multiple patterns of the type used in extended regular expressions (ERE).

expr can perform basic integer computing (like incrementing a variable). It can also be used for extracting a substring and evaluating the length of a string.

All loops use the keywords **do** and **done**. A **while** loop is used for repeatedly executing a group of commands. The **for** loop iterates through a list which can be obtained from a variety of sources including command substitution. You can use **basename** inside a `for` loop to change the extensions of files. Both **while** and `for` use **continue** and **break** to control the loop iteration.

Redirection at the **done** keyword opens the file only once. In that case, all terminal-destined **echo** statements inside the construct must be separately directed with `>/dev/tty`.

set places values into positional parameters. Every time **shift** is invoked, the left-most parameter is lost, so it should be saved in a variable before using **shift**. **set --** is recommended for use when using command substitution. To debug shell scripts, use **set -x** at the beginning so that every command line is echoed to the screen.

The *here document* (<<) is used in the same script as the command to provide nominal standard input. It can be used with both command substitution and variables.

Use **trap** as a signal handler if you want your script to respond to a signal in a specific way. You can also make a script ignore signals by using a null command list.

TEST YOUR UNDERSTANDING

16.1 If you have developed a script using the Korn shell, how will you make sure the script will use that shell even if the login shell is different?

16.2 If a script is run as **foo -l -t bar[1-3]**, what are the values of `$#` and `$*` ? Does it make any difference if the options are combined?

16.3 What is the *exit status* of a command? What is its normal value and where is the value stored?

16.4 Develop script logic that allows only romeo and henry to execute a program, and only from the terminals `tty05` and `tty06`.

16.5 A script named **test** containing the **df** and **du** commands displays nothing when executed. Why does that happen? State two ways of making the script behave properly.

16.6 Search for a pattern with **grep** and **sed** and look for a file with **find**. Test the return value of each command when it displays no output. What conclusions would you draw?

16.7 Write shell code to accept a string from the terminal, and echo a suitable message if it doesn't have at least 10 characters using (i) **case** (ii) **expr**.

16.8 Use **expr** to extract the parent directory from the absolute pathname of a file.

16.9 Write a script that accepts a filename as argument and displays the last modification time if the file exists and a suitable message if it doesn't.

16.10 Devise a script that accepts two directory names, `bar1` and `bar2`, and deletes those files in `bar2` which are identical to their namesakes in `bar1`.

16.11 Modify the script **comc.sh** (Fig. 16.9) to also accept a `.c` filename as argument. In that case, it won't work on the last modified file. The script should remove the `.c` extension in the executable.

16.12 Write a shell script that searches for a pattern (supplied as argument) in all files in the current directory and then calls up the **vi** editor with those files containing the pattern. How will you repeat the search in the current file and other files?

16.13 What will this construct do and why?—**while [5]**

16.14 Write a script that accepts one or more filenames as arguments, and converts them all to uppercase provided they exist in the current directory.

16.15 How will you make sure that a script prompts you before exiting on interruption?

FLEX YOUR BRAIN

16.1 Devise a script that takes a filename as argument (which must exist in the current directory) and locates from your home directory tree all pathnames of its links. The list should be mailed to self.

16.2 Use a script to take two numbers as arguments and output their sum using (i) **bc** (ii) **expr**. Include error-checking to test whether two arguments were entered.

16.3 Write a script that lists files by modification time when called with **lm** and by access time when called with **la**. By default, the script should show the listing of all files in the current directory.

16.4 Expand the scope of the script in 16.12 (Test Your Understanding) to perform the search recursively.

16.5 Write a script that behaves both in interactive and noninteractive mode. When no arguments are supplied, it picks up each C program from the current directory and lists the first 10 lines. It then prompts for deletion of the file. If the user supplies arguments with the script, then it works on those files only.

16.6 Display the processes in the system every 30 seconds five times using a (i) **while** loop (ii) **for** loop. What is the unusual feature of the **for** loop?

16.7 You are moving files to a handheld which accepts only 8+3 type filenames. Produce a list of those files in your current directory that fail in this test.

16.8 Write a script that displays a special listing showing the (i) permissions (ii) size (iii) filename (iv) last modification time (v) last access time of filenames supplied as arguments. Provide suitable headers using the **printf** command.

16.9 Find out the pathname of the Korn shell on your machine and then change the interpreter line in all shell scripts in the current directory that show a different pathname for **ksh**.

16.10 Add the statement `#include <stdio.h>` at the beginning of every C source file in the current directory containing `printf` or `fprintf`, if it doesn't already have it included.

16.11 Write a script that compares two directories `bar1` and `bar2` (supplied as arguments) and copies or overwrites to `bar1` from `bar2` every file that is (i) not present in `bar1` or (ii) newer than its namesake in `bar1`. (HINT: Use the **find** command.)

16.12 You have a number of C programs that contain comment lines at the beginning of each program. The lines begin with /* followed by the first line of comment, but the terminator line has */ as the *only* characters in the line. Remove these comments from all files.

16.13 Write a shell script that uses **find** to look for a file and echo a suitable message if the file is not found. You must not store the **find** output in a file.

16.14 Devise a script that allows a user to view, add, delete or modify a setting in a configuration file that contains these settings in the form *variable=value*.

16.15 Devise a script that creates a lock file which prevents more than one user from running it. The lock file must be removed before script termination or if the user presses the interrupt key.

16.16 Assume that you have a number of files, downloaded from the Internet, in the `/home/kumar/download` directory. The table of contents (TOC) is available in the file `TOC_download.txt` in the form *filename:description*. The script should check each file in the `download` directory that doesn't have a description in the TOC file and prompt the user for the description. The TOC should be updated to maintain the list in sorted condition. The script must be immune to signals.

17

Essential System Administration

As the concluding act for Part I of this book, it's time to make a visit to the world of system administration. This task is usually entrusted to a single person—the *system administrator*, also known as the *superuser* or *root user*. The administrator has vast powers, having access to practically everything. The success and stability of any UNIX installation depends, in great measure, on the effectiveness of the system administrator. Today, every user must know some of the important administrative functions that she may be called upon to perform at any time.

The job of system administration involves the management of the entire system—ranging from maintaining user accounts, security and managing the disk space to performing backups. The burden is not overwhelming though because UNIX is more easily maintained and well documented than most other systems. However, UNIX gets greatly fragmented in this area, and POSIX makes no attempt to address administrative issues. We consider the routine duties in this chapter and the more involved ones in Chapter 27.

WHAT YOU WILL LEARN

- Log in to root and become a superuser with **su**.
- The administrator's powers in changing the attributes of any file and in killing any process.
- Control access to the scheduling services, **at** and **cron**.
- Create, modify and delete user accounts with **useradd**, **usermod** and **userdel**.
- The concept of *run levels* and their role in startup and shutdown operations.
- Use **df** and **du** to report on both free and used disk space.
- Format and copy diskettes with **format**, **fdformat** and **dd**.
- Handle DOS files on diskettes with a set of "dos" commands.
- Use **cpio** to back up and restore files.
- Use **tar** to back up a directory tree and append files to an archive.

TOPICS OF SPECIAL INTEREST

- The significance of the three special file permissions bits—*SUID*, *SGID* and *sticky bit* and how the administrator uses them in enforcing security.
- Understanding how disk read/write takes place and the significance of the attributes of device files.

17.1 root: THE SYSTEM ADMINISTRATOR'S LOGIN

The UNIX system provides a special login name for the exclusive use of the administrator; it's called *root*. This account doesn't need to be separately created, but comes with every system. Its password is generally set at the time of installation of the system and has to be used on logging in:

```
login: root
password: *******[Enter]
# _
```

The prompt of root is #, unlike the $ or % used by the nonprivileged users. Once you log in as root, you are placed in root's home directory. Depending on the system, this directory could be / or /root.

On modern systems, most administrative commands are resident in /sbin and /usr/sbin, but if you are using an older system, you could find them in /etc. root's PATH list is also different from other users:

```
/sbin:/bin:/usr/sbin:/usr/bin:/usr/dt/bin
```

Since the superuser has to constantly navigate the file system, it's possible that he might inadvertently execute programs and scripts written by other users. That's why the PATH for a superuser doesn't include the current directory.

Many of the standard scripts supplied with UNIX systems for system administration work (especially the scripts related to booting) rely on the Bourne shell for execution. As an administrator, you have to carefully weigh the consequences of using the Korn shell since scripts developed under this shell may not run on another host, which may not have this shell. But you must not under any circumstances use C shell scripts. Linux uses Bash for normal and system administrative activities; there's no problem there.

17.1.1 su: Acquiring Superuser Status

Any user can acquire superuser status with the **su** command if she knows the root password. For example, the user juliet (with the home directory /home/juliet) becomes a superuser in this way:

```
$ su
Password: ********                    root's password
# pwd
/home/juliet                          Prompt changes, but directory doesn't
```

Though the current directory doesn't change, the # prompt indicates that juliet now has powers of a superuser. To be in the root directory on superuser login, use **su -l**.

Creating a User's Environment Users often rush to the administrator with the complaint that a program has stopped running. The administrator first tries running it in a simulated environment. **su**, when used with a -, recreates the user's environment without taking the login-password route:

```
su - henry                            No password required
```

This sequence executes henry's .profile (or the relevant startup scripts), and temporarily creates henry's environment. **su** runs a separate sub-shell, so this mode can be terminated by hitting *[Ctrl-d]* or using **exit**.

17.2 THE ADMINISTRATOR'S PRIVILEGES

The superuser has enormous powers, and any command invoked by him has a greater chance of success than when issued by others. The command may also behave differently. Moreover, there are several commands reserved for his exclusive use. The superuser authority is mainly derived from the power to

- Change the contents or attributes of any file like its permissions and ownership. He can delete any file with **rm** even if it is write-protected!
- Initiate or kill any process. The administrator can directly kill all processes except the ones essential for running the system.
- Change any user's password without knowing the existing one.
- Set the system clock with **date**.
- Address all users concurrently with **wall**.
- Limit the maximum size of files that users are permitted to create with **ulimit**.
- Control users' access to the scheduling services like **at** and **cron**.
- Control users' access to many networking services like Telnet, Ftp, etc.

The administrator has to use these powers with utmost caution. An apparently innocent and unplugged loophole can cause disaster if that knowledge is acquired by a mischievous person. Let's now see how the administrator exercises some of the powers listed above.

17.2.1 date: Setting the System Date

We have used **date** as a "passive" command before *(4.2)*—to display the system date. In the hands of the administrator, the same command is used with a numeric argument to actually *set* the system date. This argument is usually an eight-character string of the form *MMDDhhmm*, optionally followed by a two- or four-digit year string:

```
# date 01092124
Thu Jan  9 21:24:00 IST 2003
```

UNIX systems will continue to understand the century for some time (till the year 2038, at least). Ensure that the date is reasonably accurate as the **cron** scheduler *(10.11)* uses the clock time to run jobs.

17.2.2 wall: Communicating with Users

The **wall** command addresses all users simultaneously. Most UNIX systems don't permit users to use this command (Linux excepted), and reserve it for the sole use of the administrator:

```
# wall
The machine will be shut down today
at 14:30 hrs. The backup will be at 13:30 hrs
[Ctrl-d]
```

All users currently logged in will receive this message on their terminal. The **mesg** setting *(12.3)* is ignored by **wall**. This command is routinely executed by the administrator—especially before shutdown of the system.

17.2.3 ulimit: Setting Limits on File Size

Faulty programs or negligence can eat up disk space in no time. The **ulimit** command (now a builtin in all shells) imposes a restriction on the maximum size of a file that a user is permitted to create. Though an ordinary user can only reduce this default value, the superuser can increase it:

```
ulimit 20971510                              Measured in 512-byte blocks
```

You'll often place this statement in /etc/profile so that every user has to work within these restrictions. When used by itself, **ulimit** displays the current setting. Solaris and Linux show unlimited as the default output, but it could be different on your system.

17.2.4 Controlling Use of at and cron

The access to the use of **at** and **batch** is restricted and controlled by the files at.allow and at.deny in /etc/cron.d (/etc in Linux). If at.allow is present, only the users listed in the file are permitted to use **at** and **batch**. If it is not present, the system checks at.deny for users who are barred from using these commands. If neither file is present, only the system administrator is permitted to invoke **at** and **batch**.

The **cron** scheduler *(10.11)* is used by the administrator to make commands like **find** and **du** compile useful information about the system, or for automating the backup operations. Like **at** and **batch**, the authorization to use it is controlled in identical manner by two files, cron.allow and cron.deny, in /etc/cron.d (/etc in Linux).

17.3 MAINTAINING SECURITY

Because security in a computer system eventually involves files, a faulty file permission can easily be exploited by a malicious user in a destructive manner. As administrator, you have to ensure that the system directories (/bin, /usr/bin, /etc, /sbin etc.) and the files in them are not writable by others. We'll now discuss some important security-related features found on a UNIX system.

17.3.1 passwd: Changing Any Password

passwd prompts for the existing password when the command is used by a nonprivileged user *(4.7)* However, when the superuser uses the command, the system behaves in a more lenient manner:

```
# passwd
Changing password for root
Enter the new password (minimum of 5, maximum of 8 characters)
Please use a combination of upper and lower case letters and numbers.
New password: *********
Re-enter password: *********                          To be entered twice
Password changed.
```

Note that the system doesn't prompt for the old password this time. The administrator must closely guard the superuser password. Otherwise, the entire UNIX system may have to be reloaded! UNIX also allows the administrator the privilege of changing anybody's password without knowing it:

```
passwd henry
```

Once again, the old password is not prompted for; the new one has only to be entered twice. As users often give out their passwords to others, passwords tend to be known to others over time. What makes matters worse is that users themselves are quite averse to changing their own passwords. The **passwd** command offers features that force users to change their passwords after a specific time (not discussed in this text).

> **Note** **passwd** doesn't prompt for the old password when the command is used by the superuser for changing the root password.

17.3.2 Set-User-Id (SUID): Power for a Moment

Recall the discussions on process attributes *(10.4)* where we mentioned that sometimes the *effective UID* may not be the same as the *real UID*. The time has now come to discuss a security feature which exploits this fact. Many UNIX programs have a special permissions mode that lets users update sensitive system files—like /etc/shadow—something they can't do directly with an editor. This is true of the **passwd** program:

```
-rwsr-xr-x   1 root     shadow        34808 Nov 30 17:55 /usr/bin/passwd
```

The letter s in the user category of the permissions field represents a special mode known as the *set-user-id* (SUID). This mode lets a process have the privileges of the *owner* of the file during the instance of the program. Thus when a nonprivileged user executes **passwd**, the *effective* UID of the process is not the user's, but of root's—the owner of the program. This SUID privilege is then used by **passwd** to edit /etc/shadow.

The SUID for any file can be set only by the superuser with a special syntax of the **chmod** command. This syntax uses the character s as the permission:

```
# chmod u+s a.out ; ls -l a.out
-rwsr-xr-x   1 root     staff        2113 Mar 24 11:18 a.out
```

To assign SUID in an absolute manner, simply prefix 4 to whatever octal string you would otherwise use (like 4755 instead of 755). The *set-group-id* (SGID) is similar to SUID except that a program with SGID set allows the user to have the same power as the group which owns the program. The SGID bit is 2, and some typical examples could be **chmod g+s a.out** or **chmod 2755 a.out**.

The SUID mechanism, invented by Dennis Ritchie, is a potential security hazard. It lets a user acquire hidden powers by running such a file owned by root. As administrator, you must keep track of all SUID programs owned by root that a user may try to create or copy. The **find** command easily locates them:

```
find /home -perm -4000 -print | mail root
```

The extra octal bit (4) signifies the SUID mode, *but* **find** *treats the - before* 4000 *as representing any other permissions*. You can use **cron** to run this program at regular intervals and mail the file list to root.

> **Note** The fourth permission bit is used only when a special mode of a file needs to be set. It has the value 4 for SUID, 2 for SGID and 1 for the sticky bit. The other 3 bits have their usual significance.

17.3.3 The Sticky Bit

The *sticky bit* (also called the *saved text bit*) is the last permission bit remaining to be discussed. It applies to both regular files and directories. When applied to a regular file, it ensures that the text image of a program with the bit set is permanently kept in the swap area so that it can be reloaded quickly when the program's turn to use the CPU arrives. Previously, it made sense to have this bit set for programs like **vi** and **emacs**. Today, machines with ultra-fast disk drives and lots of cheap memory don't need this bit for ordinary files. This bit is still set for the **emacs** editor (not discussed in this text).

However, the sticky bit becomes a useful security feature when used with a directory. The UNIX system allows users to create files in /tmp and /var/tmp, but no one can delete files not owned by her. Strange, isn't it? That's possible because both directories have their sticky bits set:

```
# ls -ld /tmp /var/tmp
drwxrwxrwt   5 root      sys          377 Jan  9 13:28 /tmp
drwxrwxrwt   2 root      sys         7168 Jan  9 13:34 /var/tmp
```

The directories are *apparently* writable by all, but that extra t (sticky) bit ensures that kumar can't remove sharma's files in these directories. Using **chmod**, you can set the bit on a directory by using 1 as the additional bit:

```
# chmod 1775 bar                                         Or chmod +t bar
# ls -l bar
drwxrwxr-t   2 sumit    dialout       1024 Apr 13 08:25 bar
```

The sticky bit is extremely useful for implementing group projects. To let a group of users work on a set of files without infringing on security, you'll have to do this:

1. Create a common group for these users in /etc/group.
2. Create separate user accounts for them but specify the same home directory.
3. Make sure the home directory and all subdirectories are not owned by any of the users. Use **chown** to surrender ownership to root.
4. Make the directories group-writable and set their sticky bits with **chmod 1775**.

In this scenario, every user of the group has write permission on the directory and can create files and directories, but can only delete those she owns. A very useful feature indeed!

17.4 USER MANAGEMENT

The term *user* in UNIX is not meant to be only a person; it can represent a project or an application as well. A group of users performing similar functions may use the same username to use the system. It's thus quite common to have usernames like marketing, accounts, and so forth. For the creation and maintenance of user accounts, UNIX provides three commands—**useradd**, **usermod** and **userdel**.

When opening a user account, you have to associate the user with a group. A group usually has more than one member with a different set of privileges. People working on a common project should be able to read one another's files, which is possible only if they belong to the same group.

Creating a user involves defining the following parameters:

- A user identification number (UID) and username.
- A group identification number (GID) and group name.
- The home directory.
- The login shell.
- The mailbox in `/var/mail`.
- The password.

Most of these parameters are found in a single line identifying the user in `/etc/passwd`. We'll now create a group for a user and then add that user to the system.

17.4.1 groupadd: Adding a Group

If the user is to be placed in a new group, an entry for the group has to be created first in `/etc/group`. A user always has one primary group and may also have one or more *supplementary groups*. This file contains all the named groups of the system, and a few lines of this file reveal the structure:

```
root:x:0:root
bin:x:1:root,bin,daemon
lp:x:7:
uucp:x:14:uucp,fax,root,fnet,sumit
users:x:100:henry,oracle,image,enquiry
```

Each line contains four colon-delimited fields. Let's focus our attention on the group named users shown in the first field. This is the same name you see in the group ownership column of the listing. The second field once represented the group password but is hardly used today; it is either blank or an `x`. The third field shows the user's GID (here, 100). The last field contains a list of comma-delimited usernames (`henry,oracle,image,enquiry`) for whom this is the supplementary group. A blank at this position doesn't mean that no one is a member of this group; it's just that it's not the supplementary group for any user. Note that primary group for a user is shown in `/etc/passwd`.

To create a new group, dba, with a GID of 241, you have to use the **groupadd** command:

```
groupadd -g 241 dba                    241 is the GID for dba
```

The command places this entry in `/etc/group` which you can also insert manually:

```
dba:x:241:
```

Once an entry for the group has been made, you are now ready to add a user of this group to the system.

17.4.2 useradd: Adding a User

The **useradd** command adds new users to the system. All parameters related to the user have to be provided in the command line itself:

```
# useradd -u 210 -g dba -c "THE RDBMS" -d /home/oracle -s /bin/ksh -m oracle
# _
```

This quietly creates the user oracle with a UID of 210 and group name dba. The home directory is `/home/oracle`, and the user will use the Korn shell. The `-m` option ensures that the home directory is created if it doesn't already exist and copies a sample `.profile` and `.kshrc` to the user's home directory. The line **useradd** creates in `/etc/passwd` is shown below:

```
oracle:x:210:241:THE RDBMS:/home/oracle:/bin/ksh
```

useradd also sets up the user's mailbox and sets the `MAIL` variable to point to that location (in `/var/mail` or `/var/spool/mail`). You now have to set the new user's password with the command **passwd oracle**. Once all this is done, the oracle user account is ready for use.

17.4.3 /etc/passwd and /etc/shadow: User Profiles

All user information except the password encryption is now stored in `/etc/passwd`. This file contained the password once, the reason why it continues to be known by that name. The encryption itself is stored in `/etc/shadow`. This is now the control file used by **passwd** to ascertain the legitimacy of a user's password.

Let's take the line pertaining to oracle in `/etc/passwd`. There are seven fields here, and their significance is noted below (in the order they appear in `/etc/passwd`):

- Username—The name you use to log on to a UNIX system (oracle).
- Password—No longer stores the password encryption but contains an `x`.
- UID—The user's numerical identification (210). No two users *should* have the same UID.
- GID—The user's numerical group identification (241). This number is also the third field in `/etc/group`. Commands like **ls** read this file to print the group name.
- Comment or GCOS—User details, e.g., her name, address and so forth (The RDBMS). This name is used at the front of the email address for this user. Any mail sent from this user account will show the sender as *"The RDBMS" <oracle@heavens.com>*—assuming that the user belongs to the domain shown.
- Home directory—The directory where the user ends up on logging in (`/home/oracle`). The variable `HOME` is set by the **login** program by reading this field.
- Login shell—The first program executed after logging in. This is usually the shell (`/bin/ksh`). **login** also sets the variable `SHELL` by reading this entry, and also fork-execs the shell process *(10.4.1)*.

For every line in `/etc/passwd`, there's a corresponding entry in `/etc/shadow`. The relevant line in this file could look something like this:

```
oracle:PR1hjiDhRM2Lg:12032:::::
```

The password encryption is shown in the second field. It's impossible to generate the password from this encryption. However, an intelligent hacker can use an encryption algorithm to generate a sequence of encrypted patterns. It's quite possible that she might just find a match, so this file must be made unreadable to all but the superuser.

> **Note** The last field in `/etc/passwd` is actually the command that has to be executed when a user logs in. This is usually the shell, but the administrator may choose a different program to restrict the user's actions (like **`uucico`**).

17.4.4 `usermod` and `userdel`: Modifying and Removing Users

`usermod` is used for modifying some of the parameters set with **`useradd`**. Users sometimes need to change their login shell, and the following command line sets Bash as the login shell for the user oracle:

```
usermod -s /bin/bash oracle                    Use if chsh is not available
```

Users are removed from the system with **`userdel`**. The following command removes the user oracle from the system:

```
userdel oracle                                 Doesn't delete user's files
```

This removes all entries pertaining to oracle from `/etc/passwd`, `/etc/group` and `/etc/shadow`. The user's home directory doesn't get deleted in the process and has to be removed separately if required.

17.5 STARTUP AND SHUTDOWN

Startup After a machine is powered on, the system looks for all peripherals and then goes through a series of steps that may take up to a few minutes to complete the boot cycle. The exact sequence is system-dependent, but the first major event is the loading of the kernel (**`/kernel/genunix`** in Solaris and **`/boot/vmlinuz`** in Linux) into memory. The kernel then spawns **`init`** (PID 1) which, in turn, spawns further processes. Some of these processes monitor all the terminal lines, activate the network and printer. Eventually, **`init`** becomes the parent of all shells and system daemons.

A UNIX system boots to a specific *state* (or mode), and this state is represented by a number or letter, called the *run level*. The default run level as well as the action to take for each run level are controlled by **`init`**. We'll consider **`init`**'s role in detail later *(27.8)*, but as of now you should know these two states:

- *Single-user* mode—This mode is important for the administrator, who uses it to perform his administrative tasks, like checking or backing up individual file systems. Other users are prevented from operating the system in single-user mode.
- *Multiuser* mode—In this mode, individual file systems are mounted *(27.6)*, and system daemons *(10.3)* are also started. Printing is possible only in multiuser mode when the **`lpsched`** daemon is running.

The **who -r** command displays the run level for your system:

```
$ who -r
   .       run-level 3  Jan   9 09:39     3      0  S
```

This machine is at run-level 3, a state which supports multiuser and network operations. We'll have more to discuss about run levels and the role of **init** in Part II of the text.

Shutdown The administrator also has the duty of shutting down the machine at the end of the day (if it is ever shut down). The **shutdown** command controls this sequence. **shutdown** usually performs the following activities:

- Notifies users with **wall** about the system going down with a directive to log out. Users are then expected to close all their files and log out of the system within a minute or so. **shutdown** itself sleeps for a minute after mailing the first message and may issue a reminder or two.
- Sends signals to all running processes so they can terminate normally.
- Logs users off and kills remaining processes.
- Unmounts *(27.6.2)* all secondary file systems.
- Writes information about file system status to disk *(27.9)* to preserve the integrity of the file system.
- Notifies users to reboot or switch off, or moves the system to single-user mode.

shutdown finally displays a message that could look something like these:

```
Reboot the system now or turn power off
System halted
```

The machine can now be considered to have completed the shutdown sequence successfully. You can now turn the power off unless your machine supports a power management feature that does this job automatically.

The -g option to **shutdown** overrides the default waiting time of one minute. The command can be used in these ways:

`shutdown -g2`	*Powers down machine after 2 minutes*
`shutdown -y -g0`	*Immediate shutdown*
`shutdown -y -g0 -i6`	*Shut down and reboot*

Some systems like Solaris have the **reboot** and **halt** commands that also shut the system down without warning the users. Unless you know what you are doing, you should stick to **shutdown** if you are administering a multiuser system.

LINUX: Linux uses the -t option to override the default waiting time of one minute. **shutdown** can also be used in these ways:

`shutdown 17:30`	*Shut down at 17:30 hours*
`shutdown -r now`	*Shut down immediately and reboot*
`shutdown -h now`	*Shut down immediately and halt*

Linux also permits the use of the Windows-styled *[Ctrl][Alt][Del]* sequence to shut down the system.

17.6 MANAGING DISK SPACE

No matter how many disks are added to the system, there will always be a scramble for space. Users often forget to remove the files they no longer require. Files tend to accumulate during the day, thus slowing down the system. If this buildup is not checked, the entire disk space will eventually be eaten up. The administrator must regularly scan the disk and locate files that have outlived their utility. He needs the **df** and **du** commands for this task as well as **find** that has already been discussed *(17.6)*. All three commands can also be issued by any user.

17.6.1 df: Reporting Free Space

You are aware *(13.1)* that your operating system is supported by multiple file systems. The **df** (disk free) command reports the amount of free space available for each file system separately:

```
# df
/                (/dev/dsk/c0t0d0s0 ): 3491876 blocks   483932 files
/usr             (/dev/dsk/c0t0d0s4 ): 2434820 blocks   458466 files
/proc            (/proc             ):       0 blocks    15875 files
/dev/fd          (fd                ):       0 blocks        0 files
/etc/mnttab      (mnttab            ):       0 blocks        0 files
/var             (/dev/dsk/c0t0d0s1 ): 3881394 blocks   484212 files
/var/run         (swap              ): 2602128 blocks   109840 files
/users1          (/dev/dsk/c0t8d0s0 ): 8037576 blocks  1024196 files
/users2          (/dev/dsk/c0t9d0s0 ): 4920276 blocks   956432 files
/tmp             (swap              ): 2602128 blocks   109840 files
/export/home     (/dev/dsk/c0t0d0s7 ): 2187782 blocks   340677 files
```

There are several file systems on this Solaris machine, but you don't have control over all of them (like /proc and /etc/mnttab). The first column shows the directory where the file system is attached (mounted). The second column shows the device name of the file system. The last two columns show the number of 512-byte blocks available and the number of files that you can create.

The first line in the list refers to the root file system (/), and has 3,491,876 blocks of disk space free. It also has 483,932 inodes free, which means that up to that many additional files can be created on this file system. The system will continue to function until the free blocks or inodes are eaten away, whichever occurs earlier.

The -t (total) option includes the above output, as well as the total amount of disk space in the file system. We won't display its output, but we'll consider the informative -k option that reports in units of KB. This time, let's obtain the statistics for the / and /usr file systems:

```
$ df -k / /usr                                     Reports on / and /usr file systems
Filesystem             kbytes    used    avail capacity  Mounted on
/dev/dsk/c0t0d0s0     1986439  240501 1686345    13%     /
/dev/dsk/c0t0d0s4     2025076  807666 1156658    42%     /usr
```

You probably won't need to know anything more than what this output offers. It shows the percentage utilization also. Once you have identified the file system that needs to be investigated thoroughly, you need the **du** command that is considered next.

LINUX: The default output itself is quite informative; it shows both the total as well as the available space, but in a format that resembles the -k option used by UNIX. The -h option makes it even more readable by reporting in larger units (like MB, GB, etc):

```
$ df -h / /download
Filesystem              Size  Used Avail Use% Mounted on
/dev/hda10              4.8G  2.6G  1.9G  57% /
/dev/hda13              5.6G  985M  4.3G  18% /download
```

The block size used for reporting is usually different in Linux. **find**, **df** and **du** report in 1024-byte blocks.

Note When the space in one file system is totally consumed, the file system can't borrow space from another file system.

17.6.2 du: Disk Usage

You'll often need to find out the consumption of a specific directory tree rather than an entire file system. **du** (disk usage) is the command you need as it reports usage by a recursive examination of the directory tree. This is how **du** lists the usage of /home/sales/tml:

```
# du /home/sales/tml
11554     /home/sales/tml/forms
12820     /home/sales/tml/data
638       /home/sales/tml/database
.....
25170     /home/sales/tml                    Also reports a summary at end
```

By default, **du** lists the usage of each subdirectory of its argument, and finally produces a summary. The list can often be quite large, and more often than not, you may be interested only in a single figure that takes into account all these subdirectories. For this, the -s (summary) option is quite convenient:

```
# du -s /home/sales/tml
25170    /home/sales/tml
```

Assessing Space Consumed by Users Most of the dynamic space in a system is consumed by users' home directories and data files. You should use **du -s** to report on each user's home directory. The output is brief and yet quite informative:

```
# du -s /home/*
144208     /home/henry
98290      /home/image
13834      /home/local
28346      /home/sales
```

du can also report on each file in a directory (-a option), but the list would be too big to be of any use. You may instead look for some of the notorious disk eaters, and exceptional reporting is what you probably need. The **find** command can do this job.

> **Note** You have used **find** before *(13.7)*; the command uses the `-size` option to locate large files. Multiple selection criteria can also be specified:
>
> ```
> find /home -size +2048 -print                    Files above 1 MB
> find /home -size +2048 -size -8192 -print        Above 1 MB and below 4 MB
> ```
>
> You need to halve these figures when using Linux as **find** there uses 1024-byte blocks.

17.7 DEVICE FILES

Devices are also files, and you have seen some of these filenames in the **df** output. You open a device, read and write to it, and then close it like you do to any file. The functions for doing all this are built into the kernel for each and every device of the system. The same device can often be accessed with several different filenames. This has sometimes been done for backward compatibility and sometimes for associating a separate device with a specific function.

All device files are stored in /dev or in its subdirectories. The device names seen on one UNIX system and Linux are shown in Table 17.1. Though the device names in Linux have been known to be remarkably invariant, the same can't be said of the System V devices. If you are using Solaris or HP-UX, the names will be different. Here's a concise listing of these devices for a system running System V:

```
# ls -l /dev
total 52
brw-rw-rw-   1 root    sys       51,  0 Aug 31 07:28 cd0       CD-ROM
brw-rw-rw-   2 bin     bin        2, 64 Feb 23  1997 fd0       Default floppy drive
brw-------   1 sysinfo sysinfo    1,  0 May  7  1996 hd00      First hard disk
crw-------   2 bin     bin        6,  0 Dec  5 14:12 lp0       Printer
cr--r--r--   1 root    root      50,  0 Aug 31 07:28 rcdt0     Tape drive
crw-------   1 henry   terminal   0,  0 Oct 15 10:23 tty01     Terminal
crw-rw-rw-   2 bin     bin        5,  0 May  7  1996 tty1a     Serial port 1
```

SVR4 also has two additional directories—/dev/dsk and /dev/rdsk containing some more files. The files in those directories sometimes have equivalents (or even links) in /dev. The lists in real life are much larger than this and includes every possible device on your system—including even the main memory of your computer. This listing reveals two vital points:

- Device files can be grouped into mainly two categories depending on the first character of the permissions field (b or c).
- The fifth field—normally representing the size for other files—consists of a pair of numbers. A device file contains no data.

Device files also have permissions with the same significance. To send output to a terminal, you need to have write permission for the device, and to read a floppy, you must have read permission for the device file. The significance of the device attributes is taken up next.

17.7.1 Block and Character Devices

First, a word about disk reading and writing. When you issue an instruction to save a file, the write operation takes place in chunks or blocks. Each block here represents an integral number of disk sectors (of 512 bytes each). The data is first transferred to a *buffer cache* which the kernel later writes to disk. When you read from disk, the buffer cache is first accessed containing the most recently used data. If the data is found there, the disk access is avoided. You may also decide to ignore this facility and access the device directly. Many devices allow you to do that, and the access method is determined by the name of the device that is called up.

Note that generally the first character in the permissions field is `c` or `b`. The floppy drive, CD-ROM and the hard disk have `b` prefixed to their permissions. All data are read and written to these devices in blocks and use the buffer cache. That's why they are referred to as *block special* devices. On the other hand, the terminal, tape drive and printer are *character special* or raw devices, indicated by the letter `c`. For the latter, the read/write operations ignore the buffer cache and access the device directly.

Many devices have both a raw and a block counterpart in System V. Hard disks, floppy drives and CD-ROMs are both block and character devices. Generally, an `r` prefixed to a block device name makes it a character device. Block devices are also found separately in `/dev/dsk` and character devices in `/dev/rdsk`.

17.7.2 Major and Minor Numbers

The set of routines needed to operate a specific device is known as the *device driver*. When a particular device is accessed, the kernel calls the right device driver and passes some parameters for it to act properly. The kernel must know not only the type of device but also certain details about the device—like the density of a floppy or the partition number of the disk.

The fifth column of the previous listing doesn't show the file size in bytes, but rather a pair of two numbers separated by a comma. These numbers are called the *major* and *minor* device numbers, respectively. The major number represents the device driver; this is actually the type of device. All hard disks will have the same major number if they are attached to the same controller.

The minor number is indicative of the parameters that the kernel passes to the device driver. Often, it indicates the special characteristics of the device. For example, `fd0h1440` and `fd1h1440` represent two floppy devices attached to a particular controller. So both of them will have the same major number but different minor numbers.

You'll see a lot of 0s, 1s and other digits in the device names. Often, you'll be able to identify a device from its filename. System V device files are resident in `/dev/dsk` (and `/dev/rdsk` for raw devices). The name `/dev/dsk/f0q18dt` represents a 3.5" floppy (block) device. It is bootable (0), of quad density and has 18 sectors/track—a 1.44 MB diskette. There is also a default name for many devices; the floppy drive can be accessed by `/dev/fd0`.

> **Note** Unlike ordinary and directory files, device files don't contain any data. They merely point to the location of the device driver routines that actually operate the device.

Table 17.1 Typical Device Names (Directory: /dev)

SVR4 Device	*Linux Device*	*Significance*
`cd0` or `dsk/c0t6d0s2`	`cdrom`	CD-ROM
`fd0` or `diskette`	`fd0`	Default floppy drive
`dsk/f0q18dt`	`fd0H1440`	1.44 MB floppy
`rdsk/f0q18dt`	`fd0H1440`	1.44 MB raw floppy
`hd00` or `dsk/c0t0d0s2`	`hda`	First hard disk
`hd10` or `dsk/c1t3d0s2`	`hdb`	Second hard disk
`lp0`	`lp0`	Printer
`rcdt0` or `rmt/0`	`st0`	Tape drive
`term/1`	`tty1`	Terminal
`tty1a`	`cua0`	Serial port 1
`tty2A`	`ttyS1`	Modem port 2

17.8 HANDLING FLOPPY DISKETTES

Although the tape is the most common backup device, the floppy diskette represents the most convenient means of exchanging files between machines at work and home. For our examples, we'll be using the 3.5", 1.44 MB diskette.

17.8.1 `format` and `fdformat`: Formatting Diskettes

Before you use a floppy for backup purposes, you need to format it. This is done with the **`format`** or **`fdformat`** commands (whichever is available on your system):

```
# fdformat                                    On Solaris
Press return to start formatting floppy.
```

The `-d` option uses the DOS format.

This command formats and verifies a 1.44 MB floppy. Other systems may require you to specify the raw device name as argument:

```
format /dev/rdsk/f0q18dt                      On another UNIX system running System V
```

LINUX: Linux too uses the **`fdformat`** command for formatting a floppy. Device names in Linux generally don't vary across the different flavors; a floppy usually has the name `/dev/fd0` or `/dev/fd0h1440`, so you should use **`fdformat /dev/fd0`** (or the other device name).

17.8.2 `dd`: Copying Diskettes

`dd` (disk dump) is a versatile command that can be used to perform a variety of tasks. It is somewhat dated as some of its filtering functions have been taken over by other UNIX tools. It can be invoked by any user, but is really the administrator's tool. It has a strange command line having a series of options in the form *option=value*.

`dd` was extensively used in copying file systems, but today its role is mainly restricted to copying media—like floppies and tapes. It is not interactive (in fact, a filter), and a pair of **`dd`** commands is needed to complete the operation.

We'll now use **dd** to make a copy of a 1.44 MB floppy diskette. The first step is to create the image of the floppy on disk:

```
# dd if=/dev/rdsk/f0q18dt of=$$ bs=147456
10+0 records in
10+0 records out
```

The keywords are `if=` (input filename), `of=` (output filename) and `bs=` (block size). The above command copies the raw contents of a 1.44 MB floppy to a temporary file, $$, using a block size of 147456—exactly one-tenth the capacity of a 1.44 MB diskette.

Next, take out the source floppy from the drive and insert a formatted target floppy. A second reversed **dd** command copies this temporary file to the diskette:

```
# dd if=$$ of=/dev/rdsk/f0q18dt bs=147456 ; rm $$
10+0 records in
10+0 records out
```

You should copy your boot floppies in this way. In the same manner, you can copy a tape, but if there are two tape drives, a single **dd** command can do the job:

```
dd if=/dev/rct0 of=/dev/rct1 bs=9k
```

dd uses only raw devices—those in `/dev/rdsk` or the ones in `/dev` beginning with an `r`—like `/dev/rdiskette` or `/dev/rct0`. Linux doesn't have separate devices for the two modes but selects the right mode automatically.

17.8.3 Handling DOS Diskettes

It has now become quite common to see both Windows and UNIX systems on the desktop. UNIX today provides a family of commands (Table 17.2) that can read and write DOS floppy diskettes. These command names begin with the string `dos` in SVR4. They are modeled after UNIX commands performing similar functions.

The command required most is **doscp**, which copies files between disk and diskette:

```
doscp emp.lst /dev/dsk/f0q18dt:/per.lst
```

There are two components in the target specification—the device name (1.44 MB floppy drive) and the filename (`/per.lst`), with the `:` used as delimiter. As in **cp**, multiple file copying is also possible:

```
doscp emp[123].lst /dev/dsk/f0q18dt
```

doscat performs a simple "cat" of its arguments in the command line. When more than one filename is specified, the standard output for each is concatenated:

```
doscat /dev/dsk/f0q18dt:/CHAP01 /dev/dsk/f0q18dt:/CHAP02 > newchap
```

These commands make the newline conversions automatically *(6.13)*, but they also work with the `-r` option, in which case the files are copied or concatenated without newline conversions.

Table 17.2 shows the use of these commands with varying device names. One of them should work on your system. If `a:` and `b:` don't work, then use the appropriate file in `/dev` or `/dev/dsk`.

LINUX: The Linux "DOS" commands begin with the string `m`, and use the corresponding DOS command as the rest of the string. Here are some examples:

```
mcopy emp.lst a:
mcopy a:* .
mdir a:
mdel a:*.txt
```

Note that Linux uses the DOS drive name. All these commands belong to the "mtools" collection. For details, use **`man mtools`**.

Table 17.2 The Family of DOS Commands (Linux command name in parentheses)

Command	*Action*
`doscp /dev/fd0135ds18:/tags .`	Copies `tags` from DOS diskette (`mcopy`)
`doscat a:readme a:setup.txt`	Concatenates files `readme` and `setup.txt` in DOS diskette (`mtype`)
`dosdir /dev/dsk/f0q18dt`	Lists files in DOS diskette in DOS-style (`mdir`)
`dosls /dev/dsk/f0q18dt`	Lists files in UNIX **`ls`**-style
`dosmkdir a:bin`	Creates directory `bin` on DOS diskette (`mmd`)
`dosrmdir a:bin`	Removes directory `bin` on DOS diskette (`mrd`)
`dosrm /dev/dsk/f0q18dt:setup.inf`	Deletes file `setup.inf` on DOS diskette (`mdel`)
`dosformat b:`	Formats diskette in nonbootable drive for use on DOS systems (`mformat`)

17.9 cpio: A BACKUP PROGRAM

The importance of performing regular backups isn't usually appreciated till a crash has occurred and a lot of data has been lost. As an administrator, you are partly responsible for the safety of the data that resides on the system. It is part of your duties to decide which files should be backed up and to determine the periodicity of such backups. The effectiveness of the backup is determined by your ability to easily restore lost or corrupted data files.

We'll consider two backup programs in this chapter—**`cpio`** and **`tar`**. Both combine a group of files into an archive *(6.14)*, with suitable headers preceding the contents of each file. The backup device can be a magnetic or a cartridge tape, a floppy diskette, or even a disk file. Small systems, especially workstations, may not have the tape facility, so the floppy drive will be used here to illustrate the features of both commands.

The **`cpio`** command (copy input-output) copies files to and from a backup device. It uses standard input to take the list of filenames. It then copies them with their contents and headers to a stream which can be redirected to a file or a device. This means that **`cpio`** can be (and is) used with redirection and piping.

cpio uses two *key* options, -o (output) and -i (input), either of which (but not both) must be there in the command line. All other options have to be used with either of these key options. The **cpio** options are shown in Table 17.3. The examples in this section and the next use System V device names. Linux users should use /dev/fd0h1440, and Solaris users should use /dev/rdiskette as the device names.

17.9.1 Backing Up Files (-o)

Since **cpio** uses only standard input, you can use **ls** to generate a list of filenames to serve as its input. The -o key option creates the archive on the standard output, which you need to redirect to a device file. This is how you copy files in the current directory to a 1.44 MB floppy:

```
# ls | cpio -ov > /dev/rdsk/f0q18dt          Use /dev/fd0 in Linux
array.pl
calendar
cent2fah.pl
convert.sh
xinitrc.sam
276 blocks                                   Total size of the archive
```

The -v (verbose) option displays each filename on the terminal when it's being copied. **cpio** needs as input a list of files, and if this list is available in a file, redirection can be used too:

```
cpio -o >/dev/rdsk/f0q18dt < flist
```

Incremental Backups **find** can also produce a file list, so any files that satisfy its selection criteria can also be backed up. You'll frequently need to use **find** and **cpio** in combination to back up selected files—for instance, those that have been modified in the last two days:

```
find . -type f -mtime -2 -print | cpio -ovB >/dev/rdsk/f0q18dt
```

Since the path list of **find** is a dot, the files are backed up with their relative pathnames. However, if it is a /, **find** will use absolute pathnames.

The -B option sets the block size to 5120 bytes for input and output, which is 10 times the default size. For higher (or lower) sizes, the -C option has to be used:

```
ls *.pl | cpio -ovC51200 >/dev/rdsk/f0q18dt          100 times the default
```

Multivolume Backups When the created archive in the backup device is larger than the capacity of the device, **cpio** prompts for inserting a new diskette into the drive:

```
# find . -type f -print | cpio -ocB >/dev/rdsk/f0q18dt
Reached end of medium on output.
If you want to go on, type device/filename when ready
/dev/fd0                                             Device name entered
3672 blocks
```

Enter the device name when **cpio** pauses to take input. In this way, an archive can be split into several extents (volumes).

17.9.2 Restoring Files (-i)

A complete archive or selected files can be restored with the -i key option. To restore files, use redirection to take input from the device:

```
# cpio -iv < /dev/rdsk/f0q18dt
array.pl
calendar
cent2fah.pl
convert.sh
xinitrc.sam
276 blocks
```

When restoring subdirectories, **cpio** assumes that the subdirectory structures are also maintained on the hard disk; it can't create them in case they are not. However, the -d (directory) option overrides that.

cpio also accepts a quoted wild-card pattern, so multiple files fitting the pattern can be restored. Restoring only the shell scripts becomes quite easy:

```
cpio -i "*.sh" < /dev/rdsk/f0q18dt
```

> **Tip** A file is restored in that directory that matches its pathname. In other words, if a file has been backed up with the absolute pathname (e.g., /home/romeo/unit13), then it will be restored in the same directory (/home/romeo). However, when relative pathnames are used, files can be restored anywhere. The "relative filename" method is normally recommended because the administrator often likes to back up files from one directory and restore them in another. Make sure you use **find** with a dot, rather than a /, to specify the path list when you are using it with **cpio**.

Handling Modification Times (-m) By default, when a file is extracted, its modification time is set to the time of extraction. This could lead to problems as this file will participate in future incremental backups even though it has actually not been modified after restoration. Instead of using **touch** *(13.6.1)* to change the modification times (an impractical solution), you can use the -m option to tell **cpio** that the modification time has to be retained.

cpio compares the modification time of a file on the media with the one on disk (if any). If the disk file is newer than the copy, or of the same age, then it won't be restored; **cpio** then echoes this message:

```
"current <unit14> newer"
```

This is a useful built-in protection feature that safeguards the latest version of a file. (**tar** doesn't have this feature.) However, this can be overridden with the -u (unconditional) option.

> **Tip** If you are often moving files from one machine to another, use **cpio** instead of **tar**. You are then assured that a newer file on one machine is not overwritten by an older one from another.

17.9.3 Displaying the Archive (-it)

The -t option displays the contents of the device without restoring the files. This option must be combined with the -i key option:

```
# cpio -itv </dev/rdsk/f0q18dt
100755 henry     605  Oct 18 23:34:07 1997  cent2fah.pl
100755 henry     273  Oct 18 23:34:07 1997  check_number.pl
100755 henry     531  Oct 18 23:34:08 1997  dec2bin.pl
100755 henry     214  Oct 18 23:34:08 1997  get_home.pl
```

The files are displayed in a format resembling the listing. (Linux and Solaris output are identical to the listing.) This format shows the octal representation of the file type (10) and the permissions (0755) as well as the modification time of the file (to the nearest second!). Both file type and permissions are stored in the inode as an integral unit, and in Chapter 25 you'll learn to separate them.

17.9.4 Other Options

There are two important options that can be used with the -o and -i options:

- The -r (rename) option lets you rename each file before starting the copying process. The system presents each filename and prompts you for a response. If you enter a filename, copying is done to that file; a null response leaves the file uncopied.
- The -f option, followed by an expression, causes **cpio** to select all files *except* those in the expression:

```
cpio -ivf "*.c" </dev/rdsk/f0q18dt          Restores all except C programs.
```

cpio relies on another command (usually **find**) or a file to provide its file list. It can't accept filename arguments in the command line. A **cpio** archive is also overwritten with every invocation of the command. This is where **tar** comes in.

Table 17.3 **cpio** Nonkey Options (used with -i or -o as relevant)

Option	*Significance*
-d	Creates directories as and when needed
-c	Writes header information in ASCII character form for portability
-r	Renames files in interactive manner
-t	Lists files in archive (only with -i option)
-u	Overwrites newer file with older version
-v	Verbose option; prints list of files that are being copied
-m	Retains original file modification time
-f *exp*	Copies all files except those in *exp*
-C*size*	Sets input-output block size to *size* bytes
-A -O *device*	Appends files to *device (Solaris and Linux only)*
-H tar	Creates or reads a tar header format *(Solaris and Linux only)*
-E *file*	Extracts only those files listed in *file (Solaris and Linux only)*

17.10 tar: THE "TAPE" ARCHIVE PROGRAM

The **tar** (tape archive) command has been in existence since before the emergence of **cpio**. Today, it not only creates archives on tapes but supports floppies as well. Unlike **cpio**, **tar** doesn't normally write to the standard output (though it can be made to), but creates an archive in the media. It is a versatile command with certain exclusive features not found in **cpio**:

- It doesn't use standard input to obtain its file list. **tar** accepts file and directory names as arguments.
- It copies one or more entire directory trees; i.e., it operates recursively by default.
- It can append to an archive without overwriting the entire archive (**cpio** in Solaris and Linux also).

You have already used **tar** with its key options *(6.16)* to handle disk archives. The common key options are `-c` (copy), `-x` (extract) and `-t` (table of contents). The `-f` option additionally has to be used for specifying the device name. The **tar** options are listed in Table 17.4.

17.10.1 Backing Up Files (-c)

tar accepts directory and filenames directly on the command line. The `-c` key option is used to copy files to the backup device. The verbose option (`-v`) shows the progress of the backup:

```
# tar -cvf /dev/rdsk/f0q18dt /home/sales/SQL/*.sql
a /home/sales/SQL/invoice_do_all.sql 1 tape blocks
a /home/sales/SQL/load2invoice_do_all.sql 1 tape blocks
a /home/sales/SQL/remove_duplicate.sql 1 tape blocks
a /home/sales/SQL/t_mr_alloc.sql 10 tape blocks
```

The **a** before each pathname indicates that the file is appended. The command backs up all SQL scripts with their absolute pathnames. The same restrictions apply; they can only be restored in the same directory. However, if you choose to keep the option open of installing the files in a different directory, you should first "cd" to `/home/sales/SQL` and then use a relative pathname:

```
cd /home/sales/SQL
tar -cvf /dev/rdsk/f0q18dt ./*.sql                    Using the ./
```

The advantage of **tar** lies in that it can copy an entire directory tree with all its subdirectories. The current directory can be backed up with or without the hidden files:

```
tar -cvfb /dev/rdsk/f0q18dt 18 *                      Doesn't back up hidden files
tar -cvfb /dev/fd0 18 .                               Backs up hidden files also
```

The files here are backed up with their relative pathnames, assuming they all fit in one diskette. If they don't, **tar** in System V may accommodate them as much as possible and then quit the program without warning.

> **Tip** If you have backed up your files with absolute pathnames and now want to restore them in another directory, then use the `-C` option.

The command will also execute faster if used with a block size of 18 (i.e., 18X2X512 bytes):

```
tar -cvfb /dev/rdsk/f0q18dt 18 *.sql          ./ is really not required
```

Since both -f and -b have to be followed by an argument, the first word (/dev/rdsk/f0q18dt) after the option string -cvfb denotes the argument f or -f, and the second word (18) will line up with -b.

> **Note** **tar** is quite liberal in its handling of options. **tar cvf** is the same as **tar -cvf**. The - symbol is not required at all! However, future versions of **tar** will not support this.

Multivolume Backup (-k) For multivolume diskette backups, **tar** in Solaris (and SCO UNIX) uses a special option (-k), followed by the volume size in kilobytes. This is how the file index is backed up in SCO UNIX:

```
# tar -cvfkb /dev/rdsk/f0q18dt 1440 18 index
Volume ends at 1439K, blocking factor = 18
tar: large file index needs 2 extents.
tar: current device seek position = 0K
+++ a index 1439K [extent #1 of 2]
```

tar estimates that two 1440 KB (the argument of -k) diskettes will be required. After the first volume is full, **tar** prompts for a new volume:

```
tar: please insert new volume, then press RETURN.
```

At the time of restoration, the same option has to be used.

17.10.2 Restoring Files (-x)

Files are restored with the -x (extract) key option. When no file or directory name is specified, it restores all files from the backup device. The following command restores the files just backed up:

```
# tar -xvfb /dev/rdsk/f0q18dt 18
x /home/sales/SQL/invoice_do_all.sql, 169 bytes, 1 tape blocks
x /home/sales/SQL/load2invoice_do_all.sql, 456 bytes, 1 tape blocks
x /home/sales/SQL/remove_duplicate.sql, 237 bytes, 1 tape blocks
x /home/sales/SQL/t_mr_alloc.sql, 4855 bytes, 10 tape blocks
```

Selective extraction is also possible by providing one or more directory or filenames:

```
tar -xvf /dev/rdsk/f0q18dt /home/sales/SQL/t_mr_alloc.sql
```

Unlike **cpio**, when files are extracted, the modification times of the files also remain unchanged. This can be overridden by the -m option to reflect the system time at the time of extraction.

> **Note** Unlike **cpio**, some versions of **tar** (like in Solaris) don't read wild-card patterns. If you use **tar -xvf /dev/fd0 *.pl**, it's the shell that tries to expand the pattern, which means that the files have to reside in the current directory. However, some versions of **tar** (like in Linux) do permit the use of the wild-cards; it doesn't matter whether the files exist at all in the disk.

Table 17.4 **tar** Options

Key Options (only one to be used)	
Option	*Significance*
`-c`	Creates a new archive
`-x`	Extracts files from archive
`-t`	Lists contents of archive
`-r`	Appends files at end of archive
`-u`	Like `r`, but only if files are newer than those in archive

Nonkey Options	
Option	*Significance*
`-f` *device*	Uses pathname *device* as name of device instead of the default
`-v`	Verbose option—lists files in long format
`-w`	Confirms from user about action to be taken
`-b` *n*	Uses blocking factor *n*, where *n* is restricted to 20
`-m`	Changes modification time of file to time of extraction
`-I` *file*	Takes filenames from *file (Solaris only)*
`-T` *file*	Takes filenames from *file (Linux only)*
`-X` *file*	Excludes filenames in *file (Solaris and Linux only)*
`-k` *num*	Multivolume backup—sets size of volume to *num* kilobytes *(Solaris only)*
`-M`	Multivolume backup *(Linux only)*
`-z`	Compresses/uncompresses with **gzip** *(Linux only)*
`--bzip2`	Compresses/uncompresses with **bzip2** *(Linux only)*

17.10.3 Displaying the Archive (-t)

Like in **cpio**, the `-t` key option displays the contents of the device in a long format similar to the listing:

```
# tar -tvf /dev/rdsk/f0q18dt
rwxr-xr-x203/50      472 Jun  4 09:35 1991 ./dentry1.sh
rwxr-xr-x203/50      554 Jun  4 09:52 1991 ./dentry2.sh
rwxr-xr-x203/50     2299 Jun  4 13:59 1991 ./func.sh
```

There's something here that you ought to pay attention to. The files here have been backed up with relative pathnames. Each filename here is preceded by `./`. If you don't remember this but want to extract the file `func.sh` from the diskette, you'll obviously first try this:

```
# tar -xvf /dev/rdsk/f0q18dt func.sh
tar: func.sh: Not found in archive
```

tar failed to find the file because it existed there as `./func.sh` and not `func.sh`. Put the `./` before the filename, and get it this time. Remember this whenever you encounter extraction errors as above.

17.10.4 Other Options

There are a number of other options of **tar** that are worth considering:

- The -r key option is used to append a file to an archive. The unusual outcome of this is that an archive can contain several versions of the same file.
- The -u key option also adds a file to an archive but only if the file is not already there or is being replaced with a newer version. You can't use the -c option when using either -r or -u.
- The -w option permits interactive copying and restoration. It prints the name of the file and prompts for the action to be taken (y or n).
- Some versions of **tar** use a special option to pick up filenames from a file. You might want to use this facility when you have a list of over a hundred files, which is impractical (and sometimes, impossible) to enter in the command line. Unfortunately, this option is not standard; Solaris uses -I and Linux uses -T.

LINUX: The GNU **tar** command is more powerful than its System V counterpart and supports a host of exclusive options. Unfortunately, there is sometimes a mismatch with the options used by System V. The -M option is used for a multivolume backup (e.g. **tar -cvf /dev/fd0H1440 -M ***). There are two options (-z and -Z) related to compression that we have already discussed *(6.16.3—LINUX)*.

17.11 CONCLUSION

Even though system administration is a specialized and thankless job, modern times require all UNIX users to understand the essential concepts related to it. We discussed the routine administrative features and tools that you need to use everyday. This chapter didn't provide the forum to discuss what to do when things go wrong. That requires from the administrator an in-depth knowledge of the different components of the system.

At a deeper level, system administration also involves fixing file systems, controlling the system's services and configuring the network. With people increasingly owning machines that run Linux, it's much easier today for every user to try out these advanced features than previously. For this reason, system administration is worth a second visit, which we make in Part II of this text.

WRAP UP

The system administrator or *superuser* uses the root user account, though any user can also invoke the su command to acquire superuser powers. Most of the administrative commands are resident in /sbin and /usr/sbin. The current directory doesn't feature in the superuser's PATH.

The administrator can change the attributes of any file and kill any process. He can also change the system date and use **wall** to address all users. The administrator also control's user access to many services like **at**, **cron**, Ftp and Telnet.

For enforcing security, the superuser can change any user's password except that **passwd** doesn't prompt for the old password. The *set-user-id* (SUID) bit of a program makes its process run with the powers of the program's *owner* and not the user's. The *sticky bit* set on a directory allows users to create and remove files owned by them in that directory, but not remove or edit files belonging to others. The superuser should monitor the growth of SUID programs.

A user is identified by her UID and GID. A user can be added (**useradd**), modified (**usermod**) and removed from the system (**userdel**). User details are maintained in /etc/passwd and /etc/group. The password is stored in an encrypted manner in /etc/shadow.

During system startup, the **init** process takes the system to multiuser state, and spawns many processes that *mounts* (attaches) file systems and starts the system's daemons. **init** also spawns a **getty** at the terminals to eventually become the parent of all login shells. **shutdown** kills all processes, *unmounts* file systems and writes file system information to disk before powering down the machine.

The administrator has to monitor the disk usage and ensure that adequate free space is available. **df** displays the free disk space for each file system. **du** lists the detailed usage of each file or directory. The administrator also uses **find** to locate large files (-size).

All device files are stored in /dev. Devices can be *block special* (which use the buffer cache) or *character special* (which don't). A device file is also represented by a *major number* which represents the device driver, and *minor number* which signifies the parameters passed to the device driver. The same device can often be accessed with different filenames.

Floppy diskettes have to be formatted (**format** or **fdformat**) before they can be used. **dd** uses a character device to copy diskettes and tapes. UNIX provides an entire group of commands to handle DOS diskettes. Their names begin with the string dos (SVR4) or m (Linux).

cpio and **tar** are two commonly used backup tools. **cpio** takes a list of files from the standard input and it often depends on **find** to provide the list or for performing incremental backups. By default, it won't overwrite an older file. Wild-cards can be used to restore groups of files.

tar is more suitable for backing up a directory tree. It can append to an archive and also keep several versions of the same file. GNU **tar** adds compression to the archiving activity. Both **cpio** and **tar** can perform multivolume backups to a diskette.

TEST YOUR UNDERSTANDING

17.1 Where are the administrator's commands located?

17.2 If kumar becomes a superuser with **su**, why can't he *easily* execute commands of his current directory?

17.3 How does the behavior of the **passwd** command change when invoked by the superuser?

17.4 The letters s and t were seen in the permissions field of a listing. What do they indicate?

17.5 Why was the password encryption moved from /etc/passwd to /etc/shadow?

17.6 Explain how **ls -l** displays the name of the owner and group.

17.7 Name some services that are not available when the machine is in the single-user mode.

17.8 What is the difference between the **find** options -perm 1000 and -perm -1000?

17.9 How will you use **shutdown** to bring down the system immediately? What shortcut does Linux offer?

17.10 How can the system administrator arrange to monitor the free disk space every hour on a working day between 9 a.m. and 10 p.m.?

17.11 How will you find out the total disk usage of the current directory tree?

17.12 How do you copy all HTML files to a DOS floppy in (i) SVR4 (ii) Linux?

FLEX YOUR BRAIN

17.1 Why is the **su** command terminated with **exit**? What is the difference between **su** and **su - romeo**?

17.2 Name five administrative functions that can't be performed by a nonprivileged user.

17.3 If the administrator doesn't want romeo to use the **at** command but allow juliet to use **cron**, what does he need to do?

17.4 A program can be made to run with the privileges of its owner. Explain the feature that allows this and how you can use it make a program run with the privileges of root.

17.5 Explain what these commands do:

```
 (i) find / -perm -4000 -print
(ii) find / -type d -perm -1000 -exec ls -ld {} \;
(iii) find / -type f -size +2046 -mtime +365 -print
```

17.6 How will you arrange for a group of users to write to the same directory and yet not be able to remove one another's files?

17.7 How will you create a user guru with UID 212 and GID dialout (a new group)? guru will use Bash as his shell and be placed in the /home directory. How can you later change guru's shell to Korn without editing /etc/passwd?

17.8 A user romeo belongs to the student group, and yet /etc/group doesn't show his name beside the group name. How can that happen?

17.9 How do you display the run level for your system? What is the difference between run levels 0 and 6?

17.10 Explain the difference between (i) block and character devices (ii) major and minor numbers. Can two devices have the same major and minor numbers?

17.11 Write a shell script to copy a floppy diskette.

17.12 Specify the **tar** and **cpio** command lines that will (i) prevent files from being overwritten during restoration (ii) rename each file interactively during restoration (iii) append to an existing archive during copying.

17.13 The command **tar xvf /dev/fd0 *.c** displays an error message even though the diskette contains a number of .c files. Name two reasons that can make this happen.

PART II

For the advanced user ...

18

The X Window System

The command line and dumb terminal have for long dominated the user interface of UNIX systems. But terminals can't produce the high-quality graphics required by advanced scientific and engineering applications. Apple and Microsoft made the graphical user interface (GUI) popular, and users were also getting tired of complex command line syntaxes. This was the scene in the UNIX arena when a group of graduates at the Massachusetts Institute of Technology (MIT) came up with the X Window system.

The X Window system was developed as part of Project Athena at MIT. Once snubbed as "the Vietnam of UNIX," X (i.e., X Window) wasn't originally designed with any particular operating system in mind. However, it has now been adopted as the standard windowing system by all UNIX vendors. In 1987, MIT released X version 11—referred to as X11. It also has its own share of releases, the latest one being Relcase 6.4 (X11R6.4). X is controlled and maintained by X.Org, an organization of the Open Group.

In this chapter, we'll take a look at the X Window system (not X Windows, as most mistakenly refer to it)—the X *server* and *clients* (the tools) that are usually shipped with it. We'll examine two sides of X. First, we'll learn to handle X the way we handle any GUI, using the mouse as the navigation tool. We'll also see how X is designed and ideally suited for running in a network.

WHAT YOU WILL LEARN

- Understand the X architecture and the role of the *server* and *client*.
- How a special client, the *window manager*, determines the look and feel of all X clients.
- Learn to start X and quit an X session.
- The features of a terminal emulator program like **xterm**.
- Copy data across different windows using the mouse and **xclipboard**.
- Learn the general command line options used with X programs.
- Use some common clients like the file manager, **xclock**, **xcalc**, **xkill** and **xload**.
- Configure the file, `.xinitrc`, the startup file used by **xinit**.
- Specify X *resources* and override them with **xrdb** and the `-xrm` option.

TOPICS OF SPECIAL INTEREST

- Examine the features of the *Common Desktop Environment* (CDE) that is now common to all UNIX machines.
- Use the networked features of X to run a client on a remote machine and have the display on the local one.

18.1 X BASICS

When MIT started work on the project, they had a serious problem in their hands. People were already working with several types of graphic displays, each having its own methods for drawing lines and shapes on the screen. If an application were to write to all these displays, then there had to be several versions of the application—one for each type of display. That would be absurd, so they reasoned that a separate program should handle the display. The application would send its output to this display-handling program. This led to a very important splitting of the application itself into two components—*client* and *server*.

Client-server computing, as we know it today, is the division of labor between two computers in a network. It means somewhat different things depending on the context to which it is applied. A network application like Finger or Ftp is split up into a server and a client component—two separate programs by themselves. The database application server acts as a repository of data and the business rules, while the client (the frontend) formats the data that it obtains from the server. This frontend is installed on the user's own workstation, normally a PC. The PC's display is handled by the client running on the PC and not the server.

X reverses this paradigm, and its architecture places the responsibility of handling the display on the *server*, while the application itself runs as a *client*. X programs are thus quite portable, being free of the complexities involved in handling the terminal. To run an X client on a different terminal, all one has to do is to write the server component of X for that terminal. Future X programs can then write to this new server program.

The X server program must be able to handle not only the application's output but its input as well. If you run an X calculator program to display on a remote machine, it is obvious that the remote user should be able to use it for doing her calculations. The server thus comprises not only the display screen but also the mouse and keyboard. An X display can also comprise multiple screens on multiple monitors. In fact, many UNIX systems offer support for multiple screens.

X clients display their output on separate windows on the display. But these windows have no frames around them, so you can't move or resize them. A separate client program manages these windows. We'll be discussing the role of the window manager very shortly.

X was primarily designed to run in a network. The transmission is totally reliable; X uses the TCP protocol *(19.2.2)*. The separation of the display handling component from the application also means that you can run an X client on one machine and have the display on another. This is the most important feature of X.

18.1.1 The Window Manager

X on its own doesn't offer any window management facilities that would control the windows created by clients. Though the MIT shipment includes buttons and scrollbars, the windows wear a plain look and have no frames or menus. Left to themselves, these windows can't be moved around, resized, or positioned up or down in the window stack. The specific look and feel of X programs is determined not by the X server, but by the GUI, which is a separate product (another client) by itself. The GUI in X is known as the *window manager*.

The window manager is a special client that is built on top of the other X client programs. It ensures that all clients have the same look and feel irrespective of the vendor they come from. We have seen many window managers come and go, starting with Open Look (from AT&T and Sun), and then a period of relative stability with Motif (from OSF). The window manager used by Motif is **mwm**, which may still be available on your system.

X has a complex startup sequence, but it reads one or more startup scripts which specify the window manager that is to be called. The window manager is run only once in a single session. It can also be run manually in case the startup script doesn't specify it:

```
mwm &                                        Sometimes found in $HOME/.xinitrc
```

The window manager that is now standard on most UNIX systems is **dtwm** (desktop window manager). An X client that has its frames and borders drawn by **dtwm** is shown in Fig. 18.1. **dtwm** features a button at the top left and two on the right. The right button represented by a circle is used to *minimize* a window, i.e., convert it into an icon. The other right button shown by a "raised" rectangle (initially) is used to maximize a window. Once it is blown up full-screen, the rectangle appears depressed.

```
Terminal
Window  Edit  Options                                            Help
b.c                       h2.c                  showerrno.c
big_or_small_endian.c     h2b.c                 sigint.c
c.c                       handler.c             signal.c
ccat.c                    j6.c                  signal2.c
childenv.c                link_sort.c           signal3.c
connect.c                 lls.c                 signal4.c
d.c                       lsdir.c               signala.c
delete_open_file.c        mycat.c               status.c
dir.c                     mydup.c               unlink.c
e.c                       myfork.c              vfork1.c
ermesg.c                  mynice.c              waitpid_example.c
err_mesg.c                orphan.c              without_argc.c
faccess.c                 pipe.c                z.c
fatal.c                   pipe3.c               zombie.c
firstprog1.c              pr.c                  zombie2.c
foo.c                     process.c
fork.c                    quit.c
bash-2.03$ ls *.sh
a.sh                      emp3.sh               script.sh
create_passwd.sh          emp3a.sh              valcode.sh
dateval.sh                emp7.sh               who.sh
dentry1.sh                menu.sh
emp1.sh                   readfile_backwards.sh
bash-2.03$ █
```

Fig. 18.1 The **dtwm** Window Manager on an X Client (**dtterm**)

Once a window manager is in place, every window can be moved by dragging the window by its *title bar*, and resized by dragging any of the four corners. A window is brought to *focus* by simply clicking on it. No matter where an application is placed in the stack of overlapping windows, clicking on it always brings it to the top. You may also be able to use the Microsoft Windows technique—*[Alt][Tab]*—to select windows in a circular manner. The active window can easily be identified by the different color of its title bar.

There is a menu in **dtwm**, the Window Menu, that pops up when you click on the left button. Many of the window management functions mentioned above can also be handled by this Window Menu.

> **Tip** There is a feature of **mwm** and **dtwm** in that you can move a window without selecting it. Just press the *[Alt]* key, click on the title bar of any window and move it. The window doesn't get highlighted and yet gets moved!

18.2 THE COMMON DESKTOP ENVIRONMENT (CDE)

A number of developments have taken place that has gone a long way in making the user comfortable in any X environment. In the past, even if Motif was adopted by most vendors as the standard window manager, implementations of X still differed across vendors. The desktop appearance was not uniform, nor was the method of using the applications. This made it difficult for a user to feel at home when she encountered a different X version even though both implementations used Motif. Motif remained a standard of sorts for some time before the "desktop environment" wave changed the appearance of the entire desktop (the entire screen)—and not merely the window manager.

Basing their initiative on Motif, industry leaders IBM, HP, Sunsoft and Novell started the COSE (Common Open Software Environment) movement in 1993. They introduced the *Common Desktop Environment* (CDE)—a standard desktop that made sure once and for all that all vendors' implementations of X not only had the same look and feel for all windows, but for the entire desktop as well.

CDE uses **dtwm** as its window manager. It is similar to Motif, so if you are comfortable with Motif, you'll find little difficulty in handling CDE. The window manager has an enhanced role to play in this environment. In addition to handling windows, **dtwm** features a *Front Panel*, a *virtual Workspace Switch*, a *File Manager* and a *Trash Can* (Fig. 18.2).

From the Front Panel, you can launch subpanels by clicking on the triangular symbols on the top. The most exhaustive option list is provided by the subpanel, Programs, and you can start many X clients from here. The most commonly used clients are also provided as icons in the Front Panel itself. You can start the clock, a calendar scheduling service or the File Manager directly by clicking on their icons.

At the center of the Front Panel is the Workspace Switch. This is a set of four buttons that let you create multiple "desktops" on your machine. You can have a set of windows on one desktop, another set on another, and you can select your desktop by clicking on the respective workspace button.

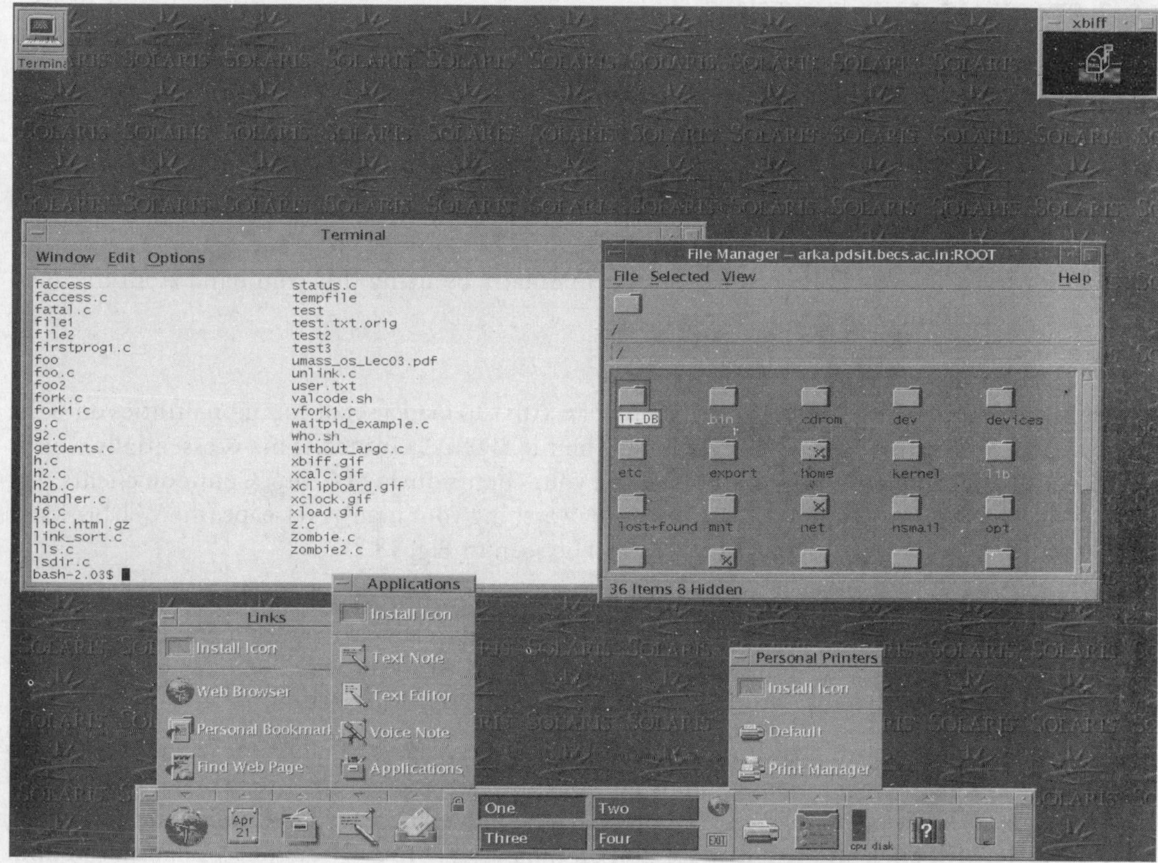

Fig. 18.2 The Common Desktop Environment

With four buttons, you can have up to four such desktops. It's like having a screen four times as large.

A menu comes up when you click one of the mouse buttons on the desktop (also known as the *root window*)—sometimes at one of the edges. Called the *Root Menu*, it offers important X applications like calendar and mail, the Web browser, terminals or the option to exit the X session.

Further discussion on CDE is beyond the purview of this text. What follows is a generic presentation of the features of X. Remember that the appearance of windows and the desktop on your systems can be different if you use a different window manager or a different desktop environment.

LINUX: Not to be left behind, Linux too is part of the "desktop" movement, and now has two products—KDE and GNOME (from GNU). Both KDE and GNOME feature many of the essential components that you see on the CDE. Linux vendors (like Red Hat and SuSE) offer both environments, and we aren't sure which one will eventually become the standard (if at all).

18.3 STARTING AND QUITTING X

Your UNIX system boots to a specific run level *(17.5)*, and this run level is selected at the time of installing the system. However, it can also be changed by modifying an entry in the file `/etc/inittab` *(27.8.2)*. Depending on your system, X will start automatically for a certain run level (3 in Solaris and 5 in Linux). This startup uses the **xdm** (X display manager) to display a graphical screen that requires you to authenticate yourself by entering your username and password. **xdm** can otherwise be run only by the root user.

If X doesn't start at boot time, you can start it manually by using this command from the shell prompt of your terminal:

```
startx
```

The command starts the X server, and *could* invoke **xinit** to load a set of common utilities onto the desktop. If X uses **xinit**, then **xinit** will read the file `$HOME/.xinitrc`. This is essentially a shell script where you can place commands to load all your clients during startup. Common clients that you may like to have on your desktop are **xbiff** (for watching your mail), Netscape (the Web browser) and a terminal emulation program. They can all be seen in Fig. 18.2.

The terminal emulation program appears as a window that's running a shell. You can fire all UNIX commands from this window—even the ones that feature as separate icons or menu items on your desktop. **xterm** is the original emulation program you'll find on all systems, but today we have better programs. We'll be considering this important X client in a separate section.

There's no standard way of quitting X. On systems where X runs as CDE (or where it is started manually), clicking the right mouse button anywhere in the desktop brings up a menu (Workspace Menu in Solaris). This menu invariably features an item named *Log out*. On Linux systems running KDE or GNOME, click on the left-most icon on the panel at the bottom to see a similar option. You may either be returned a shell prompt or the graphic authenication screen to allow you to log in again.

> **Note** X has separate functions for three mouse butttons, but if you are using a two-button mouse, then press the two buttons simultaneously to simulate the action of the middle button.

18.4 THE TERMINAL EMULATOR

The terminal emulator is the client that you'll probably be using the most. MIT shipped X with the **xterm** program, but today we have a host of emulators available. Any emulator program (like **xterm**) simply runs a shell in a window. This makes it possible to run any UNIX command. UNIX commands use a character-based display, but you can also invoke any graphical X client from the emulator's shell. This is how you run Netscape:

```
netscape &                    Run all X clients in the background
```

Since **xterm** itself is an X client, you can run create one **xterm** window from another **xterm** window:

```
xterm &
```

Generally, a user has a number of such overlapping **xterm** windows, each running a separate application. She gets the feeling of working on several machines at a time. On one window, she may use the **vi** editor to edit a program; on the other, she may compile the program. On yet another **xterm**, she may query a database. However, input to an **xterm** window is only possible when the user clicks on it or selects it by other means. The **exit** command from an **xterm** window kills the shell itself and the window associated with it.

Systems running CDE, KDE or GNOME have their own terminal emulators, though they all offer **xterm**. CDE uses **dtterm**, KDE uses **konsole** and GNOME uses **gnome-terminal**. You could see one of these emulator programs on your desktop when you log in. This client can often be invoked by clicking on some icon in the panel. **xterm** doesn't feature any menus in its title bar except the standard one provided by the window manager at the top-left corner. In contrast, the other emulators feature an number of menus in the title bar.

Using **xterm** There are three menus in **xterm** which pop up when you hold down the *[Ctrl]* key and click a mouse button. Every option has a toggling effect; a check mark appears or disappears depending on whether the option is activated or unset. The *Main Options* menu is invoked by pressing *[Ctrl]* and the left button. You can terminate the window (*Send KILL signal*) or display the window in reverse video. The *VT Fonts* Menu appears when you use *[Ctrl]* with the right mouse button. It lets you select the size of your font.

The *Enable Scrollbar* option in the *VT Options* menu (*[Ctrl]* and the middle button) places a scrollbar on the left of the window. This scrollbar contains a grayed-out *thumb* which initially occupies the entire column, but reduces in size as commands are entered. Previous commands entered at this window can be recalled by dragging the thumb with the middle button. Note that the middle button is emulated by pressing both left and right buttons in a two-button mouse.

xterm doesn't offer any special techniques to copy and paste text. There's a standard technique available that applies to all X clients, and is discussed shortly. Other emulators have an *Edit* menu that can perform these functions.

Using **dtterm** The **dtterm** emulator shown in Fig. 18.1 (located in `/usr/dt/bin` on Solaris) has three menu options. The *Edit* menu lets you copy and paste text. The *Options* menu lets you change the size of the window from 80 X 21 to 132 X 21. You can also change the size of the fonts. Another option enables you to use a scrollbar on the right (on by default).

> **Caution** If you don't affix the `&` to an X client command, the issued command becomes the child of the **xterm** window that created it. If you kill this parent window, the child window then gets terminated as well. This is not what you would want normally, so all X clients should be run asynchronously, i.e., in the background.

18.5 CUT-AND-PASTE OPERATIONS

Apart from the *Edit* menu that some X clients offer for copy-and-paste operations, X offers two techniques for this work. One uses only the mouse buttons, and the other is the **xclipboard** client—one of the native X clients that are shipped with every X system.

18.5.1 Using the Mouse Buttons

To copy text, highlight it by dragging it in the usual manner with the left mouse button; *the text automatically gets copied to a buffer*. Then, click on the other window with the left button, move the cursor to the point where you want to paste it, and click the middle button. The copied text is then pasted on this window. Using this technique, you can copy text from one window to another—perhaps for reexecuting a long command line in another window or placing text in another **vi** session. Only make sure you are in **vi**'s Input Mode before pasting text.

Instead of dragging, you can also select text by clicking multiple times on the text. Double-clicking selects a word, the triple click selects the entire line. The former is equally applicable in the Windows environment, but X selection techniques go further. For selecting a block of text in one screen, click with the left button at the starting point of text, and right click at the end of the text; the entire text gets selected. To extend the selection on either side, right-click at the respective text boundary. This technique may not work on all non-**xterm** emulators.

18.5.2 xclipboard: Advanced Copy and Paste

The standard copy and paste features has its limitations. You can copy only single sections of text at a time; you can't copy multiple sections in one shot for later pasting. This is also a problem with software running Microsoft Windows, where a user has to repeatedly switch between two files for performing this dual operation. X solves the problem with the **xclipboard** program.

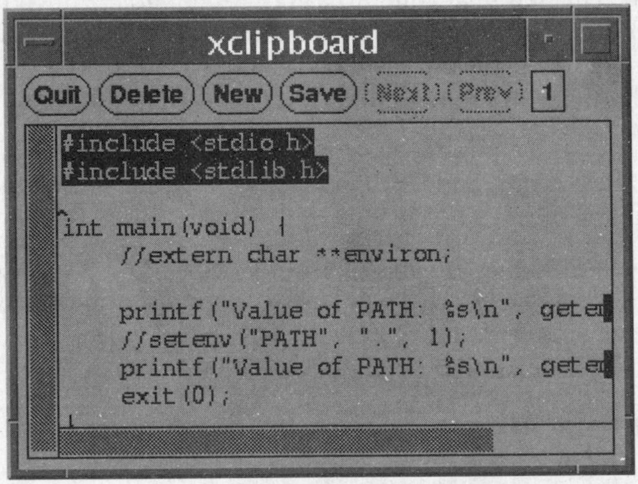

Fig. 18.3 **xclipboard**

xclipboard (Fig. 18.3) is a typical MIT X application. There are six buttons at the top of the window; the last two are grayed out initially. To use this tool, copy text from one window in the usual manner, and then paste it in the blank space on **xclipboard**. The counter at the right, which initially showed 1, continues to do so. If the text is too large to fit in the window, the scrollbars appear, and you can then drag the thumb *(18.4)* of the scrollbar with the middle button.

To repeat the copying operation with another text segment, you have to press *New* first. This clears the **xclipboard** display and advances the counter to 2. You can now paste the text that you have copied to this region. In this way, you can have multiple text sections stored in the clipboard. You can step through the various clipboard buffers by using *Next* and *Previous*. The important thing is that *once you have a text section on display on the clipboard window, that section is deemed to be copied*. You can then paste it at any place you want by using the middle button. You can delete a clipboard section (*Delete*) and even store it (*Save*) in a file. Nothing in Microsoft Windows can match this method of copying and pasting text.

18.6 RUNNING X CLIENTS REMOTELY

X was built primarily to run in a network, and in this respect, it is simply amazing. On single-user systems, the server and client run on the same machine, and you don't have to bother about controlling the display. But the beauty of X lies in running an X client on one machine and having its display on another! The X display has a very important role to play here, so let's understand it first.

18.6.1 The Display

You may decide to run a client on a remote machine, possibly because of its superior computing power, or because it's not available on your machine. As an example, consider that you want to run the **xcalc** program which is only available on a remote machine (*uranus*). However, the display of the program must appear on your local machine (*saturn*) so you can input data from your keyboard. There are two things that you have to ensure before you can make that happen:

- The server (on your machine, *saturn*) must enable others to write to its display. This is done by using the **xhost** command on the local machine.
- The client program must be directed to write its output to another display. This is achieved by setting either the `DISPLAY` variable or by using the `-display` option with the client.

We'll first use **xhost** on our local machine to enable any user on *uranus* to write to our display:

```
$ xhost +uranus
uranus being added to access control list
```

You can turn off the **xhost** setting with the - symbol or enable your display for all machines with +:

```
$ xhost -                                     Disables display for others
access control enabled, only authorized clients can connect
$ xhost +                                     Enables display for others
access control disabled, clients can connect from any host
```

You now have to run the **xcalc** program on *uranus*, the remote machine. A simple way of doing that is to log on to it using **telnet**. This networking tool is dicussed in the next chapter, but you could be using it already to work on a remote host where you have an account. There are basically two ways of running an X client remotely, and they are considered next.

18.6.2 Using the `DISPLAY` variable

`DISPLAY` is a shell variable used by X to determine where the output of an X client should be displayed. After you have logged in to *uranus* with **`telnet`**, define and export the `DISPLAY` variable at the shell prompt of a terminal emulator:

```
DISPLAY=saturn:0.0                    uranus must be able to access saturn
export DISPLAY                        by name; else use the IP address
```

The value assigned to `DISPLAY` is of the form *hostname*:*server.screen*. *saturn* is the hostname, `:0` is the instance of the X server program and `.0` is the screen number of the display. Both server and screen are usually `0` for single-user systems, and the screen number (`.0`) may be omitted. If X is running in a TCP/IP network, the hostname should either be present in `/etc/hosts` *(19.3.1)* or be accessible using DNS *(20.1)*. If it is not, you have to use the IP address *(19.1.3)* in place of the hostname.

The above setting signifies that *any* X client that will subsequently be run on *uranus* will use the display of *saturn*, rather than its own. Now you can run the program **`xcalc`** on *uranus*:

```
xcalc &
```

Just notice what you have done here. You executed **`xcalc`** on a remote machine and the calculator pops up on your local machine! X allows the use of the local keyboard with a remote client simply because the keyboard is a component of the server definition, and this server runs locally.

18.6.3 Using the `-display` Option

The other technique is to use the `-display` option offered by every X client. The parameter to this option is the complete display name—the sam e value assigned to `DISPLAY`:

```
xcalc -display saturn:0.0 &
```

Depending on the system you are using, the `-display` option may override any previous `DISPLAY` setting. If that happens on your system (as in Linux), you then don't need to use the `-display` option any more to run client programs from this emulator.

The above techniques assume that the Telnet service is enabled on the remote system; otherwise, you won't be able to log in at all. If it is not, you can use the **`rsh`** command to run a program remotely, provided it is also enabled and configured properly. **`rsh`** is discussed in Section 19.7.3 and its configuration in Section 28.9.

> **Tip** If you have a number of clients to run on a remote machine with the display on your local one, then it is preferable to use `DISPLAY`, which needs to be set only once. If `DISPLAY` is not set, then you'll have to use the `-display` option with every X client. Many Linux systems set `DISPLAY` automatically when you log in, so you don't need to use either feature at all!

18.7 COMMAND LINE OPTIONS

Most X client programs are built to handle a large number of options. Many of these options (Table 18.1) are common to practically all commands. They often take on abbreviations, which are shown in parentheses in the table. We'll discuss their significance briefly.

18.7.1 Window Position and Size (-geometry)

When you require to run a number of client programs, it is necessary to size and place them properly so that they can be easily selected. All X clients offer the `-geometry` option to determine the location and size of the client. The option is followed by a two-part component—the size of the window and the location of one of its corners from the respective edge of the screen.

For **xterm**, the size of the window has to be specified in characters, and the location (or offset) in pixels. The following command line sets up an **xterm** with a window size of 40 by 12 characters, with its top-left corner offset by 10 pixels from the left side of the display, and 20 pixels from the top:

```
xterm -g 40x12+10+20 &
```

For other clients, 40x12 would mean 40 pixels by 12 pixels—a very small window to be of any use. By default, **xterm** windows have the size 80 by 24 characters. You can have multiple **xterm**s at different areas of the screen; the size can also be omitted:

```
xterm -g -10-20 &                    Offset from lower-right corner of display
xterm -g +10-20 &                    Offset from lower-left corner
xterm -g -10+20 &                    Offset from upper-right corner
```

It should be quite obvious that when both numbers are zeros, the window is placed at the corner of the display.

18.7.2 Setting Colors (-fg, -bg and -rv)

The `-foreground` (`-fg`) and `-background` (`-bg`) options determine the respective colors of the client. You can set these colors for your terminal emulator window in this manner:

```
xterm -fg darkslategrey -bg lightblue &
```

X maintains this database of colors in the text file `/usr/lib/X11/rgb.txt`. (`/openwin/lib/X11/rgb.txt` on Solaris). This file contains several hundred color descriptions, with each line containing three numbers representing the amount of red, green and blue (the RGB values). The file also contains variations in these spellings—often with spaces between the words. Here are some typical entries in this file:

```
255 255 240          ivory
 47  79  79          dark slate gray
 47  79  79          DarkSlateGray
  0   0 128          navy blue
135 206 235          sky blue
```

The foreground and background colors can be reversed with the `-reverse` (`-rv`) option. This option comes in handy when you need to have a distinctly different appearance for a window, say the parent **xterm**.

18.7.3 Other Options

You can start any X client, but in an iconic form, with the `-iconic` option. This option is required especially when there isn't sufficient space on your desktop to accommodate all of them. You can keep your parent **xterm** window permanently iconified so that you don't kill it by mistake.

You can provide a title (`-title`) to be displayed in the title bar at the top. When running multiple instances of **xterm**, it's better that you have separate names for them, perhaps named after the machines on which they are running, or the applications running on them:

```
xterm -fg red -bg lightblue -title "Compilation"
```

The `-name` option lets you provide a name which can be identified by the server, and you'll see the name both in the title bar as well as in the icon label. *X resources understand the string provided with* `-name`. For this reason, it is often preferable to use this option rather than the `-title` option.

We'll discuss the significance of the `-xrm` option when we come to X resources *(8.10)*.

Table 18.1 Common Command Line Options Used by X Clients

Option	*Significance*
`-foreground`	Window foreground color (`-fg`)
`-background`	Window background color (`-bg`)
`-display`	The display specification of the host that will be written by the client
`-geometry`	Size and location of window (`-g`)
`-iconic`	Starts client in minimized form
`-title`	Name of window to be displayed in title bar
`-name`	The name of the application
`-xrm`	Resource specification that overrides settings of resource files
`-reverse`	Reverses foreground and background colors (`-rv`)

18.8 SOME STANDARD X CLIENTS

MIT ships X with over 50 clients, ranging from desktop accessories, font and graphic utilities to special tools related to window and resource management. Many of them have superior counterparts in the form of desktop clients. For instance, **xfm** is the original MIT file manager, but CDE provides a superior client in **dtfile**. Both KDE and GNOME offer many more clients. We can't possibly discuss most of them, so we present below the ones that are commonly used. Many of them can be seen on the CDE desktop in Fig. 18.2. Only one, **dtfile**, is a CDE client; the rest are all original MIT clients.

18.8.1 dtfile: The File Manager

We use files all the time, we copy, move and delete them several times in a day. It's no wonder that a file manager is considered by most to be the most useful X client. Windows also has a similar application, Windows Explorer, which is used by many users not only to perform the basic file-handling functions, but even to launch programs. On the CDE, the **dtfile** file manager performs similar functions (Fig. 18.4).

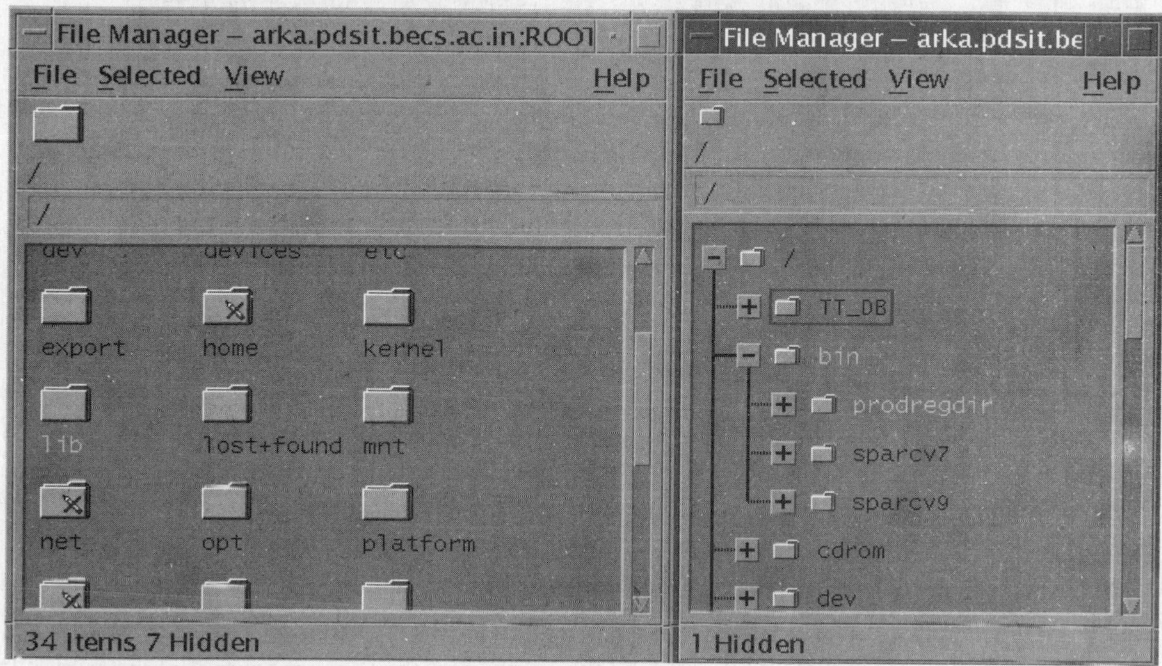

Fig. 18.4 Two Views of the **dtfile** File Manager used on CDE

18.8.2 xclock: The Analog Clock

All X distributions come with the analog clock, **xclock** (Fig. 18.5). The client has a couple of useful options, as the following command lines show:

`xclock -chime &`	*Chime sounds once for every half-hour and twice every hour*
`xclock -digital &`	*Prints date and time in character format*
`xclock -update 5 &`	*Shows a seconds dial which updates every 5 seconds*

Besides these options, there are other options to set the color of the hands.

18.8.3 xcalc: The Calculator

X also features a calculator, the **xcalc** client (Fig. 18.6). You can run it in two modes—the Texas Instruments TI-30 mode, or the Hewlett-Packard 10C mode. The first mode is emulated by using **xcalc** without arguments. There is nothing special about this calculator except that its `-rpn` option lets you use *reverse polish notation* (i.e., the HP-10C mode).

Fig. 18.5 `xclock`

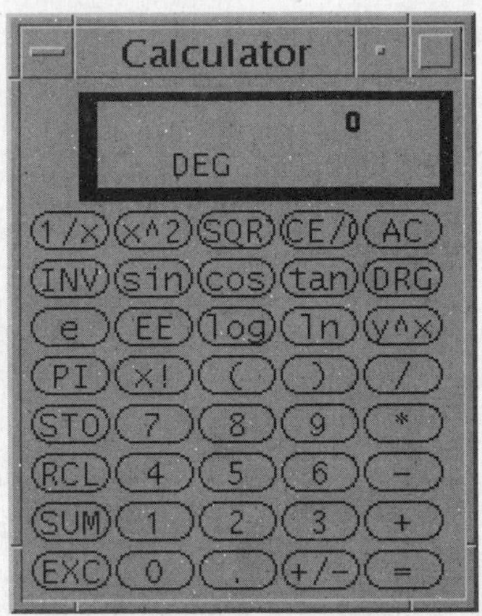

Fig. 18.6 `xcalc`

18.8.4 xbiff: Mail Intimation

This is a client that you would like to have on your desktop all the time (Fig. 18.7). **xbiff** monitors the arrival of mail by noting the modification time of the user's mailbox. The mailbox file is defined by the `MAIL` variable, which is often located in `/var/mail` or `/var/spool/mail`. **xbiff** is typically invoked like this:

```
xbiff -g -0+0 -file /home/sumit/nsmail/Inbox -update 60
```

`Inbox` is the mailbox used by Netscape (which doesn't read `MAIL`), but the location could differ on your system. The command places a picture of the mailbox on the top-right corner of the screen. It checks the modification file of `Inbox` every 60 seconds (`-update 60`). When it finds that the time has changed on arrival of a new message, it hoists the flag and darkens the window. A click on the window restores its original status (with the flag down).

Fig. 18.7 `xbiff`

Fig. 18.8 `xload`

18.8.5 `xload`: Displaying the System Load

`xload` displays a histogram of the system load average (Fig. 18.8). This is a useful program which you can run on multiple remote machines and have their histograms on your local machine. You can then run your next program on the machine with the lowest load, other things being equal (the processing power, for instance). The command should be used with two useful options—`-update` and `-jumpscroll`:

```
xload -update 15 -jumpscroll 1 &
```

By default, **`xload`** pools the machine every 5 seconds (10 in Linux). The `-update` option sets this time to 15 seconds. The `-jumpscroll` option ensures that the graph shifts to the left by 1 pixel when the histogram reaches the end on the right. This ensures smooth scrolling of the display. Because the command is most often used to run on multiple machines, the window always shows the domain name of the host (or its alias) at the top.

18.8.6 `xkill`: Killing a Window

`xterm` windows are terminated by using *[Ctrl-d]* or **`exit`** at the shell prompt. You can also use **`xkill`** to kill a single window or all windows together. When used without arguments, X displays this message:

```
Select the window whose client you wish to kill with button 1....
```

You just have to move the cursor to the window and do exactly as told. Now, if this happens to be the parent window of a number of child windows, this action will kill the child windows as well. The `-all` option lets you kill all root-level windows in one shot, except that X makes you select the root window three times, once with each button. This gives you a number of chances to change your mind.

18.9 THE STARTUP FILES

X can be customized to present a specific look and feel upon startup. The techniques depend on whether you are using CDE or not. On a system which uses **`xinit`** to start X (through the **`startx`** route), **`xinit`** looks first in `$HOME/.xinitrc`, failing which it starts the X server and loads a single **`xterm`** window with or without the window manager. From that window, you'll have to invoke other X clients to continue your session.

Generally, if you want your desktop to be loaded with a number of **`xterm`** windows and other X clients upon startup with **`xinit`**, you have to place the command sequences in `.xinitrc`. This is a Bourne shell script where every command, except the last, is placed in the background. A sample `.xinitrc` is shown below:

```
$ cat $HOME/.xinitrc
xload -load $HOME/.Xdefaults
mwm &
xclock -g 100x100-0+0 -bg tomato3 -fg white -update 1 -chime &
xterm -g -80-55 -sb -sl 300 -bg darkslategrey -fg ivory -rv -iconic &
xterm -g -0-0 -sb -sl 3000 -bg darkslategrey -fg ivory &
xterm -g +0+0 -sb -sl 3000 -bg darkslategrey -fg ivory
```

Make sure that you start the **mwm** client, otherwise you won't bc able to move or resize any of the windows.

18.10 X RESOURCES

Every X client is composed of a number of objects (*widgets*) like scrollbars, buttons etc. There are attributes (*resources*) that are associated with both a class of objects as well as individual instances of these objects. For instance, every application button has a foreground color, which is termed as the *resource* for the button. Every possible resource of every object of an application can be customized so that you need not invoke the client with complex options.

The sample file, `.xinitrc`, shown previously shows **xterm** invoked with the same set of background and foreground colors (`darkslategrey` and `ivory`), and with a scrollbar. Now, if that is how you want **xterm** to always appear, you can set these attributes in a special file, `$HOME/.Xdefaults`. This file is read by X when it is started, but can also be made to be reread when you make changes to it in the middle of a session. To customize **xterm** as above, you have to place the following entries in this file:

```
XTerm*ScrollBar: True
XTerm*saveLines: 10000
XTerm*background: darkslategrey
XTerm*foreground: ivory
```

The resourcc definition always begins with the name of the client (the class), which may be followed by either the widget hierarchy (a series of objects separated by dots) or an asterisk which matches all objects at that location. In either case, the resource attribute follows, terminated by a `:`, and then the value of the attribute. These values can be boolean (`True` or `False`), a string (`ivory`), or a number (`10000`). Henceforth, you need not use the `-sb`, `-sl`, `-fg` and `-bg` options with **xterm** if you want it to always appear with these attributes. However, you would certainly want to leave the `-geometry` option out of this, being the only variable part of the **xterm** command line.

18.10.1 xrdb: Loading the Resources

You need not quit and restart X if you have made changes to `.Xdefaults` during your session. You can simply use the **xrdb** command to signal to X that it should reread the configuration file:

```
xrdb $HOME/.Xdefaults
```

X starts with a number of defaults for these resources, some of which are specified in the application itself. There are yet others which are set in a systemwide configuration file, `/usr/dt/app-defaults`, on Solaris (`/usr/X11R6/lib/X11/app-defaults` in Linux). There could be a file named after each client in this directory. If a user has no `.Xdefaults` in her home directory, the specifications of the systemwide file are applicable when X is started. If you have created a customized `.Xdefaults`, then you should also put the **xrdb** statement in the `.xinitrc` so that clients are invoked with the right resource values.

18.10.2 The -xrm Option: Overriding the Resources

There are situations when you require not only to ignore the systemwide default settings, but also the ones you have put in your `.Xdefaults`. A specific instance of an application may also require a different setting. You can sometimes override these settings by invoking the command with suitable options. However, not all resources have corresponding option equivalents, but a special option `-xrm` can let you specify any resource value. For example, you can change the background color of **xclock** with the `-bg` option. But you can also use the resource specification for the class:

```
xclock -xrm 'xclock*background: lightblue' &
```

Besides these simple resources, there are other settings related to the translation of events. A typical event could be the interpretation of mouse clicks or movements. They are not at all intuitive, and a discussion on them is beyond the scope of this text.

18.11 CONCLUSION

Even if you are a habitual command line user, you'll often need to use X to view PDF and Postscript documents. This chapter covered X briefly simply because it is not central to the UNIX philosophy. We discussed just as much of X as is needed to use the file manager, view the documentation, handle multimedia mail attachments and browse the World Wide Web. We'll be discussing the last two functions in Chapter 20.

WRAP UP

The X Window system splits up the application into two components—*client* and *server*. The server program controls the monitor, keyboard and mouse, while the application itself is the client.

By default, X clients don't have any window management functions. A special client, the window manager, must be invoked once, at the start of an X session, to make these functions available to all windows. A window manager makes it possible to move and resize windows. The standard window manager for UNIX has been Motif (**mwm**), but it is now being replaced by **dtwm** of CDE.

The *Common Desktop Environment* (CDE) provides a standard look for both the desktop and the window manager. It features a Front Panel from which you can launch many applications. The File Manager handles the file and directory functions, and the Trash Can stores deleted files. The Front Panel also offers a Workspace Switch that lets you create virtual desktops to accommodate clients that won't fit in one screen.

X is started with the **startx** or **xinit** commands. X can also be invoked during system startup with the **xdm** command. **xdm** can otherwise be invoked by the root user only.

The most important X client is **xterm**, which displays a simple terminal window that runs a shell. Further commands can be invoked at the shell prompt of this window. CDE and other desktop environments use better terminal emulation programs.

You can copy text from any window by merely selecting it with the mouse button. The copied text is pasted back by clicking the middle button. Multiple sections of copied text can be stored in the **xclipboard** client from which it can be pasted anywhere.

X normally runs on a network, and it is possible for a client to run on one machine and have its display on another. **xhosts** controls access to the server, while the environment variable, `DISPLAY`, determines where the client should display its output. The `-display` option overrides and resets the `DISPLAY` setting.

X programs run with a number of common options. You can position and specify the size and position of a window (`-geometry`) and its foreground and background colors (`-fg` and `-bg`). You can start a program as an icon (`-icon`) and provide a name (`-name`) or title (`-title`).

There are several clients available in X. The most commonly used client is the file manager that functions like Microsoft Windows Explorer. X offers a clock (**xclock**) and a calculator (**xcalc**). **xload** displays the system load, and is often used with remote machines. **xkill** kills a window. It can kill all root-level windows in one invocation (`-all`).

X can be easily customized. You can start X clients from the file `.xinitrc`, the startup file used by **xinit**. X resources enable you to change practically any X feature. These features can be stored in `.Xdefaults`, and **xrdb** can be used any time to read this file. These settings can also be overridden with the `-xrm` option available in every X client.

TEST YOUR UNDERSTANDING

18.1 What does an X display comprise of?

18.2 Who places the frames, borders and buttons on the windows? Is it a server or a client?

18.3 Can an X client like **xterm** running on a Solaris machine display its output on a HP-UX machine?

18.4 How is text copied in an **xterm** window?

18.5 What is the function of the **xhost** command? What does **xhost +** signify?

18.6 What circumstances led to the development of the CDE?

18.7 What is the function of the four rectangles that you see on the Front Panel at the center of Fig. 18.2?

18.8 What happens if all the commands in `.xinitrc` are placed in the background?

18.9 How will you override a resource setting when invoking a client?

FLEX YOUR BRAIN

18.1 How does X solve the problem of running the same program on different displays with different characteristics?

18.2 How is the client-server mechanism in X different from others?

18.3 Explain the role of the window manager in X. Can you work without it?

18.4 Describe how text is copied using (i) the general features of X (ii) **xclipboard**.

18.5 How can romeo running Netscape on his machine *saturn* write its output on juliet's display in a remote machine *uranus*? Do both users need to run X?

18.6 Why is the `DISPLAY` variable more convenient to use than the `-display` option?

19

TCP/IP Networking

The realization that standalone computers made no sense made the network possible. When there were too many of them, people realized that standalone networks made little sense either, and that they also needed to talk to one another. This communication would not depend on the hardware, software and operating system used. What was needed was a set of standard *protocols* (rules) that could be used by all machines and networks to communicate. This set of protocols is known as *TCP/IP*.

UNIX has played a predominant role in the development of TCP/IP as a communications technology. BSD UNIX was adopted as the platform of choice for the development of TCP/IP tools and services. Today, TCP/IP is found in every major UNIX implementation as a built-in feature of its kernel. The Internet runs on TCP/IP and most of the TCP/IP tools that we discuss in this chapter also work on the Internet which is covered in the next chapter.

WHAT YOU WILL LEARN

- The basics of TCP/IP and the way it splits data into packets before reassembling them.
- The features of TCP/IP in providing for reliable transmission in a heterogeneous environment.
- Understand how a host is addressed both by its *hostname* and *IP address*.
- The *MAC address* and how a *router* uses it to effect delivery of packets.
- The function of `/etc/hosts` in resolving hostnames to IP addresses.
- Use **`telnet`** and **`rlogin`** for logging on to a remote machine.
- Transfer files with **`ftp`** and **`rcp`**, and the utility of *anonymous Ftp* sites.
- Run a command on a remote machine with **`rcp`**.
- The drawbacks of these tools and how they are improved by the *secure shell*.

TOPICS OF SPECIAL INTEREST

- The working of the four-layer TCP/IP networking model.
- The significance of *daemons*, *ports* and *sockets* in the client-server scheme.

19.1 TCP/IP BASICS

You need to know some networking jargon to understand TCP/IP. In a network, a computer is known as a *host*, sometimes a *node*. Every host has a *hostname* which is unique throughout the network. Each machine is fitted with a *network interface card* that is connected by wire to the corresponding cards in other machines. Communication between hosts normally takes place through these network interfaces. (You can also have communication through your computer's serial port.)

You must know what your machine's hostname is; use the **hostname** command:

```
$ hostname
saturn.heavens.com
```

This is a rather longish name of the type used by hosts on the Internet, where the first word actually signifies the name of the host. *heavens.com* is the name of the *domain* to which the host belongs; we'll be taking up domains later. Some systems omit the domain name from the output of the **hostname** command.

When two or more TCP/IP networks are connected together, we have an *internet*, popularly known as an *intranet*. Note that an internet is different from *the* Internet (spelled with an uppercase I), which is the supernetwork of all networks. A local internet or intranet may easily be connected to the Internet which also uses the same protocol.

There are various ways (*topologies*) of connecting machines in a network, and they employ different technologies. The most common ones are Ethernet and the Token Ring. Fig. 19.1 shows these two networks connected to each other.

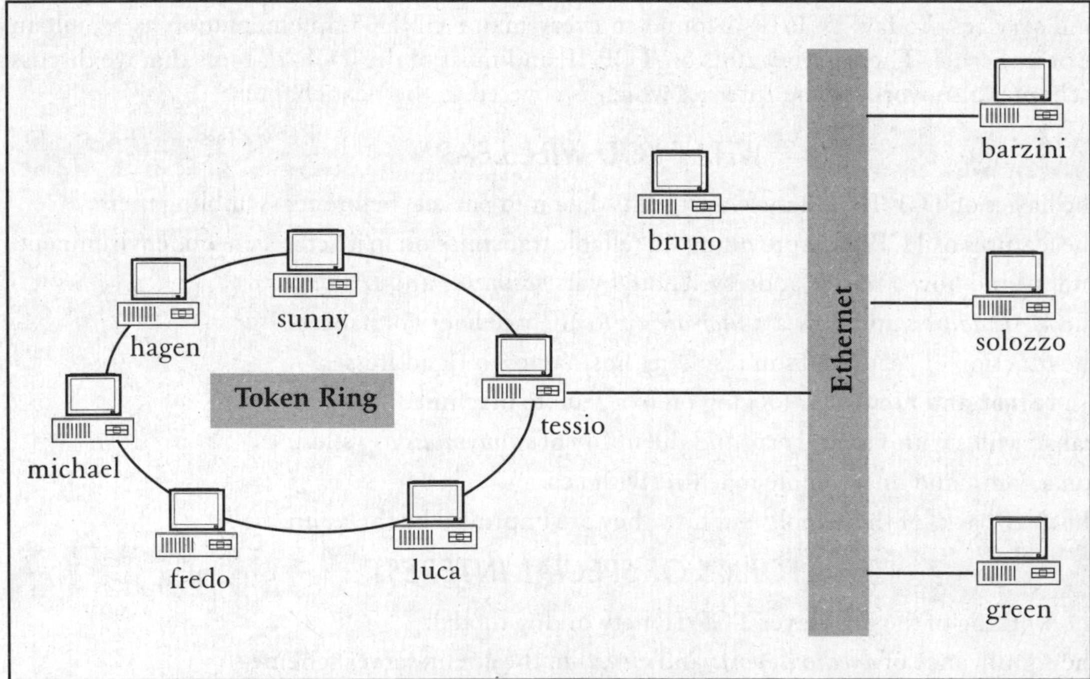

Fig. 19.1 Two Connected TCP/IP Networks

The significant feature of the Ethernet is that every host is logically connected to every other host in the same network by a thick, thin or twisted pair cable. When a message is transmitted by one of the hosts, it reaches the other host in one *hop*. On the other hand, in a token ring network, a message from machine *sunny* requires 3 hops to reach machine *fredo*. It's quite easy for host *luca* to reach out to host *hagen* because both belong to the same network. It's equally easy for host *solozzo* to send a file to host *barzini* in the Token Ring.

But when host *michael* wants to reach out to host *bruno*, it has to pass (route) its message through host *tessio*, which serves as a *gateway* or *router* for both networks. TCP/IP banishes the distinction between the two that has traditionally been made by networking technology. A router is generally a dedicated device, but a machine with two interface cards can also act as a router. The router is actually part of both networks and has two addresses—one for each interface, i.e., each network.

19.1.1 How TCP/IP Works

Unlike our telephone system, TCP/IP is a *packet-switching* system. In a packet-switched network, there is no dedicated connection between sender and receiver. Rather, the data is broken into packets, and each packet is provided with a header. This header contains the sequence number and a *checksum*, which is a simple number determining the exact information in the packet. These packets are put inside envelopes, the sender's and recipient's addresses are written on them, and the packets are sent on their way.

As the packets travel along a vast network like the Internet, they encounter routers everywhere. These are special computers or intelligent devices that look at the envelope addresses and then determine the most efficient route each packet has to take to move closer to its destination. Because the load on the network varies constantly, packets may move along different routes and arrive out of order. The packets are reassembled in the correct order from the information provided in them.

Before assembly, the checksum of each packet is calculated and checked with the number that has been sent in the packet. If the checksums don't match, the packet is corrupted and has to be resent. When all clean packets are received, they are assembled, their headers discarded and data fed to the application in their original form.

19.1.2 TCP/IP Features

A *protocol* in TCP/IP context simply means a set of rules that have to be used by two or more machines to talk to one another. The term *TCP/IP* expands to Transmission Control Protocol/ Internet Protocol, but that's not its real meaning. In fact, it's a collection of several protocols (of which TCP and IP are the most important ones). These protocols or rules are totally independent of the hardware or operating system used by the machines, and are built into the kernel.

The goals of TCP/IP were set by the US Department of Defense, and today, they are its inherent features:

- Independence of vendor, type of machine and operating system.
- The delivery of data in multiple packets.
- One-hundred percent reliability of transmission with facilities for full error control.

- Ability to divert data immediately through other routes if one or more parts of the network went down.
- Facility to connect new subnetworks without significant disruption of services

TCP/IP is also characterized by the absence of any formal specification. All TCP/IP specifications are available in the form of *RFCs* (Request for Comments)—documents that are available widely on the Internet. You can download them using *anonymous Ftp (19.6.4)* from *rs.internic.net*.

19.1.3 IP and MAC Addresses

Apart from the hostname, every host in the network has an address called the *IP address* which is used by other machines to communicate with it. This address is a series of four dot-delimited numbers (called octets), which could typically look like this:

```
192.168.0.1
```

The maximum value of each octet is 255. The IP address of a host too is independent of the networking hardware and is set at the time of booting by the system's startup scripts. TCP/IP applications can address a host by its hostname as well as its IP address:

```
telnet saturn
ftp 192.168.0.1
```

The network administrator sets the IP address of a host to make it unique not only within the network, but also in all connected networks. And if the network is connected to the Internet, it must be unique throughout the world. A network has an address too, and this address is derived from the IP address of any host in the network. This is taken up in Section 28.1.

The IP address is a somewhat convenient mechanism by which TCP/IP identifies a host, but routers can't deliver a packet by looking at the IP address alone. Every Ethernet network card has a 48-bit physical address hard-coded into the board by the hardware manufacturer. This address is unique throughout the world, and is known as the *MAC address* (Media Access Control) or *Ethernet address*. You can know the MAC address of your network card with the administrator's **`ifconfig`** command. This output on a Solaris machine shows the MAC address in the last line:

```
hme0: flags=1000843<UP,BROADCAST,RUNNING,MULTICAST,IPv4> mtu 1500 index 2
        inet 192.168.35.12 netmask ffffff00 broadcast 192.168.35.255
        ether 8:0:20:d2:f:15
```

The MAC address (`8:0:20:d2:f:15`) consists of a set of six colon-delimited hexadecimal numbers. Applications use the IP address (or domain name), but ultimate delivery of packets is made by using the MAC address. This address features in one of the layers of the TCP/IP protocol stack *(19.2.4)*.

19.1.4 Daemons, Ports and Sockets

TCP/IP and the Internet operate on the client-server principle—the division of labor between two computers connected in a network. An Ftp application is split up into a server and a client component—two separate programs by themselves. The Web server's job is to send an HTML document, which the client software (the browser) formats on the user's screen.

The server programs are called *daemons* in UNIX, and you have seen many of them in the output of the **ps** command *(10.3)*. They are not associated with any terminal and always run in the background, *listening* for input from the clients. The **httpd** daemon listens for a Web page request. The **sendmail** daemon handles your mail.

How does an Ftp packet know that it has to connect to another Ftp application at the other end and not to a Web browser? Specifying the IP address in an Ftp packet is not enough; a separate *port number* has to be included as well. This number is always associated with the Ftp service, so the packet reaches the Ftp server. Port numbers are like telephone extension numbers in an office. Specifying the office telephone number is not enough; one must know the extension number also to reach the right person.

Daemons listen for requests at certain specific port numbers assigned to them. **sendmail** listens on port 25, Ftp on 21 and Telnet on 23. *However, their client counterparts use random port numbers at their ends.* For instance, the **ftp** client (the command named **ftp** on your machine) will open a connection using some random number at its end, but the Ftp daemon will use port number 21 at the server end.

The port numbers used by the server programs are listed in `/etc/services`. The important services have these entries in the file:

```
ftp          21/tcp
telnet       23/tcp
smtp         25/tcp              # mail
www          80/tcp              # WorldWideWeb HTTP
pop3        110/tcp              # POP version 3
```

An IP address-port number pair constitutes a *socket*. Both server and client have a socket each, and communication takes places through a pair of sockets. This socket pair is sometimes called a *connection*. No two connections can have the same set of sockets. If two users with the same IP address request a Web page from the same server, their sockets will be different because the port numbers they will be using at the client end will be random—and different.

19.2 THE TCP/IP MODEL—THE FOUR LAYERS

The task of developing a set of protocols for communicating between hosts using heterogeneous hardware and different operating systems was initially taken up in the early 80s by the International Organization for Standardization (ISO). They framed the OSI model. The protocols underlying this model couldn't see the light of the day because they were based on outdated concepts and were difficult to implement. They eventually made way for TCP/IP.

The developers of TCP/IP divided the problem into four manageable pieces, or *layers* (Fig. 19.2). Each layer handles a specific function of the communication process. Since the layers are logical, and not physical, we must understand the logic that caused this division. These four layers are:

- *Application layer*, representing the application.
- *Transport layer*, which controls the reliability of transmission.
- *Internet layer*, which takes care of addressing of the data packets.
- *Network access layer*, which makes sure that IP addresses are finally converted to MAC addresses.

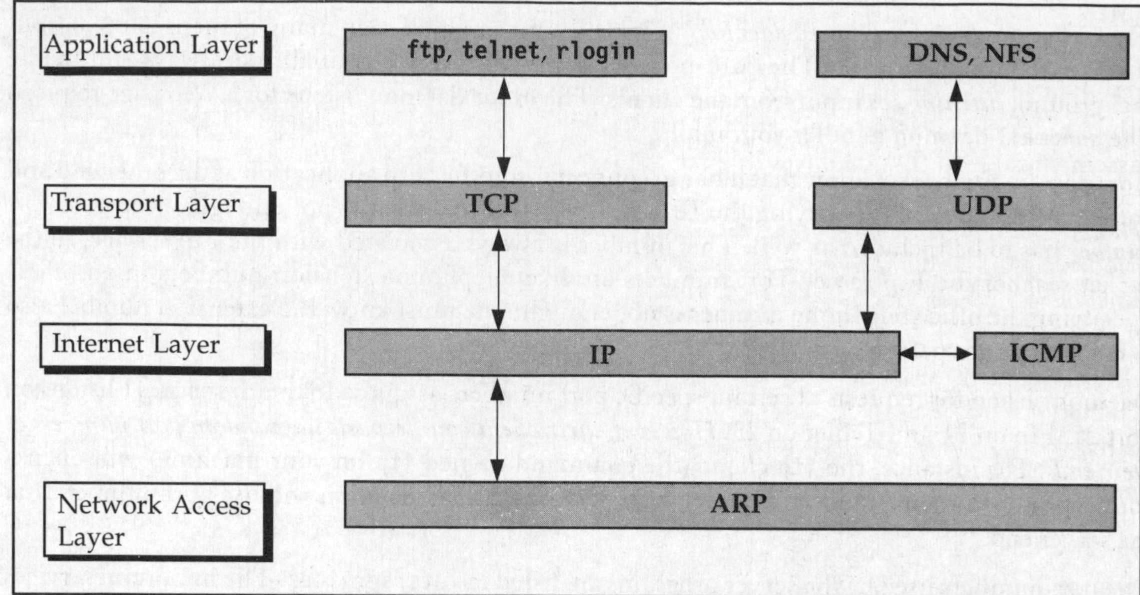

Fig. 19.2 The TCP/IP Protocol Stack

Data originates from the application at the application layer and traverses the other three layers. At the transport layer, the data is broken into chunks, which may be further split at the internet layer. These chunks have different names at the different layers, but are also universally known as *datagrams*. (A datagram is actually the chunk of the internet layer, but we'll be liberal in our definition.)

Each layer adds its own header information to the data received from the upper layer by a process known as *encapsulation*. The datagrams travel through the wire, and move up a similar set of four layers (but in the reverse direction) at the receiving end. In a similar manner, they are relieved of their headers before they are *reassembled*. We'll now take a look at the functions of the four different layers of the TCP/IP protocol stack.

19.2.1 The Application Layer

This layer contains the applications like Ftp, Rlogin, Telnet (both servers and clients), and so forth. Data originates from the application and is fed to the transport layer in the form of a stream. The application layer doesn't add any headers to this stream. This is the only layer where new services are constantly being added. DNS *(20.1)*, NFS *(28.12)*,and HTTP *(20.6.2)* and SSH *(19.8)* are some of the later additions to this layer.

19.2.2 The Transport Layer

The transport layer features two protocols—*TCP* and *UDP* (User Datagram Protocol). TCP (here, we are talking about the TCP protocol and not TCP/IP as such) is a *reliable* and *connection-oriented* mechanism for transporting data. It provides robust error detection and recovery facilities.

UDP is *unreliable* and *connection-less* in that it doesn't care whether data has reached the destination or not. An application uses either TCP or UDP and some (like NFS) use UDP instead of TCP.

TCP divides the stream it receives from the application layer into *segments*, encapsulating each with a header. The header mainly contains a checksum and a sequence number to facilitate reassembly in the right order at the other end. Since data can be lost or corrupted, or a part of the network may go down, TCP monitors the progress of the transmitted segments by waiting for *acknowledgments*. If no positive acknowledgment is received from the other side within the *timeout* period, *TCP retransmits just that segment rather than the entire data*. These features related to acknowledgment, timeout and retransmission make TCP a *reliable* protocol. These facilities are not available with UDP.

TCP is also *connection-oriented* in that it has to first satisfy itself that the remote system is ready to exchange data. This it does by way of a *three-way handshake*. It first sends a segment, waits for a positive acknowledgment from the transport layer of the remote machine, and sends one again. A *connection* is said to be established when this handshaking is successful, and TCP then proceeds with data transfer. TCP thus gives you the impression that the applications themselves are virtually connected across the network exchanging a single stream of bytes, rather than segments—more like a terminal or a telephone line.

19.2.3 The Internet Layer

The *internet layer*, also known as the *network layer*, takes care of all addressing requirements. Also, it has a limited role to play in determining the route a packet should take to reach its destination. IP is the dominant protocol in this layer and it often uses the services of *ICMP* (Internet Control Message Protocol) for its work.

When IP receives a segment from the transport layer, it first compares it with the maximum size (*MTU*, the Maximum Transfer Unit) that the next layer (i.e., the network access layer) can handle. Although IP itself can handle a datagram consisting of 65,535 bytes, the network access layer datagrams hardly ever exceed 1500 bytes. After knowing the MTU of the data, IP may have to fragment the segments into one or more *packets* or *datagrams* (the technically correct usage of the term) before it encapsulates them. If that happens, then *for every TCP segment, you may have more than one IP datagram*. The IP datagram header includes both the source and destination address (the IP addresses), and the sequence number of the fragmented segments.

These packets don't always follow the same route in the network, and need not arrive in the same order they were sent. The network doesn't even know that there is any connection between them. It is IP's job to ensure that *all packets of a TCP segment are discarded even if one of them is not received in time*. This behavior of IP is in stark contrast to the TCP protocol which will ask for retransmission of the missing segment only. IP also assigns every datagram a *TTL* (Time-to-live), which ensures that they do not move around in the network forever.

At the receiving end, IP simply unwraps the header meant for it and checks the header information only. It doesn't check the data at all, and only when the header fails the integrity test does IP use the ICMP protocol to relay an error message to the sender. IP has no way of knowing whether a message has been successfully sent or received. It is also *connection-less* because it doesn't bother to find out whether the remote host is ready to exchange data.

ICMP assists IP by providing error messages and echoing requests. If a host is unreachable, ICMP intimates the sending host. ICMP is also used by the **ping** command *(28.5)* which echoes a request to a host to test the connectivity of the network.

IP also has a limited but vital role to play in *routing* (i.e., directing) the datagrams to their proper destination. Routing and its configuration are taken up separately in Chapter 28.

> **Note** If a TCP segment is missing, it has to be transmitted. If an IP-fragmented packet of a TCP segment is missing, TCP has to send the entire segment corresponding to the datagram. IP has no mechanism of sending a single fragment.

19.2.4 The Network Access Layer

The *network access layer*, also known as the *link layer*, is the last layer in the TCP/IP protocol stack. It is also the only one which has knowledge of the underlying hardware built into it. The layer comprises the network interface card, the protocols and the details of the physical media. It accepts datagrams from the internet layer, and encapsulates them by inserting the MAC addresses of both hosts. It finally sends out a *frame* to the wire. *ARP* (Address Resolution Protocol) is the main protocol used by this layer.

We know that IP encapsulates the datagram with the source and destination addresses. Now, these are logical 32-bit addresses consisting of a sequence of four dotted numbers. The network access layer, however, understands only the MAC address, the 48-bit hard-wired address of the network card. If you change the network card of a host with another, the MAC address changes, but it will still be addressable with the same logical address. This is possible because the network access layer has a translation facility which converts all IP addresses to MAC addresses, and vice versa. ARP handles this translation.

When the network access layer receives a datagram from the internet layer, it forwards it to ARP. ARP then sends out a *broadcast* message to every host on the network, requesting an acknowledgment from the machine with this IP address. It's like crying out loud: "I have a datagram to send to machine whose IP address is `192.168.3.45`. If any machine has this address, then send me your MAC address." One machine may respond with its own corresponding MAC address, which is then used by ARP to encapsulate the datagram into a frame and send over the network. Several frames may have to reach out to the same destination, so ARP maintains a *cache* (a temporary storage area which preserves the latest information) of recently used MAC addresses. These are used for subsequent transmissions without making a broadcast each time.

19.3 RESOLVING IP ADDRESSES

IP addresses are used by many utilities like **telnet** and **ftp**. For instance, to connect to a remote site with the IP address `202.54.37.108`, you can use these applications in these ways:

```
ftp 202.54.37.108
telnet 202.54.37.108
```

Users find numbers difficult to remember, while network software understands only numbers. All machines in a network have names, and applications usually access these machines by their names rather than their IP addresses. A set of routines linked to the application called the *resolver* translates the name into its corresponding IP address. These names take two forms:

- A simple hostname (like *saturn*) which can be used by hosts to communicate among themselves in a small network. In such networks, you can connect to a host *saturn* using commands like these:

  ```
  ftp saturn
  telnet saturn
  ```

  The resolver will look up /etc/hosts (called the *hosts* file) to find out the IP address, and the command will then use it to connect to the host.

- A *fully qualified domain name* (FQDN) where the hostname is a component. *ftp.download.com* is an FQDN, where *com* is a domain, *download* is a subdomain and *ftp* is the hostname. The Internet uses only FQDNs. You can download software from the Internet using the **ftp** command like this:

  ```
  ftp ftp.download.com                    The second "ftp" is the hostname
  ```

  The resolver in this case will look up a decentralized database to determine the IP address of this FQDN. This database belongs to the *Domain Name System*, and is normally maintained on separate machines that could be spread across the globe.

Irrespective of the form used in hostnames, the resolver translates the hostname or FQDN into its corresponding IP address. The application can only run when this resolution has been performed. We consider the hosts file in the next section and DNS in the next chapter.

19.3.1 /etc/hosts: The Hosts File

In a small network, the name-address mappings are placed in /etc/hosts in each and every host of the network. This database allows the applications to look up a name and find out its corresponding IP address. A look at a sample file reveals its flexible structure:

```
$ cat /etc/hosts
# Internet host table
#
127.0.0.1       localhost
192.168.35.11   jupiter
192.168.35.12   saturn    s2             Aliases permitted
192.168.35.13   mercury
```

For each machine in the network, this table contains a line mapping the IP address to its respective hostname. It contains at least two fields for each line—one for each address. The line for *saturn* shows that TCP/IP also permits the use of aliases. This makes addressing even simpler as you can now use **telnet saturn** instead of **telnet 192.168.35.12**. And if that seems a lot of work, you can use **telnet s2** too!

The network administrator needs to maintain /etc/hosts on *all* machines in the network. Once that is done, any user can choose either the IP address, the hostname or an alias to access a host. The problem arises when a machine is added to the network. In that case the hosts file has to be changed on all machines. This could be manageable in a small network, but becomes tedious in a large one, and absolutely impossible on the Internet. The Internet uses DNS which is considered in the next chapter.

19.4 THE APPLICATIONS

With this knowledge of the functional aspects of TCP, we now proceed to discuss the well-known networking tools. Some of these tools are also used on the Internet. Initially, we'll be using these tools mostly with simple hostnames using the sample `/etc/hosts` just discussed. Though the Internet is taken up in the next chapter, we'll sometimes use FQDNs in this chapter also.

TCP/IP originally began by the development of a collection of programs called the *DARPA set*. Later, Berkeley developed an entire suite of tools known as the *r-utilities* because all their command names are prefixed with an `r`. Some of the most important applications available in the TCP/IP family are:

- **`telnet`** and **`rlogin`** for logging on to remote machines.
- **`ftp`** and **`rcp`** for file transfer.
- **`rsh`** for executing a command on a remote machine without logging in.
- The electronic mail service using **`mailx`**, **`pine`** and Netscape.
- The Network News Transfer Protocol (NNTP) that allows users to share information by posting messages to a news server.
- The Hyper Text Transfer Protocol (HTTP) of the World Wide Web which browsers like Netscape use to fetch HTML documents.
- The *Point-to-Point Protocol* (PPP) which makes all these facilities available through a telephone line.
- The *Network File System* (NFS) which lets one machine treat the file system of a remote machine as its own.

In the remaining sections of this chapter and the next, we consider the features of these TCP/IP clients and the way some of them need to be configured to be usable. However, for these applications to work, their corresponding server component must be running at the other end. For instance, you can't use **`ftp`** on your local host if the Ftp server is not running remotely. The configuration issues of some of the server applications are taken up in Chapter 28.

19.5 `telnet`: REMOTE LOGIN

Every UNIX vendor offers the **`telnet`** and **`rlogin`** utilities to connect to a remote UNIX system. **`telnet`** belongs to the DARPA command set, while **`rlogin`** is a member of the Berkeley set of r-utilities. If you have an account on a host in a local network (or on the Internet), you can use **`telnet`** with the hostname or IP address as argument:

```
$ telnet 192.168.35.12
Trying 192.168.35.12...
Connected to 192.168.35.12.
Escape character is '^]'.
```

```
SunOS 5.8
login:
```

You now have to enter your login name at this prompt, and then the password to gain access to the remote machine. As long as you are logged in, anything you type is sent to the remote machine, and your machine just acts as any other dumb terminal. Any files that you use or any commands that you run will always be on the remote machine. After you have finished, you can press *[Ctrl-d]*, or type **exit** to log out and return to your local shell.

19.5.1 Working from the telnet> Prompt

When **telnet** is used without the address, the system displays the telnet> prompt, from where you can use its internal commands. This doesn't connect you to any remote machine, but you can invoke a login session from here with **open**:

```
telnet> open saturn
Trying 192.168.35.12...
Connected to saturn.
Escape character is '^]'.
    .....
```

In the midst of a **telnet** session, you might need to check the name of a file that resides on your local machine. The "Escape character" lets you make a temporary escape to the telnet> prompt so that you can execute a command on your local machine. To invoke it, press *[Ctrl-]]* (*[Ctrl]* and the]). You can then use the **!** with a UNIX command, say **ls**, to list files on the *local* machine:

```
$ [Ctrl-]]
telnet> !ls -l *.sam
```

You can close a **telnet** session in two ways. First, you can use the shell's **exit** command, or you can escape to the telnet> prompt with *[Ctrl-]]*, close the session (**close**), and then use **quit** to exit to the local shell.

telnet is the ideal tool for administering a remote machine. Most UNIX programs still use the command line interface, and administration frequently requires editing of simple text files. This is easily done with **telnet**. You can even shut down a remote machine with **telnet**. The program is still widely used today.

> **Tip** It is sometimes difficult to find out which machine you are logged on to, especially when both machines use identical versions of UNIX. That's why the facility available in Bash to use the hostname in the prompt *(11.1.2)* becomes quite useful when using **telnet**.

19.6 ftp: FILE TRANSFER PROTOCOL

TCP/IP offers two commands for transferring files—DARPA's **ftp** (File Transfer Protocol) and Berkeley's **rcp**. **ftp** is more widely used than **rcp** and can be used to transfer both binary and text files. It offers a number of UNIX-like directory-oriented services, and many of its commands have similar names.

Like **telnet**, **ftp** can also be invoked with or without the address. This time, we'll use the hostname:

```
$ ftp saturn
Connected to saturn.
220 saturn FTP server (Version wu-2.6.1-18) ready.
Name (saturn:henry): charlie                    henry logs in as charlie
331 Password required for charlie.
Password: *********                             Enter the password
230 User charlie logged in.
Remote system type is UNIX.
Using binary mode to transfer files.
ftp> _                                          The ftp prompt
```

After establishing a connection with *saturn*, **ftp** prompts for the username and password. The local username is prompted as default (henry), and if you had pressed *[Enter]*, the system would have logged you in as henry. Some systems display the type of the remote machine's operating system and the default mode to transfer files.

Termination of **ftp** is done in two stages. First, you have to disconnect from the remote machine with **close** and then quit **ftp** either with **bye** or **quit**:

```
ftp> close                                      You can skip this if you want
221 Goodbye.
ftp> bye                                        You can use quit also
$ _
```

We have to log on to the Ftp server yet again to try out **ftp**'s internal commands that are featured in the forthcoming paragraphs.

19.6.1 Basic File and Directory Handling

ftp has all the basic facilities needed to handle files and directories on the remote machine—like **pwd**, **ls**, **cd**, **mkdir**, **rmdir** and **chmod**. You can delete a single file (**delete**), multiple files (**mdelete**) or rename a file (**rename**). However, you must at all times remember that all these commands apply only to the *remote* machine and not to the local machine.

If you have to use the operating system commands on the *local* machine, you can use the ! in the usual manner. Since the ! doesn't work with the **cd** command, **ftp** offers the **lcd** (local cd) command to do the job. The following session tells most of the story.

```
ftp> verbose                                    Turns off some ftp messages
Verbose mode off.
ftp> pwd
257 "/home/sales" is current directory.
ftp> ls
-rw-r--r--   1 sales    group       1498 Jul 25 18:34 exrc
-rw-r--r--   1 sales    group         20 Jul 25 18:37 login.sql
-rwxr-xr-x   1 sales    group     289312 Jul 25 18:22 perl
-rw-r--r--   1 sales    group    1457664 Jul 25 18:43 vb4cab.2
  .....
ftp> mkdir reports
ftp> cd reports
```

```
ftp> pwd
257 "/home/sales/reports" is current directory.
ftp> cdup                                        Equivalent to cd ..
ftp> pwd                                         This is on the remote machine
257 "/home/sales" is current directory.
ftp> !pwd                                        This is on the local machine
/home/henry/project3
ftp> delete exrc
ftp> mdelete login.sql perl vb4*                 * is interpreted on remote machine
mdelete login.sql? y
mdelete perl? y
mdelete vb4cab.2? y
```

Observe that **mdelete** prompts for each filename. This default behavior is also displayed by the **mget** and **mput** commands which are also meant to be used with multiple files.

> **Tip** If you desire to have clean output, set the **verbose** mode to `off` by using the command once or twice. The command is a toggle switch, i.e. it alternates between the two modes. By default, it is set on most systems.

19.6.2 Transferring Files

For the purpose of transfer, files can be seen as belonging to two types—*ascii* (text) and *binary*. All executables, graphics, word processing and multimedia files belong to the binary type. These files need special attention, so you should set the transfer mode to `binary` before initiating file transfer.

*Uploading (**put** and **mput**)* If you are a Web site developer, you'll frequently need to upload your Web pages and graphic files to your Web site. The **put** command sends (uploads) a single file, `penguin.gif`, to the remote machine:

```
ftp> binary
200 Type set to I.
ftp> put penguin.gif                             Copied under same name
local: penguin.gif remote: penguin.gif
200 PORT command successful.
150 Opening BINARY mode data connection for penguin.gif.
226 Transfer complete.
6152 bytes sent in 0.04 seconds (150.20 Kbytes/s)
```

You can change your destination filename, and you can also copy multiple files with **mput**:

```
put penguin.gif pelican.gif
mput t*.sql                                      * interpreted on local machine
```

By default, **mput** behaves interactively and seeks confirmation for every file has to be transferred. To make **mput** behave noninteractively, run the **prompt** command before using **mput**. You'll see the message `Interactive mode off.` **prompt** is a toggle switch; the next invocation reverses the previous mode.

*Downloading (**get** and **mget**)* To download files from the remote machine, you'll require the **get** and **mget** commands that are used in a similar manner as their "put" counterparts. This time, we'll turn off all messages with **verbose**:

```
ftp> verbose                                              Turns off noise
ftp> ls
drwxr-xr-x   14 888      999          4096 Jun 15 16:46 communicator
drwxr-xr-x    2 888      999            26 May 14 00:47 communicator_for_france
-rw-r--r--    1 888      999        323393 Sep  7 17:22 ls-lR
-rw-r--r--    1 888      999         28360 Sep  7 17:22 ls-lR.gz
   .....
ftp> binary                                               Default on most systems
ftp> get ls-lR.gz
ftp> _                                                    No statistics this time—file copied
```

Like with **put**, you can change your destination filename, and you can also copy multiple files with **mget**:

```
get ls-lR.gz netscape_filelist
mget t*.sql                                    * interpreted on remote machine
```

The **prompt** setting that works with **mput** also works with **mget** in the same way.

> **Tip** If you want to monitor the downloading of a large file, use **ftp**'s **hash** command before you use **get** or **mget**. A # will be printed whenever a block (8192 bytes in Solaris and Linux) of data has been transferred.

19.6.3 Connecting from the ftp> Prompt

ftp displays the ftp> prompt when used without an argument. You can then establish a connection with its **open** command:

```
$ ftp
ftp> open saturn
Connected to saturn.
220 saturn FTP server (Version wu-2.6.1-18) ready.
Name (saturn:sales): [Enter]
331 Password required for sales.
Password: [Enter]                                  Password not entered
530 Login incorrect.
Login failed.
```

ftp works in two stages. First, it makes a connection with the remote machine. This can be done either by invoking **ftp** with the hostname (*saturn*), or later, with the **open** command. After the connection has been established, **ftp** asks for the username and password. At both prompts, the *[Enter]* key was pressed without supplying either. This leads to an unusual situation where you have established a connection with the remote machine *without actually logging on to it.* You are still on the local machine in every sense of the term.

To log in at this stage, you have to use the **user** command and then go through the usual login sequence:

```
ftp> user charlie
331 Password required for charlie.
Password: ********
```

How does one log on to the numerous Ftp sites on the Internet where we don't have individual accounts? This question is answered in the next section.

19.6.4 Anonymous Ftp

On the Internet, there are several sites which offer trial and public domain software for downloading. There you don't have a separate account and password for every user. These sites offer a special user account, "anonymous," that has to be used for logging in. Though not always mandatory, you are also expected to provide your email address as the password. These sites are known as *anonymous Ftp* sites. You can only download files from an anonymous Ftp site. This is how you connect to the anonymous Ftp site of Netscape Corporation:

```
$ ftp ftp.netscape.com
Connected to ftp.netscape.com (64.12.168.249).
220 ftpnscp.newaol.com FTP server (SunOS 5.8) ready.
Name (ftp.netscape.com:sumit): anonymous
331 Guest login ok, send your complete e-mail address as password.
Password: sumit@cal.vsnl.net.in                    Not echoed on screen
230 Guest login ok, access restrictions apply.
Remote system type is UNIX.
Using binary mode to transfer files.
```

This time we used **ftp** with an FQDN (*ftp.netscape.com*) that represents an Internet host. Once you are in, you can use the **get** and **mget** commands to download the software you want. Note that these sites won't let you upload files to these directories or remove them.

> **LINUX:** On the Internet, file transfers sometimes get aborted, and **ftp** in Linux allows you to resume the transfer with the **reget** command. If the line drops with a file `foo` partially downloaded, you should use **reget foo** to continue the transfer from the point of failure.

19.6.5 .netrc: Using ftp Noninteractively

You always use the same username and password for anonymous Ftp sites. So why enter them every time and not take them from a file instead? **ftp** allows you to do that. It also lets you specify the authentication parameters for each host individually. The file **ftp** uses for this purpose is `$HOME/.netrc`.

Here are three entries in `.netrc`. Two of them are for hosts *jupiter* and *neptune*. The other is for all anonymous Ftp sites where you use the same username and password to log in. Each line in this file specifies the parameters for connecting to an Ftp site:

```
machine jupiter login sasol password l1u2dw3ig
machine neptune login romeo password b1e6e37nn
default login anonymous password romeo@vsnl.com
```

The first two lines apply to "private" Ftp sites where the user has individual accounts. `machine`, `login` and `password` are keywords, and each keyword is followed by its corresponding parameter. The last line contains the keyword `default` and generally applies to all other sites. Here, it is used for anonymous Ftp sites. This line has one word less than the previous ones.

Since the file contains the clear-text password, it must be made unreadable to group and others (with **chmod 600 .netrc**). Your **ftp** client will now use this file for logging on to *jupiter*, *neptune* and anonymous Ftp sites without prompting.

19.7 THE BERKELEY COMMANDS

TCP/IP is also shipped with the *r-utilities*, a comprehensive set of tools from Berkeley, featuring remote login (**rlogin**), remote copying (**rcp**) and remote command execution (**rsh**). These commands were developed for password-free access to UNIX machines only. Though they have been overshadowed by the DARPA commands, **telnet** and **ftp**, the r-utilities do possess some advantages.

To be able to use these commands without using the password (a risky facility to have in the first place), the remote machine must be configured properly. The authorization to use these tools is controlled by the files `/etc/hosts.equiv` and `$HOME/.rhosts` on the remote machine. They determine whether **rlogin** can be used without a password, and **rcp** and **rsh** be used at all. The system administrator's role in setting up the configuration files is discussed in Chapter 28.

19.7.1 rlogin: Remote Login without Password

Like **telnet**, the **rlogin** command can also be used for remote login. After you log in, you won't know which utility you used to get there:

```
$ rlogin saturn
Last login: Mon Jan 20 19:51:14 from mercury
$ _
```

Unlike **telnet**, **rlogin** doesn't prompt for the username, and the above command sequence allows a user henry to log on to a remote machine with the same username, and without supplying a password. If **rlogin** prompts for the password, then the remote machine is not properly set up for using this facility.

The reason why the r-utilities are avoided by many is that they can make access extremely insecure. For instance, user charlie on a remote machine can allow henry to log on to charlie's account without using a password! This requires henry to use the `-l` option to specify a different username:

```
rlogin -l charlie saturn                    henry logs on to saturn with username charlie
```

To log on in this manner, it's not necessary for charlie to have an account on the local machine. If the remote machine was not specifically set up for henry to log on in this manner, the system will prompt for the password, which has to be charlie's password on the remote machine.

19.7.2 rcp: Remote File Copying

rcp behaves like **cp** except that it copies files between two networked machines. Though it has been virtually replaced by **ftp**, it retains one important advantage over **ftp**: *It can copy subdirectory structures (recursive copying)*. Like **cp**, **rcp** requires both source and destination filenames to be provided:

```
rcp saturn:/home/henry/cent2fah.pl c2f.pl        Copies cent2fah.pl to c2f.pl
```

This copies a file from the remote machine *saturn*. A file on a remote machine is described to **rcp** in the form *hostname*:*filename*, using the : as delimiter. If the file has to be copied from the user's home directory, then you can shorten the command line further:

```
rcp henry@saturn:cent2fah.pl c2f.pl
```

Multiple files may be copied, but the last argument of **rcp** then has to be a directory. You can use shell wild-cards for *remote* interpretation, and the command also works both ways:

```
rcp saturn:/home/henry/"*" .                    * interpreted remotely
rcp * saturn:/home/henry                        * interpreted locally
```

Recursive Copying **rcp**'s `-r` option is used for recursive copying and remains its strongest selling point. Either of the following commands copy the entire subdirectory tree `/home/henry` to the current directory on the local machine:

```
rcp -r saturn:/home/henry .
rcp -r henry@saturn:. .                         Two dots
```

Generally, **rcp** doesn't prompt for the password. Either it works without one or it doesn't work at all. This may not be true on all systems.

19.7.3 rsh: Remote Command Execution

Sometimes, you require the resources of a larger system to run a CPU-intensive program without going through the formalities of logging in. **rsh** allows you to request a remote computer to run a particular program on that machine. It needs the machine name and the command:

```
rsh uranus ls -l                                ls -l executed on host uranus
```

Though **ls** is run remotely, the output is seen on your terminal. You have to escape the redirection character if you want to save the output in a file on the remote machine:

```
rsh uranus ls -l \> dir.lst                     > interpreted remotely
```

The absence of the \ would have saved the output in a local file. If you use wild-cards that have to be interpreted remotely, you need to quote or escape them too.

Tip You can also run a separate shell on the remote machine by using **`rsh uranus`** (without the command name). If you are using the X Window system, then you can use the `DISPLAY` variable or the `-display` option *(18.6.3)* to run X clients on the remote machine and have their display on your local machine.

19.8 CONCLUSION

The commands of the DARPA and Berkeley sets are inherently insecure because they send out the password in clear text to the network. Today, we have at our disposal, the *secure shell* (SSH) and its associated programs that encrypt the password before transmission. This prevents intruders from knowing your password. Security-conscious systems are increasingly using SSH which hopefully will replace the old programs that we have discussed in this chapter. Linux systems offer both the secure shell server (**sshd**) and its clients (**ssh**, **sftp** and **scp**), but thcy may not be available on your UNIX host.

In the next chapter, we'll discuss the newer members of the TCP/IP suite of applications. We'll take up Network News and have a second look at email and the way it handles multimedia attachments. We also have to examine in some detail the "one-stop-shop" that has integrated the important conventional applications within the framework of its own protocol—HTTP and the World Wide Web.

WRAP UP

TCP/IP is a vendor-independent suite of protocols that connects heterogeneous machines in a network. It splits data into packets and wraps each packet with a header before sending it out. If a packet is corrupt, TCP/IP ensures reliable transmission with full error control by retransmitting the packet. Packets are *routed* between hosts of two networks using a *router* or *gateway* which is part of both networks.

Every host in a network is represented by a unique *hostname* and a unique *IP address*. An IP address consists of four dot-separated octets. TCP/IP lets you access a host by both the IP address and hostname, but hostnames are easier to remember. The name-address mappings are kept in /etc/hosts on *all* machines of a small network.

TCP/IP works in the *client-server* model. The client application (like **ftp**) communicates with its server counterpart at the other end to achieve its task. The server programs are known as *daemons*, which run in the background and listen for request at certain *ports*. Servers use fixed port numbers for a service, but clients use random port numbers at their end. An IP address-port number pair constitutes a *socket*.

TCP/IP is represented by a four-layer model where each layer has a well-defined role of adding/removing header information as well as fragmenting/reassembling the data. Data from the application are broken into *segments*, then *packets* or *datagrams*, and finally *frames* at the various layers. At the receiving end, they are reassembled and the headers removed.

The DARPA set of TCP/IP applications comprise **telnet** and **ftp**. **telnet** is used to run commands on a remote machine and have the display on the local machine. It's a useful tool for administering a remote machine.

ftp is meant for file transfer. You can upload one or more files (**put** and **mput**) or download them (**get** and **mget**). *Anonymous Ftp* lets you download files from the Internet. Noninteractive operation is achieved by using the file $HOME/.netrc.

The Berkeley r-utilities offer less secure tools that don't require a password—**rlogin** for remote login, **rcp** for file copying and **rsh** for remote command execution. **rcp** allows you to copy an entire directory tree.

The *secure shell* is more secure than all these commands as it encrypts the password before it is transmitted.

TEST YOUR UNDERSTANDING

19.1 What is the difference between TCP's behavior with regard to a missing segment and IP's behavior with regard to a missing packet?

19.2 Why is TCP termed a *reliable* protocol?

19.3 Describe the mechanism by which the IP address is translated to the MAC address.

19.4 What is the significance of the *loopback address*?

19.5 What is the significance of the port number? How will you find out the port number **finger** uses?

19.6 Why is **telnet** generally used on the Internet in preference to **rlogin**?

19.7 How can you be sure whether you are working on the local machine or used **telnet** to log on to a remote machine?

19.8 If you rename **/bin/ls** to something else, will you be able to use **ftp**'s internal **ls** command?

19.9 You copied a graphics file with **ftp**, and the file appears to be corrupted. What could be the possible reason?

19.10 With which command do you upload files to an anonymous Ftp site?

19.11 When will you be compelled to use **rcp** in preference to **ftp**?

FLEX YOUR BRAIN

19.1 Describe three important features of TCP/IP. What is an RFC?

19.2 How is a TCP/IP network different from a telephone network?

19.3 What is a *socket*? Can two connections have the same pair of sockets?

19.4 Describe the role of the resolver when handling (i) simple hostnames (ii) fully qualified domain names.

19.5 How do you change the current directory on your local machine after you have logged in to a remote machine using (i) **telnet** (ii) **ftp**?

19.6 Name the sequence of commands to be executed to download *noninteractively* all PDF files from the directory /home/romeo/docs on host *pluto* to the directory /home/kumar/docs on the local machine.

19.7 When you change your local directory from inside **ftp**, will the changed directory still be in place after you quit **ftp**, and why?

19.8 How will you connect noninteractively to an anonymous Ftp site?

19.9 You have to "ftp" to your own account on another host, but when you use the **ftp** command with the hostname, you find that you have logged on to a different account. When does that happen, and how will you rectify the situation?

19.10 What does this command do? **rsh jupiter date \> .date**

19.11 Why are the advantages of SSH over **telnet** and **ftp**?

20

The Internet

The Internet owes its origin to the ARPANET network that was built in the 70s at the behest of the U.S. Department of Defense. It is a collection of a very large number of interconnected networks providing connectivity to millions of computers. The Net is often referred to as the "network of networks." It is also the biggest client-server experiment in computer history that embodies open architecture networking using TCP/IP's packet-switching technology.

Some of the TCP/IP applications used on the Net have already been discussed in Chapter 19. Ftp still remains a popular Internet service. However, the vast size of the Internet has important implications for a number of applications, especially in the way hosts are addressed and mail transported. This chapter examines these two issues and also takes on the late entrants to the Internet, including the World Wide Web.

WHAT YOU WILL LEARN

- The concept of *domains* and the Internet domain hierarchy.
- The role of *name servers*, *resolvers* and a distributed database in performing hostname-IP address mappings.
- Use Netscape Messenger to handle email.
- How Network News works and *newsgroups* are organized.
- The significance of the Web components—*hypertext*, *uniform resource locators* (URLs) and the HTML language.
- The working of the *Hyper Text Transfer Protocol* (HTTP) and its role in executing external programs.
- Use Netscape Navigator to handle Web resources.

TOPICS OF SPECIAL INTEREST

- The cooperative efforts of the *MUA*, *MTA* and *MDA* in transporting mail on the Internet.
- The *Multipurpose Internet Mail Extensions* (MIME) standard in handling mail attachments.
- How MIME technology is used to handle different media types on the Web.

20.1 THE DOMAIN NAME SYSTEM (DNS)

Because of the sheer number of hosts on the Internet, you just can't use hosts files (/etc/hosts) there. The Internet (or, rather the ARPANET, its ancestor) did have a centralized file in its teens, but its maintenance became so painful that Berkeley had to step in with the *Domain Name System* (DNS). DNS is a distributed system that is scalable easily. It introduces three key concepts:

- A hierarchical organization of hostnames.
- A distributed database for performing the name-address mappings.
- Delegation of authority to individual levels of the hierarchy.

In the Internet namespace, hosts belong to *domains*, which in turn could belong to *subdomains*, and so forth. Like in the file system, these domains and subdomains form a hierarchy with the *root* domain as the top, signified by a . (dot) (Fig. 20.1). The root domain has immediately below it a number of *top-level domains* (TLDs) or *generic domains*, like *edu* and *com*. These in turn have subdomains or second-level domains under them in the same way a directory has subdirectories under it. You can have further subdomains under these subdomains, and this nesting can descend several levels.

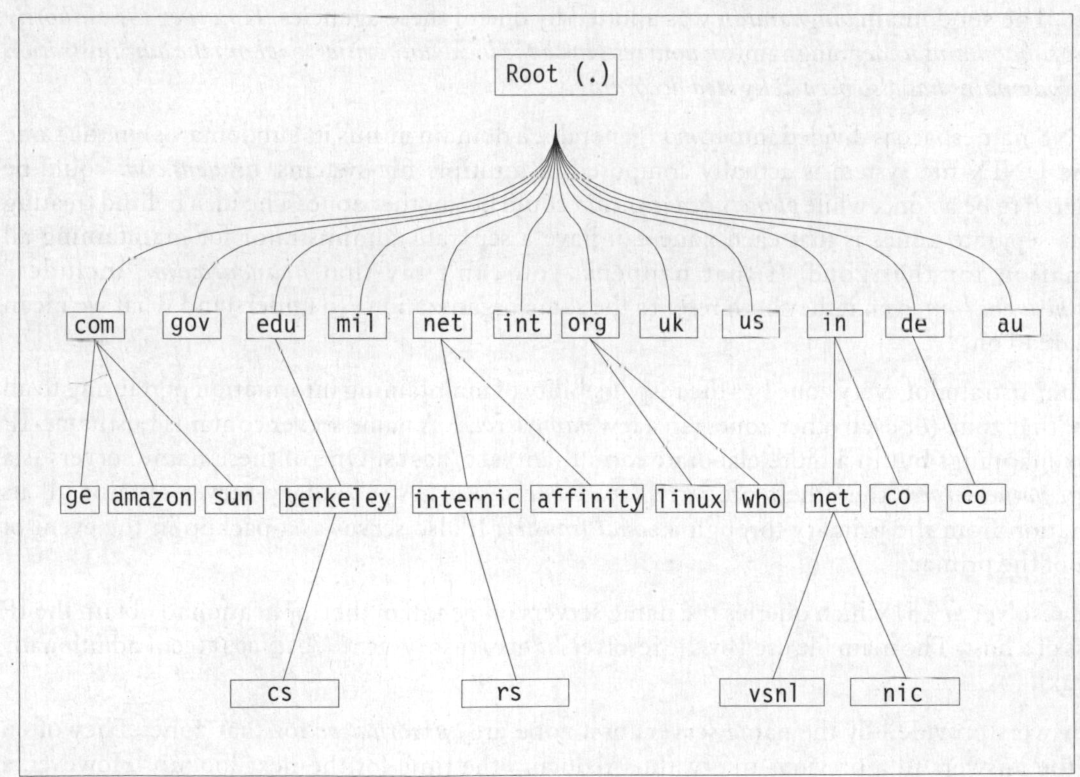

Fig. 20.1 The Internet Domain Hierarchy

For instance, if *binghamton* is a subdomain under *edu*, and *cs* a subdomain under *binghamton*, then the host *ralph* could be uniquely described as

ralph.cs.binghamton.edu.

In the hierarchy related to these dot-separated strings, *edu* is above binghamton, which in turn is above *cs*. *ralph.cs.binghamton.edu* represents a *fully qualified domain name* (FQDN) of the host *ralph*—something like the absolute pathname of a file. Another *site* (a collection of hosts of a single organization) can also have the hostname *ralph*, or the subdomain name *cs*, but the FQDN will be unique throughout the Internet.

The Net originally had eight three-character TLDs (top-level domains) allocated to organizations based on the nature of their activities. MIT is represented in the *edu* domain, but Sun Microsystems (*com*) and GNU (*org*) belong to different TLDs. Moreover, every country listed in the ISO-3166-1 specification is also represented by a two-letter *country-code top-level domain* (ccTLD) (India—*in*, Germany—*de*, France—*fr*, etc.). In late 2000, seven more TLDs have been added *(aero*, *museum*, *name*, etc.) (Table 20.1).

Typically, an organization gets one domain name and uses subdomains for its branches, subsidiaries or sites. There are agencies spread across the globe that allocate these domains without creating conflict. The subdomain *binghamton* was allotted by one of these agencies. *However, the authority to create subdomains under* binghamton *now rests with the local authorities to whom the administration of the subdomains has also been delegated accordingly*.

The DNS namespace is divided into *zones* (generally, a domain minus its subdomains) in the same way the UNIX file system is actually composed of multiple file systems. *heavens.com* could be considered to be a zone, while *planets.heavens.com* could be another zone. The idea behind treating them as separate zones is that each zone can have a separate administrator for maintaining all information for that zone. If that happens, you can't say that *heavens.com* "includes" *planets.heavens.com* even if they both refer to the same organization. To understand what we mean by this, read on.

The administrator of every zone has the responsibility of maintaining information pertaining to all hosts of that zone (or even other zones) in a few *name servers*. A name server contains hostname-IP address mappings but in a more elaborate form than `/etc/hosts`. One of these name servers is a *primary name server*; the others are *secondary name servers*. A secondary server obtains all its information from the primary through a *zonal transfer*. It also serves as a backup in the event of failure of the primary.

It's the resolver *(19.3)* which queries the name servers on behalf of the application to obtain the IP address of a host. The main file used by the resolver is `/etc/resolv.conf` (`/etc/host.conf` additionally in Linux).

The answers provided by the name servers of a zone are *authoritative* for that zone. They often cache the answers to a previous query, thus reducing the time for the next lookup. However, a name server must not give up when the address requested falls outside its zonal boundary. Instead, it must be able to contact other name servers, by *referral*, so that the FQDN finally gets resolved into the IP address.

The referral also follows a hierarchical pattern. If the local name server can't provide the address of *ralph.cs.binghamton.edu*, it will refer the matter to the server for *cs.binghamton.edu*, then *binghamton.edu*, and so forth. However, every name server must have pointers to the *root-level name servers*, so that it can contact them directly if it knows that referring the matter to the intermediate level servers would be futile. We have thirteen root-level servers on the Internet, each of which contains the IP addresses of the authoritative servers of the TLDs (*com*, *edu*, etc.).

Note FQDNs are case-insensitive; you can use *JACK.HILL.COM* in the same way you can use *jACk.HiLL.coM*. An FQDN should identify the organization easily.

Table 20.1 The Internet Domains (TLDs and cc-TLDs)

Domain Name	***Significance***
int	International Organizations
edu	Educational Institutions
gov	US Govt Organizations
mil	US Military Organizations
org	Non-profit Organizations
com	Commercial Organizations
net	Networking Organizations
arpa	Domain for Reverse Resolution
aero	Air-transport industry
biz	Businesses
museum	Accredited museums
name	Individuals; possible to have *henry.blofeld.name*
pro	Professionals
coop	Cooperatives
info	For all uses
in	ccTLD; India
uk, *ch*, *us*, etc.	Other ccTLDs; United Kingdom, Switzerland, USA, etc.

20.2 INTERNET MAIL

In Chapter 12, we examined the email system and the tools used to move mail between users on the same host. The mail programs generally need no special configuration to deliver mail in these single-host situations. However, the mechanism used to move mail on the Internet is a little complex. Unlike Telnet and Ftp, which work within a simple client-server framework, Internet mail handling requires the work of at least three agencies:

- *Mail user agent* (MUA)—For reading the mailbox and sending mail.
- *Mail transport agent* (MTA)—For transporting mail between machines.
- *Mail delivery agent* (MDA)—For delivering mail to the recipients' mailboxes.

In this three-tier arrangement, the *mail user agent* (MUA) like **mailx** or **pine** acts as the user's frontend. The MUA reads incoming mail from the mailbox and hands over outgoing mail to the *mail transport agent* (MTA).

The MTA too has two functions: it both sends and receives mail. At the sending end, the MTA identifies the recipient's address and delivers the message *directly* to the MTA at the other end. At the receiving end, the MTA passes on mail to the *Mail Delivery Agent* (MDA). Both these functions are handled universally by the *Simple Mail Transfer Protocol* (SMTP).

The MTA is not responsible for ultimate delivery of the message. It is the MDA that accepts mail from the receiving MTA and delivers it to the actual user's mailbox. This is handled by separate programs like **/usr/lib/mail.local** on Solaris and **procmail** on Linux.

A fourth tier comes in when the MTA is unable to deliver mail to the MDA. This is true for dialup lines where the user's host connects to the network intermittently. In this arrangement, users typically use their ISP's facilities to handle both incoming and outgoing mail. The ISP stores the user's mail on their server, and the user fetches the mail using a separate program. There are two protocols in use today for fetching mail—*Post Office Protocol* (POP3) and *Internet Message Access Protocol* (IMAP).

The simple character-based clients like **mailx** and **pine** can only view mail that has been delivered to the host on which they are running; they can't retrieve mail from a POP/IMAP server. It's only some of the GUI-based clients like Netscape Messenger and Mozilla that can do so. We consider Netscape next.

20.3 NETSCAPE MESSENGER: A VERSATILE MAILER

Netscape Messenger is an excellent multipurpose mail client. Even though it's mainly known as an MUA, it performs some functions of the MTA and MDA as well. It uses its built-in SMTP facilities to transport mail to an outgoing mail server. It also acts as a POP/IMAP client to fetch mail from a remote server and deliver it to its *own* mailbox (distinct from the one used by the character-based clients). In this section, we consider some of the features of this workhorse that are absent in **mailx** and **pine**.

Messenger is actually a component of the Netscape Communicator suite that is shipped with most UNIX systems. Communicator also features Navigator as the other major component—one that is used to browse Web documents. To invoke Communicator, either click on its icon on the X desktop (if available) or run this command from a terminal emulator like **xterm**:

```
netscape &
```

Either Messenger or Navigator will show up (or both). At the bottom right, you'll see the *Component Bar* containing a set of five icons, each representing a separate Communicator function. If the Messenger window doesn't show up, then you can either use *Communicator>Messenger* from the Menu Bar at the top, or click on the second icon in the Component Bar.

> **LINUX:** If you are using one of the latest versions, you may not have Netscape on your system. Red Hat offers Mozilla as a free Open Source look-alike. Practically everything discussed in this topic also applies to Mozilla. Invoke Mozilla with **mozilla &**.

20.3.1 Configuring Messenger

Unlike `mailx` and `pine`, Messenger must be configured before it can be used. The first time you invoke it, you may be prompted to enter the necessary parameters through a sequence of screens. In any case, Communicator can be customized from the *Edit>Preferences* menu. On the new window that pops up, expand the *Mail & Newsgroups* category by clicking on the triangle on its left. Two items are important in the expanded list—*Identity* and *Mail Servers*.

Now move to the *Identity* section and enter your full name and email address. This section also shows the location of the `.signature` file *(12.6.2—Tip)*, which you may like to attach with every outgoing message. Next, click on the *Mail Servers* section (Fig. 20.2). Here, you'll have to enter the FQDNs (or IP addresses) of the mail servers—both incoming and outgoing. If your mail is handled by your ISP, then enter the names of the ISP's mail servers. Your ISP may or may not use two different servers for the two types of mail. Also enter your username for both mail servers. For the incoming mail server, you'll also have to decide whether

- The password can be stored so it need not be entered every time.
- Mail is to be checked regularly and new messages automatically downloaded.
- Messages are to be left on the server. As a beginner, you should make sure that they are, so you should check this box (default: unchecked).

Once all this is done, you are ready to use Messenger.

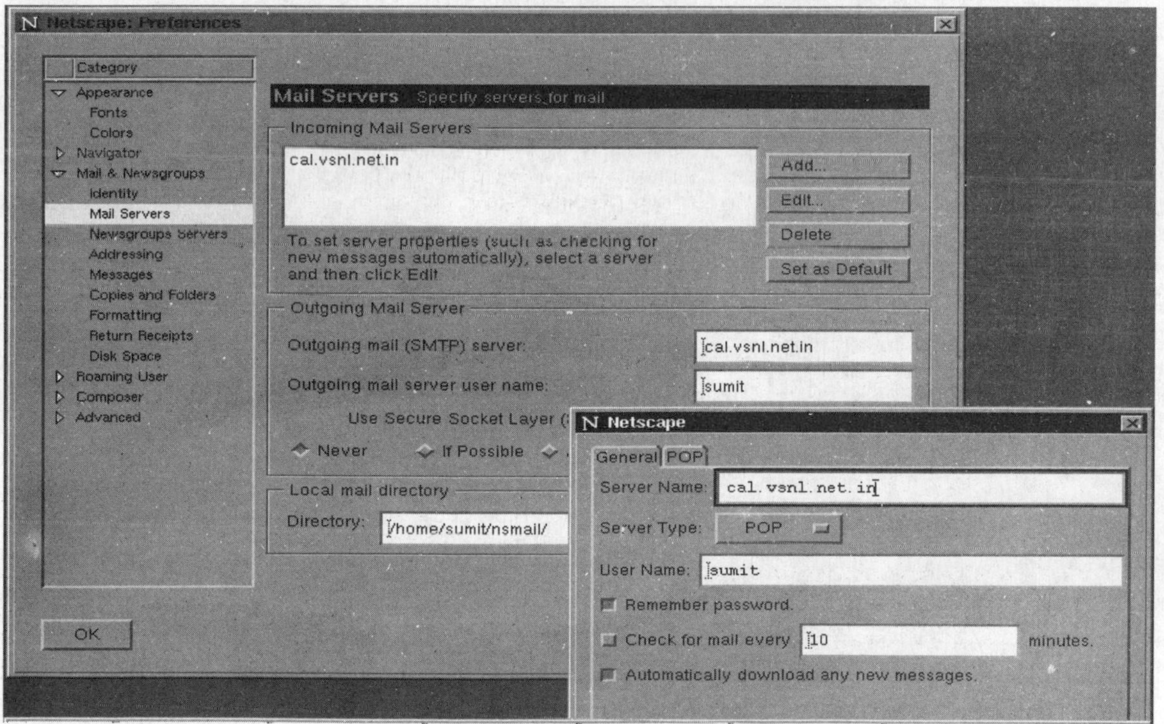

Fig. 20.2 Configuring Mail Servers in Netscape Messenger

20.3.2 Messenger: The Frontal View

From version 4.5 onwards, Messenger shows a three-pane window (Fig. 20.3). All message folders are shown on the left (the *Message Center*) along with the number of read and unread messages. You can create folders for different subjects under *Local Mail* (*File>New Folder*). The Message Center also features a separate folder for Network News, which is taken up in the next topic.

The top-right pane (*Header Pane*) shows the message headers while the bottom-right pane (*Content Pane*) displays the body of the currently selected message. Double-clicking on a message header brings up a new window with a larger viewing area. You can stretch and compress these panes with your mouse to suit your convenience. To move a message to a folder in the Message Center, simply drag the message header to the folder with your left mouse button.

At the top is the Menu Bar, followed below by the Mail Toolbar containing some clickable icons. The basic functions are all handled here, and you've encountered most of them in the character-based mailers. But Messenger is not meant only for sending email messages; a message can also be addressed to a newsgroup *(20.5)*.

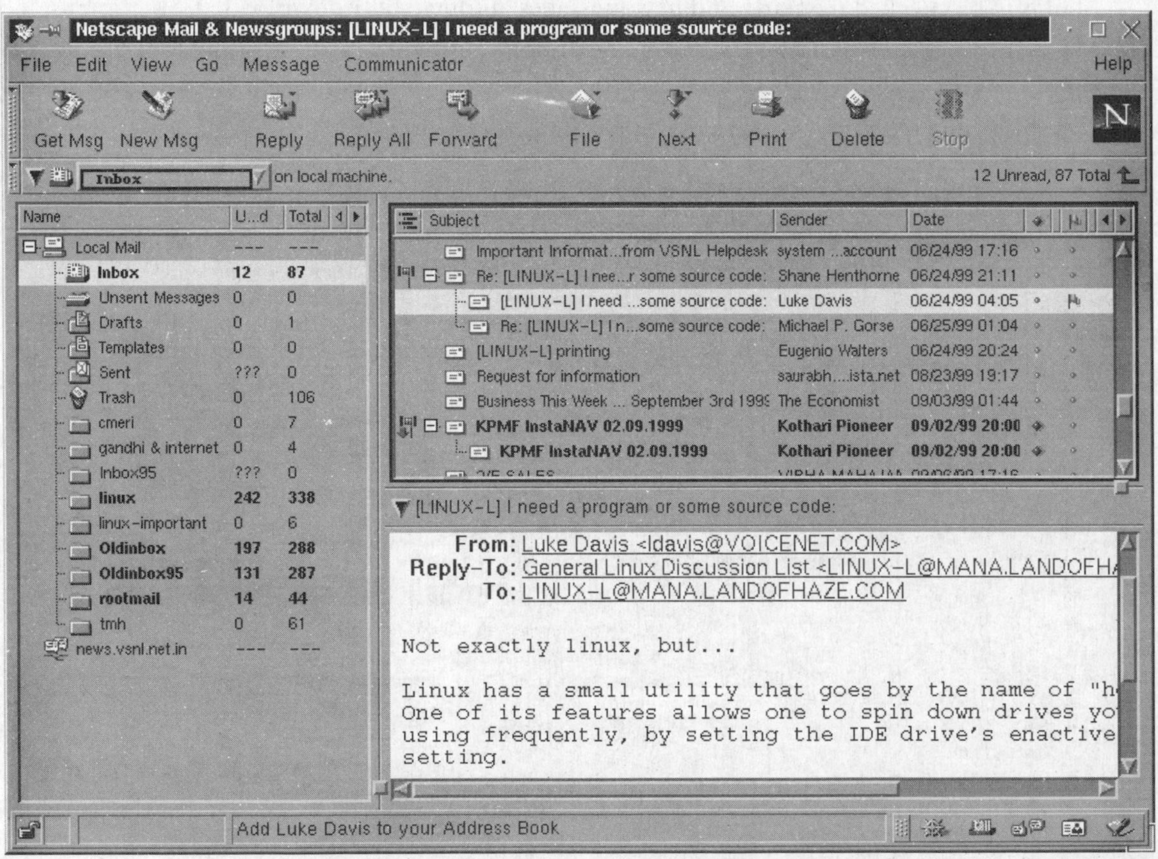

Fig. 20.3 Netscape Messenger: A Frontal View

20.3.3 Using Messenger

To download messages from a POP/IMAP server, click on *Get Msg*. All messages end up in the `Inbox` folder. You can reply to or forward a message by clicking on the respective icon in the Mail Toolbar. To compose a message, use *New Msg* to open a composition window. You can pick up the address from an address book (*Address* from the Mail Toolbar of the composition window). You can send (*Send*) a message immediately or defer it (*File>Send Later*). This feature lets you compose a group of messages offline and later send them in a bunch (*File>Send Unsent Messages*).

Messenger's address book (*Communicator>Address Book*) is well implemented (Fig. 20.4). You can initiate a mail communication from here. Just click on *New Msg*, and you'll see the composition window popping up. When you have a number of entries in your address book, you should save them in a text file (*File>Export*). You can carry this file with you wherever you go and import this list on another machine (*File>Import*).

Extending the idea of the address book is the *mailing list*, which is an alias for multiple email accounts. When a message is addressed to a list by its name, Messenger automatically performs the expansion and sends the message to all the members of the list. To create a list, click on *New List* in the address book. Give the list a name or a nickname, and then drag the entries from the address book to the mailing list window to create its members.

Messenger handles both text and binary attachments rather well—an area where **`mailx`** and **`pine`** have certain deficiencies. It displays graphics that are in GIF, JPEG and PNG format. These three formats are standard on the Web, and every GUI browser can also display them without seeking help. If Messenger can't view an attachment on its own, it will call up a *helper application* (an external program on disk), but only after the application has been registered in Netscape with *Edit>Preferences*.

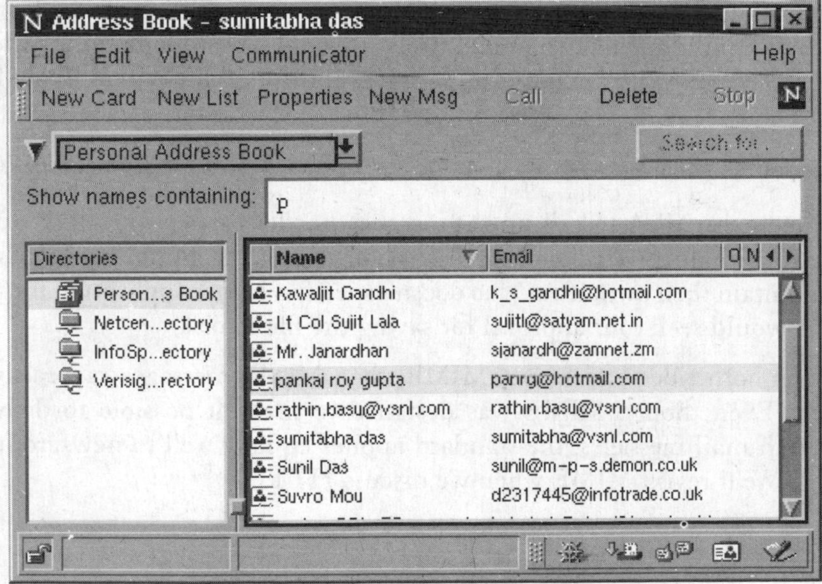

Fig. 20.4 Netscape Messenger: Address Book

20.4 MIME: HANDLING BINARY ATTACHMENTS

The original SMTP protocol allowed only 7-bit ASCII characters to form a mail message. Moreover, RFC 822 imposed a limit of 1000 characters for the maximum size of a line. As mail usage increased, the requirement to include 8-bit binary files with arbitrary line lengths was being increasingly felt. RFC 822 had to be extended by another standard, *Multipurpose Internet Mail Extensions* (MIME), that addresses these issues.

MIME extends the definition of mail to include binary files and multiple data formats in a *single* message. While RFC 822 was concerned with message headers, MIME is concerned with the format of the *content*. It also imposes no restriction on line length. Attachments containing binary data have to be encoded but the MIME standard requires two additional headers to be sent with the message:

```
Content-Type: application/pdf; name="interior.pdf"
Content-Transfer-Encoding: base64
```

The `Content-Type` header defines the *type/subtype* of the data following the header. Here, `pdf` is a subtype of `application`. For text files, you'll see `text/plain` or `text/html` as the Content-Type. Multimedia Content-Type can also be `image/jpeg` and `image/gif` for pictures, `video/mpeg` and `audio/aiff` for video and audio files, respectively. It can also be `multipart`, which means that multiple types of content can form the message body.

The `Content-Transfer-Encoding` header defines the encoding techniques used on the data. There are three well-known techniques that are used universally. `7bit` and `quoted-printable` are used for ASCII data, while `base64` is used for images, audio and video. `base64` encodes three octets of data as four six-bit characters. This consequently increases the file size by 33 percent.

These two headers provide the necessary information that would enable a MIME-compliant mail handling application at the other end to decode the content and make it available in a usable form. If the MUA can't handle a mail attachment itself, it would have to look up the file `mailcap`. This file specifies the *helper application* (an external program) for each Content-Type. Here's an entry from this file:

```
application/pdf; acroread %s
```

Note the delimiter is ;

This entry directs the MUA to call up the Acrobat Reader to view the PDF document. Many UNIX systems maintain a systemwide `mailcap` database in `/etc`, but many MUAs (like Netscape Messenger) maintain their own. If `mailcap` doesn't specify a helper application for a Content-Type, then the MUA would seek your approval for saving the file to disk.

If the MUAs on both sides understand MIME, then MIME messages can easily be exchanged between them. Even though MIME was designed to make it possible to deliver multimedia attachments with mail messages, the standard applies equally well to newsgroup messages and Web resources. We'll revisit MIME when we discuss HTTP.

20.5 NETWORK NEWS AND NEWSGROUPS

Since before the Internet, UNIX users have participated in a discussion forum known as *USENET* (Users' Network). It is a collection of *newsgroups* (discussion groups) where users pose problems on any topic. Someone somewhere usually cares to provide a suitable reply. We'll use the term *Network News* or simply *News* to mean the collection of over 100,000 newsgroups that are available on the Internet. USENET initially worked on a now-obsolete protocol named UUCP, but has since migrated to the *Network News Transfer Protocol* (NNTP), one of the application layer protocols of TCP/IP. NNTP uses port 119.

Before you can use Network News, you must have a *newsreader* client on your machine. This is a program that fetches news from a news server. You also have to *subscribe* to one or more newsgroups (Net News is free). This means that you have to tell your *newsreader* (not the server) the names of the newsgroups you would like to see on a regular basis. The newsreader keeps track of all subscribed newsgroups and article headers that have been downloaded.

News is maintained on a number of news servers by ISPs. Every news server gets *newsfeeds* from other news servers on the Internet at regular intervals by virtue of agreements which the administrators of these servers conclude among themselves. Because of the sheer volume of data generated by Network News, the news server has to *retire* (throw out) old articles to make place for new ones. It's quite possible that when you attempt to fetch the contents of a message, you'll find that it's no longer there.

You can actively participate in any newsgroup by *posting* (i.e., sending) an article or a message. Someone, in response, will post an article of her own. When a series of postings emanate from one, a particular message constitutes a *thread*. You can also be a passive news reader and just "drop in" to see what others have to say.

20.5.1 Newsgroup Naming and Conventions

Like domain names, newsgroups are organized as dot-delimited names, but in a reversed hierarchical manner. A typical newsgroup where you may pose all the problems you encounter in `perl` takes this form:

comp.lang.perl

The name on the left of the dot represents a higher level than the one on the right. Here, *comp* is the main group (computers), and *lang* (languages) is a subgroup under it. There are several newsgroups under *comp.lang* and even more under *comp*. Most newsgroups you see on the Net, especially the serious ones, can be traced back to USENET. These are the major ones that you'll see everywhere:

- *biz*—Business activities. Advertising permitted.
- *comp*—Computers. There are two major subgroups—*comp.lang* (for languages) and *comp.os* (for operating systems).
- *news*—All about USENET.
- *rec*—Recreation.

- *sci*—Group for the sciences, both hard and soft (like psychology and economics).
- *soc*—Social and cultural issues.
- *misc*—Miscellaneous group. Deals with matters not found anywhere else.
- *talk*—A free discussion on many contemporary topics.

There's often a great deal of overlap in the subjects addressed by these groups. Thus it's not uncommon for a message to be posted to multiple newsgroups. Important messages find place in the *FAQ* (Frequently Asked Questions), a compilation carried out from USENET postings by certain volunteers. For routine queries, you should look up the relevant FAQ before posting an article to a newsgroup.

Apart from the FAQ, *smileys* have their origin in USENET. These are ASCII characters (like :-)) which convey certain feelings, and when used judiciously can be remarkably effective. USENET is also responsible for the birth of the terms *foo*, *bar* and *foobar*, which are often used in the examples of this book as generic filenames.

Note Even though Netscape Messenger also handles Network News, we'll not discuss this function of Messenger in this text. If you have access to the World Wide Web, you probably would like to use your browser to access the newsgroups that are available at several sites. The well-known search engine, Google, offers comprehensive News services at *http://groups.google.com*.

20.6 THE WORLD WIDE WEB

The World Wide Web is the Internet's latest and finest service yet. It was originally conceived by Tim Berners-Lee at CERN, Switzerland, as a simple mechanism for interconnecting documents spread across the globe. It quickly went beyond the original vision of its creator, and today functions as a "one-stop shop" for practically everything that's discussed in this chapter and most of the previous one. The Web kept the traditional Internet services (email, anonymous Ftp and Net News) alive, but completely obsoleted its immediate ancestors, Archie and Gopher.

Even though the Web appears to be a conglomeration of multiple services, it works within the framework of the simple client-server model. Web service uses the *Hyper Text Transfer Protocol* (HTTP), and Web servers, also known as *HTTP servers* listen for requests at port 80. The Web's access (client) tool is called the *browser*. A Web browser fetches a document (or any *resource*) residing on Web servers and formats it using the formatting instructions provided in the document itself. It also displays pictures if they are in GIF, JPEG and PNG formats. If there's a format it can't understand, it will call up a plugin or a helper application *(20.8)* to handle it.

The World Wide Web is indeed a "web"—a vast collection of linked *hypertext* documents. This linkage is based on the understanding that if a resource is available on one server, then it makes no sense to have it on another. These links are specified by *Uniform Resource Locators* (URLs). In this way, the user "wanders and roams" without needing to know where she is, and initiates a new connection with a simple keystroke or a mouse click.

Web documents are written in the *Hyper Text Markup Language* (HTML), a text-based portable language. HTML can highlight any portion of text to be displayed with some attributes (like bold, red in color, etc.). However, HTML's real power lies in its hypertext capability. HTML text contains hypertext links (or hyperlinks) to other Web pages. Activating a link can take you to another place in the same document, another document on the same server, or any page anywhere on the Internet. Text can also link to pictures, and what's more, even pictures themselves can contain links to other pictures.

With some much jargon already introduced, it's time to understand the role they play in the functioning of the Web.

20.6.1 The Uniform Resource Locator (URL)

A resource is described by a *Uniform Resource Locator* (URL)—a form of addressing that combines the FQDN of the site and the pathname of the resource. The simplest URL is one that specifies only the FQDN of the server, and is entered through the URL window of the browser:

http://java.sun.com *Press [Enter]*

This displays the *home page* of Sun's Java site. Web servers are often configured to send the file `index.html` when you specify the FQDN as above. The home page will also show a number of hyperlinks in the form of underlined text. Clicking on a link fetches a different page, and your URL could change to something like this:

http://java.sun.com/docs/books/tutorial/information/FAQ.html

The URL syntax ranges from the simple to the complex, but in general, a URL is a combination of three or four things:

- The protocol (usually `http://`) used in transferring the resource. A Web browser supports other protocols, so you can use `ftp://` to transfer a file. You may drop the `http://` prefix when fetching a Web page because that's the default used by all browsers.
- The port number, which is not usually specified if the server uses the default port 80. The above URL is equivalent to *http://java.sun.com:80/docs/books/tutorial/information/FAQ.html*. Note the colon before the port number.
- The FQDN of the host (here, *java.sun.com*).
- The pathname of the resource (here, `docs/books/tutorial/information/FAQ.html`). This need not always be a resource to fetch, but could be a program to run on the server.

The Web has a strong UNIX tradition, so frontslashes are the rule. Like Ftp servers, Web servers also have their own root directory, which is distinctly different from the file system's root. In other words `/docs` is not under the system's root.

Note The URL string is not *fully* case-insensitive. As discussed before, the FQDN is case-insensitive; *JAVA.SUN.COM* is the same as *java.sun.com*. But whether the pathname is case-insensitive or not depends on the operating system used by the server. Most Web servers use UNIX, and UNIX is case-sensitive. If you have seen the pathname `/Docs/index.html`, then enter it just that way.

20.6.2 HTTP: The Protocol of the Web

Like the other Internet services, HTTP has separate client and server components. A Web page typically contains links to many resources that may be distributed across multiple servers. The client requests the server for a document, and the server responds by sending it. The client then extracts the URLs of the other resources from the document and then makes separate requests for each resource that has to be fetched to complete the page display. The life-cycle of a connection using HTTP/1.1 is as below:

- The client contacts the server at the FQDN specified in the URL and opens a connection at port number 80.
- The client then requests the Web server for some service. This service may be to ask for a document or to post some form data back to the server. The request consists of a request header followed by the data sent by the client.
- The server now sends a response which consists of a response header, followed by data.
- The server waits for more requests and finally closes the connection. On older HTTP/1.0 servers, the server would close the connection after each request.

Most Web servers today use HTTP/1.1 and its *Keep-Alive* feature which makes connections *persistent*. This implies that if a Web page contains five graphic files, a single connection can fetch them using Keep-Alive and not six, as was required earlier. The protocol is also *stateless* in that each connection is unaware of the other, even though thcy took place sequentially.

If the client requests a document, then the request header contains the URL of the document. It could also contain form data that has to be processed on the server end. The server's response header describes the type of data sent from the server. HTTP uses the MIME feature that was first used in email of specifying the Content-Type of the data that is to follow. For HTML documents, this is `text/html`.

20.6.3 Running External Programs

The previous URL specifications referred to static resources—files that reside on a Web server. However, a lot of content on the Web is generated dynamically, i.e., they don't exist as files on the server. Take for instance this URL which specifies a search for the string `unix system calls` on the Teoma site:

http://s.teoma.com/search?q=unix+system+calls&qcat=1&qsrc=1

Here, the string `search` following the FQDN is not the filename of a Web page, but of a *program* to be run on the server. The remaining string following the ? symbol comprise the arguments to this program, suitably encoded to avoid conflict with the characters used in the rest of the URL string. A Web server has no capacity to run these programs.

The server passes on the request to a *Common Gateway Interface* (CGI), which makes arrangements to execute the program and returns its standard output to the Web server for onward transmission back to the client. We call them *CGI programs*, and such programs could be written in any language. **`perl`** is the language of choice for CGI because of its parsing capabilities using regular expressions. However, Java servlets are being increasingly used in this domain.

20.6.4 HTML: The Language of Web Pages

Web pages are written in HTML. Even though the HTML acronym expands to HyperText Markup Language, it's not really a programming language like C, which produces binary executables from text sources. Rather, HTML uses tags to "mark up" text. It owes its origin to the **nroff/troff** suite of UNIX systems that used some of these tags several years before the Web was born. A few sample lines from a Web page show the use of these tags:

```
<BODY>
   <H1> Perl: Larry Wall's Brainchild </H1>
      <STRONG>perl</STRONG> is an interpretive language and is probably the
      best     language yet          available for text manipulation.
      <IMG SRC="perl.gif" ALIGN=LEFT VSPACE=10 HSPACE=10>
      It was created by Larry Wall, and made freely available to the world.
      <EM><STRONG> You don't have to pay for using perl</STRONG></EM>,
      It's     distributed       under the GNU General Public License,
      which means that no one can impose any restrictions on its distribution.
      You can know more about <STRONG>perl</STRONG> by visiting
      <A HREF="http://www.perl.org"> the Perl site</A>.
</BODY>
```

Each tag begins with a < and ends with a >, and most tags have some formatting capability. For instance, <STRONG> and its closing counterpart, </STRONG>, serve to boldface text. In the HTML source shown above, the word perl appears twice in boldface as shown in Fig. 20.5. The browser ignores extra spaces and blank lines, and combines multiple adjacent spaces to a single space.

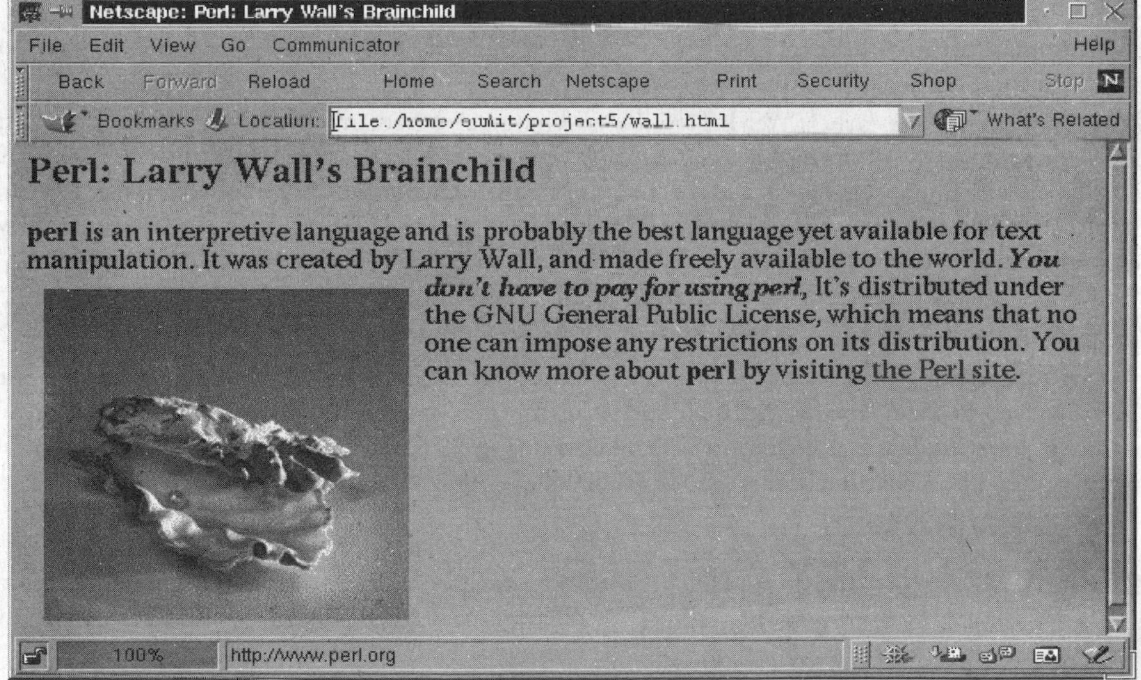

Fig. 20.5 An HTML Document Viewed with Netscape

Two tags provide the actual hyptertext capability—`<IMG>` and `<A>`. Both of them take on *attributes* in the form *attribute=value*. The `<IMG>` tag and its `SRC` attribute is used to specify a URL of a graphic. The browser fetches the graphic file from the server (which could be a different one) and displays it inline within the Web page. Here, the tag places the picture of a pearl on the page.

The anchor tag, `<A>`, and the `HREF` attribute behave in a similar manner except that they allow you to click on a section of text or an image to fetch another resource. Here, the words `the Perl site` appear underlined, indicating a hyperlink. Clicking on it replaces the current page with the home page of *www.perl.org*.

Because HTML documents are text files, they are portable and you can view them on *any* browser on *any* machine running *any* operating system. They are also small in size and thus are ideally suited for use on the Web where network bandwidth is often a severe constraint.

20.6.5 The Web Browser

The Web browser is the HTTP client. It accepts a URL either from the URL window or from a bookmark, and fetches the resource from the server. If the document contains `<IMG SRC>` tags, the browser fetches the images the tags link to—using a single Keep-Alive connection, wherever possible. Every browser is also expected to offer these features:

- Step back and forth through documents viewed in a session.
- Save HTML files (and graphics) to the local machine.
- Bookmark important URLs so they can be fetched later without actually entering the URL.
- Support other application protocols like Ftp and Telnet.
- Automatically invoke helper applications and special software (plugins) when encountering a file format it can't handle.

Like email clients, the earliest Web browsers were character-based, and the **`lynx`** browser remained popular until the advent of graphics. Netscape Navigator is the standard graphic browser for UNIX systems today. Linux users have a wider choice in Navigator, Konqueror (part of KDE) and Opera. Lately, Linux systems have been offering Mozilla instead of Navigator, which runs in practically identical manner. In the next section, we look at Navigator.

20.7 NETSCAPE NAVIGATOR: THE STANDARD UNIX BROWSER

If the **`netscape`** command shows Messenger or Composer, and not the Navigator window, then use *Communicator>Navigator* from the Menu Bar or the first icon from the Component Bar at the bottom to have the Navigator window in front of you (Fig. 20.6). You'll see a number of toolbars on this window. The Location Toolbar contains the URL window; it's here that you key in a URL:

http://www.nasdaq.com *You can drop http://*

The browser connects to the site and fetches the home page from the server. As you branch out from the home page by clicking on hyperlinks, you'll find the URL window updating its contents automatically.

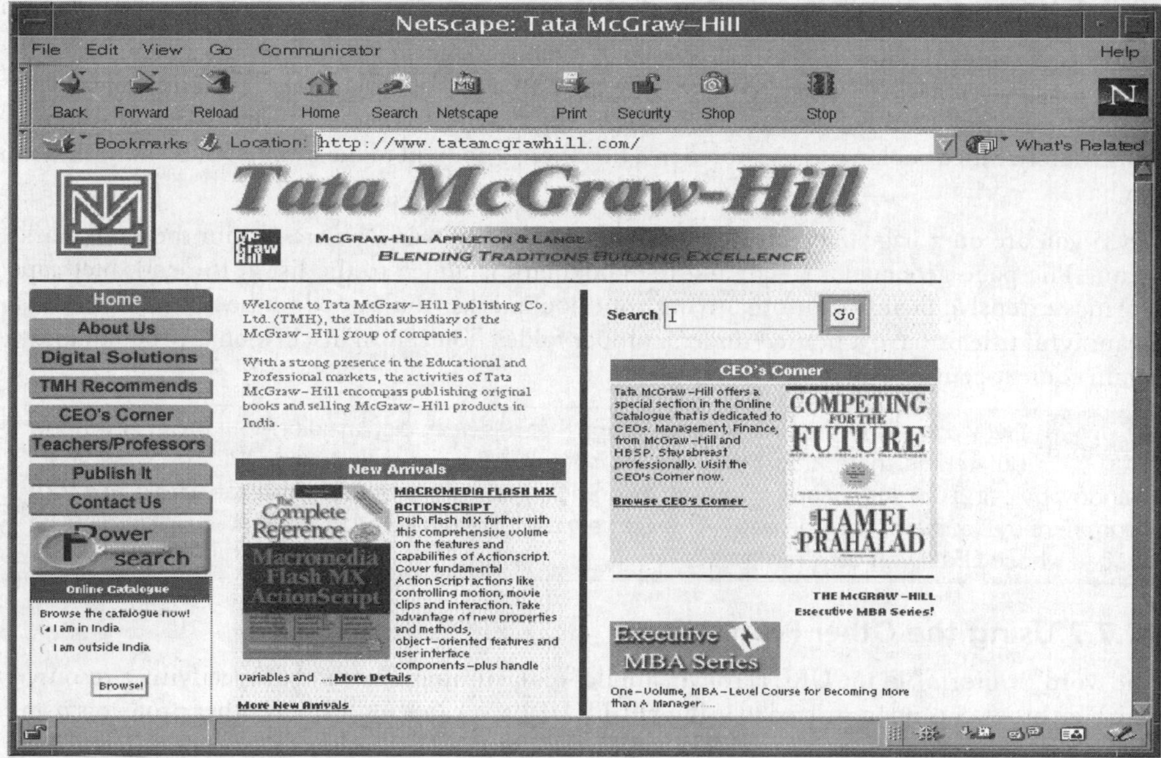

Fig. 20.6 Netscape Navigator: A Frontal View

Using the *Back* and *Forward* buttons on the Navigation Toolbar, you can step back and forth through the session. The browser remembers the sequence of the URLs visited in the current session, so you don't have to reenter a URL if you have done so once in the current session. Click on *Back* continuously and you'll arrive at the first document viewed in that session. These two buttons also store the recently visited URLs. Keep the left mouse button pressed on either button and select a visited site from the pop-up list.

Many pages like stock quotes and game scores are dynamically created, so use the *Reload* button to fetch the latest page from the server. Sometimes, this doesn't happen and data is reloaded from Netscape's internal cache. To force reloading from the network, press *[Shift]* before clicking on the *Reload* button.

You can save a page without the graphics (*File>Save As*) and later open it from your file system using *File>Open*. To save a graphic image, right-click on it and use *Save Image As*. If there are 20 images on a page, then you have to locate each one of them and use this technique. We'll discuss a better way of handling this shortly.

Note Pictures and Java applets take time to load, and on a congested network, you may need to disable the downloading of these media in the browser configuration. Use *Edit>Preferences>Advanced* and uncheck the first two boxes (*Automatically load images* and *Enable Java*).

20.7.1 Using Bookmarks and History

The *Bookmarks* icon is located on the Location Toolbar, and on clicking it, pops up a menu. Like its namesake, a bookmark marks a page by storing the URL of a Web page that is currently on view on the browser window. When you select a bookmark, you are connected to that site and resource immediately. Since bookmarks are stored in a file, there's no limit to the number of bookmarks you can have.

When you are on a page that you want bookmarked, select *Add Bookmark* from the Bookmarks menu. The page gets bookmarked, and the bookmark is added to the list at the end. Netscape provides extensive facilities for organizing your bookmarks. You can edit a bookmark to show a meaningful title or have it housed under a proper folder. You can right-click on any bookmark to obtain context-sensitive options.

> **Tip** Netscape stores the URLs of *every* page that has been displayed on your browser window but retires them after nine days by default. You can view these URLs on a separate window by using *Communicator>Tools>History* (*Go>History* in Mozilla). You can invoke any URL from here by double-clicking an entry. This is a very useful feature, and you can even use it to locate pages whose URLs you can't remember.

20.7.2 Using the Other Protocols

The word "uniform" in the URL acronym alludes to the uniform method of specifying a resource. The Web browser is not restricted to using HTTP URLs; it can handle many other protocols using prefixes like `ftp://`, `telnet://`, etc. The uniformity of the URL schemes is evident from these examples that show the usage of different protocols supported by the browser:

- *ftp://ftp.tucows.com*— When you use anonymous Ftp from the browser using this URL, you'll see a directory listing of files on the Ftp server.
- *telnet://sasolution.com*— The X Window system uses a simple **`xterm`** client which invokes **`telnet`**.
- *mailto:thathc@netscape.com*—This calls up the composition window of Netscape Messenger which you can use to send email.
- *news:comp.os.linux.networking*—This subscribes the user to the newsgroup shown (no // here).
- *file://home/henry/download/penguin.gif*—Used to view files on the local machine. Navigator presents a Windows Explorer-type interface which helps in navigation.

You'll find the `ftp://` and `mailto://` prefixes in the values used in the `HREF` attribute of the `<A>` tag. Clicking on a hyperlink may download a file from an anonymous Ftp site or open a composition window for sending mail. We'll be discussing the use of the `file` protocol next.

20.7.3 Viewing Pages Offline with All Graphics

How does one download a complete Web page with all its associated graphics in one shot? This is one of Netscape's strong features, but the job is done not by Navigator but by Netscape Composer—another component of the Communicator suite. But before you do that, create a separate directory for storing the resources that you are about to download.

When you are on a graphic-rich page, invoke the Composer's editing mode (*File>Edit Page*). You'll see a different type of window this time, and find pictures gradually appearing on this window. You don't have to wait for all of them to appear. Just call *File>Save As* and use the default HTML filename unless there's a chance of conflict. Composer now saves not only the HTML file but all its associated graphics to your disk.

Local files can be viewed in two ways—with *File>Open* or using the *file://* protocol prefix in the URL window. For example, you can enter a URL like *file://home/henry/download/wall.html* in the URL window to show the HTML file on your browser. If you have downloaded this page along with its associated graphics using Composer as detailed above, then the browser shows the graphics as well—exactly in the way you had seen it when you were connected to the Net.

> **Tip** The *file://* prefix in the URL allows you to use Navigator as a rudimentary file manager. When the last component of this type of URL is a directory, you see a directory listing somewhat similar to the Windows Explorer-like interface. Click on a directory, and you see that directory's listing. Click on an HTML, JPEG or GIF file; it's displayed straightaway. The author prefers to view files this way rather than use *File>Open*.

20.7.4 Access through Proxy

If you are in a network, you may be able to access the Net only through a *proxy server* which has direct access to the Net. The proxy server gets a page from the Net on your behalf (by proxy) and maintains a large cache for this purpose. So if someone on one machine has already requested a page once, you can retrieve it faster from the proxy cache next time. These pages reside in the cache for several days if not weeks.

Consider that the proxy server has the IP address `192.168.35.100` and is using the Squid proxy server software. You must communicate with this proxy using the port number 3128—the default port used by Squid. Move to *Edit>Preferences>Advanced>Proxies*, opt for *Manual proxy configuration* and select *View*. Enter `192.168.35.100` or the FQDN in the `HTTP Proxy:` line, and enter `3128` as the port number. You are now ready to use the proxy service.

20.8 MULTIMEDIA ON THE WEB: MIME REVISITED

Web documents today feature a variety of multimedia objects like Java applets, RealAudio, RealVideo and Shockwave technology. MIME technology *(20.4)* also applies to multimedia files on the Web. However, these files are sent by Web servers not as multipart messages but as independent files. The server sends the Content-Type to the client before it sends the file by looking up the file `mime.types` that associates the Content-Type with the file's extension, as shown below for a PDF document:

```
type=application/acrobat   exts=pdf                    Solaris
application/pdf            pdf                         Linux
```

When a browser encounters an unfamiliar data format, it first sees whether there is a *plugin* in its arsenal. A plugin is a piece of software installed ("plugged") in the browser. It is normally small in size and has the minimal features required for simple viewing (or, in case of audio and video, playing). You can't invoke a plugin separately as you can call up a helper application (explained next) like Acrobat Reader. When a file is viewed with a plugin, it appears inline with the HTML text, and not in a separate window.

If the browser is not able to locate a plugin for a specific Content-Type, it looks up `mailcap` to determine the *helper application*. This is a separate standalone application that can also be invoked separately from the UNIX command line. We saw one entry in this file in Section 20.4 that specified `acroread` (the executable for Acrobat Reader) for `application/pdf`. Unlike in Windows, UNIX Netscape doesn't have this file configured well, so you'll have to fill it up using *Edit>Preferences>Navigator>Applications*. The information you key in here make their way into both `mailcap` and `mime.types` that are maintained separately by Netscape.

> **Note** When a browser fetches a file through Ftp (using *ftp://*) or locally (using *file://*), there's no Content-Type explicitly preceding the file content. The browser must be able to guess the file's type by looking at the extension, for which it needs a `mime.types` at its end as well. That's why you can often click on a file icon on your browser window and view its contents when using these protocols.

20.9 CONCLUSION

Christopher Anderson (of The Economist) had observed that the growth of the Net is "a consequence of unleashing the power of individual creativity." UNIX users have strong reasons to feel satisfied with the development of the Internet. The open standards, the free and frank exchange of information and the offering of high-quality freeware and shareware programs available on the Net have their roots in UNIX. UNIX is the language of the Internet. In a sense, the Internet continued the good work carried put by the UNIX architects and could well turn out to be the bubble that didn't burst.

WRAP UP

Large networks and the Internet use the *Domain Name System* (DNS). Each host is represented by its *fully qualified domain name* (FQDN) which is a series of dot-delimited domain names arranged in a hierarchical manner. The hostname-IP address mappings are maintained across a number of *name servers* which are queried by the *resolver* to obtain the IP address of a host.

Internet mail is handled by three agencies. The *Mail User Agent* (MUA) is the application with which you read and compose mail. The Mail Transport Agent (MTA) transports mail to the MTA at the receiving end using the *Simple Mail Transfer Protocol* (SMTP). The *Mail Delivery Agent* (MDA) delivers the mail to the user's mailbox. Mail is fetched from a remote site with the *Post Office Protocol* (POP)—often using a dialup line.

Internet mail uses *Multipurpose Internet Mail Extensions* (MIME) to enable transmission of multimedia attachments. It uses the *Content-Type* header to determine the helper application needed to handle the content. The *Content-Transfer-Encoding* defines the encoding techniques used. *base64* is the encoding technique used for images, audio and video files.

News servers serve Network News using the *Network News Transfer Protocol* (NNTP). A news server obtains *newsfeeds* from another server. You have to *subscribe* to a newsgroup, which uses a hierarchical naming scheme similar to that used by domains. A *newsreader* is used to post and receive messages.

The Web works on the *Hyper Text Transfer Protocol* (HTTP) at port 80. The *Keep-Alive* feature allows multiple resources to be fetched in a single connection. Web documents use *hypertext* to link one document with another or any resource. A document is accessed by using a *Uniform Resource Locator* (URL) which combines the FQDN of the site with a pathname. URLs can also point to Ftp and Telnet sites.

A Web document is written in the *Hyper Text Markup Language* (HTML). An HTML document is cross-platform and can be viewed in any environment. GIF and JPEG pictures are viewed inline with the browser. All documents and graphics can be saved on the local machine so they can be viewed offline using a URL of type *file://*.

Form data is generally passed on to the *Common Gateway Interface* (CGI). A separate program processes the data, creates the HTML code and returns it to the server. **perl** is the language of choice for CGI programming.

If the browser can't handle a data format, it will either invoke a *plugin* or a *helper application*. The server looks up `mime.types` to determine the Content-Type from the file's extension and sends it in the response header. The browser uses `mailcap` to associate the Content-Type with the right helper application.

TEST YOUR UNDERSTANDING

20.1 Name three top-level domains that have added to the Internet namespace in the year 2000.

20.2 What are *root name servers* and when are they contacted? In which file are the addresses of the name servers stored?

20.3 Is the domain name *WWW.suse.COm* valid?

20.4 Explain the significance of the *MUA* and *MTA*. Whom does the MTA hand over mail to?

20.5 How are binary files included in mail messages even though SMTP handles only 7-bit data? Name the two mail headers that play an important role here.

20.6 Explain the significance of these terms: (i) newsgroup (ii) newsreader (iii) FAQ. When is a message retired?

20.7 The browser can display three types of images without needing external help. What are they?

20.8 What is *hypertext*? Is it confined to text only?

20.9 What is *HTTP*? Which port number does it use?

20.10 What are *CGI programs*? How are they invoked?

20.11 Explain how you'll use your browser to connect to the site *ftp.heavens.com* using the (i) Ftp protocol (ii) Telnet protocol?

20.12 What is the protocol used in mailing multimedia attachments?

20.13 How do you access the home page of the Web server running on your own machine?

FLEX YOUR BRAIN

20.1 Name the three important features of DNS. What advantages does DNS have over the hosts file?

20.2 What is the role of the primary and secondary name servers? What does a name server do if it can't handle an FQDN?

20.3 Explain how the general mail handling scheme changes when a user connects to the mail server over a dialup line.

20.4 What are the limitations of SMTP and RFC 822 in relation to handling mail attachments. How are they overcome by MIME?

20.5 Both DNS and Network News use a hierarchical namespace but they are interpreted in an inverse manner. Explain.

20.6 Explain the significance of each word in the acronym *URL*. What happens if you leave out the port number in the URL?

20.7 Why is HTTP called a *stateless* protocol? What is meant by the *Keep-Alive* feature?

20.8 Why is HTML particularly suitable for use on the Web compared to Word documents?

20.9 Can you use *WWW.PLANETS.COM/CATALOG.HTML* instead of *www.planets.com/catalog.html* as the URL?

20.10 To download a Web page with 10 graphics, how many connections are required in (i) HTTP 1.0 (ii) HTTP 1.1?

20.11 If a browser passes data from an HTML form to the server, how does the server handle the data?

20.12 What is a *helper application*? Explain the role of the files `mime.types` and `mailcap` when using a helper application.

20.13 What is *MIME*? Explain its role in handling of (i) email attachments (ii) Web resources.

21

awk—An Advanced Filter

The **awk** command made a late entry into the UNIX system in 1977 to augment the tool kit with suitable report formatting capabilities. Named after its authors, Aho, Weinberger and Kernighan, **awk**, until the advent of **perl**, was the most powerful utility for text manipulation. Like **sed**, it combines features of several filters, though its report writing capability is the most useful. **awk** appears as **gawk** (GNU awk) in Linux.

awk doesn't belong to the do-one-thing-well family of UNIX commands. In fact, it can do several things—and some of them quite well. Unlike other filters, it operates at the *field* level and can easily access, transform and format individual fields in a line. It also accepts extended regular expressions (EREs) for pattern matching, has C-type programming constructs, variables and several built-in functions. We'll discuss the important **awk** features in some detail because that will help you in understanding **perl**, which uses most of the **awk** constructs, sometimes in identical manner.

WHAT YOU WILL LEARN

- Understand **awk**'s unusual syntax with its *selection criteria* and *action* components.
- Split a line into *fields* and format the output with **printf**.
- Use the comparison operators to select lines on practically any condition.
- Use the ~ and !~ operators with extended regular expressions (EREs) for pattern matching.
- Handle decimal numbers and use them for computation.
- Use variables without declaring or initializing them.
- Do some pre- and post-processing with the BEGIN and END sections.
- Examine **awk**'s built-in variables.
- Use arrays and access an array element with a nonnumeric subscript.
- Use the built-in functions for performing string handling tasks.
- Make decisions with the **if** statement and its compact one-line conditional.
- Use the **for** and **while** loops to perform tasks repeatedly.

21.1 SIMPLE awk FILTERING

awk is not just a command, but a programming language too. It uses an unusual syntax that uses two components and requires single quotes and curly braces:

awk *options* '*selection_criteria* {*action*}' *file(s)*

The constituents resemble those of **find**. The *selection_criteria* (a form of addressing) filters input and selects lines for the *action* component to act upon. This component is enclosed within curly braces. The *selection_criteria* and *action* constitute an **awk** program that is surrounded by a set of single quotes. These programs are often one line long though they can span several lines as well.

The selection criteria in **awk** have wider scope than in **sed**. Like there, they can be patterns like /negroponte/ or line addresses using **awk**'s built-in variable, NR. Further, they can also be conditional expressions using the && and || operators as used in the shell. You can select lines practically on any condition.

A typically complete **awk** command specifies the selection criteria and action. The following command selects the directors from emp.lst:

```
$ awk '/director/ { print }' emp.lst
9876|jai sharma       |director |production|12/03/50|7000
2365|barun sengupta   |director |personnel |11/05/47|7800
1006|chanchal singhvi |director |sales     |03/09/38|6700
6521|lalit chowdury   |director |marketing |26/09/45|8200
```

The *selection_criteria* section (/director/) selects lines that are processed in the *action* section ({ print }). If *selection_criteria* is missing, then *action* applies to all lines of the file. If *action* is missing, the entire line is printed. Either of the two (but not both) is optional, but they must be enclosed within a pair of single (not double) quotes.

The **print** statement, when used without any field specifiers, prints the entire line. Moreover, since printing is the default action of **awk**, all the following three forms could be considered equivalent:

```
awk '/director/' emp.lst                 Printing is the default action
awk '/director/{ print }' emp.lst        Whitespace permitted
awk '/director/ { print $0}' emp.lst     $0 is the complete line
```

For pattern matching, **awk** uses regular expressions in **sed**-style:

```
$ awk -F"|" '/sa[kx]s*ena/' emp.lst
3212|shyam saksena    |d.g.m.   |accounts  |12/12/55|6000
2345|j.b. saxena      |g.m.     |marketing |12/03/45|8000
```

The regular expressions used by **awk** belong to the basic BRE (but not the IRE and TRE) and ERE variety that's used by **grep -E** *(15.3)* or **egrep**. This means that you can also use multiple patterns by delimiting each pattern with a |.

> **Note** An **awk** program must have either the selection criteria or the action, or both, but within single quotes. Double quotes will create problems unless used judiciously.

21.2 SPLITTING A LINE INTO FIELDS

awk uses the special parameter, $0, to indicate the entire line. It also identifies fields by $1, $2, $3. Since these parameters also have a special meaning to the shell, single-quoting an **awk** program protects them from interpretation by the shell.

Unlike the other UNIX filters which operate on fields, **awk** uses a contiguous sequence of spaces and tabs as a *single* delimiter. But the sample database *(14.1)* uses the |, so we must use the -F option to specify it in our programs. You can use **awk** to print the name, designation, department and salary of all the sales people:

```
$ awk -F"|" '/sales/ { print $2,$3,$4,$6 }' emp.lst
a.k. shukla        g.m.       sales      6000
chanchal singhvi   director   sales      6700
s.n. dasgupta      manager    sales      5600
anil aggarwal      manager    sales      5000
```

Notice that a , (comma) has been used to delimit the field specifications. This ensures that each field is separated from the other by a space. If you don't put the comma, the fields will be glued together.

So far, the programs have produced readable output, but that is because the file emp.lst contains fixed-length lines. Henceforth, the input for most **awk** programs used in this chapter will come from the file empn.lst which we created with **sed** in Section 15.10. This file is similar to emp.lst except that the lines are of variable length. A few lines of the file show the total absence of spaces before the |:

```
$ head -2 empn.lst
3212|shyam  saksena|d.g.m.|accounts|12/12/55|6000|6213
6213|karuna  ganguly|g.m.|accounts|05/06/62|6300|6213
```

With this file as input, we'll use **awk** with a line address (single or double) to select lines. If you want to select lines 3 to 6, all you have to do is use the built-in variable NR to specify the line numbers:

```
$ awk -F"|" 'NR == 3, NR == 6 { print NR, $2,$3,$6 }' empn.lst
3 n.k. gupta chairman 5400
4 v.k. agrawal g.m. 9000
5 j.b. saxena g.m. 8000
6 sumit chakrobarty d.g.m. 6000
```

This is **awk**'s way of implementing the **sed** instruction **3,6p**. The statement NR == 3 is really a condition that is being tested, rather than an assignment; this should appear obvious to C programmers. NR is just one of those built-in variables used in **awk** programs, and == is one of the many operators employed in comparison tests.

> **Note** **awk** is the only filter that uses whitespace as the default delimiter instead of a single space or tab.

21.3 printf: FORMATTING OUTPUT

The above output is unformatted, but with the C-like **printf** statement, you can use **awk** as a stream formatter. **awk** accepts most of the formats used by the **printf** function used in C, but in this chapter, the %s format will be used for string data, and %d for numeric. You can now produce a list of all the agarwals:

```
$ awk -F"|" '/[aA]gg?[ar]+wal/ {
> printf "%3d %-20s %-12s %d\n",NR,$2,$3,$6 }' empn.lst
  4 v.k. agrawal          g.m.         9000
  9 sudhir Agarwal        executive    7500
 15 anil aggarwal         manager      5000
```

Like in **sed**, an **awk** command is considered complete only when the quote is closed. The name and designation have been printed in spaces 20 and 12 characters wide, respectively; the - symbol left-justifies the output. The line number is three characters wide, right-justified. Note that **printf** requires an \n to print a newline after each line. Using the various formats in an **awk** program, you can have complete control over the way the output is presented.

21.3.1 Redirecting Standard Output

Every **print** and **printf** statement can be separately redirected with the > and | symbols. However, make sure the filename or the command that follows these symbols is enclosed within double quotes. For example, the following statement sorts the output of the **printf** statement:

```
printf "%s %-10s %-12s %-8s\n", $1, $3, $4, $6 | "sort"
```

If you use redirection instead, the filename should be enclosed in quotes in a similar manner:

```
printf "%s %-10s %-12s %-8s\n", $1, $3, $4, $6 > "mslist"
```

awk thus provides the flexibility of separately manipulating the different output streams. But don't forget the quotes!

21.4 THE COMPARISON OPERATORS

How do you print the three fields for the directors and the chairman? Since the designation field is $3, you have to use it in the selection criteria:

```
$ awk -F"|" '$3 == "director" || $3 == "chairman" {
> printf "%-20s %-12s %d\n", $2,$3,$6 }' empn.lst
n.k. gupta          chairman     5400
lalit chowdury      director     8200
barun sengupta      director     7800
jai sharma          director     7000
chanchal singhvi    director     6700
```

This is the first time we matched a pattern with a field. In fact, field matching is possible only in **awk** and **perl**. Here, **awk** uses the || and && logical operators in the same sense as used by C and the UNIX shell. This command looks for two strings only in the third field ($3). The second match is attempted only if (||) the first match fails.

For negating the above condition, you should use the != and && operators instead:

```
$3 != "director" && $3 != "chairman"
```

The selection criteria here translates to this: "Select those lines where the third field doesn't (!=) completely match the string director and (&&) also doesn't (!=) completely match the string chairman. Note that the match is made for the *entire* field, rather than a string embedded in the field space. We couldn't verify that because the file empn.lst has all trailing spaces trimmed. But will a similar **awk** program work on the file emp.lst which has trailing spaces attached to the strings?

```
$ awk -F"|" '$3 == "director" || $3 == "chairman"' emp.lst
$ _
```

No, it won't; the third field contains trailing whitespace, so a perfect match wasn't found. Field matching is better done with regular expressions as you'll see in the next topic.

21.4.1 ~ and !~: The Regular Expression Operators

How does one match regular expressions? Previously we had used **awk** with regular expressions in this manner:

```
awk -F"|" '/sa[kx]s*ena/' emp.lst
```

This matches the pattern saxena and saksena anywhere in the line and not in a specific field. For matching a regular expression with a field, **awk** offers the ~ and !~ operators to match and negate a match, respectively. With these operators, matching becomes more specific as seen in the following examples:

```
$2 ~ /[cC]ho[wu]dh?ury/ || $2 ~ /sa[xk]s?ena/        Matches second field
$2 ~ /[cC]ho[wu]dh?ury|sa[xk]s?ena/                  Same as above
$3 !~ /director|chairman/                            Neither director nor chairman
```

Remember that the operators ~ and !~ work only with field specifiers ($1, $2 etc.). The delimiting of patterns with the | is an ERE feature, and **awk** uses extended regular expressions. However, **awk** doesn't accept the IRE and TRE used by **grep** and **sed**.

> **Tip** To match a string embedded in a field, you must use ~ instead of ==. Similarly, to negate a match, use !~ instead of !=.

To locate only the *g.m.*s, you just can't use this:

```
awk -F"|" '$3 ~ /g.m./ { printf " .....
```

Because g.m. is embedded in d.g.m., locating just the *g.m.*s requires use of the ^ and $. These characters have slightly different meanings when used by **awk**. Rather than match lines, they are used to indicate the beginning and end of a *field*, respectively, unless you use them with $0. So, if you use the condition

```
awk -F"|" '$3 ~ /^g.m./ { printf " .....
```

you'll locate only the *g.m.*s and discard the *d.g.m.*s.

Tip To match a string at the beginning of the field, precede the search pattern by a ^. Similarly, use a $ for matching a pattern at the end of a field.

21.4.2 Number Comparison

awk can also handle numbers— both integer and floating type—and make relational tests on them. Using operators from the set shown in Table 21.1, you can now print the pay-slips for those people whose basic pay exceeds 7500:

```
$ awk -F"|" '$6 > 7500 {
> printf "%-20s %-12s %d\n", $2,$3,$6 }' empn.lst
v.k. agrawal         g.m.         9000
j.b. saxena          g.m.         8000
lalit chowdury       director     8200
barun sengupta       director     7800
```

You can also combine regular expression matching with numeric comparison to locate those, either born in 1955, or drawing a basic pay greater than 8000:

```
$ awk -F"|" '$6 > 8000 || $5 ~/45$/' empn.lst
0110|v.k.  agrawal|g.m.|marketing|31/12/40|9000|6521
2345|j.b.  saxena|g.m.|marketing|12/03/45|8000|6521
6521|lalit  chowdury|director|marketing|26/09/45|8200|6521
```

Recall that thc context address /45$/ matches the string 45 at the end ($) of the field. With these operators, you can now select lines by locating a pattern as a simple string or a regular expression, as well as by a relational test on a number.

Table 21.1 The Comparison and Regular Expression Matching Operators

Operator	*Significance*
<	Less than
<=	Less than or equal to
==	Equal to
!=	Not equal to
>=	Greater than or equal to
>	Greater than
~	Matches a regular expression
!~	Doesn't match a regular expression

21.5 NUMBER PROCESSING

awk can perform computations on numbers using the arithmetic operators +, -, *, / and % (modulus). It also overcomes one of the most major limitations of the shell—the inability to handle decimal numbers.

In any environment maintaining data for the payroll application, it's common practice to store only the basic pay in the file. This is acceptable because normally the other elements of pay can be derived from this basic pay. For the purpose of using **awk**, the sixth field will now signify the basic pay, rather than the salary. Assume that the total salary consists of basic pay, dearness allowance (@40 % of basic pay) and house rent (@15 % of basic pay). You can use **awk** to print a rudimentary pay-slip for the directors:

```
$ awk -F"|" '$3 == "director" {
> printf  "%-20s %-12s %d %d %d\n",$2,$3,$6,$6*0.4,$6*0.15}' empn.lst
lalit chowdury        director        8200 3280 1230
barun sengupta        director        7800 3120 1170
jai sharma            director        7000 2800 1050
chanchal singhvi      director        6700 2680 1005
```

21.6 VARIABLES

While **awk** has certain built-in variables, like NR and $0, representing the line number and the entire line, respectively, it also permits the user to use variables of her choice. A user-defined variable used by **awk** has two special features:

- No type declarations are needed.
- By default, variables are initialized to zero or a null string, depending on its type. **awk** has a mechanism of identifying the type of variable used from its context.

You can now use these properties to print a serial number, using the variable kount, and apply it to select those directors drawing a salary exceeding 6700:

```
$ awk -F"|" '$3 == "director" && $6 > 6700 {
> kount = kount + 1
> printf "%3d %-20s %-12s %d\n", kount,$2,$3,$6 }' empn.lst
  1 lalit chowdury        director     8200
  2 barun sengupta        director     7800
  3 jai sharma            director     7000
```

The initial value of kount was 0 (by default). That's why the first line is correctly assigned the number 1. **awk** also accepts the C-style incrementing forms:

```
kount++                                    Same as kount = kount + 1
kount += 2                                 Same as kount = kount + 2
printf "%3d\n", ++kount                    Increments kount before printing
```

> **Tip** No type declarations or initial values are required for user-defined variables used in an **awk** program. **awk** identifies their type and initializes them to zero or null strings.

21.7 THE -f OPTION: STORING awk PROGRAMS IN A FILE

You should hold large **awk** programs in separate files and provide them with the .awk extension for easier identification. Let's first store the previous program in the file **empawk.awk**:

```
$ cat empawk.awk
$3 == "director" && $6 > 6700 {
printf "%3d %-20s %-12s %d\n", ++kount,$2,$3,$6 }
```

Observe that this time we haven't used any quotes to enclose the **awk** program. You can now use **awk** with the -f *filename* option to obtain the same output:

```
awk -F"|" -f empawk.awk empn.lst
```

> **Note** If you use **awk** with the -f option, make sure the program stored in the file is not enclosed within quotes. **awk** uses single quotes only when the program is specified in the command line or the entire **awk** command line is held in a shell script.

21.8 THE BEGIN AND END SECTIONS

awk statements are usually applied to all lines selected by the address, and if there are no addresses, then they are applied to every line of input. But, if you have to print something before processing the first line, for example, a heading, then the BEGIN section can be used quite gainfully. Similarly, the END section is useful in printing some totals after the processing is over.

The BEGIN and END sections are optional and take the form

```
BEGIN { action }                                    Both require curly braces
END { action }
```

These two sections, when present, are delimited by the body of the **awk** program. You can use them to print a suitable heading at the beginning and the average salary at the end. Store this **awk** program, in a separate file **empawk2.awk** (Fig. 21.1).

```
BEGIN {
    printf "\t\tEmployee abstract\n\n"
} $6 > 7500 {         # Increment the variables for the serial number and the pay
    kount++ ; tot+= $6     # Multiple assignments in one line
    printf "%3d %-20s %-12s %d\n", kount,$2,$3,$6
}
END {
    printf "\n\tThe average basic pay is %6d\n", tot/kount
}
```

Fig. 21.1 **empawk2.awk**

Like the shell, **awk** also uses the # for providing comments. The BEGIN section here is meant to print a suitable heading, offset by two tabs (\t\t), while the END section should print the average pay (tot/kount) for those lines selected. To execute this program you have to use the -f option:

```
$ awk -F"|" -f empawk2.awk empn.lst
        Employee abstract

  1 v.k. agrawal        g.m.         9000
  2 j.b. saxena         g.m.         8000
  3 lalit chowdury      director     8200
  4 barun sengupta      director     7800

   The average basic pay is   8250
```

Caution Always start the opening brace in the same line the section (BEGIN or END) begins. If you don't do that, **awk** will generate some strange messages!

21.9 BUILT-IN VARIABLES

awk has several built-in variables (Table 21.2). They are all assigned automatically, though it is also possible for a user to reassign some of them. You have already used NR, which signifies the record number of the current line. We'll now have a brief look at some of the other variables.

Table 21.2 Built-in Variables Used by **awk**

Variable	*Function*
NR	Cumulative number of lines read
FS	Input field separator
OFS	Output field separator
NF	Number of fields in current line
FILENAME	Current input file
ARGC	Number of arguments in command line
ARGV	List of arguments

The FS *Variable* As stated elsewhere, **awk** uses a contiguous string of spaces as the default field delimiter. FS redefines this field separator, which in the sample database happens to be the |. When used at all, it must occur in the BEGIN section so that the body of the program knows its value before it starts processing:

```
BEGIN { FS="|" }
```

This is an alternative to the -F option of the command which does the same thing.

The OFS *Variable* When you used the **print** statement with comma-separated arguments, each argument was separated from the other by a space. This is **awk**'s default output field separator, and can be reassigned using the variable OFS in the BEGIN section:

```
BEGIN { OFS="~" }
```

When you reassign this variable with a ~ (tilde), **awk** will use this character for delimiting the **print** arguments. This is a useful variable for creating lines with delimited fields.

The NF *Variable* NF comes in quite handy in cleaning up a database of lines that don't contain the right number of fields. By using it on a file, say empx.lst, you can locate those lines not having six fields, and which have crept in due to faulty data entry:

```
$ awk 'BEGIN { FS = "|" }
> NF != 6 {
> print "Record No ", NR, "has ", NF, " fields"}' empx.lst
Record No 6 has 4 fields
Record No 17 has 5 fields
```

The FILENAME *variable* FILENAME stores the name of the current file being processed. Like **grep** and **sed**, **awk** can also handle multiple filenames in the command line. By default, **awk** doesn't print the filename, but you can instruct it to do so:

```
'$6 < 4000 { print FILENAME, $0 }'
```

With FILENAME, you can devise logic that does different things depending on the file being processed.

21.10 ARRAYS

awk handles one-dimensional arrays. The index for an array can be virtually anything; *it can even be a string.* No array declarations are necessary; an array is considered to be declared the moment it is used, and is automatically initialized to zero, unless initialized explicitly.

In the program **empawk3.awk** (Fig. 21.2), we use arrays to store the totals of the basic pay, da, hra and gross pay of the sales and marketing people. Assume that the da is 25%, and hra 50% of basic pay. Use the tot[] array to store the totals of each element of pay, and also the gross pay:

```
BEGIN {
    FS = "|"
    printf "%46s\n", "Basic    Da   Hra Gross"
} /sales|marketing/ {
    # Calculate the da, hra and the gross pay
    da = 0.25*$6 ; hra = 0.50*$6 ; gp = $6+hra+da

    # Store the aggregates in separate arrays
    tot[1] += $6 ; tot[2] += da ; tot[3] += hra ; tot[4] += gp
    kount++
}
END { # Print the averages
    printf "\t     Average    %5d %5d %5d %5d\n", \
    tot[1]/kount, tot[2]/kount, tot[3]/kount, tot[4]/kount
}
```

Fig. 21.2 **empawk3.awk**

Note that this time we didn't match the patterns sales and marketing specifically in a field. We could afford to do that because the patterns occur only in the fourth field, and there's no scope here for ambiguity. When you run the program, it outputs the averages of the two elements of pay:

```
$ awk -f empawk3.awk empn.lst
                         Basic    Da   Hra Gross
             Average      6812  1703  3406 11921
```

The program is too simple to require any explanation. C programmers will find the syntax quite comfortable to work with, except that **awk** simplifies a number of things that require explicit specification in C. There are no type declarations, no initializations and no statement terminators.

21.11 FUNCTIONS

awk has several built-in functions, performing both arithmetic and string operations (Table 21.3). The parameters are passed to a function in C-style, delimited by commas and enclosed by a matched pair of parentheses. In contrast to C, however, when a function is used without arguments, the () symbols need not be used.

Some of these functions take a variable number of arguments, and one (**length**) uses no argument as a variant form. The functions are adequately explained here so you can confidently use them in **perl** which often uses identical syntaxes.

There are two arithmetic functions which a programmer will expect **awk** to offer. **int** calculates the integral portion of a number (without rounding off), while **sqrt** calculates the square root of a number. **awk** also has some of the common string handling functions you can hope to find in any language. We'll review them briefly.

length **length** determines the length of its argument, and if no argument is present, then it assumes the entire line as its argument. You can use length (without any argument) to locate lines whose length exceeds 1024 characters:

```
awk -F"|" 'length > 1024' empn.lst
```

You can use length with a field as well. The following program selects those people who have short names:

```
awk -F"|" 'length($2) < 11' empn.lst
```

index **index**(*s1*,*s2*) determines the position of a string *s2* within a larger string *s1*. This function is especially useful in validating single character fields. If you have a field which can take the values a, b, c, d or e, you can use this function to find out whether this single character field can be located within the string abcde:

```
x = index("abcde","b")
```

This returns the value 2.

substr The **substr**(*stg*,*m*,*n*) function extracts a substring from a string *stg*. *m* represents the starting point of extraction, and *n* indicates the number of characters to be extracted. Because string values can also be used for computation, the returned string from this function can be used to select those born between 1946 and 1951:

```
$ awk -F"|" 'substr($5,7,2) > 45 && substr($5,7,2) < 52' empn.lst
2365|barun  sengupta|director|personnel|11/05/47|7800|2365
3564|sudhir  Agarwal|executive|personnel|06/07/47|7500|2365
4290|jayant  Choudhury|executive|production|07/09/50|6000|9876
9876|jai  sharma|director|production|12/03/50|7000|9876
```

You can never get this output with either **sed** or **grep** because their regular expressions can never match the numbers between 46 and 51. Note that **awk** does indeed possess a mechanism of identifying the type of expression from its context. It identified the date field as a string for using **substr** and then converted it to a number for making a numeric comparison.

> **Note** **awk** makes no distinction between numeric and string variables. You can use a string for numeric computations as well.

split `split(`*stg*`,`*arr*`,`*ch*`)` breaks up a string *stg* on the delimiter *ch* and stores the fields in an array `arr[]`. Here's how you can convert the date field to the format *YYYYMMDD*:

```
$ awk -F\| '{split($5,ar,"/") ; print "19"ar[3]ar[2]ar[1]}' empn.lst
19521212
19501203
19431904
   .....
```

You can also do this with **sed**, but this method is superior because it explicitly picks up the fifth field, whereas **sed** would transform the only date field that it finds.

system You may want to print the system date at the beginning of the report. For running any UNIX command within **awk**, you'll have to use the **system** function. Here are two examples:

```
BEGIN {
     system("tput clear")                    Clears the screen
     system("date") }                        Executes the UNIX date command
```

You should be familiar with all the functions discussed in this section as they are used in a wide variety of situations. We'll use them again in **perl**. **awk** features some more built-in variables and functions, and also allows the user to define her own functions.

Table 21.3 Built-in Functions in **awk**

Function	*Description*
`int(`*x*`)`	Returns integer value of *x*
`sqrt(`*x*`)`	Returns square root of *x*
`length`	Returns length of complete line
`length(`*x*`)`	Returns length of *x*
`substr(`*stg*`,`*m*`,`*n*`)`	Returns portion of string of length *n*, starting from position *m* in string *stg*
`index(`*s1*`,`*s2*`)`	Returns position of string *s2* in string *s1*
`split(`*stg*`,`*arr*`, `*ch*`)`	Splits string *stg* into array *arr* using *ch* as delimiter
`system("`*cmd*`")`	Runs UNIX command *cmd* and returns its exit status

21.12 CONTROL FLOW—THE `if` STATEMENT

awk has practically all the features of a modern programming language. It has conditional structures (the **if** statement) and loops (**while** and **for**). They all execute a body of statements depending on the success or failure of the *control command*. This is simply a condition that is specified in the first line of the construct. Since you have already been introduced to similar structures in the shell, they will be described briefly in these sections.

The **if** statement can be used when the `&&` and `||` are found to be inadequate for certain tasks. Its behavior is well known to all programmers, and has also been elaborated in Section 16.6. The statement here takes the form

```
if ( condition is true ) {
    statements
} else {                                           else is optional
    statements
}
```

Like in C, none of the control flow constructs require to use curly braces if there's only one statement to be executed. But when there are multiple actions to take, the statements must be enclosed within a pair of curly braces. Moreover, the control command must be enclosed in parentheses.

Most of the addresses that have been used so far reflect the logic normally used in the `if` statement. In a previous example, you had selected the lines where the basic pay exceeded 7500, by using the condition as the selection criteria:

```
$6 > 7500 {
```

An alternative form of this logic places the condition inside the action component rather than the selection criteria. But this form requires the `if` statement:

```
awk -F"|" '{ if ($6 > 7500) printf  .....
```

`if` can be used with the comparison operators and the special symbols ~ and !~ to match a regular expression. When used in combination with the logical operators || and &&, **awk** programming becomes quite easy and powerful. Some of the earlier pattern matching expressions are rephrased in the following, this time in the form used by `if`:

```
if ( NR >= 3 && NR <= 6 )
if ( $3 == "director" || $3 == "chairman" )
if ( $3 ~ /^g.m/ )
if ( $2 !~ /[aA]gg?[ar]+wal/ )
if ( $2 ~ /[cC]ho[wu]dh?ury|sa[xk]s?ena/ )
```

To illustrate the use of the optional `else` statement, let's assume that the dearness allowance is 25% of basic pay when the latter is less than 600, and 1000 otherwise. The `if-else` structure that implements this logic looks like this:

```
if ( $6 < 6000 )
    da = 0.25*$6
else
    da  = 1000
```

You can even replace the above `if` construct with a compact conditional structure:

```
$6 < 6000 ? da = 0.25*$6 : da = 1000
```

This is the form that C and **perl** use to implement the logic of a simple `if-else` construct. The ? and : act as separators of the two actions.

When you have more than one statement to be executed, they must be bounded by a pair of curly braces (as in C). For example, if the factors determining the hra and da are in turn dependent on the basic pay itself, then you need to use terminators:

```
if ( $6 < 6000 ) {
     hra = 0.50*$6
     da = 0.25*$6
} else {
     hra = 0.40*$6
     da  = 1000
}
```

Note There's no **endif** or **fi** terminator for the **if** statement used in **awk**. **awk** uses the { and } to define a block of code.

21.13 LOOPING WITH for

awk supports two loops—**for** and **while**. They both execute the loop body as long as the control command returns a true value. **for** has two forms. The easier one resembles its C counterpart. A simple example illustrates the first form:

```
for ( K=1 ; K<=9 ; K+= 2 )
```

This form also consists of three components; the first component initializes the value of K, the second checks the condition with every iteration, while the third sets the increment used for every iteration.

for is useful for centering text, and the following example uses **awk** with **echo** in a pipeline to do that:

```
$ echo "
> Income statement\nfor\nthe month of August, 2002\nDepartment : Sales" |
> awk '{ for (k = 1 ; k < (55 - length($0)) / 2 ; k++)
> printf "%s"," "
> print $0 }'
                    Income statement
                          for
                the month of August, 2002
                  Department : Sales
```

The loop here uses the first **printf** statement to print the required number of spaces (page width assumed to be 55). The line is then printed with the second **printf** statement, which falls outside the loop. This is a useful routine which can be used to center some titles that normally appear at the beginning of any report.

The second form of the **for** loop doesn't have a parallel in any known programming language except **perl**. It has an unusual syntax:

```
for ( k in array )
     commands
```

This form uses an array where *k* is the subscript. The unusual aspect of this form is that the subscript here is not restricted to integers, but can even be a string! This makes it very simple to display a count of the employees, grouped according to designation (the third field). Since designation happens to be the third field, you can use $3 as the subscript of the array kount[]:

```
$ awk -F"|" '{ kount[$3]++ }
> END { for ( desig in kount)
> print desig, kount[desig] }' empn.lst
g.m.        4
chairman    1
executive 2
director  4
manager     2
d.g.m.      2
```

The program here analyzes the database to reveal the break-up of employees, grouped on the basis of designation. The array kount[] takes as its subscript nonnumeric values like g.m., chairman, executive, etc. for is invoked in the END section to print the subscript (desig) and the number of occurrences of the subscript (kount[desig]). Note that you don't need to sort the input file to print this report!

> **Note** The same SQL-style logic has already been implemented by using three commands in a pipeline—**cut**, **sort** and **uniq** *(14.8.1)*. That one used only a single line of code!

21.14 LOOPING WITH while

The **while** loop has a similar role to play; it repeatedly iterates the loop till the control command succeeds. For example, the previous **for** loop used for centering text can be easily replaced with a **while** construct:

```
k = 0                                          k first initialized
while (k < (55 - length($0))/2) {
    printf "%s", " "
    k++
}
print $0
```

The loop here prints a space and increments the value of k with every iteration. The condition (k < (55 - length($0))/2) is tested at the beginning of every iteration, and the loop body performed only if the test succeeds. In this way, the entire line is filled with a string of spaces before the actual text is printed with **print $0**.

Note that the **length** function has been used with an argument ($0). This **awk** understands to be the entire line. Since **length**, in the absence of an argument, uses the entire line anyway, $0 can be omitted. Similarly, **print $0** may also be replaced by simply **print**.

21.15 CONCLUSION

awk, like **sed**, violates the do-one-thing-well philosophy that generally characterizes all UNIX tools. Although presented in this chapter as a utility filter, it's more of a scripting language. At the time of its entry, you didn't have regular expressions in other languages. You couldn't intermingle strings with numbers. Partly because of the absence of type declarations and initializations, an **awk** program is often a fraction of the size of its C counterpart.

awk has been completely overwhelmed in sheer power by **perl**—the latest and most notable addition to the UNIX tool kit for several years. There is nothing that any UNIX filter can do and which **perl** can't. In fact, **perl** is even more compact, is faster, and in every sense better than them. This chapter was prepared for you to understand **perl** better because so many of the constructs are also used there. **perl** is taken up in Chapter 22.

WRAP UP

The **awk** filter combines features of several filters. **awk** can manipulate individual fields ($1, $2, etc.) in a line ($0). It uses **sed**-type addresses and the built-in variable NR to determine line numbers. Lines are printed with **print** and **printf**. The latter uses format specifiers to format strings (%s), integers (%d) and floating point numbers (%f). Each **print** or **printf** statement can be used with the shell's operators for redirection and piping.

awk uses all the comparison operators (like >, ==, <= etc.). The special operators ~ and !~ are used to match regular expressions or negate a match with specific fields. The ^ and $ are used to anchor a pattern at the beginning or end of a *field* rather than the line.

awk can perform numeric computation. It overcomes a shell limitation by handling decimal numbers. Variables are used without initializing them or declaring their type. **awk** accepts x++ as a way of incrementing variables.

awk can take instructions from an external file (-f). In this case, the program must not be enclosed within quotes. The BEGIN and END sections are used to do some pre- and post-processing work. A report header is generated by the BEGIN section, and a numeric total is computed in the END section.

awk's built-in variables can be used to specify the field delimiter (FS), the number of fields (NF) and the filename (FILENAME). **awk** uses one-dimensional arrays where the array subscript can be a string as well.

awk has a number of built-in functions, and many of them are used for string handling. You can find the length (**length**), extract a substring (**substr**) and find the location (**index**) of a string within a larger string. The **system** function executes a UNIX command.

The **if** statement uses the return value of its control command to determine program flow. **if** also uses the operators || and && to handle complex conditions. The first form of the **for** loop uses an array and can be used to count occurrences of an item using a nonnumeric subscript. The other form resembles its C counterpart. The **while** loop repeats a set of instructions as long as its control command returns a true value.

perl is better than **awk**.

TEST YOUR UNDERSTANDING

21.1 What is the difference between **print** and **print $0**?

21.2 What is wrong with this statement? **printf "%s %-20s\n", $1, $6 | sort**

21.3 Print only the odd-numbered lines of a file.

21.4 How do you delete all blank lines (including those that contain whitespace) from a file?

21.5 Use **awk** to locate lines longer than 100 and smaller than 150 characters.

21.6 Find out recursively the files in your home directory that have been last modified on January 6 of the current year at the 11th hour.

21.7 Find out the total space usage of ordinary files in the current directory.

21.8 Use a **for** loop to center the output of the command **echo "DOCUMENT LIST"**, where the page width is 55 characters.

21.9 Repeat the previous exercise with a **while** loop.

FLEX YOUR BRAIN

21.1 Display from /etc/passwd a list of users and their shells for those using the Korn shell or Bash. Order the output by the shell used.

21.2 Find out the next available UID in /etc/passwd after ignoring all system users placed at the beginning and up to the occurrence of the user nobody.

21.3 The **tar** command on one system can't accept absolute pathnames longer than 100 characters. How can you use **find** and **awk** to generate a list of such files?

21.4 Invert the name of the individual in emp.lst *(14.1)* so that the last name occurs first.

21.5 Use a script to kill a process by specifying its name rather than the PID.

21.6 How can you print the last field of a line even if all lines don't contain the same number of fields? Assume the field delimiter is the **:**.

21.7 List the users currently using the system along with a count of the number of times they have logged in.

21.8 Write an **awk** sequence in a shell script which accepts input from the standard input. The program should print the total of any column specified as script argument. For instance, *prog1* | *awk_prog* 3 should print the total of the third column in the output of *prog1*.

22

perl—The Master Manipulator

perl is UNIX's latest major acquisition, and one of its finest. Developed by Larry Wall, it's often hailed as the "Swiss Army Officer's Knife" of the UNIX system, in that it does several things well. It was meant to expand to a Practical Extraction and Report Language, but has gone far beyond its original purpose. In **perl**, Wall invented a general-purpose tool which is at once a programming language and the mother of all filters. **perl** is standard on Linux and also offered on Solaris 8. However, it is free, and executables are available for all UNIX flavors (*http://www.perl.com*).

perl combines the power of some of the most powerful UNIX tools—the shell, **grep**, **tr**, **sed** and **awk**. In fact, there's nothing these tools can do, which **perl** can't. It has all the control structures that you could possibly have seen anywhere. It has a host of other features related to handling of files, directories, processes, and so on, most of whom have counterparts in UNIX and C. **perl** also knows all the regular expressions that we have discussed so far. In spite of offering so much, **perl** is faster than the shell and **awk**.

WHAT YOU WILL LEARN

- Gain an overview of a sample **perl** program.
- Use **chop** to remove the last character of a line or variable.
- Use the escape sequences and the concatenation operators.
- Use the superior string handling features.
- Specify loops both in command line and inside script for reading files.
- Use the **foreach** loop for working with a list.
- Use *lists* and *scalar* arrays and their operators.
- Split and join a line with **split** and **join**.
- Use **grep** to search an array.
- Handle *associative arrays* with a nonnumeric subscript.
- Handle substitution with regular expressions, the **s** and **tr** commands.
- Use *filehandles* to access a file or stream.
- Test the file attributes.
- Develop *subroutines* for repeated use.

TOPICS OF SPECIAL INTEREST

- The significance of the default variable, $_, and how its presence can be felt everywhere.
- The special regular expression characters and escape sequences that **perl** uses for pattern matching.

22.1 perl PRELIMINARIES

A **perl** program runs in a special interpretive mode; the entire script is compiled internally in memory before being executed. Unlike other interpreted languages like the shell and **awk**, script errors are generated before execution itself. With this simple one-liner you can test whether **perl** is in your PATH:

```
$ perl -e 'print ("GNUs Not Unix\n") ;'
GNUs Not Unix
```

perl doesn't behave like a filter here in printing the GNU acronym, but more like **echo**. Unlike **awk**, printing isn't **perl**'s default action, so you have to specify it explicitly. Like in C, all **perl** statements end with a semicolon.

perl can do a lot of useful things from the command line when used with the -e option. However, most **perl** programs are big—often very big—and are better placed in .pl files. The program, **sample.pl** (Fig. 22.1), shows the use of variables and computation.

```
#!/usr/bin/perl
# Script: sample.pl - Shows use of variables
print ("Enter your name: ") ;
$name = <STDIN> ;                                # Input from the keyboard
print (  "Enter a temperature in Centigrade: "  ) ;
$centigrade=<STDIN> ;                            # Whitespace unimportant
$fahrenheit=$centigrade*9/5 + 32 ;               # Here too
print "The temperature $name in Fahrenheit is $fahrenheit\n" ;
```

Fig. 22.1 **sample.plC**

We used the interpreter line as the first line in all our shell scripts *(16.1)*; we'll use a similar line for all our **perl** scripts as well. **perl** variables need the $ prefix both in the definition ($name = <STDIN>), as well as in evaluation (The temperature, $name .....). <STDIN> is a *filehandle* (a logical name for a file) representing the standard input. Note that the last **print** function doesn't use parentheses. *In general, functions in* **perl** *require the parentheses only when their omission leads to ambiguity.* Handling decimal numbers also seems to be no problem.

Let's execute this program in the same way we execute a shell script. This means that we need to use **chmod** to make the script executable first. We'll also enter a lot of spaces before keying in the actual input:

```
$ chmod +x sample.pl ; sample.pl
Enter your name:                              stallman
Enter a temperature in Centigrade:                            40.5
The temperature                                 stallman
in Fahrenheit is 104.9
```

Note that **perl** reads the spaces provided before `stallman` but not those entered before the number `40.5`.

> **Note** You can also execute a **perl** script using **perl** *scriptname*. In that case, you don't need to provide the interpreter line in the first line of the script.

22.2 THE chop FUNCTION: REMOVING THE LAST CHARACTER

Why did **perl** show the output in two lines? That's because it included the newline generated by *[Enter]* as part of `$name`. (The shell's **read** statement doesn't do that.) So `$name` is now actually `stallman\n` (ignoring the spaces at the front). In many instances, we need to remove the last character—especially when it's a newline. This is done by the **chop** function which is used in the program, **name.pl** (Fig. 22.2).

```
#!/usr/bin/perl
# Script: name.pl - Demonstrates use of chop
print ("Enter your name: ") ;
$name = <STDIN> ;
chop ($name) ;                              # Removes newline character from $name
if ( $name ne "" ) {
    print ("$name, have a nice day\n" ) ;
} else {
    print ("You have not entered your name\n" ) ;
}
```

Fig. 22.2 **name.pl**

The **if** conditional here differs from its namesake in C and **awk** in that the curly braces are *always* required—whether it's one or multiple statements to be executed. **chop** removes the last character all right, but here it also assigns the "chopped" value to the same variable. This time, you'll find the output in a single line:

```
$ name.pl
Enter your name: larry wall
larry wall, have a nice day
There are other ways of using chop:
chop ($name = <STDIN>) ;                 Reading and assigning together
$lname = chop($name) ;                   lname stores last character chopped
```

The first statement combines, in C-style, both reading and chopping in a single statement. The second one is a special case of the **substr** function for extracting the last character of a string.

> **Tip** You should remember to use **chop** whenever you read a line from the keyboard or a file unless you deliberately want to retain the newline character.

22.3 VARIABLES AND OPERATORS

As you would have already seen, **perl** variables have no type and need no initialization. Strings and numbers can be as large as the machine permits. These are some of the variable attributes that one should remember:

- When a string is used for numeric computation or comparison, **perl** immediately converts it into a number.
- If a variable is undefined, it is assumed to be a null string and a null string is numerically zero.
- If the first character of a string is not numeric, the entire string becomes numerically equivalent to zero.

perl uses the same set of operators as **awk** for numeric comparison *(21.4.2)* with `==`, `!=`, `>`, `<`, `>=` and `<=`. For string comparison, you'll have to use similar operators the shell uses—`eq`, `ne`, `gt`, `lt`, `ge` and `le` (without the hyphen).

When **perl** compares strings, it has to match the ASCII values of each character starting from the left. Thus, `b` is greater than `aa1234` because the first character producing a mismatch, i.e., `b` is greater than `a` in the ASCII collating sequence. Similarly, `a` is greater than `Z`.

You can use practically any character as a variable's value—including all the escape sequences we know. In addition, **perl** has some special ones that convert the case of a string. The following assignments show the versatility of **perl**'s variables:

```
$x = $y = $z = 5 ;                  Multiple assignments
$name = "larry\t\twall\n" ;         Two tabs and newline
$y = "A" ;   $y++ ;                 This becomes B
$z = "P01" ; $z++ ;                 This becomes P02!
$todays_date = `date` ;             Uses command substitution
$name = "steve jobs" ;
$result = "\U$name\E" ;             $result is STEVE JOBS
$result = "\u$name\E" ;             $result is Steve jobs
```

There are some unusual things to observe here. The escape sequences `\U` and `\u` convert to uppercase the entire string and the first character, respectively. The end of the affected area is marked by `\E`.

perl also offers the C and **awk** feature of conditional assignment, using the `?` and `:`. The following assignment determines whether February has 28 or 29 days:

```
$feb_days = $year % 4 == 0 ? 29 : 28 ;
```

perl can also set the return value of a comparison to a variable. The following statement sets the value of `$x`, depending on the result of the comparison:

```
$x = $y == $z ;
```

The return value of a comparison (here, `$y == $z`) is non-zero if the result of the comparison is true. Here, `$x` has the value 1 if `$y` and `$z` are equal; otherwise it has the value 0. *Note that* **perl** *deviates from the general UNIX feature of using zero to signify a true return value.*

22.3.1 The Concatenation Operators . and x

Unlike in the shell, the expression xy (or ${x}${y}) isn't interpreted as variable concatenation. Rather, **perl** uses the . (dot) operator for concatenating variables:

```
$ perl -e '$x=maruti ; $y=".com" ; print ($x . $y . "\n") ;'
maruti.com
```

Note that $y itself contains a dot, so it had to be placed within quotes. For the sake of readability, it's preferable to have whitespace on either side of the dot operator.

perl uses the x operator to repeat a string. The following statement prints 40 asterisks on the screen:

```
$ perl -e 'print "*" x 40 ;'
****************************************
```

The string to print isn't restricted to a single character; it can even be an expression. This operator is most useful in printing rulers for reports.

22.4 THE STRING HANDLING FUNCTIONS

perl has all the string functions that you could have possibly seen anywhere. **length** and **index** play their usual role *(21.11)*, but the **substr** function is quite versatile. The following examples tell the story:

```
$x = "abcdijklm" ;
print length($x) ;                  This is 9
print index($x,j) ;                 This is 5
substr($x,4,0) = "efgh" ;           Stuffs $x with efgh
print "$x" ;                        $x is now abcdefghijklm
$y = substr($x,-3,2) ;              Extracts from right
print "$y" ;                        $y is kl
```

substr can do more than what it is normally expected to do; it can extract characters from the *right* of the string, and insert or replace a string. Here, **substr($x,4,0)** stuffs the string $x with efgh without replacing any characters; 0 denotes nonreplacement. **substr($x,-3,2)** extracts two characters from the third position on the *right*.

There are four functions for changing the case of text. **uc** converts to uppercase its entire argument, while **ucfirst** converts only the first character to uppercase:

```
$name = "larry wall" ;
$result = uc($name)                 $result is LARRY WALL
$result = ucfirst($name)            $result is Larry Wall
```

The functions **lc** and **lcfirst** perform opposite functions of their "uc" counterparts. Apart from converting case, **perl** can filter the contents of variables in the same way UNIX filters manipulate text. We'll be discussing the **tr** and **s** functions later—two important functions that **perl** uses for substitution.

22.5 SPECIFYING FILENAMES IN COMMAND LINE

Unlike **awk**, **perl** provides specific functions to open a file and then perform I/O operations on it. However, using special symbols, these actions can occur "beneath the hood." Here are two ways of reading dept.lst:

```
perl -e 'print while (<>)' dept.lst          File opening implied
perl -e 'print <>' dept.lst                  As above but loop also implied
```

<> generally represents a null filehandle—representing the filenames supplied as arguments to the command. The contents of dept.lst are printed till **while** is able to read input (<>). But **perl** also has a -n option which implies this loop:

```
perl -ne 'print' dept.lst                    -en won't work here!
```

Both **perl** forms can be used with multiple files for concatenation. The advantage of this form is that you can use simple one-line conditionals in the command line itself. Here is a bare-bones **grep** command at work:

```
$ perl -ne 'print if /\bgupta/' emp.lst
5423|n.k. gupta        |chairman |admin      |30/08/56|5400
```

This one-line conditional uses the regular expression /\bgupta. **perl** uses an enlarged regular expression set (Table 22.1), where \b is used to match on a word boundary. This eliminated sengupta and dasgupta from the output. We'll see more of **perl**'s regular expressions later.

The above **perl** statement could have been placed in a script. This time, a loop is implied, so we have to use **perl** with the -n option in the interpreter line:

```
#!/usr/bin/perl -n
print if /\bgupta/ ;
```

We often need to do some processing outside the loop—like printing a heading or a total. The -n option doesn't allow that, so we have to set up the while loop inside the script:

```
#!/usr/bin/perl
printf ("%30s", "LIST OF EMPLOYEES\n") ;
while (<>) {
   print if /\bgupta|ag+[ar][ar]wal/ ;              Using an extended RE
}
print "\nREPORT COMPLETE\n" ;
```

What you see above is something that we do many a time: print a heading before the detail and then something after the detail.

> **Tip** For pure filtering, use **perl -n** as the interpreter name at the beginning of the script. No explicit **while** loop is then required. If you have headers and footers to print, then drop the -n option and set up a **while** loop inside the script.

22.6 $_: THE DEFAULT VARIABLE

The previous programs used **print** without specifying what to print; **perl** automatically understood it to be the entire line. **perl** assigns the line read from input to a special variable, `$_`, often called the *default variable*. This is an extremely important variable, and you must understand its magical properties if you want to write compact code.

Suppose you have to prefix a line number to every line. This is where you need $_ to explicitly specify the line. The comments in the script, **grep1.pl** (Fig. 22.3) show what **perl** does internally with $_.

```
#!/usr/bin/perl
# grep1.pl: Extracts the From: headers from the mailbox
while (<>) {                                  # Actually ($_ = <>)
    chop() ;                                  # chop($_)
    if (/From:.*\@velvet.com/) {              # if ($_ =~ /From:.*\@velvet ...)
        $slno++ ;
        print ($slno . "  " . $_ . "\n") ;
    }
}
```

Fig. 22.3 **grep1.pl**

<>, **chop** and pattern matching operate on $_ by default, the reason why it isn't explicitly specified anywhere except in the **print** statement. Though its function is difficult to define exactly, it often represents the last line read or the last pattern matched. We used it with the **print** statement only because it had to be concatenated with `$slno`; otherwise **print** also operates on $_ by default. The program locates the email addresses of all senders from the *velvet.com* domain:

```
$ grep1.pl $HOME/mbox
1  From: "Caesar, Julius" <Julius_Caesar@velvet.com>
2  From: "Goddard, John" <John_Goddard@velvet.com>
3  From: "Barnack, Oscar" <Oscar_Barnack@velvet.com>
```

You can reassign the value of $_. Since many **perl** functions operate on $_ by default, you may often want to set $_ to the expression you are working with. This allows you to use these functions without specifying either $_ or any variable name as argument.

22.7 CURRENT LINE NUMBER ($.) AND THE RANGE OPERATOR (..)

perl stores the current line number in another special variable, `$.` ($ followed by a dot). You can use it to represent a line address and select lines from anywhere in a file:

```
perl -ne 'print if ($. < 4)' foo                    Like head -n 3
perl -ne 'print if ($. > 7 && $. < 11)' foo         Like sed -n '8,10p'
```

But **perl** has shortcuts to these commands too. Use its range operator, `..` (2 dots):

```
perl -ne 'print if (1..3)' foo
perl -ne 'print if (8..10)' foo
```

For selecting multiple segments from a file, you can use multiple **print** statements, or you can use compound conditions:

```
if ((1..2) || (13..15)) { print ; }
```

Unlike `$_` which can be reassigned, `$.` always retains the current line number. If all input lines are passed through, you can use `$.` to number lines; a separate variable like `$slno` is not required.

22.8 LISTS AND ARRAYS

Lists and arrays lie at the very heart and soul of **perl**. **perl** has a large number of functions that can manipulate them. The following is an example of a list:

```
( "Jan", 123, "How are you", -34.56, Dec )
```

A list may either be assigned to an array or formed into a set of variables. These arrays are of two types—*scalar lists* and *associative arrays*. We'll be looking at scalar lists in this section. Let's assign the following list to an array `@month`:

```
@month = ("Jan", "Feb", "Mar") ;                    $month[0] is Jan
```

This sets up a three-element array, `@month`, from a list. This size is not fixed; **perl** automatically increases the size of the array when you add another element to it. The first value, `$month[0]`, yields the string `Jan`. Note that even though the array itself is defined with the `@` symbol, each individual element is accessed with `$mon[`*n*`]`. Array assignment is also quite flexible in **perl**. You can use the range operator or even assign values selectively:

```
@x = (1..12) ;
@month[1,3..5,12] = ("Jan", "Mar", "Apr", "May", "Dec") ;
```

The first example assigns the first 12 integers (`1..12`) to the first 12 elements of the array `@x`. In the second example, note that `$month[4]` is now `Apr` and `$month[2]` is null if it wasn't defined previously. The script, **ar_in_ar.pl** (Fig. 22.4), illustrates some features of **perl** arrays.

```
#!/usr/bin/perl
# Script: ar_in_ar.pl - Shows use of arrays
@days_between = ("Wed", "Thu") ;
@days= (Mon, Tue, @days_between, Fri) ;             # No quotes, OK
@days[5,6] = ("Sat", "Sun") ;
$length = @days ;                                   # @days becomes array length here
@r_days = reverse @days ;                           # Reverses the array

print ("The third day of the week is $days[2]\n") ;
print ("The days of the week are @days\n") ;
print ("The days of the week in reverse are @r_days\n") ;
print ("The number of elements in the array is $length\n") ;
print ("The last subscript of the array is $#days\n") ;
```

Fig. 22.4 **ar_in_ar.pl**

Observe that **perl** permits a second array (@days_between) to become a part of another array @days. **perl** also offers a smart way of choosing your own subscripts (@days[5,6] = ...). With **reverse**, you can reverse the array too.

The length of the array can be determined from two functions—$#days and @days. $#days actually stores the last subscript of the array. The actual length of the array is stored in @days *when it is placed on the right side of an assignment*. Because the index of an array starts from 0, $length is one greater than $#days:

```
$ ar_in_ar.pl
The third day of the week is Wed
The days of the week are Mon Tue Wed Thu Fri Sat Sun
The days of the week in reverse are Sun Sat Fri Thu Wed Tue Mon
The number of elements in the array is 7
The last subscript of the array is 6
```

Note that @days evaluates differently depending on the way it is used. **print @days** displays all the elements, but when @days is assigned to a variable ($length = @days), it becomes the length of the array!

22.8.1 Reading a File into an Array

The easiest way to fill up an array is to read a file into it. Each line becomes an element of the array:

```
@line = <> ;                    Reads entire file from command line
print @line ;                   Prints entire file
```

The entire file is read with a single statement (@line = <>), and each element of the array, @line, contains a line of the file (including the newline).

> **Note** When you read a file into an array, every element will have newline as the last character. The **chop** function, when applied to arrays, removes the newline from each and every element of the array, and not just the last element.

22.8.2 ARGV[ ]: Command Line Arguments

perl also uses command line arguments which are stored in the system array @ARGV[ ]; the first argument is $ARGV[0]. Note that the command name itself *isn't* stored in this element; it is held in another system variable, $0. The next program, **leap_year.pl** (Fig. 22.5), expects a year as the argument string and determines whether it's a leap year or not.

We used the **die** function to simply print its argument and exit a script. **die** is most often used to handle errors in opening a file or in discarding erroneous user input. Note that the value of @ARGV (without the subscripts) equates to the length of the array. You also see here the rather unusual use of the **substr** function. Let's run the program:

```
$ leap_year.pl
You have not entered the year
$ leap_year.pl 2004
```

```
2004 is certainly a leap year
$ leap_year.pl 1997
1997 is not a leap year
```

There is one drawback with the above script; you have to invoke the program five times if you want to subject five numbers to leap year checks. This can be taken care of by the **foreach** loop which is taken up soon.

```
#!/usr/bin/perl
# Script: leap_year.pl - Determines whether a year is a leap year or not
die ("You have not entered the year\n") if (@ARGV == 0 ) ;
$year = $ARGV[0] ;                                    # The first argument
$last2digits = substr($year, -2, 2) ;                 # Extract from the right
if ($last2digits eq "00") {
    $yesorno = ($year % 400 == 0 ? "certainly" : "not" ) ;
}
else {
    $yesorno = ($year % 4 == 0 ? "certainly" : "not" ) ;
}
print ("$year is " . $yesorno . " a leap year\n") ;
```

Fig. 22.5 `leap_year.pl`

22.8.3 Modifying Array Contents

perl has a number of functions for manipulating the contents of an array. For deleting elements at the beginning or end of an array, **perl** uses the **shift** and **pop** functions:

```
@list = (3..5, 9) ;                 This is 3 4 5 9
shift(@list) ;                      The 3 goes away, becomes 4 5 9
pop (@list) ;                       Removes last element, becomes 4 5
```

The **unshift** and **push** functions add elements to an array. Let's apply them to the residual value of `@list` at the end of the previous example:

```
unshift(@list, 1..3) ;              Adds 1, 2 and 3—1 2 3 4 5
push (@list, 9) ;                   Pushes 9 at end—1 2 3 4 5 9
```

The **splice** function can do everything these four functions can do. Additionally, it uses up to four arguments to add or remove elements at any location of the array. The second argument is the offset from where the insertion or removal should begin. The third argument represents the number of elements to be removed. If it is 0, elements have to be added. The new replaced list is specified by the fourth argument (if present):

```
splice (@list, 5, 0, 6..8) ;        Adds at 6th location—1 2 3 4 5 6 7 8 9
splice (@list, 0, 2) ;              Removes from beginning—3 4 5 6 7 8 9
```

We'll be using some of these functions later in another script after we have examined the **foreach** loop and the **join** function.

22.9 foreach: LOOPING THROUGH A LIST

perl provides an extremely useful **foreach** construct to loop through a list. The construct borrowed from the C shell has a very simple syntax:

```
foreach $var (@arr) {
   statements
}
```

In spirit, this works like the **for** loop of the shell as well. Each element of the array *@arr* is picked up and assigned to the variable *$var*. The iteration is continued as many times as there are items in the list. The program, **square_root.pl** (Fig. 22.6), uses **foreach** to calculate the square root of some numbers.

```
#!/usr/bin/perl
# square_root.pl - Finds the square root of each command line argument
print ("The program you are running is $0\n") ;
foreach $number (@ARGV) {                # Each element of @ARGV goes to $number
    print ("The square root of $number is " . sqrt($number) . "\n") ;
}
```

Fig. 22.6 square_root.pl

Every element in the array @ARGV is assigned to the variable $number. You can now supply as many arguments to the script as you like:

```
$ square_root.pl 123 456 25
The program you are running is ./square_root.pl
The square root of 123 is 11.0905365064094
The square root of 456 is 21.3541565040626
The square root of 25 is 5
```

We have previously noted $_ making its presence felt everywhere, and this is no exception. In the above example, you need not use $number at all. **foreach** stores each item in $_, and **sqrt** works on it as well:

```
foreach (@ARGV) {                                    $_ is the default variable
    print ("The square root of $_ is " . sqrt() . "\n") ;
```

It's not that **foreach** is used with named arrays only. It can be used with lists generated by UNIX commands as well. You can use command substitution to generate the list:

```
foreach $file (`ls`) {
```

This loop construct picks up each file in the current directory and assigns it to the variable $file. We'll use this feature later in the chapter.

Note **perl** has a **for** loop as well. This construct performs its enclosing code block three times:

```
for ($i=0 ; $i<3 ; $i++) {
```

22.10 split: SPLITTING INTO A LIST OR ARRAY

CGI programmers using **perl** need to understand two important array handling functions—**split** and **join**. **split** breaks up a line or an expression into fields. These fields are assigned either to variables or an array. Here are the two syntaxes:

```
($var1, $var2, $var3....     ) = split(/sep/,stg) ;
@arr = split(/sep/,stg) ;
```

split takes up to three arguments but is usually used with two. It splits the string *stg* on *sep*, but here *sep* can be a literal character or a regular expression (which could expand to multiple characters). *stg* is optional, and in its absence, $_ is used as default. The fields resulting from the split are assigned either to the variables *$var1*, *$var2* and so on, or to the array *@arr*.

22.10.1 Splitting into Variables

We'll now use the first syntactical form in our next program, **3_numbers.pl** (Fig. 22.7), to assign three numbers, taken from the keyboard, to a set of variables.

```
#!/usr/bin/perl
# Script: 3_numbers.pl - Splits a string on whitespace
print ("Enter three numbers: " ) ;
chop ($numstring = <STDIN>) ;
die ("Nothing entered\n") if ($numstring eq "") ;
($f_number, $s_number, $l_number) = split (/ /, $numstring) ;
print ("The last, second and first numbers are ") ;
print ("$l_number, $s_number and $f_number.\n" ) ;
```

Fig. 22.7 **3_numbers.pl**

To understand how **split** breaks up the variable $numstring and assigns three new variables, let's run this program twice:

```
$ 3_numbers.pl
Enter three numbers: [Enter]                    Nothing entered
Nothing entered
$ 3_numbers.pl
Enter three numbers: 123 345 567
The last, second and first numbers are 567, 345 and 123.
```

When the three numbers are entered, $numstring acquires the value 123 345 567\n, from where the newline is subsequently chopped off. **split** acts on this string using a *single* space as delimiter, and breaks it up into three variables.

22.10.2 Splitting into an Array

What do you do when there are a large number of fields in a line? In that case, it's better to split it up into an array, rather than variables. The following statement fills up the array @thislist:

```
@thislist = split(/:/, $string) ;
```

`$string` is often the last line read, in which case we can replace it with `$_` or rather, drop it altogether:

```
@thislist = split(/:/) ;                    split uses $_ by default
```

In the next program, **rep1.pl** (Fig. 22.8), we print some specific fields from the sample database with the last name shown before the first name. We need to use **split** twice—first on the | delimiter and then again on the space that separates the first and last name. The program selects the first four lines and also a total of the salary field for the selected lines.

```
#!/usr/bin/perl
# Script: rep1.pl - Uses split twice; prints with first and last name reversed
while (<>) {
   chop;
   @field = split (/\|/) ;   # $_ is used by default
   if (1..4) {               # Lines 1 to 4
      $dept = $field[3] ; $name = $field[1] ; $salary = $field[5] ;
      ($f_name, $l_name) = split(/ +/, $name);
      $name = $l_name . ", " . $f_name ;     # Reusing $name

      $totsal += $salary ;
      printf ( "%3d %-20s %-11s %4d\n", $., $name, $dept, $salary) ;
   }
}
printf("%35s %5d\n", "Total Salary: ", $totsal) ;
```

Fig. 22.8 rep1.pl

The second **split** was used to enable the subsequent reversal of the first and last names with a comma between them. We also use the range operator (`..`) to print only the first four lines, and `$.` to print the current line number as serial number:

```
$ rep1.pl emp.lst
  1 shukla, a.k.          sales        6000
  2 sharma, jai           production   7000
  3 chakrobarty, sumit    marketing    6000
  4 sengupta, barun       personnel    7800
                       Total Salary:  26800
```

split can also be used without an explicit assignment, in which case it populates the built-in array, `@_`:

```
split (/:/) ;                               Fills up the array @_
```

split gets shortened further. The array `@_` has the elements `$_[0]`, `$_[1]` and so forth. You should get used to this form also as you'll see it used in many programs.

> **Note** When **split** is used as a statement without an array name (rather than as an assignment on the right of the =), the built-in array, `@_`, is used. Moreover, when **split** is used with the null string (//) as delimiter, it stores *each* character of the string as a separate element.

22.11 join: JOINING A LIST

The **join** function acts in an opposite manner to **split**. It combines all array elements into a single string. It uses the delimiter as the first argument. The remaining arguments could be either an array name or a list of variables or strings to be joined. This is how you provide a space after each day:

```
$weekstring = join (" ", @week_array) ;
$weekstring = join (" ", "Mon", "Tue", "Wed", "Thu", "Fri", "Sat", "Sun") ;
print $weekstring ;
```

Either statement should produce this output:

```
Mon Tue Wed Thu Fri Sat Sun
```

split and **join** often go together. The next program, **rep2.pl** (Fig. 22.9), splits each line of our sample database on the |, adds a century prefix to the date and then joins all the fields back. The script is well documented to require elaboration.

```
#!/usr/bin/perl -n
# Script: rep2.pl - Uppercases the name and adds century prefix to the date

@line = split (/\|/) ;                                  # $_ is assumed
($day, $month, $year) = split(/\//, $line[4]);          # Splits date field
$year = "19" . $year ;                                  # Adds century prefix
$line[4] = join("\/", $day, $month, $year);             # Rebuilds date field
$line = join("\|", @line);                              # Rebuilds line
print $line;
```

Fig. 22.9 **rep2.pl**

Let's now print the first three lines of our transformed database by running the program:

```
$ rep2.pl emp.lst | head -n 3
2233|a.k. shukla      |g.m.     |sales     |12/12/195 |6000
9876|jai sharma       |director |production|12/03/1950|7000
5678|sumit chakrobarty|d.g.m.   |marketing |19/04/1943|6000
```

Joining on a specified delimiter has common applications in everyday programming. Even though we used **join** on a specific delimiter in our examples, the next section uses **join** without any delimiter to perform a very useful task.

22.12 dec2bin.pl: CONVERTING A DECIMAL NUMBER TO BINARY

We'll now consolidate our knowledge of array-handling functions by developing a script, **dec2bin.pl** (Fig. 22.10). This script accepts a decimal number as an argument and converts it to binary. You are probably aware that, to do that, you have to repeatedly divide a number (rather the quotient) by 2, and then reverse all the collected remainders. We need the **unshift** function here to perform this reversal by filling up an array with the remainder bit that arises from every division.

```
#!/usr/bin/perl
# Script: dec2bin.pl -- Converts decimal numbers to binary
foreach $number (@ARGV) {
    $original_number = $number ;
    until ($number == 0 ) {
        $bit = $number % 2  ;                         # Find the remainder bit
        unshift (@bit_arr, $bit) ;                    # Insert bit at beginning
        $number = int($number / 2 ) ;
    }
    $binary_number = join ("", @bit_arr) ;            # Join on nothing!
    print ("The binary number of $original_number is $binary_number\n") ;
    splice(@bit_arr, 0, $#bit_arr+1) ;                # Delete all array elements
                                           # Can also use $#bit_arr = -1 ;
}
```

Fig. 22.10 **dec2bin.pl**

Like the shell, **perl** also uses the **until** loop with the same meaning. The **join** function is used simply to concatenate all digit strings (0 or 1) that are stored in the array, `@bit_arr`, without using a delimiter at all! The **foreach** loop lets you supply as many numbers as you want in a single invocation of the script:

```
$ dec2bin.pl 2 7 65 191 255
The binary number of 2 is 10
The binary number of 7 is 111
The binary number of 65 is 1000001
The binary number of 191 is 10111111
The binary number of 255 is 11111111
```

You can use this program for determining whether two hosts are in the same subnet *(28.2)* by converting their network addresses to binary.

22.13 grep: SEARCHING AN ARRAY FOR A PATTERN

perl has a **grep** function, and you can guess what it does; it searches an array for a pattern. **grep** returns an array too which stores the array elements found in another array. This is how you search the array `@dept_arr` for the pattern `marketing`:

```
@found_arr = grep (/marketing/, @dept_arr) ;
```

If **grep** succeeds, the matched lines will be stored as separate elements in `@found_arr`. You can then check the variable `$#found_arr` for success or failure, which you'll remember, stores the last index of the array. By definition, this is -1 if the array is null. Using this principle, our next script, **search_array.pl** (Fig. 22.11), accepts a pattern from the user and searches an array that was previously populated by reading the file `dept.lst`.

```
#!/usr/bin/perl
# Script: search_array.pl - Searches array for a string or regular expression
@dept_arr = <> ;                          # Read file into array
for ($i=0 ; $i<3 ; $i++) {                # Can use only three times
    print ("Enter a code to look up: ") ;
    chop ($code = <STDIN>) ;
    @found_arr = grep (/^$code/, @dept_arr) ;          # Search at beginning
    if ($#found_arr == -1 || $code eq "") {            # -1 means null array
        print ("Code does not exist\n") ;
        next ;                              # Go to beginning of loop
    }
    split (/\|/, $found_arr[0]) ;           # Split first element only
    print ("Code = $code    Description = $_[1]\n") ;
}
```

Fig. 22.11 **search_array.pl**

We split the first array element of `@found_arr` to extract the code and description separately. The **for** loop ensures that the program prompts for the code only thrice. It then prints the code description if it finds a match:

```
$ search_array.pl dept.lst
Enter a code to look up: 05
Code = 05     Description = production
Enter a code to look up: 99
Code does not exist
Enter a code to look up: 02
Code - 02     Description = admin
```

It makes a lot of sense to store a table in an array, rather than access its disk file repeatedly. **grep** enables table lookups, and is extremely useful for report writing purposes. Like its UNIX counterpart, **grep** also accepts regular expressions for pattern matches, but more of these expressions later.

22.14 ASSOCIATIVE ARRAYS

perl uses yet another type of array—the *associative array*. It alternates the array subscripts and values in a series of comma-delimited strings. For instance, the associative array `%region` could be defined like this:

```
%region = ("N", "North", "S", "South", "E", "East", "W", "West") ;
```

This array uses the `%` symbol to prefix the array name. This assignment creates an array of four elements where the subscript precedes the value in the array definition. The array subscript, which can also be a string, is enclosed within a pair of curly braces rather than [ ]. For instance, `$region{"N"}` produces `North`. CGI programmers must feel totally at home with associative arrays.

We use an associative array, `%region`, in the program, **region.pl** (Fig. 22.12) to expand region codes. The program shows how to use two associative array functions, **keys** and **values**.

```
#!/usr/bin/perl
# Script: region.pl - Uses an associative array
%region = ("N", "North", "S", "South", "E", "East", "W", "West") ;
foreach $letter (@ARGV) {
   print ("The letter $letter stands for $region{$letter}" . "\n" );
}
@key_list = keys(%region) ;                               # List of subscripts
print ("The subscripts are @key_list\n") ;
@value_list = values %region  ;                           # List of values
print ("The values are @value_list\n") ;
```

Fig. 22.12 **region.pl**

keys stores the list of subscripts in a separate array (here, `@key_list`), while **values** holds the value of each element in yet another array (here, `@value_list`). Let's test the script by supplying a couple of single-character strings:

```
$ region.pl S W
The letter S stands for South
The letter W stands for West
The subscripts are S E N W
The values are South East North West
```

There are important implications here. You can separately extract both the keys and their values from an associative array. You can also present these values in the same way the **set** statement shows all environment variables:

```
foreach $key (keys %region) {
    print "$key" . "=" . "$region{$key}\n" ;
}
```

We found out the value of each key and stored it in turn in the variable `$key`. It's then a simple matter to use it as the subscript of `%region`. The element `$region{$key}` stores the value of each key as shown by this output:

```
S=South
E=East
N=North
W=West
```

Normally, **keys** returns the key strings in a random sequence. To order the list alphabetically, you'll often find the **sort** function used with **keys**. You can have both a normal and a reverse sort:

```
foreach $key (sort(keys %region)) {
@key_list = reverse sort keys %region   ;              No ( )—OK
```

> **Note** **Note: perl**'s built-in array, `%ENV`, stores all the shell's environment variables. For instance, `$ENV{'PATH'}` contains the value of the shell's `PATH`. You can easily access these variables using the techniques discussed here.

22.14.1 Counting Number of Occurrences

Associative arrays are extremely useful in counting the number of occurrences of an item. From the sample database, you can create a report showing the number of people in each department. We tried a similar exercise before with **awk** *(21.13)*, and we'll do it again with **perl**. For a programming language, this is quite some work, but a small **perl** program, **count.pl** (Fig. 22.13), does the job.

```
#!/usr/bin/perl
# Script: count.pl - Counts frequency of occurrence of an item
while (<>) {
    split (/\|/) ;                          # | has to be escaped
    $dept = $_[3] ;                         # Department is fourth field
    $deptlist{$dept} += 1 ;                 # Same as ++
}
foreach $dept (sort (keys %deptlist)) {
    print ("$dept: $deptlist{$dept}\n") ;
}
```

Fig. 22.13 **count.pl**

The program is divided into two parts. The **while** construct first filters out the values of `$dept` for each line read, and increments the counter of the respective element of the array `%deptlist`. After all input has been read, the **foreach** construct assigns each value of the key from `%deptlist` to the variable `$dept`. `$deptlist{$dept}` now contains the accumulated total for each key. This sorted output shows the power of **perl**:

```
$ count.pl emp.lst
accounts  : 2
admin     : 1
marketing : 4
personnel : 2
production: 2
sales     : 4
```

With only a few lines of **perl** code you have been able to list out the department-wise distribution of people.

22.15 REGULAR EXPRESSIONS AND SUBSTITUTION

perl offers a grand superset of *all* possible regular expressions that are found in the UNIX system (except the ones specified by POSIX). You have already used some of them for pattern matching. **perl** understands both basic and extended regular expressions (BRE and ERE) and has some of its own too. You must know regular expressions and the **sed** and **tr** commands very well before you can appreciate the material that is presented in this section.

22.15.1 The s and tr Functions

The **s** and **tr** functions handle all substitution in **perl**. The s function is used in the same way as the **s** command in **sed**. **tr** translates characters in just the same way the UNIX **tr** command does, but with a slightly different syntax. This is how we use them:

```
s/:/-/g ;                                   Sets $_ when used this way
tr/a-z/A-Z/ ;                               In UNIX, you use tr '[a-z]' '[A-Z]'
```

In either case, you are setting the system variable, $_. Often, you'll split a line into fields and then use one of these functions for transforming the fields. In that case, you'll have to use the operator, =~, for performing a match and !~ for negating it:

```
$line =~ s/:/-/g ;                          $line is reassigned
$name =~ tr/a-z/A-Z/ ;                      Here too
```

s and **tr** also accept flags. s accepts the g flag (shown above) for global substitution, and yet another (e) for indicating that the replaced pattern is to be evaluated as an expression. **tr** uses all the UNIX **tr** options as flags—s squeezes multiple occurrences, c complements and d deletes the character *(14.9.1)*.

The next program, **rep3.pl** (Fig. 22.14), takes the last two digits of the year as user input, and then selects those lines where the year of birth (embedded in the fifth field) matches this input. It then performs some transformation on the selected lines before printing them.

```
#!/usr/bin/perl
# Source: rep3.pl - Uses the s and tr functions for substitution

print("Last two digits of date of birth: ");
$yearin = <STDIN> ;
chop($yearin);                  # Remove \n else comparison will fail later

$found = 0;
while (<>) {
   @line = split(/\|/) ;
   $name = $line[1] ; $emp_id = $line[0] ;

   split(/\//, $line[4]);                   # Splits date field
   $year =  $_[2] ;                         # 2-digit year extracted ...

   if ($year eq $yearin)  {                 # .. and compared with user input
      $found = 1;
      $name =~ tr/a-z/A-Z/ ;                # Name field changed to uppercase
      $emp_id =~ s/^/9/ ;                   # Adds a "9" prefix to the first field
      $line[0] = $emp_id ;                  # Reassign elements of @line with
      $line[1] = $name;                     # the two changes made by tr and s

      $_ = join(":", @line) ;               # Assigning to $_ allows use of next
                                            # two s functions without using =~
      s/\s *:/:/g ;                         # Removes whitespace before delimiter
      s#/#-#g ;                             # Delimiter in date is now the -
      print ;                               # Print $_
   }
}
print("Year 19" . $yearin . " not found\n") if $found eq 0 ;
```

Fig. 22.14 rep3.pl

We split up the sample database as usual, and then again split the date field to extract the two-digit year. This year string is compared with user input for every line read. If the match succeeds, two changes are made at field level, and two more at global level. At the field level, the name is converted to uppercase, and the prefix 9 is added to the emp_id. Both require the use of the regular expression matching operator, `=~`. The fields are joined before the global changes are carried out. We also change the delimiter to a colon when joining.

To use the **s** and **tr** functions on the entire line (globally), we need to make sure that `$_` is properly set. The **join** function cleverly achieves this by assigning its return value to `$_`. The **s** function first removes all spaces before the delimiter, which has now become a : on account of the previous join. The next s function changes every / in the line to a -. This affects only the date field, and rather than place a \ before the /, it's better to change the delimiter used by **s** to a #. The statement is more readable too.

We'll run the script with two inputs—one that exists and one that doesn't exist:

```
$ rep3.pl emp.lst
Last two digits of date of birth: 45
96521:LALIT CHOWDURY:director:marketing:26-09-45:8200
92345:J.B. SAXENA:g.m.:marketing:12-03-45:8000
$ rep3.pl emp.lst
Last two digits of date of birth: 60
Year 1960 not found
```

22.15.2 Identifying Whitespace, Digits and Words

perl also offers some escaped characters to represent whitespace, digits and word boundaries (Table 22.1). Here are three commonly-used ones:

`\s` — A whitespace character
`\d` — A digit
`\w` — A word character

All these escaped characters also have uppercase counterparts that negate their lowercase ones. Thus, `\D` is a nondigit character. We have already used the anchoring sequence `\b` for matching a pattern on a word boundary *(22.5)*, and the `\s` in the previous program to match whitespace.

The following statement uses the anchoring characters, ^ and $, to check whether `$stg` consists only of word characters :

```
if ($stg =~ /^\w+$/) {                    Same as ($stg =~ /^[a-zA-Z0-9_]+$/)
```

And this statement locates all lines that contain IP addresses. Since dots separate the octets, we need to escape the dots too for perfect matching:

```
if (/\d+\.\d+\.\d+\.\d+/) {
```

You can often compact your regular expressions by using these characters. In the next example, we'll be using some of these escape sequences.

Table 22.1 Additional Regular Expression Sequences Used by **perl**

Symbols	*Significance*
`\w`	Matches a word character (same as `[a-zA-Z0-9_]`)
`\W`	Doesn't match a word character (same as `[^a-zA-Z0-9_]`)
`\d`	Matches a digit (Same as `[0-9]`)
`\D`	Doesn't match a digit (Same as `[^0-9]`)
`\s`	Matches a whitespace character
`\S`	Doesn't match a whitespace character
`\b`	Matches on word boundary
`\B`	Doesn't match on word boundary

22.15.3 The IRE and TRE Features

perl accepts the IRE and TRE used by **grep** and **sed** *(15.11)*, except that the curly braces and parentheses are not escaped. For instance, this is how you locate lines longer than 512 characters using an IRE:

```
perl -ne 'print if /.{513,}/' foo                    No \ before { and }
```

You can enclose part of a pattern within parentheses and use them anywhere in the program with $1, $2, etc. This is **sed**'s TRE *(15.11.3)* implemented in **perl**. The repeated pattern could be \1 if it is specified in a pattern search with 2 /s, or $1 if the ~= operator is used.

The next example, **rep4.pl** (Fig. 22.15), changes the form of reporting for the date format of the sample database. It uses a TRE to report in the form *dd-mon-yyyy* format where *mon* is a three-character month name.

```
#!/usr/bin/perl -n
# Script: rep4.pl - Reports a date in format dd-mon-yyyy using a TRE
@month[1..12] = ("Jan", "Feb", "Mar", "Apr", "May", "Jun",
                 "Jul", "Aug", "Sep", "Oct", "Nov", "Dec") ;
split (/\|/) ;              #
$_[4] =~ /(\d+).(\d+).(\d+)/ ;  # Splits up into $1, $2 and $3
$_[4] = join ("-", $1, $month[$2], "19$3") ;
$_ = join(":", @_);
print ;
```

Fig. 22.15 **rep4.pl**

We split the database yet again, and store the split fields in the default array, `@_`. Each of the three components of the date field can be represented by the TRE `(\d+)`, which signifies one or more occurrences of a digit. **perl** TREs are more readable than their UNIX counterparts; they don't use the `\s` before the `(` and `)`. The three groups get the tags $1, $2 and $3. Using $2, we extract the month name form the array `@month`. Finally, we join the elements of the `@_` array on the : delimiter. Here are the first three lines of output:

```
$ rep4.pl emp.lst | head -n 3
2233:a.k. shukla       :g.m.      :sales      :12-Dec-1952:6000
9876:jai sharma        :director  :production:12-Mar-1950:7000
5678:sumit chakrobarty:d.g.m.     :marketing  :19-Apr-1943:6000
```

Look at the fifth field showing a date format that is also used by Oracle. The TRE in **perl** is unique in another way; **perl** stores these groupings ($1, etc.) in memory till the next grouping is done.

22.15.4 Editing Files In-Place

Instead of writing to the standard output or to a separate file, **perl** can edit and *rewrite* the input file itself. With **sed**, you would have redirected the output to a temporary file and then renamed it back to the original file. For a group of files, you would have used a **for** loop as well. Not so for **perl**; the `-i` option can edit multiple files in-place:

```
perl -p -i -e "s/<B>/<STRONG>/g" *.html *.htm
```

This changes `<B>` in all lines where they occur in all HTML files to `<STRONG>`. The files themselves are rewritten with the new output. If in-place editing seems a risky thing to do, you can back the files up before undertaking the operation:

```
perl -p -i.bak -e "tr/a-z/A-Z/" foo1 foo2 foo3 foo4
```

This first backs up `foo1` to `foo1.bak`, `foo2` to `foo2.bak`, and so forth, before converting all lowercase letters in each file to uppercase.

22.16 FILE HANDLING

So far, we have been specifying the input filenames from the command line. **perl** also provides the low-level file handling functions that let you hard-code the source and destination of the data stream in the script itself. A file is opened for reading like this:

```
open (INFILE,  "/home/henry/mbox") ;                 Don't forget the quotes!
```

`INFILE` here is a *filehandle* (a shorthand representation) of the file `mbox` (file presumed to be in current directory if a pathname is not used). Once a file has been opened, functions that read and write the file will use the filehandle to access the file.

A file is opened for writing with the shell-like operators, `>` and `>>`, having their usual meanings:

```
open (OUTFILE, ">rep_out.lst") ;
open (OUTFILE, ">>rep_out.lst") ;
```

perl's filehandles can be associated with pipelines also. To shell programmers, the meanings of these statements should be quite obvious:

```
open (INFILE, "sort emp.lst |" ) ;                  Input from sort output
open (OUTFILE, "| lp" ) ;                           Output to print spooler
```

The next script, **rw.pl** (Fig. 22.16), uses **open** to obtain two filehandles to read one file and write another. It also uses the **print** statement with a filehandle as argument to write output to a file without using redirection. Both files are explicitly closed at the end with **close**.

```
#!/usr/bin/perl
# Script: rw.pl -  Shows use of low-level I/O available in perl
open (FILEIN, "desig.lst") || die ("Cannot open file") ;
open (FILEOUT, ">desig_out.lst") ;
while (<FILEIN>) {                          # Till there are lines in the file
    print FILEOUT if (1..3) ;               # Can also use if ($. < 4 )
}
close (FILEIN) ;
close (FILEOUT) ;
```

Fig. 22.16 rw.pl

The statement **while (<FILEIN>)** reads a line at a time from the file represented by the FILEIN filehandle, and stores it in $_. Every time the <FILEIN> statement is executed, the next line is read. You can read and print a single line in this way:

```
$_ = <FILEIN> ;                    Assign to $_
print ;                            print uses $_ by default
```

Even if you don't close the files before terminating the script, **perl** closes them on its own. When we run the script without arguments, the output doesn't come to the terminal this time, but goes to the file desig_out.lst.

> **Tip** If a number of **print** statements have to write to the same filehandle (say, FILEOUT), then you can assign this filehandle as the default using **select (FILEOUT) ;**. Subsequent **print** statements don't need to use the FILEOUT argument in that case.

22.17 FILE TESTS

perl has an elaborate system of file tests. It overshadows the capabilities of the Bourne shell—and even the **find** command in some ways. The following statements test some of the most common attributes of a file:

```
$x = "rdbnew.lst" ;
print "File $x is readable\n" if -r $x ;
print "File $x is executable\n" if -x $x ;
print "File $x has non-zero size\n" if -s $x ;
print "File $x exists\n" if -e $x ;
print "File $x is a text file\n" if -T $x ;
print "File $x is a binary file\n" if -B $y ;
```

's file tests go further; it can tell you a file's modification and access times very accurately. The script, **when_last.pl** (Fig. 22.17), uses the C- and **awk**-like **printf** statement with its standard formats. It detects files which were modified less than 2.4 hours ago.

```
#!/usr/bin/perl
# Script: when_last.pl - Finds files that are less than 2.4 hours old
foreach $file (`ls`)  {
   chop ($file) ;
   if (($m_age = -M $file) < 0.1) {           # tenth of a day i.e., 2.4 hours
       printf "File %s was last modified %0.3f days back \n", $file, $m_age ;
   }
}
```

Fig. 22.17 **when_last.pl**

`-M $file` returns the time elapsed in hours since `$file` was last modified. It's a general **perl** feature (an idea borrowed from C) that you can make a test (`< 0.1`) and assignment (`$m_age = ...`) at the same time. Let's observe the output:

```
$ when_last.pl
File bf2o.sh was last modified 0.063 days back
File profile.sam was last modified 0.082 days back
File when_last.pl was last modified 0.000 days back
```

It seems that the last file has just been modified; three decimal places are not enough. You have to increase the length of the **printf** format if you need to know the exact time.

Apart from testing file attributes, **perl** can manipulate files and directories very easily. It uses **chmod**, **chown**, **chgrp**, **chdir** (like **cd**), **mkdir**, **rmdir**, **rename** (like **mv**), **link**, **unlink** (like **rm**) and **umask** in the same way. It can also open directories with directory filehandles. The UNIX system call library also uses functions having these names, as you'll discover in Chapter 25.

22.18 SUBROUTINES

perl handles subroutines—both as procedures and functions that return values. Subroutines are called by the & symbol followed by the subroutine name. A subroutine's arguments are stored in the array `@_`. Variables inside the subroutine can be declared as `local` to make them invisible in the calling program.

Many applications require the user to supply a username and password. Since this involves executing the same amount of code twice, it becomes an ideal candidate for a subroutine. The program, **input.pl** (Fig. 22.18), uses the subroutine **take_input**, which accepts the prompt string as an argument, validates the input for word characters and returns the value that was input.

The subroutine arguments are accepted into the system array, `@_`, and then reassigned to the two local variables `$prompt` and `$flag`. What is checked in the subroutine is just the number of arguments passed (`@_ == 2`). When you pass two arguments to it, the UNIX **stty** command blanks out the display during password entry.

last is **perl**'s equivalent of the shell's **break** statement that exits a loop. (**perl** also uses **next** instead of **continue**.) Here, control breaks out of the loop when there is at least one word character in the input. This is how you can ensure that the password is not displayed:

```
#!/usr/bin/perl
# Script: input.pl - Shows use of subroutines
system ("tput clear") ;                    # Executes the UNIX command
$username = &take_input ("Oracle user-id: ") ;
$password = &take_input ("Oracle password: ", "noecho") ;
print "\nThe username and password are $username and $password\n" ;
system ("sqlplus $username/$password @query.sql >/dev/null" ) ;

sub take_input {
   local ($prompt, $flag) = @_ ;              # @_ stores arguments of subroutine
   while (1)   {                              # (1) is always true
      print ("$prompt") ;
      system("stty -echo") if (@_ == 2 ) ;  # Echo mode off
      chop ($name = <STDIN>) ;
      system("stty echo") if (@_ == 2 ) ;   # Echo mode on
      last if $name =~ /\w/ ;                # Quit the loop if $name has at
   }                                          # least one word character
   $name ;                                    # return $name will also do
}
```

Fig. 22.18 **input.pl**

```
$ input.pl
Oracle user-id: !@#$%^&*                        Nonword characters
Oracle user-id: scott
Oracle password: *****                          Password not echoed
The username and password are scott and tiger
    .... Executes SQL*Plus script query.sql ....
```

The last statement in the program (`$name`) is typically **perl**'s way of returning a value. You should store frequently used subroutines in separate files. Instruct the calling program to read a file containing a subroutine by placing the **require** statement at the beginning. If you save the **take_input** subroutine in the file **oracle_lib.pl**, you should do these two things:

- Insert the statement **require "oracle_lib.pl" ;** in the calling program immediately after the line specifying the **perl** interpreter.
- Place the statement **1;** at the end of the file containing one or more subroutines. The **perl** documentation requires every "required" file to end with a true value. Any nonzero value is a true value in **perl**, so **1;** returns true.

In the above example, you can use `$_[0]` instead of `$prompt` and `$_[1]` in place of `$flag`. You can also drop the word `local` when assigning the subroutine arguments in case you want the variables to be visible outside the subroutine.

22.19 CONCLUSION

perl has specific functions for inter-process communication which have not been skimmed at all here. Its object-oriented tools and networking functions have been ignored. It has several options and many more functions that let you do things with the minimal amount of code. **perl** is a real gold mine of techniques; every day some one discovers a new feature in it. The UNIX spirit lives in **perl**. Think of a strong UNIX feature; it is there in **perl**. Browse the Web; you are most likely invoking a CGI program written in **perl**. **perl** is the pride of UNIX.

WRAP UP

perl is a superset of **grep**, **tr**, **sed**, **awk** and the shell. It can be used from the command line with the -e option, but a **perl** program is better placed in a file with the interpreter specified in the first line.

Input is read from the keyboard by assigning <STDIN> to a variable. **perl** reads everything that is entered including spaces and the newline character. The last character of a line is removed by **chop**.

Variables need the $ both for assignment and evaluation. They need no type declarations and can store a number with a very high degree of precision. Variable values can include the escape sequences. You can capitalize the first character of a string (\u) or the entire string (\U).

The **.** is used for string concatenation. x is used for repetition. **substr** extracts a string both from right and left, and also inserts a string. **uc** and **ucfirst** convert into uppercase the entire argument and the first character, respectively.

perl uses the -n option to set up an implicit loop for reading files. An explicit loop can also be set up with the symbols <>—representing the filenames specified in the command line. **while (<>)** is quite often used inside a script to read a file.

$. stores the current line number, and the range operator (..) specifies a group of lines.

$_ is the *default variable* used by many **perl** functions. It stores the last line read or the last pattern matched. **print**, **chop**, **split**, pattern matching and substitution operate on $_ by default.

perl uses *lists* and arrays extensively. @arr, when assigned to a variable, represents the length of the array. $#arr stores the last subscript of the array. @ARGV[ ] stores all command line arguments, but the command name is available as $0.

The **foreach** construct loops through an array and assigns each element in turn to a variable. The list can also be provided by command substitution.

split breaks up a list into variables or an array. @_ is the default array, and whitespace the default delimiter. Elements of a split line can be glued together with **join**. Elements can be deleted from an array (**shift** and **pop**) or inserted (**unshift** and **push**). **splice** can do everything at any array location.

The *associative array* uses the % symbol and alternates the array subscript and value in a series of comma-delimited values. The subscript of this array can also be a character string. The **keys** function extracts these subscripts, and **values** filters out the values. **sort** may be used to order the extraction.

perl accepts all regular expressions used by all UNIX commands, and has some of its own. Now you can match a digit (\d), a word character (\w), the beginning of a word (\b) and a whitespace character (\s). The uppercase counterparts negate the lowercase ones.

The **s** and **tr** functions are used for substitution and character translation in the same way done in **sed** and **tr**. The operators =~ and !~ are used to match regular expressions with variables. Files can be edited "in-place" with the -i option, and can be optionally backed up with a separate extension.

The IRE and TRE work in the same way as before except that the \ is not required before the () and {} characters. A grouped pattern can also be reproduced elsewhere with $1, $2 and so on, till the next grouping is done.

perl uses a *filehandle* to access a file. A filehandle can represent a pipeline as well. **print** also uses a filehandle to write to a file. The **select** *filehandle* statement makes **print** use that filehandle as the default. **perl**'s file tests can store the age of a file (modification and access) to several places of decimals.

Subroutines are invoked with an &, and its arguments are stored in the array, `@_`. Subroutines can be held in an external file but must have the statement **1;** placed at the end of the file. The calling program "includes" subroutines placed in an external file with the **require** statement.

TEST YOUR UNDERSTANDING

22.1 Number all lines of a file, separating the line from line number by a tab.

22.2 Print the string `UNIX` 20 times without using a loop.

22.3 How do you list the line in `/etc/passwd` that has 1 as the UID?

22.4 How will you print *only* the first occurrence of a string in a file?

22.5 Use **perl** to show all lines containing the string `director` and the next line.

22.6 Ask the user repeatedly to enter a number, and when the user enters 0, print the total of all numbers entered so far.

22.7 How will you convert all characters in a file to uppercase without using shell redirection?

22.8 Write a program that prompts a user to input a string and a number, and prints the string that many times, with each string on a separate line.

22.9 By default, file reading, chopping and pattern matching operate on (i) `$.` (ii) `$_` (iii) `@_` (iv) None of these.

FLEX YOUR BRAIN

22.1 How do you double-space a file with **perl**?

22.2 Instead of numbering lines, add the letters `A.`, `B.`, `C.` and so on at the beginning of every line.

22.3 Capitalize the first character of every word in a file.

22.4 How will you use a **perl** script to convert a binary number supplied as argument to decimal?

22.5 Accept a four-digit year from the keyboard and then check whether it's a leap year or not. (Note: Years ending with 00 must be divisible by 400.)

22.6 Devise a script which lists the usage of words (in the form *word*`:` *count*) in its argument files.

22.7 How will you use **find** and **perl** to delete all files modified more than a year back? What is the advantage of using this method compared to using **find** with `-exec rm`?

22.8 Change the interpreter line to `#!/usr/local/bin/perl` in all **perl** scripts in the current directory.

22.9 A closing HTML tag starts with /. For instance <b> is closed with </b>. Convert all these tags comprising single words (without attributes) to uppercase. (Tags like `<img src=` .... must not get converted.)

23

Advanced vi

In this chapter, we consider some of the advanced features of the **vi** editor. After having worked with **vi** for some time, you'll find it helpful to know these features. Many of them aren't available in other editors with the possible exception of **emacs**. Editing can be very productive if you customize your editor to suit your requirements, and we'll do that in this chapter. With **vi** you can move mountains with only a few keystrokes, but only if you have gone through Chapter 8 thoroughly.

WHAT YOU WILL LEARN

- The use of *operator-command* combinations to delete, move and copy text.
- Change screen text by running (filtering) a UNIX command on it.
- Edit multiple files and switch from one file to another. Split the window in **vim**.
- Recover up to nine complete line deletions using the *numbered buffers*.
- Use *[Ctrl-v]* to enter any control character and *[Esc]*.
- Place cursor on or near any character.
- Mark text and access any mark. Toggle between two marked locations.
- Customize the editor's environment by defining abbreviations and key maps and setting variables.

TOPICS OF SPECIAL INTEREST

- Copy or delete multiple text sections to 26 separate *named buffers* and restore them in another file.
- Use the mapping feature to compile programs and execute shell and **perl** scripts without leaving the editor.

23.1 OPERATORS

Most of the useful functions in the Command Mode are derived from a combination of an *operator* and a command. This is probably **vi**'s strongest feature, and opens up a new domain of commands for you to work with. With operators, you can frame a command for practically any situation. There are only a few operators, and you must know at least the following ones:

d — Delete
c — Change
y — Yank (copy)
! — Filter to act on text

An operator alone can't perform any function unless it is combined with a command or itself. When used with itself (i.e., twice), it can handle a very specialized function. In Chapter 8, you've seen how these specialized functions were performed by using **dd** and **yy** to delete and copy a line, respectively. All these operators also take a repeat factor which greatly enhances their power. The power of **vi** is mainly derived from the ease with which you can frame commands of your own using these operators.

Note	An operator, when doubled by itself, (like **dd**, **cc**, **yy** and **!!**), acts only on the current line.

23.1.1 Deleting and Moving Text (d, p and P)

You know how to delete characters and lines with **x**, **X** and **dd** *(8.5.1)*. **dd** is really a combination of the **d** operator with itself. **vi** can perform some complex deletion when this operator is combined with a command of the Command Mode.

Suppose you wish to delete all text from the present cursor position to the end of the line. You can frame the command yourself if you recall the primary commands that are used in the Command Mode. Since the command to move to the end of a line is **$**, you can combine the **d** operator with the **$** to delete from the cursor position to the end of the line:

d$ *Deletes rest of line*

Note how a specialized function could be devised by following a simple set of rules. Taking the cue from here, the command to delete a word should be equally simple—**dw. dG** should delete text from current position to the end of file. A repeat factor applies here too; **3dw** deletes three words, and **5dd** deletes five lines, including with the current line.

For using operators to move text, there are no special considerations involved. We have deleted text using the **dd**, **x** and **X** commands and then placed the deleted text at a different location with the **p** and **P** commands. Recall *(8.5.2)* that **p** and **P** behave differently depending on whether the deletion affects entire lines or parts of lines. When working with entire lines, **p** puts text *below* the cursor and **P** places it *above*. However, when you delete a word with **dw**, you can put the deleted word only to the *left* (with **p**) or *right* (with **P**) of the cursor position, and not above or below the current line.

23.1.2 Yanking Text (y)

The **y** operator yanks (or copies) text. It is used in the same way the **d** operator is combined with another command or by itself. You can yank a word, a group of words, line segments or even entire lines with this operator. Moreover, the **p** and **P** commands act in the same way for putting the copied text at its destination.

For instance, to yank five lines of text, move the cursor to the first of these lines and press

```
5yy
```

Next, move the cursor to the new location, and press

`p` *or* `P`

to place the copied text below or above the current line, respectively. When you yank words, **p** and **P** have the same significance as with the **d** operator; **p** puts text on the right of the cursor location, while **P** puts it on the left.

23.1.3 Changing Text (c)

Text is changed with the **c** (change) operator. This operator too is combined with a command to indicate the boundaries of replacement. If **dw** deletes a word, **cw** changes it. This is the only operator which functions in the Input Mode. The change operation thus has to be terminated with *[Esc]*.

When you use **c** with a Command Mode command, you are taken to the Input Mode. But this time the boundary limiting your area of operation could be indicated by a **$**. If you change three words with **3cw**, a **$** should appear at the end of the third word (Linux excepted). The inserted text overwrites the characters delimited by the **$** that temporarily appears on the screen. If the replaced text is larger, then once the cursor moves up to the **$** marker, further insertion shifts existing text to the right.

To change text from the present cursor position up to the end of a line, use

`c$` *or* `C`

To change entire lines, use

```
cc
```

Now that you know the use of the two operators discussed so far, how can you frame a command to change text from the current position to the first occurrence of a pattern? For instance, you may like to change the contents of the rest of this section, i.e., till the heading of the next section (entitled `Filtering Text`). Since searching is done with the */pattern* sequence, combine this sequence with the operator and it does the job:

`c/Filtering Text/`*[Enter]*

When you use this command, all text starting from the current cursor position, up to, but not on to, the string `Filtering Text` will be deleted, and **vi** will switch to the Input Mode. Enter the changed text and press *[Esc]*. Some systems don't show the $, but simply remove the defined text the moment the change command is entered.

23.1.4 Filtering Text (!)

vi has a marvelous feature of allowing a UNIX filter to act on text that's on display at your terminal. Can you sort the contents of your editing window without leaving the editor? Yes, that is possible with the **!** operator and the UNIX **sort** command. In general, filtering text on the screen requires three steps:

1. Move to the beginning of the text to be acted upon and type **!**.
2. Move to the other end of the text using any navigation command like **G**.
3. Enter the UNIX command to act on the text. The text on the screen should change immediately.

Table 23.1 A Few Specimen Operator-Command Combinations

Command	*Function*
`d$` or `D`	Deletes from cursor to end of line
`5dd`	Deletes 5 lines
`d/}`	Deletes from cursor up to first occurrence of }
`d30G`	Deletes from cursor up to line number 30
`df.`	Deletes from cursor to first occurrence of a dot
`y$` or `Y`	Yanks from cursor to end of line
`3yw` or `y3w`	Yanks three words from cursor position
`5yy`	Yanks five lines
`yG`	Yanks from cursor to end of file
`y?case`	Yanks from cursor up to first occurrence of string `case` in reverse direction
`c0`	Changes from cursor to beginning of line
`c$` or `C`	Changes from cursor to end of line
`3cw` or `c3w`	Changes three words
`cc`	Changes current line
`!Gsort`	Sorts all lines from current cursor position to end of file
`!!tr '[a-z]' '[A-Z]'`	Converts current line to uppercase

For instance, to sort lines 21 to 40 of a file, move the cursor to the first character of line 21 (with **21G**), and then press the following sequence:

`!40Gsort`*[Enter]*

Nothing appears on the screen till the second address (**40G**) is entered. After you enter the word `sort`, the last line could look like this:

`:21,40!sort` *You executed an ex Mode command!*

After you press *[Enter]*, the 20 specified lines are sorted and the output replaces the current contents. You have just executed the ex Mode command **:21,40!sort** without knowing it. You can enter this command directly as well. You can save the change if you want or undo it (with **u**) if it didn't do exactly what you wanted.

Like the other operators, the **!**, when doubled, uses the command following it to operate on the current line. This is how you use **tr** to change the case of the text of the current line to upper:

```
!!tr '[a-z]' '[A-Z]'
```

To make editing work very productive and satisfying, you must have thorough knowledge of the commands that are used to control cursor positioning. After that, it's easy to perform any text manipulation by using the right operator-command combination, employing a repeat factor wherever necessary. You shouldn't now find it difficult to understand the significance of these combinations listed in Table 23.1.

> **Note** Doubling an operator (like **dd**, **yy** and **cc**) also constitutes a special command, which always acts on the current line. Three operator-command combinations also have synonyms—**D** (**d$**), **Y** (**y$**) and **C** (**c$**). They act on text from the current position to the end of line.

23.2 THE ex MODE: HANDLING MULTIPLE FILES

This mode offers some facilities not seen in the Command Mode, especially those related to handling multiple files. You can work with multiple files in **vi**, and easily switch from one file to another. As a programmer, you need to know multiple file-handling techniques since you'll often need to move or copy text from one program to another. The basic file handling commands are already known to you *(8.3)*; the advanced ones (Table 23.2) are discussed in this section.

23.2.1 Switching Files

You may sometimes require to ignore all the unsaved changes you made. If you were quitting **vi** and then invoking it once again, you don't need to do that anymore. **vi** allows you to reload the last saved version of the file with

`:e!` *Like Revert in Microsoft Windows*

You can also edit multiple files without leaving the editor. While editing one file, you can easily switch to another by using its **:e** command:

`:e note2` *Temporarily leaves current file and starts editing* `note2`.

You can return to the original file by using one of these sequences:

[Ctrl-^] *Toggle between current and previous file*
`:e#` *Same*

This has a toggling effect; the next time you use either of these sequences, you'll switch to the other file again. The first sequence is easier to execute and you should use it whenever you use **vi** with multiple files.

Using **vi** *with Multiple Filenames* When **vi** is used with multiple filenames, say with **vi note[1-4]**, it throws out a message `4 files to edit`, and loads the first file (`note1`) into the buffer. You can switch to the next file, viz. `note2`, by using

```
:n                                      Next file in command line
```

You can go on in this manner and without leaving the editor till you have encountered the last file. At any stage, you can move back to the first file specified in the command line by "rewinding" the file list:

```
:rew                                    Back to first file in command line
```

When you switch from one file to another, there is a protection mechanism which prevents the switch if changes have been made to the file. The system displays a terse message:

```
No write since last change (:edit! overrides)
```

Just as the command **:q!** quits the editor after discarding all changes, the **:e! #** command similarly switches to the last edited file after discarding the changes made to the current file. You can also use **:n!** or **:rew!** in the same vein.

23.2.2 Inserting File and Command Output

With most Windows text editors, there's no easy way of inserting the contents of one file at a certain location in another file. You have to open the file, use something like *Select All* from the *Edit* menu, copy the entire text with *[Ctrl-c]*, switch to the original file, and then paste the contents with *[Ctrl-v]*. That involves a great deal of work by UNIX standards.

With **vi**, you don't have to visit the other file at all. Just insert its contents at the present cursor location:

```
:r note1                                Inserts file note1
```

You can also place the output of a command in your file. Use **:r** like before, but instead of specifying the filename, enter the command name preceded by the `!`:

```
:r !date                                Inserts output of date command
```

This is a very useful feature for documentation authors, who need to feature command output in their text. There's no need to save this output in a file and then read in the file.

> **Tip** There is a useful shortcut available in the Command Mode to toggle between two files; use *[Ctrl-^]* (Control-caret). For this to work at all times, make the ex Mode setting **:set autowrite** or **:set aw**. This ensures that the file is saved automatically before the switch occurs.

LINUX: Splitting the Window

You can split the screen into multiple windows in **vim**. The window can be empty or it can contain a file—even a copy of the same file. To view the same file in two separate windows, use the **:sp** (split) command in the ex Mode:

```
:sp                                     Splits existing window in two
```

In this situation, changes made to the buffer in one window are also seen in the other window. You can also create a new window not associated with any file:

`:new` *New blank window*

In either case, you'll see the screen split into two. You can move between the two windows by using this command:

[Ctrl-w][Ctrl-w] *Cycles through windows*

In any window (empty or otherwise), you can open a new file by using **:e** *filename*. You can also increase or decrease the vertical size of a window:

[Ctrl-w]+ *Increases size of current window*
[Ctrl-w]- *Reduces size of current window*

To make the current window the only window on the screen and close all other windows, use

`:on` *Removes all other windows*

You can kill the current window and move to the other window (if any):

`:q`

Note that when you have multiple windows on, **:q** will quit editing from the current window and close it. To apply the save, quit and exit commands to all windows in **vim**, you have to append an a to the existing commands. To quit all windows without saving, use **:qa**. To save all buffers and quit, use **:xa**.

Table 23.2 ex Mode Commands for File Handling

Command	*Function*
`:r note`	Reads file `note` below current line
`:r !head -3 dec2.pl`	Reads first three lines of `dec2.pl` below current line
`:w >> note1`	Appends buffer contents to file `note1`
`:e note1`	Stops editing current file and edits file `note1`
`:e! note1`	As above, but after abandoning changes made to current file
`:e!`	Loads last saved edition of current file (Like *Revert* in Microsoft Windows)
`:e#`	Returns to editing most recently edited file
`:n`	Edits next file (if **vi** is invoked with more than one filename)
`:rew`	Rewinds file list to start editing from first file specified in command line

23.3 STORING MULTIPLE TEXT SECTIONS: NAMED BUFFERS

So far, we have moved a single section of text by deleting it from the original location and putting it in the new one. **vi** actually stores the deleted text in an unnamed buffer. This technique has two limitations. First, you can use only one buffer at a time. Second, when moving text from one file to another (using **:e** *filename*), the contents of this special buffer are lost (Linux excepted).

Actually, **vi** has 26 special *named buffers*, but by default we don't use them. These buffers are named after the characters of the alphabet, and their use is fairly straightforward. Just precede the editing operation (deletion or yank) with a **"** (double quote) and the buffer name, say **a**. Thus, to yank four lines into this buffer named a, you should simply use

```
"a4yy                                      Copies 4 lines into buffer a
```

Now navigate to the desired location, press **"**, the buffer name (**a**) and **p** or **P** to put back the text:

```
"ap                                        Use P to put text above
```

You can delete or copy another section of text into another buffer, say **b**, and restore the same with **"bp** (or **"bP**). In this way, you have access to 26 buffers to hold 26 sections of text. Windows and the mouse can't do this! However, the X Window System and its **xclipboard** client *(18.5.2)* can do even better than this. Note that you can now toggle between the two files using *[Ctrl-^]* or **:e#**.

Moving Text from One File to Another Using this feature of named buffers, you can now copy and move text freely across a file, and even from one file to another. This is how you copy text across two files:

```
"a10yy                                     Copy 10 lines into buffer a
:e bin2dec.pl                              Switch to file bin2dec.pl
30G                                        Move to line 30
"ap                                        Put the 10 lines after line 30
```

The only precaution you need to take here is that, on no account, should you exit **vi** to open a second file. The buffer contents are lost when you leave **vi**.

> **Note** If you perform an operation on a named buffer which already contains some text, the contents of the buffer are overwritten. **vi** uses the uppercase letters to append to these buffers—**"Ayy** instead of **"ayy**.

23.4 UNDOING MULTIPLE LINE DELETIONS: NUMBERED BUFFERS

Even though the **u** command can undo only the last editing action, we often need to restore a number of recent deletions. **vi** makes it possible to restore up to the last nine *complete* line deletions using its *numbered buffers*. These buffers are numbered 1 to 9. The most recent deletion is stored in the buffer numbered 1, the next-most in the buffer numbered 2, and so forth. These buffers are accessed by prefixing the buffer number with a **"**. *Entire lines, when deleted, are stored in these buffers; parts of lines can't be stored.*

To restore the most recently deleted group of lines, move the cursor to your desired location and use

```
"1p                                        Restores most recent deletion
```

And if that's not the text you expected to restore, you can undo the last restoration with **u**, and then use **"2p** to see whether the desired text is stored in the buffer numbered 2. You can go on like this, using the nine numerals available, and undo up to nine deletions.

LINUX: Even though Linux can undo and redo *all* editing actions, this feature is still useful in that environment.

23.4.1 The Dot (`.`) Command: Restoring the Previous Deleted Line

The above technique of undoing deletions can be quite tedious, especially when you are doing a mass restoration. As a shortcut, `vi` offers the `.` command to restore the contents of any buffer. The command generally repeats the last editing instruction *(8.7)*, but behaves differently when used on a numbered buffer. Every time it is pressed, it steps through the buffer set to restore the contents of the *next* buffer.

To use this command here, you have to first restore at least one deletion using, say **`"1p`**. If that's not the block you are looking for, you can undo the restoration with **`u`**, and then press

to restore the contents of the next numbered buffer, i.e., the one numbered 2. You can issue a series of dots to step through the various buffers, each dot followed by **`u`**, until you spot the one you have been looking for. For instance, if the desired text to be undeleted resides in the buffer numbered 4, you can start with buffer number 1, and then issue the following sequence of commands:

```
"1pu.u.u.
```

This feature lets you retrieve entire groups of deleted lines, which you may like to restore after you have changed your mind.

Note This facility to restore line deletions from numbered buffers applies only to *entire* lines. You can't hope to restore three words deleted with **`3dw`** unless it was the last editing action performed.

23.5 ENTERING CONTROL CHARACTERS (*[Ctrl-v]*)

If you write shell scripts to send some escape sequences to your printer or terminal, then you would need to enter control characters. In `vi`, some of these characters are directly enterable, but generally a control character has to be preceded by another control character for it to be interpreted properly.

`vi` uses *[Ctrl-v]* to precede any control character. For instance, to enter *[Ctrl-h]*, you have to first press *[Ctrl-v]* and then *[Ctrl-h]*. You'll then see this on the screen:

```
^H                                  Just one character here
```

Even though you feel you are seeing a ^ (caret) and an `H`, there's only a single character out there. You can position the cursor only on the ^ and not on the `H`; that's how you identify control characters anyway.

The same technique can be adopted for entering the *[Esc]* character. Press *[Ctrl-v][Esc]*, and you'll see the *[Esc]* character looking like this:

```
^[                                  Just one character here
```

This too is a single character; you can place your cursor only on the ^. If your version of **vi** doesn't let you enter the *[Esc]* character as advised above, then you can use this: *[Ctrl-v][Ctrl-[ ]* (Control with [). The *[Esc]* character may need special treatment in **vi** since it is the terminator of the Input Mode.

23.6 SEARCHING FOR A CHARACTER

There's a special facility to take the cursor *near* or to a specific character in the current line. This is done with the **f** and **t** keys, with either key followed by the character to be searched for. To move the cursor forward to the first occurrence of the character, use

```
f
```

followed by the character. For instance, **f.** moves the cursor to the first period following the current cursor position. This is a convenient way of moving to the end of a sentence when editing a document. **t** also acts in a similar fashion, except that the cursor is positioned a single character *before* the occurrence.

F and **T** perform the respective functions as their lowercase counterparts, but in the reverse direction. The repeat factor works with all these characters. For example, **2f}** places the cursor on the second occurrence of the } in the line. However, all these characters restrict their activities to the current line only.

The character search is repeated by using the **;** (semi-colon) and **,** (comma) characters. Table 23.3 lists the character search and repeat commands.

Table 23.3 The Character Search and Repeat Commands

Command	*Action*
f*ch*	Moves cursor forward to first occurrence of character *ch* in current line
t*ch*	Moves cursor forward onto but before first occurrence of character *ch* in current line
;	Repeats search in same direction along which previous search was made with f or t
,	Repeats search in a direction opposite to that along which previous search was made with f or t

23.7 MARKING TEXT

You can mark up to 26 positions (labeled a to z) in the file, and later locate them. The **m** command is used for marking lines, while the **'** (single quote) command locates a marked line. Any alphabetic character can be used in combination with **m** and **'** for marking and locating different portions of text.

To mark any portion of a file with the label a, move the cursor to the required location and press

```
ma
```

An invisible mark is left at the corresponding point in the file. You can move back to this mark from any point in the file simply by using a **'** in combination with the character used to mark that location, in this case a:

```
'a                                                  Moves to mark a
```

The **'** when doubled by itself toggles the motion of the cursor between its present and immediately previous locations. If you had first moved to a mark a with **'a** and then to mark b with **'b**, you can return to the mark a with **''** (two single quotes) and then again move back to mark b with the same command.

This also applies to those situations where the cursor is not explicitly moved away from a line. If you have moved to a line with **30G** and then to the end of the file with **G**, you can alternate between these two locations by using **''** (two single quotes).

23.8 CUSTOMIZING vi

vi can be tailored to behave in a way desirable to the user. For instance, you may like to define (or redefine) some of the keys to represent a command sequence which you may be using quite often, or abbreviate frequently used words or phrases into short strings. There are three ex Mode commands—**set**, **map** and **abbr**—which make the editor behave exactly in the way you would like it to.

vi reads the file ~/.exrc only once, upon startup, and its behavior is determined by statements placed in that file. We have used some of these commands already (like **:set showmode**, **:set aw**, etc.). In the following paragraphs, we'll learn to place some more commands in this file. Keep in mind that you have to restart **vi** whenever you make changes to .exrc. Linux users using **vim** need to edit ~/.vimrc and not ~/.exrc.

23.8.1 The set Command

The general **vi** environment is determined by its variable settings. These variables are controlled by the **:set** command. We have met this command already in this chapter and in Chapter 8 on two occasions:

```
:set showmode
:set autowrite                                      Or :set aw
```

set is used with a variable name (like showmode). The variable in the second example takes on an abbreviation, which means that you can also use **:set aw**. Many of these variables can have the string no prefixed to their name, in which case the setting is deactivated. For instance, noautowrite (or noaw) negates autowrite (or aw). Other variables are of the form *variable=value*. Let's take a look at some of these variables.

*Automatic indentation (*autoindent*)* Programmers need to provide indentation to their code for easier readability. Nested **if** statements along with their corresponding **fi**s should appear at the right indentation. This aspect is taken care of when you use the following **set** statement:

```
:set autoindent                                     Or :set ai
```

When this option is set, an *[Enter]* in the Input Mode places the cursor in the next line at the current indentation.

Numbering Lines (`number`) The `number` setting shows all lines duly numbered. This makes it easier to debug programs. However, the line numbers are not preserved when the file is saved. To reverse this setting (i.e., switching back to the `nonumber` option), you simply have to prefix the string `no` to the option:

```
:set nonumber
```

Ignoring case in Pattern Searches (`ignorecase`) The search commands (not the substitution ones) may or may not pursue a case-insensitive search. That depends on the `ignorecase` setting. By default, this is generally off, but you can turn it on with **`:set ignorecase`**.

No Regular Expressions in Search (`nomagic`) You may sometimes need to despecialize the regular expression characters when searching for a pattern. In that case you should use this setting:

```
:set nomagic                Searching with /g* will now show g*
```

By default, the setting is `magic`, i.e., the characters `*`, `.`, etc. retain their special meanings.

See Matching } *or*) (`showmatch`) Another option, especially useful for C and **`perl`** programmers, enables the programmer to see momentarily the matching bracket to a) or }. The `showmatch` option helps you locate matching brackets:

```
:set showmatch
```

When text is entered in the Input Mode, the moment a) or } is entered, the cursor will jump to its matching counterpart, and stay there for a fraction of a second before returning to its current location. If a match is not found, it responds with a beep.

Setting Tab Stops (`tabstop=`*n*) Too many nested programming constructs often cause a line to wrap around. To some extent, this can be alleviated by changing the default tab setting (8 spaces). You can reduce this value, say to 4, with **`:set tabstop=4`**.

Table 23.4 `set` Options

Option	*Abbreviation*	*Significance*
`autoindent`	`ai`	Next line starts at previous indented level
`autowrite`	`aw`	Writes current file automatically whenever switching files with `:n` or `:e`
`ignorecase`	`ic`	Ignores case when searching for patterns
`magic`		Treats regular expression characters as special when searching for patterns
`number`	`nu`	Displays line numbers on screen
`showmatch`	`sm`	Shows momentarily match to a) and }
`showmode`		Displays a message when **`vi`** is in Input Mode
`tabstop`	`ts`	Sets tabs for display (default: 8 spaces)
`wrapscan`	`ws`	Continues pattern search by moving to other end of a file so that entire file is scanned

Most options can be reversed as discussed (except the ones that take a parameters like `tabstop`), using the option prefix `no`. All settings made with set are displayed with the **`:set all`** command. Some of the important **`set`** options are shown in Table 23.4.

23.8.2 map: Mapping Keys of Keyboard

The **`map`** command lets you assign the undefined keys or reassign the defined ones so that, when such a key is pressed, it expands to a command sequence. It's particularly useful to convert a sequence of keystrokes into a macro. The command **`:map`** is followed by the key which needs mapping, and the key sequence which is mapped.

You may, for instance, like to have the writing of the buffer achieved with a single keystroke. This is normally done with **`:w`***[Enter]*, but you can use the **`map`** command to condense this sequence to the character `g` by using the following command:

```
:map g :w^M                                   ^M signifies the [Enter] key
```

This mapping also includes the *[Enter]* key, which **`vi`** understands as *[Ctrl-m]* (shown as `^M`). This character is entered by first pressing *[Ctrl-v]* and then *[Ctrl-m] (23.4)*. Once **`g`** has been mapped, when you press it in the Command Mode, the buffer is written.

There are other useful mappings you can create for yourself. If you have been working with **`vi`** for a long time, then by now you probably know that the letters `g`, `q`, `v`, `K`, `V` and `Z` are undefined. You can map **`v`** to write the current line into the buffer named `a`. You can also use **`V`** to restore it:

```
:map v "ayy                                   Copies current line into buffer a
:map V "ap                                    Restores the line when pressing V
```

You can map keys in the Input Mode also, in which case, you can press the mapped key while entering or changing text itself. You can use one of the function keys, say *[F2]*, and map it to the function. For instance, this mapping

```
:map! #2 ^[:w^M                               Function key [F2] is #2
```

lets you save the file in the Command Mode. The string `^[` is actually the *[Esc]* character.

The **`:map`** command displays the mapped environment. **`:unmap`** cancels a Command Mode map and **`:unmap!`** cancels an Input Mode map.

> **Tip** Did you know that you can compile your C program or execute a shell or **`perl`** script from inside the editor with a single keystroke? **`vi`** understands the current file as `%`, so **`cc %`** compiles the current file. Let's map the function key *[F3]* to invoke this function:
>
> ```
> :map #3 :!cc %^M                  [F3] now compiles current C program
> ```
>
> The symbols **`:!`** invoke a temporary shell escape which is used to run **`cc`** (the C compiler). To invoke a shell or **`perl`** script, make this mapping of the function key *[F4]*:
>
> ```
> :map #4 :!%^M                     [F4] now executes current script
> ```
>
> These are two important mappings used by the author. Note scripts need to have executable permission, so you should first use **`:!chmod 755 %`** to assign this permission. You don't have to leave **`vi`** for this task either.

23.8.3 abbr: Abbreviating Text Input

The **abbreviate** command (itself abbreviated to ab) is used to expand short strings to long words. The syntax is similar to **map** except that the string that is mapped can consist of more than one character. While writing this text, the following abbreviations were used:

```
:ab re regular expression
:ab me metacharacter
```

This indicates that when you enter the word re, followed by a key which is neither alphanumeric nor the _ (underscore) character, you'll see the words `regular expression` in place of the string.

> **Tip** Store all sets, maps and abbreviations in the file $HOME/.exrc ($HOME/.vimrc for **vim**). **vi** reads this file on startup and executes its instructions as ex Mode commands to set the environment for the session. Carry this file with you wherever you go; it could be your most precious possession.

23.9 CONCLUSION

In this chapter, we had a second look at the **vi** editor to discover some of its advanced features. We saw how operators serve both to select text and pass commands to act on the selection.. C programmers will also find the features of copying or moving multiple sections of text from one file to another quite useful. But you still require to customize the editor and it won't be long before you realize that there's one file that you should never fail to back up—the .exrc (or .vimrc).

WRAP UP

vi's power lies in its operators. By combining an operator with a Command Mode command, you can delete (**d**), yank (**y**), change (**c**) and filter (**!**) text in practically any manner. When the operator is used doubly, the operation affects the current line only.

Using the ex Mode, you can switch to an alternate file (**:e**), return to the last edited file (**:e#**) and revert to the last saved version (**:e!**). You can also invoke **vi** with multiple filenames, edit each file in turn (**:n**), and rewind the file list (**:rew**) to start from the beginning. **vi** normally doesn't allow a change of file if changes in the current file are not saved unless the ! suffix is used. You can also read in another file or command output (**:r**).

vim in Linux can split the window (**:sp**) in two (or more) so that you can display two different (or same) files on them. You can also create a new window (**:new**) and toggle between two windows (*[Ctrl-w][Ctrl-w]*). Any ex Mode command (like **:q**) applies to the current window unless suffixed with a, when it applies to all windows (like **:qa**).

You can use up to 26 buffers to store text, using the " to precede the buffer name. **"ayy** stores the current line in the buffer a and the stored text can be placed—even in another file—with ", the buffer name and p (**"ap**). You can also undo up to nine sets of deletions of *complete* lines using the numerals 1 to 9. The **.**, when used for restoring deleted lines, steps through the buffer and restores the previous line deletion.

You can enter control characters (using *[Ctrl-v]* first) and then the character. The *[Esc]* character is inserted using *[Ctrl-v][Ctrl-[]*.

The cursor can placed on (**f**) or near (**t**) a character in the current line. **f.** places the cursor at the end of a sentence. Up to 26 areas in a text can be marked using **m** and a letter. The **'** and the letter is used to access any marked portion. The **''** command serves to toggle between two positions.

You can abbreviate (**:ab**) long strings to short ones so that they are automatically expanded when they are input. You can map a frequently used command sequence to a single key, both in the Command Mode (**:map**) and the Input Mode (**:map!**). Use *[Ctrl-m]* to signify *[Enter]*.

With the **:set** command, you can ensure that a file is saved before switching (`autowrite`). You can make searches case-insensitive (`ignorecase`) and turn off the significance of regular expressions (`nomagic`). The no prefix reverse a setting.

All **:ab**, **:map** and **:set** commands should be placed in `$HOME/.exrc` (or `.vimrc` for **vim**) so that they are always available on startup.

TEST YOUR UNDERSTANDING

23.1 What is the difference between the commands **/*** and **f***?

23.2 Frame a command to delete the first two sentences of a line. How will you do that for subsequent lines?

23.3 How can you edit a second file without leaving **vi**, and then toggle between the two files?

23.4 How will you ensure that **vi** automatically saves a file when moving from one file to another?

23.5 How are **d** and **y** different from the Command Mode commands?

23.6 How will you copy 5 lines of text from one file to another?

23.7 You copied 20 lines in one file, then switched to another file with **:e foo**, but when you tried to paste these lines back with **p**, it didn't work. Why?

23.8 How will you do the following? (i) revert to the last saved version of a file (ii) read in the entire contents of another file at the beginning of the current file.

23.9 How will you compile a C program without leaving the editor?

23.10 You defined an abbreviation re to expand to `regular expression` and when you try to input the word `re-rating`, you find the expansion getting in the way. What do you do?

23.11 Map the first function key to search for `loop`, and copy into the buffer a all text following it up to but not including the string `end loop`.

FLEX YOUR BRAIN

23.1 How do you copy from the current cursor position to the following? (i) the character under the cursor (ii) the beginning of line (iii) 10 words (iv) the current sentence and the next.

23.2 How will you delete the following? (i) text from the current cursor position to the end of the file (ii) the entire contents of the file.

23.3 How do you move to the 100th line and then write the remaining lines (including that line) to a separate file?

23.4 How do you do the following? (i) invert the case of all characters in the current line (ii) convert to uppercase the entire line (iii) convert to uppercase all text up to the end of file.

23.5 How will you copy two groups of ten and five lines each from one file to another?

23.6 You have inadvertently deleted three groups of lines with **10dd**, **5dd** and **dd** (in that order). How will you restore the 10 deleted lines?

23.7 What are the two functions of the dot command?

23.8 Write a map which removes all trailing spaces in a line.

23.9 Use one of the unused keys to create a map that locates the next blank line (which may or not contain spaces) and deletes it.

23.10 Explain the significance of the following **set** options: (i) `autoindent` (ii) `showmode` (iii) `magic`.

23.11 How can you number all lines which are (i) saved (ii) not saved, when saving the file?

24

Advanced Shell Programming

You have already discovered the basic features of the shell—both as an interpreter and as a scripting language. But the shell is more than just an interpreter or a language. It is also a process, an environment which makes itself available to the programs that it executes. It is necessary that you understand the environmental changes that take place when the shell executes a program, especially a shell script. You should also know how to change these environmental parameters.

Advanced knowledge of shell programming is needed by the system administrator, who has to constantly devise scripts that monitor and correct system functioning. A detailed knowledge of the shell's subtle features is also necessary if you aspire to be an expert script writer. The following discussions mostly assume the Bourne shell, but the special features of the Korn and Bash shells are also examined here.

WHAT YOU WILL LEARN

- How the shell uses a second shell to execute a shell script.
- When and how commands are executed in the current shell and a sub-shell.
- Make variables visible in sub-shells with **export**.
- Use `let` and `(( ))` for computation in the Korn shell and Bash.
- Use arrays supported by the Korn shell and Bash.
- Handle strings with the built-in facilities of the Korn shell and Bash.
- Evaluate variables in different ways depending on whether they are set or not.
- Merge the standard output and standard error streams with the symbols 1>&2 and 2>&1.
- Understand how *shell functions* are superior to aliases.
- Use **eval** to evaluate a command line twice and produce generalized prompts and variables.
- Overlay the current program with another and handle multiple streams with **exec**.

TOPICS OF SPECIAL INTEREST

- The situations that demand execution of a command in the current shell. Use of the dot command for this purpose.
- Devise useful shell functions required for everyday use.
- Access files with file descriptors, using **exec**, in the same way system calls and library functions access them.

24.1 SHELLS AND SUB-SHELLS

When the shell executes a shell script, it first spawns a sub-shell, which in turn executes the commands in the script. When script execution is complete, the child shell withers away and returns control to the parent shell. You can also *explicitly* invoke a sub-shell to execute a shell script. The command representing the shell itself (**sh**, **ksh** or **bash**) can be used to read the statements in **join.sh**:

```
sh join.sh          Shell also accepts a script name as argument
sh < join.sh        It's standard input can also be redirected
```

Thus a shell script run with **sh**, **ksh** or **bash** need not have executable permission. This technique, however, is applicable for executing only shell scripts and not executables. You certainly can't use **sh < a.out**.

Even though the shell accepts a script name as argument, we generally don't run shell scripts in the way shown above. We simply key in the script name from the shell prompt and run it as an executable. In this case, the current shell uses a sub-shell of the same type to execute it. However, if the script contains the interpreter line in this form:

```
#!/usr/bin/ksh
```

then, even though the login shell may be Bourne, it will use the Korn shell to execute the script. Specification of the interpreter line also helps us identify the shell the script is meant to use. We have specified the interpreter line in every script used in Chapter 16; we'll continue this practice in this chapter also.

24.2 ( ) AND { }: SUB-SHELL OR CURRENT SHELL?

The shell uses two types of operators to group commands. You must understand clearly the consequences of using one in preference to the other:

- The ( ) Statements enclosed within parentheses are executed in a sub-shell.
- The { } Statements enclosed within curly braces are executed in the current shell only.

You have used the first type *(9.5.2)* to collectively redirect the standard output of two commands with a single redirection symbol in a manner similar to this:

```
( a.sh ; b.sh ; c.sh ) > d.sh
```

Sub-shell considerations are not important here, so we can use either form, but some applications require us to run a set of commands *without* spawning a child shell. To consider an example, let's use both grouping operators with the **cd** and **pwd** commands. Check your current directory and then change it with **cd**:

```
$ pwd
/home/kumar
$ ( cd progs ; pwd )
/home/kumar/progs
$ pwd
/home/kumar                         Back to original directory
```

Working from a sub-shell, **cd** changed the working directory (one of the environmental parameters) to /home/kumar/progs. The parent (login shell) can't adopt this change, so the original directory is back in place. The same command group—this time using the {} operators—tells a different story:

```
$ pwd
/home/kumar
$ { cd progs ; pwd ; }
/home/kumar/progs
$ pwd
/home/kumar/progs                        Directory change is now permanent
```

The two commands have now been executed without spawning a shell; no separate environment was created, and the change of directory became permanent even after the execution of the command group. Note that we need to precede the closing brace with a ; if both { and } appear in the same line.

An often-used sequence used by many shell scripts checks the number of arguments supplied with the command, and then terminates the script with **exit** if the test fails. For instance, a sequence like this:

```
if [ $# -ne 3 ] ; then
    echo "You have not keyed in 3 arguments"
    exit 3
fi
```

can be easily replaced with this sequence using curly braces:

```
[ $# -ne 3 ] && { echo "You have not keyed in 3 arguments" ; exit 3 ; }
```

Why can't we use ( ) instead of { } here? The **exit** statement can terminate a script only if it runs in the same shell that's running the script. This is the case when **exit** runs inside the { }, but not when it runs inside ( ). An **exit** inside ( ) will stop executing the remaining statements in the group, but it doesn't automatically terminate a script.

24.3 export: EXPORTING SHELL VARIABLES

By default, the values stored in shell variables are local to the shell, i.e., they are available only in the shell in which they are defined. They are not passed on to a child shell. But the shell can also *export* these variables (with the **export** statement) recursively to all child processes so that, once defined, they are available globally. You have used this statement before, but now you should understand why you have done so.

Consider a simple script which displays the value of a variable x, assigns a new value to it and then displays the new value again:

```
$ cat var.sh
echo The value of x is $x
x=20                                 # Now change the value of x
echo The new value of x is $x
```

First assign 10 to x at the prompt and then execute the script:

```
$ x=10 ; var.sh
The value of x is                    Value of x not visible in a sub-shell
The new value of x is 20
$ echo $x                            Value set inside the script doesn't
10                                   affect value outside script
```

Because x is a *local* variable in the login shell, its value can't be accessed by **echo** in the script, which is run in a sub-shell. To make x available globally, you need to use the **export** statement before the script is executed:

```
$ x=10 ; export x
$ var.sh
The value of x is 10                 Value in parent shell now visible here
The new value of x is 20
$ echo $x                            Value reset inside script (child shell)
10                                   is not available outside it (parent shell)
```

When x is exported, its assigned value (10) is available in the script. But when you export a variable, it has another important consequence; a reassignment (x=20) made in the script, i.e., a sub-shell, is not seen in the parent shell which executed the script.

You must export the variables you define unless you have strong reasons not to let sub-shells inherit their values. To know whether you have already done so, use **export** without arguments. It lists all environment variables (which are already exported) and user-defined variables (like x) that you have exported. The **env** command also lists exported variables.

Note A variable defined in a process is only local to the process in which it is defined, and is not available in a child process. But when it is exported, it is available recursively to all child processes. However, when the child alters the value of the variable, the change is not seen in the parent.

24.4 RUNNING SCRIPT IN THE CURRENT SHELL: THE . COMMAND

Variable assignments made in the shell's startup file (.profile or .bash_profile) are *always* seen in the login shell. It's obvious that the profile is executed by the login shell without creating a sub-shell, but how? If you thought that the .profile was executed by grouping it with the curly braces:

```
{ .profile ; }
```

then you'll be disappointed to see that there is no executable permission for the file:

```
$ ls -l .profile
-rw-r--r--   1 kumar    group          727 Feb 27 23:02 .profile
```

There's a special command which is used to execute any shell script without creating a sub-shell—the . (dot) command. This means that you can make changes to .profile and execute it with the . command *without requiring to log out and log in again*:

```
. .profile
```

Many users have the impression that you must log out and log in if you have made any change to the .profile. You actually don't need to do that; simply execute the edited file with the . command. You'll need this facility later to execute files containing shell functions.

> **Note** The dot command executes a script without using a sub-shell. It also doesn't require the script to have executable permission.

24.5 let: COMPUTATION—A SECOND LOOK (KORN AND BASH)

Korn and Bash come with a built-in integer handling facility that totally dispenses with the need to use **expr**. You can compute with the **let** statement which is used here both with and without quotes:

```
let sum=256+128                      No whitespace after variable
let sum="256 + 128"                  No whitespace after variable
```

If you use whitespace for imparting better readability, then quote the expression. In either case, sum is assigned the result of the expression:

```
$ echo $sum
384
```

Let's see how **let** handles variables. First define three variables; a single **let** does it:

```
$ let x=12 y=18 z=5
$ let z=x+y+$z                       $ not required by let
$ echo $z
35
```

let permits you to get rid of the $ altogether when making an assignment. Since this computational feature is built-in, scripts run much faster than when used with **expr**. Later, we'll be using **let** in place of **expr** in one of our scripts.

A Second Form of Computing with ((*and*)) The Korn shell and Bash use the (( )) operators that replace the **let** statement itself:

```
$ x=22 y=28 z=5
$ z=$((x+y + z))                     Whitespace is unimportant
$ echo $z
55
$ z=$((z+1))                         Can also use z=$((z+=1))
$ echo $z
56
```

POSIX recommends the use of ((and)) rather than **let**, and this form is likely to become a standard feature of the shells. It's easier to use too because a variable doesn't have to be preceded by the $. The entire arithmetic operation, however, needs to be preceded by a single $.

24.6 ARRAYS (KORN AND BASH)

Korn and Bash support one-dimensional arrays where the first element has the index 0. Here's how you set and evaluate the value of the third element of the array prompt:

```
$ prompt[2]="Enter your name: "
$ echo ${prompt[2]}
Enter your name:
```

Note that evaluation is done with the curly braces, and `prompt[2]` is treated just like a variable. It, however, doesn't conflict with a variable `prompt` that you may also define in the same shell. When a group of elements needs to be assigned, you can use a space-delimited list using either of these two forms:

```
set -A month_arr 0 31 29 31 30 31 30 31 31 30 31 30 31
month_arr=(0 31 29 31 30 31 30 31 31 30 31 30 31)
```

Bash accepts both, but older versions of Korn use only the first form. In either case, the array stores the number of days available in each of the 12 months. The first element had to be deliberately assigned to zero for obvious reasons. Finding out the number of days in June is simple:

```
$ echo ${month_arr[6]}
30
```

Using the @ or * as subscript, you can display all the elements of the array as well as the number of elements. The forms are similar except for the presence of the # in one:

```
$ echo ${month_arr[@]}
0 31 29 31 30 31 30 31 31 30 31 30 31
$ echo ${#month_arr[@]}                                  Length of the array
13
```

Can we use arrays to validate an entered date? The next script, **dateval.sh** (Fig. 24.1), does just that. It takes into account the leap year changes (except the one that takes place at the turn of every fourth century).

The first option of the outer **case** construct checks for a null response. The second option uses the expression `$n/$n/$n` to check for an eight-character string in the form *dd/mm/yy*. Using a changed value of `IFS`, the components of the date are set to three positional parameters and checked for valid months. The second **case** construct makes the leap year check and then uses an array to validate the day. The **continue** statements take you to loop beginning whenever the test fails the validity check.

Now, let's test the script:

```
$ dateval.sh
Enter a date: [Enter]
No date entered
Enter a date: 28/13/00
Illegal month
Enter a date: 31/04/00
Illegal day
Enter a date: 29/02/01
2001 is not a leap year
Enter a date: 29/02/00
29/02/00 is a valid date
[Ctrl-c]
```

Since the script has no exit path at all, we had to use the interrupt key to terminate execution.

```
#!/usr/bin/ksh
# Script: dateval.sh - Validates a date field using an array
IFS="/"
n="[0-9][0-9]"
set -A month_arr 0 31 29 31 30 31 30 31 31 30 31 30 31
while echo "Enter a date: \c" ; do
  read value
  case "$value" in
        "") echo "No date entered" ; continue ;;
  $n/$n/$n) set $value
            let rem="$3 % 4"
            if [ $2 -gt 12 -o $2 -eq 0 ] ; then
                 echo "Illegal month" ; continue
            else
                 case "$value" in
         29/02/??) [ $rem -gt 0 ] &&
                        { echo "20$3 is not a leap year" ; continue ; } ;;
                     *) [ $1 -gt ${month_arr[$2]} -o $1 -eq 0 ] &&
                        { echo "Illegal day" ; continue ; } ;;
                 esac
            fi;;
          *) echo "Invalid date" ; continue ;;
  esac
  echo "$1/$2/$3" is a valid date
done
```

Fig. 24.1 **dateval.sh**

24.7 STRING HANDLING (KORN AND BASH)

Korn and Bash don't need **expr** as they have adequate string handling features themselves. Unlike **expr**, they use wild-cards but not regular expressions. All forms of usage require curly braces to enclose the variable name along with some special symbols. The subtle variations in their forms make them difficult to remember and sometimes uncomfortable to work with.

Length of String The length of a string is easily found by preceding the variable name with a #. Consider this example:

```
$ name="vinton cerf"
$ echo ${#name}
11
```

You can now use this expression with an **if** statement to check the length of a string. This built-in feature is not only easier to use than its corresponding **expr** version *(16.9.2)*, but is also comparatively faster:

```
if [ ${#name} -gt 20 ] ; then                          Korn and Bash
```

This form should appear familiar to you as **perl** uses a similar form to evaluate the length of an array *(21.10)*.

24.7.1 Extracting a String by Pattern Matching

You can extract a substring using a special pattern matching feature. These functions make use of two characters—# and %. Their selection seems to have been based on mnemonic considerations. # is used to match at the beginning and % at the end, and both are used inside curly braces when evaluating a variable.

To remove the extension from a filename, previously you had to use an external command—**basename** *(16.12.2)*. This time, you can use a variable's ${*variable%pattern*} format to do that:

```
$ filename=quotation.txt
$ echo ${filename%txt}
quotation.                                          txt stripped off
```

The % symbol after the variable name deletes the *shortest* string that matches the variable's contents at the *end*. Had there been two %s instead of one, the expression would have matched the longest one. Let's now use %% with wild-cards to extract the hostname from an FQDN:

```
$ fqdn=java.sun.com
$ echo ${fqdn%%.*}
java
```

You'll recall that **basename** can also extract the base filename from a pathname. This requires you to delete the longest pattern which matches the pattern */, but at the beginning of the variable's value:

```
$ filename="/var/mail/henry"
$ echo ${filename##*/}
henry
```

This deletes the segment, /var/mail—the longest pattern that matches the pattern */ at the beginning. The pattern matching forms of Korn and Bash are listed in Table 24.1.

Table 24.1 Pattern Matching Operators Used by Korn and Bash

Form	*Evaluates to segment remaining after deleting*
${*var#pat*}	Shortest segment that matches *pat* at beginning of $*var*
${*var##pat*}	Longest segment that matches *pat* at beginning of $*var*
${*var%pat*}	Shortest segment that matches *pat* at end of $*var*
${*var%%pat*}	Longest segment that matches *pat* at end of $*var*

24.8 CONDITIONAL PARAMETER SUBSTITUTION

To continue on the subject of variable evaluation, you can evaluate a variable depending on whether it has a null or defined value. This feature is known as *parameter substitution*, and is available in the Bourne shell also. It takes this general form:

```
${<var>:<opt><stg>}
```

This time, the variable <*var*> is followed by a colon and any of the symbols +, -, = or ? as <*opt*>. The symbol is followed by the string <*stg*>. In all cases barring one, this doesn't alter the value of the variable, but only determines the way it is *evaluated*. This evaluation can be done in four ways.

The + Option Here, *var* evaluates to *stg* if it is defined and assigned a nonnull string. This feature can be used to set a variable to the output of a command, and echo a message if the variable is nonnull:

```
found=`ls`
echo ${found:+"This directory is not empty"}
```

ls displays nothing if it finds no files, in which case the variable found is set to a null string. However, the message is echoed if **ls** finds at least one file.

The - Option Here, *var* is evaluated to *stg* if it is undefined or assigned a null string (the opposite of the + option). You can use this feature in a program which prompts for a filename, and then uses a default value when the user simply presses *[Enter]*:

```
echo "Enter the filename : \c"
read flname
fname=${flname:-emp.lst}                    Instead of using if [ -z $flname ]
```

If flname is null or is not set, it *evaluates* to the string emp.lst. The value of flname, however, still remains null. This compact assignment dispenses with the need for an **if** conditional.

The = Option This also works similarly except that it goes a step further and *makes the assignment* to the variable that is evaluated. With the = option, you can use parameter substitution with a command without making the intermediate assignment:

```
echo "Enter the filename : \c"
read flname
grep $pattern ${flname:=emp.lst}                    flname is now assigned
```

Note that in the last statement, the variable flname itself got assigned (provided it was either unset or set to a null string). This feature is most useful in initializing a loop which iterates as long as a counter inside the loop matches the control command in the **while** command line. The following statements

```
x=1 ; while [ $x -le 10 ]
```

can now be combined in one:

```
while [ ${x:=1} -le 10 ]
```

The ? Option It evaluates the parameter if the variable is assigned and nonnull, otherwise it echoes the string following it. Additionally, the shell is killed. This is quite useful in terminating a script if the user fails to respond properly to shell directives:

```
echo "Enter the filename : \c"
read flname
grep $pattern ${flname:?"No filename entered"}
```

If no filename is entered here, the message No filename entered is displayed. The script is also aborted without the use of an explicit **exit** command.

Apart from the = operator, the other operators can also be used with positional parameters. You can now easily set a variable to some default if the script is invoked without an argument:

```
flname=${1:-emp.lst}                    $1 is null if script invoked without arguments
```

You can now compress some of the earlier scripts to even shorter command sequences. You'll see some of these applications later in the chapter.

> **Note** Only the = option actually assigns a value to a variable; the others merely control the way the variable is evaluated.

24.9 MERGING STREAMS

You have seen the utility of redirecting a loop at the **done** keyword *(16.11)*. This also meant redirecting individual statements inside the loop to `/dev/tty` when these statements needed to send output to the terminal. When there are a large number of such terminal-destined statements, separately using `>/dev/tty` with each one of them can be quite tedious. The shell offers a simple solution to this problem.

Though the standard output and standard error are two separate streams, the shell lets you merge the two so that they can be collectively manipulated. Once you do that, you effectively have a single stream, which you can subsequently use with any of the shell's redirection and piping symbols. This is done with the `&` operator following the redirection symbol. When the **echo** statement is placed in a script in this way:

```
echo "None of the patterns found" 1>&2
```

then, irrespective of the destination of the rest of the script, the output of this statement will always come to the destination of the standard error. It's like saying: "Send the standard output to the destination of the standard error". Since the default file descriptor for standard output is 1, you can also use `>&2`.

The notation `1>&2` merges the standard output with the standard error, which, in the absence of further redirection, is connected to the terminal. However, when you redirect the standard error of the entire script in this way:

```
emp8.sh > sclist 2> errlist
```

all script statements having the symbols `1>&2` affixed, will actually write to `errlist`. The rest of the script output will, however, be saved in `sclist`.

For the reverse situation, i.e., sending the standard error to the destination of the standard output, the notation becomes `2>&1`. You may require this to be done on many occasions, especially when a job is run in the background, and you still want the error messages to be held in the same file that contains the actual output.

24.10 SHELL FUNCTIONS

A *shell function* is like any other function; it executes a group of statements as a bunch. Optionally, it also returns a value. This construct is available in most modern shells where you can use them to condense important routines to short sequences. The syntax is simple:

```
function_name() {
    statements
    return value                                  Optional
}
```

The function definition is followed by (), and the body is enclosed within curly braces. On invocation, the function executes all *statements* in the body. The **return** statement, when present, returns a value representing the success or failure of the function (and not a string value).

Let's consider a simple application. When viewing the listing of a large number of files in a directory, you are often compelled to use **ls -l | more**. This command sequence is an ideal candidate for a shell function, which we'll name ll:

```
$ ll() {                       Function defined in the command line
> ls -l $* | more              is available in current shell only
> }
```

Like shell scripts, shell functions also use command line arguments (like $1, $2, etc.). $*, "$@" and $# also retain their usual significance in functions. Even though you need the () in the function definition, you must not use them when invoking the function. You can now invoke the function with or without arguments:

```
ll                             Executes ls -l | more
ll ux3rd??                     Executes ls -l ux3rd?? | more
```

We have used the **ll** function more like a procedure, but a shell function can also return its exit status with the **return** statement. This exit status can be gathered from the shell parameter, $?.

Shell functions can be defined at a number of places:

- At the beginning of every script using them. Since shell statements are executed in the interpretive mode, a shell function must precede the statements that call it.
- In the .profile so that they are available in the current session.
- In a separate "library" file so that other applications can also use them.

Since the above function is often required, it's better you create a file **mainfunc.sh** to hold it. You then have to place the following entry at the beginning of every shell script that needs to use it:

```
. mainfunc.sh                  Functions available in the current shell
```

Caution The positional parameters made available to shell scripts externally are not available *directly* to a shell function. To make them available, store these parameters in shell variables first.

24.10.1 Generating a Filename from the System Date

As a system administrator, you'll often require to maintain separate files for each day of a specific activity. These filenames can be derived from the system date, so you can easily identify a file pertaining to a certain day. It's a good idea to have this value echoed by a shell function **dated_fname**, which in turn gets it from the **date** output:

```
dated_fname() {
    set -- `date`
    year=`expr $6 : '..\(..\)'`              Picks up last two characters from year
    echo "$2$3_$year"
}
```

When you invoke the function, **echo** displays a string derived from the current date:

```
$ dated_fname
Jan28_03
```

This string can be used to frame filenames that are needed not more than once a day. Oracle users can easily use this function to have a system-generated dump filename for the **exp** command:

```
exp scott/tiger file=`dated_fname`
```

This will generate the export dump file `Jan28_03.dmp`. Place this function definition in the library file **mainfunc.sh** that we created previously. We'll use this file later—after we have added two more functions to it.

24.10.2 To Continue or Not to Continue

We'll now consider a shell function which actually returns a value. Recall the sequence used at the end of the script, **dentry1.sh** *(16.17.2)*, which prompts the user for a `y` to continue, or an `n` to terminate the outermost loop. This routine is very often used inside shell scripts, and it's a good idea to convert this into a function, **anymore**:

```
anymore() {
     echo "\n$1 ?(y/n) : \c" 1>&2                Prompt supplied as argument
     read response
     case "$response" in
       y|Y) echo  1>&2 ; return 0 ;;
         *) return 1 ;;
     esac
}
```

The function uses its argument `$1` to determine what the entire prompt will look like. When this function is invoked with the string `Wish to continue`, you are prompted for a response:

```
$ anymore "Wish to continue"

Wish to continue ?(y/n) : n
$ echo $?
1                                  Same value as specified in return statement
```

We'll make use of the return value of this function later in the chapter.

24.10.3 Validating Data Entry

Consider the script, **dentry1.sh** *(16.17.2)*, where you used a **while** loop to repeatedly prompt the user for a valid entry. This sequence can also be easily converted into a shell function, **valid_string**. We expect the function to check two things—first that something is entered at all, and whether it exceeds a certain length:

```
valid_string() {
    while echo "$1 \c"  1>&2 ; do
        read name
        case $name in
            "") echo "Nothing entered"  1>&2 ; continue ;;
             *) if [ `expr "$name" : '.*'` -gt $2 ] ; then
                    echo "Maximum $2 characters permitted" 1>&2
                else
                    break
                fi ;;
        esac
    done
    echo $name
}
```

The function takes two arguments—the prompt string and the maximum number of characters permitted. We'll place this function in our library file, **mainfunc.sh**, and call it from the script **user_passwd.sh** (Fig. 24.2).

```
#!/bin/sh
# Script: user_passwd.sh - Uses a shell function
. mainfunc.sh                        # Script containing valid_string function

user=`valid_string "Enter your user-id :" 16`
stty -echo                           # Password not to be echoed
password=`valid_string "Enter your password:" 5`
stty echo                            # Turns on echoing facility
echo "\nYour user-id is $user and your password is $password"
```

Fig. 24.2 user_passwd.sh

This small script accepts the user's name and password, which can't exceed 16 and 5 characters in length, respectively. A sample session shows how shell functions can reduce script size:

```
$ user_passwd.sh
Enter your user-id : robert louis stevenson
Maximum 16 characters permitted
Enter your user-id : scott
Enter your password:
Nothing entered
Enter your password: *****                                Doesn't show on screen
Your user-id is scott and your password is tiger
```

Invocation of a shell function reduces disk I/O since the function is resident in memory. On the other hand, when you execute a shell script, the shell first scans the disk for the script file. However, you must take care to see that you don't keep a lot of functions in memory as that would eat up CPU resources. Shell functions are better than aliases in every way, and they work in the Bourne shell also.

Tip If a number of shell functions are used by multiple programs, you should place all of them in a single "library" file, and store the file at a convenient location. At the beginning of every script which requires these functions, insert a statement that executes the library file with the dot command.

24.11 eval: EVALUATING TWICE

The previous script requires that you set the variable names (`$user` and `$password`) for reading each input. We would prefer to have a more general script where the variable name itself can be generated by the script on the fly. We would store the prompts as variables and read the input as "numbered variables".

First define a couple of prompts at the prompt and then attempt to issue the first prompt with a numbered variable:

```
$ prompt1="Employee id : " ; prompt2="Name : " ; prompt3="Designation : "
$ x=1
$ echo $prompt$x
1
```

Instead of echoing `Employee id :` , it simply echoes the value 1, viz. the value of `x`. This happens because the shell evaluates the command line from left to right. It first encounters the `$` and evaluates `$prompt`; obviously `$prompt` is undefined. The shell then evaluates `$x`, which has the value 1.

The shell's **eval** statement evaluates a command line twice. The first pass ignores any metacharacter escaped with a \. The second pass ignores the \ and evaluates the metacharacter normally. This is exactly what we require the shell to do in our previous example. If we escape the first `$` (like `\$prompt$x`), the first pass will evaluate `$x` first so that we have `prompt1`, and the second pass then evaluates `$prompt1`. This is done by prefixing the **echo** command with **eval**:

```
$ x=1 ; eval echo \$prompt$x
Employee id :
```

We have a numbered prompt; we now need to use a numbered variable to read the input. For instance, the responses against numbered prompts can also be held in variables `value1`, `value2`, `value3`, etc. The following sequence does it for the second prompt:

```
$ { x=2
> eval echo \$prompt$x '\\c'
> read value$x                                    This has no problems
> eval echo \$value$x
> }
Name : rahul verma
rahul verma
```

Let's consider another application of **eval**. We can access a positional parameter with $1 or whatever, but can we access the last parameter directly? Since we have the value of $# available, we can use the services of **eval**:

```
$ tail -1 /etc/passwd
martha:x:605:100:martha mitchell:/home/martha:/bin/ksh
$ IFS=:
$ set `tail -1 /etc/passwd`    set -- not required here
$ eval echo \$$#
/bin/ksh
```

Look, using **eval**, we don't even have to know the number of fields in a line of /etc/passwd. In the next section, we'll use the services of **eval** both to generate prompts as well as to read user input.

24.11.1 A Generalized Data Entry Script with eval

We'll now use the **eval** feature to accept inputs into six fields with a generalized script, **dentry2.sh** (Fig. 24.3). There are six prompts defined at the beginning of the script as numbered variables, and an inner **while** loop issues all of them in turn. The values are read into the variables value1, value2, etc., and appended to the variable $rekord, using the | as delimiter each time.

```
#!/bin/sh
# Script: dentry2.sh - Uses eval and shell functions

trap 'echo "Program interrupted"; exit' HUP INT TERM
. mainfunc.sh          # Invokes functions valid_string() and anymore ()

prompt1="Employee id : " ; prompt2="Name : " ; prompt3="Designation : "
prompt4="Department : " ; prompt5="Date birth : " ; prompt6="Basic pay : "
rekord=

flname=`valid_string "Enter the output filename: " 8`
while true ; do
   while [ ${x:=1} -le 6 ] ; do                       # x first set to 1
      eval echo \$prompt$x '\\c' 1>&2
      read value$x
      rekord="${rekord}`eval echo \\$value$x`|"
      x=`expr $x + 1`
   done
   echo "$rekord"
   anymore "More entries to add" 1>&2 || break
done > $flname
```

Fig. 24.3 **dentry2.sh**

Note how the use of shell functions has kept the script size small. Here's a sample interaction:

```
$ dentry2.sh
Enter the output filename : newlist

Employee id : 2244
Name : prakash kumar
Designation : director
Department : marketing
Date birth : 27/02/44
Basic pay : 6700

More entries to add ?(y/n) : y

Employee id : 4789
Name : v.k. singh
Designation : manager
Department : personnel
Date birth : 21/12/46
Basic pay : 6500

More entries to add ?(y/n) : n
```

When you see `newlist`, you will find two records with an extra | at the end of each:

```
$ cat newlist
2244|prakash kumar|director|marketing|27/02/44|6700|
4789|v.k. singh|manager|personnel|21/12/46|6500|
```

Now, this is amazing; thanks to **eval**, we have managed to read six user responses into six variables with a minuscule script!

24.12 THE exec STATEMENT

Your study of the mechanism of process creation *(10.4)* led you to the **exec** system call—one that overlays a forked process. This property has some importance to shell scripters who sometimes need to overwrite the current shell itself with another program's code. This is something we haven't done yet, but if you precede any UNIX command with **exec**, the command overwrites the current process—often the shell. This has the effect of logging you out after the completion of the command:

```
$ exec date
Tue Jan 28 21:21:52 IST 2003                    Shell no longer exists!
login:
```

Sometimes, you might want to let a user run a single program automatically on logging in and deny her an escape to the shell. You can place the command in the `.profile`, duly preceded by **exec**. The shell overlays itself with the code of the program to be executed, and when command execution is complete, the user is logged out (since there's no shell waiting for it).

24.12.1 Using exec to Create Additional File Descriptors

exec has another important property; it can redirect the standard streams for an entire script. If a script has several commands whose standard output go to a single file, then instead of using separate redirection symbols for each, you can use **exec** to reassign their default destination like this:

```
exec > foundfile                                    Can use >> also
```

What's the big deal you might say; one could redirect the script itself. But **exec** can create several streams apart from the standard three (0, 1 and 2), each with its own file descriptor. For instance, you can create a file descriptor 3 for directing all output and associate it with a physical file `foundfile`:

```
exec 3>invalidfile
```

In system call parlance *(25.2.1)*, you have *opened* this file to generate the file descriptor 3. Subsequent access to this file can be made by using this file descriptor. You can now write the file by merging the standard output stream with the file descriptor 3:

```
echo "This goes to invalidfile" 1>&3
```

With this powerful I/O handler, you should now be able to handle files in a simpler and more elegant way. Let's design a script which reads emp-ids from a file. It then searches `emp.lst` and saves in three separate files the following:

- The lines found.
- The emp-ids not found.
- Badly formed emp-ids.

First, here's the file that contains the emp-ids. It contains two three-digit emp-ids which should be trapped by the script:

```
$ cat empid.lst
2233
9765
2476
789
3564
9877
0110
245
2954
```

The script, **countpat.sh** (Fig. 24.4), divides the standard output into three streams and redirects them to three separate files. It requires four arguments—the file containing the patterns and the files for the three streams.

The standard output streams are merged with the file descriptors 1, 3 and 4 using **exec**. Note that we have also set $1 as the source of all standard input. This means that the **read** statement in the loop will take input from $1—the file containing the patterns. Once all file writing is over, the standard output stream has to be reassigned to the terminal (**exec >/dev/tty**), otherwise the message `Job Over` will also be saved in the filename passed to $2.

This script is quite clean and has two statements using the merging symbols. The **grep** statement uses the standard output's file descriptor, so no merging is required. The script takes four arguments and diverts the output into three of them:

```
#!/bin/sh
# Script: countpat.sh -- Uses exec to handle multiple files
#
exec > $2                          # Open file 1 for storing selected lines
exec 3> $3                         # Open file 4 for storing patterns not found
exec 4> $4                         # Open file 5 for storing invalid patterns
[ $# -ne 4 ] && { echo "4 arguments required" ; exit 2 ; }
exec < $1                                  # Redirecting input
while read pattern ; do
     case "$pattern" in
        ????) grep $pattern emp.lst ||
           echo $pattern not found in file 1>&3 ;;
            *) echo $pattern not a four-character string 1>&4 ;;
     esac
done
exec >/dev/tty                   # Redirects standard output back to terminal
echo Job Over
```

Fig. 24.4 **countpat.sh**

```
$ countpat.sh empid.lst foundfile notfoundfile invalidfile
Job Over
```

The message appears on the terminal instead of going to any of these files. Now, just have a look at the three files and see for yourself what has actually happened:

```
$ cat foundfile
2233|a.k. shukla     |g.m.     |sales     |12/12/52|6000
2476|anil aggarwal   |manager  |sales     |05/01/59|5000
3564|sudhir Agarwal  |executive|personnel |07/06/47|7500
0110|v.k. agrawal    |g.m.     |marketing |12/31/40|9000
$ cat notfoundfile
9765 not found in file
9877 not found in file
2954 not found in file
$ cat invalidfile
789 not a four-character string
245 not a four-character string
```

This then is the power of **exec**. It can open several files together, and access each one separately in the same way **perl** uses its own filehandles and system calls use file descriptors. It is always preferable to use file descriptors instead of filenames because using **exec**, you can keep them open, and this makes I/O operations efficient.

24.13 CONCLUSION

We examined the shell's environment and discussed some of the useful features of the Korn and Bash shells. We also discussed two advanced features, **eval** and **exec**, that are available in the Bourne shell also. Like **sed**, it takes time to master them, but they are extremely useful tools. The **eval** feature is indeed unique, but knowing **exec** will help you understand how file I/O actually takes place. In the next chapter, we take up this subject in our study of the UNIX system calls.

We have finally come to the end of our journey with the shell. Along with **awk** and **perl**, the shell too has to be taken seriously if the power of the UNIX system is to be exploited to the hilt.

WRAP UP

Every shell script is executed in a sub-shell, which inherits a number of environmental parameters from its parent. You can run a shell script by using **sh** *script_name*. The grouping operators ( ) run a group of commands in a sub-shell but the { } don't spawn one.

The variables defined in the parent shell are inaccessible in the child shell unless they are exported. However, when the child alters the value of a variable, the changed value is not seen by the parent. The **.** command is used to execute a shell script without using a second shell.

Shell variables can be evaluated in a conditional manner, depending on whether they are assigned a nonempty value. The = operator additionally assigns a value to the variable, while ? prints an error message and exits the shell.

The shell has a mechanism for merging the standard output and standard error streams using the symbols 1>&2 and 2>&1. Using this mechanism, it is possible to treat standard output as standard error, and vice versa.

Shell functions let you condense important and repetitive sequences so that they are available everywhere. Unlike aliases, they accept command line arguments and also return a true or false value.

eval is used to process a command line twice. This makes it possible to simulate arrays and execute variables. **exec** overlays the current shell when prefixed to a command. It can be used to deny a user entry into the shell. It is also used to associate file descriptors with physical filenames.

TEST YOUR UNDERSTANDING

24.1 If you define a variable at the command prompt, how can you make its value available in a shell script?

24.2 Invoke the **script** command and define a variable at the prompt. Now quit **script** with **exit**, and then echo the value of this variable. What do you see and why?

24.3 If a directory change is made inside a shell script, why is the original directory restored after the completion of the script? How can you overcome this problem?

24.4 Write a shell function, **size()**, which lists *only* the total size of the files supplied as arguments (all files without arguments).

24.5 Why can't you use the **exit** statement inside a function to return control to the calling program?

24.6 What will this statement do? `flname=${1:-emp.lst}`

24.7 Write a shell function for **rm** which goes to the interactive mode whenever you use it with more than one filename.

24.8 Write a shell function that removes the current directory by invoking the function from there.

24.9 How will you make sure that a specific program is executed immediately on logging in, and the user is logged out when the program finishes?

FLEX YOUR BRAIN

24.1 Write a script which accepts an anonymous Ftp site (like *ftp.heavens.com*) and any number of **ftp** commands (like `"cd pub"`, `"get cp32.tar.gz"`) as arguments. It should then connect to this Internet site, log in automatically, and execute the **ftp** commands.

24.2 Why won't the **exit** command, when placed in a shell script like this, terminate the script? How do you get over this? `(` *statements*`; exit )`

24.3 Invoke the **su** command (if you know the root password), and then run **ps -t** with the terminal name. What conclusion would you draw?

24.4 Write a shell function that locates a directory, supplied as argument, in the home directory tree and switches to it. Will the same code work if placed in a shell script?

24.5 What is wrong with this statement? How do you modify it to execute correctly?

```
[ $# -ne 2 ] && echo "Usage: $0 min_guid max_guid" ; exit
```

24.6 You have to run a job at night and need to have both the output and error messages in the same file. How will you run the script?

24.7 How can you extract the last command line argument to a script using (i) arrays (ii) **eval**?

24.8 Write a script to copy files to a directory only when they don't exist there. The filenames are supplied as arguments and the last argument is the directory. You are allowed to use only one external command (**cp**) and exploit the features of the Korn and Bash shells. (HINT: Use the **eval** statement to identify the directory name.)

24.9 Modify the above script using **exec** so that every successful copy writes a message (of your choice) to one file and an unsuccessful copy saves the error message generated by **cp** to another file.

25

Systems Programming I—Files

Now that you know what the UNIX system has to offer, some questions should be playing in your mind already. How are files and processes handled by the kernel and shell? Since UNIX is written in C, can we use the same functions that are internally used by UNIX commands? The answers to these questions lie in the system call library that is available to a C programmer working in the UNIX environment. In this chapter and the following, we look at files and processes from the system programmer's point of view.

Because of the multiprogramming nature of UNIX, a single resource is often shared by multiple processes. As a UNIX programmer, you are required to use your existing knowledge of the C language to devise programs and applications that ensure that resources are shared in the way they are meant to, and without causing conflict. This chapter takes up file internals and their associated system calls; the next chapter does the same for processes. The knowledge you acquire from them will help you write new tools and improve the existing ones.

WHAT YOU WILL LEARN

- The basics of *system calls* and *library functions*.
- Perform file I/O with **open**, **read**, **write**, **lseek** and **close**, using a *file descriptor*.
- How system call errors are handled and reported with **perror** and **strerror**.
- Navigate a directory structure with **chdir** and **getcwd**.
- Read directory entries with **opendir** and **readdir**, and examine the `dirent` structure.
- The combined role of the `stat` structure and **stat** system calls in retrieving inode information.
- Use `S_IFMT` and the `S_IS`*xxx* macros to determine the file type.
- How to use symbolic constants to test each permission bit of a file.
- Use **access** to test a file's access rights, and how the SUID bit affects file access.
- Understand how **unlink** works and the consequences of using it with an open file.

TOPICS OF SPECIAL INTEREST

- Why it is important to properly set the size of the buffer used by **read** and **write**.
- The three-table scheme that comes into play when a file is opened, and how the scheme changes when a file is accessed by multiple processes.

25.1 SYSTEM CALL BASICS

C was created by Dennis Ritchie to *rewrite* the UNIX operating system in that language. To access the services available in the operating system, all UNIX systems offer around 200 special functions called *system calls*. A system call is a routine built into the kernel and performs a very basic function that requires communication with the CPU, memory and devices. All activities related to file handling, process and memory management and maintenance of user and system information are handled by the kernel using these system calls. These calls offer a high-level interface for us to use without requiring us to know the gory details of the functioning of these resources. As mentioned before, all UNIX and Linux systems have one thing in common; they use the same system calls.

When you execute a C program, the CPU runs in *user mode* till a system call is invoked. In this mode, the process has access to a limited section of the computer's memory, and can execute a restricted set of machine instructions. However, when the process invokes a system call, the CPU switches from user mode to a more privileged mode—the *kernel mode* (*supervisory mode* in operating system parlance). In this mode, it's the kernel that runs on behalf of the user, but it has access to any memory location and can execute any machine instruction. After the system call has returned, the CPU switches back to user mode. Process modes are explained in the next chapter.

A programmer knowing ANSI C should have no difficulty in using system calls provided she knows well the UNIX commands that internally use these calls. Many commands and system calls share the same names; the **chmod** command invokes the **chmod** system call.

25.1.1 System Calls and Library Functions

If you are a C programmer and have not used system calls, then you have must have used the *library functions*—a set of functions available in the standard library that is shipped with the C compiler for all UNIX and non-UNIX systems. On UNIX systems, these library functions are built on top of the system calls. The C standard library offers separate functions to read a block of data (**fread**), a line (**fgets**) and a single character (**fgetc**). All these functions ultimately invoke the only system call available for reading input—**read**. The library functions provide convenient interfaces that take care of some things that we may not like to bother about.

Does all this mean that we use only library functions and not system calls? No. Library functions are specialized and often don't provide the finer control features offered by system calls. For instance, **fopen**can create a file in read or write mode but can't set the file permissions (in **chmod**-style) which **open** does easily. A library function can't tell you the size of a file which the **stat** system call does by looking up a structure associated with the inode. Further, some file types (like a socket) can be read with only system calls.

Even though libraries don't contain the *code* for system calls, they contain, for every system call, a *wrapper* routine that ultimately invokes the corresponding system call in the kernel. For instance, the **open** system call is built into the kernel but is invoked by a library function of the same name. Every system call is represented by a number, and when a call is invoked, a special instruction—called a *trap*—switches control to the kernel (the kernel mode) and transmits this number to the kernel. The kernel uses this number to look up a table that points to the address in memory containing the code of the system call.

There are significant overheads associated with system calls and mode switches (user mode to kernel mode, and vice versa), so we'll have to use these calls judiciously. It's advantageous to direct the **read** system call to read a large block of data in a single invocation rather that read in small blocks with multiple invocations. This is sometimes difficult to achieve, so we'll also be using library functions whenever it's expedient to do so.

25.1.2 Anatomy of a System Call

Many of the system calls are written in C but a few of them are written in assembly language. Irrespective of the way they are implemented, the user-level interface is C-like, and for all practical purposes, system calls behave like C functions. You can pass arguments (generally, not exceeding five) of all types (`int`, `char`, `struct`, pointers, etc.) to these calls and also make them return values.

Like library functions, system calls use a mix of primitive and derived data types as can be seen from the prototype declaration of this **`write`** call:

```
ssize_t write(int fd, const void *buf, size_t count);
```

The third argument is of type `size_t` and the return type is of `ssize_t`. Generally, C uses **`typedef`** to ultimately translate them to the primitive types. For instance, `size_t` and `ssize_t` could ultimately be typedef'd to `unsigned int` and `int`, respectively on your machine. On another machine, they could represent `unsigned long` and `long`, respectively. `int` itself could be 16 bits on one machine and 32 bits on another. By using the derived types, `size_t` and `ssize_t`, rather than the primitive types in our programs, we are assured that appropriate mapping will be performed by the compiler. We need not bother *much* about these variations.

Originally, some system calls used a buffer of type `char`, but today, we are permitted to use a *generic buffer*, which is represented by a pointer of type `void *`. In the prototype for **`write`** shown above, `void` **buf* represents a generic buffer which can be for `char * buf`, `int *buf`, etc. We don't need to cast this generic buffer to the type that we actually use in our program.

Unlike library functions that often return null on error, system calls generally return `-1`. On error, a system call also sets a static (global) variable, `errno`, to a numeric value representing the error. There's a text message associated with every error number, and we'll learn to identify the cause of the error and print these messages. Some system calls, however, never return an error and some never return at all.

25.1.3 Atomic Operations

When you program in this multiprogramming environment, there's one thing that you have to keep in mind at all times: Multiple processes can contend for a single resource—like a file. There can be serious consequences in using two system calls (**`open`** and **`lseek`**) to append to a file when one would have sufficed (**`open`**). It's possible that a process is taken out of the CPU after **`open`** and before **`lseek`**, and a second process could overwrite the file in this period.

Wherever possible, you need to take care that certain critical operations are performed in an *atomic* manner. An atomic operation comprises multiple actions that are either performed in their entirety or not at all. Using two system calls in succession can't be an atomic operation because that allows a second process to run in between. In this chapter and the next, we'll note the instances of atomic behavior as and when we encounter them.

> **Tip** The UNIX man documentation features system calls and library functions in Sections 2 and 3, respectively. Sometimes, the same name represents both a UNIX command and a system call (like **read**, **write** and **exec**), so calling **man** without the section number would wrongly display the man page for the command. (**man read** shows the man page for the shell's built-in **read** command.) You must use **man 2 read** (or **man -s2 read** on Solaris). The documentation is complete and very well-explained.

25.2 OPENING AND CLOSING A FILE

In this chapter, the file-related system calls are divided into the following three categories:

- I/O-oriented calls that perform read-write operations and control the file offset pointer.
- Directory-related calls that access and manipulate directory entries or navigate a directory tree.
- Attribute-related calls that can access and change file attributes.

We begin our discussion on system calls with the ones related to file I/O. These comprise the **open**, **read**, **write**, **close** and **lseek** calls. Since UNIX treats even pipes and sockets as files, all these calls (barring **lseek**) are used with these objects also. Directories are files too, but we'll be using library functions rather than these system calls to handle directories for reasons that are explained later.

In this group, it's only **open** that accesses a file by its pathname. **open** returns a *file descriptor* (a small integer) which is used as an argument by the other four calls. We'll then use these calls to copy a file and also display its contents in reverse order.

25.2.1 open: Opening and Creating a File

You don't need to open a file to access its attributes, but you can't read or write a file unless you first open it. **open** has two forms; the first form assumes that the file exists, and the second one creates it if it doesn't. Both forms can be expressed by this syntax:

```
int open(const char *path, int oflag, ... );
```

open returns the file descriptor as an `int`. This is the lowest number available for allocation. Since every program always finds the three standard files (having the descriptors 0, 1 and 2) open, we don't need to open these files from our programs (though we can close them). Normally, the first **open** in your program should return the file descriptor 3.

The first argument (*path*) is a pointer to a character string that represents the file's pathname (either absolute or relative). The second argument (*oflag*) is used to set the *mode* of opening (read, write or read-write), which is conveniently represented by three symbolic constants. When opening a file one and only one of the following modes must be specified:

`O_RDONLY`	Opens file for reading.
`O_WRONLY`	Opens file for writing.
`O_RDWR`	Opens file for reading and writing.

These constants are defined in the file `fcntl.h` in `/usr/include`, so you need to place the statement **`#include <fcntl.h>`** at the top of your program. For added functionality, you'll often need to use one or more of the following *status flags* (also defined in `fcntl.h`) as components of *oflag*:

`O_APPEND`	Opens file in append mode (only if file opening mode is `O_WRONLY` or `O_RDWR`).
`O_TRUNC`	Truncates file to zero length (Same conditions as above).
`O_CREAT`	Creates file if it doesn't exist.
`O_EXCL`	Generates an error if `O_CREAT` is also specified and the file also exists.
`O_SYNC`	Synchronizes read-write operations. Ensures that **`write`** doesn't return till the data is written to disk (Explained later).

These status flags are used with the bit-wise OR operator, |, along with the mode of opening. Here are some ways you can use **`open`** with a file that exists:

```
int fd;                                               The file descriptor
fd = open("/etc/passwd", O_RDONLY);                   Read only
fd = open("foo.txt", O_WRONLY | O_APPEND) ;           Like the >> symbols
fd = open("../foo.txt", O_WRONLY | O_TRUNC) ;         Similar to the > symbol
```

The first **`open`** call above sets the *file offset pointer* to the beginning of the file. This pointer determines where in the file the subsequent read or write will take place. In the second call, the file is opened for writing but only by appending (`O_APPEND`), which sets the offset pointer to EOF. A subsequent write call here doesn't overwrite this file but increases its size. The third call truncates a file's contents (`O_TRUNC`) and positions the offset pointer at the beginning.

If the file doesn't exist, then you need to use the status flag, `O_CREAT` (and sometimes, `O_EXCL` also), to create the file. (Previously, the **`creat`** system call was used for this function.) In that case, you'll have to specify the absolute permissions of the file as the third argument. This argument can be specified as an octal number in the same way used by **`chmod`**, except that you'll have to prefix the number with a `0` (like `0644` instead of `644`). However, you are advised to use the symbolic constants provided in `sys/stat.h`. They are displayed in a tabular form below:

Permission	*User*	*Group*	*Others*	*All*
Read	`S_IRUSR`	`S_IRGRP`	`S_IROTH`	`S_IRWXU`
Write	`S_IWUSR`	`S_IWGRP`	`S_IWOTH`	`S_IRWXG`
Execute	`S_IXUSR`	`S_IXGRP`	`S_IXOTH`	`S_IRWXO`

Since each permission is represented by a separate bit, you need to OR these constants (bit-wise) to obtain the desired permissions. For instance, `0644` is the same as

```
S_IRUSR | S_IWUSR | S_IRGRP | S_IROTH
```

To open a file for writing after truncation (O_TRUNC), while ensuring that the file is created if it doesn't exist (O_CREAT), you need to specify the permissions as the third argument:

```
fd = open("foo.txt", O_WRONLY | O_CREAT | O_TRUNC,          Second argument is 01101
          S_IRUSR | S_IWUSR | S_IRGRP | S_IROTH) ;          Permissions are 0644
```

This is how the shell opens a file or overwrites one that exists when it sees the > symbol. Note that the bit-wise OR of the opening mode and status flags equates to octal 01101. That's why we must use symbolic constants; we can't remember these numbers.

The status flag, O_EXCL, provides protection from overwriting an existing file. If used at all, then it must be combined with O_CREAT (O_CREAT | O_EXCL). With the two flags set in this way, **open** will return an error (-1) if the file exists. We can use this mechanism to test for the existence of a file.

Note The file may not be created with the exact permissions you specify with **open** and the O_CREAT flag. The specified permissions get reduced by the umask value of the process. There's a separate system call named **umask** for handling this function and is discussed in Section 25.5.

Tip The O_EXCL feature comes in handy when you devise a scheme to let two processes share a file, foo, in a cooperative manner. To make the scheme work as an *advisory* form of file locking, both programs must agree to first create a lock file (with the same name) before they write to foo, and then remove the lock file they are done with foo. If all cooperating programs use the O_EXCL flag in their **open** calls that attempt to create the lock file the first **open** will succeed and the others will fail. Adherence to this agreement ensures that a file is not written simultaneously by two or more processes.

Caution If you are using numbers (like 644) rather than the symbolic constants to represent the permissions, don't forget to prefix a 0 to the number. We are using octal numbers here, and even though the **chmod** command doesn't require the 0 prefix (it does it internally), you'll have to be careful when using **open** (and the **chmod** system call as well).

25.2.2 close: Closing a File

A program automatically closes all open files before termination, but it's good practice to close them explicitly when you no longer require them. The **close** system call closes a file:

```
int close(int fd);
```

close returns 0 if successful and -1 otherwise. It actually deallocates the file descriptor for that process and makes it available for the next **open** (if there is one). When the **unlink** call is invoked to delete a file, the kernel can actually delete it only when the file is closed. This is discussed in Section 25.10.3.

When the same file is opened by two processes A and B (or by two **open** calls in the same program), the kernel simply assigns two separate file descriptors for them. If you use **close** in process A, you would simply release the descriptor for process A; process B would still find the file open. How all this happens will be described soon with reference to three tables maintained by the kernel for every open file.

Note Even though every process inherits copies of the open file descriptors of the three standard files from its parent, you can close any of them explicitly in your program. Yes, you can use **close(1);** to close the standard output file and then open a disk file to return 1 as the descriptor value. The implications of a file having descriptor values that are normally associated with the three standard streams will be examined in the next chapter.

25.3 USING THE I/O CALLS

The standard library offers a host a functions for reading (like **fread**, **fgets**, **fgetc** and **scanf**) and writing (like **fwrite**, **fputs**, **fputc** and **printf**), but only two system calls are actually at work here—**read** and **write**. These calls share a similar syntax that makes use of a user-defined buffer for reading and writing. We'll soon learn how the size of the buffer impacts disk I/O operations, so let's begin with **read**.

25.3.1 read: Reading a File

You need the **read** call to read a file using a file descriptor returned by a prior **open**. The prototype declaration for **read** is shown below:

```
ssize_t read(int fildes, void *buf, size_t nbyte);
```

read attempts to read *nbyte* characters from the file descriptor *filedes* into the buffer *buf*. *buf* represents a pointer to a generic buffer (which could be any of the primitive data types, often char). *nbyte* is generally the size of the buffer itself. The call returns the number of characters read.

If you have to process every character you read, then declare *buf* as a char variable and then pass its address to **read**:

```
int fd, n; char buf ;
while ((n = read (fd, &buf, 1)) > 0)                fd obtained from a prior open
```

The number of characters read as returned by this call (here, n) is generally equal to the number requested (here, 1). However, in a general situation, the two will not match when **read** encounters EOF, in which case it returns the number of characters that it could *actually* read. Network congestion and signals can also affect the return value of **read**.

For these reasons, we simply check for a positive integer return value and run **read** in a loop till it encounters EOF. Reading 100 characters with a single character buffer (as above) would require 100 system call invocations, which is rather expensive. If you don't need to process each character individually, then you should use an array. If it's a character array, then read into this array as many characters as its size:

```
#define BUFSIZE 100
int n; char buf[BUFSIZE];
while ((n = read(fd, buf, BUFSIZE)) > 0)
```

This **read** call is more efficient than the previous one as a single invocation reads in 100 characters in a *single* mode switch (user mode to kernel mode). We'll shortly discuss the factors that help determine the size of the buffer buf that was used with **read**.

25.3.2 write: Writing a File

You need the **write** call to write a file that has previously been opened with **open**. The prototype declaration of **write** is virtually identical to that of **read**:

```
ssize_t write(int fildes, const void *buf, size_t nbyte);
```

Each invocation of **write** writes *nbyte* number of bytes from the generic buffer *buf* to the file descriptor *filedes*. **write** returns the number of characters written, which *must* be equal to the number requested. However, if the disk fills up while a **write** is in progress or if the file size exceeds the system's limit, **write** returns -1.

As in **read**, you can write one character at a time in which case you should declare buf as a char variable:

```
char buf ;
write(fd, &buf, 1));                          fd obtained from a prior open
```

For writing data in chunks of characters, say, 8192 bytes, buf should be declared as a character array for holding that many characters, and **write**'s third argument should represent the size of this array:

```
#define BUFSIZE 8192
int n; char buf[BUFSIZE];
n = write(fd, buf, BUFSIZE));
```

The determination of the buffer size for both **read** and **write** depends on the device written to (terminal, hard disk, etc.) and the size of the kernel buffer maintained in memory. We are coming to that soon.

> **Note** When reading and writing the standard streams, we should use the symbolic constants, STDIN_FILENO, STDOUT_FILENO and STDERR_FILENO as the file descriptors rather than the integers, 0, 1 and 2, that they represent. These symbolic constants are defined in unistd.h.

25.3.3 ccp.c: COPYING A FILE

Our first program, **ccp.c** (Fig. 25.1), copies the file /etc/passwd to passwd.bak in the user's current directory. The source file is opened in the read-only mode (O_RDONLY). The destination file is opened in the write mode (O_WRONLY), is created if it doesn't exist (O_CREAT) and truncated if it does (O_TRUNC). Each **open** returns a file descriptor which should have the values 3 and 4 in this program.

For copying operations, both **read** and **write** need to use the same buffer. We set up a loop that attempts to read 1024 bytes into buf (an array of 1024 characters) from the descriptor fd1. The return value of **read** is next used by **write** to save the same buffer to disk using file descriptor fd2. The loop terminates when **read** returns 0 (on EOF). The descriptors are explicitly closed before exiting the program.

The program doesn't do any error checking and works only if ideal conditions prevail. Let's now compile this program with **cc** (or **gcc**) and then run the executable **a.out**. A byte-by-byte comparison of the two files with **cmp** confirms the faithfulness of the copy:

```
/* Program: ccp.c -- Copies a file with the read and write system calls */

#include <fcntl.h>                  /* For O_RDONLY, O_WRONLY, O_CREAT etc. */
#include <sys/stat.h>               /* For S_IRUSR, S_IWUSR, S_IRGRP etc. */
#define BUFSIZE 1024                /* May not be the right size here */

int main(void) {
    int fd1, fd2;                   /* File descriptors for read and write */
    int n;                          /* Number of characters returned by read */
    char buf[BUFSIZE];              /* BUFSIZE should be carefully chosen */
    fd1 = open("/etc/passwd", O_RDONLY);
    fd2 = open("passwd.bak", O_WRONLY | O_CREAT | O_TRUNC,
               S_IRUSR | S_IWUSR | S_IRGRP |S_IWGRP| S_IROTH);   /* Mode 664 */

    while ((n = read(fd1, buf, BUFSIZE)) > 0)    /* Return value of read is */
        write(fd2, buf, n) ;                     /* used by write as argument */

    close(fd1);
    close(fd2);
    exit(0);                      /* This would have closed all file descriptors */
}
```

Fig. 25.1 **ccp.c**

```
$ cc ccp.c
$ a.out
$ cmp /etc/passwd passwd.bak
$ _                                          Prompt returns—files identical
```

You need not always write data to disk; you can write to the standard output also. So if we replace fd2 in the **write** statement with 1 (rather, STDOUT_FILENO), we can use the program as a simple **cat** command. The second **open** and **close** calls won't then be required.

Note The library function **fopen** doesn't return a file descriptor, but a pointer to a FILE structure. The other functions like **fread** and **fwrite** access the file through this pointer. Beneath the hood, these functions actually run the corresponding system calls, **open**, **read** and **write**, and the file descriptor is embedded in the FILE structure as a separate member. You can retrieve this descriptor from this structure (with the **fileno** library function) if you have used **fopen** to open a file.

25.3.4 lseek: Positioning the Offset Pointer

The **lseek** call moves the file offset pointer to any point you specify. **lseek** doesn't do any physical. I/O, but it determines the position in the file where the next I/O operation will take place. Here's its syntax:

```
off_t lseek(int fildes, off_t offset, int whence);
```

The *offset* and *whence* arguments together control the location of the file's offset pointer. *offset* signifies the position (positive or negative) of this pointer relative to *whence*, which can take one of three values:

SEEK_SET Offset pointer set to beginning of file.
SEEK_END Offset pointer set to end of file.
SEEK_CUR Offset pointer remains at current location.

With some restrictions, *offset* can be a positive or negative integer, so it is represented by a signed data type. For instance,

```
lseek(fd, 10, SEEK_CUR)                    Descriptor fd obtained from prior open
```

moves the pointer forward by 10 characters from its current position, and

```
lseek(fd, -10, SEEK_END)                   Negative offset
```

sets the pointer 10 characters before the end of file. You can't have a negative *offset* with *whence* set to SEEK_SET, but strangely enough you can have a positive *offset* with *whence* at SEEK_END. In this case, the pointer moves beyond EOF, thus creating a *sparse* file—also called a file with a "hole". Sparse files find use in database applications.

lseek returns the position of the pointer in bytes from the beginning of the file. This return value can be used to determine the size of the file:

```
size = lseek(fd, 0, SEEK_END);             This returns the file size
```

Unlike **read** and **write**, which work with practically all file types, **lseek** works only with those files that are capable of seeking. It doesn't work with the terminal file or with a socket or pipe, and is mainly used for disk files.

Tip There are two ways of appending data to a file. You can use **open** with the O_APPEND status flag which positions the file's offset pointer to EOF. Alternatively, you can use **open** (without the flag) followed by **lseek(fd, 0, SEEK_END)**. The former technique is an atomic operation *(25.1.3)* and is recommended for use, but the latter is not.

25.3.5 reverse_read.c: Reading a File in Reverse

You can't read a file from the end to the beginning using the standard UNIX utilities (except **perl**), but using **lseek** in a C program, **reverse_read.c** (Fig. 25.2), you can. You have to first move the file pointer to one character before EOF to allow the last character to be read. Subsequently, every time you read one character, you must move the pointer back by two positions. This action needs to be performed in a loop till the beginning of file is reached.

The program accepts the input filename as argument and writes to the standard output. Observe that by moving the file offset pointer to one character before SEEK_END (EOF), we effectively captured the size of the file from **lseek**'s return value. size in the program is initially one less than the file size, a fact that is taken into account in the control command of the **while** loop.

```
/* Program: reverse_read.c -- Reads a file in reverse - uses lseek  */

#include <fcntl.h>                          /* For O_RDONLY */
#include <unistd.h>                         /* For STDOUT_FILENO */

int main(int argc, char **argv) {
   char buf;                                /* Single-character buffer; will make */
   int size, fd;                            /* I/O inefficient. See Section 25.4 */

   fd = open(argv[1], O_RDONLY);
   size = lseek(fd, -1, SEEK_END);          /* Pointer taken to EOF - 1 ... */
   while (size-- >= 0) {                    /* ... so size = file size - 1 */
      read(fd, &buf, 1);                    /* Read one character at a time */
      write(STDOUT_FILENO, &buf, 1);        /* and write it immediately */
      lseek(fd, -2, SEEK_CUR);              /* Now move file pointer back */
   }                                        /* by two characters */
   /* exit(0); */                           /* Done deliberately */
}
```

Fig. 25.2 **reverse_read.c**

Unlike in **ccp.c**, where we picked up data in chunks, this application demands that we read *one* character at a time. Hence, we use a single-character buffer with **read** and **write**. While **read** advances the pointer one byte forward, the next **lseek** takes it back by two bytes.

This program isn't syntactically correct; it does the job all right but terminates with an error. Let's run it on /etc/hosts.equiv, which contains hostnames derived from our solar system. Finally, we'll check the exit status:

```
$ a.out /etc/hosts.equiv
... A blank line ...                  The terminating \n of the last line
retipuj                               This is jupiter
yrucrem                               mercury
htrae                                 earth
nrutas                                saturn
$ echo $?
132
```

Why did the program terminate with a non-zero exit value? Look at the **while** loop closely and you'll find that in the last iteration, **lseek** runs with a negative offset at the beginning of the file. The second argument to **lseek** then becomes invalid. We didn't see any error message because we didn't trap it. Later, we'll rewrite this program after incorporating error-handling features.

25.3.6 truncate and ftruncate: Truncating a File

The O_TRUNC flag used with **open** truncates a file to zero bytes, but needs to open the file too. The **truncate** and **ftruncate** calls can truncate a file to any length. They are used like this:

```
int truncate(const char *path, off_t length);
int ftruncate(int fildes, off_t length);
```

truncate needs the pathname (*path*) as argument, but **ftruncate** works with the file descriptor (*fildes*) of an open file. Both truncate the file to *length* bytes. These calls are often used in combination with **lseek** to overwrite a certain segment of a file. You can truncate a file to any desired length and then use **lseek** to take the pointer to the location of truncation so that you can start writing from there.

> **Note** Many of the system calls discussed in this chapter have two, and sometimes, three versions. There's a "normal" version (like **truncate**) that uses the pathname, and a "f"-prefixed version (like **ftruncate**) that uses the file descriptor as argument. You can use either version if the file is open, but only the normal version if the file is not.

25.4 BUFFERED AND UNBUFFERED I/O

Before we move away from file I/O, we need to know something about the way disk I/O actually takes place. The **read** and **write** calls never access the disk directly. Rather, they read and write to a pool of buffers maintained by the kernel for this purpose, called the *buffer cache (17.7.1)*. If the kernel buffer is found to be empty during a read, the kernel instructs the disk controller to read data from disk and fill up the cache. **read** *blocks* (waits) while the disk is being read and even relinquishes control of the CPU.

To ensure that a single invocation of **read** gathers all bytes stored in the kernel buffer, the size of the latter and the buffer used by **read** (`char buf[BUFSIZE]` in the previous example) should be equal. Improper setting of the buffer size can make your program inefficient. So if each kernel buffer stores 8192 bytes, then `BUFSIZE` should also be set to 8192; there's no point choosing a figure larger than this.

In the context of disk I/O, **write** also uses the buffer cache but it differs from **read** in one way; it returns *immediately* after the call is invoked, and doesn't wait for the actual writing to take place. The kernel writes the buffer to disk *later* at a convenient time. Database applications often can't accept this, in which case you should open a file with the `O_SYNC` status flag to ensure that **write** doesn't return till the kernel has finally written the buffer to disk.

Unlike the standard library functions, the **read** and **write** calls are unbuffered when they interact with the terminal. When you use **write** to output a string to the terminal, the string appears on your display as soon as the call is invoked. On the other hand, the standard library functions (like **printf**) are line buffered when they access the terminal. That means a string is printed on the terminal when the newline character is encountered.

> **Note** The size of the kernel buffer is set at the time of installation of the operating system, and varies across systems. It's inconvenient to write programs that explicitly specify buffer sizes that are file system- and machine-dependent; we can't then have portable applications. This is where library functions come in. They use a buffer in the `FILE` structure and adjust its size *dynamically* during runtime using **malloc**. If you are apprehensive that `BUFSIZE` can change, then use the library functions rather than the system calls. The previous program, **reverse_read.c**, is terribly inefficient as it uses single-character buffers. We should use library functions here.

25.5 umask: MODIFYING FILE PERMISSIONS DURING CREATION

The permissions that you specify with **open** (when used with the O_CREAT flag) are modified by the umask value that is set in your shell. This mask, you'll recall *(13.5)*, reduces the default file and directory permissions (666 and 777, respectively) by the value of the mask. The **umask** system call kills two birds with one stone; it sets the mask to the value specified as argument, but it also returns the previous value of the mask:

```
mode_t umask(mode_t cmask);
```

Unlike the shell's **umask** statement, however, *the* **umask** *call can't display the current value of the mask without changing it*. To use a workaround, store the current mask by changing it to some arbitrary value, display the returned value and finally restore the saved mask. In our next program, **umask.c** (Fig. 25.3), we change the mask, print its old value and then create two files with two different settings of the mask.

```
/* Program: umask.c -- Changes umask twice and checks effect on permissions */

#include <stdio.h>
#include <fcntl.h>

int main(void) {
   mode_t old_mode, new_mode;

   old_mode = umask(0);                           /* No mask */
   printf("Previous umask value: %o\n", old_mode);

   open("foo1", O_RDONLY | O_CREAT, 0777);        /* Create file using new mask */
   umask(old_mode);                               /* Revert to previous mask */
   open("foo2", O_RDWR | O_CREAT, 0764);          /* Create file using old mask */
   exit(0);
}
```

Fig. 25.3 **umask.c**

In this program, we first set the mask to 0 and save its previous value in old_mode. After printing the previous value of the mask, we create a file with permissions 777. Next, we restore the old mask and then create another file with permissions 764. The output makes for some interesting reading:

```
$ a.out
Previous umask value: 22
$ ls -l foo?
-rwxrwxrwx   1 sumit    sumit          0 Dec  1 12:01 foo1
-rwxr--r--   1 sumit    sumit          0 Dec  1 12:01 foo2
```

Note that we could create a file foo1 with all permissions; this is something we can't do from the shell. The permissions of foo2 are 744, which isn't what you get when you subtract 022 from 764. A umask value of 022 indicates that a file will be created with the write permission bit absent for group and others. A simple arithmetic subtraction (764 - 022) would result in write permission for others—something that wasn't intended!

Note The restrictions placed by **umask** in no way affect our ability to change the permissions later with the **chmod** system call. **chmod** is taken up in Section 25.13.1.

25.6 HANDLING ERRORS

We haven't checked for errors in any of our previous programs. But errors can occur for a host of reasons—a resource not available, the receipt of a signal, I/O operational failures or invalid call arguments. A system call returns -1 on error, so to create robust code, we should always check for this condition (unless we are certain that this check isn't really necessary).

When a system call returns -1, the kernel sets the static (global) variable, errno, to a positive integer. This integer is associated with an error message and is represented by a symbolic constant. For instance, ENOENT has the value 2 and signifies No such file or directory. The number of messages available on your system is available in the extern variable, sys_nerr. The message strings can be printed with the library functions, **strerror** and **perror**.

25.6.1 Using strerror

The library function, **strerror**, uses the error number as its argument and returns a pointer to the string representing the error:

```
char *strerror(int errnum);
```

The program, **show_errors.c** (Fig. 25.4), uses **strerror** to print all the error messages used by your system. A **for** loop iterates as many times as the value of sys_nerr, and **strerror** prints the message for each value of *errnum*.

```
/* Program: show_errors.c -- Uses strerror to print all error messages */

#include <stdio.h>

int main(void) {
    int i;
    extern int sys_nerr;                /* Total number of error messages */

    for (i =0; i < sys_nerr; i++)
        printf("%d: %s\n", i, strerror(i));
    printf("Number of errors available: %d\n", sys_nerr);
    exit(0);
}
```

Fig. 25.4 **show_errors.c**

The output obtained on a Solaris system is suitably edited to show the most common messages from the top of the list:

```
$ a.out
0: Error 0
1: Not owner
2: No such file or directory
3: No such process
4: Interrupted system call
5: I/O error
13: Permission denied
17: File exists
22: Invalid argument
Number of errors available: 151
```

Solaris shows 151 possible error messages. To see how errno gets set, let's now modify the program in Fig. 25.2 by replacing the line containing the last occurrence of **lseek** with these two lines:

```
if ((lseek(fd, -2, SEEK_CUR)) == -1)
    fprintf (stderr, "\nerrno = %d, Message = %s\n", errno, strerror(errno));
```

When you run the program now on the same file, /etc/hosts.equiv, you should additionally see this error message at the end of output:

```
errno = 22, Message = Invalid argument
```

lseek eventually was called with an "invalid argument", which set errno to 22.

25.6.2 Using perror

Let's take a cue from the previous output to write a program, **show_errno.c** (Fig. 25.5), that attempts to open a non-existent file (non_existent_file), an unreadable file (/etc/shadow) and create a file that exists (the current program file, show_errno.c). This time, we use **perror** to print the error messages. **perror** follows this syntax:

```
void perror(const char *s);
```

Unlike **strerror**, **perror** doesn't use errno as argument; so it can only print the message associated with the current value of errno. The function takes a character string, *s*, as argument, and prints the string, a colon, a space followed by the message associated with errno.

In this program, we check the return value of **open** every time we use it. The first **open** should fail because non_existent_file won't (hopefully) exist in your directory. The second **open** tries to open /etc/shadow, which is unreadable to all except root. The third **open** uses O_CREAT | O_EXCL to create this source file itself; obviously it will fail. Here's the output of this program:

```
$ a.out
non_existent_file: No such file or directory
shadow: Permission denied
show_errno.c: File exists
```

perror doesn't print errno, but you know their values from the output of the program prior to the previous one. These error numbers are associated with symbolic constants defined in <sys/errno.h>. A subset of these constants, their errno values and the message strings are shown in Table 25.1. Henceforth, we'll be using error checking in most of our programs and sometimes check for specific error conditions.

```
/* Program: show_errno.c -- Displaying system call errors with perror */

#include <fcntl.h>

int main (int argc, char **argv) {
    int fd;
    char* filename = "non_existent_file";  /* This file must not exist */

    fd = open(filename, O_RDONLY);             /* File descriptor assigned first */
    if (fd == -1)                              /* and then checked */
        perror("non_existent_file");
    if ((fd = open ("/etc/shadow", O_RDONLY)) == -1)   /* Both combined here */
        perror("shadow");
    if ((fd = open ("show_errno.c", O_WRONLY | O_CREAT | O_EXCL, 0744)) == -1)
        perror("show_errno.c");
    exit(0);
}
```

Fig. 25.5 show_errno.c

Caution You must check the value of errno *immediately* after a system call returns an error, and before you do anything else. The behavior of errno in the event of a successful call is undefined. Some systems leave it unchanged, but some don't. If necessary, save the value of errno in a separate variable if you need this value later in your program.

Table 25.1 Significance of Symbolic Constants Associated with errno

Symbolic Constant	errno	*Message*
EPERM	1	Not super-user
ENOENT	2	No such file or directory
ESRCH	3	No such process
EINTR	4	Interrupted system call
EIO	5	I/O error
EACCES	13	Permission denied
EEXIST	17	File exists
ENOTDIR	20	Not a directory
EISDIR	21	Is a directory
ENOSPC	28	No space left on device
ESPIPE	29	Illegal seek
EROFS	30	Read only file system

25.6.3 reverse_read2.c: Reverse Reading a File with Error Handling

Now let's use our knowledge of error handling to improve our previous program (Fig. 25.2) that reads a file in reverse order. The program, **reverse_read2.c** (Fig. 25.6), employs three types of error handling techniques and provides five exit points. It checks for possible error conditions in most of the system calls used, but lets some of them off only because there's hardly a way they could generate errors.

```
/* Program: reverse_read2.c -- Reads a file in reverse - uses error handling  */

#include <fcntl.h>                      /* For O_RDONLY */
#include <unistd.h>                     /* For STDOUT_FILENO */
#include <errno.h>                      /* For ENOENT, errno, etc. */
#include <stdio.h>                      /* For ENOENT, errno, etc. */

int main(int argc, char **argv) {
    int size, fd;
    char buf;                                       /* Single-character buffer */
    char *mesg = "Not enough arguments\n";

    if (argc != 2) {                    /* Our own user-defined error message */
       write(STDERR_FILENO, mesg, strlen(mesg));  /* Crude form of error */
       exit(1);                                   /* handling using write */
    }                                             /* Use fprintf instead */

    if ((fd = open(argv[1], O_RDONLY)) == -1) {
       if (errno == ENOENT) {                     / *Checking for specific error*/
          fprintf(stderr, "%s\n", strerror(errno)); /* perror is better */
          exit(2);
       } else {
          perror(argv[1]);                      /* Using two library functions */
          exit(3);                              /* perror and exit. Often the */
       }                                        /* preferred way */
    }

    lseek(fd, 1, SEEK_END);                     /* Pointer taken to EOF + 1 first */
    while (lseek(fd, -2, SEEK_CUR) >= 0) {      /* and then back by two bytes */
       if (read(fd, &buf, 1) != 1) {            /* A signal can create error here */
          perror("read");
          exit(4);
       }
       if (write(STDOUT_FILENO, &buf, 1) != 1) { /* Disk may run out of space */
          perror("write");
          exit(5);
       }
    }
    close(fd);                             /* Can have error here too */
    exit(0);                               /* exit doesn't return - hence no error */
}
```

Fig. 25.6 **`reverse_read2.c`**

The first form of error handling uses **write** with a character string, but gives no indication of the nature of the error. The second form checks for a specific type of error (here, ENOENT), and is useful in situations where program flow depends on the nature of the error. But this form uses **fprintf** and **strerror** to print the error message; it's inconvenient to use it this way. The third form uses the library functions, **perror** and **exit**, three times in a consistent manner which justifies their conversion to a function.

Observe that this time **lseek** takes the offset pointer beyond EOF before moving back from there. The program provides five abnormal exit points having different values of the exit status (1 to 5). If the program generates an error, you can know the exit route it took by examining the value of $?. So let's run it in a number of ways:

```
$ a.out ; echo $?
Not enough arguments
1
$ a.out /etc/shdaow ; echo $?
No such file or directory                    Printed with strerror; this is ENOENT
2
$ a.out /etc/shadow ; echo $?
/etc/shadow: Permission denied               Printed with perror; this is EACCES
3
```

Note how the program returned three different exit values when the command line arguments to the program were either wrongly specified or the input file was unreadable. Let's use the right file now:

```
$ a.out /etc/hosts.equiv                     Displays same output as
... A blank line ...                         program in Fig. 25.2.
retipuj
yrucrem
htrae
nrutas
$ echo $?
0                                            Normal exit from program.
```

It's often the case that when you use **perror** to print the error message, you also quit the program immediately thereafter. Henceforth, we'll be using the **quit** function to handle most error conditions. Enter this definition for **quit** in a file, **quit.c**:

```
#include <stdio.h>
void quit (char *message, int exit_status) {
    perror(message);
    exit(exit_status);
}
```

quit uses **perror** to print the message associated with errno. The same message could be used by multiple **quit** invocations, so we additionally provide the exit status as the second argument. We can gather this exit status from the shell by examining $?. Create the object code, **quit.o**, for this function with **cc -c quit.c**.

25.7 FILE SHARING

Things start to get complex when we realize that UNIX is a multiprogramming system, which allows multiple processes to use the same file. It's also possible for a parent process to open a file and make its file descriptor available to the child. That's similar to the way the shell handles redirection, so we need to understand the structural changes that take place in memory when a file is opened.

The inode contains only static data about a file, but when a file is opened, the dynamic attributes come into play. These attributes comprise the mode of opening (like `O_RDONLY`), the status flags (like `O_CREAT`, `O_APPEND`, etc.), the file offset, and so forth. The kernel maintains three data structures in memory that contain all information about an open file that a process needs to access:

- The *file descriptor table*—This structure contains all allocated file descriptors for a process. Each entry points to the file table.
- The *file table* —It contains all the parameters that are supplied at the time of opening a file. It also contains the file offset. This table points to the vnode table.
- The *vnode table*—This contains all inode information, and can be considered as an approximation of the inode in memory (in-core inode).

Even though the file descriptor table is a per-process structure (only one table per process), the other two tables are not. It's possible to have multiple file tables for the same file (with multiple **open**s) or for multiple processes to access the same file table and vnode table (by replicating file descriptors). Both tables maintain a *reference count* field that signifies the number of pointers to the table. In the following sections, we'll examine these tables and their relationship as depicted in Fig. 25.7. This knowledge is essential to our understanding of processes that is taken up in the next chapter.

25.7.1 The File Descriptor Table

The kernel returns a non-negative integer, the file descriptor, to the process that opens the file. This file descriptor is stored along with a flag in the *file descriptor table*. This table is maintained separately for every process that runs in the system as a component of a separate structure called the *u area* (discussed in next chapter). The u area contains all attributes of the currently running process.

The shell's three standard files occupy the first three slots (0, 1 and 2) in the file descriptor table. If you close, say, descriptor number 1, the kernel will allocate this number to the next file that is opened. We'll use this behavioral property in the next chapter to implement redirection. The flag, `FD_CLOEXEC`, is not used by **open**, but by a powerful system call named **`fcntl`** to determine whether the descriptor will be closed when the process does an exec *(10.4)* to run a separate program. By default, a descriptor is not closed when the process does an exec.

25.7.2 The File Table

Every entry in the file descriptor table points to a *file table*. This table contains all data that are relevant to an opened file. More specifically, it contains

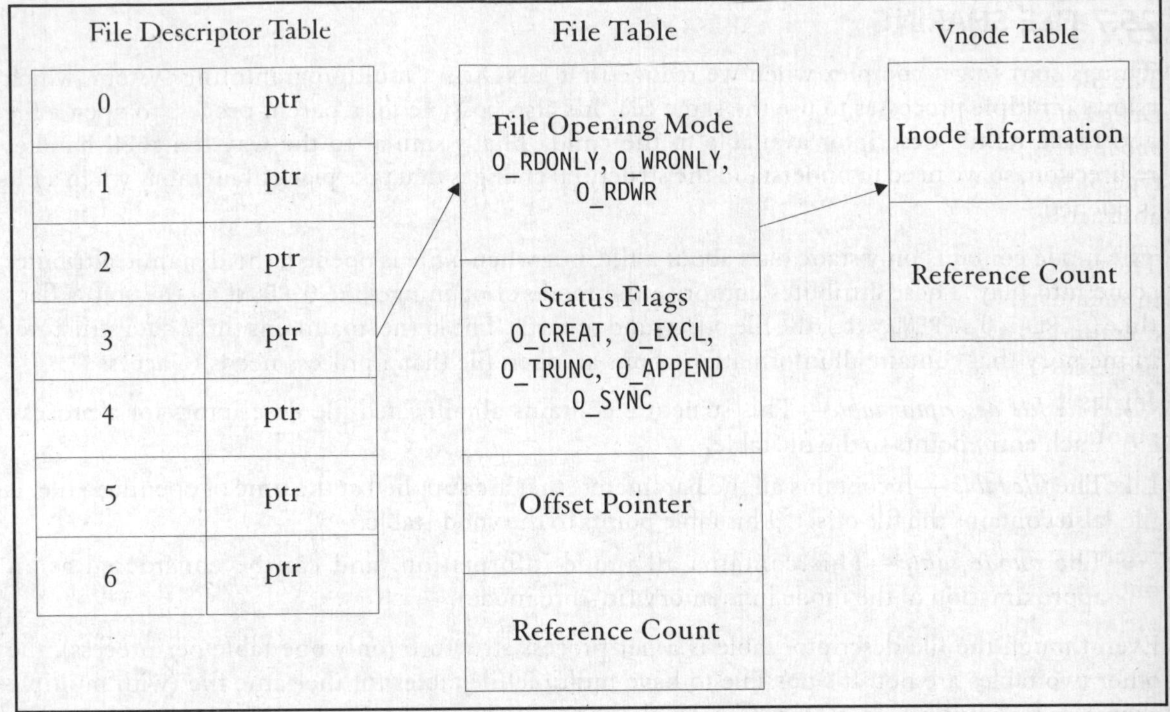

Fig. 25.7 File Sharing—The Three Tables

- The mode of opening (like `O_RDONLY`).
- The status flags (like `O_CREAT`, `O_TRUNC`, etc.).
- The offset pointer location that determines the byte position to be used by the next read or write operation.
- A reference count that indicates the number of processes or calls that point to this table.

Every symbolic constant used as the second argument to **open** is made available in the file table. Since the file descriptor table and file table appear to share a one-to-one relationship, you could ask this: Why can't the mode, flags and offset be kept in the file descriptor table rather than in the file table? The answer is that UNIX also allows two or more file descriptors to point to the same file table entry (many-to-one). This happens when you duplicate the file descriptor (with the **dup** and **dup2** system calls) and when you create a process (with **fork**). We'll consider the implications of this replication in the next chapter.

The file's status flags (though not its mode) can be changed by the **fcntl** system call—the same call that controls the `FD_CLOEXEC` flag in the file descriptor table. The reference count field tracks the number of descriptors pointing to the file table (in a many-to-one situation). The kernel releases the table from memory only when there's no descriptor pointing to it, i.e. when the reference count has dropped to zero.

25.7.3 The Vnode Table

The file table contains a pointer to the *vnode table*, the third table in the scheme. Maurice Bach (*The Design of the UNIX Operating System*, Prentice Hall) calls this the *inode table*, but that is because the *vnode* originated after the book was written. That was when UNIX systems supported only a single type of file system. Today, we have multiple file system types on the same machine, so the vnode abstraction was created to make it possible to access the inode in a file-system independent way.

The vnode table contains all information present in the inode except that this structure is maintained in memory. It's often called the *in-core inode* (Bach). There's only a single copy of the vnode in memory. The inode on disk is updated from the information in the vnode by the kernel. If two processes open the same file, or the same program opens the same file twice, there would be separate entries in the file descriptor tables and two separate file table structures, but both structures would point to the same vnode table (Fig. 25.8).

Like the file table, the vnode table also maintains a reference count field that signifies the number of file table entries that point to this table. When a file is deleted, the kernel has to first check the reference count to see whether any process still has the file open. If the reference count is at least one, the kernel can't delete the file and release the inode *though it will delete the directory entry for the file.* This unusual action is discussed later *(25.10.3)*.

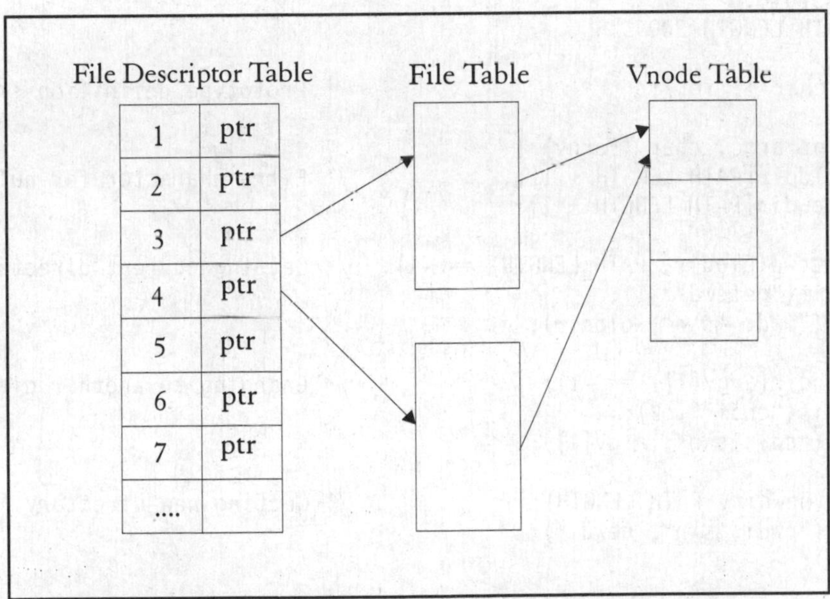

Fig. 25.8 When a File is Opened Twice in the Same Process

25.8 DIRECTORY NAVIGATION

There are two system calls that perform the action of the **cd** command. They are **chdir** and **fchdir**, which use a pathname and a file descriptor, respectively as argument:

```
int chdir(const char *path);
int fchdir(int fildes);
```

We'll be using **chdir** in our next example. The current directory is obtained by the **getcwd** library function. Some UNIX systems feature other functions (like **getwd**), but POSIX recommends the use of **getcwd** which must use this syntax only:

```
extern char *getcwd(char *buf, size_t size);
```

Here, *buf* is defined as a character array of *size* bytes. After invocation of **getcwd**, the pathname of the current directory is made available in *buf*. If *buf* is null, **getcwd** creates the buffer using **malloc** and returns a pointer to it. This form of usage is discouraged by POSIX.

The next program, **dir.c** (Fig. 25.9), uses **chdir** to switch to a directory. It also invokes **getcwd** to obtain the pathname of the current directory, both before and after the switch. The buffers that store the directory pathnames are provided with one extra slot for storing the null character.

```
/* Program: dir.c -- Directory navigation with chdir and getcwd */

#include <stdio.h>
#define PATH_LENGTH 200

void quit(char *, int);                          /* Prototype definition */

int main(int argc, char **argv) {
    char olddir[PATH_LENGTH + 1];                /* Extra character for null */
    char newdir[PATH_LENGTH + 1];

    if (getcwd(olddir, PATH_LENGTH) == -1)       /* Getting current directory */
        quit("getcwd", 1);
    printf("pwd: %s\n", olddir);

    if ((chdir(argv[1]) == -1))                  /* Changing to another directory */
        quit("chdir", 2);
    printf("cd: %s\n", argv[1]);

    getcwd(newdir, PATH_LENGTH);                 /* Getting new directory */
    printf("pwd: %s\n", newdir);
    exit(0);
}
```

Fig. 25.9 **dir.c**

The program makes use of the **quit** function that we just developed. We'll now have to link the object code for **quit.o** with this program using

```
cc dir.c quit.o
```

Let's now use the generated executable, **a.out**, to switch to the directory /usr/include/sys. The program prints the current directory both before and after the switch:

```
$ a.out /usr/include/sys
pwd: /users1/home/staff/sumit
cd: /usr/include/sys
pwd: /usr/include/sys                    Change of directory inside program ...
$ pwd
/users1/home/staff/sumit                 ... is not available outside it
```

After completion of the program, we also ran the shell's **pwd** command. As explained previously *(10.4)*, a change of environment inside a program is not available outside it.

25.9 READING A DIRECTORY

Directories are also files, and they can be opened, read and written in the same way as regular files. The format of a directory is not consistent across file systems—and even across different flavors of UNIX. Using **open** and **read** to list directory entries can be a grueling task. UNIX offers a number of library functions to handle a directory:

```
DIR *opendir(const char *dirname);            Opens a directory
struct dirent *readdir(DIR *dirp);            Reads a directory
int closedir(DIR *dirp);                      Closes a directory
```

Note that we can't *directly* write a directory; only the kernel can do that. These three functions take on the role of the **open**, **read** and **close** system calls as applied to ordinary files. Being library functions, they encapsulate the file descriptors they actually work with. **opendir** takes *dirname* as the pathname and returns a pointer to a DIR structure (whose structure need not bother us). The other two functions use the address of this structure as argument.

A directory maintains the inode number and filename for every file in its fold. Expectedly, these two entities are members of the dirent structure that is returned by **readdir**. Every invocation of **readdir** fills up this structure with information related to the next directory entry (i.e., the next filename). POSIX doesn't specify the internal format of a directory, but it requires the dirent structure (defined in <dirent.h>) to provide at least these two members:

```
struct dirent {
    ino_t  d_ino                              Inode number
    char   d_name[]                           Directory name
};
```

Both Solaris and Linux have at least two more members (signifying the record length and the offset of the directory entry), but we'll ignore them to keep our programs portable. UNIX systems usually have the upper limit for d_name[] set to 256, so filenames can't exceed 255 characters (one element of the array to be reserved for the terminating null).

25.9.1 `lls.c`: Listing Filenames in a Directory

Let's now use the three functions and the `dirent` structure in out next program, **`lls.c`** (Fig. 25.10), to list for every file in a directory, its inode number and filename. This program also uses the **`quit`** function, so you should remember to link **`quit.o`** when you compile the program.

```
/* Program: lls.c -- Uses readdir to populate a dirent structure */

#include <dirent.h>
#include <stdio.h>

int main(int argc, char **argv) {
    DIR *dir;                                      /* Returned by opendir */
    struct dirent *direntry;                       /* Returned by readdir */

    if ( (dir = opendir(argv[1])) == NULL)         /* Directory must exist and */
        quit("opendir", 1);                        /* have read permission */

    while ((direntry = readdir(dir)) != NULL)      /* Till there are entries */
        printf("%10d %s\n", direntry->d_ino, direntry->d_name);

    closedir(dir);
    exit(0);
}
```

Fig. 25.10 `lls.c`

We first define two pointers of type `DIR` and `struct dirent`. **`opendir`** returns the pointer, `dir`, of type `DIR`, and **`readdir`** uses this pointer to return another pointer, `direntry`, of type `struct dirent`. The members of this structure are accessed using the pointer notation ->. The partial output of the program shows the inode number and filename of all files in the root directory:

```
$ a.out /
         2 .                                   Program shows hidden files also
         2 ..
      6784 usr
     13568 var
     20352 export
     54272 etc
     67840 dev
         5 lib
    407040 sbin
  ......
```

This is how **`ls -ia /`** displays the contents of the root directory. There are three other functions available for handling directories. The **`rewinddir`** function rewinds the directory list so you can start reading it from the beginning with **`readdir`**. **`telldir`** returns the current location of the `DIR` pointer. This location (a `long int` in Solaris) can be used as an argument to **`seekdir`** to set the position of the pointer to a specific location.

> **Note** In the output of the previous program, both directories . and .. represent root, which has the inode number 2.

25.10 MODIFYING ENTRIES IN DIRECTORY

Even though we can't directly edit a directory, we can use functions to add, remove or modify entries in a directory. In this section, we take up the following system calls:

- **mkdir** and **rmdir**—These calls have the same significance as the commands of the same name.
- **link**, **symlink** and **unlink**—**link** behaves like the **ln** command, but only to create a hard link. **symlink** creates a symbolic link. **unlink** removes a directory entry which can be used to remove a file (or a link) and a symbolic link. **unlink** doesn't remove a directory.
- **rename**—Like **mv**, this call is used to modify the name in a directory entry.

Every function in this group uses a syntax that is identical to the simplest form of its corresponding UNIX command. They are, therefore, considered briefly in the following paragraphs.

25.10.1 mkdir and rmdir: Creating and Removing Directories

Like a regular file, a directory also has an entry in its parent directory. The **mknod** system call can be used by the superuser to create a directory, but a nonprivileged user can use the **mkdir** and **rmdir** calls to create and remove a directory:

```
int mkdir(const char *path, mode_t mode);
int rmdir(const char *path);
```

The second argument to **mkdir** sets the permissions the directory will have on creation. (**open** also uses this *mode* as its third argument when invoked with the O_CREAT flag.) The permissions are also modified by the umask setting. Note that the parent directory needs to have write permission for a directory to be created in it. The directory also needs to be empty to be removable with **rmdir**.

25.10.2 link and symlink: Creating a Hard and Symbolic Link

Unlike the **ln** command which creates both hard and symbolic links, the system call library has two separate functions, **link** and **symlink**, for these tasks. Both require two arguments:

```
int link(const char *path1, const char *path2);
int symlink(const char *path1, const char *path2);
```

Here, both **link** and **symlink** create a directory entry with the name *path2* for an existing file *path1*. **symlink** creates a new inode for *path2* also. **link** doesn't create an inode but simply updates the link count of the existing inode for *path1* by one.

25.10.3 unlink: Removing a Link

The **unlink** call reverses the action of **link** and **symlink**. It removes the directory entry for the file (the argument) and decrements the link count in its inode by one. The syntax is simple:

```
int unlink(const char *path);
```

Although **link** doesn't create a symbolic link, **unlink** removes one, but not the file it points to; that has to be done separately. A file is considered to be removed when its link count in the inode has dropped to zero. When that happens, the kernel frees the inode and the associated disk blocks for fresh allocation, *but provided the file is closed also*. We need to understand exactly how the kernel responds to an **unlink** call.

There's one important thing that you need to remember when you use **unlink** on a file which has a single link count: If the file has been opened by another program or by code in your own program, the kernel will remove the directory entry all right, but it won't delete the file as long as at least one file descriptor points to the file. So it's possible to issue an **unlink** command immediately after an **open** and then read the file like this:

```
fd = open("foo", O_RDONLY);
unlink("foo");                          This file won't be removed
while ((n = read(fd, buf, BUFSIZE)) > 0)   till it is closed.
```

Here, foo will be deleted only after it is closed or on termination of the program, which closes all open file descriptors. You can read the file even after issuing **unlink** since its descriptor still points to the file table, and ultimately to the vnode table. But the kernel has already removed the directory entry for the file, so another **open** on this file will fail. Note because the file is open, both the file table and vnode table are available in memory, the reason why the file can be read even after the "unlink."

Tip The facility to "unlink" a file immediately after opening it can be used gainfully in a program having multiple exit points. If your application requires doing I/O on a temporary file and then deleting it before program termination, then unlinking the file at an early stage makes sure your file is ultimately deleted. In the interim, this "unlinking" doesn't affect I/O operations on the file in any way.

25.10.4 rename: Renaming a File, Directory or Symbolic Link

The **rename** call is used for renaming any type of file. Like **mv**, it can work with the three types of files shown in the section header, and follows this syntax:

```
int rename(const char *old, const char *new);
```

Here, **rename** modifies the directory entry by replacing the filename *old* with *new*. When operated on regular files or symbolic links, the behavior of **rename** is identical to that of **mv**. However, **rename** differs from **mv** when it comes to handling directories:

- If *old* is a directory and *new* exists as a directory, **rename** simply removes *new* and moves *old* to *new*. **mv** makes *old* a subdirectory of *new*.
- If *old* is a regular file, *new* can't be a directory. **mv** doesn't operate with this constraint.

You'll recall how simply you used the command **mv *.c workc** to move all C source files to the workc directory. To emulate this function in your C program, you'll have to call **rename** as many times as there are C programs.

25.11 READING THE INODE: stat

We now move on to the vnode table to access the information available in the inode. The inode contains all file attributes (except the filename), and to get these attributes, we must access the `stat` structure. The information in this structure is obtained by a system call having the same name as the structure. Let's first examine the members of the `stat` structure as mandated by POSIX:

```
struct stat {
    ino_t       st_ino          Inode number
    mode_t      st_mode         Mode (type and permissions)
    nlink_t     st_nlink        Number of hard links
    uid_t       st_uid          UID (owner)
    gid_t       st_gid          GID (group owner)
    dev_t       st_rdev         Device ID (for device files)
    off_t       st_size         File size in bytes
    time_t      st_atime        Last access time
    time_t      st_mtime        Last modification time
    time_t      st_ctime        Last time of change of inode
    blksize_t   st_blksize      Preferred block size for I/O
    blkcnt_t    st_blocks       Number of blocks allocated
};
```

The `ls` command looks up this structure to gather the file attributes, and the `dirent` structure for the filename. You can do that too with the **stat** system call (or with its two derivatives, **fstat** and **lstat**). All three calls use an address to a `stat` structure as their second argument as shown below:

```
int stat(const char *path, struct stat *buf);
int fstat(int fildes, struct stat *buf);
int lstat(const char *path, struct stat *buf);
```

stat requires the pathname as the first argument, and **fstat** requires a file descriptor. **stat** follows symbolic links, so if a file `foo` is symbolically linked to a file `bar` (`foo->bar`), doing a "stat" on `foo` will actually populate the `stat` structure with the attributes of `bar`. **lstat** behaves exactly like **stat** for ordinary files and directories, but it doesn't follow symbolic links, so an "lstat" on `foo` actually extracts the attributes of `foo`. We'll be using **lstat**, rather than **stat**, for the examples in this book.

Some of the members of the `stat` structure need some processing before they can be displayed in a meaningful format. `stat` (the structure) stores the three time stamps in seconds elapsed since the Epoch (January 1, 1970), so we'll use the library function, **ctime**, to display the time stamps in the Internet format. We need to process the `st_mode` member too, but before we do that, let's first write a program that prints some of these members.

25.11.1 attributes.c: Displaying Some File Attributes

Our next program, **attributes.c** (Fig. 25.11), uses **lstat** to populate the `statbuf` variable of type `struct stat`. It uses the **ctime** function to format the time stamps by passing the address of the respective member (`st_mtime` or `st_atime`) as argument. The program shows how easy it is to display file attributes.

```
/* Program: attributes.c -- Uses lstat call and
                              struct stat to display file attributes*/
#include <stdio.h>
#include <sys/stat.h>

void quit(char *, int);

int main(int argc, char **argv) {
   struct stat statbuf;                    /* We'll use lstat to populate this */

   if (lstat(argv[1], &statbuf) == -1)
      quit("Couldn't stat file", 1);

   printf("File: %s\n", argv[1]);
   printf("Inode number: %d \n", statbuf.st_ino);
   printf("UID: %d    ", statbuf.st_uid);
   printf("GID: %d\n", statbuf.st_gid);
   printf("Type and Permissions: %o\n",  statbuf.st_mode);
   printf("Number of links: %d \n", statbuf.st_nlink);
   printf("Size in bytes: %d\n", statbuf.st_size);
   printf("Blocks allocated: %d\n", statbuf.st_blocks);
   printf("Last Modification Time: %s", ctime(&statbuf.st_mtime));
   printf("Last Access Time: %s\n", ctime(&statbuf.st_atime));
   exit(0);
}
```

Fig. 25.11 **attributes.c**

All numeric data are printed in decimal (with %d) except the file type and permissions, which are formatted in octal. When we run this program with the filename /etc/passwd as argument, we see all attributes that **ls** also shows us with its various options (except that you require separate invocations of **ls** to display each time stamp):

```
$ a.out /etc/passwd
File: /etc/passwd
Inode number: 54412
UID: 0    GID: 3
Type and Permissions: 100755
Number of links: 1
Size in bytes: 10803
Blocks allocated: 22
Last Modification Time: Tue Nov 19 16:29:13 2002
Last Access Time: Tue Nov 26 19:57:01 2002
```

Observe the line that displays the file type and permissions as a single number in octal (100755). Unfortunately, UNIX doesn't have separate members for them in stat, so we need to mask out one attribute to obtain the other. This is what we are going to do next.

25.11.2 S_IFMT: Manipulating the st_mode Member

The st_mode member of stat combines the file type with its permissions in a space of 16 bits. The organization of these bits is shown below:

Bits	*File Attribute*
1-4	Type
5-7	SUID, SGID and Sticky bit permissions
8-10	Owner permissions
11-13	Group permissions
14-16	Other permissions

The four most significant bits contain the file type. We need 12 bits (and not 9) to represent a file's permissions completely. Recall that 3 separate bits are needed to set the SUID, SGID and the sticky bit *(17.3.2)*. In the previous example, the file type is represented by the octal number 100000 and the permissions by 755.

To extract these components separately, we need to use the S_IFMT mask. When an AND operation is performed with st_mode and this mask, it returns the file type. An inverse AND operation (with ~) returns the permissions. This is how you'll be using S_IFMT in your programs:

```
mode_t file_type, file_perm;
file_type = statbuf.st_mode & S_IFMT;                    Bits 1-4
file_perm = statbuf.st_mode & ~S_IFMT;                   Bits 5-16
```

Once you are able to separate the two components with this mask, you can identify files of a specific type or ones having (or not having) a specific permission. Checking file types for numeric values is not very convenient, so UNIX provides a number of macros that make our task simpler.

Table 25.2 The S_IS*xxx* Macros

Macro	*Returns True if File Type is*
S_ISREG	Regular
S_ISDIR	Directory
S_ISBLK	Block special
S_ISCHR	Character special
S_ISLNK	Symbolic link
S_ISFIFO	FIFO
S_ISSOCK	Socket

25.11.3 Using the S_IS*xxx* Macros to Determine File Type

All UNIX systems provide a set of macros beginning with S_IF (often called the S_IF*xxx* macros) that simplify the work of checking for file types, but modern UNIX systems make this task even simpler with the S_IS*xxx* macros (Table 25.2). Each S_IS*xxx* macro uses the st_mode member as argument and returns true or false. For instance, S_ISREG checks for a regular file, and S_ISDIR checks for a directory. This is how you determine whether a file is a directory:

```
if (S_ISDIR(buf.st_mode)) printf("File is a directory\n");
```

These macros actually mask out the file type from `st_mode` with `S_IFMT` and then checks the residual value. We'll make use of the `S_IFMT` and `S_ISDIR` macros in our next program.

25.11.4 `lsdir.c`: Listing Only Directories

ls has no option to list only directories, but using the directory handling functions and the information in the `stat` structure, we can devise a program that does just that. This program, **lsdir.c** (Fig. 25.12), uses the `S_IFMT` mask and the `S_ISDIR` macro to display the file type, permissions and the name of every subdirectory of the directory name provided as argument. We are not recursively examining directories here.

As we have done in a previous program, **lls.c** (Fig. 25.10), we first have to obtain a pointer to a `DIR` structure with **opendir**, and then use **readdir** to return a pointer (`direntry`) to a `dirent` structure. *However, this time we must change to the directory with* **chdir** *before we use* **readdir**.

```
/* Program: lsdir.c --
                        Lists only directories - Uses S_IFMT and S_ISDIR macros */
#include <sys/types.h>
#include <sys/stat.h>
#include <stdio.h>
#include <dirent.h>

int main(int argc, char *argv[]) {
   DIR *dir;
   struct dirent *direntry;                /* Returned by readdir() */
   struct stat statbuf;                    /* Address of statbuf used by lstat() */
   mode_t file_type, file_perm;

   if ((dir = opendir(argv[1])) == NULL)
      quit("Couldn't open directory", 1);
   if ((chdir(argv[1]) == -1))             /* Change to the directory before */
      quit("chdir", 2);                    /* you starting reading its entries */

   while ((direntry = readdir(dir)) != NULL) { /* Read each entry in directory*/
      if (lstat(direntry->d_name, &statbuf) < 0) { /* dname must be in */
         perror("lstat");                          /* current directory */
         continue;
      }
      if (S_ISDIR(statbuf.st_mode)) {              /* If file is a directory */
         file_type = statbuf.st_mode & S_IFMT;
         file_perm = statbuf.st_mode & ~S_IFMT;
         printf("%o %4o %s\n", file_type, file_perm, direntry->d_name);
      }
   }
   exit(0);
}
```

Fig. 25.12 **lsdir.c**

Next, we extract the filename from direntry (direntry->d_name) and then use **lstat** to populate a stat structure (statbuf) with the attributes of the file. From this structure, we extract the st_mode member (statbuf.st_mode) and then use it with the S_ISDIR macro to filter out only directories. For each directory we find, we mask its st_mode value with S_IFMT and ~S_IFMT to obtain the file type and permissions. We print both along with the filename.

Note that the **chdir** call is essential because the d_name member of the dirent structure evaluates to a filename without slashes. Without **chdir**, **lstat** would look for the file in the current directory (when it shouldn't be). Let's run this program with the root directory as argument; a censored list is shown below:

```
$ a.out /
40000  755 .
40000  755 ..
40000  700 lost+found
40000  755 usr
40000  755 var
40000  755 export
40000  755 etc
40000  755 sbin
40000 1777 tmp                    The 1 shows the sticky bit is set
40000  755 .dt
```

The first character of the first field shows 4 (representing a directory) as the file type; the other four octal digits (here, 0000) have been masked out (with S_IFMT). The second field shows the file's permissions. Note the entry for tmp; it shows the sticky bit set for the directory. You now have a command that lists only directory names but also includes those beginning with a dot.

25.12 CHECKING A FILE'S ACCESS RIGHTS

There are a couple of mechanisms for checking a file's access rights. You can check each permission bit that's embedded in stat.st_mode, but that doesn't always have much meaning. A user running a program would often like to know whether she has the necessary access permissions without knowing the category (user, group or others) to which she belongs. We'll be discussing two ways of checking whether a file has the necessary permissions:

- By testing the individual members of the st_mode member of the stat structure. All the 12 permission bits can be tested in this way.
- Using the **access** system call, which looks at the *real* UID and *real* GID of the user running the program, and determines whether the file is accessible by the "real" user.

Both techniques have their advantages and limitations, but they can sometimes appear to contradict each other, so you must know the relationship between ownership and permissions well. We'll also make use of the SUID bit to highlight the distinction between real UID and effective UID, a point that was first raised in Section 17.3.2.

25.12.1 check_all_perm.c: Checking All 12 Permission Bits

In this section, we'll devise means to check every permission bit that's available in `stat.st_mode`. Recall from Section 25.11.2 that the `S_IFMT` mask has to be used in this way to extract the permissions from `st_mode`:

```
file_perm = statbuf.st_mode & ~S_IFMT;
```

To test for a specific permission, we need to AND `file_perm` with the symbolic constant that represents the permission. The expression returns true if the permission bit is on. For instance, to test a file for read permission for the others category, we should use this statement:

```
if (file_perm & S_IROTH)
```

Note that this is something we couldn't do with shell programming where all permission tests were applicable only to the *user* running the script. Let's use this feature to develop a program that tests a file for all 12 permissions. This program needs two functions to be developed. The first function, **`print_permissions`**, prints a file's permissions:

```
#include <stdio.h>
#include <sys/stat.h>
#include <unistd.h>

void print_permissions(char *fname, struct stat *addbuf) {
    if (lstat(fname, addbuf) < 0) {
        perror("stat");
        exit(1);
    } else
        printf("File: %s  Permissions: %o\n", fname, addbuf->st_mode & ~S_IFMT);
}
```

`print_permissions` takes the filename and address of a `stat` structure as its two arguments. It uses the **`lstat`** system call to populate the `stat` structure, `addbuf`. It prints the permissions obtained by masking `st_mode` with `~S_IFMT`. Store this code in the file **`print_permissions.c`**, and compile it with **`cc -c print_permissions.c`** to generate **`print_permissions.o`**.

The next function, **`check_permissions`**, ANDs the expression representing all permissions with the symbolic constant representing a specific permission. If the result is true, a message is printed on the terminal:

```
void check_permissions(int perm, int flag, char *message) {
    if (perm & flag)
        printf("%s\n", message);
}
```

`check_permissions` uses three arguments—the permissions portion of `stat.st_mode` (like 0644), the permission to be tested (like `S_IRUSR`) and a message. Store this function too in a separate file, **`check_permissions.c`**, and then use **`cc -c check_permissions.c`** to generate the object code for it.

Our main program, **check_all_perm.c** (Fig. 25.13), makes use of both functions. It initially uses **print_permissions** to display a file's permissions and then calls **check_permissions** 12 times in a loop. For compactness, the program uses two arrays. perm_flag[ ] holds the numeric values of the 12 permissions (like perm_flag[0] = S_IRUSR, i.e., 0400). *mesg[ ] is an array of pointers to character strings, each representing a permission-specific message that is printed. By delegating some tasks to the two functions, the program has become fairly easy to comprehend.

```
/* Program: check_all_perm.c -- Checks all 12 permission bits of a file */

#include <stdio.h>
#include <sys/stat.h>
#include <fcntl.h>

void print_permissions(char *, struct stat *) ;
void check_permission(int, int, char *);

int main(int argc, char *argv[]) {
   int i, fd, perm;
   char *filename = argv[1];
   struct stat statbuf;
   mode_t perm_flag[] = {S_IRUSR, S_IWUSR, S_IXUSR, S_IRGRP, S_IWGRP, S_IXGRP,
                         S_IROTH, S_IWOTH, S_IXOTH, S_ISUID, S_ISGID, S_ISVTX };

   char *mesg[] = {"User-readable", "User-writable", "User-executable",
                   "Group-readable", "Group-writable", "Group-executable",
                   "Others-readable", "Others-writable", "Others-executable",
                   "SUID bit set", "SGID bit set", "Sticky bit set" };

   print_permissions(filename, &statbuf);

   perm = statbuf.st_mode & ~S_IFMT;
   for (i = 0; i < 12; i ++)
      check_permissions(perm, perm_flag[i], mesg[i]);
}
```

Fig. 24.13 **check_all_perm.c**

Assuming that we have previously created the object files of the functions, let's compile this program first:

```
cc check_all_perm.c check_permissions.o print_permissions.o
```

Before running the program with each of the files, /usr/bin/passwd (the **passwd** command) and /etc/shadow, let's observe their listing:

```
$ ls -l /usr/bin/passwd /etc/shadow
-r--------    1 root     root         1055 Nov 21 15:59 /etc/shadow
-r-s--x--x    1 root     root        15368 May 28  2002 /usr/bin/passwd
```

The s in the permissions field of the listing of **passwd** shows thc SUID bit set. This is the bit that makes **passwd** run with the powers of root, the program's owner, even when it is invoked by a nonprivileged user. Let's see whether the output of the program matches the information in the permissions field:

```
$ a.out /usr/bin/passwd
File: /usr/bin/passwd  Permissions: 4511                    SUID is 4
User-readable
User-executable
Group-executable
Others-executable
SUID bit set
```

The first octal digit (4) in the four-octet permissions string signifies the presence of the SUID bit. The second octal digit (5) shows that the file has read and executable permission for the user. Now run this program on the other file:

```
$ a.out /etc/shadow
File: /etc/shadow  Permissions: 400
User-readable
```

True, the file is user-readable, but as a non-root user we can't read this file. More often than not, we need to know whether a file is accessible to *us* irrespective of the user category to which we belong. This is what **access** does and it is taken up in the next topic.

25.12.2 access: Checking the Owner's Permissions

The **access** system call looks at the real UID and real GID of the process, and lets you know whether the "real" user has the necessary access rights. It uses this syntax:

```
int access(const char *path, int amode);
```

The first argument is the pathname and *amode* specifies the access permission to be tested, which can be one or more of these four values:

R_OK—Read permission OK
W_OK—Write permission OK
X_OK—Execute permission OK
F_OK—File exists

Checking for specific permissions makes sense only when the file exists, and **access** is frequently used with F_OK to make the test for existence before continuing with the program. The program, **faccess.c** (Fig. 25.14), makes this check for multiple files.

The program uses a **for** loop to iterate through a list of command line arguments representing filenames. For each argument, it performs all four tests with **access**. We'll now find out the access rights a nonprivileged user has to /etc/passwd and /etc/shadow, and compare the output with the listing:

```
/* Program: faccess.c --
                Determines a file's access rights using the read UID and GID */
#include <unistd.h>

void quit(char *, int);
int main(int argc, char *argv[]) {
    short count;
    for (count = 1; count < argc; count++) {
        printf("%s: ", argv[count]);

        if (access(argv[count], F_OK) == -1)
            quit("File not found", 1);
        if (access(argv[count], R_OK) == -1 )
            printf("Not readable  ");
        if (access(argv[count], W_OK) == -1)
            printf("Not writable  ");
        if (access(argv[count], X_OK) == -1)
            printf("Not executable  ");

        printf("\n");
    }
    exit(0);
}
```

Fig. 25.14 **faccess.c**

```
$ ls -l /etc/passwd /etc/shadow
-r--r--r--   1 root     sys          9953 Nov 28 15:30 /etc/passwd
-r--------   1 root     sys          5425 Nov 28 15:30 /etc/shadow
$ a.out /etc/passwd /etc/shadow
/etc/passwd: Not writable  Not executable
/etc/shadow: Not readable  Not writable  Not executable
```

The listing shows that passwd is readable by all, but shadow is unreadable by group and others. It's obvious that the user running the program belongs to one of these two categories (probably, others), so **access** fails in the read test on shadow. This also implies that an attempt to open the file using the program represented by the **source, reverse_read2.c** (Fig. 25.6), should also fail:

```
$ reverse_read2 /etc/shadow
/etc/shadow: Permission denied
```

Yes, it does. **reverse_read2** here is the executable of **reverse_read2.c**. The story's not over yet; there's a way of making the file readable *with the same program* even though **access** will still fail in the read test. This is where the SUID bit comes in and is taken up next.

> **Note** You can OR the symbolic constants used by **access** to test for multiple permissions. For instance, **access("foo", R_OK | W_OK)** tests for both read and write permission.

25.12.3 How SUID Affects File Access

To continue with the exercise of making shadow readable by a nonprivileged user, let's assume for the two programs, **reverse_read2** and **faccess** (the executables for **reverse_read2.c** and **faccess.c**), considered in this section, that user sumit executes them and also owns them initially. To make **reverse_read2** work, we'll have to do two things—both from the root account:

1. Set the SUID bit of **reverse_read2**:

```
# chmod u+s reverse_read2 ; ls -l reverse_read2
-rwsr-xr-x   1 sumit    staff        7588 Feb 13 16:04 reverse_read2
```

2. Surrender the ownership of the file to root:

```
# chown root reverse_read2 ; ls -l reverse_read2
-rwsr-xr-x   1 root     staff        7588 Feb 13 16:04 reverse_read2
```

Now return from the superuser mode to the usual nonprivileged mode. With two important attributes changed, when you run this program now, *it's effective UID this time becomes the owner of the file, i.e. root*. And since root has permissions to open /etc/shadow, the program can now read the file:

```
$ read_reverse2 /etc/shadow
                                                  Blank line
::::::56021:2CLXPgOdqjMPz:mahtrap
::::::03021:UGqdYyX2fYEs/:atnasus
::::::60021:*:ptf                                 The ftp user
  ......
```

The SUID bit has made all the difference here; it enabled us to read shadow. But what happens if we try out a similar exercise with **faccess**? Let's go through the usual steps of using **chmod** and **chown** before running the program:

```
# chmod u+s faccess ; ls -l faccess
-rwsr-xr-x   1 sumit    staff      7464 Dec  7 19:00 faccess
# chown root faccess ; ls -l faccess
-rwsr-xr-x   1 root     staff      7464 Dec  7 19:00 faccess
# [Ctrl-d]                                        Quit superuser mode
$ echo $LOGNAME                                   What is our real UID?
sumit                                             Real UID is still sumit, and
$ faccess /etc/shadow                             sumit has no access to the file
/etc/shadow: Not readable  Not writable  Not executable
```

Unlike **reverse_read2**, the behavior of **faccess** is unaffected by the setting of the SUID bit. Even though **open** in **reverse_read2** could open the file, **access** in **faccess** still fails in spite of the fact that both **faccess** and **reverse_read2** have identical ownership and permission settings.

Setting SUID doesn't make any difference to the **access** system call since it uses the real UID, and not the effective UID, to determine the access rights. The real UID is still sumit (since sumit has run **faccess**), and sumit doesn't have access rights to /etc/shadow. It makes no difference to **access** that **faccess** is running with root as its effective UID.

> **Note** From the preceding discussions, we can conclude that there's no point in using **access** to check a file's access rights if the program using it has its SUID bit set. In such circumstances, it makes sense to use **open** and check whether it fails.

25.13 MODIFYING FILE ATTRIBUTES

Finally, let's terminate this chapter with a discussion on file attribute manipulation. The `stat` structure is useful for accessing a file's attributes but it can't be used to set them except in an indirect manner. To change these attributes, the system call library offers a number of calls, some of whom have identical command names:

- **link** and **unlink**—For creating a hard link and removing both a hard and symbolic link. This has already been discussed.
- **chmod** and **fchmod**—For changing file permissions.
- **chown**—This handles both ownership and group ownership.
- **utime**—This changes the file's modification and access times.

Each call in the list sets one or two file attributes to absolute values. Some of them (like **chmod** and **utime**) can be used in a relative manner also. For doing that, the general principle is to obtain the current value of the attribute from the `stat` structure and then add to or subtract from it.

25.13.1 chmod and fchmod: Changing File Permissions

There's nothing special to mention about these two calls except note that **chmod** identifies a file by its pathname while **fchmod** uses a file descriptor:

```
int chmod(const char *path, mode_t mode);
int fchmod(int fildes, mode_t mode);
```

The second argument (*mode*) represents the permissions and can be used by ORing any number of the symbolic constants listed in Section 25.2.1. For instance, to set permissions in an absolute manner, this is how you should use the **chmod** call:

```
chmod ("foo", S_IRUSR | SIWUSR | S_IRGRP)                Same as chmod 640 foo
```

Unlike the **chmod** command, the **chmod** system call can't be used *directly* to set relative permissions. You'll have to first extract the current permissions from `st_mode` and then use **chmod** with the bit-wise

- OR combination of the existing permissions and the specific permission to be assigned.
- AND combination of the existing permissions and the complement of the specific permission to be removed.

To consider an example, you can assign execute permission to `foo` in two steps:

```
lstat("foo", &statbuf);
chmod("foo", statbuf.st_mode | S_IXUSR);                 Adding a permission
```

To remove a permission, you have to use the AND operator with the complement of the permission. The first example below removes the user's execute permission, while the second one removes all permissions for the user:

```
chmod("foo", statbuf.st_mode & ~S_IXUSR);
chmod("foo", statbuf.st_mode & ~(S_IRUSR | S_IWUSR | S_IXUSR));
```

In a previous example *(25.12.3)*, we used the command **chmod u+s reverse_read2** to add SUID permission to the **reverse_read2** program. This can also be done in your C program but only if the program is run from the superuser account:

```
chmod("reverse_read2", statbuf.st_mode | S_ISUID);
```

> **Note** You may be wondering why we didn't use S_IFMT to extract the permissions from st_mode before applying **chmod**. Fortunately, **chmod** also accepts the entire st_mode (which includes the file type) as its second argument. However, you can't use this advantage to change the file's type. A file's type simply can't be changed in any way.

25.13.2 chown: Changing Ownership

Like its command counterpart, the **chown** system call is used to change both the owner and group owner. As with **stat**, there are three versions. One uses a pathname, the other a file descriptor and the third doesn't follow symbolic links:

```
int chown(const char *path, uid_t owner, gid_t group);
int fchown(int fildes, uid_t owner, gid_t group);
int lchown(const char *path, uid_t owner, gid_t group);
```

owner and *group* are represented by the numeric UID and GID, respectively. To change either the owner or group owner, set the unchanged argument to -1 (the first time we encounter -1 as an argument to a system call). Here are two examples:

```
chown("foo", 512, 100);          UID changed to 512, GID to 100
fchown(4, -1, 100);              UID unchanged, GID changed to 100
```

If the **chown** command can be used only by the superuser on your system, then the same restriction applies to the **chown** system call siblings also. Similarly, your system may permit changing your GID to only another group to which you also belong (supplementary group).

25.13.3 utime: Changing the Time Stamps

The last system call that we take up is **utime**. This call is used to change a file's modification and access times. It takes two arguments:

```
int utime(const char *path, const struct utimbuf *times);
```

The first argument is obviously the pathname. The second argument represents a pointer to a structure of type utimbuf. (Note the missing 'e'.) This structure contains two members of type time_t:

```
struct utimbuf {
    time_t actime                    Last access time
    time_t modtime                   Last modification time
};
```

These two members store the last access and modification time in seconds since the Epoch. To obtain the existing values for a file, you need to "stat" it and then examine the `st_atime` and `st_mtime` members in the `stat` structure. But to set them to different values, you'll have to populate the `utimbuf` structure before using **`utime`**.

25.13.4 atimemtime.c: Creating a File with Identical Time Stamps

Can you create a file having the same time stamps as another file using UNIX commands? It's not as easy as you might think, but our next C program, **`atimemtime.c`** (Fig. 25.15), makes the task look simple. It requires two filenames as arguments; the time stamps of the first file are used to set the stamps for the second.

```
/* Program: atimemtime.c --
                          Sets a file's time stamps to those of another file */
#include <sys/stat.h>
#include <fcntl.h>
#include <utime.h>

void quit(char *, int);
int main(int argc, char **argv) {
   struct stat statbuf;          /* To obtain time stamps for an existing file */
   struct utimbuf timebuf;       /* To set time stamps for another file */

    if (lstat(argv[1], &statbuf) == -1)
        quit("stat", 1);

    timebuf.actime  = statbuf.st_atime;   /* Setting members of timebuf with */
    timebuf.modtime = statbuf.st_mtime;   /* values obtained from statbuf */

    if (open(argv[2], O_RDWR | O_CREAT, 0644) == -1)
        quit("open", 2);
    close(argv[2]);                     /* Previously used open only to create it */

    if (utime(argv[2], &timebuf) == -1)   /* Sets both time stamps for file */
        quit("utime", 3);                 /* that was just created */
    exit(0);
}
```

Fig. 25.15 **`atimemtime.c`**

We first use **`lstat`** to fill up `statbuf` with the attributes of an existing file (`argv[1]`). Next, we populate the `utimbuf` structure with the two time stamps obtained from the previous **`lstat`** call. We open a second file (`argv[2]`), creating it if necessary, and then use **`utime`** to change its time stamps to the values in `timebuf`. This operation can be performed even if the file is not open; the file was opened simply to make sure that it's created if it doesn't exist.

Let's use this program to create a file with the same time stamps as one of the profiles—like `.profile`. Let's first see its time stamps:

```
$ cd ; ls -l ~/.profile ; ls -lu ~/.profile
-rw-r--r--   1 sumit    staff           61 Dec 12 20:14 .profile
-rw-r--r--   1 sumit    staff           61 Feb  2 12:33 .profile
```

The last access time for this file (obtained with **ls -lu**) is generally the time we logged in, and it's a good idea to save this time by creating another file with identical time stamps. We'll move the **a.out** executable to the home directory before running it:

```
$ mv a.out $HOME; cd ; a.out .profile .logintime
$ ls -l .logintime ; ls -lu .logintime
-rw-r--r--   1 sumit    staff            0 Dec 12 20:14 .logintime
-rw-r--r--   1 sumit    staff            0 Feb  2 12:33 .logintime
```

Note that the time stamps for the two files are identical. Using a C program, we have done something which we couldn't do using the UNIX commands and the shell.

25.14 CONCLUSION

In this chapter, we looked at the file system from a system programmer's point of view. We can now understand how commands like **cat** and **chmod** actually work. Moreover, using system calls we could do things that just can't be done using UNIX commands alone.

Though we discussed file descriptors, we didn't manipulate them. We must be able to open files in one process and pass on the descriptors to the child. We need to manipulate these descriptors to implement redirection and piping. To understand how all that is done, we need to know the process well. The programmer's view of the process is presented in the next chapter.

WRAP UP

A *system call* is a routine built in the kernel to perform a specific function that requires communication with the system's hardware. It switches the CPU to *kernel mode* from *user mode*. It generally returns -1 on error. *Library functions* are built on top of the system calls, but can't do everything system calls can do. System calls and library functions are documented in sections 2 and 3, respectively, of the UNIX manual.

open returns a *file descriptor* that is used by the other I/O calls. It sets the opening *mode* (O_RDONLY, O_WRONLY or O_RDWR) and *status flags* that can create (O_CREAT) or truncate (O_TRUNC) a file or allow data to be appended (O_APPEND). File permissions specified with O_CREAT are modified by the shell's umask setting unless the **open** call is preceded by **umask(0)**.

read and **write** use a user-defined buffer whose size should be set equal to the size of the kernel buffer for best performance. **lseek** simply moves the file offset pointer, and can take it beyond EOF to create a *sparse* file. Unlike **read**, **write** returns immediately even though the actual writing can take place later (unless **open** is used with O_SYNC).

All system calls set a global variable, errno, to a numeric value whose associated text can be printed with **perror** and **strerror**.

The kernel maintains three tables in memory when a file is opened. The *file descriptor table* stores all open descriptors along with a flag that determines whether the descriptor will be closed on an exec. The descriptor table points to a *file table* that stores the opening mode, status flags and the file offset. This table points to the *vnode table* that contains the inode information. The last two tables also maintain a reference count field.

Directories are usually handled with library functions because of the nonstandard format of the directory structure. **opendir** opens a directory to return a pointer to a DIR structure, which is subsequently used as argument by **readdir**. This function reads a directory entry to return a pointer to a dirent structure that contains the filename and inode number as its members. **chdir** changes the current directory and **getcwd** returns the pathname of the current directory.

Files can be hard linked (**link**) and symbolically linked (**symlink**), but **unlink** removes both. When **unlink** is invoked on an open file, the kernel removes the directory entry but its data blocks are deallocated only when the file is closed.

The inode information is maintained in the stat structure which is populated by **stat**, **lstat** and **fstat**. The file type and its permissions are maintained in a single field, st_mode, which can be split up into separate components using the S_IFMT mask. The S_IS*xxx* macros can be used to test for specific file types.

access tests a file's access rights (which includes the test for its existence) using the *real* UID and *real* GID of the process. The SUID bit affects accessibility. Setting this bit on a program and changing its ownership to root gives the program the power of the superuser.

The **chmod** and **chown** calls do the same jobs as their command counterparts. **utime** is used to set a file's access and modification time stamps using a structure of type utimbuf.

TEST YOUR UNDERSTANDING

Incorporate error checking wherever possible and relevant. File I/O operations are to be performed using only the **read** *and* **write** *system calls and not library functions.*

25.1 Explain the difference between *system calls* and *library functions*. What happens in the CPU when a system call is invoked?

25.2 What is a *file descriptor* and what is it used for? Name the system calls that return a file descriptor.

25.3 Specify how the **open** call is used to emulate the function performed by the shell's (i) > (ii) >> symbols.

25.4 Group the following symbolic constants into two categories and explain the significance of the categories: (i) O_RDONLY (ii) O_CREAT (iii) O_SYNC (iv) O_RDWR (v) O_TRUNC (vi) O_APPEND (vii) O_WRONLY. What is the role of the O_SYNC flag when using **write**?

25.5 What is the difference between the *file descriptor table* and *file table*? Will each entry in the descriptor table have a separate file table associated with it?

25.6 Write a program that displays the contents of a file in uppercase on the terminal using only system calls. The filename is supplied as argument. How will you find out the ASCII values of the alphabetic characters using another program?

25.7 How will you create a (i) file with permissions 666 (ii) directory with permissions 777? Use only symbolic constants to represent the permissions.

25.8 Write a program that accepts a directory name as argument and then checks whether it exists as a directory. If it doesn't exist or exists as an ordinary file, then remove the file and then create the directory. Also change to that directory and display the current directory.

25.9 Write a program that lists from the current directory all ordinary filenames whose size exists 100,000 bytes. Also remove all files whose size is 0 bytes.

25.10 Write a program that removes the read, write and execute permissions for others in all files owned by the user running the program. The directory name is provided as argument. (HINT: Use **getuid** to obtain your own UID.)

FLEX YOUR BRAIN

Incorporate error checking wherever possible and relevant. File I/O operations are to be performed using only the **read** *and* **write** *system calls and not library functions.*

25.1 Explain what an *atomic operation* is. How do you open a file and (i) truncate it if it exists (ii) create it if it doesn't? What is the advantage of using **open** to create a file instead of **creat** which is designed for only that purpose?

25.2 Write a program that copies a file and accepts the source and destination as its two arguments. The destination can also be a directory.

25.3 Modify the program in 25.6 (Test Your Understanding) so that it displays the output in lowercase when invoked by the name **lower** and uppercase when invoked by **upper**. What else do you need to do to run it?

25.4 Explain why the selection of the buffer size used by **read** and **write** is crucial in writing efficient programs.

25.5 Devise an advisory locking mechanism which allows two programs **lock1.c** and **lock2.c** to read a file `foo` only if the file `.lockfile` doesn't exist. Both programs will first create the file if it doesn't exist, and remove it before termination.

25.6 Write a program to split the contents of a file into multiple files so that each file contains at most 10,000 bytes. Name the files `foo.1`, `foo.2` and so forth.

25.7 Explain fully whether the following statement is true or not: It is possible to read and write a file even after it is deleted.

25.8 Write a program that moves a group of files to a directory. The file names are provided as arguments and the last argument is a directory. Provide adequate checks to ensure that the files exist and have the file type they are expected to. If the last argument doesn't exist, then create a directory by that name.

25.9 Write code to create a file `foo1` with the same permissions, modification time and access time as another file, `foo2`.

26

Systems Programming II— Process Control

The process abstraction enables us to understand the activities that take place in the computer. In this chapter—the second devoted to systems programming—we examine processes from the C programmer's point of view. We find here answers to some old questions. How can one program run another? How do we manipulate the shell's standard streams? How can we handle signals in our programs? We'll learn to do all that in this chapter, but only after we have enlarged our existing knowledge of processes acquired in Chapter 10.

To master the techniques of process control, we'll discuss the process control mechanism and associated data structures maintained by the kernel. We'll examine in some detail the fork-exec-wait cycle that will enable us to create processes using the system call library. We handled file descriptors in the previous chapter, but here we'll make use of the kernel's descriptor replicating properties to implement two important shell features—redirection and piping. Finally, we'll examine the elaborate signal handling mechanism and develop code that generates and handles signals.

WHAT YOU WILL LEARN

- Examination of the different segments of the *virtual address space* of a process and the role of the *Memory Management Unit* (MMU) in address translation.
- The other process abstractions—*user mode* and *kernel mode*, *context* and *context switching*.
- Analyze the control information held in the *proc* and *u area* structures.
- Use **fork** to create a process and study the environmental changes in the child.
- Terminate a process with **_exit** and **exit**, and examine the significance of the *exit status*.
- Use **wait** and **waitpid** to wait for a change of status in the child and gather its exit status from the process table.
- How the system handles *orphan* and *zombie* processes.
- Replace the existing process address space with a new program using the *exec* family of functions.
- Understand the attributes of a pipe and create a pipeline using the **pipe** system call.
- The basics of signal handling and the concept of signal *disposition*.
- Install *signal handlers* with **signal** and generate signals with **kill**.

TOPICS OF SPECIAL INTEREST

- Using **fork**, exec and **wait**, emulate shell behavior in executing a user-specified command line.
- Perform shell-like redirection using the **dup** and **dup2** system calls.
- Use **pipe** to run two commands in a pipeline.

26.1 PROCESS ABSTRACTIONS

Rather than consider a process as simply an instance of a program, it helps to to treat it as a sequence of instructions executed by the CPU. This act of execution involves constant interaction with the operating system and hardware. It also involves placing important parameters related to the current process in the CPU's hardware registers. The kernel preempts a process when its time slice expires (with some exceptions), and saves its state before it directs the next process to occupy the CPU and start running.

UNIX being a multiprogramming system, the kernel has to maintain several processes in memory, even though only one will be running at a time on a uniprocessor system. The kernel also maintains a number of data structures in memory, and we'll discuss the significance of two important ones—the *proc* structure and the *u area*—later in the chapter. To understand how the kernel manages processes, we'll have to understand some of the fundamental process abstractions—the *virtual address space*, process *modes* and *context*. They are considered next.

26.1.1 The Virtual Address Space

In general, processes have their origin in executable program files on disk. When you execute a C program that has been correctly compiled, the program loader transfers the binary code from the on-disk program to memory. That's not enough; the kernel has to create additional space in memory as and when needed by the process (for invoking functions, for instance). This collection of memory locations that the process can access is referred to as its *virtual address space*. This space is organized into a number of segments (Fig. 26.1):

- The *text segment* This segment contains the instructions to be executed. It is populated by a similar segment that is read in from the program's disk file. The text segment is marked read-only and can't be changed by the program. Multiple instances of one program will share this segment; three users running **vi** will all use a single text segment.
- *Initialized and uninitialized data segments* The initialized data segment represents the constants, global and static variables used in the program. Like for the text segment, the program's disk file contains the image of the initialized data segment. The program's header, however, specifies the *size* of the uninitialized data segment (often called the *bss* segment) which is created only during runtime.
- The *stack* The stack stores the arguments and local variables of functions as well as the address to return to. It grows and shrinks in size as functions are invoked and complete execution. Each time your program performs a function call, information about the location of the call, its arguments and local variables required in the function are created and saved in a block of data called a *stack frame*. The stack frames are manipulated using *push* and *pop* instructions.

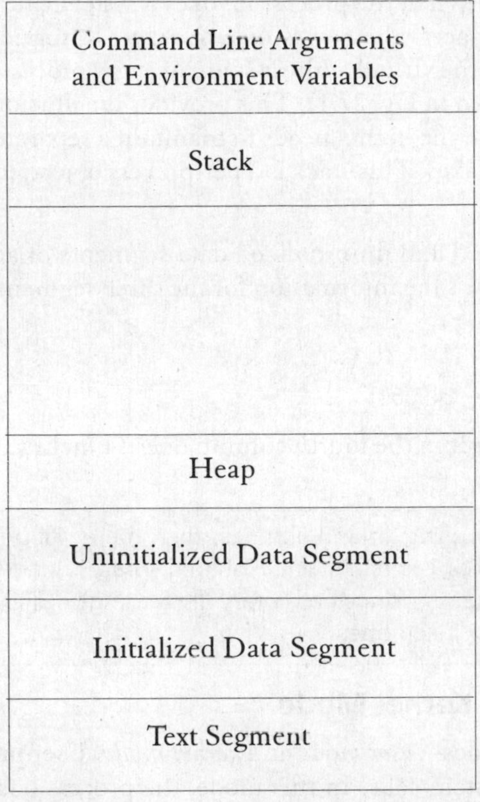

Fig. 26.1 The Process Virtual Address Space

- The *heap* This segment is used to dynamically allocate memory during program runtime (using functions like **sbrk**, **malloc** and **calloc**). The heap and stack are separated by unallocated space, and they grow at the expense of each other.
- Command line arguments and environment variables. These are generally found as the first entries in the stack (top in figure). Every process has an environment of its own though most of it is inherited from its parent.

The addresses of the process segments (text, data, stack, etc.) created by the linker are *virtual* because they don't point to physical memory locations. It is possible for all programs to have their virtual address space begin from address 0 and yet run without conflict. At runtime, the *Memory Management Unit* (MMU) converts these virtual addresses to nonconflicting physical memory locations using a set of *address translation maps*. The MMU contains a set of hardware registers that point to the translation maps of the currently running process. When the process changes, the MMU loads the registers with the translation maps of the next process. Because every process has its own set of translation maps, one process can't access another's address space.

The preceding discussions actually featured the *user address space*. It is a rather simplistic view because it ignores the kernel. When the process invokes a system call, the kernel runs on behalf of the user in its own address space—the *kernel address space*—to service the call. Since there's only one kernel running, a part of the virtual address space of every process also includes the kernel text and data structures (not shown in Fig. 27.1). This provides the illusion that every process includes a copy of the kernel. However, the kernel needs to maintain a separate stack—the *kernel stack*—to handle the function calls it makes. This stack is a per-process object; it is maintained separately for each process.

The size of the text, initialized and uninitialized data segments of any program can be obtained with the **size** command. Here's the information for the three segments (in that order) for the **nawk** command:

```
$ size /usr/bin/nawk
108255 + 18370 + 22438 = 149063
```

Note that the total requirement in the fourth column doesn't include the memory required by the stack and heap.

Note If your program is using shared libraries, then there will be a separate segment for it, located between the heap and stack. A shared library is loaded only once, but its address space is shared by all programs using that library. Increasingly, UNIX systems are using shared libraries rather than statically linked ones.

26.1.2 User Mode and Kernel Mode

A process can run in two modes—*user mode* and *kernel mode*. User programs run in user mode as long as they don't invoke system calls. In this mode, the process has access only to its own user address space described earlier. It can't access the kernel address space or even the address space of another process.

However, when the process invokes a system call, the processor moves to a more privileged mode—the kernel mode. In this mode, it's the kernel that is running on behalf of the user process and thus has access to the kernel's data structures. Once the system call returns, the processor switches back to user mode. (This view is actually an over-simplification. The kernel may not allow the current process to continue after the system call returns; it may schedule another process to run instead.)

It's not only a system call that switches the processor to kernel mode; *interrupts* and *exceptions* are also handled in this mode. Certain events that are external to the current process could request the attention of the CPU. This is an asynchronous event and causes what is known as an interrupt. For instance, when an I/O operation completes, the disk controller sends an interrupt to the kernel.

On the other hand, exceptions are generated as a direct result of the processor executing an instruction. A divide-by-zero operation in the processor is a synchronous event which generates an exception. A special instruction (called a *trap*) is required to invoke a system call. The kernel treats interrupts and exceptions in a uniform way; it suspends the current process and handles the exception.

26.1.3 Context Switching

Yet another process abstraction is its *context*. This represents the entire environment available to the process when it is running. You could treat the process context as the sum total of all information related to the running process that needs to be saved before the process vacates the CPU. This context has two components:

- *Hardware context* The CPU has a set of high-speed hardware registers which maintain important information on the state of the currently running process. One of them (the *program counter*) stores the address of the next instruction to be fetched. Yet another (the *stack pointer*) stores the address of the top-most element of the stack. Besides, the MMU registers that provide pointers to the translation maps of a process are also part of the hardware context.
- *Software context* This comprises the process address space and data structures that maintain the credentials of the process—like its PID, UID, file creation mask, table of file descriptors, signal handling information, and so forth. Most of this information is maintained by the kernel in two important structures—*proc* and *u area*—which will feature several times in this chapter.

When the time slice allotted to a process expires, the scheduler preempts the process to allow another one to occupy the CPU. The kernel saves the contents of the hardware registers in the *process control block* (a component of the u area—to be discussed shortly) and then makes a *context switch*. This switch also involves loading the MMU registers with pointers to the translation maps of the new process. With the previous state of the process restored by the context switch, the next process can resume execution from the point it was preempted.

Note When a process invokes a system call, there's a change of *mode* (user to kernel); the process remains the same. But when one process makes way for another, there's a change of *context*. A context switch is more expensive than a mode switch.

26.1.4 Process States

From the time a process is created and till it dies, a process can be in one of several states. The **ps -l** command (**ps aux** in Linux) lists many of these states:

```
$ ps -l
F S   UID   PID  PPID  C PRI NI      ADDR     SZ    WCHAN TTY      TIME CMD
19 T    0     0     0  0   0 SY       ?       0         ?         0:01 sched
 8 S    0     1     0  0  41 20       ?      97       ? ?         0:00 init
19 S    0     3     0  0   0 SY       ?       0       ? ?         0:26 fsflush
 8 O    0  1915  1912  0  51 20       ?     234         pts/7     0:00 ps
 .......
```

Observe the second column which shows many of these states as single-letter abbreviations (as S, O, T, Z etc.). We present below the various states of a process in an approximate sequence of its life cycle. At any instant, the process table shows a process as belonging to one of these states:

- *Created* This is the first stage every process has to go through when it is created with the **fork** system call. The process is not ready to run yet.
- *Ready-to-run* (or *Runnable*) In this state, nothing stops the process from running except that it has not yet been selected by the scheduler. A process can be in this state either in memory or in swapped state on disk. In case of the latter, the process has to first move to the ready-to-run state in memory before it can run.
- *Running* A process can be running in two modes here—user mode and kernel mode. However, after a process exits kernel mode (which it enters from user mode), it doesn't automatically revert to user mode. The kernel could preempt the process and place it in the ready-to-run state.
- *Sleeping* A process sometimes doesn't have anything to do in the kernel mode. When performing I/O for instance (using **read**) or when waiting for another process to complete (using **wait**), the process *voluntarily* gives up control of the CPU and moves to the sleeping state. The process is said to *sleep* on an event and when the event occurs, the kernel wakes up the sleeping process, which could then move to the ready-to-run state.
- *Suspended* A process can be suspended by pressing a key (usually, *[Ctrl-z]*) or by sending it the SIGSTOP signal.
- *Zombie* When a child dies, its address space is deallocated and it is immediately transformed into a zombie. (A zombie is a dead creature that is reanimated by magic.) The process remains in this state till the parent waits to receive its exit status. We'll consider zombies when we take up the **wait** system call.

Note that every process has to switch to the running mode only from the ready-to-run state. When a process relinquishes control of the CPU to execute an I/O or wait operation, the process has to move to the ready-to-run state before it can run again.

Note Even though normal UNIX functioning requires the kernel to preempt a process when its time quota expires, this is not so when the process is executing an I/O-bound system call. Generally a system call is allowed to complete, but if it keeps the CPU idle (when waiting for an I/O operation to complete, for instance), the process *voluntarily* gives up control of the CPU and moves to the sleeping state. The process is said to *block* (wait); we have a voluntary, not a preemptive context switch here.

26.2 proc AND u area: THE PROCESS CONTROL STRUCTURES

ps looks up two important per-process structures maintained by the kernel to obtain control information pertaining to one or more processes. We have alluded to these structures before in this chapter:

- The *proc* structure, which contains control information for a process that the kernel may need to look up any time—even when the process is not running.
- The *u area* (also known as user area) also contains control information, but on the currently running process.

Both structures are accessible only in the kernel mode. The proc structure is fairly large, occupying a thousand bytes or more, and contains the complete details of a process—either directly or through pointers to other structures. Among the important attributes are:

- The PID and PPID of the process.
- Location of the u area if it is not part of the proc structure itself.
- The state of the process—whether running, runnable, sleeping, zombie, and so forth.
- The scheduling priority. The kernel's process scheduler uses this value to determine the process that has to run next.
- The *pending signals mask*. This is a list of signals pending against the process. The process can know that it has received a signal only when it "peeks" into this field.

The global *process table* that we often refer to is simply an array of proc structures. Every active process is represented as an element of this array. Unlike the u area, which can be swapped to disk (for systems where it is maintained as a separate structure), the proc structure is always available in memory.

The u area contains process control information that the kernel needs to access only when the process is running. A forked child process also has a copy of this structure, the reason why the child's environment has a lot in common with it's parent's. Some of the important information held in the u area are:

- The real and effective UID and GID of the process.
- The *process control block* (PCB) that stores the saved hardware context including the contents of the MMU registers.
- A pointer to the proc structure for the process.
- Information on the current system call—its arguments, return value, etc.
- The file descriptor table with pointers to the respective file tables.
- The file creation mask.
- Pointers to the vnodes of the current directory, root directory and controlling terminal.
- Memory management information like the size of the text, data and stack segments.
- CPU usage information.
- A signal *disposition* table. It specifies the action to take when the process receives a signal.

In traditional UNIX implementations, the proc and u area were maintained as separate structures. In those days when memory was tight, its usage was optimized by having the u area as a separate structure that could even be swapped out to disk when memory ran low. With plentiful memory now available on modern systems, it no longer makes sense to maintain this division. Accordingly, both Solaris and Linux have the u area embedded in the proc structure in their latest implementations.

Note Both proc and u area maintain important data related to signals. A process knows that it has received a signal by looking up the pending signals mask in proc, but it is the u area that specifies the action to be taken in its disposition table. These are important events in the process life cycle, which we can fully appreciate when we take up signal handling at the end of this chapter.

26.2.1 process.c: Looking Up Some Process Credentials

Our first program, **process.c** (Fig. 26.2), displays some parameters that are held in the proc and u area structures. It displays the PID and PPID of the current process along with the ownership credentials. Six system calls are used here, and their names reflect their function.

```
/* Program: process.c -- Lists process and user credentials
                          The PID, PPID, real and effective UIDs and GIDs */

#include <stdio.h>
int main(void) {
     printf("PID : %4d, PPID: %4d\n", getpid(), getppid());
     printf("UID : %4d,  GID: %4d\n", getuid(), getgid());
     printf("EUID: %4d, EGID: %4d\n", geteuid(), getegid());
     exit(0);
}
```

Fig. 26.2 **process.c**

The process obtains its own PID and its parent's PID using the **getpid** and **getppid** calls. The program also prints the effective UID and GID, which normally are equal to the real UID and GID:

```
$ a.out
PID : 1035, PPID: 1028
UID :  102,  GID:   10
EUID:  102, EGID:   10
```

Real UID and GID are the same as their effective cousins

To understand how the SUID bit affects the effective UID, let's set the SUID bit of this executable from the superuser account and transfer the ownership to root. Confirm your actions by observing the listing:

```
# chmod u+s a.out ; chown root a.out ; ls -l a.out
-rwsr-xr-x    1 root      sumit       12211 Dec 17 09:49 a.out
```

Now quit the superuser mode and run the program again. The effective UID now becomes the owner of the file (root, whose UID is 0):

```
$ a.out
PID : 1041, PPID: 1028
UID :  102,  GID:   10
EUID:    0, EGID:   10
```

Recall that we had carried out a similar exercise with the program represented by **reverse_read2.c** in the previous chapter *(25.12.3)*. The SUID setting there allowed a nonprivileged user to read a file that is otherwise readable only by root.

26.3 CREATING A PROCESS

The basic mechanism of process creation was discussed in Section 10.4; we need to examine the concepts in some detail now. The entire process life cycle is built around four system calls—**fork,** exec (not a system call really), **wait** and **_exit**. It's important for the systems programmer to know how to create processes because many important functions can't be performed in a single process. For instance, to build a pipeline you need to create at least two processes.

26.3.1 fork: Replicating the Current Process

The forking mechanism uses the **fork** system call to create a process. Except for PIDs 0, 1, 2, and possibly 3, which the kernel creates "by hand", every process in the system owes its creation to **fork**. It has a simple syntax but returns in an unusual manner:

```
pid_t fork(void);
```
Creates child process

After **fork** returns, the parent and child now have different PIDs and PPIDs, and that's probably the only major difference between them. At this point, there are two processes with practically identical constituents, and they both continue execution at the statement *following* **fork** (code before **fork** ignored by child). To be able to distinguish between the original and its replica, **fork** returns twice with two different values:

- Zero in the child, which is safe because no process can be created with that PID.
- The PID of the child in the parent, so the parent can later access the child with this PID.

When **fork** is invoked, the kernel replicates the address space of the current process (its text, data, stack, etc.). The kernel also allocates a new proc structure for the child. Some fields of this structure are copied from the parent, and some are initialized to zero or other values. The kernel copies the u area of the parent but makes some changes here as well. Because the child runs in its own address space, it maintains an environment that is distinct from its parent's. We'll soon demonstrate this.

The u area contains the file descriptor table, which means that the child has separate copies of all descriptors allocated in the parent. *However, the original descriptor and its copy share the same file table.* This means that the file offset pointer set by an I/O operation in the parent is seen by the child using a copy of the descriptor. However, subsequently changing the entries of the descriptor table in one process won't have any effect on the other. We'll discuss the effect of **fork** on signal handling when we take up exec.

UNIX systems impose limits on the number of processes a user can create. Further, the size of the process table also places restrictions on the total number of processes that the machine can support. If an attempt to fork a process violates either of these restrictions, **fork** returns -1.

26.3.2 fork.c: A Simple Child Creation Program

You may find the behavior of **fork** a little confusing initially, so let's demonstrate its effect with a simple program, **fork.c** (Fig. 26.3). We simply fork a process and then use and **getppid** to obtain the PID and PPID of both parent and child.

Since **fork** returns two different values, we need to examine this return value to distinguish between parent and child. Observe from the output below that the first and second **printf** statements are executed in the parent, and the third one in the child. The final **printf** is executed by both processes. We'll discuss the significance of the **sleep** call after observing the output:

```
/* Program: fork.c -- A simple fork
                      Shows PID, PPID in both parent and child */
#include <stdio.h>
#include <sys/types.h>

int main (void) {
    pid_t pid;

    printf("Before fork\n");
    pid = fork();                    /* Replicates current process */

    if (pid > 0) {                   /* In the parent process; make sure */
        sleep(1);                    /* that parent doesn't die before child */
        printf("PARENT -- PID: %d PPID: %d, CHILD PID: %d\n",
                   getpid(), getppid(), pid);
    }
    else if (pid == 0)               /*In the child process */
        printf("CHILD -- PID: %d PPID: %d\n", getpid(), getppid());
    else {                           /* pid must be -1 here */
        printf("Fork error\n");
        exit(1);
    }

    printf("Both processes continue from here\n");      /*In both processes */
    exit(0);
}
```

Fig. 26.3 fork.c

```
$ a.out
Before forking
CHILD -- PID: 1556 PPID: 1555
Both processes continue from here                   This statement runs in child ...
PARENT -- PID: 1555 PPID: 1450, CHILD PID: 1556
Both processes continue from here                   ... as well as in parent
```

Note that the parent is aware of the PID of three generations, while the child has knowledge of two. In this program run on Solaris, the child runs first, but there's no guarantee that it will happen on every system. POSIX doesn't specify any sequence either. On Linux, the parent runs before the child, so you can't write programs based on the assumption that one runs before the other. We deliberately introduced the **sleep** call to ensure that the parent doesn't die before the child. The consequences of letting the parent die first are examined in Section 26.6.

Note As mentioned before, the process address space also provides for kernel text and data structures *(26.1.1)*. These structures include the kernel's I/O buffers (used by standard library functions like **printf**) allocated to the process. Forking copies the pointers to these buffers as well, which means that the same buffers are available to the child. This creates problems when using functions like **printf** with **fork**. Let's now understand how **printf** and **write** differ in their use of these buffers.

Unlike **write**, **printf** is *line-buffered* when writing to the terminal. This means that the buffer contents are written to the terminal only when a newline is encountered. **printf** is, however, *fully-buffered* when writing to disk; the buffer is written when it is full. You'll find the above program to behave differently when its output is redirected to a file. We'll see later how exec handles these buffers.

26.3.3 getenv and setenv: Handling Environment Variables

Forking also transmits the parent's environment to the child since environment variables are constituents of the process address space. These variables are available in the environ[] variable, which you may need to define in your C program like this:

```
extern char **environ;
```

Like argv[] (used as the second argument to **main**), this represents a pointer to an array of pointers to char, except that this array stores pointers to environment variable strings of the form *name=value*. POSIX specifies two functions, **getenv** and **setenv**, to obtain and set these values:

```
char *getenv(const char *name);
int setenv(const char *envname, const char *envval, int overwrite);
```

getenv returns a pointer to the value of a variable, whose string representation is passed to it as the *name* argument. For instance, you can obtain the current value of PATH in this manner:

```
char *path = getenv("PATH");                    Obtains value from environ[] variable
```

setenv uses three arguments; the first two are used to pass the variable name and value. The third argument, *overwrite*, determines whether an existing value of a variable will be overwritten. If the variable is already defined and *overwrite* is nonzero, its existing value is updated. However, the value is left alone if *overwrite* is zero. This is how you can reset the PATH variable to include only the current directory:

```
setenv("PATH", ".", 1);
```

BSD created **setenv**, and even though POSIX recommends its use, it is not available on many SVR4 systems including Solaris. If you don't find **setenv** on your machine, then use SVR4's **putenv** (not preferred by POSIX) which accepts a pointer to char as its only argument. The strings pointed to are of type *name=value*. The previous **setenv** call can be replaced with **putenv("PATH=.")**.

26.3.4 childenv.c: Studying the Environment

The following program, **childenv.c** (Fig. 26.4), demonstrates how the parent is affected by three changes made to a child's environment. First, we'll set a variable x in the parent and change it in the child. Next, we'll reset the environment variable PATH and change the current directory in the child. Henceforth, we'll be using a **switch** construct to separate parent code from child code.

We first obtain and print the current directory using **getcwd**. The **switch** statement tests for three possible types of return values from **fork**. The first checks for a **fork** error. Next, **switch** checks for a child, where we make three changes to the child's environment. We set x to 200, the PATH variable to a dot (with **setenv**), and change the current directory (with **chdir**). We also print some of the old and changed values as seen in the child.

```
/* Program: childenv.c -- Changes child's environment and then checks
                          the effect in parent */
#include <stdio.h>
#include <sys/types.h>
#define PATH_LENGTH 30

int main (void) {
    pid_t pid;
    int x = 100;
    char newdir[PATH_LENGTH + 1];      /* Additional space required for \0 */

    getcwd(newdir, PATH_LENGTH);       /*Get current directory before fork */
    printf ("BEFORE FORK -- Current directory: %s\n", newdir);

    pid = fork ();
    switch (pid) {
      case -1:
          perror("fork");                                  /* fork error */
          exit(1);                                         /* Parent exits */
      case 0:    /* Child */
          printf("CHILD -- Inherited value of x: %d\n", x);
          x = 200 ;                                        /* Change x in child */
          printf("CHILD -- Changed value of x: %d\n", x);
          printf("CHILD -- Inherited value of PATH: %s\n", getenv("PATH"));
          setenv("PATH", ".", 1);  /* Change PATH here; use putenv("PATH=.") */
                                   /* if setenv() not supported */
          printf ("CHILD -- New value of PATH: %s\n", getenv("PATH"));
          if (chdir("/etc") != -1) {                       /* "cd" to /etc */
              getcwd(newdir, PATH_LENGTH);                 /* Do a "pwd" */
              printf("CHILD -- Current directory changed to: %s\n", newdir);
          }
          break;
          exit(0);
      default:    /* Parent */
          sleep(2);                                      /* Allow child to complete */
          getcwd(newdir, PATH_LENGTH);                   /*Getting new directory */
          printf("PARENT -- Value of x after change by child: %d\n", x);
          printf("PARENT -- Current directory is still: %s\n", newdir);
          printf("PARENT -- Value of PATH is unchanged: %s\n", getenv("PATH"));
          exit(0);
    }
}
```

Fig. 26.4 **childenv.c**

Once again, we let the parent sleep for two seconds to ensure that the child dies before the parent continues beyond **fork**. Let's now check whether the changes made in the child's environment are visible in the parent:

```
$ a.out
BEFORE FORK -- Current directory: /users1/home/staff/sumit
CHILD -- Inherited value of x: 100
CHILD -- Changed value of x: 200
CHILD -- Inherited value of PATH: /usr/bin::/usr/local/bin:/usr/ccs/bin
CHILD -- New value of PATH: .
CHILD -- Current directory changed to: /etc
PARENT -- Value of x after change by child: 100
PARENT -- Current directory is still: /users1/home/staff/sumit
PARENT -- Value of PATH is unchanged: /usr/bin::/usr/local/bin:/usr/ccs/bin
```

It shouldn't surprise us that the changes made in the child are not visible in the parent; x still has the value 100, PATH retains its old value and the current directory remains /users1/home/staff/sumit. A child process maintains its own copies of these parameters..

Putting a parent to sleep for an arbitrary time interval isn't a satisfactory method of ensuring that the child dies before the parent. Ideally, in most situations, the parent should *wait* for the death of the child. This it does by invoking **wait**, which is taken up soon after discussing **exit** and **_exit**.

26.4 _exit AND exit: EXPLICIT PROCESS TERMINATION

Except for some daemon processes that live as long as the machine is up, most processes will eventually die. When a process dies, the kernel closes all open files and frees all memory associated with the process (like the address space and u area). Whether or not it also frees the process table entry (the proc structure) depends on whether the parent has waited for the child's death. Before we get into what exactly the parent waits for, let's first understand that a process can terminate in any of the following ways:

- By falling through to the end of the program. This happens when you don't include an explicit **exit** or **return** call in **main**. The process then invokes an implicit **return**.
- By an explicit **return** statement in the **main** function.
- By the **exit** function or **_exit** system call anywhere in the program.
- On receipt of a signal which may terminate the process.

We'll discuss signal handling later; in this section, we examine the **exit** library function and **_exit** system call. We have used **exit** in every C program used in this text. It's time to see what exactly **exit** does and how it differs from **_exit**. **_exit** is one of the four basic system calls used in the process life cycle. Both **_exit** and **exit** share an identical syntax:

```
void _exit(int status);
void exit(int status);
```

Both functions work in a manner similar to the shell's built-in **exit** command that is used in shell scripts. The **_exit** call closes all open files and terminates a process but doesn't bother about performing other cleanup operations. We generally avoid its use because **exit** internally calls **_exit** but not before it has

- Invoked all exit handlers that have been registered with the **atexit** function (not discussed in this text).
- Flushed all output streams.
- Removed all temporary files created with the **tmpfile** library function. **tmpfile** (not discussed in this text) creates a temporary file with a unique name which won't conflict with any filenames that you have.

When a process terminates by any of the methods described at the beginning of the section, the kernel sends a signal (SIGCHLD) to the parent informing it of the child's death. If termination is on account of invoking **exit** (or **_exit**), the argument used with **exit** eventually finds its way to the proc structure in the process table. This value, called the *exit status*, is picked up by the parent by invoking the **wait** or **waitpid** system call. We'll soon discuss how this value is actually extracted from an argument used with **wait** or **waitpid**.

> **Note** The shell's **exit** command and the **exit** and **_exit** calls in a C program often return control to the shell. In the shell, the exit status is stored in the shell variable `$?` (`status` in the C shell).

26.5 WAITING TO PICK UP CHILD'S EXIT STATUS

After a process has forked a child, more often than not, it is followed by a call to exec. You know what exec does; it replaces the child's address space with that of a new program *(10.4)*. We'll be taking up exec shortly, but note that regardless whether a call to exec is finally made or not, the two processes run independently. So what does the parent do while the child executes? It can do two things:

- Wait to gather the child's exit status.
- Continue execution without waiting for the child (and pick up the exit status later, if at all).

The first is the normal shell behavior when we enter a command. The shell exhibits its nonwaiting role when it runs a job in the background. The two system calls involved in waiting are **wait** and **waitpid**. **waitpid** is much more powerful than **wait** and can also emulate **wait** behavior by using a special syntax. We take up **wait** first.

26.5.1 wait: Waiting for Death of Child

When a child terminates, its exit status is placed along with other information in the process table. The parent picks up this exit status using the **wait** system call. The call uses a pointer to an `int` variable as its only argument:

```
pid_t wait(int *stat_loc);
```

When there's at least one child process running, **wait** blocks till a child dies. It then returns the PID of the first dying child and places its exit status in *stat_loc*. The kernel writes a process accounting record to a log file and clears the slot in the process table that was allocated to the child. The parent then resumes operation with the statement following **wait**. The exit status of other children (if any) can't be obtained by the parent when they die unless it invokes **wait** again—and as many times as there are children.

The variable *stat_loc*, representing the *termination status*, doesn't contain only the exit status but some other things as well—like the process state and the signal that caused the process to be in that state. Separate macros are available to obtain the complete information. The exit status itself is stored in the least eight significant bits of *stat_loc*. The WEXITSTATUS macro used with *stat_loc* as argument fetches this value.

> **Note** Even though we explained the use of **wait** with reference to a dying child, **wait** is not merely concerned with death of a process but a change in its state. This can be caused by, say, a signal suspending a process. The termination status stores both the state and the signal responsible for the change. Apart from WEXITSTATUS, there are other macros available to fetch additional information from *stat_loc*. For more details, use **man 2 wait** or **man -s2 wait**.

26.5.2 wait.c: Using wait and WEXITSTATUS

In this program, **wait.c** (Fig. 26.5), the parent opens a file and writes one line of data to it. After forking, the child writes one more line to the same file. This should be possible since the child inherits the parent's file descriptors. Meanwhile, the parent waits for the child to die, and when it does, it invokes the WEXITSTATUS macro to gather the exit status from the process table. Finally, the parent writes a third line to the file.

```
/* Program: wait.c -- Uses wait to obtain child's termination status.
                      The WEXITSTATUS macro fetches the exit status. */
#include <stdio.h>
#include <fcntl.h>
#include <sys/wait.h>
   int main (int argc, char **argv) {
   int fd, exitstatus;
   int exitval = 10;              /* Value to be returned by child */

   fd = open(argv[1], O_WRONLY | O_CREAT | O_TRUNC, 0644);
   write(fd, "Original process writes\n", 24);      /* First write */
     switch(fork()) {
      case 0:
          write(fd, "Child writes\n", 13);         /* Second write */
          close(fd);              /* Closing here doesn't affect parent's copy */
          printf ("CHILD: Terminating with exit value %d\n", exitval);
          exit(exitval);          /* Can also use _exit(exitval) */
     default:
          wait(&exitstatus);      /* Waits for child to die */
          printf ("PARENT: Child terminated with exit value %d\n",
                 WEXITSTATUS(exitstatus));         /* Extracting exit status */
          write(fd, "Parent writes\n", 14);        /* Third write */
          exit(20);               /* Value returned to shell; try echo $? */
   }
}
```

Fig. 26.5 wait.c

This time, we used the **write** call three times in this program. In each case, we had to specify as **write**'s third argument, the length of the string written to the file. The filename itself is obtained as a command line argument. We have raised concerns about the sequence of operations before—whether the parent runs first or the child runs first after the fork. Once we use **wait**, such concerns disappear as the parent can't continue execution till the child dies.

Let's now run this program with a filename as argument and then observe the sequence in which the three lines appear:

```
$ a.out foo
CHILD: Terminating with exit value 10
PARENT: Child terminated with exit value 10
$ cat foo
Original process writes
Child writes
Parent writes
```

This sequence (child first and then parent)—observed both in the display as well as in the file's contents—is invariant across all UNIX and Linux machines. We have been able to run the parent in synchronism with the child. We have also achieved a rudimentary form of *inter-process communication* (IPC); the parent knows the child's exit status.

26.5.3 waitpid: A More Powerful Waiting Mechanism

wait suffers from a number of limitations. It blocks till a child dies, and there's nothing that the process invoking it can do till that happens. Further, if a parent spawns several children, **wait** returns the moment one of them dies; it can't wait for a process with a specific PID to die. Finally, **wait** can't handle *process groups* (discussed in the next section).

Overcoming these limitations is important in process management, and for these reasons the use of **waitpid** is recommended over **wait**. **waitpid** takes three arguments:

```
pid_t waitpid(pid_t pid, int *stat_loc, int options);
```

The second argument, *stat_loc*, has the same significance as in **wait**; the termination status of the process is stored there. The *options* setting enables **waitpid** to run in nonblocking mode, but there are other functions. The *pid* can take four types of values:

- If *pid* is -1, **waitpid** blocks till a child dies or changes state.
- If *pid* > 0, **waitpid** waits for a specific process with *pid* as its PID.
- If *pid* = 0, **waitpid** waits for any process belonging to the same *process group* as the process invoking the call. (Process groups are explained in the next section.)
- If *pid* < -1, **waitpid** waits for any process whose PGID is the same as the absolute value of *pid* (PGID is *process group-id*, and is explained in the next section).

The behavior of **waitpid** is also controlled by the *options* setting. This can be zero or a bit-wise OR of the constants WNOHANG, WUNTRACED and WCONTINUED. We consider only the two following settings of *options*:

- If *options* is 0, **waitpid** blocks till the child changes state, but the behavior of the process is also influenced by the way *pid* is specified.
- If *options* is set to WNOHANG, **waitpid** behaves in a nonblocking manner; it returns immediately regardless whether a child has changed state or not.

For emulating **wait(&status)**, we need to use **waitpid(-1, &status, 0)**. The advantages of using **waitpid** over **wait** now seem quite obvious. **waitpid** need not block till a child dies, it can wait for a child with a specific PID to die and it can also handle process groups. We'll use **waitpid** in an example later in the chapter.

26.6 PROCESS GROUPS

waitpid works with process groups, so let's understand what they are. Every process belongs to a *process group* (a Berkeley feature that lets you control a group of processes working for a common cause). Each process in the group has the same *process group-id* (PGID). The group has a leader whose PGID is the same as its PID. UNIX provides tools—both at command and system call level—to manipulate process groups. The **waitpid** system call can be made to wait for any member of a process group to die. The **kill** system call can also send a signal to all processes in a process group.

The shell's handling of the process groups of its children depends on whether it supports job control. In the Bourne shell, a command run from the shell has the same PGID as the shell itself. That is not so in the other three shells (C shell, Korn and Bash) supporting job control where every command is placed in its own process group. A pipeline that represents a job in these three shells also forms a process group.

You can have several process groups in a *session*, but only one of them would be a *foreground process group*; the rest would be *background process groups*. A foreground process group is directly connected to the session's controlling terminal. This means that you can use your keyboard to input data to the processes in the group as well as send them signals. When you press *[Ctrl-c]*, all processes in the foreground process group receive the SIGINT signal and respond accordingly (usually, terminate).

A background process group can't be sent signals from the terminal though they can receive signals by other means (with **kill**, for instance). A background process group may or may not be allowed to write to the terminal depending on how the system is set up, but if it tries to read from the terminal, then the terminal driver notices this and immediately issues a signal to suspend the process group. This explains why you can't use the **vi** editor in the background with **vi foo &**.

26.7 ZOMBIES AND ORPHANS

Though the normal shell behavior is to wait for a child to die, that is not always practicable. With most shells today supporting job control, it is usual for a process or process group to be in the background or remain in a suspended state. However, there are two things that can happen if the parent doesn't wait for the child to die:

- The child dies while the parent is still alive.
- The parent dies while the child is still alive.

If the child dies first, the normal rules apply; the kernel empties the address space and all registers associated with the process, but retains an entry in the process table that contains the child's exit status and some accounting usage information. The child is said to be in a *zombie* state, and recall this is one of the states *(26.1.4)* a process can be in.

A zombie is actually not a process at all, so you can't kill it. It can be considered to be simply a remnant of a process. Zombies are not harmful, but too many zombies can eat into the available slots of a process table, which is of a finite size. The only reason for a child to remain in the zombie state is the "hope" that the parent may eventually call **wait** or **waitpid** to pick up the exit status and clear the process table slot. The **ps** output shows zombie processes as the string <defunct> in the last column. If too many zombie processes develop on a machine, a system reboot may be required to clear them.

The situation changes significantly when the parent dies before the child. The child then becomes an *orphan* since the parent isn't just there to pick up its exit status. The kernel clears the process table slot of the parent, but before doing so, it checks whether there are any processes spawned by the parent that are still alive. When it finds one, it makes **init** its parent by changing the PPID field of the child in the proc structure. This is what happens when we run a job with **nohup** and then kill the shell by logging out *(10.6.2)*.

The following program, **orphan.c** (Fig. 26.6), also creates an orphan but doesn't require us to log out. Here, the parent exits immediately after creating the child. The child sleeps for two seconds to let the parent die and then prints a message.

```
/* Program: orphan.c -- Creates an orphan by letting child sleep for 2 minutes
                        Parent doesn't call wait and dies immediately */
#include <stdio.h>
int main(void) {
    int pid;
    if ((pid = fork()) > 0)          /* Parent */
       exit(10);                     /* Parent exits without calling wait */
    else if (pid == 0) {             /* Child */
       sleep(2);                     /* Lets parent die in this time frame */
       printf("CHILD: Adopted by init now, PPID: %d\n", getppid());
       exit(0);
    }
}
```

Fig. 26.6 **orphan.c**

After running the program, let's check the exit status as returned by the program to the shell:

```
$ a.out
   ...no response for 2 seconds...
CHILD: Adopted by init now, PPID: 1
$ echo $?
10
```

Note how **init** acquired the parentage of the child process. It's the parent, not the child, that returned the exit status to the shell. The child returned its own exit status to **init** *without* **init** *waiting for it*. **init** is so designed that it can run numerous child processes without blocking, but is smart enough to collect the exit status of its children as and when they die. You can do that too in your programs.

> **Note** **init** relies on a signaling mechanism to know when a shell dies. When a user logs out, her shell terminates and the kernel sends a `SIGCHLD` signal to **init**. **init**'s signal handler then immediately fork-execs a **getty** at that terminal to display the `login` prompt. This has already been discussed before *(10.4.1)*.

26.8 exec: THE FINAL STEP IN PROCESS CREATION

Forking is an essential phase of process creation, but more often than not, we don't stop at fork. We want to run a separate program in a forked process. This is done by doing an *exec*. This operation replaces the entire address space of a process (the text, data and stack) with that of the new program. Since the stack is also replaced, the call to exec doesn't return unless it results in an error. The forking mechanism is responsible for creating processes, but it's exec that actually executes programs on a UNIX system.

Many of the attributes inherited during a fork don't change with an exec. For instance, the previous program's file descriptors, the current and root directory, umask settings and the environment remain the same (though file descriptors can be closed if we want, and a different environment can be specified). Since no new process is created, the PID doesn't change across an exec. However, note the contrasting behavior of exec compared to **fork** with regard to the following:

- exec preserves the *pending signals mask* stored in the proc structure *(26.2)*. The term is used to mean a list of signals that have been been received but not delivered to a process. **fork** clears the pending signals mask.
- exec modifies the signal *disposition* stored in the u area *(26.2)*. The term is used to describe the action a process takes on receipt of a signal. The exact nature of change is discussed in Section 26.12.2 (in the Note). **fork** retains the existing disposition.
- exec overwrites the kernel's I/O buffers, so make sure that you flush them before using exec. **fork** inherits all I/O buffers which creates problems when using **printf** *(26.3.2—Note)*.

The exec operation can be performed by six members of a family of one system call and five library functions, which we'll refer to simply as "exec" or the "exec family". There's no system call named exec; rather, there's only one—**execve**, on top of which five library functions are built.

The entire set can be grouped into two parts, which we'll call the "execl" set and the "execv" set, because the function names begin with the string exec followed by either an `l` or a `v`. Two of the members also have the names **execl** and **execv**; the other four are simple derivatives of them and have more similarities than differences.

> **Tip** First, commit to memory this simple statement: The `l` in **execl** (and its variants) represents a fixed *list* of arguments, while the `v` in **execv** (and its variants) signifies a *variable* number of arguments.

26.8.1 execl: The Key Member of the "l" Series

As noted in the Tip above, **execl** is used with a list comprising the command name and its arguments:

```
int execl(const char *path, const char *arg0, ... /*, (char *) 0 */);
```

The syntax may appear daunting, but it is not; in fact, it is quite simple. We use **execl** when we know the number of arguments in advance. The first argument is the pathname (*path*) which could be an absolute or a relative pathname. The arguments to the command to run are represented as separate arguments beginning with the name of the command (**arg0*). The ellipsis representation in the syntax (... /*) points to the varying number of arguments.

To consider an example, here's how we use **execl** to run the **wc -l** command with the filename foo as argument:

```
execl("/bin/wc", "wc", "-l", "foo", (char *) 0);
```

execl doesn't use PATH to locate **wc**, so we must specify the pathname as its first argument. *The remaining arguments are specified exactly in the way they will appear as* **main**'s *arguments in* **wc**. So, argv[0] in **wc**'s **main** is wc, the name of the command itself.

Why a Null Pointer is Required To understand why we follow the argument list with a null pointer ((char *) 0), let's first understand how arguments are passed to a C program. By convention, we use this syntax for **main** when a program is run with arguments:

```
int main(int argc, char **argv) {
```

The startup routine that eventually runs **main** populates argv[] (pointer to an array of pointers to char) with the string arguments specified in the command line. A null pointer is also placed at the end of the array. The number of arguments (excluding the null pointer) is then evaluated and assigned to argc. When **main** runs, it knows the number of arguments passed to it.

When we use exec to run a program, there's no provision to specify the number of arguments (no argc); exec has to fill up argc "by hand." The only way for **execl** to know the size of the argument list is to keep counting till it encounters the null pointer. That's why this pointer must be specified in every member of the **execl** series.

```
/* Program: execl.c -- Uses execl to run wc */
#include <stdio.h>
int main (void) {
    execl ("/bin/wc", "wc", "-l", "-c", "/etc/passwd", (char *) 0);
    printf ("execl error\n");
}
```

Fig. 26.7 **execl.c**

Let's use **execl** in our next program, **execl.c** (Fig. 26.7), to run the **wc -l -c** command with /etc/passwd as argument. Because a successful **execl** never returns, the **printf** statement is not executed:

```
$ a.out
     166    9953 /etc/passwd
```

We can also use NULL in place of (char *) 0. Note that to be able to use **execl**, we must know the number of arguments in advance because each argument is specified as a separate argument to **execl**. Often, the size of the argument list is known only at runtime. The solution is **execv**, which we'll take up next. We'll take up the two derivatives of **execl** (**execlp** and **execle**) after we have covered **execv**.

26.8.2 execv: The Key Member of the "v" Series

To be able to run a command with any number of arguments, you must use one of the functions of the "execv" set. In this section, we discuss the **execv** function before we discover the advantages that are often found in its variants. **execv** needs an array to work with:

```
int execv(const char *path, char *const argv[]);
```

Like in **execl**, *path* represents the pathname of the command to run. The second argument is a pointer to an array of pointers to char (of the same type as **main**'s argv[]). The array has to be populated by addresses that point to strings representing the command name and its arguments in the form they are passed to the **main** function of the program to be exec'd. In this case also, the last element of *argv*[] must be a null pointer.

```
/* Program: execv.c -- Stuffs all command line arguments to an array
                       to be used with execv */
#include <stdio.h>
int main (int argc, char **argv) {
   char *cmdargs[] = { "grep", "-i", "-n", "SUMIT", "/etc/passwd", NULL };
   execv ("/bin/grep", cmdargs);                      /* Execute another program */
   printf ("execv error\n");
}
```

Fig. 26.8 execv.c

We'll use **execv** in the next program, **execv.c** (Fig. 26.8), to run the **grep** command with two options to look up the author's name in /etc/passwd. In this program, we populate the array cmdargs[] with the strings comprising the command line to be executed by **execv**. Note that the first argument to **execv** still remains the pathname of the command. Here's the run:

```
$ a.out
15:sumit:x:102:10::/users1/home/staff/sumit:/usr/bin/bash
```

You might say that this sequence could have been run by **execl** also, but observe the way we used **execv** in the program. Since we pass the address of an array element as its second argument (cmdargs being the same as &cmdargs[0]), it implies that we can input *any* command line during runtime. Our next program will be used in that way.

26.8.3 exec_and_fork.c: Running exec in a Child Process

The previous two programs used **execl** and **execv** in the current process. We normally don't use exec like this; often we do an exec in a child process so that the parent is free to do what it likes. In the following program, **exec_and_fork.c** (Fig. 26.9), the command line to execute is specified as the program's arguments. We also fork a process, run **execv** in the child and then make the parent wait for the child's death.

```
/* Program: exec_and_fork.c.c --
                              Uses fork, exec and wait to run a UNIX command */
#include <stdio.h>
#include <wait.h>

int main (int argc, char **argv) {
   int returnval ;                       /* Used by wait */

   switch(fork()) {
      case 0:                            /* Run command in child */
         if ((execv (argv[1], &argv[2]) < 0)) {
             fprintf(stderr, "execl error\n");
             exit(200);
         }
      default:                           /* In the parent */
         wait(&returnval);               /* After the command has completed ... */
         fprintf(stderr, "Exit status: %d\n", WEXITSTATUS(returnval));
         exit (0);
   }
}
```

Fig. 26.9 exec_and_fork.c

Here we take advantage of the facilities available in a program's startup routine to fill up **main**'s argv[]—including the null pointer at the end. We didn't bother about including the null pointer here because that is automatically done when you pass command line arguments to a program. Instead, we pass the absolute pathname of the command to run as the first argument, and the *entire* command line as the remaining arguments. This command line is accessed by **execv** as the address of argv[2]. The program doesn't terminate immediately after exec in the way the previous two programs did:

```
$ a.out /bin/grep grep -i -n SUMIT /etc/passwd
15:sumit:x:102:10::/users1/home/staff/sumit:/usr/bin/bash
Exit status: 0
```

The shell does a similar thing with our input except that we don't provide input to the shell in the way we did above. Even if we ignore this program's inability to handle redirection and wild-card interpretation, it still has the following drawbacks:

- We need to know the location of the command file because neither **execl** nor **execv** will use PATH to locate it.
- The command name is specified twice—as the first two arguments.
- These calls can't be used to run a shell script but only binary executables.
- The program has to be invoked every time we need to run a command.

To be able to run programs in a simpler and easier way, we need to discuss the derivatives of **execl** and **execv**. There are four of them, and after we examine them in the next section, we 'll use one of them to design a rudimentary shell program that has none of the limitations presented above.

26.8.4 The Other Members of the "l" and "v" Series

execlp *and* **execvp** The requirement to provide the pathname of the command makes the previous exec calls somewhat inconvenient to use. Fortunately, help is at hand in the form of the **execlp** and **execvp** functions that use PATH to locate the command. They behave exactly like their other counterparts but overcome two of the four limitations discussed in the previous section. First, the first argument need not be a pathname; it can be a command name. Second, these functions can also run a shell (or **awk** or **perl**) script. Here's their syntax:

```
int execlp(const char *file, const char *arg0, ... /*, (char *)0 */);
int execvp(const char *file, char *const argv[]);
```

Note that *pathname* has now become *file*; the other arguments remain the same. To show how **execlp** works, just replace the line containing the **execl** call in the program **execl.c** (Fig. 26.7), with this one:

```
execlp("wc", "wc", "-l", "foo", (char *) 0);
```

Now the first and second arguments are the same. To run the program, **execv.c** (Fig. 26.8), that uses **execv**, just change **execv** to **execvp** without disturbing the arguments. When running it, the first two command line arguments can again be the same. You'll find these calls easier to work with.

> **Note** To run shell, **awk** or **perl** scripts with exec, use **execlp** or **execvp**. By default, exec spawns a Bourne shell to read the commands in the script, but you can override that by providing an interpreter line at the top of the script. For instance, if you have #!/bin/ksh as the interpreter line, exec will call up the Korn shell.

execle *and* **execve** All the previous four exec calls silently pass the environment of the current process to the exec'd process by making available the environ[] variable to the overlaid process. Sometimes, you may need to provide a different environment to the new program—a restricted shell, for instance. In that case we need to use the remaining members of the exec family, **execle** and **execve**:

```
int execle(const char *path, const char *arg0, ... /*,
          (char *) 0, char *const envp[]*/);
int execve(const char *path, char *const argv[], char *const envp[]);
```

Unlike the other four members, both **execle** and **execve** use an additional argument to pass a pointer to an array (*envp*[ ]) of environment strings (of the form *variable=value*) to the program. It's *only* this environment that is available in the exec'd process, not the one stored in environ[ ].

We are back to *path* once again; these functions behave more like **execl** and **execv** in that they use the command pathname as the first argument. However, they retain one advantage of **execlp** and **execvp**: They can run a shell script too provided the script contains an interpreter line The last one, **execve**, is the only system call in the exec family; the others internally invoke **execve**.

26.9 shell.c: A PROGRAM WITH A SHELL-LIKE CAPABILITY

We'll now round up discussions on process creation by devising a program, **shell.c** (Fig. 26.10), that mimics the shell's behavior in executing a command that is input by the user. The parent repeatedly displays a prompt, and **execvp** is run with user input in a child process. To keep things simple, we define arrays of fixed sizes so that the following restrictions apply: Command lines can't be longer than 200 characters and the number of arguments can't exceed 40. The program doesn't permit use of the special characters, so no redirection and piping are allowed.

The program first initializes the arrays, buf and clargs, and then prints the Shell> prompt. It then reads user input into the buffer buf. The program terminates if the user enters **exit**. The **strtok** (string tokenizer) function then parses the command line (buf, its first argument) on whitespace (DELIM, its second argument). The function is a little unusual; in the first call, it returns the first word which is assigned to clargs[0]. However, subsequent calls to **strtok** will return the other words only if the first argument is null. After clargs[ ] is populated with the words extracted from user input, a null pointer is automatically added because it's only by doing that can control break out of the **while** loop. The program now knows the number of elements of clargs[ ] to read.

Next, the process forks and runs **execvp** in the child, using the arguments that were obtained with **strtok**. The parent waits for the child's death and prints the exit status every time a command is run. Here's a sample run:

```
$ a.out
Shell> grep joker /etc/passwd
Exit status of command: 1                     grep returns 1 if pattern not found
Shell> date
Mon Mar 10 16:18:28 IST 2003
Exit status of command: 0
Shell> pwd                                    Is this the shell builtin?
/users1/home/staff/sumit
Exit status of command: 0
Shell> ls -lu /usr/bin/pwd                    Now check the access time of on-disk pwd
-r-xr-xr-x   1 root     bin                   4360 Mar 10 16:18 /usr/bin/pwd
Exit status of command: 0                     Disk file has just been accessed!
Shell> exit
$ _
```

This "shell" runs all external commands using **execvp**. Note how the program correctly prints the exit status after executing each command. The exec calls can't execute shell builtins (because there's

```
/* Program: shell.c - Accepts user input as a command to be executed. Uses
                      the strtok library function for parsing command line */
#include <stdio.h>
#include <unistd.h>
#include <string.h>                          /* For strtok */
#include <wait.h>

#define BUFSIZE 200                          /* Maximum size of command line */
#define ARGVSIZE 40                          /* Maximum number of arguments */
#define DELIM "\n\t\r "                      /* White-space delimiters for strtok */

int main (int argc, char **argv) {
    int i, n ;
    char buf[BUFSIZE+1];                     /* Stores the entered command line */
    char *clargs[ARGVSIZE];                  /* Stores the argument strings */
    int returnval ;                          /* Used by wait */
    for (;;) {                               /* Loop forever */
        n = 1;
        for (i = 0; i <ARGVSIZE; i++)        /* Initialize both the argument array */
            clargs[i] = "\0";                /* with address of NULL character */
        for (i = 0; i <= BUFSIZE; i++)       /*... and buffer that stores command */
            buf[i] = '\0';                   /* with NULL characters */
        write(STDOUT_FILENO, "Shell> ", 7);  /* Display a prompt */
        read(STDIN_FILENO, buf, BUFSIZE);    /* Read user input into buf */
        if (!strcmp(buf, "exit\n"))
            exit(0);                         /* Terminate if user enters exit */
                                             /* Now parse buf to extract the */
        clargs[0] = strtok(buf, DELIM);      /* first word */
                                             /* Continue parsing till ... */
        while (clargs[n] = strtok(NULL, DELIM))
            n++;                             /* ... all words are extracted */

        switch(fork()) {
           case 0:                           /* Run command in child */
              if ((execvp(clargs[0], &clargs[0])) < 0)
                  exit(200);                 /* We'll check this value later */
           default:                          /* In the parent */
              wait(&returnval);              /* After the command has completed ... */
              printf("Exit status of command: %d\n", WEXITSTATUS(returnval));
        }                                    /* line, so next command can work with */
    }                                        /* an initialized buffer and argument */
}                                            /* array. */
```

Fig. 26.10 `shell.c`

no shell here), so every command that we input must exist as an on-disk executable. This must be true for the **pwd** command also, and we confirmed this by checking the last accessed time for the file and comparing it with the **date** output.

Tip As can be seen from the code of the previous program, it's tedious to parse a line into word-strings and then populate an array with pointers to these strings. You can make the shell do this work for you by passing the shell itself as the first two arguments to **execlp**. All shells support a -c option that takes a command line as argument to be executed. For instance, you can run the **ls** command *with wild-cards and redirection to save the output* by using **sh -c "ls *.c > list"**. To use this with **execlp,** we need to use **execlp("sh", "sh", "-c", "ls *.c > list")**. The first three arguments will always be the same; the entire command line can be supplied as a single fourth argument!

Note Often, you'll find it more convenient to use the **system** library function which is built on top of the **fork**, exec and **wait** calls. Like the -c option offered by shells, **system** takes the entire command line (which can also be a shell builtin or a shell script) as a single argument. The function uses a shell (by default, Bourne) to execute it, and also makes use of PATH. Like **sh -c, system** also works with redirection—for instance, **system("ls -lu /etc/passwd > foo")**.

26.10 FILE DESCRIPTOR MANIPULATION

The previous program can't handle redirection or connect two commands in a pipe. To be able to do that, we must first understand a special feature available in the UNIX kernel to manipulate file descriptors. You'll recall that the kernel always allocates the lowest available integer as the new file descriptor when you open a file. This implies that if you close standard output and then open a disk file foo, the descriptor for the file would be 1:

```
close(STDOUT_FILENO);                              Next open returns 1 as file descriptor
open("foo", O_WRONLY | O_CREAT |O_TRUNC, S_IRUSR | S_IWUSR);
printf("This statement goes to foo; standard output redirected\n");
```

Place these three statements in a program with the necessary **#include** statements (fcntl.h, sys/stat.h and unistd.h), and you'll find that the output of the **printf** statement has been "redirected" to foo. This isn't the way the shell actually performs redirection, but it has an important message to convey:

> *If you want to perform a read or write operation on a file* foo *using a specific file descriptor that is already allocated to* bar, *then close* bar *before you open* foo. foo *should then get the descriptor that was previously allocated to* bar.

We'll now see how this concept is used to implement redirection and piping.

26.10.1 dup: Duplicating a File Descriptor

At the outset, let's clearly understand the difference between opening a file twice and duplicating the descriptor of an open file. When a file is opened twice—either in the same or in a different process—the two file descriptors point to *separate* file table entries. This means that they have their own separate file offsets. However, when you duplicate a file descriptor, both descriptors point to the *same* file table, which means that they share the same offset. This behavior—also shared by **fork** *(26.3.1)*—is required to achieve redirection and piping.

We'll consider here two system calls that duplicate file descriptors—**dup** and **dup2**. The first one has a very simple syntax:

```
int dup(int fildes);
```

Here, **dup** duplicates the file descriptor *filedes* and returns the lowest numbered descriptor available for allocation. Assuming that the standard descriptors 0, 1 and 2 are allocated, and there's no other file open in that process, **dup(1)** will return the value 3. This is one way of creating another handle to access standard output.

Let's use this feature in our next program, **dup.c** (Fig. 26.11), to run any filter that obtains input from redirected standard input and writes to redirected standard output. The program accepts the first argument as the input filename, the second argument as the output filename, and the remaining arguments as the command line to be executed.

```
/* Program: dup.c -- Uses dup to achieve both input and output redirection
                    Closes standard streams first before using dup */
#include <unistd.h>
#include <stdio.h>
#include <sys/stat.h>
#include <fcntl.h>
#define MODE600 (S_IRUSR | S_IWUSR)

int main(int argc, char **argv) {
    int fd1, fd2;
    fd1 = open(argv[1], O_RDONLY);
    fd2 = open(argv[2], O_WRONLY | O_CREAT | O_TRUNC, MODE600);

    close(STDIN_FILENO);
    dup(fd1);                       /* This should return descriptor 0 */
    close(STDOUT_FILENO);
    dup(fd2);                       /* This should return descriptor 1 */

    execvp(argv[3], &argv[3]);      /* Execute any filter */
    printf("Failed to exec filter");
}
```

Fig. 26.11 **dup.c**

We use **dup** to replicate the file descriptors that are returned by opening the two files (argv[1] and argv[2]). Because we closed the respective standard streams previously, we *should* get them back by using **dup**. Let's now use the program to run **wc** (the third argument) to save the word count of /etc/passwd (the first argument) in passwd.cnt (the second argument):

```
$ a.out /etc/passwd passwd.cnt wc -l
$ cat passwd.cnt
     37 /etc/passwd
```

We have said this before as a UNIX user *(9.5.1)*, and we say this again—this time as a systems programmer: **wc** didn't open /etc/passwd but obtained its input from the standard input. We have achieved the effect of redirection except that we didn't use the < and > symbols and relied on the program to identify the first two arguments as the filenames to be used for redirection.

26.10.2 dup2: A Better Way of Replicating a Descriptor

The reason why we used the word "should" (twice in the program annotations and once in the paragraph prior to the previous one) is that we assume that nothing untoward will occur after **close** and before **dup**. However, this behavior is not guaranteed; a signal handler (covered later) could create a file in this time interval. In that case, that file will be allocated the descriptor that we wanted from **dup**. The program will then fail.

To overcome this problem, we use the **dup2** system call that uses two arguments:

```
int dup2(int fildes, int fildes2);
```

dup2 replicates *filedes* to *filedes2* and returns it. If *filedes2* is already open, **dup2** closes it first. **dup2** thus combines the actions of **close** and **dup** that were used in succession in the previous program, except that **dup2** performs both functions as a single atomic operation *(25.1.3)*; a signal can't interrupt an atomic operation that is partially complete.

There are two problems with the previous program. First, doing an exec in a single process leaves us with nothing more to do since exec doesn't return. Further, by closing standard output, we ensured that we can't write to the terminal again. Ideally, files to be used for redirection should be opened in a separate child process. The child should manipulate the descriptors before exec'ing the program which uses these descriptors.

To fall in line with the shell's approach to redirection, let's repeat the previous exercise, using **dup2** this time. In this program, **dup2.c** (Fig. 26.12), file opening, descriptor manipulation and also the exec are done in a child process. The parent simply forks and waits for the child to die. The program uses the **quit** function developed in the previous chapter to handle error messages.

To demonstrate how the parent correctly obtains the exit status of the command run by the child, let's use the program to run **grep** twice:

```
$ a.out /etc/passwd passwd.cnt grep joker
Exit status: 1                                joker not found in /etc/passwd
$ a.out /etc/passwd passwd.cnt grep sumit
Exit status: 0                                sumit found in /etc/passwd
$ cat passwd.cnt
sumit:x:500:500:sumitabha das:/home/sumit:/bin/bash
```

grep here is used only with the pattern as argument; it obtained its input from the standard input, which was redirected using **dup2** to originate from /etc/passwd. Further, the standard output of **grep** was also redirected with **dup2** to passwd.cnt.

```
/* Program: dup2.c -- Opens files in the parent and uses
                      dup2 in the child to reassign the descriptors */
#include <unistd.h>
#include <stdio.h>
#include <sys/stat.h>
#include <fcntl.h>
#include <wait.h>

#define OPENFLAGS (O_WRONLY | O_CREAT | O_TRUNC)
#define MODE600 (S_IRUSR | S_IWUSR)

void quit (char *message, int exit_status) ;

int main(int argc, char **argv) {
   int fd1, fd2, rv, exit_status;

   if (fork() == 0) {                  /* Child */
      if ((fd1 = open(argv[1], O_RDONLY)) == -1)
         quit("Error in opening file for reading\n", 1);
      if ((fd2 = open(argv[2], OPENFLAGS, MODE600)) == -1)
         quit("Error in opening file for writing\n", 1);
      dup2(fd1,0);                     /* Closes standard input simultaneously */
      dup2(fd2,1);                     /* Closes standard output simultaneously */
      execvp(argv[3], &argv[3]);       /* Execute command */
      quit("exec error", 2);
   } else {                            /* Parent */
      wait(&rv);                       /* Or use waitpid(-1, &rv, 0) */
      printf("Exit status: %d\n", WEXITSTATUS(rv));
   }
}
```

Fig. 26.12 **dup2.c**

26.10.3 fcntl: Recommended over dup and dup2

POSIX calls **dup** and **dup2** "redundant" functions, and advocates the use of the **fcntl** system call. Space constraints don't permit a thorough examination of this versatile system call, but you should at least know that descriptor replication is one of **fcntl**'s numerous functions. Here are the **fcntl** equivalents to **dup** and **dup2**:

dup *and* **dup2**	**fcntl** *Equivalents*
fd = dup(*filedes*);	fd = fcntl(*fildes*, F_DUPFD, 0);
fd = dup2(*fildes*, *fildes2*);	close(*fildes2*); fd = fcntl(*fildes*, F_DUPFD, *fildes2*);

Note that **fcntl** loses its atomicity when emulating **dup2**, because it is preceded by the **close** call. POSIX recommends the use of signal blocking to avoid this problem.

fcntl can also manipulate information held in the file descriptor table and file table. Every file descriptor is associated with a flag that determines whether the descriptor will be closed across an exec. By default, descriptors remain open, but a prior call to **fcntl** can reverse this behavior. **fcntl** can also change the file's status flags (though not its opening modes) while it is open.

> **Note** There are basically two ways of duplicating a file descriptor—using **fork**, and using **dup** and **dup2** (or their **fcntl** equivalents). **fork** makes a copy of the parent's descriptor available in the child, while **dup** and **dup2** do the same in the current process. In either case, the end result is that both original and copy share the same file table, i.e. the same file offset, opening modes and status flags.

26.11 pipe: INTER-PROCESS COMMUNICATION

UNIX has very elaborate schemes for two processes to communicate with each other. At a very rudimentary level, we have seen how the child communicates its exit status to the parent. Later in this chapter, we'll see how the kernel sends a signal to another process. At a more advanced level, UNIX offers shared memory, semaphores and message queues for *inter-process communication* (IPC). In this section, we discuss the piping mechanism available in the shell.

To understand how a pipe enables one process to send its standard output to another's standard input, imagine doing a similar thing using a disk file instead. One process could write to the file and the other could read from it. This just won't work because if the reader is faster than the writer, it will often catch up with the writer and read EOF. There's no flow control mechanism that would make one process block till the other has completed its job. Besides, the size of the file grows as the data continues to flow from the writer to the reader. Operating system theorists have a name for this—the *producer-consumer* problem.

The pipe solves both these problems. It is a half-duplex communication channel, which means that data flows in only one direction. It is a type of file which can be used with **read** and **write**, but it's created with the **pipe** system call:

```
int pipe(int fildes[2]);
```

pipe takes an array of 2 integers as its only argument, which it populates with two file descriptors. Whatever is written to *fildes*[1] can be read from *fildes*[0]; the significance of 0 and 1 have been retained in the pipe as well. A call to **write** on *fildes*[1] populates a fixed-sized buffer (about 4-8 KB), while a call to **read** on *filedes*[0] drains the buffer so the next **write** can fill it up again.

If the buffer is found to be empty during a read, the operation will block till the buffer is written. Similarly, a write to a buffer that has not yet been read will block too. The data is read on first in-first out basis (FIFO), and expectedly, the pipe's file type is FIFO which can be checked with the S_ISFIFO macro.

Although a pipe is most commonly shared by two processes, a trivial example shows its use in a single process:

```
int n, fd[2];
char buf[100];
pipe(fd);                                    Fills up fd[2] with 2 descriptors
write(fd[1], "abcdefgh", 8 );                Writing to one file descriptor
n = read(fd[0], buf, 100);                   and reading it back from another
write(STDOUT_FILENO, buf, n);                Printing what was read from pipe
```

The **pipe** call here generates two file descriptors, fd[0] and fd[1]. We simply write the string abcdefgh to fd[1] and read it back from fd[0], and then write the same string to the standard output. There's not much to learn from here except that numerous possibilities open up when a pipe is used by two processes. This is taken up next.

26.11.1 Using pipe with fork

To make **pipe** work in tandem with **fork**, the usual procedure is to create the pipe before forking a process. Because **fork** duplicates all open descriptors, a call to **pipe** before a **fork** connects two descriptors to each end of the pipe. To use the pipe, we don't need all four of them, but only one at each end. Data here can flow in either direction, but assuming that the parent writes to the pipe and the child reads it, then we must close the pipe's read end in the parent and the write end in the child. This is what the program, **pipe.c** (Fig. 26.13), does.

```
/* Program: pipe.c -- Shares a pipe between two processes.
                      We want the data to flow from the parent to the child */
#include <stdio.h>
#include <unistd.h>

void quit(char *, int);
int main(void) {
   int n, fd[2];                            /* fd[2] to be filled up by pipe() */
   char buf[100];                           /* Buffer to be used by read() */

   if (pipe(fd) < 0)                        /* fd[0] is read end */
      quit("pipe", 1);                      /* fd[1] is write end */

   switch (fork()) {                        /* Pipe has four descriptors now */
      case -1: quit("Fork error", 2);
       case 0: close(fd[1]);                /* CHILD-Close write end of pipe */
               n = read(fd[0], buf, 100);   /* and read from its read end */
               write(STDOUT_FILENO, buf, n);
               break;
      default: close(fd[0]);                /* PARENT-Close read end of pipe */
               write(fd[1], "Writing to pipe\n", 16); /* write to write end */
   }
   exit(0);
}
```

Fig. 26.13 **pipe.c**

The **pipe** call returns two descriptors, fd[0] and fd[1], which should have the values 3 and 4 in this program. This example assumes data flowing from parent to child, so the parent doesn't need the read end (fd[0]), while the child doesn't need the write end (fd[1]), the reason why these descriptors have been closed. The program outputs the string that's written to the pipe:

```
$ a.out
Writing to pipe
```

This is the string **write** wrote to fd[1] and **read** gathered from fd[0]. In real-life though, you use separate programs on either side of the shell's pipe symbol, |. So you'll naturally expect to be able to do a similar thing with **pipe**. This means that you have to connect the standard output of one program to fd[1] and the standard input of the other to fd[0]. How does one do that?

26.11.2 pipe2.c: Running UNIX Commands in a Pipe

The next program, **pipe2.c** (Fig. 26.14), addresses this issue. Apart from closing the unneeded file descriptors associated with the pipe, the program also uses **dup2** to replicate the other descriptors—both in the parent and the child. We reverse the data flow here—from the child to the parent—just to prove that the direction of flow is irrelevant.

```
/* Program: pipe2.c -- Runs two programs in a pipeline
                       Child runs cat, parent runs tr */
#include <unistd.h>
#include <stdio.h>

void quit (char *message, int exit_status) ;
int main(void) {
   int fd[2];                               /* To be filled up by pipe() */

   if (pipe(fd) < 0)                        /* Now have four descriptors for pipe */
      quit("pipe", 1);
   switch (fork()) {
      case -1: quit("fork", 2);

       case 0: close(fd[0]);                     /* CHILD - Close read end first */
               dup2(fd[1], STDOUT_FILENO);   /* Connect stdout to  write end */
               close(fd[1]);                     /* and close original descriptor */
               execlp("cat", "cat", "/etc/hosts.equiv", (char *) 0);
               quit("cat", 3);

      default: close(fd[1]);                     /* PARENT - Close write end first */
               dup2(fd[0], STDIN_FILENO);    /* Connect stdin to read end */
               close(fd[0]);                     /* and close original descriptor */
               execlp("tr", "tr", "'[a-z]'","'[A-Z]'", (char *) 0);
               quit("tr", 4);
   }
}
```

Fig. 26.14 pipe2.c

To understand how the program works, let's first examine the sequence of statements that are executed in the child process. We first close (`fd[0]`), the descriptor for the read end of the pipe. We don't need it since the child writes (not reads) to the pipe. Next, we replicate `fd[1]` with **dup2** to give us the descriptor used by standard output. At this stage, the file descriptor for standard output points to the write end of the pipe. This means we don't need the original descriptor (`fd[1]`) that was connected to the same end of the pipe, so we close it.

Having now closed both the original read and write ends of the pipe, we are left with only the descriptor for standard output that is now connected to the pipe's write end. Invoking **execvp** to run the **cat** command ensures that **cat**'s output is connected to the pipe's write end.

If we apply a similar line of reasoning to the statements in the parent, we'll end up in a situation where the standard input of **tr** is connected to the read end of the pipe. We have been able to establish a pipeline between **cat** and **tr**. On running the program, you should see the entries in `/etc/hosts.equiv`, but after conversion to uppercase:

```
$ a.out
SATURN
EARTH
MERCURY
JUPITER
```

Compare this output with that obtained from the program, **reverse_read2.c** (Fig. 25.2), which displayed the contents of `/etc/hosts.equiv`, but in reverse order.

A pipe is meant for one-way communication, and that's how we used it in these examples. The two programs that we considered lead us to an obvious conclusion: Two processes can use a pipe for communication only when they share a common ancestor. In these cases, the ancestor is the process represented by **a.out**, but in the UNIX command line, the shell is the common ancestor of all processes in a pipeline (not strictly true).

You can also effect two-way communication using two pipes, but that would require closing most of the file descriptors connected to them. UNIX also offers facilities for two unrelated processes to communicate with each other. Besides, UNIX offers *named pipes* (which also have FIFO as the file type, but are also called *FIFO*s. We'll not dwell on these features in this text.

26.12 SIGNAL HANDLING

Signals represent a primitive way of performing inter-process communication. We were introduced to signals in Chapter 10 where we used them to kill processes. But generally speaking, a signal is a mechanism used by the kernel to communicate the occurrence of an event to a process. The process often responds by terminating itself, but there are other actions the process can take—ignore it or invoke a user-defined function for instance. The action that a signal will take on receipt of a signal is known as its *disposition*.

A signal is represented by an integer and its symbolic name. For instance, `SIGINT` represents the signal number 2, and you'll recall having used signal names (without the `SIG` prefix) as arguments to the **kill** *(10.8.1)* and **trap** *(16.15)* commands. We must use signal names rather than their numbers in our programs because the same signal is sometimes represented by two different names on SVR4 and BSD systems. The name-number translation map is defined in `<signal.h>` (`<bits/signum.h>` in Linux).

The event that generates a signal can take place in the hardware, in the operating system or elsewhere. To be more specific, signals can be generated from the following sources:

- The keyboard There are three signals that have their origin in the keyboard, and they all affect the current foreground job (or process group). *[Ctrl-c]* generates the `SIGINT` signal which terminates the process. *[Ctrl-\]* generates `SIGQUIT` which directs a process to produce a core dump (a file named `core` in the current directory). *[Ctrl-z]*, the suspend key, sends `SIGTSTP` to all processes of the foreground process group in a shell that supports job control.
- From the hardware Signals can be generated on account of an arithmetic exception (`SIGFPE`), an illegal instruction (`SIGILL`) or a memory access violation (`SIGSEGV`). They all result in termination of the process.
- From a C program The system call library offers some functions that generate signals. The `alarm` system call generates `SIGALRM` after the expiry of a specified time. The **abort** call generates `SIGABRT` which terminates a process. The **raise** and **kill** functions can generate any signal.
- From other sources When a child dies, the kernel sends the `SIGCHLD` signal to the parent. When a background job tries to read from the terminal, the terminal driver generates the `SIGTTIN` signal and stops the process. You can also send many of these signals using the **kill** command, a technique with which you are familiar by now.

Signals can be *synchronous* or *asynchronous*. An asynchronous signal is one over which you have no control; it is often caused by events not directly connected with the execution of program instructions. For instance, a user can press *[Ctrl-c]* to generate `SIGINT` any time. On the other hand, a division by zero that arises on account of the CPU executing a process instruction generates the `SIGFPE` signal in a synchronous manner. However, the disposition of a signal is not influenced by the synchronous nature or otherwise of the signal.

26.12.1 Signal Disposition

How a process responds to a signal depends on how things are set up in the program representing the process. This could be a little confusing to understand at first, so let's first simply matters by noting that none of the programs considered in the previous chapter as well as the ones of this chapter (up to this point) has any code that handles signals. If any of their processes receives a signal, there are mainly three things that it can do with it:

- *Ignore the signal.* The process continues running as if nothing has happened. This is true of the `SIGCHLD` signal that is sent to the parent when a child dies. The parent actually ignores the signal, but user-defined code in the parent often invokes **wait** or **waitpid** to pick up the exit status of the child.
- *Terminate the process.* This is the default disposition of most signals. For instance, `SIGINT` and `SIGHUP` terminate the process. Both *[Ctrl-c]* and **kill -s INT** generate `SIGINT`. Signals generated by hardware errors also usually terminate a process.

- *Suspend (stop) the process.* This happens when you press *[Ctrl-z]* from the keyboard (which generates SIGTSTP) or send the SIGSTOP signal from your program. The kernel also suspends a background process when it tries to read from the terminal.

One of these would be the default disposition for a particular signal. However, you can override the default action and *catch* the signal using the **signal** system call. Contrary to what you would like to believe, this call doesn't generate a signal but only specifies its disposition. Using **signal**, you can do these things:

- *Ignore the signal.* Even if the default disposition may not ignore a signal, you can still ignore it in your program.
- *Restore the default (in case the default was changed earlier).*
- *Invoke a signal handling function.* This function is automatically invoked when the process receives a signal for which the invocation of the signal handler is the current disposition.

In the remaining sections of this chapter, we'll discuss how the **signal** call is used to specify all the three possible dispositions presented above. The last one—invoking a signal handling function—will be the focus of attention.

> **Note** Irrespective of the action you take, there are two signals that you can neither ignore nor catch by invoking a signal handler. They are SIGKILL and SIGSTOP. It's necessary for the superuser to have the powers to kill any process (with SIGKILL) or stop it (with SIGSTOP). If the superuser didn't have these powers, runaway processes could bring life to a standstill.

26.12.2 How the Kernel Handles Signals

Like a process, a signal has to go through a number of phases in its own life cycle. A signal is first *generated* and then *delivered* to a process. A signal is considered to be delivered when the signal disposition has occurred—even if the disposition is to ignore the signal. Till the signal is delivered, it is considered to be *pending*.

When a signal is sent to a process, the kernel sets a bit in the pending *signals mask* field of the proc structure to indicate that a signal of a specific type has been received by the process. This field has a bit reserved for each type of signal. There's no provision in the process table to detect the receipt of multiple instances of the same signal. A process merely knows that it has received at least one instance of that signal. It is also not guaranteed that a signal A that is generated before signal B will be disposed of before B.

A process generally doesn't come to know instantly that it has received a signal but only at certain specific times. The kernel checks up the pending signals mask before the process returns from kernel mode to user mode. The check is also made when a process moves to runnable state. When the process knows that it has received a signal, it checks up the signal disposition table maintained in the u area *(26.2)*. Accordingly the process decides to ignore, terminate or invoke a signal handler.

The kernel gets cautious when the process is in the midst of execution of a system call. When a process blocks and moves to the sleeping state, whether or not it is awakened depends on the reason that caused the process to change to that state. If the process is sleeping on the completion of a disk I/O, the kernel allows the system call to complete before performing signal delivery. However, if the process is waiting to take input from the terminal, the kernel will abort the call and wake up the process. That is reasonable because waiting for terminal input could be a wait forever.

26.12.3 The System Calls

This chapter discusses the signal handling mechanism that has been in use ever since BSD modified the SVR4 implementation. These signals are considered *unreliable* for reasons that are discussed later. The adverse qualification need not deter you from using them; these calls work very well on most occasions. These are the calls that we are going to discuss:

- **`signal`** This call doesn't send a signal, but specifies the disposition—how a process should behave when it receives a signal.
- **`kill`** This call behaves in identical manner to the **`kill`** command. Like "signal", the name "kill" is a misnomer too; it's **`kill`** that sends a signal, but it doesn't necessarily kill a process. A library function, **`raise`**, uses **`kill`** to send any signal to the current process.
- **`alarm`** The **`alarm`** call is used in the next example to set a timer that generates the `SIGALRM` signal after the timeout period. The library function **`sleep`** uses **`alarm`**.
- **`pause`** This is like the shell's **`read`** statement. It holds up program execution till a signal is received.

The important signals are listed along with their default disposition in Table 26.1. We'll now take up some of these calls in developing programs that handle signals. We begin with a detailed examination of the **`signal`** call.

Table 26.1 Signals and Default Disposition

Signal Name	*Significance*	*Default Action*
`SIGINT`	Terminal interrupt (*[Ctrl-c]*)	Terminate
`SIGQUIT`	Terminal quit (*[Ctrl\]*)	Terminate with core dump
`SIGTSTP`	Terminal stop (*[Ctrl-z]*)	Stop
`SIGABRT`	Abnormal termination (`abort` call)	Terminate
`SIGCHLD`	Change of child's status	Ignore
`SIGCONT`	Continue stopped child	Continue
`SIGALRM`	Timer (set by **`alarm`** call); sends signal after expiry of timeout period	Terminate
`SIGHUP`	Hangup signal	Terminate
`SIGTERM`	Software termination	Terminate
`SIGPIPE`	Write to pipe with read ends closed	Terminate
`SIGILL`	Illegal instruction	Terminate with core dump
`SIGFPE`	Arithmetic exception	Terminate with core dump
`SIGSEGV`	Segmentation violation; process attempts to access memory outside its own address space	Terminate with core dump
`SIGKILL`	Sure kill	Terminate; can't be caught
`SIGSTOP`	Process stop	Stop; can't be caught

26.13 `signal`: INSTALLING A SIGNAL HANDLER

A signal's disposition is set with the **signal** system call. The call *installs* a handler by specifying it as one of its two arguments. Installation makes the program aware of the action to take. **signal** returns the previous handler as shown by the syntax:

```
void (*signal(int sig, void (*func)(int)))(int);
```

This is how the POSIX prototype indicates that **signal** takes two arguments—the signal number (*sig*) and a pointer to a signal handling function (**func*). The handler takes one argument, the signal number (the second `int`), and returns nothing (the second `void`). **signal** itself returns a pointer to the previous handler, which takes one argument (the final `int`) and also returns nothing (the first `void`).

If you find this too much to accept, then consider this comforting syntax taken from the Linux man page:

```
sighandler_t signal(int signum, sighandler_t handler);
```

Strictly speaking, the second argument to **signal** need not always be a pointer to a signal handling function; it can also be one of these two values:

`SIG_IGN`	Ignore the signal.
`SIG_DFL`	Revert to the default disposition.

So a signal handler can specify either a handler or one of the two constants shown above as disposition for the signal. Here are two typical signal installations:

```
signal(SIGALRM, alrm_handler);          Installs a handler
signal(SIGINT, SIG_IGN);                Changes default disposition to ignore
```

The first example installs the **alrm_handler function** which is invoked by the process when it receives `SIGALRM`. The second example sets the disposition to ignore on receipt of `SIGINT`. This means that the interrupt key can't terminate this program. You can make use of this protective feature to place this statement at the beginning of a critical section of code that you wouldn't like to be interrupted. You can then revert to the default disposition by placing this statement after the critical code section:

```
signal(SIGINT, SIG_DFL);                Restores the default disposition
```

Signal handlers are executed in the user mode. Let's now write our first signal handling program to catch the `SIGALRM` signal.

26.13.1 Catching the SIGALRM Signal

This program, **signal.c** (Fig. 26.15), uses the **alarm** call to set up a timer which times out in 5 seconds. The program prompts the user for a filename which is displayed if the user inputs it in 5 seconds. If the user is late in responding, `SIGALRM` is generated, which invokes a signal handler to set the default filename to `foo`.

```
/* Program: signal.c -- Waits for 5 seconds for user input and then
                        generates SIGALRM that has a handler specified */
#include <stdio.h>
#include <unistd.h>
#include <signal.h>
#define BUFSIZE 100

void alrm_handler(int signo);                   /* Prototype declarations for */
void quit (char *message, int exit_status); /* signal handler and quit */

char buf[BUFSIZE] = "foo\0";                    /* Global variable */
int main (void) {
    int n;
    if (signal(SIGALRM, alrm_handler) == SIG_ERR)   /* signal returns SIG_ERR */
        quit("sigalrm", 1);                          /* on error */

    fprintf(stderr, "Enter filename: ");
    alarm(5);                                   /* Sets alarm clock; will deliver */
    n = read(STDIN_FILENO, buf, BUFSIZE);       /* SIGALRM in 5 seconds */
    if (n > 1)                                  /* Will come here if user inputs */
        printf("Filename: %s\n", buf);          /* string within 5 seconds */
    exit(0);
}

void alrm_handler(int signo) {             /* Invoked with process receives SIGALRM */
    signal(SIGALRM, alrm_handler);         /* Resetting signal handler */
    fprintf(stderr, "\nSignal %d received, default filename: %s\n", signo, buf);
    exit(1);
}
```

Fig. 26.15 **signal.c**

We declare the prototype of the **alrm_handler** function before the **main** section. In the program body, we install this function with **signal**, checking for SIG_ERR, the only error that **signal** can return. The user is prompted for a filename, and the **alarm** timer sets off immediately thereafter. The filename is displayed if it is entered in the timeout period. But if the timeout occurs, SIGALRM is generated which leads to the execution of **alrm_handler**. This function prints the signal number and the default filename. It also explicitly terminates the program with **exit**.

Before we discuss what the second **signal** call is doing in this function, lets' execute this program twice—with and without a filename. We'll then verify the correctness of the signal number with the **kill -l** output:

```
$ a.out
Enter filename: signal.log
Filename: signal.log
$ a.out
Enter filename:                               Nothing entered in 5 seconds
```

```
Signal 14 received, default filename: foo
$ kill -l | grep 14                          What is signal 14?
13) SIGPIPE      14) SIGALRM      15) SIGTERM      16) SIGUSR1
```

Note We have observed that both the proc and u area contain important data related to signals *(26.2)*. The information stored in these two structures change with **fork** and exec, and has already been examined in Section 26.8. Let's review briefly the statements made there.

While **fork** clears the pending signals mask, it doesn't change the signal disposition. exec retains the signals mask but sets the disposition of any signal that is caught to SIG_DFL (default). For other signals, exec leaves them undisturbed. Remember that SIGKILL and SIGSTOP can't be caught or ignored.

26.13.2 Why signal is Unreliable

Why did we reinstall the signal handler in the same handling function? We need to move back in time a bit to discover that the original signals in System V were unreliable in that a signal's disposition was reset to the default before the handler was invoked. A second signal of the same type would then be subject to the default disposition. However, if we require the disposition to be persistent, we must reinstall the handler at the beginning of the handling function.

This approach works most of the time, but there's a finite probability of it leading to a *race condition.* In this situation, two or more events act on the same resource and the sequence in which they are serviced determines the eventual outcome of the race. Here, if a second signal of the same type arrives *after* the disposition is reset to the default and *before* the handler is reinstalled, the default action will be taken. If the default action is to terminate the process, the handler won't be given a chance to reinstall itself.

Linux used BSD signals, and they are different; the signal disposition is not reset to the default. If you are running this program on Linux, you need not reinstall the handler. However, reinstallation is a safe thing to do because you are assured that the disposition is persistent regardless of the system the program is running on. However, all signals that are handled by **signal** are unreliable for other reasons also; a signal can get lost and can't be blocked.

Note POSIX recommends the use of *reliable* system calls for which it provides the interface for a large number of them. In the POSIX system, it's **sigaction** and not **signal** that sets a signal's disposition. A POSIX signal can be *blocked* and can be delivered only when it is *unblocked* (both with **sigprocmask**). We are constrained to drop discussions on the POSIX signal handling functions in this edition.

26.13.3 Catching Terminal-generated Signals

Having seen how **signal** is used to handle SIGALRM that is generated in the program, and how the signal handler is reinstalled every time it is called, let's use these ideas in the program, **signal2.c** (Fig. 26.16), to develop two signal handlers for the SIGINT and SIGTSTP signals that are sent from the keyboard. We'll also ignore the SIGQUIT signal.

```
/* Program: signal2.c -- Handles SIGINT and SIGTSTP generated from terminal
                         Requires two [Ctrl-c]s to terminate */
#include <stdio.h>
#include <unistd.h>
#include <signal.h>

void quit (char *message, int exit_status) ;
void tstp_handler(int signo);                /* Handler for [Ctrl-z] */
void int_handler(int signo);                 /* Handler for [Ctrl-c] */
int n, count = 0;

int main (void) {
    signal(SIGTSTP, tstp_handler);           /* Disposition for these two signals */
    signal(SIGINT, int_handler);             /* set to enter respective handlers */
    signal(SIGQUIT, SIG_IGN);                /* Disposition set to ignore */

    fprintf(stderr, "Press [Ctrl-z] first, then [Ctrl-c]\n");
    for (;;)
        pause();                             /* Will return on receipt of signal */
}

void tstp_handler(int signo) {
    signal(SIGTSTP, tstp_handler);                      /* Not entirely reliable */
    fprintf(stderr, "Can't stop this program\n");       /* same signal can reset */
}                                                       /* disposition to default */

void int_handler(int signo) {                           /* Will terminate program */
    signal(SIGINT, int_handler);                        /* on second invocation */
    (++count == 1) ? printf("Press again\n") : quit("Quitting", 1);
}
```

Fig. 26.16 **signal2.c**

Using three **signal** calls we set the disposition of three different signals. Since we are using unreliable signals, we reset the signal handlers every time we invoke them. Note the use of SIG_IGN in one **signal** call which sets the disposition to ignore for SIGQUIT. *[Ctrl-z]* generates SIGTSTP, but we catch it to display a message but without stopping the process. We also catch *[Ctrl-c]* (SIGINT), but to terminate it only when the key is pressed twice.

The **for** loop makes the **pause** system call run in a loop. **pause** simply suspends execution till it receives any signal, in which case it returns with the EINTR error. Let's now run this program by pressing all the three key sequences in turn:

```
$ a.out
Press [Ctrl-z] first, then [Ctrl-c]
[Ctrl-\]                                         Signal ignored
[Ctrl-z]
Can't stop this program                          From tstp_handler
[Ctrl-c]
```

```
Press again                                    From int_handler
[Ctrl-c]
Quitting: Interrupted system call              From int_handler
```

All three signal handlers can be seen at work here. So far, we have been handling signals; in the next section, we'll use **kill** to generate them.

> **Note** When a process is executed in the background with &, the disposition of SIGINT is set to SIG_DFL (default), the reason why *[Ctrl-c]* can't terminate a background process. When a process is run with **nohup**, the disposition of SIGHUP is also set to SIG_DFL; the process then won't terminate when the shell is killed (which generates SIGHUP).

26.14 killprocess.c: THE FINAL PROGRAM USING kill

Before we take up the final program featured in this chapter, we have a new system call to discuss—**kill**. Like its command counterpart, the **kill** system call sends a signal to one or more processes:

```
int kill(pid_t pid, int sig);
```

Generally, we obtain the PID of the child using **pid = fork()**, and then use, say, **kill(pid, SIGTERM)** to kill the child with SIGTERM. The *pid* in the syntax doesn't always represent a single PID; like in **waitpid** *(26.5.3)*, *pid* can take on four types of values with identical meaning. This means that you can send a signal to a process group also.

It's time for consolidation; so let's demonstrate the combined use of the fork-exec-wait and signal handling mechanisms. The program, **killprocess.c** (Fig. 26.17), runs a command that is input by the user and prints the exit status if the command completes in 5 seconds. If it doesn't, then the parent uses **kill** to send a SIGTERM signal to kill the child process.

This time we use a single signal handling function to handle both SIGCHLD and SIGALRM. The parent forks a child which then uses **execvp** to run a user-specified program supplied as one or more command line arguments. Note that this time the parent doesn't wait for the child's death after the fork. It starts a timer with **alarm(5)**, which on expiry issues the SIGALRM signal. The parent issues **pause**, which returns on receipt of any signal.

One of two signals can wake up the parent here—either SIGCHLD or SIGALRM. In the signal handling function, we take into account two other possibilities; the child may or may not complete execution in 5 seconds. If it does, SIGCHLD is issued and **death_handler** invokes **waitpid** to pick up the exit status of the child. Otherwise, **death_handler** waits for SIGALRM and then kills the process with SIGTERM.

We'll run the program twice—once with a program that completes in 5 seconds and then with one that doesn't:

```
$ a.out date
Thu Apr  3 14:49:57 IST 2003
Child dies; exit status: 0
Parent dies
```

```
/* Program: killprocess.c -- Uses fork and exec to run a user-defined program
                              and kills it if it doesn't complete in 5 seconds.*/

#include <stdio.h>
#include <sys/types.h>
#include <sys/wait.h>
#include <signal.h>

pid_t pid;
int main (int argc, char **argv) {
    int i, status;
    void death_handler(int signo);        /* A common signal handler this time */

    signal(SIGCHLD, death_handler);       /* death_handler is invoked when a */
    signal(SIGALRM, death_handler);       /* child dies or an alarm is received */

    switch (pid = fork()) {
        case -1: printf("Fork error\n");
        case  0: execvp(argv[1], &argv[1]);    /* Execute command */
                 perror("exec");
                 break;
        default: alarm(5);     /* Will send SIGALRM after 5 seconds */
                 pause();      /* Will return when SIGCHLD signal is received */
                 printf("Parent dies\n");
    }
    exit(0);
}

void death_handler(int signo) {          /* This common handler picks up the */
    int status;                          /* exit status for normal termination */
    signal(signo, death_handler);        /* but sends the SIGTERM signal if */
    switch (signo) {                     /* command doesn't complete in 5 seconds */
      case SIGCHLD: waitpid(-1, &status, 0);    /* Same as wait(&status); */
                    printf("Child dies; exit status: %d\n",
                            WEXITSTATUS(status));
                    break;
      case SIGALRM: if (kill(pid, SIGTERM) == 0)
                        fprintf(stderr, "5 seconds over, child killed\n");
    }
}
```

Fig. 26.17 signal.c

```
$ a.out find /home -name a.out -print
/home/sumit/personal/project8/a.out
/home/sumit/personal/books_code/glass_ables/12/a.out
/home/sumit/personal/books_code/stevens_c/ch08/a.out
    ...after 5 second time interval ......
5 seconds over, child killed
Parent dies
```

When we use **kill** to send a signal to a process group (a pipeline, for instance), then we must specify as **kill**'s first argument, the negative value of the PGID of all processes comprising that group. For instance, if the PGID of a process group is 350, then you should use **kill(-350, SIGTERM)** to kill all processes in that group. Though we ignored process groups in Chapter 10, the **kill** command can also be used to send a signal to a process group.

kill can be used to send a signal to the current process also. You need to use **getpid** to specify the PID here, but the **raise** library function does this work for us. **raise(SIGTERM)** is equivalent to **kill(getpid(), SIGTERM)**.

26.15 CONCLUSION

We covered some of the basic process internals in this chapter and the system calls that are used for process control. Space constraints don't permit inclusion of topics covering the advanced forms of IPC—like semaphores, message queues and shared memory. But the message is clear; there are a lot of places you can go from here. Pursuing IPC eventually leads us to the world of socket programming. You should also learn the fully reliable signal handling mechanism that is mandated by POSIX and offered by Solaris and Linux.

WRAP UP

A process runs in its own *virtual address space* comprising the text, data, heap and stack segments. The virtual addresses are translated into physical addresses at runtime by the *Memory Management Unit* (MMU). Part of the process address space is also reserved for the kernel which uses a separate stack for each process.

A program also has a *context* that comprises the contents of the hardware registers, the process address space as well as process control information. Within a context, a process can run either in *user mode* or *kernel mode*, the latter being used when the kernel runs on the user's behalf while servicing a system call. The kernel performs a *context switch* to preempt one process to let another use the CPU.

A process can be in one of several *states*. It needs to first move to *ready-to-run* (or *runnable*) state before it can actually run. A process can also *sleep* on an event (like waiting for I/O to complete) or be *suspended*. The *zombie* state is an intermediate stage a process has to go through before it finally dies.

Process control information is available in kernel data structures. The *process table* is an array of *proc* structures containing information that the kernel may need to know any time (like its PID and state). Information on the currently running process (like the UIDs, GIDs and the file descriptor table) is stored in the *u area*.

The **fork** system call creates a process by replicating the existing address space. **fork** returns twice—zero in the child and its own PID in the parent. The child has a separate copy of the parent's environment, and hence changes made in it don't affect the parent. Even though file descriptors are also replicated, they share the same file table.

The environment variables are available in the variable, `environ[]`. A variable can be set with **setenv** or **putenv** and retrieved with **getenv**.

A process exits by invoking the **_exit** system call. We use the **exit** library function because it flushes all output streams and removes all temporary files. The argument used with either function is available in the proc structure which is retrieved by the parent with the **wait** or **waitpid** system calls. Unlike **wait**, **waitpid** can wait for a specific child to die and also need not block till the child dies.

If the parent dies before the child, the child turns into an *orphan*, which is immediately adopted by **init**. If the parent is alive but doesn't invoke **wait**, the child is transformed to a *zombie*. A zombie is a dead process whose address space has been freed but not the entry in the process table.

The exec family of functions replaces the complete address space of the current process with that of a new program. **execl** and **execlp** work with a fixed list of arguments; the latter uses PATH to locate the program. **execv** and **execvp** work in a similar manner, but with a variable list. Shell and **perl** scripts can be run by **execlp** and **execvp**. A successful exec doesn't return.

dup replicates a file descriptor and returns the lowest unallocated value. **dup2** allows us to choose the descriptor we want by closing it if it is already open. In either case, original and copy both share the same file table. These calls are required to implement redirection. POSIX recommends the use of **fcntl** rather than **dup** or **dup2**.

pipe creates a buffered object that returns two file descriptors. Data written to one descriptor can be read back from the other. To create a pipeline of two commands, first create a pipe before a **fork**, then use **dup2** to replicate the pipe's descriptors in both parent and child so as to connect standard input and standard output to the two ends of the pipe. Finally, close all unneeded descriptors.

A *signal* is a mechanism by which a process is made aware of the occurrence of an event. A signal can be generated from the keyboard, by exceptions occurring in the hardware or by the **kill** system call. When a process receives a signal, it may allow the default *disposition* to occur, ignore the signal or invoke a *signal handler*. Every signal handler is *installed* with the **signal** call. The signals SIGKILL and SIGSTOP can't be caught. While the proc stores the pending signals mask, the signal disposition is available in the u area.

A process also belongs to a *process group*. The processes in a pipeline belong to a single process group. While **waitpid** can wait for the death of any member of a group, **kill** can send a signal to all members.

TEST YOUR UNDERSTANDING

26.1 Name the system calls discussed in this chapter that return one or more file descriptors.

26.2 What is the significance of the stack and heap segments in the address space of a process? Why does the kernel need a separate stack for each process?

26.3 What is *kernel mode*? Does a separate process run in this mode?

26.4 Write a program that forks twice. Display the PIDs and PPIDs of all three processes.

26.5 Redirect the output of **fork.c** (Fig. 26.3) to a file. How do the contents of the file differ with the output obtained on the terminal without redirection? Explain with reasons.

26.6 Write a program that accepts two small numbers (< 50) as arguments and then sums the two in a child process. The sum should be returned by the child to the parent as its exit status and the parent should print the sum.

26.7 Write a shell script containing only one statement: **exit 123456**. Now run the script and issue **echo $?** from the shell. Explain why the value provided in the script differs with $?.

26.8 Write a program that uses **write** to output the message `hello dolly` to the standard error. Manipulate file descriptors in such a way that it is possible to save the error message using **a.out > foo** and not with **a.out 2>foo**.

26.9 Use the **kill** command to find the number of signals available on your system and then write a program that ignores all of them. Is it possible to do so?

FLEX YOUR BRAIN

26.1 In the virtual address space of a process, which segments are loaded directly from the program file on disk? How and when are the other segments created?

26.2 Explain which of these process attributes change with a fork and exec: (i) PID (ii) PPID (iii) kernel I/O buffers (iv) pending signals mask (v) signal disposition (vi) file descriptors.

26.3 What is *context switching*? Explain the role of the *Process Control Block* when making a context switch.

26.4 What are the structural changes that take place in memory when (i) a file is opened twice (ii) its descriptor is replicated. In how many ways can you replicate the descriptor?

26.5 Modify the program in 26.6 (Test Your Understanding) so that process A creates B and B creates C. The summation should be performed in C and the result returned to B as the exit status. B should double the summed value and return the product to A as the exit status. Will the program work with large numbers?

26.6 Name three advantages **waitpid** has over **wait**. Why can't a background process be terminated with the interrupt key?

26.7 Explain the difference in treatment meted out by the kernel to zombies and orphans.

26.8 Write a program that prompts for a command line to be executed and then uses an exec function to run it. The command line can contain shell metacharacters including redirection and piping symbols. (HINT: Take advantage of the shell's **-c** option.)

26.9 Write a program that runs the **ls -lids** command, but specifies a separate environment for the exec'd process. The new environment should only specify the `HOME` and `PATH` variables. Prove that the `MAIL` and `TERM` variables are not available in the new process.

27

Advanced System Administration

In this revisit to the system administrator's domain, we take a closer look at the ways and means a UNIX system should be administered. The routine duties of an administrator, like monitoring the disk space and taking backups, have already been discussed in Chapter 17. But administration also involves handling problems, and system problems can be quite grave and unexpected. The file system might crash, a new terminal or printer may not operate, or a user may delete a supposedly secure file. To handle every eventuality, the system administrator must have thorough knowledge of practically every system component.

The administrator is also responsible for the installation of all system peripherals. He has to often devise scripts for automating some operations that need to be carried out regularly. He must also be able to configure the system's initialization scripts. All these functions are system-dependent, and it's no wonder that POSIX doesn't address administrative issues. Since you could have easier access to a Linux machine for testing these functions, many examples in this chapter use a Linux system.

WHAT YOU WILL LEARN

- Enforce password aging with **passwd** so that passwords are changed regularly.
- Restrict a user's activities with the *restricted shell*.
- The concept of a *partition* and *file system* and the functions of its four components.
- Create a partition and a file system on a Linux machine with **fdisk** and **mkfs**.
- *Mount* and *unmount* file systems with **mount** and **umount**, and examine their configuration file, /etc/fstab.
- Check and repair file systems with **fsck**.
- The significance of **init** *run levels*, and how they control startup and shutdown.
- How **init** uses /etc/inittab and *rc* scripts to start and stop the system's daemons.
- Administer a System V printer with **lpadmin** and control the print spooler.
- Consider the other options of **find** that aid in the backup process.

TOPICS OF SPECIAL INTEREST

- How the inode keeps track of all disk block addresses allocated to a file.
- The different types of file systems that you'll find on UNIX machines.

- A detailed examination of the behavior of **init** and the organization of the *rc* files and scripts responsible for starting and stopping services.
- How the **xargs–find** combination can often speed up execution time.

27.1 MAINTAINING SECURITY

The administrator must exercise diligence in enabling access to some of the system's services. At times, he has to prevent some users from using a specific service. Modern times have seen several instances of hackers who manage to get into a system mainly because of the negligence of the administrator.

27.1.1 Password Aging

Systems having /etc/shadow use an elaborate scheme for administering the change of password. It is called *password aging* which should be used by the administrator to force users to change their passwords after a predetermined time. A line in this file contains several fields containing the attributes of the user's password. Most of these fields can be updated by using the **passwd** command with suitable options.

The -n option sets its argument equal to the minimum number of days for which a password has to be retained. The -x option sets the maximum limit. Here are some examples of their usage for the user oracle:

```
passwd -n 12 oracle          Minimum 12 weeks before password can be changed
passwd -x 24 oracle          Maximum 24 weeks before password must be changed
```

In the interests of security, it may be sometimes necessary for you to lock a user account. You can do that with **passwd**'s -l (lock) option. The -u option restores the account. You can also force a user to change her password at the next login with the -f option.

27.1.2 Restricted Shell

To restrict the activities of a user, you should set up the user account with a special restricted shell. This shell once had the name **rsh**, but today **rsh** represents the command with which you remotely run a program. The better shells today have restricted versions—**rbash** and **rksh**. Either of them has to be specified in the last field of /etc/passwd. A user with a restricted shell can't do any of the following things:

- Use the **cd** command, which means that she can't change directories.
- Redefine the PATH, which makes it impossible to access commands placed in other directories.
- Redefine the SHELL so the user can't change to a nonrestricted shell.
- Use a pathname containing a /, which means a command can't be executed with either a relative or an absolute pathname.
- Use the > and >> operators to create or append to files.

In this environment, a user can only execute programs in the directories specified in a new unchangeable PATH. This generally is set to only the current directory. If the user needs to run some of the system commands in /bin and /usr/bin, place links of those commands in the user's restricted directory.

Some commands have shell escapes (like **vi** and **mailx**), and some versions of UNIX let you use these escapes to execute any UNIX command by using the absolute pathname. Make sure these commands don't behave in that manner on your system. If they do, disallow their use.

> **Note** If you don't have a separate restricted shell on your system, use the standard shells with the -r option to enforce that behavior (**sh -r**, **bash -r** or **ksh -r**). Since you can't put these entries in /etc/passwd, run a normal shell there and use **exec** to execute them from the startup file. Make sure to set the PATH to just one directory.

27.1.3 Allowing a User to Shut Down Only

Shutting down the system requires root privilege, and the administrator is not expected to divulge the root password to anyone. There's still a way of allowing a user to shut down the system without allowing her direct access to the shell. The trick is to first create an ordinary user account (say shut) with **useradd**:

```
useradd -u 210 -g group -s /bin/sh -d /home/shut -m shut
```

Next, you have to confer root status on this user by changing the UID in /etc/passwd from 210 to 0, the one used by root. This can't be done directly by **useradd** because it won't permit reuse of the root UID, and must be done manually by editing /etc/passwd. The **shutdown** command must be placed in the user's .profile (preferably with an exec prefix) so that she can't do anything else.

27.2 PARTITIONS AND FILE SYSTEMS

The system administrator must understand the file system internals well because it is his job to maintain it in a healthy and correct state. He must display his efficiency in fixing inconsistencies that tend to crop up from time to time, and ensure that loss of data is minimum. When the system refuses to boot, he must not panic and reinstall the entire system. In this section and the following ones, we discuss the tools UNIX provides for performing this job.

Like other operating systems, UNIX requires a formatted hard disk. Normally, the formatting operation lies outside the operating system's domain. It marks the defective tracks so read-write operations avoid them. This operation was once carried out by special utilities supplied by the vendor. Today, disks (both IDE and SCSI) come preformatted, so this is one thing you don't have to bother about.

After the disk has been formatted, the next step is to divide it into *partitions*. Each partition can be considered to be a logically independent disk that is accessed by its own device file. Dividing a disk into a number of partitions has a number of distinct advantages:

- Separate partitions prevent potential encroachment conflicts that may arise between the various data areas.

- If there's corruption in one area, other areas are effectively shielded from this evil influence.
- If the system has an adequate number of partitions, each partition can be backed up separately onto a single volume of tape.

After the disk has been partitioned, it's still not ready for use. A *file system (13.1)* has to be created on each partition. Unlike a partition, a file system is organized in the form of a directory structure with its own root. But it also has space set aside (outside the directory structure) for maintaining information (like inodes) on the files it stores. Every file system has these four components:

- The *boot block*—This block contains a small boot program and the partition table.
- The *superblock*—It contains global information about the file system. Additionally, it also maintains a free list of inodes and data blocks that can be immediately allocated by the kernel when creating a file.
- The *inode blocks*—This region contains the inode for every file of the file system.
- The *data blocks*—All data and programs created by users reside in this area.

The operating system usually resides on multiple file systems, and every file system has these four components. At the time of booting, these file systems combine (using a technique known as *mounting*) and appear to the user as a single file system. In the forthcoming sections, we'll use the **fdisk** command to create partitions, **mkfs** to create file systems and the **mount** and **umount** commands to mount and unmount file systems. Before we do that, let's briefly discuss the significance of the four file system components.

> **Note** The words *partition* and *file system* are often used synonymously, especially when a partition contains a single file system. However, this is not always the case. Some systems like Solaris break up a partition into *slices*, with a file system in each slice. Linux allows the creation of an *extended* partition, with multiple *logical* partitions in each extended partition. Each logical partition then contains a file system. In this way, it's possible to have multiple file systems in a single partition.

27.2.1 The Boot Block

The first block of a file system is known as the *boot block*, containing a small bootstrap program—often referred to as the *Master Boot Record* (MBR). The program is loaded into memory when the system is booted (hence the name). It may, in turn, load another program from the disk, but eventually it loads the kernel into memory. However, the bootstrapping program is read in from the boot block of only one file system (the main one, called the *root* file system). For other file systems, this block is simply kept blank.

27.2.2 The Superblock

The boot block is followed by the *superblock*, the "balance sheet" of every UNIX file system. It contains global file information about disk usage and availability of data blocks and inodes. Its information should, therefore, be correct for healthy operation of the system. This is mainly what it contains:

- The size of the file system.
- The block size used by the file system.
- The number of free data blocks available and a partial list of immediately allocable free data blocks.
- Number of free inodes available and a partial list of immediately usable inodes.
- Last time of updating.
- The state of the file system (whether "clean" or "dirty").

The kernel maintains a copy of the superblock in memory and reads and writes this copy when controlling allocation of inodes and data blocks. It also periodically updates the disk copy with the contents of the memory copy. Because the two copies are not in *sync* (one more recent than the other), the integrity of the file system is compromised when the power to the machine is improperly cut off. The **sync** command (discussed later) writes the memory copy to disk and ensures that the disk copy is never newer than the memory copy. When booting, the system checks for a possible mismatch between the two and accordingly brands the file system "dirty" or "clean".

UNIX refuses to boot if the superblock is corrupt. To overcome this problem, many systems (like Solaris and Linux) have multiple superblocks written on different areas of the disk. If one superblock is corrupt, the system can be directed to use another.

Note The kernel always maintains a copy of the superblock in memory. The in-memory copy actually contains the latest and correct file system status rather than its disk copy.

27.2.3 Inode Blocks

This is the area containing all inodes. When a file is created, an inode is allocated here. Even though the inode contains all file attributes (except its name), it doesn't store the inode number. Since the inodes are laid out sequentially, the kernel uses simple arithmetic to identify the inode by using the inode number as the index in this "array" of inodes, i.e. by its position in this list. The **ls** command looks up a directory to know the inode number of a file, and then reads the inode to obtain the file's attributes.

Apart from file attributes, the inode contains an array of 13 to 15 pointers to disk block addresses. Most of them are actual addresses of disk blocks containing the file's data. The other pointers hold addresses of disk blocks that don't contain the file's remaining data but the *addresses* of the other data-bearing disk blocks. We'll elaborate on this point later, but be assured that this array of 13 to 15 pointers ultimately keep track of *every* disk block used by a file.

When a file is opened, the kernel copies its inode from disk to memory. Like for the superblock, the kernel works with the memory copy which is maintained in a structure known as *vnode*. A perpetually running process (named **update** or **bdflush**) uses **sync** periodically to write this memory copy to disk.

27.2.4 Data Blocks

All file data are stored in the data blocks, which occupy most of the file system. Most UNIX tools like **find**, **df** and **du** assume a block size of 512 bytes (1024 in Linux). **find** interprets the argument used with `-size` as the number of 512-byte blocks. **df** and **du** report on disk usage in 512-byte blocks. We often call this the *physical* block size, being the size of a disk sector—the smallest addressable disk area.

The physical block is useful for reporting purposes only. However, disk allocation takes place using a different block size—often 1024 bytes. We call this the *logical* block size and it is set at the time of installation of the system. This block size also determines the largest file size that the system can accommodate. However using an entire block for read/write operations means that even if you have to write three bytes of data into a 1024-byte disk block, 1021 bytes will simply be wasted. A pity, but that is the price one has to pay for having a well-organized and consistent file system.

There's yet another block size, the one *actually* used for doing I/O. As we have discussed before *(25.4)*, all disk I/O takes place through a pool of buffers maintained by the kernel, and a command like **cat** never accesses the disk directly. Even though your logical block size could be 1024 bytes, the size of each kernel buffer could be 8192 bytes on your system. The kernel will then read in 8192 bytes from disk and write that many bytes in a single I/O operation. This is the size we use in our C programs for the buffer used by **read** and **write** *(25.3)*. The `st_blksize` member of `stat` *(25.11)* also points to this figure.

Even though disk blocks are numbered consecutively, you'll often find a file's data are arranged in noncontiguous blocks. When a file expands, the kernel may not find its adjacent blocks free. The remaining data then have to be written to the next free block, wherever it may be. This, no doubt, leads to disk *fragmentation*, and consequently increases the overheads of read/write operations. However, this fragmentation also allows files to be enlarged or reduced at will, and helps keep wastage to a minimum.

27.2.5 The Block Addressing Scheme

The discussions in this section are drawn up with reference to the standard file system (ufs) used by Solaris, but the concepts are applicable universally. We'll also assume a logical block size of 1024. We'll now see how the array of 15 disk block addresses maintained in the inode suffice to keep track of a file's data blocks.

The first 12 entries contain the addresses of the first 12 blocks of the file. However, if a file is only three blocks large, the first three entries are utilized and the remaining entries are flushed out with zeroes. This arrangement suffices for most files which are below 12 KB (12 X 1024) in size.

The three entries from the 13th onward don't point to direct blocks but only to indirect ones. The 13th entry itself has the address of a *single indirect block* which contains many more direct block addresses. When the file size increases further, the 14th entry points to a *double indirect block*, which contains the addresses of single indirect blocks. The 15th and final entry points to a *triple indirect block*, which points to double indirect blocks. Ultimately, all these direct and indirect blocks store all the blocks used by a file. A simplified view of the organization of data blocks is depicted in Fig. 27.1.

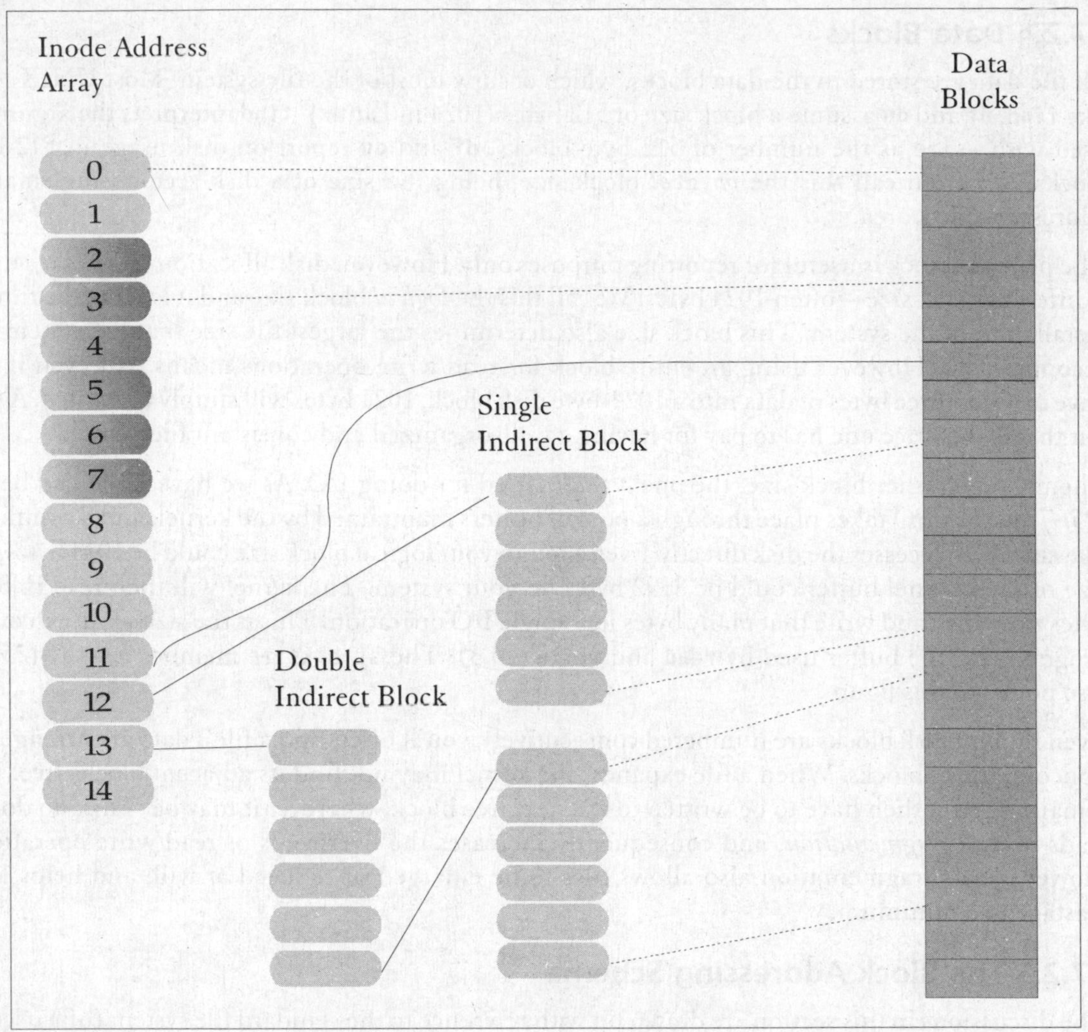

Fig.27.1 The Block Addressing Scheme

> **Note** The maximum size of a file in the ufs file system discussed above is 2 GB on a 32-bit machine (using 32-bit disk sector addressing). Now that UNIX has gone 64-bit, it's now possible to have file sizes exceeding several terabytes (1 TB = 1000 GB).

27.3 THE STANDARD FILE SYSTEMS AND THEIR TYPES

The preceding discussion related to a single file system. In real life, modern UNIX systems are invariably set up with multiple file systems, each meant for a specific purpose. If you have multiple disks, every such disk must have at least one file system on it. However, a single file system, until recently, could not span multiple disks. In general, most UNIX systems will always have these file systems:

- The *root* file system This file system is present in every UNIX system. It contains the bare-bones UNIX—the root directory, the `/bin`, `/etc`, `/dev` and `/lib` directories, i.e., all the tools and utilities that are just sufficient to keep the system going. When the system is booted in single-user mode, this is the only file system available to the system administrator.
- The *boot* file system This contains the UNIX kernel and other boot programs.
- The *swap* file system When the system memory is heavily loaded, the kernel moves processes out of memory and to this file system. When these swapped processes are ready to run, they are loaded back to memory. Users can't access this file system directly.

Apart from these essential file systems, your computer would in all probability have additional ones. System files should be kept separate from data files created by users, and hence a separate file system is usually made for them. You might have a `/home` or `/export/home` file system to house all users. You could also have `/usr`, `/var` and `/tmp` as separate file systems.

Initially, there were only two types of file systems—the ones from AT&T and Berkeley. Over time, many more file system types have made their entry into the UNIX system. You need to know the following file systems which you'll encounter often:

- *s5* Before SVR4, this was the only file system used by System V, but today it is offered by SVR4 by this name for backward compatibility only. This file system uses a logical block size of 512 or 1024 bytes and a single superblock. It also can't handle filenames longer than 14 characters.
- *ufs* This is how the Berkeley Fast File System is known to SVR4 and adopted by most UNIX systems. Because the block size here can go up to 64 KB, performance of this file system is considerably better than s5. It uses multiple superblocks with each cylinder group storing a superblock. Unlike s5, ufs supports 255-character filenames, symbolic links and disk quotas.
- *ext2* or *ext3* This is the standard file system on Linux. It uses a block size of 1024 bytes and, like ufs, uses multiple superblocks and symbolic links.
- *iso9660* or *hsfs* This is the standard file system used by CD-ROMs. It features DOS-style 8+3 filenames, but since UNIX uses longer filenames, hsfs also provides Rock Ridge extensions to accommodate them.
- *msdos* or *pcfs* Most UNIX systems also support DOS filesystems. You can create this file system on a floppy diskette and transfer files to it for use on a Windows system. Some systems like Linux can also directly access a DOS file system on the hard disk.
- *swap* This file system has already been discussed.
- *bfs* The boot file system. This is used by SVR4 to host the boot programs and the UNIX kernel. Users are not meant to use this file system.
- *proc* or *procfs* This can be considered a pseudo-file system maintained in memory. It stores data of each running process and appears to contain files, but actually contains none. Users can obtain most process information including their PIDs directly from here.

Some of these file systems have certain unique characteristics, but we'll ignore them. Besides the above, UNIX vendors also have their own proprietary file systems, but they also support most of the types discussed above. Commands handling file systems (like **mkfs** and **mount**) use an option to describe the file system, the reason why you should know the file system you are using.

27.4 fdisk: CREATING PARTITIONS

UNIX fragmentation becomes quite evident when it comes to creating partitions. Different versions of UNIX use different tools for partitioning a disk. Though the principles are broadly similar, there are significant differences in details. The system administrator probably won't allow you to create or delete partitions on his system, so we'll create them on a Linux system using the **fdisk** command which operates differently from the command of the same name used in DOS.

Let's use **fdisk** to create a partition on the first IDE hard disk to hold the Oracle RDBMS software. Modern versions of Linux require the device name of the hard disk as argument:

```
fdisk /dev/hda
To print the partition table, use the p command:
Disk /dev/hda: 255 heads, 63 sectors, 784 cylinders
Units = cylinders of 16065 * 512 bytes
   Device Boot    Start       End    Blocks   Id  System
/dev/hda1   *         1       217   1743021    5  Extended
/dev/hda2           218       478   2096482+   7  HPFS/NTFS
/dev/hda4           620       784   1325362+  83  Linux native
/dev/hda5             1         5     40099+  82  Linux swap
/dev/hda6             6       217   1702858   83  Linux native
```

This 6.5 GB disk contains 784 cylinders of 160652 X 512 bytes each and containing a number of partitions. Partitions in Linux behave more like their DOS counterparts. As stated before, you can create a *primary* partition with one file system in it, or an *extended* partition containing multiple *logical* partitions.

Linux has a simple scheme for naming partition devices. The first IDE hard disk as a whole is represented by /dev/hda, while individual partitions in this disk take on names hda1, hda2, and so forth. hda2 here is a primary partition housing an NTFS file system used by Windows; this disk contains another operating system also. The second hard disk will have the name /dev/hdb with similar numeric extensions.

Observe that partition 1 (hda1) uses the same cylinders as partitions 5 (hda5) and 6 (hda5). hda1 is an extended partition containing a logical partition hda6 and the swap partition, hda5. There's another Linux system on partition 4 (hda4). The active partition is indicated by an * in the second column. We also have cylinders between 479 and 619 unused, so we can use that space to create a partition. This will be partition 3.

The **fdisk m** command shows you all its internal commands of which the following subset should serve our purpose:

```
Command (m for help): m
Command action    Condensed list
   a   toggle a bootable flag
   d   delete a partition
   l   list known partition types
   m   print this menu
   n   add a new partition
```

```
p   print the partition table
q   quit without saving changes
w   write table to disk and exit
```

To create a partition, we have to use the **n** command, supply the partition number and the starting and ending cylinder numbers:

```
Command (m for help): n                                        Adding a partition
Command action
  l   logical (5 or over)                                      Note this
  p   primary partition (1-4)
p                                                              Opting for primary partition
Partition number (1-4): 3
First cylinder (479-784, default 479): 479                     Choosing default
Last cylinder or +size or +sizeM or +sizeK (479-619, default 619): 619
```

Linux is smart enough to suggest default cylinder values, but we preferred to enter the values explicitly. Now use **p** again to view the new partition:

```
Device      Boot  Start    End    Blocks    Id  System
/dev/hda1    *       1     217   1743021     5  Extended
/dev/hda2          218     478   2096482+    7  HPFS/NTFS
/dev/hda3          479     619   1132582+   83  Linux native           New partition
/dev/hda4          620     784   1325362+   83  Linux native
/dev/hda5            1       5     40099+   82  Linux swap
/dev/hda6            6     217   1702858    83  Linux native
```

We now have a new partition, hda3, occupying over 1 GB of space. Now that the partition table has been modified, we have to write it to the boot block with the **w** command. You *may* be prompted to reboot the system which will make the new file system available for use.

Note To have multiple file systems on one Linux partition, you must first have an extended partition and then create multiple logical partitions on this extended partition.

27.5 mkfs: CREATING A FILE SYSTEM

Now that we have created a partition, we need to create a file system on this partition to make it usable. Though frontend tools are available today, they generally operate through **mkfs**—the universal file system creation tool. Sticking to Linux and the partition that we created recently, we'll use **mkfs** with the -t option to specify the type of file system:

```
# mkfs -t ext2 /dev/hda3
mke2fs 1.14, 9-Jan-1999 for EXT2 FS 0.5b, 95/08/09
Linux ext2 filesystem format
Filesystem label=
283560 inodes, 1132582 blocks
56629 blocks (5.00%) reserved for the super user
First data block=1
Block size=1024 (log=0)
Fragment size=1024 (log=0)
```

```
139 block groups
8192 blocks per group, 8192 fragments per group
2040 inodes per group
Superblock backups stored on blocks:
        8193, 16385, 24577, 32769, 40961, 49153, 57345, 65537, 73729, 81921,
        90113, 98305, 106497, 114689, 122881, 131073, 139265, 147457, 155649,
    ..... Condensed list .....
Writing inode tables: done
Writing superblocks and filesystem accounting information: done
```

This creates an ext2 file system—the standard Linux file system that uses a block size of 1024 bytes. Note the multiple superblocks that are uniformly (8192 blocks) spaced apart. The ufs and ext2 file systems also use fragments to minimize wastage; discussion on this is beyond the scope of this text. For details, look up *System Performance Tuning* (O'Reilly & Associates) by Mike Loukides.

mkfs in Linux acts as a frontend to **mke2fs** which actually creates the file system. Since we didn't specify the number of blocks, **mkfs** used default values for the number of inodes and data blocks. The increase of one can only be achieved at the expense of the other. The file system fills up whenever either figure is reached. Generally, you won't need to disturb the default values unless you are handling a huge number of very small files.

> **Tip** From the output of the **mkfs** command you should keep a record of the block addresses that contain copies of the superblock. If the main superblock gets corrupt, then you would need to use **fsck** with an alternate superblock number.

27.6 MOUNTING AND UNMOUNTING FILE SYSTEMS

A file system is a self-contained entity with its own tree structure and root directory. It just sits there in a standalone mode; the main file system doesn't even know of its existence. These file systems unite to become a *single* file system at the time of booting. The root file system then becomes the *main* file system, and its root directory is also the directory of the unified file system. This happens by a process known as *mounting*, when all these secondary file systems *mount* (attach) themselves to the main file system at different points.

The UNIX **mount** and **umount** commands are used for mounting and unmounting file systems. The point at which mounting takes place is called the *mount point*. This is usually an empty directory. After mounting you see a single file system instead of two separate ones. You can then copy and move files between the two file systems.

27.6.1 mount: Mounting File Systems

The **mount** command is used to mount file systems. When mounting a new file system, it takes two arguments—the device name of the file system and the mount point. Before mounting a file system, an empty directory (say, `/oracle`) must first be made available in the main file system. The root directory of the new file system has to be mounted on this directory.

mount uses an option to specify the type of file system. This option varies across UNIX flavors. This is how we use **mount** to mount a file system on the /oracle directory on Solaris and Linux systems:

```
mount -F ufs /dev/dsk/c0t3d0s5 /oracle          Solaris
mount -t ext2 /dev/hda3 /oracle                 Linux
```

After the device is mounted, the root directory of the file system created by **mkfs** loses its separate identity. It now becomes the directory /oracle and is made to appear as if it's part of the main file system. The user now sees a single file system in front of her, quite oblivious of the possibility that a file moved from /oracle to /home may have actually traversed two hard disks!

Even though **mount** here used the device name and mount point as its arguments, we'll soon learn to set things up in a way that allows **mount** to be used with one argument. The mount point (/oracle) is normally an empty directory, but if it is not, then its files can't be seen if a file system is mounted on this mount point. The files are seen again when the file system is unmounted.

27.6.2 umount: Unmounting File Systems

Unmounting is achieved with the **umount** command (note the spelling!), which requires either the file system name or mount point as argument. The file system that we just created and mounted can be unmounted by using any of these commands:

```
umount /oracle                 Specify either mount point or
umount /dev/hda3               device name—here a Linux device
umount /dev/dsk/c0t3d0s5       ... and a Solaris device here
```

Unmounting a file system is not possible if you have a file open in it. Further, just as you can't remove a directory unless you are placed in a directory above it, you can't unmount a file system unless you are placed above it. If you try to do that, this is what you'll see:

```
# pwd
/oracle
# umount /dev/hda3
umount: /oracle: device is busy
```

Now move out of the mount point (/oracle) and then repeat the **umount** command; it should work now.

27.6.3 /etc/fstab: Configuring mount

Observe the **df** command output shown in Section 17.6.1, and you'll find that it shows the free space for every file system separately. These file systems have to be mounted for **df** to be able to report on them, and this mounting takes place during system startup. They are also unmounted when the system is shut down. The system's initialization scripts run the **mount** and **umount** commands with the -a (all) option to mount all file systems that are listed in **mount**'s configuration file.

This file is generally /etc/fstab (file system table), but Solaris uses the SVR4-styled /etc/vfstab having a different format. There are some minor differences in options too. We'll consider a few lines of /etc/fstab on an old Linux system:

```
# Mount device  Mount Point   File System Type   mount Options
/dev/hda5       swap          swap               defaults           0     0
/dev/hda6       /             ext2               defaults           1     1
/dev/hda2       /dosc         vfat               defaults           0     0
/dev/hda3       /oracle       ext2               defaults           1     2
/dev/hdc        /mnt/cdrom    iso9660            ro,noauto,user     0     0
/dev/fd0        /floppy       auto               noauto,user        0     0
none            /proc         proc               defaults           0     0
```

When you use **mount -a**, all file systems listed in this file are mounted sequentially (unless explicitly specified otherwise). At system startup, the same command is executed, so you always find mounted file systems available on your machine. The shutdown sequence runs **umount -a**.

Each line in /etc/fstab provides the mounting specifications for a single file system. The list includes the floppy drive and CD-ROM too. The first two columns show both the arguments used by **mount**—the device name and mount point. Once you have placed an entry for a file system in this file, you can then use **mount** with simply one argument:

```
mount /dev/hda3                                      Both these commands
mount /oracle                                        will now work
```

Let's briefly describe the other entries in fstab. The noauto option implies that the file system is mounted manually and not with **mount -a**. The user option implies that you can issue the command as an ordinary user. A 1 in the fifth field indicates that the file system has to be backed up (dumped) with the **dump** command. The sixth field shows the order in which the file systems are to be checked by the **fsck** command during a system boot.

mount, when used by itself, lists all mounted file systems. This output is seen on a Solaris system:

```
# mount
/ on /dev/dsk/c0t0d0s0 read/write/setuid/largefiles on Thu Apr 20 10:00:10 2000
/proc on /proc read/write/setuid on Thu Apr 20 10:00:10 2000
/dev/fd on fd read/write/setuid on Thu Apr 20 10:00:10 2000
/oracle on /dev/dsk/c0t0d0s3 setuid/read/write/largefiles on Thu Apr 20 10:00:15
2000
/u01 on /dev/dsk/c1t3d0s1 setuid/read/write/largefiles on Thu Apr 20 10:00:15 20
00
/u02 on /dev/dsk/c1t3d0s3 setuid/read/write/largefiles on Thu Apr 20 10:00:15 20
00
/u03 on /dev/dsk/c1t3d0s4 setuid/read/write/largefiles on Thu Apr 20 10:00:15 20
00
```

This list will generally be the same as that specified in fstab (here, vfstab), but **mount** obtains this information from /etc/mnttab (Solaris) or /etc/mtab (Linux).

27.6.4 mount Options

The third column in /etc/fstab shows the type of file system that **mount** needs to know. When mounting file systems not listed in this file, **mount** works with a default file system type (ufs in Solaris and ext2 in Linux), but if the file system you are mounting is of a different type, you need to use an option (-F in Solaris and -t in Linux):

```
mount -F hsfs -r /dev/dsk/c0t6d0s0 /cdrom          CD-ROM — Solaris
mount -F pcfs /dev/diskette /floppy                DOS diskette — Solaris
mount -t iso9660 /dev/cdrom /mnt/cdrom             CD-ROM — Linux
mount -t vfat /dev/hda1 /windows                   Windows partition — Linux
mount -t msdos /dev/fd0 /floppy                    DOS diskette — Linux
```

mount can be run with a number of special options which themselves are preceded by the -o option. Many of these options are file system-specific. These options are grouped together with the comma as delimiter. Although they are used here with Linux device names, most of the options are universally applicable:

```
mount -o ro /dev/sdb3 /usr/local                   Read only
mount -o exec /dev/cdrom /mnt/cdrom                Allows binary execution
mount -o rw,remount /dev/hda3 /home                Remounts in read-write mode
```

The first one mounts a file system in read-only mode; **mount** has a synonym for it though—the -r option. The second one lets you run executable files directly from the CD-ROM itself (exec). If you have mounted a file system as read-only, then to remount it as read-write, you don't need to unmount it first. Just use the rw and remount options together.

27.7 fsck: FILE SYSTEM CHECKING

The built-in UNIX feature of delaying the updating of the disk superblock and the inode blocks by their memory copies *(27.2.3)* leaves a lot of scope for file system inconsistency. If the power goes off before the superblock is written to disk, the file system loses its integrity. There are many discrepancies that could lead to file system corruption, and the most common ones are listed below:

- Two or more inodes claiming the same disk block.
- A block marked as free but not listed in the superblock.
- A used block marked as free.
- An inode neither marked free nor in use, or having a bad block number that is out of range.
- Mismatch between the file size specified in inode and the number of data blocks specified in the address array.
- A corrupt superblock containing erroneous summary data.
- A file not having at least one directory entry or having an invalid file type specified in the inode.

The **fsck** (file system consistency check) command is used to check and repair a damaged file system. The command generally acts as a frontend to the file system-specific program (like **fsck_ufs** or **fsck.ext2**) that actually does the job. It's generally run when a file system fails to mount. On many systems including Solaris, file systems are marked as "dirty" or "clean." **fsck** then checks only the dirty file systems during the next startup. The command can also be used with the name of the file system as argument:

```
# fsck /dev/rdsk/c0t3d0s5
** /dev/rdsk/c0t3d0s5
Phase 1 - Check Blocks and Sizes
Phase 2 - Check Pathnames
Phase 3 - Check Connectivity
Phase 4 - Check Reference Counts
```

fsck conducts a check in five phases, and the output above is obtained when the file system is consistent. However, when it is corrupt, messages and questions are seen on the system console, which you have to answer correctly. This is what **fsck** does in each phase:

- *Phase 1* Validates the inodes for correctness of format and the block numbers for bad and duplicate blocks. **fsck** declares a block BAD if the block number is out of range and DUP if it is claimed by another inode.
- *Phase 2* Checks all directory entries, starting from root, for OUT OF RANGE inode numbers detected in Phase 1. **fsck** corrects the errors either by removing the entire directory or the file.
- *Phase 3* Looks for unreferenced directories and stores their files in `/lost+found` for later examination. The files here are named after their inode numbers. You must make sure this directory is always available on every file system because **fsck** won't create it on its own.
- *Phase 4* Checks the link count as stored in the inode with the directory entries, and prompts for the file's removal or reconnection (to the `/lost+found` directory), depending on the extent of damage caused. **fsck** then compares the free inode count it computes with the figure stored in the superblock.
- *Phase 5* Finally, **fsck**'s free-block count is compared with the figure maintained in the superblock. A salvage operation may be carried out with the user's approval, which will replace the erroneous free block list with a newly computed one.

When used without options, **fsck** prompts you before repairing any damage that it has detected. It's generally safe to answer every question with a `y`. **fsck -y** (`-a` in Linux) assumes that all answers are in the affirmative, and proceeds without waiting for any response. On Solaris systems, **fsck -m** performs no rectification but merely detects flaws.

The administrator should always perform the **fsck** check with the file systems in unmounted condition. Since the root file system can't be unmounted, the check on this file system should be made in single-user mode.

If the superblock is corrupt beyond repair, then **fsck** must be used with the `-b` option (`-o b=`*n* in Solaris, where *n* is the block number) to specify an alternate superblock number. This list is displayed by **mkfs** when initializing the file system. Occasionally, the file system is so corrupt that rectification simply becomes impossible, and reinstallation of the system remains the only alternative.

Tip **fsck** often outputs the inode numbers of files which it considers suspect in integrity. You should note down these numbers for further investigation. You should also have a look in the `/lost+found` directory if you find a file missing after a system crash.

27.8 SYSTEM STARTUP AND `init`

Normally, there are no problems with either the startup or shutdown procedure. Both are run by automated shell scripts which are changed quite infrequently. Yet, the administrator needs to know the exact sequence of steps that the system follows during the two events. Things do go wrong, especially during startup, and he must be able to fix them. For that, he needs to have detailed knowledge of the system process cycle, and the role played by the initialization scripts in `/etc`. These are taken up in the following topics.

There are several processes which are initiated at system startup. The kernel is loaded into memory, and it then starts spawning further processes. The most important of these is **`/sbin/init`** having PID 1, which is responsible for the birth of all subsequent processes. You must know the behavioral pattern of **`init`** for two vital reasons:

- It controls the system *run levels* (states), and decides which processes to run for each run level. Most of these processes are daemons *(10.3)*, and they keep running all the time.
- It spawns a **`getty`** process at every terminal so that users can log in.

Recall the output of the **`ps -e`** command *(10.3)* which showed many of these processes. **`lpsched`** (**`lpd`** in Linux) monitors the line printer spooler for jobs that have been queued up for printing. **`inetd`** is the master Internet daemon, which spawns further daemons as and when required. Most daemons have **`init`** as their parent. We are going to discuss **`lpsched`** in this chapter and **`inetd`** in the next.

27.8.1 `init` Run Levels

As just mentioned, **`init`** controls the run level of a UNIX system. Each run level is normally a single digit (0 to 6), or an s or S. A distinct set of processes (mostly, daemons) is scheduled to run in each of these states. The significance of a few of these run levels shown below is system-dependent. Normally, the system would be in any one of these run levels:

- 0—System shutdown.
- 1—System administration mode (local file systems mounted).
- 2—Multiuser mode (NFS not available).
- 3—Full multiuser mode.
- 5—The graphical environment mode in Linux
- 6—Shutdown and reboot mode.
- s or S—Single-user mode (file systems mounted).

When the system is booted, **`init`** first enters the run level 1 or S, which places the system in single-user mode. This mode is used by the administrator to perform his administrative tasks, like checking the file system or taking an offline backup. You can't use either the printer or the terminals because their corresponding system daemons (**`lpsched`** and **`getty`**) are not running. The role of run level 1 is system-variant; on many systems, 1 and S have identical roles.

Depending on your system, the normal multiuser mode is implemented in either of the two run levels—2 or 3. You can change your run level by using the **init** command(or, preferably its link, **telinit**) with the run level as argument:

```
init 2                                   Switches to multiuser mode
init 3                                   Can also use telinit 3
```

Both **init 0** and **init 6** are used to shut down the system. When the run level 6 is specified, the system will be shut down and immediately rebooted. Run level 1 keeps the machine in shutdown state so that power can be switched off.

> **Tip** To know the run level you are in, use the **who -r** command. Linux users can also use the **runlevel** command from the root account.

27.8.2 Using /etc/inittab

To understand how **init** works, you must familiarize yourself with the contents of /etc/inittab. **init** takes all its instructions from this file. Its fields determine the processes that should be spawned for each of the **init** states, and the programs to run at the communication ports. Each line of the file contains four fields as revealed by a few sample lines taken from a Solaris system:

```
fs::sysinit:/sbin/rcS sysinit   >/dev/msglog 2<>/dev/msglog </dev/console
is:3:initdefault:
s0:0:wait:/sbin/rc0         >/dev/msglog 2<>/dev/msglog </dev/console
s1:1:respawn:/sbin/rc1      >/dev/msglog 2<>/dev/msglog </dev/console
s2:23:wait:/sbin/rc2        >/dev/msglog 2<>/dev/msglog </dev/console
s3:3:wait:/sbin/rc3         >/dev/msglog 2<>/dev/msglog </dev/console
s6:6:wait:/sbin/rc6         >/dev/msglog 2<>/dev/msglog </dev/console
```

All the things you see happening on startup owe their ultimate origin to entries like these. A typical inittab entry takes this form:

label:*run_levels*:*action*:*command*

label is simply used to identify the entry, and has no real significance. The second field, *run_levels*, shows the run levels for which this line is applicable. The *action* and the *command* (with all its arguments) to execute comprise the last two fields.

Let's now examine one of the lines of inittab. The line with the label s2 provides this directive: "For run levels 2 or 3, run the **/sbin/rc2** program and wait for it to complete before moving on to the other lines of this file." msglog is a special file that is used for logging all messages.

When **init** is executed with a specific run level as argument, it reads all lines that match that run level, and executes the commands specified there in sequence. A blank run level (here, in the first line) means the command has to be run for all run levels. **init** also obtains the default run level by reading the line that shows initdefault as the action. Here, the system boots to run level 3.

respawn and wait are two of the actions that **init** understands. There are others, and here are some of the important ones:

- sysinit—Used for initializing the system. The system may check the "dirtiness" of file systems, activate swap partitions and set the hostname. It may also ask for input from the administrator.
- respawn—Makes sure a process restarts on termination. This is always required for the **getty** process.
- boot—Executes only when inittab is read the first time. **init** ignores any run-level fields placed here.
- off—Kills process if it is running.
- ctrlaltdel—Executes shutdown command (Linux only).

Using **telinit q** As administrator, you can also insert or modify statements in /etc/inittab. You can change the default run level, or add and modify entries when adding a new terminal or modem to the system. But then you have to use the **telinit** command to let **init** reread its configuration file:

```
telinit q                                    A directive to init
```

init and **telinit** are symbolically linked, and in most cases, they can be used interchangeably. However, **telinit** uses the -t option to indicate to **init** the number of seconds that **init** has to wait before it starts killing processes—something that happens during system shutdown.

27.8.3 init and getty

/etc/inittab will always have at least one line that specifies running a program to produce a login prompt on the console and other terminals (if supported). We deliberately didn't include this line in the sample lines shown previously, because Solaris uses a nonstandard program for handling this function. Rather these lines from a Linux machine illustrate the relationship between **init** and the **mingetty** (the "getty" of Linux) program:

```
1:2345:respawn:/sbin/mingetty tty1
2:2345:respawn:/sbin/mingetty tty2
```

Either line provides this directive: "For run levels 2, 3, 4 or 5, run the **mingetty** program with (tty1 or tty2 as argument), and recreate (respawn) the process when it dies, i.e., when the user logs out." It's because of lines like these that you see the login: prompt on your terminal. Recall from Section 10.4.1, that the **getty** process execs **login**, which in turn execs a shell.

LINUX: Because of /etc/inittab, you can have multiple *virtual* consoles on your Linux machine. Use *[Ctrl][Alt]* and a function key to bring up a new screen. In this way, you can have multiple login sessions on a single machine.

27.8.4 The *rc* Scripts

init and /etc/inittab completely control the way the system is booted and powered down. Moreover, when the system changes a run level, **init** looks up inittab to find out the processes that should and shouldn't be running for the new run level. It first kills the processes that shouldn't be running and then spawns those that should be.

Every inittab specifies the execution of some *rc* (run command) scripts placed in /etc or /sbin. These scripts have the names **rc0**, **rc1**, **rc2**—one for each run level. This is evident from the following lines in /etc/inittab that were also shown at the beginning of Section 27.8.2:

```
s0:0:wait:/sbin/rc0            >/dev/msglog 2<>/dev/msglog </dev/console
s2:23:wait:/sbin/rc2           >/dev/msglog 2<>/dev/msglog </dev/console
s3:3:wait:/sbin/rc3            >/dev/msglog 2<>/dev/msglog </dev/console
```

init executes the script specific to that run level. However, **rc2** runs in both states 2 and 3. Each rc script further specifies the execution of a series of scripts in the directory /etc/rc*n*.d. This means that for run level 2, **init** executes **/etc/rc2**, which in turn executes the scripts in /etc/rc2.d.

Now, let's turn our attention to the scripts in the /etc/rc*n*.d directories. These directories host two types of files as shown by this listing of /etc/rc2.d:

```
K07dmi            S69inet             S74xntpd       S90wbem
K07snmpdx         S70uucp             S75cron        S92volmgt
K16apache         S71ldap.client      S75savecore    S93cacheos.finish
K28nfs.server     S71rpc              S76nscd        S94ncalogd
S01MOUNTFSYS      S72autoinstall      S80lp          S95ncad
S20sysetup        S72slpd             S85power       S99dtlogin
S21perf           S73cachefs.daemon   S88sendmail
```

The scripts here fully initialize the system by mounting file systems, setting up the network and activating the other daemons. They are executed in two batches. When the system enters run level 2, **rc2** executes (in ASCII sequence) all scripts beginning with K (the "kill" scripts) with the stop argument. This kills all processes that shouldn't be running at this level. It then executes the scripts beginning with S (the "start" scripts) with the start argument. If you look up the **rc2** script, you'll find two **for** loops doing that.

Because a daemon may run in more than one run level, the files that you see above are actually symbolic links pointing to the actual scripts placed in /etc/init.d. For instance **S88sendmail** is a symbolic link to **/etc/init.d/sendmail**. The files in /etc/init.d have similar names but with the three-character prefix chopped off. To ensure that **sendmail** doesn't run at run level 2, simply remove the symbolic link for **sendmail** (here, **S88sendmail**) in /etc/rc2.d.

As system administrator, you must understand how these scripts work. You should also be able to identify the script that starts a specific service. The filenames generally provides the clue, but sometimes you may need to use **grep** to look for the names of specific daemons (like **httpd**, **sendmail**, **lpsched**, **inetd**, etc.) in these files.

Note A script in rc*n*.d beginning with S is meant to start a service, while one beginning with K is meant to kill one. The kill scripts are executed before the start ones. They are all run from the corresponding **/etc/rc***n* (or **/etc/rc** with the argument *n* in Linux) script where *n* signifies the run level.

LINUX: The rc Files

The initialization files in Linux were originally based on BSD, but now have a strong System V flavor. However, the rc files and directories here are all under one roof—/etc/rc.d. Moreover, instead of using **rc*n***, Linux uses a single file, **rc**, with different arguments as shown below in these lines from /etc/inittab:

```
l0:0:wait:/etc/rc.d/rc 0
l1:1:wait:/etc/rc.d/rc 1
l2:2:wait:/etc/rc.d/rc 2
```

All scripts in the rc*n*.d directories are executed from **/etc/rc.d/rc**. The sequence for Linux goes like this: For switching to run level *n*, **init** executes **/etc/rc.d/rc** *n*, which executes the scripts in /etc/rc.d/rc*n*.d.

27.9 SHUTDOWN AND THE sync OPERATION

The administrator uses the **shutdown** command to bring the system down. The command uses its -i option to direct **init** to change its run level. The possible **init** levels for this are 0, 1 and 6. The corresponding rc script is then invoked, and so are the kill scripts. File systems are unmounted and processes are killed, and the system is placed in single-user mode, rebooted or simply powered down. At run level 1, the machine is not technically shut down since all processes normally active in the single-user mode continue to live.

shutdown also performs a very important task; it invokes **sync** to write all memory resident data to disk. This includes the superblock, inodes and data blocks that are cached in memory. The **update** daemon calls **sync** every thirty seconds during normal system operation. When the command is entered manually, the prompt is returned, signifying that writing has been scheduled; the actual writing could take place later. The **sync** system call also behaves in this manner, but the standard C library offers the **fsync** function that doesn't return till the buffer is actually written.

There's one occasion when **sync** must not be used. When **fsck** rebuilds the file system, the in-memory copies of the superblock and other tables may sometimes contain old and inaccurate information. In this unusual case, the information on the disk is more *recent* than the memory copy. **fsck** may then flash the following message:

```
***** BOOT UNIX (NO SYNC!) *****
```

The file system has developed a serious problem here and the system warns you that if you use **sync** to write the incorrect memory information to disk, all the good work done by **fsck** would be lost. Instead, you should *immediately press the reset button without using* **sync**, and reboot the system. This must be done before the next **sync** operation automatically writes this incorrect information to disk.

27.10 PRINTER MANAGEMENT

Printer administration is an important part of the administrator's job. UNIX provides a spooling subsystem featuring a number of commands that ensure that spooling takes place in an orderly manner. This involves managing the print queues, adding and removing printers, starting and stopping the service, and administering specific printers. The administration commands are different for SVR4 and Linux.

When a user uses **lp** to print a file, the file is spooled and submitted to a queue. Spooling in SVR4 is performed by the **lpsched** daemon. The daemon is invoked by one of the start scripts in the `rc`*n*`.d` directories when the system moves to multiuser mode. The moment printing activity ceases, you should use this sequence to first check whether **lpsched** is running:

```
ps -e | grep lpsched
```

If it's not running, look for the "start" script in `rc2.d` or `rc3.d` that has the string `lp` embedded in it. In the listing of `rc2.d` shown in Section 27.8.4, there's a script named **S80lp**. Simply execute it with the command **./S80lp start**.

The "lp" suffix refers to the once-popular line printers, which have been made obsolete today by laser and inkjet printers. However, just as the suffix has remained unchanged so has the basic technology. The printers of today are mostly bitmap devices whose resolution is measured in dots per inch. UNIX systems were not designed to handle printers that print dots, rather than complete characters.

Modern printers accept input that is formatted in a *page description language* (PDL). Today, these PDL options have narrowed down to just two—Adobe's Postscript and Hewlett Packard's PCL. UNIX commands don't produce output in Postscript format, so the character data is passed through an *interface program*. This program acts like Microsoft's print driver, and provides the control codes used by the printer. It often calls up an external program like Ghostscript (**gs**) to finally print the file.

Apart from **lp**, the spooling system consists of these major components; you'll find some of them in `/usr/lib` and some in `/usr/sbin`:

- User commands like **cancel** (for canceling jobs) and **lpstat** (for monitoring the print queue). A user can cancel only jobs submitted by her.
- The administrator's commands like **lpadmin**, **lpsched**, **lpshut**, **accept** and **reject**, **enable** and **disable**.

The chief command in the set is the **lpadmin** program. The command is used to add or remove a printer, or modify its configuration. **lpadmin** treats the final recipient of the print output as the *destination* rather than a *printer*. This destination may be a single printer or a class of similar printers. If three jobs are fired to the same class, **lpsched** would direct them to separate printers of that class.

27.10.1 Adding a Printer

Let's now use **lpadmin** to add a printer to the system. If **lpsched** is running, you have to stop it first with **lpshut** (Solaris excepted) and then use **lpadmin** to install the printer:

```
# lpshut
Print services stopped
# lpadmin -p pr1 -m epson -v /dev/lp0
```

This assigns the name *pr1* to the printer having the model type epson and attached to the device /dev/lp0. This also copies the interface program for the printer from the model directory (often, under /usr/spool/lp) to the interfaces dirctory. Standard interface programs are kept in the model directory, and the installation process copies the right one to the interfaces directory.

The interface program is actually a shell script invoked by **lpsched** with a number of arguments. These include the username, number of copies, filenames and the job-id. The script takes input from the specified filenames, formats it to suit the printer for which it is designed and dispatches it to the standard output. This output is redirected to the device file that was set when configuring the printer with the -v option.

Now start **lpsched**, direct **lp** to start accepting requests, and then enable the printer:

```
# lpsched
Print services started.
# accept pr1
destination "pr1" now accepting requests
# enable pr1
printer "pr1" now enabled                    Printer now installed and ready
```

The printer configuration can be changed by using the -p *printer_name* option. When a similar printer is added to the system, the -e option is used to copy the interface program of an existing printer. The -x option removes a printer from the system provided there are no jobs queued on that printer. The -d option is used to set the default printer. The following command lines show their usage:

```
lpadmin -x pr1                     Removes printer pr1
lpadmin -ppr1 -m HPLaserJet        Uses interface program of HPLaserJet
lpadmin -ppr1 -e pr3               Uses interface program used by pr3
lpadmin -ppr1 -v /dev/lp1          Installs and attaches printer to /dev/lp1
lpadmin -d pr1                     Sets default printer to pr1
```

Of these, only the last sequence actually adds a printer to the system; the others modify its configuration including setting of the default printer.

27.10.2 lpstat: Obtaining Printer and Job Status

lpstat has a number of options that provide the status information of printers and jobs. The -r option shows whether **lpsched** is running:

```
# lpstat -r
scheduler is running
```

Without options, **lpstat** shows the status of all requests submitted by the user who executed the command. The administrator can also obtain the list of jobs lined up for a specific printer:

```
# lpstat -ppr1                                      Can also use -p pr1
pr1-323     kumar     345670     Jan 10 13:26       on laser
pr1-324     kumar       3659     Jan 10 13:30
pr1-325     sharma     23678     Jan 10 13:40
```

The scheduler is stopped with **lpshut** and started with **lpsched**. When **lpsched** is restarted, all suspended jobs will start printing from the beginning.

27.10.3 accept and reject: Controlling Spooling

A number of commands control the spooling activity. You often have to resort to their use when the traffic is high or a printer is down. You must be able to control input coming to the spooler and divert jobs from one printer to another.

The **cancel** command *(6.6.2)* is used to cancel any job. However, when the spooler traffic is high, you should use the **accept** and **reject** commands to control input to the spooler itself. **reject** inhibits spooling, and if the -r option is used to specify the reason, a user attempting to print a job on a "rejected" printer will see the reason as the message:

```
# reject -r"Spooler very busy" laser epson
destination "laser" will no longer accept requests
destination "epson" will no longer accept requests
```

The **accept** command is used to permit spooling. This command has to be run every time a new printer is added to the system. However, both **accept** and **reject** can't affect the status of pending jobs.

27.10.4 enable and disable

accept allows spooling, but that doesn't automatically imply that jobs will be printed. For that to happen, the target printer has to be enabled, which is also done once—when a printer is added. But there are situations when a particular printer has to be shut down, for instance, when there is a jamming of paper. The **disable** command halts printing activity on the printer:

```
disable -r"Jamming of paper; just a minute" lwriter
```

Unlike **reject**, **disable** doesn't prevent jobs from being submitted to the spooler nor does it abort printing of a current job. All jobs meant for a disabled printer can only be printed when the printer is enabled with **enable**.

LINUX: The lpd System

Linux uses the older Berkeley print system. It's somewhat crude and isn't as comprehensive as the AT&T system. Jobs here are printed with the **lpr** command *(6.6—Linux)* and uses the **lpd** daemon. Compared to its SVR4 counterpart, the printing system has fewer commands in its arsenal:

- User commands like **lprm** (for canceling jobs) and **lpq** (for monitoring the print queue).
- The administrator's command, **lpc**, which takes care of all printer and spooling functions that are performed by separate commands in SVR4.

Unlike AT&T's **lpadmin**, Linux doesn't have a command line tool to install a printer. Linux systems offer menu-based software for configuring a printer. Most of the input you provide through frontends ultimately end up in a text file—/etc/printcap. This database stores all printer attributes like its name, the interface script, spool directory, device file and so on. Further discussion on the **lpr** system is beyond the scope of this text.

27.11 BACKUPS

Some files are modified more often than others, while some are not accessed at all for months, if not years. How often the data changes in the system influences the backup strategy and determines the frequency of backup. The classical theory is that there should be a complete backup of all files once a week, and a daily incremental backup of only those files that have been modified. This routine can vary depending on the size and nature of installation, but can be used as a rough thumb rule.

27.11.1 Using `find` for Incremental Backups (-newer)

The **find** command *(13.7)* can match a file with practically every attribute. You can use it for performing incremental backups. First, you have to stamp a zero-byte file with the present system date and time whenever you go in for a backup. Subsequent backups will only select those files newer than this file. The following script lines show a simple implementation:

```
find /home -newer .last_time -print | cpio -o > /dev/rct0
touch .last_time
```

These two lines can be used together any time, and **touch** ensures that the last backup time is stored in the file's modification time stamp. You can use **tar** too, using command substitution:

```
tar -cvf /dev/rct0 `find /home -type f -newer .last_time -print`
touch .last_time
```

The type has to be specified as `f` because if it is not, **find** shows the directory as part of its output, which is interpreted by **tar** to include all files of the directory. This means files would be backed up twice.

27.11.2 Using `find` for Backing Up File Systems

In addition to the routine backups, you must back up individual file systems. Backing up the root file system generally requires other file systems to be unmounted so that **find** doesn't find any files in their mount points. Using **find**'s `-mount` option, you can perform a backup of just the root file system without traversing the other file systems, *while keeping them mounted*:

```
find / -depth -mount -mtime -1 -print | cpio -ocvB -O /dev/rct0
```

This backs up the files of the root file system that have been modified in less than a day; **find** doesn't traverse the other file systems. The `-depth` keyword makes sure the files in the directories are acted upon before the directory itself. If the `-mtime` keyword is omitted, then the pipeline sequence makes a complete backup of the root file system.

Whenever peripherals are added or removed from the system, the configuration files in the root file system are changed. You must have a complete backup of both the boot and root file systems after the system has been fully configured. You can then go in for incremental backups as and when the system configuration changes.

If the system crashes and UNIX has to be reinstalled, you wouldn't obviously like to go through the tedious process of installing all peripherals separately. You can avoid that if you first install the *minimal* components of the operating system from the installation media, and then restore just the boot and root file systems from the backup.

Tip You must back up the root file system on tape immediately after installation of the system. Subsequently, you must take further backups (normally, incremental) whenever the root system files are modified.

27.11.3 xargs: Building a Dynamic Command Line

There's one problem with using **find**'s -exec operator *(13.7.3)* with a UNIX command. If **find** produces a list of 200 files for removal, **rm** has to be executed 200 times. **xargs** comes to our rescue here as it lets **rm** (or, for that matter, any UNIX command) be used just once with 200 filenames as arguments.

xargs is one of UNIX's dark horses—a command not well appreciated or understood. It breaks up data supplied as standard input into a list, and provides this list to the command used as its argument. The following command lines do the same thing except that the second one does it much faster:

```
find /usr/preserve -mtime +30 -exec rm -f {} \;
find /usr/preserve -mtime +30 -print | xargs rm -f
```

xargs here obtains the file list from **find** and supplies a *single* set of arguments to **rm**. So even if **find** selects 30 files, **rm** is executed only once.

Commands usually have limits on the number of arguments they can handle. **xargs** uses the -n option to provide the specified number of arguments for a single invocation of the command:

```
find / -name core -size +1024 -print | xargs -n20 rm -f
```

If **find** locates 100 files, **rm** will be invoked five times—each time with 20 filenames as arguments. Isn't this a useful tool?

27.11.4 Maintaining a Table of Contents

It's always preferable to maintain a file list for every backup. When a user asks for a particular file to be restored, you can first look up these lists so that you know exactly which tape has to be used. Both **tar** and **cpio** use the -v option to display each filename as it is being accessed; the output only has to be redirected to a separate file. You can always use a filename based on the current date, but the system also can do that for you quite easily:

```
tar cvf /dev/rct0 /home > homelist_`date "+%d%b%y"`
find /home -depth -print | cpio -ov > /dev/rct0 2>homelist_`date "+%d%b%y"`
```

Either of these commands can produce a file typically named homelist_17Nov03. A **grep** command can now be used, suitably framed with a regular expression, to look for any file. If the files are quite big, then they should be kept in compressed form. Apart from these selective lists, you must periodically maintain a complete list of *all* files of the system:

```
ls -lRF / > file_system.lst
```

Restoration with a wrong **tar** or **cpio** option often disturbs the file's attributes. A file's original attributes can be looked up from this list.

27.12 CONCLUSION

You can well imagine that system administration is demanding but not daunting. A system administrator must be productive and prompt in his actions. Fortunately, UNIX provides a wealth of tools that are always at his disposal. Today, most systems have elaborate GUI-based applications that take some load off the administrator. If you aspire to be an administrator yourself, then you must be able to see what's happening behind the big picture. If you can, then you are administrator already.

WRAP UP

For enforcing security, the administrator should enforce *password aging* to force users to change their passwords regularly. For certain users, he may assign a restricted shell so that the user can execute only a fixed set of commands.

A UNIX *file system* is held in a *partition* and consists of the *boot block*, *superblock*, inode and data blocks. The boot block contains boot information, while the superblock contains global information on the file system, including details of free inodes and free data blocks.

The inode contains 13 to 15 disk block addresses that keep track of all blocks used by a file. Most of these addresses point directly to the data blocks, but some do so indirectly through *indirect* blocks.

Every UNIX system will have the swap and root file systems. Most systems today use the ufs file system which permit multiple superblocks, symbolic links and disk quotas. Linux uses the ext2 and ext3 file systems. There are different file system types for CD-ROMs (hsfs or iso9660), DOS disks (pcfs, vfat or msdos) and a pseudo-file system for processes (proc or procfs).

On Linux systems, **fdisk** is used to create, delete and activate partitions. Linux allows the creation of one *extended* partition to hold multiple *logical* partitions. Solaris allows multiple *slices* in a partition. **mkfs** creates file systems and is often used with frontend tools.

Each file system is unknown to the root file system until it is *mounted* (**mount**). **mount** takes mounting instructions from `/etc/fstab` (`/etc/vfstab` in Solaris). **umount** unmounts file systems. **fsck** checks the integrity of file systems—generally in unmounted condition. It corrects inconsistencies by either deleting files or moving the unconnected ones to `/lost+found`. The root file system must be checked in single-user mode.

The **init** daemon maintains the system at one *run level*. The single-user mode (S or 1) is used for checking file systems. The multiuser mode (2 or 3) starts the system daemons and activates the network. **init** reads `/etc/inittab` which contains instructions to run **getty** at all terminals and the system's *rc* scripts. Processes are killed with the "K" scripts and started with the "S" ones.

shutdown uses **sync** to write the memory contents of the superblock to the file system. Sometimes, when the disk status is newer, "syncing" should not be done.

The **lpsched** daemon monitors and activates the print queue. **lpadmin** is used to add, modify and set the default printer. **lpstat** displays the status of print requests. **accept** makes the print queue ready for accepting jobs, and **reject** inhibits spooling altogether. The printer must be enabled (**enable**) for printing, but sometimes has to be disabled (**disable**).

The administrator exploits **find**'s `-newer` option for incremental backups, and `-mount` for backing up the root file system without traversing the other file systems. He should have a table of contents for each backup so that he knows beforehand which tape contains a requested file. **xargs** is a handy companion to **find** as it enables the file list to be used by a command as its argument list.

TEST YOUR UNDERSTANDING

27.1 How will you ensure that the password is changed after every four weeks?

27.2 A user after logging in is unable to change directories or create files in her home directory. How can that happen?

27.3 Discuss the significance of the boot, root and swap file systems.

27.4 Explain the function of the following commands: (i) **fdisk** (ii) **mkfs** (iii) **fsck**.

27.5 When can **mount** work with only one argument? When is unmounting of a file system not possible?

27.6 Where is the file system mounting information kept in (i) SVR4 (ii) Linux?

27.7 What is *run level*? How do you determine and set the default run level of your system?

27.8 What should you do immediately after you have made changes to `/etc/inittab`?

27.9 Where are the startup scripts for multiuser operation located in (i) SVR4 (ii) Linux?

27.10 Devise a sequence using **find** and **xargs** that removes all files named `a.out`. The **rm** command should work with 20 filenames in each invocation.

FLEX YOUR BRAIN

27.1 Name five features of the restricted shell.

27.2 Why do we install the UNIX system on multiple partitions?

27.3 What facilities do UNIX systems offer to counter superblock corruption?

27.4 Discuss the role of the **sync** command in maintaining the system in a consistent state. When must you not use **sync**?

27.5 Name the important features of the ufs file system. What is the significance of the proc file system?

27.6 What are the precautions you need to take when using **fsck**? What does **fsck** normally do with an unconnected file?

27.7 Describe the two main functions of **init**. What is the significance of run levels 0, 1 and 6?

27.8 You plan to use **tar** to back up all files you have worked with today. How do you plan the backup activity?

27.9 What is the significance of the "start" and "kill" scripts? How are they organized on (i) an SVR4 system (ii) Linux?

27.10 Devise a sequence which shows whether the printer daemon is running irrespective of whether the system is using SVR4 or Linux.

27.11 What is a *page description language* (PDL)? Name two common PDL languages in use. Explain the significance of the *interface script*.

27.12 What is the difference between **accept** and **enable** as the terms are applied to printing in SVR4?

28

TCP/IP Network Administration

Network administration is becoming increasingly important as the age of standalone machines is drawing to a rapid close. In large installations, the network administrator is often different from the UNIX system administrator. At one time, the network administrator had to be an expert of several networking software (like IPX/SPX from Novell or DECnet from Digital). Fortunately, administrators in newer installations don't face this problem as it's now TCP/IP all the way.

A certain amount of TCP/IP theory has been provided at the beginning of the chapter. We'll learn to set up a simple TCP/IP network and configure it to access hosts in other networks. We'll set up the basic Internet services with the Internet daemon and also connect to the Internet using a dialup line. This chapter also introduces two late entrants to the TCP/IP family—PPP and NFS.

WHAT YOU WILL LEARN

- The concept of the *network address* and the different classes of network addresses.
- The significance of the *subnet mask* in splitting a network into multiple ones.
- Install the network interface card and configure it with **ifconfig**.
- Troubleshoot a network with **ping**.
- The role of IP in routing packets, and create routes using **route**.
- Display the network statistics with **netstat**.
- The behavior of **inetd**, the Internet daemon, in controlling other daemons like the ones for Ftp and Telnet.
- Configure a host to enable the Berkeley r-utilities.
- The characteristics of the *Point-to-Point Protocol* (PPP).
- The concept of the *Network File System* (NFS) and its configuration.

TOPICS OF SPECIAL INTEREST

- Use **telnet** to check whether a service is running.
- The complete setup procedure that connects a Linux machine to the Internet with **minicom** and **dip**.

28.1 NETWORK ADDRESSES

The IP address of a host consists of two portions—a *network address* and a *host address*. All nodes in the network have the same network address, while the host address is unique to the host only. The network address may occupy one to three octets from the left, and the remaining are used as host addresses. For instance, the address 193.200.35.160 has 193.200.35 as the network address and .160 as the host address. By convention, we fill up the host portion with zeroes when specifying a network address, so 193.200.35 is actually read as 193.200.35.0.

Who allocates the network and host addresses? Internet network addresses and domain names are allotted by certain *registrars* (agencies) at the behest of the *Internet Corporation for Assigned Names and Numbers* (ICANN). However, some IP addresses are just not used on the Internet. For instance, the network address 192.169.35.0 is used on the Internet, but 192.168.35.0 is not. This network address can be used by any organization; we are coming to these reserved addresses shortly.

Regardless whether the network address is distributed by the Internet authorities or the local administrator, the host address is always allotted locally. The administrator may either assign *static* IP addresses to a host or let a DHCP server assign one *dynamically* from its pool of host addresses. In this chapter, we consider only static IP addresses that are assigned with the **ifconfig** command.

28.1.1 A, B and C Class Networks

Since each octet has 8 bits, the IP address space ranges from 0.0.0.0 to 255.255.255.255. In this space, you can theoretically have 2 ^ 32, i.e., 4 billion addresses, but all are not valid IP addresses that can be assigned to hosts. Moreover, the explosive growth of the Internet was not anticipated by its architects, and the designers presumed that the 32-bit scheme was more than adequate. We should switch to a different scheme (IPv6) soon, but we must know the existing one well.

Though the concept is getting outdated, it's still worth knowing that networks belong to certain *classes*. The number of octets reserved for the network address and the value of the first octet determine the class to which the network belongs. The three classes (Table 28.1) are:

- *Class A* —This address takes the form *N.H.H.H* where *N* signifies the network address and *H* indicates the host address. N here takes the values between 1 and 126. These addresses *were* allotted to very large corporations and institutions but are no longer assigned now. With 24 bits available for *H*, a Class A network can theoretically handle up to 16 million hosts (but actually can't).
- *Class B*—It uses the first two octets (i.e., *N.N.H.H*) as the network address, and has the values between 128 and 191 in the first octet, and any value for the second octet. You can have over 64,000 hosts on a Class B network.
- *Class C*—Here, the network address uses up the first three octets (*N.N.N.H*). The first octet varies from 192 to 223, and the second and third octets can take on any values. The number of hosts on this network is limited to 254.

You can easily tell the type of network by looking at the first octet. For instance, 148.27.3.12 is a Class B address, and 192.142.3.67 is a Class C address. 148.27.0.0 is the network address in one, and 192.142.3.0 in the other.

Table 28.1 The Network Classes and Reserved Addresses

Network Class	*Value of First Octet*	*Subnet Mask*	*Network Addresses for Intranets*
A	1-126	255.0.0.0	10.0.0.0 - 10.255.255.255
B	128-191	255.255.0.0	172.16.0.0 - 172.31.255.255
C	192-223	255.255.255.0	192.168.0.0 - 192.168.255.255

28.1.2 Reserved Addresses

Even though an octet can vary from 0 to 255, you can't use all the values because some of them are set aside for other purposes. Some are used by TCP/IP itself for its own purposes, while the *Internet Assigned Numbers Authority* (IANA) mandates that some addresses are to be used only by local intranets. When allotting IP addresses, you'll have to keep these points in mind:

- *Every network itself has an address* This means that the host part of the address can never have 0 in any of the octets.
- *Every network needs a separate broadcast address* You'll recall *(19.2.4)* that the ARP protocol at the network access layer *broadcasts* an ARP request to to all hosts to determine the destination's MAC address. Its address is selected by setting all octets in the host portion of the address to 255. For instance, the host address `158.37.3.23` (Class B) belongs to the network address `158.37.0.0`. It uscs the broadcast address `158.37.255.255`, which thus can't be assigned to any host.
- *A separate address is needed for loopback* The address `127.0.0.1` is also never used, being the *loopback* or the *localhost* (i.e., this host) address of the host. It allows all networking services to run properly on a standalone host, i.e., one without a network card. A message sent to this address by any host is not transmitted but "looped back" to the same host.
- *The addresses used on the Internet should not be used in the local network even if the network is not connected to the Internet.* A block of addresses from each class has been reserved for use by local internets and is shown in the last column of Table 28.1.

With this background, you should be able to set the addresses for a network. For instance, you could choose the Class C address `192.168.5.0` as your network address. In that case, you can have host addresses between `192.168.5.1` and `192.168.5.254`. The network and broadcast addresses then become `192.168.5.0` and `192.168.5.255`, respectively, and are unavailable for allocation.

28.2 SUBNETS

Every TCP/IP frame traversing the network goes out to all machines, so the network traffic grows as the number of networked machines increases. Even though Class A and B networks permit the creation of millions and thousands of hosts, respectively, you shouldn't, and sometimes can't, have too many hosts in a single network. In that case, you need to break up the network into *subnets*, and use routers to connect the subnets.

Consider the case of a company, Hill Textiles, who have been assigned the network address `147.35.0.0`, and now want to split the network into two subnets. This is a Class B address, where the network and host addresses have 16 bits each. If a third octet is "borrowed" by the network address, this single Class B address becomes a series of "Class C"-type addresses, with the network portion varying from `147.35.0` to `147.35.254`. Hill Textiles can then internally have 255 Class C network addresses without requiring to obtain a separate network address for each. For instance, they can have two subnets with the network addresses `147.35.3.0` and `147.35.5.0`. All this makes perfect sense to TCP/IP.

This division into two subnets has no significance to a computer outside the network. It doesn't care to know whether `147.35.3.45` is a Class B or an internally "sub-netted" Class C address. Rather, it will simply look at the first octet and treat all frames addressed to `147.35` as belonging to a Class B network. However, knowledge of the borrowed bits is necessary for Hill Textiles, who have to treat `147.35.3` and `147.35.5` as two different networks and route the frames accordingly.

TCP/IP associates every network address with the *subnet mask*. This mask is also represented as a series of four octets, where the individual bits of the network portion of the address are set to 1. For instance, if you borrow the entire third octet from the host address to be used in the network address, the network would then have `255.255.255.0` as the subnet mask. All networks have a subnet mask that determines whether it is subnetted or not. Without subnetting, `147.35.3.0` represents a Class B network with the subnet mask `255.255.0.0`.

Borrowing an entire octet for the purpose of subnetting makes sense only when you really require a large number of subnets. Now, Hill Textiles needs to have only two subnets. There's no need to borrow the entire third octet; only the first two bits are sufficient. TCP/IP also allows this; you can use any number of bits from the host address. When two bits of the third octet are borrowed, the subnet mask in binary notation changes to

```
11111111 11111111 11000000 00000000
```

This in decimal becomes `255.255.192.0`. So now 14 bits remain for the host address.

The subnetting story doesn't stop here. Further, when Hill Textiles allocate the addresses of its machines, they have to take care that in one subnet *the first two bits of the third octet should be identical (but not* 11*)*. Thus it can easily have addresses `147.35.86.23` and `147.35.118.34` for two machines in the same subnet because the first two bits of the third octet for both machines are set to 01. (86 is 01010110 and 118 is 01110110.) It is equally possible to have another subnet where the respective bits are 10.

Note Even though there can be four combinations of 0s and 1s with two borrowed bits, the number of subnets you can have here is actually restricted to 2 because the bits 00 are reserved for the network address, and 11 for the broadcast address. For three borrowed bits, the number is 8 - 2 = 6.

28.3 SETTING UP THE NETWORK INTERFACE CARD

You need an Ethernet card on every machine that has to be connected in a network. The UNIX system identifies the network interface at the time of booting just as it identifies hard disks and

CD-ROM drives. Most systems install the interface along with the necessary drivers at the time of system installation, but vendors also providc specific tools to add a card later.

When you set up your network card, the system may try to set two hardware parameters automatically, but you'll have to provide them if it can't. In general, these are the parameters that have to be set if your UNIX machine has to function properly in the network:

- The I/O address (a hardware parameter).
- The interrupt vector (a hardware parameter).
- The IP address.
- The subnet mask.
- The broadcast address.
- The gateway address.
- The hostname.
- The domain name.

The I/O address is a hexadecimal number (typically 0x300). IRQ is an integer (typically 2 or 9). If your machine sets values for these parameters automatically, then you need not bother. Otherwise, you have to set them yourself on the card before you proceed. For PCs, you may have to run a small DOS program provided by the manufacturer after the card is inserted into the machine. You have to make sure the I/O address and IRQ don't conflict with the ones used by the other devices of your system (like the keyboard, hard disks and serial ports).

The machine must identify the card correctly at the time of booting so we can then take up the software part of the configuration. You must now define sets of four octets—for IP address, subnet mask, broadcast address and gateway address. This information is used by the **`ifconfig`** and **`route`** commands at the time of startup. The machine also uses the **`hostname`** command to set your machine's FQDN from the input you provide. The subnet mask and broadcast address are often determined automatically by the system from the IP address you provide when your network is not subnetted.

You have to provide the gateway address only if your machine is connected to a gateway or router. A gateway may sometimes be the only way for your host to connect to the Internet or to another network. It's generally a dedicated device, but you can make your computer behave like a gateway if it has two network interface cards, and provide each with an IP address that belongs to the respective network.

28.4 `ifconfig`: CONFIGURING THE NETWORK INTERFACE

Since TCP/IP is independent of the network hardware, the IP addresses are not built into the kernel, but rather reside in the networking software. You have to use the **`ifconfig`** command to set the IP address of your interface. The command is used like this:

```
ifconfig eth0 192.168.0.3
```

The syntax requires the command to be followed by the interface name (here, `eth0`) and the IP address. This not only sets an IP address to the interface, but also brings it up. On non-Linux machines, this command is adequate to prepare your machine for use on the network. **ifconfig** doesn't set the interface permanently as it doesn't change any of the system's files. The command has to be run from the startup scripts every time the system is booted.

ifconfig optionally uses the subnet mask and the broadcast address as arguments. We didn't provide them here as they are not required if the network is not subnetted. If your network conforms to the class rules (A, B or C), then **ifconfig** computes the subnet mask and broadcast address automatically. For subnetted networks, the netmask and broadcast parameters have to be provided separately. This is how we have to use **ifconfig** for one of the hosts in a subnet:

```
ifconfig le0 147.35.3.45 netmask 255.255.192.0 broadcast 147.35.63.255
```

It's a different interface (`le0`) we are using this time. The broadcast address also has been specified even though it could have been derived from the subnet mask. (The corresponding bits of the host part of both always add up to 255.)

To know more about all the interfaces on your system, depending on the system you use, you may simply have to use **ifconfig** (as in Linux) or provide the `-a` option. This output was obtained on a Solaris machine:

```
# ifconfig -a
le0: flags=4043<UP,BROADCAST,RUNNING,MULTICAST> mtu 1500
      inet 147.35.3.45 netmask ffffff00 broadcast 192.168.0.255
      perf. params: recv size: 4096; send size: 8192; full-size frames: 1
      ether 00:20:18:62:47:e0
lo0: flags=4049<UP,LOOPBACK,RUNNING,MULTICAST> mtu 8232
      inet 127.0.0.1 netmask ff000000
      perf. params: recv size: 57344; send size: 57344; full-size frames: 1
```

The output is system-variant, but you can know all the static parameters of the interface from this output. **ifconfig** here not only tells you the IP address of your machine but also its status. The system is UP, supports BROADCASTs and is currently RUNNING. Note that it also shows you the MAC address of the interface card (`00:20:18:62:47:e0`).

There seems to be yet another interface, `lo0`; this is the loopback interface which every host must have. Even though **ifconfig** was not explicitly used to set its IP address to `127.0.0.1`, it was actually done at the time of system installation.

ifconfig doesn't merely set or display the interface attributes. It can also be used to activate and deactivate the interface. Sometimes that is necessary if the IP address has to be changed. The command is used in these ways:

```
ifconfig eth0 down                    Interface disabled
ifconfig eth0 up                      Interface enabled
ifconfig eth0 192.168.0.5 up          Interface set and up
```

ifconfig ensures that you'll be able to connect to all hosts in the same network (provided they too are set up properly), but you still won't be able to connect to hosts in another network. For that to happen, your system must be provided with a route to the network. Routing is considered shortly.

28.5 ping: CHECKING THE NETWORK

Once the network card has been configured and the addresses set, you have to send packets to a machine known to be working in the network. The command people use most in troubleshooting a network is the **ping** (Packet Internet Groper) command. The command sends 56-byte packets to a remote destination which answers back on receipt:

```
# ping -s earth                                          Solaris; Linux doesn't need -s option
PING earth: 56 data bytes
64 bytes from earth.pdsit.becs.ac.in (192.168.35.140): icmp_seq=0. time=0. ms
64 bytes from earth.pdsit.becs.ac.in (192.168.35.140): icmp_seq=1. time=0. ms
64 bytes from earth.pdsit.becs.ac.in (192.168.35.140): icmp_seq=2. time=0. ms
64 bytes from earth.pdsit.becs.ac.in (192.168.35.140): icmp_seq=3. time=0. ms
[Ctrl-c]                                                Display interrupted by pressing this key
----earth PING Statistics----
5 packets transmitted, 5 packets received, 0% packet loss
round-trip (ms)  min/avg/max = 0/0/0
```

That there has been no "packet loss" only confirms the connectivity between the local and remote hosts. "Pinging" a host doesn't require any server process to run at the other end. However, a successful **ping** output doesn't necessarily imply that the services themselves are running. For instance, if **inetd** is not started up on the remote machine, neither **ftp** nor **telnet** will work even if **ping** reports success.

28.6 ROUTING

A packet needs to be handled by a router if it is destined for a host in another network. Each host in the network maintains a *routing table* in the kernel that contains at least three fields—the name of the interface, the destination address and the IP address of the router. When IP receives a packet, it uses the subnet mask to extract from it the network portion of the destination address. It then compares this address with every entry in the table. (Note that an IP packet doesn't contain this mask.)

If IP finds the address in the routing table, it routes the packet through the gateway specified there. If not, then IP has to send the packet through a *default route*, which is also specified in the table. IP, thus, only specifies the route to the *network* rather than the route to the *host* itself. This is one of the most important features of IP.

Every network has a minimal routing table even if there is actually no router present. For small-sized networks, the network administrator can create a *static* routing table when there are limited routes to a host.

However, the Internet uses *dynamic* routing since there are often several routes to a host on it. Over there, routing daemons (like **routed**) communicate with other routing daemons on other machines to build dynamic routing tables. Routes are adjusted dynamically if the network topology changes or parts of the network go down. Routing protocols can also decide the most cost-effective route to a host. They make IP look "intelligent."

28.6.1 route: Building a Static Routing Table

The **ifconfig** command builds a minimal routing table which is good enough for hosts on the same network (Linux excepted). To forward packets to a host in another network, the routing information for the gateway has to be added to the routing table. If dynamic routing is not involved, the administrator has to manually build a static routing table. This is done with the **route** command.

To demonstrate how to set up a static routing table, let's consider the Class C network 192.168.0.0 which has the address 192.168.0.10 for the host *sunny*. The network has two gateways—*michael* (192.168.0.1) which accesses the Internet, and *fredo* (192.168.0.20) which is connected to another network 172.16.1.0. We'll have to configure the routing table on *sunny* to install the routes through the two gateways. We assume that the network interfaces on *michael* and *fredo* have already been configured with **ifconfig**.

We'll use the **route** command on *sunny* to first install the route to the non-Internet gateway (on *fredo*):

```
route add 172.16.1.0 192.168.0.20
```

We added a route (add) 172.16.1.0 to the routing table and specified that the gateway to be contacted for forwarding packets is 192.168.0.20 (the address of *fredo*).

Since *michael* acts as the gateway to the Internet, it obviously handles more routes (not necessarily traffic), and should, therefore, be set as the default gateway. This is done using the keyword default instead of a specific route:

```
route add default 192.168.0.1
```

Once you set up the default route this way, all packets not meant for the local network and for 172.16.1.0 are forwarded to this gateway (192.168.0.1). You can then have unhindered access to the Net. This assumes, of course, that the gateway machine is configured as a *firewall* to support *IP forwarding* or as a proxy server (not considered in this book) and has allowed this host to forward packets to this machine.

To remove a route, the delete keyword is used. The routes created above can be deleted by simply replacing the add keyword with delete:

```
route delete 172.16.1.0 192.168.0.20
route delete default 192.168.0.1
```

LINUX: Linux uses a slightly different syntax for the **route** command; it uses the keyword gw to indicate a gateway. The **route add** and **route delete** commands in Linux would have to be entered as:

Linux uses gw

```
route add 172.16.1.0 gw 192.168.0.20
route add default gw 192.168.0.1

route delete 172.16.1.0 gw 192.168.0.20
route delete default gw 192.168.0.1
```

Expectedly, **route** doesn't need to know the subnet mask as long as the network is not subnetted. But when it is, the subnet mask has to be specified with the `netmask` keyword. Sometimes you have to use the keyword `net` with the destination address to make **route** understand that we are referring to a *network* route. Occasionally, you may require to specify a *host* route, in which case the `host` keyword has to be used. Linux and Solaris use `-net` and `-host` instead.

As with **ifconfig**, these **route** statements will be valid as long as the machine is up. They will have to be executed every time the system is booted, so they are invariably kept in the system's startup scripts.

28.7 netstat: DISPLAYING THE NETWORK PARAMETERS

The **netstat -rn** command displays the routing table. The `-r` option lists the table, and `-n` prints the numeric form of the IP addresses. After executing the two **route add** statements in the previous section, this is what the table looks like on a Linux system:

```
# netstat -rn
Kernel IP routing table
Destination     Gateway         Genmask         Flags   MSS Window  irtt Iface
172.16.1.0      192.168.0.20    255.255.255.255 UGH       0 0          0 eth0
192.168.0.10    0.0.0.0         255.255.255.255 UH        0 0          0 eth0
192.168.0.0     0.0.0.0         255.255.255.0   U         0 0          0 eth0
127.0.0.0       0.0.0.0         255.0.0.0       U         0 0          0 lo
0.0.0.0         192.168.0.1     0.0.0.0         UG        0 0          0 eth0
```

The first line shows that any packet destined for the network `172.16.1.0` is forwarded to the machine with the IP address `192.168.0.20`. The `G` under *Flags* indicates a gateway; if it is absent, then the hosts are directly connected. Providing a network address here makes sense as it reduces the size of the routing table.

The third line shows that packets meant for the network `192.168.0.0` are forwarded to the machine `0.0.0.0`—the machine whose routing table is displayed. This machine is using its own interface to communicate with other machines of the same network. If a packet's destination address doesn't match any of the entries in the first column, then the last line is decisive. Since the destination here is `0.0.0.0`, the default gateway `192.168.0.1` will be used. Here, `0.0.0.0` represents addresses not matched by any previous addresses (like the `*` used by **case**). Sometimes, you may see the word `default` in this position.

You can see that every host in a network has two interfaces—the Ethernet address (here, `eth0`) and the loopback address (`lo0`). All the interfaces are up and running (Flag shows `U`). `H` indicates that you can reach only a single host through the route. A packet meant for the localhost (`127.0.0.0`) uses the same machine (`0.0.0.0`) as its gateway. If you have understood all this, then you should be able to conclude that the machine on which this command was run has the IP address `192.168.0.10`.

> **Note** If a machine is not connected to any host, the routing table displays only a single entry for the loopback interface. The presence of this route in the routing table means that you can use TCP/IP tools on that host.

28.8 inetd: THE INTERNET DAEMON

In the remaining sections of this chapter, we take up the configuration issues related to some common server applications and one client application (PPP). Space constraints don't permit discussion on the other important server applications like DNS, Mail and Web services, but the ones we are going to discuss will prepare us well for the complexities associated with configuration of the TCP/IP services. We begin with the common and oldest services like Ftp and Telnet.

UNIX has a large number of daemons, each listening at a specific port number for a request from its respective client. Can we afford to run all these daemons constantly even though some of them may not be used most of the time? Certainly not, it makes sense to invoke them as and when required. The **inetd** daemon solves this problem. Modern Linux systems no longer use **inetd**, but **xinetd**, which allows greater flexibility in configuring each service individually.

Many TCP/IP daemons like those for the Telnet and Ftp services are not started *directly* by the system's startup scripts, but by the master Internet daemon, **inetd**. **inetd** listens on *multiple* ports for any connection requests. When it detects one, it launches the program that's defined for that port in its configuration file, /etc/inetd.conf. This file contains one line for each service:

```
ftp     stream  tcp6  nowait root   /usr/sbin/in.ftpd     in.ftpd
telnet  stream  tcp6  nowait root   /usr/sbin/in.telnetd  in.telnetd
talk    dgram   udp   wait   root   /usr/sbin/in.talkd    in.talkd
finger  stream  tcp6  nowait nobody /usr/sbin/in.fingerd  in.fingerd
#tftp   dgram   udp6  wait   root   /usr/sbin/in.tftpd    in.tftpd -s /tftpboot
```

The first column shows the service. The protocol it uses is shown in the third column. Three services here use the tcp6 protocol, which is simply the TCP protocol used on IPv6 (the new generation TCP/IP that uses 128-bit IP addresses). tcp6 can also handle IPv4 (the one that uses 32-bit addresses) requests. (Similarly, udp6 uses the UDP protocol on IPv6.) If your machine doesn't support IPv6, you'll see tcp (or udp) in this column.

If the fourth column shows nowait, it means that multiple connections can be made for the same service. The previous-to-last column shows the absolute pathname of the server program. If the server program is used with arguments, then they are shown in the last column. Here the commented line shows that **in.tftpd** is used with two arguments.

UNIX systems start up with a number of **inetd**-based services, some of which may not be required at all. In that case, it's better to comment the line related to the service. You can now understand why the Trivial File Transfer Protocol (Tftp) doesn't run by default on most UNIX systems.

Now, which port number does the Ftp server (**in.ftpd**) use? This number is determined by a lookup of /etc/services. This file is related to inetd.conf through their first fields—the service name. The file contains two fields:

```
ftp         21/tcp
telnet      23/tcp
smtp        25/tcp
pop3        110/tcp
pop3        110/udp
```

The port number has the protocol tag affixed to it. A lookup of this table not only determines the port number used by a service but also the protocol. Many services in this file have two entries—one for TCP and the other for UDP.

LINUX: Even though today's Linux systems continue to offer **inetd**, they also offer **xinetd**, the extended Internet daemon. This server provides multithreaded support in some cases and also maintains a separate configuration file for each service in /etc/xinetd.d. We show below the configuration file for Telnet (named telnet):

```
service telnet
{
        disable = yes
        flags               = REUSE
        socket_type         = stream
        wait                = no
        user                = root
        server              = /usr/sbin/in.telnetd
        log_on_failure      += USERID
}
```

You'll find most of the fields in inetd.conf present here. The line to watch out is the one specifying the variable disable. On many Linux systems, most of the **xinetd** services are disabled by default, so to enable the Telnet service on this machine, set disable = no, and then restart **xinetd** using **/etc/rc.d/init.d/xinetd restart**.

28.8.1 Using telnet to Check Whether a Service is Running

To know whether a particular service is running on a host, you can use the port number as the second argument to **telnet**. For instance, to check whether the mail service is running on the host *cal.vsnl.net.in*, use 25 (the port number used by SMTP in /etc/services) as an additional argument to **telnet**:

```
$ telnet cal.vsnl.net.in 25
Trying 202.54.9.25...
Connected to cal.vsnl.net.in.
Escape character is '^]'.
220 kolkata.vsnl.net.in ESMTP Postfix
```

The ESMTP service is running, and you can see SMTP-related messages emanating from the server. ESMTP is an enhanced form of SMTP, the application protocol used to transport mail. Here, you'll have to use ESMTP's **quit** command to quit **telnet**.

28.9 ENFORCING SECURITY FOR THE BERKELEY r-UTILITIES

Berkeley created the r-utilities to make it easier (and less secure) to access a remote machine. A properly configured system allows password-free access to these tools. UNIX provides two levels of authorization at

- The system level which applies to all users of a host. Authorization here is controlled by the file `/etc/hosts.equiv` on the remote machine.
- The user level where any user can set access restrictions to her account in the file `$HOME/.rhosts`.

UNIX systems don't come with any entries in these configuration files, so you have to insert them before you can use the r-utilities. Considering system-level authorization first, if henry tries from his machine *saturn* to access his own account on the remote host *uranus*, the remote system will first check its own `/etc/hosts.equiv` file for *user equivalence* of henry on both machines. Each line of this file typically contains one field or two separated by whitespace:

```
localhost          We'll ignore this line
saturn             No password required for like-to-like accounts
saturn charlie     charlie has more powers
```

The second line, containing only `saturn`, implies that all users on the local machine can access their like-to-like accounts on the remote machine without using a password. The host is said to be *trusted*, and the users are said to have *user equivalence* with their respective accounts in the remote host. The user charlie has additional access privileges. He can access *any* account without using a password!

Unhindered access is something no administrator would generally allow as it presents a potential security hazard. A better idea would be to enforce access at the user level with the file `~/.rhosts`. This file is edited by the concerned user.

If charlie on *saturn* needs to access henry's account on *uranus* without using a password, and without using `/etc/hosts.equiv` on *uranus*, henry needs to have a `$HOME/.rhosts` file in *uranus* containing this entry:

```
saturn charlie
```

However, if the line contains just the word `saturn`, then only the same user (i.e., henry) can log in without a password. The guiding principle is this: When there are two fields in a line of `.rhosts`, the corresponding user is trusted; otherwise, the same user is trusted.

Tip It's always preferable to enforce security at the user level. The safest and most restrictive entry would be to have just the hostname in `~/.rhosts` of the concerned user.

28.10 pppd: THE POINT-TO-POINT PROTOCOL (PPP)

Your computer may not have a network card, or you may be living where the only means of communication with the outside world is the telephone. Today, you can link up two machines through the serial ports (COM1 and COM2 in DOS) and run TCP/IP on this link. A special protocol makes this possible—the *Point-to-Point Protocol* (PPP). In the sphere of serial port communication, PPP has replaced SLIP and UUCP (the protocol that powered USENET in its teens), which have already seen their best days. Today, it's the standard way users access the Net using a modem on their computer's serial port (though, it too is making way for newer technologies).

PPP is an unusual protocol. It sets up a connection between two hosts, using its own set of IP addresses so the other protocols like FTP and TELNET can run thereafter. Since there's no network interface card here, PPP frames, and not Ethernet frames, are exchanged at both ends. PPP is also a client-server application except that the same program, **pppd** (in `/usr/sbin`), has to be invoked with different options to run either as client or server. In this section, we'll discuss the BSD PPP package, which is used by Linux and many UNIX systems (but not Solaris).

We assume you are logged in as root user since running **pppd** from an ordinary user account requires some configuration. If you are connecting to your ISP, you have to start the **pppd** process on your local machine like this:

```
/usr/sbin/pppd /dev/ttyS0 115200 crtscts modem defaultroute noipdefault -detach
```

`/dev/ttyS0` is the modem device attached to the first serial port (COM1), and the port speed (here 115,200 bauds, i.e., bits per second) is set to three times the maximum speed the modem can handle. There's a reason behind this *(28.11.2)*. The command sets up another interface (`ppp0`) whose attributes can be displayed by the **ifconfig** and **netstat -rn** commands.

You need to run PPP between your computer (client) and your ISP's (server) to access the Internet. If the client PPP interface is set up without a separate IP address (as above), then the server has to provide this before establishing the link. If you always have to use **pppd** with a fixed set of options, then you may keep most of these options in **pppd**'s configuration file, `/etc/ppp/options`. This file holds one option per line.

pppd has a complex command line, and you'd better know the complete syntax in case you have to start the process manually using a tool like **minicom**. You must also understand why the command above is invoked with these options:

- Since PPP uses all 8 bits, hardware flow control must be used (`crtscts`) so the system can adjust the flow of the stream.
- Software flow control must be switched off. We don't want the characters *[Ctrl-s]* and *[Ctrl-q]* to be interpreted by the modem as the start and stop characters. This is assured as **pppd** here is not using the `xonoff` option.
- The default route (`defaultroute`) for any IP packet not meant for the local network has to be routed through the PPP interface.
- Most ISPs feature dynamic addressing, which means the server has to provide the client's IP address (`noipdefault`). PPP also allows you to set the IP address yourself.
- **pppd** must not be allowed to be detached from the terminal (`-detach`) or else the connection will not persist.

We'll not consider the server's options as we can safely assume your ISP knows what they are doing. However, if you set up a PPP connection between your machines at home and work, then you must know the server options too.

Note PPP doesn't have separate client and server programs. It is neither started by the system's startup scripts nor handled by **inetd**. **pppd** can run as server or client depending on the options used.

If you are using **pppd** from an ordinary user account, then you may have to set its SUID bit *(17.3.2)*. This is easily done by using **chmod a+s /usr/sbin/pppd**. Some versions of Linux merely expect the user to belong to the same group as the one that owns **pppd**.

28.11 USING PPP TO CONNECT TO THE INTERNET

We'll now use a Linux machine to connect to an ISP—and through their gateway—to the Internet. You'll have to connect a modem to a serial port (say, COM1) and use it to dial out to the ISP. Modem installation in Linux is a straightforward affair; just set up a symbolic link between `/dev/modem` and `/dev/ttyS0` (assuming you are using the first serial port). The listing of `/dev/modem` should look like this:

```
lrwxrwxrwx   1 root      root                  10 Dec  5 08:44 /dev/modem -> /dev/ttyS0
```

ISPs normally use UNIX machines, and you have to log on to their computer using a username and password that have been registered with them. Once logged in, the PPP process has to be started at the server end. If the ISP's machine doesn't do it automatically (normally it does), then you have to start it. After that, you have to quit the ISP's machine *without resetting the modem* and then start PPP on your machine.

The ISP's PPP process generally allots your IP address—often dynamically from its pool of addresses. After you have started **pppd** on your machine, the link is established between your computer and the ISP's host. This link also provides you with a default route (the `defaultroute` option in **pppd**) to the Net. Your computer then becomes part of the Internet. The ISP's machine has no further role to play except to provide the PPP link which remains till we hang up.

Your ISP will also maintain one or more name servers *(20.1)* for you. These are machines that perform hostname-IP address resolution. Access to the name service is necessary because all domain names must be resolved and their IP addresses inserted inside the PPP packets before they move out of your machine. The ISP will also normally offer email services and maintain a news server so you can access newsgroups.

28.11.1 Specifying the Name Server and Resolver

Your ISP should provide you with the IP addresses of their name servers. You now need to modify two files on your Linux system. Simply insert these two lines in `/etc/host.conf`:

```
order hosts bind                                   Name service enabled with BIND
multi on
```

A resolver is a client *(19.3)* which acts on behalf of the application to request a name server to convert an FQDN to the IP address. The resolver on UNIX systems uses the configuration file `/etc/resolv.conf`. Place your ISP's name server addresses in this file (the ones shown here are used by the author's ISP):

```
nameserver 202.54.1.30                             The IP addresses of the primary
nameserver 202.54.9.1                              and the secondary name servers
```

This completes the resolver configuration. Your machine now knows it has to use BIND (after `/etc/hosts` fails) to resolve FQDNs, and it also knows which machines to contact for this purpose. BIND is the name Berkeley gave to the Domain Name Service (DNS) that ISPs need to maintain at their end.

28.11.2 Connecting with `minicom`

To connect to the Net, you'll use two character-based tools. Eventually, you'll learn to pass all input to the remote end through a script, but you must know what strings to expect from that side. So just dial out, observe the prompts and input the appropriate strings. **`minicom`** is an ideal tool for this purpose as it can be used with the Hayes' "AT" commands. These are strings starting with `AT`, which can dial a modem and perform some initializations too.

Before you dial out, make sure you have set the modem speed to the highest throughput that it can handle. Most modems and ISPs support data compression, which has the effect of increasing the modem's rated speed—often by a factor of 4. This means that you can safely use 115,200 bps (bits per second) as the speed for a 56 kbps (kilo bits per second) modem. If you are using **`minicom`** and a 33.6 or 56 kbps modem, invoke **`minicom -s`** and then set the serial port speed to the inflated figure. Save the settings before you quit **`minicom`** and then reenter normally.

You now have to use a couple of "AT" commands. First, reset the modem with **`atz`**, and then dial out with **`atdt`**, followed by the telephone number of the ISP. Input the usual things at the two prompts requiring user verification. We assume the ISP starts the **`pppd`** process automatically. Here's the **`minicom`** display which shows the dialup and login procedure:

```
Welcome to minicom 2.00.0

OPTIONS: History Buffer, F-key Macros, Search History Buffer, I18n
Compiled on Jun 23 2002, 16:41:20.

Press CTRL-A Z for help on special keys

AT S7=45 S0=0 L1 V1 X4 &c1 E1 Q0
OK
atdt172228
CONNECT 33600/ARQ/V34/LAPM/V42BIS
Welcome to VSNL Kolkata

Username: sumit
Password: ************
..!.........4).....~}#.!}!}"}  }?}!}$}%."}&}%}&.4)}!}"}(}"}1}$}%.
[17;80H}
[Ctrl-a]q                                       Doesn't reset the modem
```

The "junk" you see are simply the PPP packets generated at the server end. The last line shows us quitting **`minicom`**, this time with *[Ctrl-a]* **q**. You now have to start the PPP client program on your machine. You have already seen the entire command line earlier, you now need to execute this command from the root account like this:

```
# /usr/sbin/pppd /dev/ttyS0 57600 crtscts modem defaultroute noipdefault -detach
Using interface ppp0
Connect: ppp0 <--> /dev/ttyS0
local  IP address 219.65.197.165
remote IP address 203.200.163.143
```

Since this line can take some time to type in, you should run it from a shell script. The ISP here features *dynamic IP addressing*; your machine is allotted the IP address `219.65.197.165` dynamically from the ISP's pool. This has no relevance to the actual IP address that sumit may have in his local network. The next time sumit logs in, his IP address for the PPP interface would be different.

The display of the two IP addresses generally points to a successful connection, and the modem lights should start blinking. Now that the link is up, you can freely use your machine's **ftp** and **telnet** commands and your Web browser to communicate with machines on the Internet. You are now on the Net.

To kill the **pppd** client and drop the line, use the interrupt key. Better still would be to run the **pppd** client in the background and then kill it with **killall pppd**. If the **pppd** command fails to work, and doesn't make the modem lights blink on invocation, then skip to Section 28.11.4.

28.11.3 Using dip

The **minicom** experience will also help us develop a **dip** script. On examining the **minicom** output, you'll note that the two strings you should be expecting are `Username:` and `Password:`. The strings you should send in return are shown beside them. We'll develop a **dip** script using this information.

Among the character-based dialing tools, **dip** is available on a wide variety of UNIX systems like SunOS, AIX, Ultrix and Linux. It has rudimentary programming constructs and provides logic for error-handling. It can be programmed to perform redialing too. Here's the script that you should use with the expect-send strings derived above:

```
# cat dipdial.dip              Customary to use .dip extension
get $local 0.0.0.0             Local IP address is dynamic
port modem                     The symbolic link should be set up
speed 115200                   Recommended for a 56 kbps modem
reset
flush
send atdt172226\r              Can also use dial 172226
sleep 2
wait CONNECT                   The CONNECT message comes from the server
wait name: 20                  Wait up to 20 seconds for name: prompt
send sumit\r
wait word:
send a9h4uil\r                 Password is visible!!
mode PPP                       pppd at server started automatically; starts pppd at client
exit
```

This script needs little explanation as most of it has been provided already. Note that the *[Enter]* key is represented here by `\r`—the carriage return sequence understood by the **echo** command also. We used substrings to allow for minor variations in the prompt strings. For instance, `name:`

takes care of both `username:` and `Username:`. The `if` statement ensures that the modem will redial if errors are encountered. Note that **dip** starts the **pppd** process at the client end with a simple statement (`mode PPP`). This has the effect of starting the **pppd** command line shown earlier.

After you have saved this in a file, `dipdial.dip`, you have to run the **dip** command:

```
/usr/sbin/dip -v dipdial.dip
```

That's all there is to it. This should dial the modem, log you in, start PPP processes at both ends and return you the prompt. You are now on the Internet. Use **dip -k** to terminate **pppd**. If this method works, then drop the `-v` (verbose) option because that displays your password on the screen.

Tip If you have a pulse-dialing telephone system, use **atdp** instead of **atdt**. If you use a slower modem, say, 14.4 kbps, set the speed to 38,400. If your modem won't dial, try using **atx3dt** instead of **atdt**. If all this fails, try the **wvdial** and **wvdialconf** commands if they are available on your Linux system. **wvdialconf** can often configure these settings for you.

28.11.4 After Establishing the Link

It's possible that **dip** went through without a hitch, but you are still unable to connect to a remote site. In that case, you should first test whether your PPP interface is up by using **netstat -rn** or **route -n**:

```
# netstat -rn                                        Can also use route -n
Kernel IP routing table
Destination       Gateway           Genmask           Flags   MSS Window  irtt Iface
203.200.163.143 0.0.0.0           255.255.255.255 UH      40 0           0 ppp0
127.0.0.0         0.0.0.0           255.0.0.0         U       40 0           0 lo
0.0.0.0           203.200.163.143 0.0.0.0           UG      40 0           0 ppp0
```

You should now see two lines pertaining to `ppp0`. The second one shows the effect of using the `defaultroute` option with the **pppd** command. "Ping" the server, and if this works, then try pinging a known host with, say, **ping www.google.com**. If **ping** doesn't produce the usual output, then check the speed set for the modem in the dialing script.

Note You may sometimes get the message that the modem is locked. In that case, the error message will tell you to delete the file `/var/lock/LCK..modem`. Follow the directive.

28.12 THE NETWORK FILE SYSTEM

The facility to log on remotely and transfer files using TCP/IP is often not enough. It's impractical to transfer a large database. It would be much better if the remote file system could be mounted on a directory in the local file system so the user wouldn't need to access the remote system with any special commands. Sun Microsystems felt this need and pioneered the concept of the *Network File System* (NFS), which has since been ported to all flavors of UNIX.

A network file system mounts a remote file system on a local directory. This provides the illusion that they are locally connected. For instance, if the `/datab` file system on host *fredo* is mounted locally on the directory `/oracle`, you'll not know whether `/oracle` is a local or a remote file system. No special commands are necessary to access these files on the remote (mounted) file system.

The NFS facility is useful for some reasons. Instead of encouraging users to make copies of files (as in **ftp**), NFS allows users working on several computers to share files. This means you can have a number of large disks on a few computers that can be accessed by others. It also makes system maintenance and backup easier because the administrator needs to back up and maintain a single set of files rather than back up identical copies on multiple machines.

Unlike local mounting, NFS is not restricted to mounting only file systems. *It allows you to mount any remote directory even if the directory doesn't constitute a separate file system*. Users may be allowed read or read-write permission on a directory. You can also specify the hosts permitted to use the facility. However, NFS doesn't set permissions at the user level. If you have allowed access to a host, then you are trusting all users on that host. This makes NFS somewhat insecure, especially when providing write access.

28.12.1 Setting Up NFS

NFS is handled mainly by two daemons, **mountd** and **nfsd**, on the server side (**rpc.mountd** and **rpc.nfsd** in Linux). **mountd** validates the user request, while **nfsd** actually serves the client by mounting and unmounting file systems. On the client side, the commands are the same (**mount** and **umount**), but used here with some modifications.

Most systems use BSD-type NFS, which *exports* file systems rather than Sun's Solaris which *shares* them. In this chapter, we'll discuss the BSD system that is also used by Linux.

When the client issues a mount request, **mountd** looks up the server's `/etc/exports` file for verifying the access rights of the client. This file contains a line for every "exported" directory that can be mounted remotely. It can also specify the type of access permitted and the hosts authorized to mount the directory. Here are some typical entries from `/etc/exports`:

```
/                                            Read-write access to root for all hosts!
/project3/doc
/java/programs    -ro                        Read-only access to all hosts
/hrd/html   -access=fredo:tessio             Access only to hosts fredo and tessio
/prog/html   -rw=michael                     Read-write access to host michael
```

LINUX: The format in Linux is different; it follows the directory name with a space-delimited list of one or more hosts. Each hostname is accompanied by the type of permission in parentheses. The first two lines are the same on this system too, and are thus not shown:

```
/java/programs   (ro)                        Read-only access to all
/hrd/html   fredo(rw) tessio(rw)
/projects        *.heavens.com(rw)           All hosts in heavens.com domain
```

While the first line specifies read-only permission for all machines, the second one provides read-write access to the hosts *fredo* and *tessio*. The last line allows read-write access to all hosts in the *heavens.com* domain.

Once the directory is mounted, access is controlled by **nfsd**. Make sure that both **mountd** and a sufficient number of **nfsd** processes are running, and then export the directories in /etc/exports with the **exportfs** command:

```
exportfs -a                                    Red Hat uses same command
```

If your system doesn't have the **exportfs** command, then you need to locate the script that contains statements starting the **mountd** and **nfsd** daemons. This is the script named **nfs** in /etc/rc.d/init.d on modern Red Hat systems..

Once the server is ready, the client simply has to execute the **mount** command. This time we have to specify the file system type as nfs. Here, we try a soft mount (soft) in the background (bg) in read-only mode:

```
mount -r -F nfs -o soft,bg sunny:/project3/doc /fredo/project3
```

Soft mounting ensures that the client doesn't retry the operation if mounting fails. This mode is recommended for reading documentation. Here, even though the directory was available for mounting in read-write mode, **mount**'s -r option makes sure that /etc/exports is overruled. You can also use the remount option, which along with the other **mount** options, has already been discussed *(27.6.4)*.

Like local file systems, NFS file systems can also be specified in /etc/fstab. **mount** then need not be used with such a complex set of options. The above mounting action can be performed automatically at boot time if fstab contains this entry:

```
sunny:/project3/doc  /fredo/project3 nfs ro,soft,bg 0 0
```

NFS is the most common way of sharing files across the network. It can be quite cost-effective in that it is often used to store a single copy of software on a mountable file system. The advantage here is that updates to the software are carried out at only one place. Some organizations use NFS to export the mail spool directory, /var/mail, for centralizing their mail.

28.13 CONCLUSION

Network maintenance has today become an important administrative function. We considered some of the basic networking functions in this chapter. We learned to enable and disable the commonly used services like Telnet and Ftp. If your network is connected to the Internet, you need to set up a DNS server, a mail server and one for hosting your Web site. The author expects users to configure all these services themselves.

WRAP UP

Every host in a network has a common *network address* and *broadcast address* that is used to address all hosts. On the Internet, network addresses are categorized into Class A, B and C. A host can communicate with itself using the *loopback address*, 127.0.0.1.

The *subnet mask* shows whether any bits have been borrowed from the host address to form part of the network address. IP uses this mask to determine whether a packet belongs to the current network or not.

ifconfig sets the IP address and the subnet mask of the network interface. It is also used to activate and deactivate an interface. **ping** and **netstat** are used to check the connectivity of the network. **route** builds the kernel's routing table to indicate the gateways that have to be used for routing packets destined for external networks.

Many TCP/IP services like Telnet, Ftp and Pop3 are invoked by **inetd** (or **xinetd** in Linux) by reading entries in `/etc/inetd.conf`. **inetd** listens on multiple ports representing these services, and invokes the functional daemon when it receives a request. **telnet** can be used with a port number as argument to check whether a service is running. Port numbers are listed in `/etc/services`.

The Berkeley r-utilities can be used only if proper authorization is provided at the server end. System level authorization is controlled by `/etc/hosts.equiv`. Authorization can also be enforced at the user level with `$HOME/.rhosts`.

The *Point-to-Point Protocol* (PPP) makes TCP/IP facilities available on a telephone line. **pppd** uses hardware flow control, but not software flow control. Most ISPs use **pppd** to provide dynamic IP addresses at both ends of the link.

To connect to the Internet, the name server addresses have to be specified in `/etc/resolv.conf`. **minicom** can dial out to the ISP but the **pppd** daemon has to be started manually. **dip** is script-based that uses expect-send string pairs to automate the login procedure. PPP connectivity should be checked with **netstat -rn** and **ping**.

The *Network File System* (NFS) lets you mount a remote file system or a directory on a local directory with the same commands used for handling local file systems (**mount** and **umount**). Directories along with their access rights are maintained in `/etc/exports`. NFS provides no user-level access..

TEST YOUR UNDERSTANDING

28.1 Explain the role of ICANN.

28.2 Name the class of network to which these IP addresses belong: (i) 202.54.9.1, (ii) 107.35.45.78, (iii) 34.67.102.34.

28.3 Can you have 11.23.34.45 and 172.26.0.6 as IP addresses of hosts on the Internet?

28.4 If a Class C address uses the first three bits of the fourth octet to form part of the network address, what will be its subnet mask?

28.5 What are the two hardware parameters of the network interface card that you may need to set manually before configuring TCP/IP on your machine?

28.6 How do you find out your machine's MAC address?

28.7 Which of these programs don't need a server process to run at the remote end? **ftp**, **telnet**, **ping**, **rcp** and **finger**

28.8 How do you find out the IP address of your router?

28.9 If `/etc/hosts.equiv` on a host *neptune* contains just the word `mars`, how do you interpret the entry? If you now remove this entry, what do you think will happen?

28.10 What protocol is mostly used in a TCP/IP dialup connection, and which command activates the service?

28.11 With which Hayes-modem command do you dial on a connection that uses tone dialing?

28.12 What does /etc/exports contain, and how can you make **mountd** read this file after you have made changes to it?

FLEX YOUR BRAIN

28.1 What is the significance of (i) broadcast and (ii) loopback? What addresses do they use?

28.2 If you are setting up a Class C intranet, what would the first two octets be if you were following the official guidelines?

28.3 What does the routing table on your machine contain? Explain the significance of the *default route*.

28.4 Your machine is connected to another one with the IP address 192.168.0.1 which is connected to the Internet. Assuming that the gateway machine allows you to pass packets to the Internet, how will you set up routing on your machine in (i) SVR4 and (ii) Linux?

28.5 How will you disable the Ftp service on (i) UNIX (ii) modern implementations of Linux?

28.6 You are able to connect to an Ftp site on the Internet using only the IP address but not the FQDN. What setting have you forgotten to make considering that the name service is running in your network?

28.7 You are unable to either send mail to your ISP's mail server or fetch it from its POP server. How do you check whether the relevant services are running on your ISP's host?

28.8 How should the remote machine on *neptune* be configured for use of the r-utilities if user henry on *mars* is to be allowed to access (i) any account (ii) only his own account without using a password?

28.9 Explain the significance of the following options used with **pppd**: (i) `crtscts` (ii) `defaultroute` (iii) `-detach`.

28.10 You need to connect to an Ftp site on the Internet from a script but have to make sure the word ppp0 shows in the **netstat -rn** output before executing the **ftp** command. How do you do that?

28.11 Use a single-line **perl** program to change the password of all your .dip scripts from s1o3n5y8 to j2n98d0k2.

28.12 How will you use mount on an SVR4 system to access a remote directory /usr/doc on host *uranus* in read-only mode?

Appendix **A**

The C Shell—Programming Constructs

The C shell was developed at the University of California, Berkeley by Bill Joy, the architect of **vi**. Both the Korn shell and Bash have drawn heavily from the features of this shell. Linux offers a vastly superior C shell as Tcsh. In this appendix we cover its programming constructs.

Computation

The C shell can handle integers for computations. Variable assignment is made with **set** or **@**:

```
% set x=5
% @ y = 10                                  A space after @
% @ sum=$x + $y
% @ product = $x * $y
% @ quotient = $y/$x                        Space around / required
@: Badly formed number
% @ quotient = $y / $x
```

Incrementing numbers is done in these ways:

```
@ x = $x + 1
@ x++
@ x ++
```

The @ must be followed by whitespace even if the = need not have any around it. There must also be whitespace on either side of the operand (i.e., the +, -, *, / and % symbols). Variable values are echoed normally with the **echo** statement.

Arrays

The C shell has a number of variables—some unique to itself and some having similar counterparts in the other shells. You have learned how to set and evaluate these variables in Chapter 9, but note that one variable (path) is set a little differently:

```
set path = (/bin /usr/bin /usr/local/bin /usr/dt/bin .)
```

The above list is actually an *array* supported by this shell. path is normally referred to as a variable, but it can also be considered to be an array of five elements. The first element is accessed by $path[1], the second by $path[2], and so on. The number of elements in the array is indicated by the parameter $#, followed immediately by the variable (or array) name. Let's look at a few examples:

```
% echo $path
/bin /usr/bin /usr/local/bin /usr/X11R6/bin .
% echo $path[3]
/usr/dt/bin
% echo $#path
5
```

Values can be put into an array with the **set** statement and **shift** also works with arrays:

```
% set numb = ( 9876 2345 6213 )          Like set 9876 2345 6213
% echo $numb[1]
9876
% echo $#numb                            Entire list stored in $numb[*]
3
% shift numb                             Uses array name too
% echo $numb[1]
2345
```

Executing a Script

By default, scripts written in the C shell language are executed by the Bourne shell. (Linux uses Bash to execute a Tcsh script.) There are two ways of getting around this; either execute the script with the **csh** command, or place the interpreter specification at the beginning of every C shell script:

```
csh script_name
#!/bin/csh
```

Most C shells support the more convenient second form, but if your version doesn't support it, then the only option left is to use the **csh** command itself.

The if Statement

The **if** statement has a different form here. First, the keyword **then** must be in the *same* line as **if**. Second, the statement terminator is **endif** and not **fi**. Finally, the condition being tested has to be usually enclosed in a matched pair of parentheses:

```
% cat filesize.csh
#!/bin/csh
# Program: filesize.csh - Converts file blocks to size in bytes
if ( $#argv != 2 ) then          # Condition tested with != instead of -ne
    echo Two parameters required
else
    @ size = $1 * 512
    echo Size of $2 is $size bytes
endif
% filesize.csh 124 tulec04
Size of tulec04 is 63488 bytes
```

Numeric comparison is made with the C-like operators >, == and !=, etc., rather than the ones Bourne uses (-gt, -lt etc.). $#argv (and not $#) is set to the number of arguments passed to a script. The arguments are individually accessed with $argv[1], $argv[2] etc. To maintain compatibility with the other shells, the C shell also lets you access them as $1 and $2, and so forth.

You can have single-line conditionals when there is no **else** clause:

```
if ( $#argv == 2 ) @ size = $1 * 512 ; echo Size of $2 is $size bytes
```

When executing a UNIX command as the control command, the command itself should be surrounded by a matched pair of curly braces and not parentheses:

```
if { grep "director" emp.lst } then
```

Finally, remember, that there is no **test** statement or its [ ] equivalent in this shell. However, some of the file attributes can be tested here. You can use **if (-r foo)** to test if the file foo is readable, **if (! -d bar)** to check whether bar is not a directory, and so on.

The switch Statement

The **switch** statement (like **case**) matches an expression for more than one alternative, and uses the keywords **endsw**, **case** and **breaksw**. This three-option menu provides a simple example:

```
% cat menu.csh
#!/bin/csh
set choice = $1                        # Option supplied as argument to script
switch ($choice)                       # Like case $choice
case 1:
   ls -l
   breaksw                             # Stops further matching
case 2:
   ps -f
   breaksw
case 3:                                # Can also use default: for the last option
   exit
   breaksw
endsw
```

case has a different use here and is terminated by a colon. **breaksw** breaks control out of the construct after a match is found and the matching actions performed. If this word is not provided, the actions related to *all* options are performed. This makes no sense in most cases, so make sure it's there. Often the last **case** option is used to perform some action—usually aborting the program. In that case, the specific value of the variable choice doesn't matter and you can use the **default** keyword.

The while and foreach Loops

There are two loops—**while** and **foreach** (instead of **for**). Both loops have three major differences with their counterparts in the other shells:

- The loop condition (or the list) is to be enclosed within parentheses.
- The **do** keyword is not used.
- The loop is terminated with end instead of **done**.

Let's consider the **while** loop first. We'll enter a simple sequence at the prompt:

```
% set x = 5                          PS2 for C shell is a ?
% while ( $x > 3 )                   Can also use while { true }
?   ps -f
?   sleep 5
? end
```

The **foreach** loop also has differences with its Bourne rival, but has been emulated by **perl**. The keyword **foreach** replaces **for**, and the **in** keyword is not required. The example in Section 16.12 can be reframed like this:

```
% foreach file (chap20 chap21 chap22 chap23)
?    cp $file ${file}.bak
?    echo $file copied to $file.bak
? end
```

There are other ways of using a list:

```
foreach item ( `cat clist` )
foreach fname ( *.c )                All C programs in current directory
foreach fname ( $* )                 Script arguments
```

The repeat Statement

If a single command has to be repeated a finite number of times, you can use the **repeat** statement:

```
% repeat 3 date
Sat Apr 26 10:46:25 IST 2003
Sat Apr 26 10:46:25 IST 2003
Sat Apr 26 10:46:25 IST 2003
```

The goto Statement

You can use the **goto** statement also. Though this construct is hardly used by programmers today, it's often the best way to wriggle out if used with caution. Let's consider this script:

```
% cat gotoexamp.csh
#!/bin/csh
if ( $#argv == 0 ) then                # No arguments entered
    goto endblock
else
    grep $1 emp.lst
    exit
endif
endblock:
echo "You have not keyed in an argument"
```

The **exit** statement makes sure that control doesn't "fall through" after completion of **grep** and execute the **echo** command. If you don't place it there, the error message will appear irrespective of whether an argument was supplied or not.

The onintr Statement

The **onintr** statement (**trap** in other shells) specifies the commands to be executed when a interrupt signal is sent to the script. It is normally placed at the beginning of a shell script:

```
% cat onintr.csh
#!/bin/csh
onintr cleanup
cut -c1-10 index > $$
cut -c21- index > $$.1
paste $$ $$.1 > pastelist
rm $$ $$.1
exit                            # Required to stop intrusion into cleanup
cleanup:
rm $$ $$.1
echo "Program interrupted"
```

Like the **goto** statement, the **onintr** statement is followed by a label. Execution branches to that label when the interrupt key is pressed. You may also like to ignore the signal and continue processing. In that case, you should make the program immune to such signals by using **onintr** with a -:

```
onintr -
```

The C Shell has been completely superseded in power and versatility by the Korn shell and Bash who have more powerful programming constructs. If you are looking for an improved C shell, then use the Tcsh shell.

Appendix B
Programming Tools—make and ar

UNIX is written in C, and C was invented for rewriting UNIX. It's therefore no wonder that every UNIX system offers a very useful set of programming tools. In this appendix, we discuss two important ones—**make** and **ar**. Before we take up these programs, we need to examine the three phases a C program has to pass through before a standalone executable is created:

- *Compiling* Even though we use the term *compiling* to signify all three phases, compilation actually converts the C source code (in the `.c` files) to assembly language.
- *Assembling* The assembled code is transformed into object code by the *assembler*. A file containing object code has the `.o` extension. However, this code doesn't include the code of functions.
- *Linking* The object code is finally linked by the *linker* with other object files and libraries that contain code used by functions. This phase produces a single executable file, which by default is named **a.out**.

The **cc** compiler (or GNU's **gcc**) used on UNIX systems can combine all these phases in a single invocation. For instance, if the code to be compiled is distributed across a number of files, the following command could generate **a.out**:

```
cc a.c b.c c.c                          Creates a.out; no .o files
```

cc calls the assembler (a program named **as**) to create the `.o` files before it invokes the linker (a program named **ld**) to create a single executable. We can also invoke **ld** directly, but its syntax is a little awkward; we can leave this job to **cc**. After **ld** has created the executable (by default, **a.out**), **cc** removes the `.o` files. This is not always desirable; let's understand why.

Let's assume that a program **a.c** contains **main** and calls functions defined in **b.c** and **c.c**. We also assume that these functions are used by other programs also, so it makes sense to generate their object files which can later be linked to other programs. The `-c` option to **cc** generates object files only:

```
cc -c b.c c.c                           Creates .o files only; no a.out
```

Here, **cc -c** generates **b.o** and **c.o**, but doesn't proceed beyond the assembler stage. It doesn't invoke the linker to create **a.out**. To do that, we need to invoke **cc** again but with **a.c** and the object filenames as arguments. You can either have the default name **a.out** for the executable or use the -o option to specify the name you want the executable to have:

```
cc a.c b.o c.o                  Default executable is a.out
cc -o run a.c b.o c.o           Executable here is named run
```

There's one variation possible in the above sequence. We can create an object file for the program containing the **main** function also (here, **a.c**). In that case, we can run **cc -c a.c b.c c.c** to generate three object files and **cc a.o b.o c.o** to create the executable.

Even though object files can't be executed directly, they have two important functions from the developer's point of view:

- Because **b.o** is created from **b.c**, one can compare their last modification times to determine whether the source has changed after the object file was created. The **make** program handles this function.
- We can combine a set of .o files to form a *library* or *archive* so that we can specify one file rather than several .o files to generate the final executable. Library creation is the job of the **ar** command.

In the following paragraphs, we take up **make** and **ar**.

make—Program Maintenance

Programs contain functions which are best kept in separate files. The advantage of doing that becomes apparent when implementing large programming projects. We devise functions for two reasons:

- For imparting modularity to our code. This makes programs comprehensible which consequently helps in debugging them.
- Enable their reuse. The same function can be used by another program.

A change in the source code of a function (or a header file used by it) necessitates a recompilation of all programs using that function (or header file). When there are simply too many source and object files that *depend* on the function, keeping track of these dependencies becomes an impossible task. The **make** command does this job for us.

make shortens program compilation time by recompiling only those sources (.c and .h files) that have changed. It looks up a *makefile* (a control file) that specifies two things:

- How a program or object file is related to other files. For instance, **a.out** could be related to **a.o**, **b.o** and **c.o**.
- The command to execute when a file, on which another file depends, changes. This could be to run the **cc** command to regenerate the object files.

make by default use a file named makefile in the user's current directory. The file contains a set of *rules*. Each rule is of the following form:

target: *dependency_list*
    command_list

Here, *target* is generally an executable or an object file which depends on the files in *dependency_list*. If any of the files in this list change, then *target* has to be rebuilt. The command to rebuild the target is provided in *command_list*. The rule syntax is simple except that you need to keep in mind that *command_list* is preceded by a tab (spaces here won't do).

In many of the programs used in Chapters 25 and 26, we used the **quit** function. Assuming that the source code of this function is available in **quit.c** and its object code in **quit.o**, the make rule for **quit.o** is this:

```
quit.o: quit.c                          The dependency
    cc -c quit.c                        The command to execute—tab before cc
```

The first line states that **quit.o** depends on **quit.c**. If **quit.c** is modified, then it needs to be recompiled with the **cc** command shown in the second line. **make** monitors the modification time of both files, and when it sees at least one file in *dependency_list* to be newer than *target*, it runs the **cc** command.

Enter these two lines of code in a file named makefile in your current directory. Next use **touch** to change the modification time of **quit.c** and then run **make**:

```
$ touch quit.c                          Not necessary if quit.o doesn't exist
$ make
cc -c quit.c                            make runs cc
```

To understand the versatility of **make**, let's consider the program, **check_all_perm.c**, used in Fig. 24.13 (Chapter 25). The program uses two functions, **check_permissions** and **print_permissions**, whose source files have the same name (but with .c). We have modified the contents of these files to understand **make** better. All three files also use header files, so let's view each set of source and header file in turn. First, let's view the set comprising **check_permissions.c** and **check_perm.h**:

```
$ cat check_permissions.c
#include "check_perm.h"

void check_permissions(int perm, int flag, char *message) {
    if (perm & flag)
        printf("%s\n", message);
}
$ cat check_perm.h
#include <stdio.h>

void check_permissions(int, int, char *);
```

The header file here describes the prototype of the function and also contains a #include line. The next set we need to look at are the files for the function, **print_permissions**:

```
$ cat print_permissions.c
#include "print_perm.h"

void print_permissions(char *fname, struct stat *addbuf) {
    if (stat(fname, addbuf) < 0) {
        perror("stat");
        exit(1);
    } else
        printf("File: %s  Permissions: %o\n", fname, addbuf->st_mode & ~S_IFMT);
}
$ cat print_perm.h
#include <sys/stat.h>
#include <unistd.h>

void print_permissions(char *, struct stat *) ;
```

The main program, **check_all_perm.c**, uses the two header files shown above but it also uses a third one named **check_all.h**:

```
$ cat check_all_perm.c
#include "check_all.h"
#include "check_perm.h"
#include "print_perm.h"

int main(int argc, char *argv[]) {
    int i, fd, perm;
    char *filename = argv[1] ;
    struct stat statbuf;
    mode_t perm_flag[] = { S_IRUSR, S_IWUSR, S_IXUSR, S_IRGRP, S_IWGRP, S_IXGRP,
                           S_IROTH, S_IWOTH, S_IXOTH, S_ISUID, S_ISGID, S_ISVTX
                         };

    char *mesg[] = {"User-readable", "User-writable", "User-executable",
                    "Group-readable", "Group-writable", "Group-executable",
                    "Others-readable", "Others-writable", "Others-executable",
                    "SUID bit set", "SGID bit set", "Sticky bit set"
                   };
    print_permissions(filename, &statbuf);
    perm = statbuf.st_mode & ~S_IFMT;

    for (i = 0; i < 12; i ++)
        check_permissions(perm, perm_flag[i], mesg[i]);
}
$ cat check_all.h
#include <stdio.h>
#include <sys/stat.h>
#include <fcntl.h>
```

Observe the dependency of the main program on the two functions it calls. There is also a dependency between a source file and its corresponding object and header files. Keeping these points in mind, let's proceed to place four rules in our makefile. This file is called makefile, the default file used by **make**:

```
$ cat makefile
# Rule 1
check_all_perm: check_all_perm.o check_permissions.o print_permissions.o
	cc -o check_all_perm check_all_perm.o check_permissions.o \
	print_permissions.o

# Rule 2
check_all_perm.o: check_all_perm.c check_all.h
	cc -c check_all_perm.c

# Rule 3
print_permissions.o: print_permissions.c print_perm.h
	cc -c print_permissions.c

# Rule 4
check_permissions.o: check_permissions.c check_perm.h
	cc -c check_permissions.c
```

make permits the use of the \ in splitting a line into two. It also uses the # as the comment character. Each rule is separated from the other by a blank line. This is a requirement on some systems, but your system may not need a blank line as a delimiter of rules.

make rules are organized in the form of a hierarchical dependency tree. The ultimate target is placed in the first rule which lists three object files as its dependencies. These dependencies in turn form separate targets of their own and are shown as three separate rules following the first rule. **make** scans the makefile from top to bottom and then works back right to the top, issuing the necessary commands whenever it finds the modification time of any of the dependencies to be later that it associated target. If an object file doesn't exist then **make** creates one.

Let's first remove all object files in this directory (if any), so **make** gets a chance to run all four commands:

```
$ rm *.o ; make
cc -c check_all_perm.c
cc -c check_permissions.c
cc -c print_permissions.c
cc -o check_all_perm check_all_perm.o check_permissions.o print_permissions.o
```

make runs the **cc** command for each of the four rules. The object files that **make** creates can now be considered to be up-to-date. When you issue **make** again, you'll find that there's nothing left for it to do:

```
$ make
`check_all_perm' is up to date.
```

We'll now make changes in the makefile presented above to illustrate the features of **make**. We'll take advantage of **make**'s built-in rules to shorten the code and then understand how macros help in designing better makefiles.

Removing Redundancies

The makefile that we just worked upon has a number of redundancies. We generally have the same name for both source and object file, and **make** is intelligent enough to understand that if the target and the dependency have the same basename, then *command_list* need not be specified. In other words, if **foo.c** has **foo.o** as its dependency, then you don't need to specify **cc -c foo.c** in *command_list*. In the next makefile, we have dropped *command_list* from the last three rules:

```
$ cat makefile2
check_all_perm: check_all_perm.o check_permissions.o print_permissions.o
    gcc -o check_all_perm check_all_perm.o check_permissions.o \
    print_permissions.o

check_all_perm.o: check_all_perm.c check_all.h

print_permissions.o: print_permissions.c print_perm.h

check_permissions.o: check_permissions.c check_perm.h
```

Since we are no longer using the default makefile, **make** needs to be used with the `-f` option to specify the makefile it has to use:

```
make -f makefile2
```

make is more intelligent than what we have observed. If the source file itself is omitted in the dependency, **make** assumes that the base source filename is the same as the object file. For instance, if we have **foo.o** as the target and don't specify **foo.c** as its dependency, **make** assumes it and runs **cc** accordingly. Before we view the next makefile that shows the changes, let's understand that **make** is not merely concerned with compiling C programs.

make runs a UNIX command after making the dependency test. It can compile any program written in any language provided the compilation process generates separate target files that can be compared with their sources. We can use **make** to run Fortran programs, but Java has the "make" feature builtin. The **javac** compiler makes sure that all dependent source files are automatically compiled before it generates the `.class` file that is used by the **java** interpreter. Our next makefile incorporates the observations made in this and the preceding paragraph:

```
$ cat makefile3
check_all_perm: check_all_perm.o check_permissions.o print_permissions.o
    gcc -o check_all_perm check_all_perm.o check_permissions.o \
    print_permissions.o

check_all_perm.o: check_all.h

print_permissions.o: print_perm.h

check_permissions.o: check_perm.h
```

```
clean:                                  # No dependency list here
   rm *.o

tar:                                    # ... and here
   tar -cvf progs.tar *.c *.h
```

There's no change in the first rule, but the next three contain a lot of hidden information. To consider the second rule, **check_all_perm.o** depends on **check_all_perm.c** (assumed by **make** since there's no .c file specified), and if that file or **check_all.h** is modified, **make** will run the command **cc -c check_all_perm.c** to generate **check_all_perm.o**. The significance of the last two rules is taken up next.

Cleaning Up and Backup

make is not restricted to compilation; it can run any command. For instance, you can instruct **make** to remove all object files or even perform a backup with **tar**. The last two rules of the previous example make for some interesting reading. There are no dependencies associated with the targets clean and tar. *But* **make** *this time has to be used with the target as an argument.*

When **make** is invoked with the clean argument, it removes all .o files, and when invoked with tar, it creates the archive progs.tar using **tar**. Let's issue two **make** commands to illustrate this behavior:

```
$ make -f makefile2 clean
rm *.o
$ make -f makefile2 tar
tar -cvf progs.tar *.c *.h
a check_all_perm.c 1K
a check_permissions.c 1K
a print_permissions.c 1K
a check_all.h 1K
a check_perm.h 1K
a print_perm.h 1K
```

The command **make clean** is often run at the beginning to remove all object files in the current directory. This is usually followed by a "regular" **make** that forces compilation of all programs.

Macros

Makefiles can be very big, and you'll often have a group of filenames used repeatedly in the dependency list. Moreover the **cc -c** command is also used very frequently. When we encounter similar situations in shell scripts and C programs, we store repeatedly used data in variables or use #define. The advantage with this approach is that if the data changes, then we simply change the variable or #define setting; the rest of the code can be left undisturbed.

make can also emulate this behavior with its *macros*, sometimes called *variables*. A macro is of the form *macroname* = *value* and is defined at the beginning of the makefile. A macro is invoked in a rule with $(*macroname*) or ${*macroname*}.

To consider an application of a macro, consider that even though we have used the **cc** compiler here, some systems may instead use GNU's **gcc**. To be able to run the same makefile on another system that uses **gcc** and without making major changes in the body of the makefile, we simply define a macro CC = gcc, and then use it in a rule as $(CC). Our next makefile uses a number of macros:

```
$ cat makefile4
CC = gcc
SOURCES = check_all_perm.c check_permissions.c print_permissions.c
OBJECTS = check_all_perm.o check_permissions.o print_permissions.o
HEADERS = check_all.h print_perm.h check_perm.h

check_all_perm: $(OBJECTS)
    $(CC) -o check_all_perm $(OBJECTS)

check_all_perm.o: check_all.h

print_permissions.o: print_perm.h

check_permissions.o: check_perm.h

clean:
    rm $(OBJECTS)

tar:
    tar -cvf progs.tar $(SOURCES) $(HEADERS)
```

In this makefile, we have defined four macros. One of them defines the compiler and the other three macros group all files into three categories. Note that even though the compiler has changed here, we can still continue to omit the command list in three rules—a practice continued from makefile3. This is because one of these macros—CC—is a **make** builtin. **make** uses the compiler defined in CC (by default, **cc**), and if that is reassigned to **gcc**, **make** will use **gcc** as the compiler *even for commands that implement its built-in rules*:

```
$ make -f makefile4 clean
rm check_all_perm.o check_permissions.o print_permissions.o
$ make -f makefile4
gcc    -c  check_all_perm.c
gcc    -c  check_permissions.c
gcc    -c  print_permissions.c
gcc -o check_all_perm check_all_perm.o check_permissions.o print_permissions.o
```

The advantage of using macros in the rules for the clean and tar targets should be obvious. This time **make** doesn't delete all .o files or back up all .c and .h files, but only the ones that are defined in the makefile.

Apart from CC, there are two more macros that are built into **make**. CFLAGS lists the options that have to be additionally used in compilation. LDFLAGS determines the options to be used by the linker. We'll revisit **make** after we have learned to build a library file using **ar**.

ar—Building a Library (Archive)

Even though our sample makefile didn't feature too many files, in real-life projects that will not be the case. You'll often have hundreds of files to deal with. Specifying all object files in a makefile could be quite tedious for the programmer. It's better to group them into a library or an archive. All UNIX systems are shipped with the library file **libc.a** which contain the object code for all the commonly used functions like **printf**. You too can create a library of your own with the **ar** command. An archive must have the extension `.a`.

The **ar** command is used in a manner similar to **tar**; it can be used to add object files to an archive, extract and delete them, and even view the archive's table of contents. The command uses the following options:

- `-r` Adds a file if it is not present in the archive or replaces an existing one.
- `-q` Appends a file at the end of the archive.
- `-x` Extracts a file from the archive.
- `-d` Deletes a file in the archive.
- `-t` Displays the table of contents of the archive.

Like **tar**, **ar** is also used with the `-v` option to produce a verbose output. We can use options without the hyphen also, but POSIX requires **ar** options to be prefixed with a hyphen, the reason why we'll use hyphenated options. We'll also see how we can use **make** to maintain an archive.

Let's stick to the example files used in the section on **make**, and create an archive named **permissions.a** containing three object files—**check_permissions.o**, **print_permissions.o** and **quit.o**. Let's first use the `-r` option to add two of them to the archive:

```
$ ar -rv permissions.a print_permissions.o check_permissions.o
a - print_permissions.o
a - check_permissions.o
ar: creating permissions.a
ar: writing permissions.a
```

Without the `-v` option, **ar** does its work silently. The first argument is the name of the library file to be created, and the `-r` option creates one if it doesn't already exist. We can add one more object file, but this time we need to use the `-q` option:

```
$ ar -qv permissions.a quit.o                    Appending to archive
a - quit.o
ar: writing permissions.a
```

Now the archive contains three object files, and we can verify this by using the `-t` option to view the table of contents:

```
$ ar -tv permissions.a
rw-r--r--    102/    10   1000 Apr 24 18:22 2003 print_permissions.o
rw-r--r--    102/    10    788 Apr 24 18:22 2003 check_permissions.o
rw-r--r--    102/    10    676 Apr 24 19:50 2003 quit.o
```

We can now safely delete all three object files from the directory. This time, our compilation command becomes simpler; instead of specifying three object files, we can simply specify the name of the archive:

```
cc check_all_perm.c permissions.a
```

At any stage we can extract any or all these object files using the `-x` option. By default all files are extracted but to extract a particular object file, we need to specify its name:

```
$ ar -xv permissions.a quit.o
x - quit.o
```

We can also delete an object file in the archive; a subsequent display of its table of contents confirms the action that we have taken:

```
$ ar -dv permissions.a quit.o
d - quit.o
ar: writing permissions.a
$ ar -tv permissions.a
rw-r--r--   102/    10    1000 Apr 24 18:22 2003 print_permissions.o
rw-r--r--   102/    10     788 Apr 24 18:22 2003 check_permissions.o
```

Maintaining an Archive with make

Having all object files in a single library reduces our typing load, but what happens when the source code for these object files are modified? We need to use **make** all right, but using **ar** in the command line to maintain an archive can still be quite tedious. **make** is the answer yet again; it can both recompile the source files and replace the archive entries with their newer versions. For doing this, **make** uses this syntax for an object file placed in an archive:

archive_name(*object_file*)

The object file is placed in parentheses and is preceded by the library name. The following makefile takes care of compiling and archiving:

```
$ cat makefile5
CC = gcc
check_all_perm: check_all_perm.o permissions.a(check_permissions.o) \
                permissions.a(print_permissions.o)
    $(CC) -o check_all_perm check_all_perm.o permissions.a

check_all_perm.o: check_all.h

permissions.a(print_permissions.o):  print_perm.h

permissions.a(check_permissions.o):  check_perm.h
```

Observe the changed specification of the object files. The makefile entries are a little longer this time, but **make** here has some additional work to do—run **ar** to recreate the archive. Just change the source code in **print_permissions.c** and then run **make** like this:

```
$ make -f makefile5
gcc    -c -o print_permissions.o print_permissions.c
ar rv permissions.a print_permissions.o
r - print_permissions.o
ar: writing permissions.a
rm -f print_permissions.o
gcc -o check_all_perm check_all_perm.o permissions.a
```

Note that **make** here performs its usual compilation tasks but it also invokes **ar** to maintain the archive with the updated versions of the object files.

Using the -l Option to cc

UNIX library files have the `lib` prefix, and the `-l` option to **cc** (or **gcc**) requires us to specify only a portion of the library name (without the `lib` prefix and `.a`). For instance, to link the library **libm.a** (containing the mathematical functions like **pow**) with your program, we need to use **cc foo.c -lm**. The compiler prefixes `lib` and suffixes `.a` to the argument used with `-l` (here, `m`). We don't need to specify the location of the library file because the compiler by default looks up `/lib` and `/usr/lib` to locate all library files.

This approach can also work for us, albeit in a modified manner. To be able to use the `-l` option we need to rename the library file from **permissions.a** to one having the `lib` prefix, say **libperm.a**. If this library is placed in the current directory, we need to also use the `-L` option to indicate that:

```
$ mv permissions.a libperm.a
$ cc check_all_perm.c -lperm -L"."
$ _
```

The `-L` option to **cc** allows us to place all user-created libraries in a separate directory. The `-I` option points to the location of all include files, but only those that are specified with the `<` and `>` enclosures. By default, the compiler looks for such include files in `/usr/include`. Since we have used statements line `#include "check_all.h"` and not `#include <check_all.h>`, we don't need to use this option for the examples used in this appendix. The `-l`, `-I` and `-L` options are frequently used in makefiles.

Static and Shared Libraries

We created a *static* library here. When a program is compiled and linked to a static library, the object code of the library is included in the executable. Several programs may use the same function, which means that the same library code gets included in all these programs. This bloats the code size and eats into the disk space. This also means that if the code for the function changes, all programs that have the functions statically linked to them, have to be recompiled. Even though **make** can do this work for us, compilation of several hundred programs can still take a lot of time.

C also supports *shared* libraries (also called shared objects), and the compiler can be instructed to create one. In contrast to a static library, a program using a shared library loads the library code only during runtime. Once it is loaded, a single copy of the library code is kept in memory for other programs to use. Programs using shared libraries could be a little slower, but the executables are smaller since they don't include library code. A change in function code (provided the signature is not altered) doesn't necessitate recompilation of those programs using the function. Shared libraries are increasingly being used by modern UNIX systems. In fact, Solaris no longer offers static libraries. Further discussion on shared libraries is beyond the scope of this text.

Appendix C

Solutions to Test Your Understanding

CHAPTER 1

1.1 The ASCII value.

1.2 So that other people can't see it, otherwise they can use it to gain unauthorized access to the system.

1.3 When the prompt returns.

1.4 No, it doesn't. UNIX is insensitive to the presence of spaces around the >, < and | symbols.

1.5 The number of files in the current directory.

1.6 Since the * matches all files in the current directory, both **echo** and **ls** produce the same output, except that **echo**'s output is quite cluttered.

1.7 The command in double quotes evaluates the variable and displays its value, but the other command in single quotes simply displays the quoted string.

1.8 The shell first scans the entire command and its arguments for metacharacters. If it sees symbols like the *, it selects those filenames that match the pattern. If it sees the >, it creates the file following the >. Finally, it directs the kernel to execute the command.

CHAPTER 2

2.1 Because it is written in C, a high level language.

2.2 The Open Group owns the UNIX trademark. POSIX and the Single UNIX Specification are two current standards in use.

2.3 The **vi** editor, C shell, symbolic links and TCP/IP.

2.4 Sun, IBM, Digital.

2.5 X Window System.

2.6 The Free Software Foundation is responsible for the development of most of the application tools and the shell. The kernel was created by Linus Torvalds.

2.7 The **man** command on the machine and newsgroups and FAQs on the Internet.

CHAPTER 3

3.1 Normally not; UNIX is case-sensitive.

3.2 That is because the commands there are most often used by users and would be located faster.

3.3 By a dot.

3.4 **cd** and **pwd** are the internal commands of the shell.

3.5 An option is also an argument but generally begins with a hyphen.

3.6 The secondary prompt is generally a > or ?, and appears when the *[Enter]* key is pressed before the command specification is complete.

3.7 A program that displays text on the screen a page at a time. **more** and **less** are two standard pagers used by **man**.

3.8 Linux; its commands often have double-hyphenated options.

3.9 *[Ctrl-c]* or *[Delete]*

CHAPTER 4

4.1 12 days were skipped in September for adjustment purposes.

4.2 `cal 1752 | more`

4.3 `date +"%Y%m%d"`

4.4 `echo "\007"` or `echo -e "\007"`

4.5 Yes, you can; two or more users can log in with the same username.

4.6 The password is stored in encrypted form in the file `/etc/shadow`.

4.7 Make the setting `scale=3`.

4.8 Use the **`script session.lst`** command at the beginning of your login session.

4.9 First enter the command **`stty echo`**. If that doesn't work, try **`stty sane`**.

CHAPTER 5

5.1 255 characters. The / and null can't be used as filename characters.

5.2 There are three ways: (i) `cd ; pwd` (ii) `echo $HOME` (iii) Locate the sixth field in the line pertaining to your username in `/etc/passwd`.

5.3 The command **`cd ../../mail`** will take you there with the minimum number of keystrokes.

5.4 It simply switches to the home directory.

5.5 You have to use **`mkdir -p share/man/cat1`**. The `-p` option creates all subdirectories in one shot.

5.6 The directory `c_progs` is not empty or the command is executed in the directory itself.

5.7 `/bin/echo`

5.8 `ls -F`

5.9 `ls -laR /`

CHAPTER 6

6.1 It will display the same file three times in succession.

6.2 Use **`cp -r bar1 bar2`**. If `bar2` exists, then `bar1` becomes a subdirectory of `bar2`.

6.3 The contents of the file are displayed on the terminal.

6.4 `rm -rf foo`

6.5 (i) `bar1` becomes a subdirectory of `bar2` (ii) `bar1` is renamed to `bar2`.

6.6 `lp -d arjun -n3 /etc/passwd`

6.7 Create a file with these characters, and then use **`od -bc foo`**.

6.8 `comm -12 foo1 foo2`

6.9 The two files are identical.

CHAPTER 7

7.1 2048 on systems where the size of a disk block is 1024 bytes.

7.2 (i) 756 (ii) 640 (iii) 124

7.3 (i) `r-xrw-rwx` (ii) `rw--w--wx` (iii) `r--w--x`

7.4 He can read but not write unless he changes the permissions.

7.5 The owner of the file.

7.6 You can create a directory in `/tmp` (permissions—`rwxrwxrwt`) but not in `/bin` (`rwxr-xr-x`). group and others can't write in `/bin`, but they can write in `/tmp`.

7.7 No, she can't, because the owner's permissions override her group's.

7.8 On a BSD-based system, only the superuser can use **`chown`** to change the owner of a file. However, a user can change her own group with **`chgrp`** but only to one to which she also belongs.

7.9 Recursively changes (i) the owner of all files in the current directory, including the hidden files (ii) the group of all files but doesn't include the hidden files.

CHAPTER 8

8.1 Take the cursor to the end of `has` using **`e`** multiple times and then press **`sve`***[Esc]*.

8.2 (i) `0` (ii) `o`

8.3 `:q!`

8.4 `:x`, `:wq` and `ZZ`

8.5 `40|`

8.6 Use **`0`**, **`5w`**, **`4s`**, enter `counter` and press *[Esc]*.

8.7 (i) 7 (ii) 2

8.8 Only (iii) and (iv) because they change the contents of the editing buffer. (i) and (ii) merely perform navigation without changing the buffer in any way.

8.9 Take the cursor to `t` and then use **`xp`**.

8.10 Use **`5J`** with the cursor on the top-most line.

8.11 **`n`** repeats a search in the same direction the original search was made, which could be forward or back. **`N`** operates in a reverse manner.

8.12 Because you pressed an `o` before pressing the dot.

CHAPTER 9

9.1 The command lists all files where a dot occurs anywhere in the filename. It could end with a dot but not begin with one.

9.2 The command **`rm .[!.]*`** removes all files beginning with a dot, followed by a non-dot character, and then anything else. Effectively, the expression matches all files beginning with a dot except `.` and `..`. **`rm *`** doesn't remove these files.

9.3 `chap[a-cx-z]`

9.4 Yes, because `3` has a higher value than `e` in the ASCII collating sequence.

9.5 `*[!0-9]`

9.6 When there is only one file in the current directory and that file is also a directory.

9.7 The terminal, redirection and pipe.

9.8 The command **ls -lRa $HOME > home.tar** saves the listing of the current directory structure in file home.tar.

9.9 They expect input from the standard input, the terminal by default. Press *[Ctrl-d]* to send EOF and return to the shell.

9.10 Use the command **echo >** *[Enter]*. Precede the space with a backslash. When you use **ls | od -bc**, you'll find the octal value 040 at that position.

9.11 (ii) 9.12 (iv)

CHAPTER 10

10.1 The PID is a unique number assigned to a process by the kernel. The PPID is the PID of the parent.

10.2 The **init** process with the PID 1, and the parent of all shells.

10.3 ps -e (SVR4) and ps aux (Linux) 10.4 Shell scripts. 10.5 cd, pwd, echo

10.6 ps -f -u timothy (ps --user timothy in Linux) 10.7 The -s KILL option.

10.8 Use **kill $!**, which should work on most shells. 10.9 kill -l

10.10 First press *[Ctrl-z]* to suspend the process and escape to the shell prompt. Enter **fg** to continue the suspended process and bring up vi once again.

10.11 The **find** command runs at 21:30 hours every day.

10.12 Use the **time** command with both and note the real time.

CHAPTER 11

11.1 It is set by /etc/passwd, being the directory you are placed in when logging in. However, when you reassign the value of HOME, cd used without an argument will take you to the new value of $HOME. However, the home directory continues to be what has been specified in /etc/passwd.

11.2 The file vt220 will be available in /usr/share/lib/terminfo/v on Solaris systems.

11.3 PATH=$PATH:. 11.4 alias lh="ls .[!.]*" 11.5 (i) r (ii) !!

11.6 (i) r tar sh=pl (ii) !tar:s/sh/pl 11.7 set -o vi

11.8 The next command should be **more $_**. 11.9 cd ~henry

11.10 /etc/profile is executed when a user logs in, and before her own .profile is executed.

11.11 No, Bash will read only .bash_profile.

11.12 First use **cd /usr/include**, then **cd ../lib**. Now, every time you use **cd -**, the current directory toggles between the two.

11.13 Yes, using **cp ~henry/* .** in the Korn and Bash shells.

CHAPTER 12

12.1 You have to leave behind your leave details in the files `.plan` and `.project`.

12.2 Make the setting **mesg n** in your `.profile`.

12.3 `/var/mail` (SVR4) and `/var/spool/mail` (Linux)

12.4 **mailx** is used without arguments when checking for incoming mail and with one or more arguments when sending mail.

12.5 `ps -e | mailx charlie`

12.6 That the message has been viewed.

12.7 `pine -I a`

12.8 Because it can handle multimedia files as attachments.

CHAPTER 13

13.1 The filename.

13.2 `ln *.c bar`

13.3 False, **rm** removes both.

13.4 False, a symbolic link has a separate inode.

13.5 (i) `ln foo1 foo2` (ii) `ln -s foo1 foo2`. If you delete the hard link `foo2`, then the link count drops to 1 and the file exists. If `foo2` is a symbolic link, then deleting it only removes the link, the main file still exists.

13.6 Remove the read permission from the directory for others.

13.7 The directory was writable by group and others.

13.8 Use **umask 006** in your `.profile`.

13.9 False, the access time of a file is not changed by a lookup of the inode.

13.10 It sets the modification and access time to the current time. The administrator uses **touch** to change these times whenever he finds files to wrongly stamped. Wrong time stamps can result in inclusion or exclusion of a file from a backup.

13.11 `touch -m 09301030 foo`

13.12 (i) `find /bin /usr/bin -name "z*" -print`

(ii) `find /bin /usr/bin \( -name "*.html" -o -name "*.java" \) -print`

13.13 `find /home/henry -type f -print | wc -l`

13.14 The access time of `foo` doesn't change when using the >> symbols, even though the file has been modified.

CHAPTER 14

14.1 `pr -t -d foo`

14.2 `ls | pr -t -3`

14.3 **head** picks up 10 lines from each file, but precedes each group with a header that shows the filename.

14.4 Run **a.out** in the background with `&` and then use **tail -f foo** if `foo` is the name of log file.

14.5 `head -10 foo | tail +5`

14.6 No, you can use only one of the options, `-c` and `-f`.

14.7 `sort -t"|" -k 5.4 emp.lst`

14.8 We first have to cut out the date field. Then a second **cut** extracts the year:

```
cut -d"|" -f5 emp.lst | cut -c7- | sort | uniq -c
```

14.9 `cut -d"|" -f4 emp.lst | sort -u | pr -t -n`

14.10 If the repeated lines are adjacent, simply use **uniq foo**. Otherwise, use **sort -u foo**.

14.11 `tr '[a-z]' '[A-Z]' < emp.lst`

CHAPTER 15

15.1 (i) **grep** searches for a in files b and c. (ii) The command doesn't work because <HTML> is not quoted, and the shell interprets the < and > symbols as the redirection characters.

15.2 It searches for an asterisk at the beginning of the line. Because the * loses its special meaning when not preceded by a character, the \ isn't really required.

15.3 (i) The longest pattern starting with a and ending with b, as close to the left of the line as possible. (ii) The } as the only character in the line.

15.4 (i) `sa[kx]s?ena` (ii) `raj[ei]e?[vb]` (iii) `SIG(STOP|TSTP)`

15.5 `grep pattern foo | tail -1`

15.6 `grep -v director emp.lst | sort -t"|" -k 5.5 -r | cut -d"|" -f2,3 | head -1`

15.7 `grep -E "^[0-9]+\.[0-9]+ |^[0-9]+\.[0-9]+\.[0-9]+ " chap??`

15.8

```
lsdir() {
    ls -l | grep "^d"
}
```

15.9 `cat * | grep -E "f?printf"`

15.10 (i) `sed -n '3,10p' foo` (ii) `sed -n '$!p' foo`

15.11 We can use any numeral as a "temporary" character for **sed**:

```
sed -e 's/_/9/g' foo -e 's/-/_/g' -e 's/9/-/g' foo
```

15.12 `sed 's/Linux/Red Hat &/g' foo`

15.13 `sed 's/^/  /' foo`

15.14 Look for the locations where the | occurs and then use the TRE:

```
sed 's/\([^|]*|\)\([^ ]*\) \([^|]*\)/\1\3 \2/' emp.lst
```

CHAPTER 16

16.1 Use `!/bin/ksh` as the interpreter line or run the script with **ksh** *script_name*.

16.2 $# is initially 5. If the options are combined, $# becomes 4.

16.3 The exit status of a command is the value that is returned to the caller before termination. A command returns a value 0 on successful termination. The exit status is available in the shell parameter, `$?`.

16.4

```
case $LOGNAME in
  henry|romeo) case `tty` in
               *tty0[56]) ;;
                         *) echo "You cannot use this terminal" ; exit
               esac ;;
            *) echo "You are not authorized to use script" ; exit ;;
esac
```

16.5 **test** is a shell builtin and thus the script doesn't execute. The script can still be run with **sh test** or **./test**.

16.6 Only **grep** returns a false exit status if the pattern is not found; **sed** and **find** don't.

16.7 (i)
```
echo "Enter a long string: \c"
read name
case $name in
??????????*) ;;
          *) echo "String shorter than 10 characters"
esac
```
(ii) The **case** construct in (i) can be replaced with this:
```
if [ `expr "$name" : '.*'` -lt 10 ] ; then
    echo "String shorter than 10 characters"
fi
```

16.8
```
expr "$x" : '\(.*\)/[^/]*'
```

16.9
```
file=$1                        # Save the filename before it gets lost with set
if [ -f $file ] ; then               # If file exists
    set -- `ls -l $file`
    echo "The last modification time of $file is $6 $7 $8"
else
    echo "File not found" ; exit 2
fi
```

16.10
```
cd $1
for file in * ; do
    if [ -f ../$2/$file ] ; then
        cmp $file ../$2/$file >/dev/null 2>/dev/null && rm ../$2/$file
    fi
done
```

16.11 Replace the assignment to `lastfile` at the beginning of the script with this:
```
case $# in
    1) lastfile=$1 ;;
    0) lastfile=`ls -t *.c | head -1` ;;
    *) exit ;;
esac
case $lastfile in
*.c) ;;
   *) exit;;
esac
```

16.12 Use this script, and then use **:n** to call up the next file and the **n** key to locate each occurrence of the pattern. (**n** repeats the last pattern search in **vi**.)
```
pattern="$1"
set -- `grep -l "$pattern" conapp??`
[ $# -gt 0 ] && vi +/"$pattern" "$@"   || echo "$1 not found"
```

16.13 This displays an error as 5 is not a command.

16.14
```
for file in $* ; do
     ufile=`echo $file | tr '[a-z]' '[A-Z]'`
     mv $file $ufile
done
```

16.15 Place the following statement at the beginning of the script:
```
trap 'echo -e "Do you wish to quit? \c" ; read reply ; [ $reply == y ] \
&& exit' 1 2 15
```

CHAPTER 17

17.1 In /sbin and /usr/sbin.

17.2 Because the PATH for a superuser doesn't include the current directory.

17.3 It doesn't ask for the old password.

17.4 s indicates that the SUID bit is set and t signifies the sticky bit.

17.5 The password encryption was world-readable in /etc/passwd of older systems. This made it vulnerable to attack by hackers. However, /etc/shadow is not world-readable.

17.6 **ls** obtains the numeric UID and GID from the inode and then looks up /etc/passwd for the name representation of UID and /etc/group for the name representation of GID.

17.7 Printing, network services and user logins are not available in single-user mode.

17.8 -perm 1000 matches a file having exactly those permissions, but -perm -1000 matches only 1 (the sticky bit) and ignores the other three octal digits.

17.9 Use **shutdown -y -g0**. Linux allows us to use *[Ctrl][Alt][Del]*.

17.10 He should place the following statement in /var/spool/cron/crontabs/root:
```
00 09-22 * * 1,2,3,4,5 df -t
```

17.11 du -s .

17.12 (i) doscp *.htm *.html /dev/fd0 (ii) mcopy *.htm *.html a:

CHAPTER 18

18.1 The screen, keyboard and mouse.

18.2 The window manager client takes care of window management.

18.3 Yes, by using the -display option of the client or the DISPLAY variable before invoking the client.

18.4 Merely by selecting it with the mouse.

18.5 **xhost** determines whether other hosts can write to the current machine's display. **xhost +** enables the display to be written by all hosts.

18.6 The nonuniformity of the desktop made a user feel uncomfortable when changing to a different machine.

18.7 To provide four separate virtual desktops.

18.8 The commands will all be executed and then X will be terminated.

18.9 By using the -xrm option with the resource string.

CHAPTER 19

19.1 When a segment is missing, just the segment has to be retransmitted, but when a packet is missing, the entire packet has to be retransmitted.

19.2 TCP monitors transmission of segments with an elaborate system of timeouts and retransmission facilities. These ensure that a missing or corrupted segment will make reassembly impossible.

19.3 The ARP protocol at the network access layer makes a broadcast to all machines in the network asking one of them to respond with the MAC address that corresponds to the IP address that it broadcasts. After a host has responded, ARP includes the MAC address in the packet header.

19.4 It simulates a network without actually connecting to one. The functionality of the TCP/IP tools can be tested with the loopback address if there is no network.

19.5 The port number specifies the application that is responsible for the generation of the packet and the one that is meant to receive it. Look up `/etc/services` and you will find that **`finger`** uses port 79.

19.6 **`rlogin`** is used with UNIX systems only, whereas **`telnet`** works with most multiuser systems.

19.7 Use the **`hostname`** command.

19.8 No, **`ftp`** uses **`/bin/ls`**.

19.9 You did not use `ftp`'s **`binary`** command before starting the transfer, and the machine's default mode is not binary.

19.10 You can't upload files to an anonymous Ftp site.

19.11 **`rcp`** must be used to copy a directory structure between a local and a remote UNIX machine; **`ftp`** can't copy directories.

CHAPTER 20

20.1 *aero*, *biz*, *pro* are three new entrants.

20.2 Root name servers contain the names of the authoritative name servers of the top-level domains. All name servers contact the root servers when they are unable to resolve an FQDN.

20.3 Yes, because DNS is indifferent to case.

20.4 The MUA hands over outgoing mail to the MTA which connects directly to its peer at the destination to transmit the message. The MTA finally invokes the MDA to deliver the mail to the user's mailbox.

20.5 The original SMTP protocol used 7-bit ASCII for mail messages. Binary attachments had to be encoded using `base64` to make this possible. The MIME standard requires such encoded data to be preceded by the headers `Content-Type` and `Content-Transfer-Encoding`.

20.6 (i) A discussion group on the Internet to which users can subscribe. (ii) A client program that interacts with a news server to post and fetch messages (iii) Frequently Asked Questions—a document that is prepared and maintained by one or more volunteers and periodically posted to the newsgroup. Old messages are retired to free disk space.

20.7 GIF, JPEG and PNG.

20.8 Hypertext is a system of organizing information by which references can be made to other documents in the same or different server. The concept is not restricted to text only but applies to images as well.

20.9 Hyper Text Transfer Protocol—the application protocol used on the Web to serve Web resources. The port number used by HTTP is 80.

20.10 A CGI program is a separate program that accepts a request passed by the HTTP server. The server invokes the program which does all the processing work, creates fresh HTML code and passes it back to the server.

20.11 (i) *ftp://ftp.heavens.com* (ii) *telnet://ftp.heavens.com*

20.12 MIME **20.13** Use the URL *http://localhost*.

CHAPTER 21

21.1 They are identical; both print the entire line.

21.2 The **sort** command must be placed within double quotes.

21.3
```
awk '{ x= NR % 2 ; if ( x == 1 ) print }' foo
```

21.4
```
awk '$0 !~ /^ *$/' foo
```

21.5
```
awk 'length > 100 && length < 150' foo
```

21.6
```
ls -lR $HOME | awk ' $6 ~ /^Jan/ && $7 ~ /^6/ && $8 ~ /^11/'
```

21.7
```
find . -type f -ls | awk '{tot += $7} END { print tot}'
```

21.8
```
echo "DOCUMENT LIST" | \
awk '{ for (k = 1 ; k < (55 - length($0)) / 2 ; k++)
           printf "%s"," "
       print $0 }'
```

21.9
```
echo "DOCUMENT LIST" | \
awk '{ k = 0
       while (k < (55 - length($0))/2) {
          printf "%s", " " ; k++
       }
      print $0
}'
```

CHAPTER 22

22.1
```
perl -ne 'print "$.\t" . $_' foo
```

22.2
```
perl -e 'print "UNIX" x 20 . "\n" ;'
```

22.3
```
#!/usr/bin/perl
open(INFILE, "/etc/passwd");
while (<INFILE>) {
      split(/:/);
      print if ($_[2] == 1);
}
```

22.4
```
#!/usr/bin/perl
open (INFILE, "$ARGV[1]") ;
while (<INFILE>) {
      if (/$ARGV[0]/) {
            print ; exit ;
      }
}
```

22.5
```
perl -ne 'print if /director/ ? ($x=2) : (--$x> 0)' emp.lst
```

22.6
```
#!/usr/bin/perl
$number = 1 ;
while ( $number != 0 ) {
      print ("Enter a number: ") ;
   $number = <STDIN> ;
   chop ($number) ;
   if ( $number != 0 ) {
      $total+= $number ;
   }
}
print "The total is $total\n" ;
```

22.7
```
perl -p -i -e "tr/[a-z]/[A-Z]/" foo
```

22.8
```
#!/usr/bin/perl
print "String : ";
$a = <STDIN>;
print "Number of times : ";
chop ($b = <STDIN>);
$c = $a x $b;
print "The result is : \n$c";
```

22.9 (ii)

CHAPTER 23

23.1 `/*` searches the entire file for an asterisk, while **`f*`** looks for it in the current line only.

23.2 Use **`0`** first to move to the beginning of the line. Then use **`2df.`** For subsequent lines, you can repeat the operation with the dot.

23.3 Use **`:e foo`** to open foo, and then use *[Ctrl-^]* to toggle between the two files.

23.4 Make the setting **`:set autowrite`** in `.exrc`.

23.5 Any operator like **`d`** and **`y`** can only work when it is used with a Command Mode command or by itself.

23.6 Use the command **`"a5yy`** on the first of the lines to be copied. Bring up the second file with **`:e`** *filename*, move to the right location, and then press **`"ap`**.

23.7 You should have used **`"a20yy`** for copying and **`"ap`** for pasting.

23.8 (i) `:e!` (ii) `:0r foo`

23.9 `:!cc %`

23.10 Unabbreviate it: `:unab re`*[Enter]*

23.11 `:map #1 /loop^M^M"ay/end loop^M`

CHAPTER 24

24.1 Export the variable with **export**.

24.2 **script** runs a separate sub-shell, and a variable defined in a sub-shell is not visible in the parent shell.

24.3 The current directory is one of the environmental parameters inherited by a child process. Since the child cannot alter the environment of its parent, the original directory has to be restored after the death of the script, which is executed in a sub-shell. To make the change permanent, execute the script with the . command.

24.4 `size() { ls -l $* | awk '{ tot += $5 } END {print tot}' }`

24.5 A shell function always executes in the current shell. An **exit** statement will terminate the shell itself, and may log the user out.

24.6 If the script is invoked without any argument, $1 would be null and `flname` would be set to `emp.lst`.

24.7
```
rmi() {
    [ $# -gt 1 ] && option="-i"
    rm $option $*
}
```

24.8
```
rd() {
        dir=`pwd`
        cd ..
        rm -r $dir
}
```

24.9 Run the program from the `.profile` with **exec**.

CHAPTER 25

Incorporate error checking wherever possible and relevant. File I/O operations are to be performed using only the **read** *and* **write** *system calls and not library functions.*

25.1 System calls are built into the kernel but library functions are built on top of them. When a system call is invoked, the processor switches to the kernel mode and returns to the user mode when the call returns.

25.2 A file descriptor is an integer that is allocated when a file is opened. It is used by all system calls that perform some operation on the file—like **read**, **write**, **close**, **lseek**. **open**, **dup** and **dup2** return a file descriptor.

25.3 (i) `fd = open("foo", O_WRONLY | O_TRUNC) ;`

(ii) `fd = open("foo.txt", O_WRONLY | O_APPEND) ;`

25.4 (i), (iv) and (vii) are opening mode flags, the rest are status flags. A file can be opened in one of the modes, but each mode can be associated with one or more status flags. `O_SYNC` ensures that **write** doesn't return till the physical write to disk has completed.

25.5 The file descriptor table contains all allocated file descriptor entries. Each entry points to its associated file table which contains the file's mode flags, status flags, file offset pointer and reference count. Each file descriptor is associated with a separate file table entry except when **dup**, **dup2** and **fork** are used.

25.6

```
#include <fcntl.h>
#include <unistd.h>
int main(int argc, char **argv) {
    int fd, n;
    char u ;
    fd = open(argv[1], O_RDONLY);
    while ((n = read(fd, &u, 1)) > 0) {
        if (u >=97 && u <= 122)    /* Testing for lowercase alphabet */
            u -= 32;              /* and changing it to uppercase */
        write(STDOUT_FILENO, &u, 1);
    }
    close(fd);
}
```

The following program displays the ASCII values of the alphabets:

```
#include <stdio.h>
int main(void) {
    char c ;
    for (c ='A'; c <= 'Z'; c++)
        printf("%d\n", c);
    for (c ='a'; c <= 'z'; c++)
        printf("%d\n", c);
}
```

25.7 (i)

```
umask(0);
fd = open("foo", O_WRONLY | O_CREAT, S_IRUSR | S_IWUSR | S_IRGRP |
                 S_IWGRP | S_IROTH | S_IWOTH);
```

(ii)

```
umask(0);
mkdir("foofoo", S_IRWXU | S_IRWXG | S_IRWXO);
```

25.8

```
#include <sys/stat.h>
#include <stdio.h>
#include <unistd.h>
int main(int argc, char **argv) {
    struct stat statbuf;
    int exists = 1;
    if ((access(argv[1], F_OK) == 0)) {
       lstat(argv[1], &statbuf);
       if (S_ISREG(statbuf.st_mode)) {
          unlink(argv[1]);
          exists = 0;
       }
    } else
       exists = 0;
    if (exists == 0)
         mkdir(argv[1], S_IRWXU | S_IRGRP | S_IXGRP | S_IROTH | S_IXOTH);
}
```

25.9
```
#include <sys/types.h>
#include <sys/stat.h>
#include <stdio.h>
#include <dirent.h>
int main(void) {
    DIR *dir; off_t size;
    struct dirent *direntry;  struct stat statbuf;
    if ((dir = opendir(".")) != NULL)
       while ((direntry = readdir(dir)) != NULL)
            if (lstat(direntry->d_name, &statbuf) == 0)
               if (S_ISREG(statbuf.st_mode))
                  if ((size = statbuf.st_size) > 100000)
                     printf("%s: %d\n", direntry->d_name, size);
                  else if (size == 0)
                     unlink(direntry->d_name);
}
```

25.10 Assuming that the files are available in the current directory, this program should work:

```
#include <sys/types.h>
#include <sys/stat.h>
#include <stdio.h>
#include <dirent.h>
int main(void) {
    DIR *dir; off_t size;
    struct dirent *direntry;  struct stat statbuf;
    if ((dir = opendir(".")) != NULL)
         while ((direntry = readdir(dir)) != NULL)
             if (lstat(direntry->d_name, &statbuf) == 0)
                 if (getuid() == statbuf.st_uid)
                     chmod(direntry->d_name, statbuf.st_mode & ~S_IRWXO);
}
```

CHAPTER 26

26.1 **dup**, **dup2** and **fcntl**.

26.2 The stack stores the local variables and arguments of a function while the heap memory is used when a process needs to create memory dynamically. Since the kernel may be concurrently executing on behalf of several processes, it needs a separate stack for each process.

26.3 A mode of the processor where any machine instruction can be executed. No separate process runs in this mode.

26.4
```
#include <sys/types.h>
#include <stdio.h>
int main(void) {
    pid_t pid, pid2;
    if (fork() > 0)
        fork();
    printf("PID: %d PPID: %d\n", getpid(), getppid());
}
```

26.5 The statement `Before fork` occurs twice in the file because I/O buffers are copied during a fork. When using the standard library functions, standard output is line-buffered when connected to the terminal and fully-buffered when writing to a file.

26.6
```
#include <stdio.h>
#include <fcntl.h>
#include <sys/wait.h>
int main (int argc, char **argv) {
          int a, b, c, status;
          switch(fork()) {
              case 0:
                  a = atoi(argv[1]);
                  b = atoi(argv[2]);
                  c = a + b ;
                  exit(c);
              default:
                  wait(&status);
                printf("The sum of the two numbers is %d\n", WEXITSTATUS(status));
                  exit(20);
          }
}
```

26.7 The exit status is actually 8 bits long, and the value set inside the shell script is a large value. `$?` only stores the last 8 bits.

26.8
```
#include <unistd.h>
int main (void) {
   dup2(STDOUT_FILENO, STDERR_FILENO);
   write(2, "Hello Dolly\n", 12);
   exit(0);
}
```

26.9 The output of this program will always show two lines for the `SIGKILL` and `SIGSTOP` signals:
```
#include <stdio.h>
#include <signal.h>
int main (void) {
     int i;
     for (i = 1; i <= 32; i++)
          if (signal(i, SIG_IGN) == SIG_ERR)
               printf("Signal %d can't be ignored\n", i);
}
```

CHAPTER 27

27.1 The command **`passwd -x 28`** *username* forces a user to change a password every four weeks.

27.2 The user is running a restricted shell.

27.3 The boot file system contains the UNIX kernel, the root file system contains the essential utilities that keep the system running and the swap file system stores the process images when they can't be held in memory.

27.4 (i) **`fdisk`** creates, modifies and deletes partitions. (ii) **`mkfs`** creates a file system.

(iii) **fsck** makes a consistency check of one or more file systems.

27.5 **mount** can work with only one argument when the mount point and device name are specified in /etc/fstab. Unmounting is not possible when the user executing **umount** is placed in a directory inside the file system, or any user has a file open in it.

27.6 (i) /etc/vfstab (ii) /etc/fstab

27.7 Run level is the state the system is in; some services run only at specified run levels. The default run level is set in the line containing initdefault in /etc/inittab.

27.8 telinit q

27.9 (i) /etc/rc*n*.d (ii) /etc/rc.d/rc*n*.d where *n* is the run level.

27.10 find / -name a.out -print | xargs -n20 rm -f

CHAPTER 28

28.1 The Internet Corporation for Assigned Names and Numbers (ICANN) is responsible for allocation of IP addresses and domain names.

28.2 (i) Class C (ii) Class A (iii) Class A

28.3 You can have the first one, but the second one is reserved for internets.

28.4 255.255.255.224 (128 + 64 + 32 = 224)

28.5 The IRQ and the I/O address.

28.6 ifconfig -a

28.7 ping

28.8 Use **netstat -rn** and look at the IP address in the Gateway column of that line that shows a G in the Flags column.

28.9 Any user on *mars* can use **rlogin** to log on to her own like-to-like account in *neptune* without using a password. The user can also execute the **rcp** and **rsh** commands to access *neptune*. If the entry is removed, the user will now need a password for **rlogin** but may not be able to use **rcp** and **rsh** at all.

28.10 The Point-to-Point protocol used by the pppd command.

28.11 atdt

28.12 /etc/exports shows the directories that can be mounted remotely, and specifies the access rights of the client. You can use the **exportfs -a** command to make the changed information available to the **mount** daemons. If the command is not available, you have to invoke the relevant start script in the rc*n*.d directory with the restart argument.

Appendix **D**

Glossary

absolute pathname A pathname which begins with a /, indicating that the file has to be referenced in an absolute manner—from root. See also **relative pathname**.

access time One of the time stamps of a file stored in the inode representing the date and time a file was last accessed. A file is considered to be accessed if it is read, written or executed, and the access time is displayed by **`ls -lu`**.

action A component of an **sed**, **awk** or **perl** instruction which acts on text specified by an address. It normally uses a single character to represent an action for **sed**, but could be a complete program in case of **awk** and **perl**. Also known sometimes as **internal command**.

address A component of an **sed**, **awk** or **perl** instruction which specifies the lines to be affected by the action. The specification could be made with a single line number or a range of them, or with a regular expression or a pair of them, or any combination of the two.

alias Term used to refer to a command sequence or a hostname by another name. Aliasing is available in **csh**, **bash** and **ksh** to abbreviate long command sequences. DNS and /etc/hosts use aliasing to associate a host with meaningful names.

Anonymous ftp A public Ftp site where users use the login name anonymous and the email address as the password to gain access. Most downloadable software are hosted in these sites. Doesn't permit uploading of files.

archive Term used to a store a group of files as a single unit—either on magnetic media or as a single disk file. Refers to such units created by **tar**, **cpio** and **zip**.

argument The words following a command. It can be an option, an expression, an instruction, a program or one or more filenames. Options can also have their own arguments.

ASCII collating sequence The sequence used by ASCII (American Standard Code for Information Interchange) to number characters. Control characters occupy the top slots, followed by numerals, uppercase letters, and then lowercase. Sequence followed by **sort**, **ls**, the character class used by wild-cards and regular expressions and any UNIX command which sorts its output.

atomic operation Multiple actions that must be performed in entirety or not at all. The use of one system call (like **dup2**) in place of two (like **close** and **dup**) is recommended because a system call represents an atomic operation.

attachment A file that is sent along with an email message. Attachments can be binary files and can be viewed by a mail client either **inline** or using a **plugin** or a **helper application**.

background job One or more related processes that run without being waited for by their parent. A command, when terminated by the & symbol runs in the background. When preceded by **nohup**, a background job continues to run even after the user logs out of the system.

block device A hard disk, tape unit or floppy drive where output is written into and read from in units of blocks rather than bytes. Data reading is also attempted first from a buffer cache. Is indicated by the character b in the first character of the permissions field of the listing. See also **character device.**

boot block A special area in every file system. For the main file system, this block contains the boot procedure and the partition table, while for others it is left blank.

broadcast A message relayed by the ARP protocol to all machines in a network to get the MAC address of a machine. The host portion of the IP address is set to 255 for determining the broadcast address.

browser A program used to view HTML pages of the World Wide Web. Common Web browsers include Netscape and Internet Explorer (for Microsoft Windows and selected UNIX flavors). Linux is shipped with Netscape, Mozilla and Konqueror.

BSD UNIX A flavor of UNIX from the University of California, Berkeley. Berkeley rewrote the entire UNIX system from scratch and introduced a number of enhancements like the vi editor, C shell, r-utilities, PPP and symbolic links. TCP/IP was first available on BSD UNIX.

buffer A facility offered by many applications to hold frequently requested information in memory, rather than on disk, thus speeding up data transfer. Used by vi to make a copy of a file before editing. Netscape uses a buffer to store recently retrieved Web pages. Buffers are used for reading and writing data to disk and storing superblock and inode data.

buffer cache A pool of buffers maintained by the kernel to store data when doing I/O. All programs read from and write to these buffers unless explicitly directed to skip them. The kernel writes data from buffer to disk later rather than immediately.

cache Same as **buffer** .

character The smallest unit of information. The press of a key generates a single character, while ASCII has a set of 256 of them.

character device A terminal or printer where output is written into and read from in streams of characters. Is indicated by the character c in the first character of the permissions field of the listing. See also **block device.**

child process The process created by the parent process. The created process inherits some of the environmental parameters of its parent, but environmental changes made in the child are not available in the parent.

client-server Term used in TCP/IP to refer to a networked arrangement that allows two processes to run in a cooperative manner. The client process requests a service from a server process, generally running on a different host. X Window treats the concept in a reverse manner. See also **X server** and **X client**.

command Normally the first word entered at the prompt. It is usually an executable file, but can also include the built-in statements (also known as **internal commands**) of the shell and some other commands (like `mailx`, `vi`, etc.)

command failure The **exit status** returned by a command on unsuccessful completion. A value greater than 0 indicates failure and 0 signifies success. See also **command success**.

command line A complete sequence of a command, its options, filenames and other arguments that are specified at the prompt of the shell. The shell executes a command only when it encounters a complete command line.

Command Mode One of the three modes available in the `vi` editor to let keystrokes be interpreted as commands to act on text. When a key is pressed in this mode, it doesn't show up on screen but its effect does. See also **Input Mode** and **ex Mode**.

command substitution A feature of the shell which executes a command enclosed within a pair of backquotes (``) and uses its standard output to form the arguments of another command. Double quotes enable command substitution but not single quotes.

command success The **exit status** returned by a command on successful completion. A value of 0 indicates success, any other value signifies failure. See also **command failure**.

Common Desktop Environment (CDE) A standardized look and feel of the entire desktop under the X Window system now adopted by most UNIX vendors. It features a Front Panel from where applications can be launched, a File Manager and a Workspace Switch to allow the use of multiple desktops. The window manager `dtwm` used by CDE is based on Motif.

Common Gateway Interface (CGI) The interface offered by a Web server to pass on form data to an external application. The application processes the data and sends back the results to the server. `perl` is the most common language used for CGI.

concatenate The combination of two or more entities. Term used in connection with the `cat` command and shell variables.

context address A form of addressing used by `sed`, `awk` and `perl` which uses a regular expression enclosed by a pair of /s. The lines containing the expression are affected by the action.

context switch The changing of the process context achieved by loading the registers used by the Memory Management Unit (MMU) with the translation maps of the new process. A context switch occurs when the time quantum allocated to a process expires but it can also occur when the process invokes an I/O bound system call.

control command A command used in the command line of a shell, `awk` and `perl` conditional or loop to determine the control flow of the construct.

control file A text file where some programs take their instructions from. `$HOME/.exrc`, `/etc/sendmail.cf`, `/etc/inittab` and `/etc/inetd` are some of the control files to be found on a UNIX system.

cron The chronograph of the UNIX system. It executes the commands listed in a **crontab** file at a frequency that is specified by the various fields in the file. Is widely used for scheduling noninteractive jobs.

crontab A control file named after the user-id containing all instructions that need to be executed periodically, and their frequency of execution. The **cron** command looks at this table every minute to execute any command scheduled for execution.

current directory The directory in which the user is placed after using the **cd** command with an argument. Usually is set to the home directory during login time. See also **home directory.**

daemon A process that runs continuously without a user specifically requesting it. It is usually not associated with a specific terminal. **cron**, **init**, **inetd**, **lpsched** and **sendmail** are important daemons which keep the system running.

DARPA set The original set of TCP/IP utilities developed at the behest of DARPA and includes **telnet** and **ftp.**

default route Term used in connection with routing to provide a default exit path for all packets not meant for the local network. PPP uses it as an option (`defaultroute`) to guide all packets meant for the Internet to the `ppp0` interface. Every host also maintains a routing table that provides a similar default route.

device driver A set of routines built into the kernel to handle all devices. The kernel identifies the device driver from the device name used as argument to a command. The parameters passed by the kernel to the device driver are indicated by the **major number** and **minor number** of the device.

device file A file that represents a device. Provides a communication channel so that any interaction with the file actually results in activation of the physical device.

directory file A file that houses other files and subdirectories. Maintains the inode number and filename for every file in its fold. Writing to a directory file is possible only by the kernel.

DNS Same as **domain name system.**

domain A common string used by several hosts as part of their fully qualified hostnames. Examples of top-level domains on the Internet are *com*, *edu*, *org* etc.

domain name system (DNS) A service available on the Internet that uses domains and zones to uniquely describe the name of a host. Also provides facility to convert these hostnames to IP addresses, and vice versa. The database containing the mappings is distributed in a large network with consequent delegation of authority.

empty regular expression A null string signified by two /s, which indicates that the string to be acted upon is the same as the last string searched. It is used by **sed** in performing substitution.

encapsulation A process by which information is added to a packet in a TCP/IP network while moving down the protocol stack. Each layer adds its own header and trailer at the sending end, which are stripped off at the receiving end.

encryption A method of encoding a string of characters into a seemingly random character sequence. Used for storing the password of every authorized user of the system.

environment variable A shell variable that determines the nature of the environment of a user. Some of them are automatically set by the shell, though they can also be reassigned by the user. `HOME`, `TERM` and `SHELL` are common environment variables.

escape sequence A character preceded by a \ which imparts a special meaning to itself. Escape sequences are used by **`echo`**, **`printf`**, **`awk`** and **`perl`**. For instance, `\t` represents a tab, and `\n` implies a newline.

escaping The use of the \ immediately before a character to indicate that the following character should be treated literally. This property is used by the shell and some filters. In most cases, it removes the special meaning of a character, but sometimes is also used to emphasize it. See also **quoting**.

Ethernet address Same as **MAC address**.

exception An event that occurs on account of the processor executing an instruction (like divide-by-zero) Exceptions occur synchronously and are handled by the kernel.

exec The mechanism used by a process to overwrite itself with the code of the new program. Usually follows the **fork** operation. Represents a family of six C functions that actually do the job. Also a shell built-in statement that generates file descriptors and assigns them to physical files.

exit status A value returned by a program after execution. A value 0 indicates successful (true) execution, while any other value indicates unsuccessful (false) execution. In a C program, the **`wait`** system call directs the parent to pick up the child's exit status.

ex Mode A mode available in the **`vi`** editor to let **ex** commands be used to act on text. An indispensable mode for substitution, handling multiple files and customizing the editor. In **`vi`**, the mode is invoked by pressing a colon. Also known as **Last Line Mode**. See also **Command Mode** and **Input Mode**.

export A built-in shell command which makes the environment of the parent process available in the child process. The statement is used with variables.

extended regular expression (ERE) An enhanced regular expression used by **`grep -E`**, **`egrep`**, **`awk`** and **`perl`** which enables the specification of multiple patterns and permits the use of groups. Uses the metacharacters ?, +, (,) and |.

FAQ A collection of frequently asked questions that are maintained on Net News on virtually every topic.

file A container for storing information. An ordinary file contains data. A directory file contains filenames. A device file provides the interface to access a physical device. A symbolic link points to the file that actually contains the information.

file attributes A set of parameters stored in the inode which describe the characteristics of a file. They consist of the type, ownership, permissions, time stamps, size, number of links and an array disk block addresses.

file descriptor A small integer that is returned by the **open** system call when a file is opened. All file descriptors are maintained in the file descriptor table, and each descriptor in the table points to the **file table**. The first three entires are usually allocated to the shell's standard streams.

file offset pointer The location within the file where the next read or write operation will take place. This location is maintained in the **file table** and is updated every time a read or write operation on the file takes place.

file ownership One of the attributes of a file. The user creating or copying a file is generally the owner as well. The owner of a file has certain privileges which are denied others. Ownership can be surrendered only by the superuser on a BSD-based system.

file permission A three-tiered protection mechanism which determines the read, write and executable permissions of a file. These permissions are available to three categories of users—**user**, **group** and **others**. The permissions can be altered only by the owner of the file with **chmod**.

file system A hierarchical structure of files and directories having its separate root directory. Every hard disk has at least one file system on it, which is attached to the main file system with the **mount** command.

file table A structure maintained in memory that contains the file's opening modes, status flags, position of the offset pointer and a reference count field. Two file descriptors point to the same file table when the process forks or when it replicates a descriptor using **dup**, **dup2** or **fcntl**.

file time stamps A set of three dates and times representing the date of last modification, access and change of inode of a file. This information is stored in the inode and revealed with various options to **ls**.

File Transfer Protocol (FTP) A TCP/IP application protocol that transfers files between two remote machines. Also features a command by that name.

filter A UNIX command which uses standard input and standard output. It takes a character stream as input, manipulates its contents, and generates a similar stream as output. The shell's redirection and piping features can be used with these commands.

foreground job An environment where a **job** runs with its parent waiting for its execution to complete. You can run only one job in the foreground.

fork The mechanism of process creation by replicating the address space of the existing process. The copied process inherits the open files of its parent, the current directory and the exported variables. A fork is usually followed by an **exec**. Features a system call by that name.

FQDN See **fully qualified domain name.**

fragmentation A process by which packets are broken down into smaller units at a layer in the TCP/IP protocol stack. This usually happens before encapsulation because the network can handle only small packets.

free list A list of inodes maintained in the superblock of the file system which can be released by the kernel immediately for creating or appending to a file.

Free Software Foundation Same as **GNU**.

fully qualified domain name (FQDN) A set of dot-delimited strings representing the domains and sub-domains to which the host belongs. The FQDN of a host (like *www.altavista.com*) is unique on the Internet.

gateway A computer that belongs to multiple networks. A gateway routes packets from one network to another. See **router**.

getty A process that runs at every free terminal to monitor the next login. Is spawned by `init` and execs the `login` program whenever a user tries to log in..

GNU An organization founded by Richard Stallman which expands to **G**NU's **N**ot **U**NIX, but now known as the Free Software Foundation. Many of the tools available on Linux have been developed by GNU or distributed under its license. The GNU license requires all developers to make the source code public.

graphical user interface (GUI) The component of the X Window system that controls its look and feel. GUI looks are determined by a special client—the **window manager**.

group A category of user understood by the **chmod** command when handling file permissions. More than one user may belong to a group, and one set of file permissions is associated with this category. See also **owner** and **others**.

group-id (GID) The group name or number of the user, which is allotted by the system administrator when creating a user account. The name and its numeric representation are maintained in `/etc/group`, while the numeric value is also available in `/etc/passwd`. See also **user-id**.

hard link See **link**.

helper application An external program that is invoked by a browser to handle a special file format that it can't handle itself. Unlike a **plugin**, a helper application views files in a separate window. The file's extension, content type and the external program needed to handle it are specified in `mime.types` and `mailcap`.

here document A form of standard input used by many commands using the << symbols. The input to the command forms part of the command line itself. It is especially useful when used with commands which don't accept the input filename as an argument.

history The facility to store, recall and execute previous commands in **csh**, **bash** and **ksh**. Also features a command by that name in these shells.

home directory A field specified in `/etc/passwd` to indicate the directory where a user is to be placed on login. Also used by the **cd** command when used without arguments. Same as **login directory**.

home page Term used to refer to the first page presented to the user on connecting to a Web site.

host A computer or a device in a network having a separate IP address.

hostname The name of a host which is unique in the network. Often used on the Internet with a series of dot-delimited strings to represent a **fully qualified domain name.** Features a command by that name which both displays and sets the hostname.

hosts file Refers to the file `/etc/hosts` that contains the hostname-IP address mappings.

hypertext A link placed in one document with the `<A HREF>` tag which points to a location in another document in the same machine or another. The World Wide Web is a collection of these documents. See also **Web page**.

Hyper Text Markup Language (HTML) The universal language for coding Web documents. It is characterized by the presence of tags which can transfer control to another document in another machine. HTML documents can be used to view animation or video or play audio.

Hyper Text Transfer Protocol (HTTP) The application protocol that retrieves HTML documents from hosts on the Web. It is *stateless* in that a connection has no knowledge of the state of the previous connection. HTTP 1.1 supports **keep-alive** (persistent) connections.

infinite loop A **`while`**, **`until`** or **`for`** loop which never terminates. The **`break`** (**`last`** in **`perl`**) statement is used to switch control out of the loop.

init A process having the PID number 1, which is responsible for the creation of all major processes of the system. **`init`** runs all the system's daemons and the **`getty`** process at the terminal ports. It takes its instructions from `/etc/inittab`. It can also be used as a command to set the system to a specific run level.

inline The placement of a graphic beside the text in a browser window without using a separate window or application. GIF and JPEG files are displayed inline by a graphic browser.

inode A structure maintained in a special area of the disk for storing the attributes of a file. This table contains for every file its permissions, ownership details, time stamps and number of links. However, it doesn't contain the filename.

inode number A number identifying an inode for a file which is unique in a single file system. It is displayed with the `-i` option of **`ls`**.

in-place editing Term used in **`perl`** to edit a file and write the output back to the same file without using redirection.

Input Mode One of the three modes of the **`vi`** editor. In this mode, any key depression is interpreted as input and displayed on the screen. The mode is terminated by pressing *[Esc]*. See also **Command Mode** and **ex Mode.**

instruction A combination of an address and an action. The address specifies the lines to be affected by the action. See also **address** and **action.**

interface program A program that filters data for printing. The interface program formats the data, supplies the codes needed by the printer and often calls up an external application to print the file.

internal command Name given to a sub-command of many UNIX tools like **vi**, **more**, **mailx** and **sed** commands, and the shell.

Internet The super network of networks connected by the TCP/IP protocol with facilities of email, file transfer, remote login, Net News and the World Wide Web. All the major networks of the world are connected in this way. See also **World Wide Web.**

internet Two or more networks connected by the TCP/IP protocol. All the Internet facilities like Ftp, Telnet, Web browsing and email are also available on an internet. Same as **intranet.**

internet address Same as **IP address.**

internet daemon A daemon that listens on multiple ports and invokes the other daemons for Ftp, Telnet and the POP service. Available as the file **inetd** or **xinetd**, and can be used to enable or disable a service.

Internet Protocol (IP) An important member of the TCP/IP protocol suite which handles routing of packets. IP provides a route to the network rather than a route to the host. It has no error-detection or recovery facilities.

interrupt The sending of a signal (SIGINT) to a process with the intention of terminating it. A specific key is assigned this job, usually *[Ctrl-c]* or *[Delete]*, though it can be reassigned with the **stty** command.

interval regular expression (IRE) A regular expression that uses a single or a comma-delimited pair of numbers, enclosed by a matched pair of escaped curly braces (\{ and \}). The two numbers indicate the minimum and maximum number of times that the single character preceding it can occur. Used by **grep**, **sed** and **perl** commands. **perl** drops the \ in its implementation.

intranet Same as **internet.**

IP address A string of four dot-delimited octets used to describe the logical address of a machine in a TCP/IP network. All fully qualified domain names are converted to this address before data can reach the host. Same as **internet address.**

iteration The repeating of a loop's instruction set. The statements inside the loop are repeated as long as the condition specified in the command line of the loop remains true. Term is used in connection with the **while**, **until** and **for** loops.

job A group of processes working toward a common goal. A pipeline is a simple example of a job. All processes in a job have the same process group-id (PGID).

job control A feature provided in most shells (except Bourne) of moving jobs between foreground and background and suspending them. A suspended job can be moved to foreground and background with **fg** and **bg**, respectively.

keep-alive connection A feature available in HTTP 1.1 that allows multiple resources to be fetched in a single (persistent) connection. The server holds the connection for a certain time to allow further requests. Persistent connections speed up Web access.

kernel The part of the UNIX operating system which is responsible for the creation and management of files and processes. Is loaded into memory when the machine is booted and interacts directly with the machine hardware. All system calls are built into the kernel.

kernel mode A mode of the CPU used by the kernel when it runs on behalf of the user process. In this mode, the kernel can access any memory location. A switch from **user mode** to kernel mode takes place when the user program invokes a system call.

kill The change of state of a process by sending a signal to it. UNIX also features a command and system call by the name, which uses a signal number and the process PID to kill or suspend a process.

kill script An **rc script** beginning with `K` that is used to kill a service. See also **start script**.

Last Line Mode Same as **ex Mode**.

library function A C function available in the standard library that performs most of the common programming tasks. Library functions encapsulate the **system calls** they internally use and often provide more convenient interfaces that the ones offered by system calls.

line A sequence of characters terminated by the newline character.

line address A form of addressing used by **sed, awk** and **perl** to specify a single line or a group of contiguous lines. It requires a single line number or a pair of them to limit the boundaries of the text.

link A file attribute stored in the inode that allows a file to be referred to by more than one name. One of the attributes of a file that is maintained in the inode. Same as **hard link**. See also **symbolic link.**

listing The output obtained with the **ls -l** command showing seven attributes of a file.

logical block The minimum number of bytes allocated for one disk write operation. The logical block size is an integral multiple of the sector size (512 bytes) which is called the **physical block**.

login A process that overlays the **getty** program when the user enters a login name. It execs the shell process on successful login.

login directory Same as **home directory.**

login name Same as **user-id**.

loopback address A fictitious network interface available in every machine. It "loops back" a message addressed to `127.0.0.1` and allows all networking services to run on a standalone host.

MAC address A 48-bit address of the network interface card, which is unique throughout the world. All IP addresses have to be converted to these addresses before they can be understood by the receiving machine. Same as **Ethernet address**.

magic Term used in **vi** to refer to the special meaning of a character used in a regular expression. The magic is turned off by using the ex Mode command `set nomagic`.

mailbox A text file named after the username, usually in `/var/mail` (`/var/spool/mail` in Linux) that contains all mail received by the user. Binary attachments are held in this file in encoded form.

Mail Delivery Agent (MDA) The agency responsible for delivering mail to the user. Receives a mail message from the **Mail Transport Agent** and appends it to a text file in `/var/mail` (`/var/spool/mail` in Linux).

Mail Transport Agent (MTA) The agency responsible for transporting mail across a network. One MTA hands over mail to another MTA before the mail can be delivered. SMTP is the standard protocol used by MTAs.

Mail User Agent (MUA) The client program that is used to send and receive mail. The MUA looks at the spool directory in `/var/mail` (`/var/spool/mail` in Linux) for locating received mail. It hands over outgoing mail to the **Mail Transport Agent.** **`mailx`**, **`elm`**, **`pine`** and Netscape Messenger are the common MUAs.

major number One of the parameters of the listing of a device file which indicates the device driver required to access the device. Similar devices have the same major number. See also **minor number.**

man page The UNIX documentation as viewed by the **`man`** command. Every command, system configuration file, system call and library function is associated with a man page.

mbox A secondary file where a mail message is saved after it has been viewed. Many character-based mail clients use `$HOME/mbox` as the default mbox.

metacharacter The name given to a group of characters which means something special to the shell. The shell acts on these characters before executing the command. The meaning of any of these characters is reversed by preceding it with a \. The concept also extends to special characters used by certain commands as part of their syntax.

minor number One of the parameters of the listing of a device file which indicates the special characteristics of the device. Can be interpreted to mean the parameters passed on to the device driver. See also **major number.**

modem A device (**mo**dulator-**dem**odulator) that converts analog signals to digital, and vice versa. Used for connecting to the Internet or any TCP/IP network through a telephone line.

modification time One of the time stamps of a file stored in the inode which represents the date and time the contents of a file were last modified. One of the attributes displayed by the listing.

mounting The process of attaching a standalone file system to the main file system. Its root directory after mounting becomes the directory of the file system at which mounting took place. Also features a command by the name, and is used by the system during booting to integrate all standalone systems with the main file system.

Multipurpose Internet Mail Extensions (MIME) A standard used on the Internet to encode and decode binary files. Also useful in encoding multiple data formats in a *single* mail message. Features two headers—Content-Type and Content-Transfer-Encoding. Used to mail multimedia attachments.

name server A dedicated service used on the Internet to convert the fully qualified domain name of a host into its IP address and vice versa. A name server is queried by a **resolver**. It may either have the answer or provide the address of another name server.

Network File System (NFS) A TCP/IP application that lets users mount a directory of a remote file system on a local directory. Access rights are controlled by `/etc/exports` on the remote system.

Network News Transfer Protocol (NNTP) The TCP/IP protocol used to handle Net News or newsgroups. One news server fetches news from another news server. Netscape Messenger also acts as an NNTP client.

newline The character generated by hitting *[Enter]* or *[Ctrl-j]*. Used as the delimiter between two lines, and forms one of the characters of **whitespace**.

newsgroup An offline discussion group on the Internet which originates from the UNIX-based USENET. News messages are fetched in two stages—first the headers and then the contents. News uses the NNTP protocol. Netscape Messenger also handles newsgroups.

nonprivileged user An ordinary user having no superuser privileges.

option A string normally starting with a -, which changes the default behavior of a command. It also forms one of its arguments. Multiple options can generally be combined with a single - symbol. Some commands use options beginning with a + symbol, and some don't use either.

ordinary file The most common file of the UNIX system represented by programs, data and text. It contains as much data as one puts into it but doesn't contain the end-of-file mark nor any of the file's attributes. Also known as **regular file**.

orphan A process whose parent has died. Orphans are adopted by **`init`**.

others A category of user understood by the **`chmod`** command when handling file permissions. A user who is neither the owner of a file nor belongs to the group of the group owner, is in this class. One set of file permissions is associated with this category. See also **owner** and **group**.

overlay Same as **exec**.

owner The creator of a file having complete authority of determining its contents and permissions. Understood as **user** by the **`chmod`** command when handling file permissions. The string and numeric representations are stored in `/etc/passwd`. See also **group** and **others**.

packet Term applied to describe a fragmented unit of data in a TCP/IP network. Sometimes used synonymously with **datagram**.

pager A tool that displays output one screen at a time. **`more`** and **`less`** are the standard pagers on UNIX and Linux systems.

parent process-id (PPID) The **process-id** of the parent process which is stored in the process table for every process.

partition A contiguous area of the hard disk that holds a file system. Data from one partition can't spill over to another partition. Linux can have a single extended partition that can hold multiple logical partitions.

password aging A system of setting conditions for change of password. Usually, there is a maximum and minimum time for this change. Is implemented by using options with the **passwd** command.

password A supposedly secret code used by every user at the time of logging in. The code is not flashed on the terminal, but is stored in an encrypted manner in /etc/shadow. Also features a command with a similar name (**passwd**) to change the password.

PATH A shell variable that contains a colon-delimited list of directories that the shell will look through to locate a command invoked by a user. The PATH generally includes /bin and /usr/bin for nonprivileged users and /sbin and /usr/sbin for the superuser.

pathname A sequence of one or more filenames using a / as a delimiter. All except the last filename have to be directories. See also **relative pathname** and **absolute pathname.**

pending signals mask A field maintained in the proc structure that shows the signals that have been received for a process. The kernel looks up this field at certain specific times and then looks up the signal disposition table to determine the action to be taken.

physical block The unit used by several UNIX commands for quantifying data stored in disk. For most systems this expands to 512 bytes (1024 in Linux).

ping The sending of packets to a remote host to check the connectivity of the network. Also features a command by that name.

pipe A buffered object that allows one-way data transmission through its two ends using flow control. Whatever is written to one end is read from the other. Features a system call by that name and is required create a **pipeline.**

pipeline A sequence of two or more commands used with the | symbol so the input of one command comes from the output of the other. See also **pipe.**

plugin A small program that is installed in a browser to handle special file formats which can't be handled by the browser. Unlike a **helper application,** a plugin can't be invoked separately.

Point-to-Point Protocol (PPP) A TCP/IP protocol that runs on the serial port— often through a modem. Users usually connect to the Internet through a PPP link between their machines and their ISPs. Represented by the **pppd** command which can run both as server and client.

port number A number used to identify a TCP/IP application and defined in /etc/services. Servers use fixed port numbers but clients use random port numbers. A packet has two port numbers, one for each end of the channel. See also **socket.**

positional parameters The external arguments to a shell script which are read into a series of special variables designated as $1, $2, $3, etc. $* and "$@" represent the entire string and $# signifies the number of parameters set.

POSIX A set of standard interfaces that are based on the UNIX operating system. POSIX compliance ensures that a set of programs developed on one machine can be moved to another without recoding. POSIX.1 represents the standard for the application programming interface for the C language. POSIX.2 provides the interface for the shell and utilities.

Post Office Protocol (POP) The TCP/IP protocol used for fetching mail from an offline mail server. POP is often used over a dialup line to fetch Internet mail. The POP server is invoked by the internet daemon (`inetd`). Netscape has the POP client built-in, but **`fetchmail`** is the standard POP client for Linux systems.

proc structure A structure maintained by the kernel that contains control information about the process like its PID, PPID, state and signal handling data. The process table is a collection of proc structures. Also contains a pointer to the **u area**, another structure that contains information about the currently running process.

process An instance of a running program and created by the **`fork`** system call. Usually is followed by an **exec**. Most of the shell's internal commands are executed without creating a process.

process address space The memory locations that a process can access and includes the text, data, heap and stack segments. The address space also has space for the kernel's text and data.

process birth Term used to refer to the creation of a process. The process is created when the command representing it is invoked and dies when command execution is complete. The **`fork`** system call gives birth to a process.

process context The complete environment that is seen by the process when it runs. Includes a hardware context (the state of the CPU registers) and a software context (the address space, process credentials). The kernel saves the context of the current process before running a new one.

process death Term used to refer to the termination of a process. The process dies when the command representing it has completed execution. Frees entire address space and the process table entry.

process group A collection of processes having some common attributes. In shells supporting job control, each job or process is placed in its own process group. A process group can be suspended and killed by sending a signal to the leader of the group.

process group-id (PGID) A common number allotted to a group of processes. The group leader has its PGID equal to the PID. See also **process group.**

process-id (PID) A unique number allotted to a process by the kernel when it is born.

profile A startup file used and maintained by every user. Has the name `.profile` or `.bash_profile` in the home directory. The instructions contained in this file are executed during login time without spawning a sub-shell. However, `/etc/profile` (no dot) is executed first before the user's own profile.

prompt A string that shows the position of the cursor. The appearance of a prompt generally indicates that the previous command has completed its run. Can be customized by setting the value of the shell variable PS1.

quoting The principle of enclosing a group of characters in single or double quotes to remove their special meaning. Though the shell ignores all special characters enclosed in single quotes, double quotes permit evaluation of $ as a variable and ` for **command substitution.**

race condition A situation where two or more events contend for the same resource and the eventual outcome is determined by the sequence in which the events are serviced.

rc script A set of shell scripts available in an `rc`*n*`.d` directory (where *n* indicates the run level) in `/etc` that are used to set a machine to a specific run level. These scripts run the daemons that should run for that level and kills the ones that shouldn't. See also **start script** and **stop script**.

recursion A characteristic feature of some UNIX commands to descend a specified directory to access all subdirectories under this directory, and beyond. **`ls`**, **`rm`**, **`chmod`**, **`chown`** and **`chgrp`** use a special option to do that, while **`find`** and **`tar`** do it compulsorily.

redirection Term used in the shell to reassign the standard input and standard output of a command. The default source and destination of a data stream can be redirected to point to a disk file.

regular expression An ambiguous expression formed with some special and ordinary characters, which is expanded by a command (and not by the shell) to match more than one string. Conceptually similar to the shell's wild-cards, a regular expression can match a pattern at a certain location in a line and should be quoted to prevent its interpretation by the shell.

regular file Same as **ordinary file**.

relative pathname A pathname which specifies the location of a file using the symbols `.` and `..` to refer to the current and parent directories, respectively. See also **absolute pathname.**

remote login Connecting to a remote machine using a username and password. All commands entered after logging in are actually executed on the remote machine. See also **`telnet`**.

repeat factor A feature available in the **`vi`** editor and the **`more`** and **`less`** commands of using a number to prefix any command. It usually repeats the command that number of times.

resolver A set of library routines used by a TCP/IP application to query a **name server** for resolving a domain name to the IP address. Is represented by the file `/etc/resolv.conf`.

root The top-most directory in every file system which has no parent. Is indicated by the `/` symbol. Also signifies a user who uses the login name root to log on to the superuser account.

root name server A server running **DNS** that specifies the name servers of the top-level domains like *.com*, *.edu*, *.org* etc. Thirteen of them handle all top-level name server queries on the Internet.

router A special device that routes packets from one network to another. It functions like a gateway.

routing The sending of packets to a gateway or a router when the packet belongs to a different network. The routing table also provides a default route for all packets that can't be matched with explicit routes.

run level Term used to refer to the various states that a UNIX system can be in. The run level is determined by the argument of the **`init`** command and the action to be taken is specified in `/etc/inittab`. Different **rc scripts** are executed depending on the value of this run level.

r-utilities A set of TCP/IP tools developed by Berkeley as alternatives to the DARPA set. The tools include `rlogin`, `rcp` and `rsh`. Access to a remote system through these utilities is controlled by `/etc/hosts.equiv` and `$HOME/.rhosts` on the remote machine.

server See **client-server architecture**.

set-user-id (SUID) A special mode of a file indicated by the letter s in the permissions field. The effective user-id of a process having this bit set is the owner of the file and not the user running the program. This property lets users modify important system files by using a specific command, rather than directly.

shell The command interpreter of the UNIX system, which runs perpetually at every logged-in terminal. The shell processes a user request and interacts with the kernel to execute the command. It also possesses a programming capability.

shell function A group of statements executed as a bunch in the current shell. A shell function accepts parameters and can return only a boolean value.

shell script An ordinary file containing a set of commands, which is executed in an interpretive manner in a sub-shell. All the shell's internal commands and external UNIX commands can be specified in a script.

signal The notification made by the kernel that an event has occurred. This event can be on account of the hardware, the keyboard or is generated by a program. A signal has a default disposition (action to take) but it can be overridden by a user-defined **signal handler**. Signals `SIGKILL` and `SIGSTOP` can't be ignored or handled otherwise. See also **signal disposition** and **signal handler**.

signal disposition The action that is to be taken when a signal occurs. Every signal has a default disposition, maintained in the signal disposition table, which could be to terminate, stop the process or to ignore the signal. The disposition can be changed by using a **signal handler** except for the `SIGKILL` and `SIGSTOP` signals.

signal handler A user-defined function in a C program that catches a signal and makes it behave in a manner that is different from the default. Signals `SIGKILL` and `SIGSTOP` can't be caught.

signature file A file named `.signature` in a user's home directory. It is used to enter a person's details that must accompany every mail message. Most mail user agents are configured to automatically attach the file with every outgoing message.

Simple Mail Transfer Protocol (SMTP) The TCP/IP protocol used to transport email data across the Internet. The SMTP client communicates with the SMTP server at the other end and *directly* delivers the message. `sendmail` is the most common implementation of SMTP.

sleep Term used to refer to the temporary suspension of a process. Also features a command and library function by that name.

socket A combination of a port number and an IP addresses. Both source and destination hosts use a socket each for communication. No two connections can have the same pair of sockets. See also **port number**.

spawn The creating of a child process. However, most of the internal statements of the shell are executed without creating a process. See also **process birth**.

standard error The destination used by the diagnostic output stream to write its output. Includes all error messages generated by UNIX commands. The default destination of this stream is the terminal but can be redirected to any file.

standard input The source opened by the shell to accept information as a stream of characters. By default, the keyboard is assigned this source, but it can also come from a file, a pipeline or a **here document**.

standard output The destination used by commands to send output to. Used by all UNIX commands which send output to the terminal. The default destination can also be reassigned to divert output to another file or a pipeline.

start script An **rc script** beginning with S that is used to start a service. See also **kill script**.

sticky bit A special mode assigned to a file or a directory and indicated by the letter t in the permissions field. The executable code of an ordinary file gets stuck in the swap area once it has been executed. A directory with the sticky bit set can be shared by a group of users, where one user can't delete or modify another user's files.

stop script An **rc script** beginning with K that is used to stop a service. See also **start script**.

subnet mask The IP address of a host in a TCP/IP network which has all the bits of the network address set to 1. The mask determines whether a network is subnetted or not.

subroutine A group of statements executed as a bunch in **perl**—like a shell function. Subroutines use arguments which are stored in the array @_. **perl** uses the & symbol to call a subroutine.

sub-shell A second shell created by the parent shell. It is normally required for executing a shell script or a group of commands with the () operators. Changes made in a sub-shell are not available in the parent.

superblock A special area in every file system which contains important information on the file system. Includes a list of free data blocks and inodes. Disk copy is regularly updated with the memory copy by the **sync** command.

superuser Same as **system administrator**.

suspend The process of stopping of a job. The job may later be resumed, either in the background or foreground. This feature is available in **csh**, **ksh** and **bash**.

swapping The process of moving currently inactive processes from memory to the swap area of the disk (swapping out). Also refers to the transfer of these processes from the temporary area to memory when ready for execution (swapping in). The swap area is organized in a series of contiguous blocks as a separate file system.

symbolic link A file which points to the location of another file or directory. Unlike hard links, a symbolic link can link files across file systems. Can be used to link directories also. See also **link**.

sync Term used to describe the synchronization of the superblock and inodes with their respective memory versions. Also features a command by that name which the kernel uses to write the memory data to disk.

system administrator The person responsible for the management of system resources. The administrator can change any file attribute and kill any user process. Uses a special user account (generally, root) to perform administrative duties. Also known as **superuser**.

system call A basic routine defined in the kernel which performs the basic operations of the computer like opening a file and creating a process. All UNIX commands and library functions are written in terms of system calls. All UNIX systems use the same system calls. Processor switches from **user mode** to **kernel mode** when executing a system call.

system process A process which runs in the system during booting without being specifically requested for by a user. **init**, **getty**, **cron** and **lpsched** are some of the system processes. See also **daemon.**

tab A single character which simulates a contiguous set of spaces. Is generated by hitting a specific key or *[Ctrl-i]* and forms one of the characters of **whitespace.** Useful for aligning columns.

tagged regular expression (TRE) Term used to indicate the grouping of a regular expression with an escaped pair of parentheses, \(and \). This group is repeated elsewhere in the line by using the tag *n* or $*n* (**perl**), where *n* is a number between 1 and 9. Used by **grep**, **sed** and **perl** commands.

TCP/IP Expands to Transmission Control Protocol/Internet Protocol—a collection of protocols used for networking computers using different operating systems and different hardware. Ensures reliable transmission with full error-correction facilities. TCP and IP are two of the most important protocols in this suite.

telnet A TCP/IP application that enables a user to log on to a remote machine after supplying a username and password. After logging in, the user can use the remote machine as if it is a local one. All files are created on the remote machine.

The Open Group Owner of the UNIX standard and the originator of the Single UNIX Specification. Includes X/OPEN in its fold. Also maintains the X Window system.

thread Term used to group messages exchanged in response to one another. Threads are encountered both in email and newsgroup messages. Many mail user agents and newsreaders like Netscape can organize and view messages by threads.

toggle switch A command that reverses the effect of its immediate previous invocation.

top-level domain (TLD) Any domain under the root (.) domain which has not been allotted to a specific country. TLDs comprise the generic domains *com*, *edu*, *org*, *net*, *museum*, *biz*. etc. Domains allocated to countries are known as **country code top-level domains** (cc-TLDs).

Transmission Control Protocol (TCP) One of the most important protocols of the TCP/IP family responsible for transporting data. It breaks data into segments and assembles them at the other end. The transmission is wholly reliable as lost segments are retransmitted.

trusted host A host that is trusted by a remote host to access its resources. When a host is trusted, all users of the host are also trusted. Trusted hosts are a security threat in a network.

u area A structure that contains information on the currently running process like its UID, GID and the file descriptor table. Forking copies the u area. Modern UNIX systems have the u area embedded in the **proc structure.**

umask A number maintained in the shell that determines a file's default permissions. This number is subtracted from the system's default to obtain a file's actual permissions. The value can be displayed and set by using a command of the same name.

Uniform Resource Locator (URL) A string of characters that specifies a resource on the Web. Comprises the protocol, the FQDN of the site and the path name of the file. `http://` is the standard protocol prefix used in the URL, but can be `ftp://` or `telnet://` as well.

unmounting The process of disengaging a file system from the main file system. All files systems must be unmounted before conducting an integrity check on it and before the system is shut down. The **`umount`** command performs this unmounting.

user equivalence Term used in the context of the r-utilities to control a user's access to a like-to-like account on a remote host. If a user has user equivalence, then she is allowed to use **`rlogin`** to log in to her own account in a remote host without using a password.

user-id (UID) The name used by a user to gain access to the system. A list of authorized names is maintained in `/etc/passwd` along with their numeric representations. Also known as **login name** and **username**. See also **group-id.**

user mode A mode of the CPU when running a program. In this mode, the program has no access to the memory locations used by the kernel. See also **kernel mode.**

username Same as **user-id.**

virtual console A system of using multiple screens and logins from a single UNIX machine. A new screen is opened by using *[Alt]* and a function key.

vnode table The image of the inode in memory. Contains apart from the inode information, a reference count that shows the number of processes that point to the table. A file can't be entirely deleted as long as this table is open.

wait Term used to refer to the inaction of a parent process while a child is running. Normally the parent waits for the death of the child to pick up its **exit status.** Also features a shell built-in command and a system call by that name.

wake Term used to indicate the termination of a dormant activity when an event occurs. The kernel wakes up a sleeping process when a specific event has occurred (like the completion of I/O).

Web page An HTML document containing text and graphics that is presented in the form of a page at every Web site. A Web page has links with other pages—often on different machines. Pages can be used to create forms for user input.

Web server A TCP/IP application that runs the HTTP protocol. The World Wide Web serves all resources through Web servers.

whitespace A contiguous sequence of spaces, tabs or newlines. The default value of the IFS variable. Used as delimiter by the shell to parse command line arguments and by the **set** statement to assign its arguments to positional parameters.

wild-card A special character used by the shell to match a group of filenames with a single expression. The * and ? are commonly used wild-cards used for framing expressions.

window manager The special X client program which controls the look and feel of all X clients. It puts a frame around every window and enables window sizing and movement. Until the **dtwm** of CDE took over, **mwm** was the most popular window manager program.

word A contiguous string of characters not containing whitespace. **wc** can count words and **vi** also enables cursor movement using a word as a navigational unit. Special regular expressions used by GNU filters and **perl** can match words. A quoted string is understood by the shell as a single word irrespective of the number of actual words that it may contain.

World Wide Web A service on the Internet featuring a collection of linked documents and images. The browser (client) fetches theses resources from a Web server using the HTTP protocol. The **hypertext** feature transports users to another document at the click of a mouse.

wraparound A feature provided by the **vi** editor for resuming the search for a pattern from the other end of a file. The entire file is thus searched irrespective of the cursor position at the time of commencement of search. Can be suppressed in **vi** by using the ex Mode command `set nowraparound`.

X client An X program which performs a specific function and uses the X server for display. **xterm** and **xclock** are common X clients found in every X Window system.

X server The program in X Window which controls the display including the monitor, mouse and keyboard. X clients write their output to this program. If the display changes, only the server needs to change and not the clients.

X Window System The graphical component of the UNIX system. X clients write their output to the server which is responsible for their display on separate windows. Netscape requires this system to handle mail and browse the Web.

zipped file Any file that is compressed with the **gzip**, **zip** or **bzip2** commands. They are decompressed with **gunzip**, **unzip** and **bunzip2**.

zombie A dead process whose exit status has not been picked up by its parent using **wait**. Zombies clog the process table and can't be killed.

zone That part of a domain that is administered separately and handled by its own name server. The name server for a zone is authoritative for that zone.

Appendix E

Bibliography

There's an abundance of material on UNIX available both in print as well as on the Internet. Apart from the UNIX documentation, the following textbooks and journals served as handy references:

General Reading

UNIX System V: A Practical Guide, 3rd Edition by Mark G. Sobell (Addison-Wesley), 1995, Menlo Park, California

UNIX System V Release 4: An Introduction, 2nd Edition by Kenneth Rosen, Richard Rosinski & James Farber (Osborne McGraw Hill), 1996, Berkeley, California

Harley Hahn's Student Guide to Unix by Harley Hahn (The McGraw-Hill Companies), 1996, Berkeley, California

Your UNIX: The Ultimate Guide by Sumitabha Das (Tata-Mcgraw-Hill), 2001, New Delhi

The UNIX Operating System by Kaare Christian & Susan Richter (John Wiley), 1993, New York

UNIX: The Textbook by Syed Mansoor Sarwar, Robert Koretsky and Syed Aqeel Sarwar (Addison-Wesley Longman), 2001

UNIX Made Easy—UNIX and Linux Basics and Beyond by John Muster (Tata McGraw-Hill), 2002, New Delhi

Running Linux, Third Edition by Matt Welsh, Matthias Kalle Dalheimer and Lar Kaufman (O'Reilly & Associates), 1999, Sebastopol, California

Topical Reading

Advanced UNIX — A Programmer's Guide by Stephen Prata (SAMS), 1986, New Delhi

Learning the Korn Shell by Bill Rosenblatt and Arnold Robbins (Shroff Publishers and Distributors), 2002, Mumbai

Learning the bash Shell by Cameron Newham and Bill Rosenblatt (O'Reilly & Associates), 1998, Sebastopol, California

Programming Perl by Larry Wall, Brett McLaughlin, Jon Orwant (O'Reilly & Associates), 2000, Sebastopol, California

Learning Perl by Randal Schwartz (Shroff Publishers and Distributors), 2001, Mumbai

The X Window System User's Guide—Motif Edition by Valerie Quercia and Tim O'Reilly (O'Reilly & Associates), 1993, Sebastopol, California

References

UNIX in a Nutshell by Arnold Robbins (Shroff Publishers and Distributors), 1998, Mumbai

The UNIX Programming Environment by Brian Kernighan & Rob Pike (Prentice Hall of India), 1984, New Delhi

The Design of the UNIX Operating System by Maurice Bach (Prentice Hall of India), 1986, New Delhi

UNIX Internals—The New Frontiers by Uresh Vahalia (Pearson Education Asia), 1996, New Delhi

Solaris Internals—Core Kernel Architecture by Jim Mauro and Rochard McDougall (Sun Microsystems Press), 2001, Palo Alto, California

UNIX Power Tools by Shelley Powers, Jerry Peek, Tim O'Reilly and Mike Loukides (Shroff Publishers and Distributors), 2002, Mumbai

Systems Programming

Advanced Programming in the UNIX Environment by W. Richard Stevens (Pearson Education Asia), 1993, New Delhi

UNIX for Programmers and Users by Graham Glass and King Ables (Prentice Hall), 1993, Upper Saddle River, New Jersey

Beginning Linux Programming by Richard Stones and Neil Matthew (Shroff Publishers and Distributors), 1999, Mumbai

System and Network Administration

UNIX System Administration Handbook by Evi Nemeth, Garth Snyder, Scott Seebass and Trent Hein (Pearson Education), 2001, Addison-Wesley Longman (Singapore) Pte Ltd., New Delhi

Essential System Administration by AEleen Frisch (Shroff Publishers and Distributors), 2002, Mumbai

TCP/IP Network Administration by Craig Hunt (Shroff Publishers and Distributors), 2002, Mumbai

Journals and Papers

The UNIX Time-Sharing System by Dennis Ritchie & Ken Thompson (Bell System Technical Journal, Vol 57, No 6), 1978, Murray Hill, New Jersey

UNIX Implementation by Ken Thompson (Bell System Technical Journal, Vol 57, No 6), 1978, Murray Hill, New Jersey

A Retrospective by Dennis Ritchie (Bell System Technical Journal, Vol 57, No 6), 1978, Murray Hill, New Jersey

The UNIX Shell by Steve Bourne (Bell System Technical Journal, Vol 57, No 6), 1978, Murray Hill, New Jersey

Awk - A Pattern Scanning and Processing Language Programmer's Manual by Alfred Aho, Peter Weinberger & Brian Kernighan (Computing Science Technical Report No 118 of AT&T Bell Labs), Murray Hill, New Jersey

Index

V

W

X

Z